A Practical

Handbook of

Software

Construction

CODE

COMPLETE

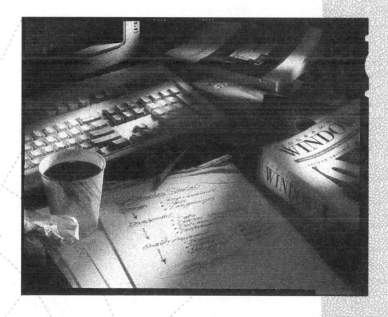

Microsoft
P R E S S

STEVE McCONNELL

What The Press Says About Code Complete

"Buy it and use it liberally."
Ed Nisley—*Computer Applications Journal*

"Thorough, fact-filled, and witty....the definitive book on software construction that belongs on every software developer's bookshelf."
Warren Keuffel—*Software Development*

"An exhaustive manual, covering just about everything any programmer should know."
PC Magazine

"Steve McConnell does for software engineering what Michael Abrash did for optimization in Zen of Assembly Language."
PC Techniques

"Every programmer should read this outstanding book."
T.L. (Frank) Pappas—*Computer*

"An invaluable $35 reference."
Peter Coffee—*PC Week*

"Anyone who programs professionally ought to read it."
Jim Kyle—*Windows Tech Journal*

"Don't stop to read the rest of this review. Just run out and buy it."
IEEE Micro

"Code Complete should be required reading for anyone who plans to begin or continue a career in software development."
Tommy Usher—*C User's Journal*

PUBLISHED BY
Microsoft Press
A Division of Microsoft Corporation
One Microsoft Way
Redmond, Washington 98052-6399

Library of Congress Cataloging-in-Publication Data
McConnell, Steven C.
    Code complete : a practical handbook of software construction /
  Steven C. McConnell.
      p. cm.
  Includes bibliographical references and index.
  ISBN 1-55615-484-4
    1. Computer Software--Development--Handbooks, manuals, etc.
  I. Title.
  QA76.76.D3M39   1993
  005.1--dc20   92-41059
                                    CIP

15   QUM   1 0 9

Distributed to the book trade in Canada by Macmillan of Canada, a division
of Canada Publishing Corporation.

Distributed to the book trade outside the United States and Canada by
Penguin Books Ltd.

Penguin Books Ltd., Harmondsworth, Middlesex, England
Penguin Books Australia Ltd., Ringwood, Victoria, Australia
Penguin Books N.Z. Ltd., 182–190 Wairau Road, Auckland 10, New Zealand

British Cataloging-in-Publication Data available.

Apple and Macintosh are registered trademarks of Apple Computer, Inc. The X Window
System is a trademark of the Massachusetts Institute of Technology. Microsoft is a
registered trademark and Microsoft QuickBasic and Windows are trademarks of
Microsoft Corporation. OS/2 and Presentation Manager are registered trademarks
licensed to Microsoft Corporation. UNIX is a registered trademark of UNIX Systems
Laboratories. Smalltalk is a registered trademark of Xerox Corporation.

Acquisitions Editor: Michael Halvorson
Project Editor: Erin O'Connor
Technical Editor: Jeff Carey

Contents

CONSTANT CONSIDERATIONS

QUALITY IMPROVEMENT

Checklists

Reference Tables

Preface

> **The gap between the best software engineering practice and the average practice is very wide—perhaps wider than in any other engineering discipline. A tool that disseminates good practice would be important.**
>
> *Fred Brooks*

MY PRIMARY CONCERN IN WRITING this book has been to narrow the gap between the knowledge of industry gurus and professors on the one hand and common commercial practice on the other. Many powerful programming techniques hide in journals and academic papers for years before trickling down to the programming public.

Although leading-edge software-development practice has advanced rapidly in recent years, common practice hasn't. Many programs are still buggy, late, and over budget, and many fail to satisfy the needs of their users. Researchers in both the software industry and academic settings have discovered effective practices that eliminate most of the programming problems that were prevalent in the seventies and eighties. Because these practices aren't often reported outside the pages of highly specialized technical journals, however, most programming organizations aren't yet using them in the nineties. Sridhar Raghavan and Donald Chand found that it typically takes 5 to 15 years for a research development to make its way into commercial practice (1989). This handbook shortcuts the process, making key discoveries available to the average programmer now.

Who Should Read This Book?

The research and programming experience collected in this handbook will help you to create higher-quality software and to do your work more quickly and with fewer problems. This book will give you insight into why you've had problems in the past and will show you how to avoid them in the future. The programming practices described here will help you keep big projects under control and help you maintain and modify software successfully as the demands of your projects change.

Experienced programmers

This handbook serves experienced programmers who want a comprehensive, easy-to-use guide to software construction. Because this book focuses on implementation, the part of the software-development cycle familiar to all programmers, it makes powerful software-development techniques understandable to self-taught programmers as well as to programmers with formal training.

Self-taught programmers

If you haven't had much formal training, you're in good company. About 100,000 new programmers enter the profession each year (Boehm and Pappaccio 1988), but only about 40,000 computer science degrees are awarded each year (NCES 1991). From these figures it's a short hop to the conclusion that most programmers don't receive a formal education in software development. Many self-taught programmers are found in the emerging group of professionals—engineers, accountants, teachers, scientists, and small-business owners—who program as part of their jobs but who do not necessarily view themselves as programmers. Regardless of the extent of your programming education, this handbook can give you insight into effective programming practices.

Students

The counterpoint to the programmer with experience but little formal training is the fresh college graduate. The recent graduate is often rich in theoretical knowledge but poor in the practical know-how that goes into building production programs. The practical lore of good coding is often passed down slowly in the ritualistic tribal dances of systems architects, analysts, project leads, and more-experienced programmers. Even more often, it's the product of the individual programmer's trials and errors. This book is an alternative to the slow workings of the traditional intellectual potlatch. It pulls together the helpful tips and effective development strategies previously available mainly by hunting and gathering from other people's experience. It's a hand up for the student making the transition from an academic environment to a professional one.

Key Benefits of This Handbook

Whatever your background, this handbook can help you write better programs in less time and with fewer headaches.

Complete software-construction reference. This handbook discusses general aspects of construction such as software quality and ways to think about programming. It gets into nitty-gritty construction details such as steps in building a routine, ins and outs of using data and control structures, debugging, and code-tuning techniques and strategies. You don't need to read it cover to cover to learn about these topics. The book is designed to make it easy to find the specific information that interests you.

Ready-to-use checklists. This book includes checklists you can use to assess your software architecture, design approach, module and routine quality, variable names, control structures, layout, test cases, and much more.

State-of-the-art information. This handbook describes some of the most up-to-date techniques available, many of which have not yet made it into common use. Because this book draws from both practice and research, the techniques it describes will remain useful for years.

Larger perspective on software development. This book will give you a chance to rise above the fray of day-to-day fire fighting and figure out what works and what doesn't. Few practicing programmers have the time to read through the dozens of software-engineering books and the hundreds of journal articles that have been distilled into this handbook. The research and real-world experience gathered into this handbook will inform and stimulate your thinking about your projects, enabling you to take strategic action so that you don't have to fight the same battles again and again.

Concepts applicable to any procedural language. This book describes techniques you can use to get the most out of whatever language you're using, whether it's Pascal, C, C++, Ada, Basic, Fortran, COBOL, or another procedural language.

Code examples. The book contains about 500 examples of good and bad code. I've included so many examples because I learn best from examples. I think other programmers learn best that way too.

The examples are in multiple languages because mastering more than one language is usually a watershed in the career of a professional programmer. Once a programmer realizes that programming principles transcend the syntax of any specific language, the doors swing open to knowledge that truly makes a difference in quality and productivity.

In order to make the multiple-language burden as light as possible, I've avoided esoteric language features except where they're specifically discussed. You don't need to understand every nuance of the code fragments to understand the points they're making. If you focus on the point being illustrated, you'll find that you can read the code regardless of the language. I've tried to make your job even easier by annotating the significant parts of the examples.

Access to other sources of information. This book collects much of the available information on software construction, but it's hardly the last word. Throughout the chapters, "Further Reading" sections describe other books and articles you can read as you pursue the topics you find most interesting.

Where Else Can You Find This Information?

This book synthesizes construction techniques from a variety of sources. In addition to being widely scattered, much of the accumulated wisdom about construction resides outside written sources (Hildebrand 1989). There is nothing mysterious about the effective, high-powered programming techniques used by expert programmers. In the day-to-day rush of grinding out the latest project, however, few experts take the time to share what they have learned. Consequently, programmers may have difficulty finding a good source of programming information.

The techniques described in this book fill the void after introductory and advanced programming texts. After you have read *Introduction to C, Advanced C,* and *Advanced Advanced C,* what book do you read to learn more about programming? You could read books about the details of PC, Macintosh, or UNIX hardware or operating-system functions, or about the details of another programming language—you can't use a language or program in an environment without a good reference to such details. But this is one of the few books that discusses programming per se. Some of the most beneficial programming aids are practices that you can use regardless of the environment or language you're working in. Other books generally neglect such practices, which is why this book concentrates on them.

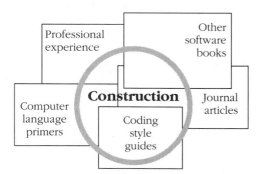

The information in this book is distilled from many sources.

The only other way to obtain the information you'll find in this handbook would be to plow through a mountain of books and a few hundred technical journals and then add a significant amount of real-world experience. If you've already done all that, you can still benefit from this book's collecting the information in one place for easy reference.

Why This Handbook Was Written

The need for development handbooks that capture knowledge about effective development practices is well recognized in the software-engineering community. A report of the Computer Science and Technology Board stated that the biggest gains in software-development quality and productivity will come from codifying, unifying, and distributing existing knowledge about effective software-development practices (CSTB 1990). The board concluded that the strategy for spreading that knowledge should be built on the concept of software-engineering handbooks.

The history of computer programming provides more insight into the particular need for a handbook on software construction.

The topic of construction has been neglected

At one time, software development and coding were thought to be one and the same. But as distinct activities in the software-development life cycle have been identified, the best minds in the field have spent their time analyzing and debating methods of project management, requirements analysis, design, and testing. The rush to study these newly identified areas has left code construction as the ignorant cousin of software development.

The neglect of code construction has been exacerbated by the perception that coding is the dirtiest grunt work of the software-development world. An entry-level programmer in a large organization is typically assigned to code routines that have been specified and designed by someone higher up on the corporate ladder. After a few years, the programmer will be promoted to requirements analysis or project management, and a few years after that may proclaim with pride that it has been years since he or she has had to write any code.

Construction is important

Another reason construction has been neglected by researchers and writers recently is the mistaken idea that, compared to other software-development activities, construction is a relatively mechanical process that presents little opportunity for improvement. Nothing could be further from the truth.

Construction typically makes up about 80 percent of the effort on small projects and 50 percent on medium projects. Construction accounts for about 75 percent of the errors on small projects and 50 to 75 percent on medium and large projects. Any activity that accounts for 50 to 75 percent of the errors presents a clear opportunity for improvement.

Some commentators have pointed out that although construction errors account for a high percentage of total errors, construction errors tend to be less expensive to fix than those caused by analysis and design, the suggestion being that they are therefore less important. The claim that construction errors cost less to fix is true but misleading because the cost of not fixing them can be incredibly expensive. Gerald Weinberg reported that the three most expensive programming errors of all time cost hundreds of millions of dollars each and that each was a one-line, coding-level mistake (1983). Errors in those single lines might be less expensive to fix than errors in analysis or architecture, but an inexpensive cost to fix obviously does not imply that fixing them should be a low priority.

The irony of the shift in focus away from construction is that construction is the only activity that's guaranteed to be done. Requirements can be assumed rather than analyzed; architecture can be shortchanged rather than designed; and system testing can be abbreviated or skipped rather than fully planned and executed. But if there's going to be a program, there has to be construction, and that makes construction a uniquely fruitful area in which to improve development practices.

No comparable book is available

In light of construction's obvious importance, I was sure that someone else would already have written a book on effective construction practices. The need for a book about how to program effectively seemed obvious. But I found that only a few books had been written about construction and then only on parts of the topic. Some were written 15 years ago or more and employed relatively exotic languages such as ALGOL, PL/I, and Ratfor. Some were written by professors who were not working on production code. The professors wrote about techniques that worked for student projects, but they often had little idea of how the techniques would play out in full-scale development environments. Still other books trumpeted the authors' newest favorite methodologies but ignored the huge repository of mature practices that have proven their effectiveness over time.

In short, I couldn't find any book that had even attempted to capture the body of practical techniques available from professional experience, industry research, and academic work. The discussion needed to be brought up to date for current programming languages, interactive environments, and leading-edge development practices. It seemed clear that a book about programming needed to be written by someone who was knowledgeable about the theoretical state of the art but who was also building enough production code to appreciate the state of the practice. I conceived this book as a full discussion of code construction—from one programmer to another.

Acknowledgments

Thanks first to the hardworking people at Microsoft Press for their efforts on this unusually exacting project—especially Erin O'Connor, Mike Halvorson, Arlene Myers, Peggy Herman, Jeff Carey, Alice Smith, Lisa Theobald, Jennifer Harris, Zaafar Hasnain, Pat Forgette, Shawn Peck, Judith Bloch, Eric Stroo, Barbara Runyan, Steve Murray, Katherine Erickson, Jeannie McGivern, Lisa Sandburg, Connie Little, Margarite Hargrave, Sally Brunsman, Carol Luke, Ruth Pettis, Kim Eggleston, Dean Holmes, Jennifer Vick, and Wallis Bolz. Credit also goes to the people at the Bellevue Lake Hills Public Library and the Microsoft Library for processing literally hundreds of requests for hard-to-find books and journal articles.

The work of several software researchers has significantly influenced this book, and they should be acknowledged: Barry Boehm, Capers Jones, Gerald Weinberg, Tom Gilb, Harlan Mills, David Card, Frank McGarry, Robert Grady, Bill Curtis, Ben Shneiderman, Elliot Soloway, and Victor Basili. Many other people in the field deserve recognition, but the people I've singled out here have been collecting hard data from real-world projects to provide a concrete answer to the question What makes for effective software development? It is the work of these people that will ultimately change software development from a trial-and-error trade into a true engineering discipline.

One aspect of writing this book that I've thoroughly enjoyed has been the counsel of an exceptional group of reviewers. Each reviewer commented on the areas he or she felt most qualified to critique, so I've been at the intellectual crossroads of their best thinking. Their comments have improved the book significantly and have also improved me as a programmer.

Thanks to the people who reviewed chapters in their early stages: Tammy Forman, Bill Kiestler, Mike Klein, Margot Page, Peter Páthe, Jack Woolley, Joey Wyrick, and Mike Zevenbergen.

Several more people reviewed the manuscript from start to finish. Thanks to Tony Pisculli, especially for comments about the book's organization; to Dave Moore, especially for discussions about software development at Microsoft; to Pat Forman, especially for her sensitivity to time-pressure and maintenance issues; and to Robert L. Glass, especially for pointers to related information.

I'd also like to acknowledge several people with whom I had key conversations while the book was in its early stages and who also reviewed the manuscript. Thanks to Wayne Beardsley for helping to set the tone and direction of the book while the contents were still evolving, to Brian Daugherty for pointing out redundancies and preventing the book from being 500 pages longer, to Hank Meuret for paying special attention to code examples and coding details, to Greg Hitchcock for rooting out passages in which I embraced software-engineering dogma without asking enough questions, and to Al Corwin for his vigorous defense of the better software-engineering practices.

Extra thanks go to Tony Garland for his particularly thorough and perceptive review. His comments improved nearly every page, and he often reminded me that construction practices deserved more attention than they had recently received. His comments, like those of all the other reviewers, embodied the ideal of constructive criticism.

Each reviewer disagreed with at least a few of the recommendations I've made in these pages. Because I believe this kind of book should bear the distinctive technical signature of a single person rather than the bland stamp of a large committee, I made the final decision about how each issue should be resolved. Thus, in spite of other people's significant contributions, I bear the intellectual responsibility for errors in content or technical judgment. If you have any comments, please feel free to contact me care of Microsoft Press, on the Internet as stevemcc@construx.com, or at my web site at http://www.construx.com/stevemcc.

Tacoma, Washington
New Year's Day, 1993

1

Welcome to Software Construction

Contents

Related Topics

YOU KNOW WHAT "CONSTRUCTION" MEANS when it's used outside software development. "Construction" is the work "construction workers" do when they build a house, a school, or a skyscraper. When you were younger, you built things out of "construction paper." In common usage, "construction" refers to the process of building. The construction process might include some aspects of planning, designing, and checking your work, but mostly "construction" refers to the hands-on part of creating something.

1.1 What Is Software Construction?

Developing computer software can be a complicated process, and in the last 15 years, researchers have identified numerous distinct activities that go into software development. They include

- Problem definition
- Requirements analysis
- Implementation planning
- High-level design, or architecture

- Detailed design
- Construction, or implementation
- Integration
- Unit testing
- System testing
- Corrective maintenance
- Functional enhancements

If you've worked on informal projects, you might think that this list represents a lot of red tape. If you've worked on projects that are too formal, you *know* that this list represents a lot of red tape. It's hard to strike a balance between too little and too much formality, and that's discussed in a later chapter.

If you've taught yourself to program or worked mainly on informal projects, you might not have made distinctions among the many activities that go into creating a software product. Mentally, you might have grouped all of these activities together as "programming." If you work on informal projects, the main activity you think of when you think about creating software is probably the activity the researchers refer to as "construction."

This intuitive notion of "construction" is fairly accurate, but it suffers from a lack of perspective. Putting construction in its context with other activities helps keep the focus on the right tasks during construction and appropriately emphasizes important nonconstruction activities. Figure 1-1 illustrates construction's scope and place in the classic software life-cycle model.

KEY POINT

As the figure indicates, construction is mostly coding and debugging but also involves elements of detailed design and unit testing. If this were a book about all aspects of software development, it would feature nicely balanced discussions of all activities in the development process. Because this is a handbook of construction techniques, however, it places a lopsided emphasis on construction and only touches on related topics. If this book were a dog, it would nuzzle up to construction, wag its tail at design and testing, and bark at the other development activities.

Construction is also commonly known as "implementation." Other names for it are "coding and debugging," as in the classic model shown in Figure 1-1, and "programming." "Coding" isn't really the best word because it implies the mechanical translation of a preexisting design into a computer language; construction is not at all mechanical and involves substantial creativity and judgment. Throughout the book, I use "implementation" and "programming" interchangeably with "construction."

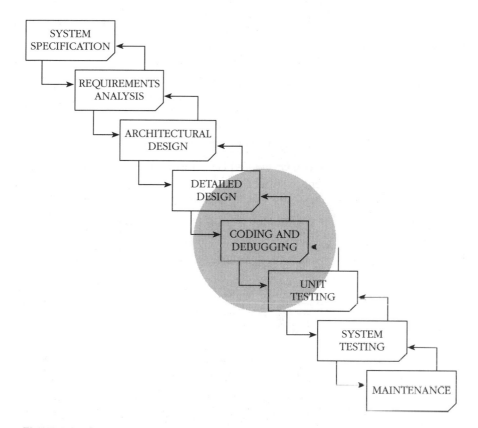

Figure 1-1. *Construction activities are shown inside the gray circle. Construction focuses on coding and debugging but also includes some detailed design and some unit testing. It comes after architectural design and before system testing and maintenance.*

In contrast to Figure 1-1's flat-earth view of software development, Figure 1-2 on the next page shows the round-earth perspective of this book.

Figure 1-1 and Figure 1-2 are high-level views of construction activities, but what about the details? Here are a few of the specific tasks involved in construction:

- Verifying that the groundwork has been laid so that construction can proceed successfully
- Designing and writing routines and modules
- Creating data types and naming variables
- Selecting control structures and organizing blocks of statements
- Finding and fixing errors

- Reviewing other team members' low-level designs and code and having them review yours
- Polishing code by carefully formatting and commenting it
- Integrating software components that have been built separately
- Tuning code to make it smaller and faster

Figure 1-2. *This book focuses on detailed design, coding, debugging, and unit testing in roughly these proportions.*

For an even fuller list of construction activities, look through the chapter titles in the table of contents.

With so many activities at work in construction, you might say, "OK, Jack, what activities are *not* parts of construction?" That's a fair question. Important nonconstruction activities include management, requirements analysis, software architecture, user-interface design, system testing, and maintenance. Each of these activities affects the ultimate success of a project as much as construction—at least the success of any project that calls for more than one or two people and lasts longer than a few weeks. You can find good books on each activity; many are listed in the "Further Reading" sections throughout the book and in the "Where to Go for More Information" chapter at the end of the book.

1.2 Why Is Software Construction Important?

Since you're reading this book, you probably agree that improving software quality and developer productivity is important. Many of today's most exciting projects use software extensively: The space program, aeronautics, medical life-support systems, movie special effects, high-speed financial analysis, and scientific research are a few examples. If you agree that improving software development is important in general, the question for you as a reader of this book becomes Why is construction an important focus?

Here's why:

CROSS-REFERENCE
For details on the relationship between project size and the percentage of time consumed by construction, see "Activity Proportions and Size" in Section 21.2.

Construction is a large part of software development. Depending on the size of the project, construction typically takes 30 to 80 percent of the total time spent on a project. Anything that takes up that much project time is bound to affect the success of the project.

Construction is the pivotal activity in software development. Analysis and design are done before construction so that you can do construction effectively. System testing is done after construction to verify that construction has been done correctly. Construction is at the center of the software-development process.

CROSS-REFERENCE
For data on variations among programmers, see "Individual Variation" in Section 22.5.

With a focus on construction, the individual programmer's productivity can improve enormously. A classic study by Sackman, Erikson, and Grant showed that the productivity of individual programmers varied by a factor of 10 to 20 during construction (1968). Since their study, their results have been confirmed by several other studies. The wide gap in productivity between the average and the best suggests that there is great potential for the average programmer to improve.

Construction's product, the source code, is often the only accurate description of the software. On many projects, the only documentation available to programmers is the code itself. Requirements specifications and design documents can go out of date, but the source code is always up to date. Consequently, it's imperative that the source code be of the highest possible quality. Consistent application of techniques for source-code improvement makes the difference between a Rube Goldberg contraption and a detailed, correct, and therefore informative program. Such techniques are most effectively applied during construction.

Construction is the only activity that's guaranteed to be done. The ideal software project goes through careful requirements analysis and architectural design before construction begins. The ideal project undergoes comprehensive, statistically controlled system testing after construction. Imperfect, real-world projects, however, often skip analysis and design to jump into construction. They drop testing because they have too many errors to fix and they've run out of time. But no matter how rushed or poorly planned a project is, you can't drop construction; it's where the rubber meets the road. Improving construction is thus a way of improving any software-development effort, no matter how abbreviated.

Key Points

- Software construction occurs between architectural design and system testing.
- The main activities in construction are detailed design, coding, debugging, and unit testing.
- Other common terms for "construction" are "implementation" and "programming."
- The quality of the construction substantially affects the quality of the software.
- In the final analysis, your understanding of how to do construction determines how good a programmer you are, and that's the subject of the rest of the book.

2

Metaphors for a Richer Understanding of Programming

Contents

Related Topic

COMPUTER SCIENCE HAS SOME OF THE MOST COLORFUL language of any field. In what other field can you walk into a sterile room, carefully controlled at 68°F, and find viruses, Trojan horses, worms, bugs, bombs, crashes, flames, twisted sex changers, and fatal errors?

These graphic metaphors describe specific software phenomena. Equally vivid metaphors describe broader phenomena, and you can use them to improve your understanding of the software-development process.

The rest of the book doesn't directly depend on the discussion of metaphors in this chapter. Skip it if you want to get to the practical suggestions. Read it if you want to think about software development more clearly.

2.1   The Importance of Metaphors

Important developments often arise out of analogies. By comparing a topic you understand poorly to something similar you understand better, you can come up with insights that result in a better understanding of the less-familiar topic. This use of metaphor is called "modeling."

The history of science is full of discoveries based on exploiting the power of metaphors. The chemist Kekulé had a dream in which he saw a snake grasp its tail in its mouth. When he awoke, he realized that a molecular structure based on a similar ring shape would account for the properties of benzene. Further experimentation confirmed the hypothesis (Barbour 1966).

The kinetic theory of gases was based on a "billiard-ball" model. Gas molecules were thought to have mass and to collide elastically, as billiard balls do, and many useful theorems were developed from this model.

The wave theory of light was developed largely by exploring similarities between light and sound. Light and sound have amplitude (brightness, loudness), frequency (color, pitch), and other properties in common. The comparison between the wave theories of sound and light was so productive that scientists spent a great deal of effort looking for a medium that would propagate light the way air propagates sound. They even gave it a name—"ether"—but they never found the medium. The analogy that had been so fruitful in some ways proved to be misleading in this case.

In general, the power of models is that they're vivid and can be grasped as conceptual wholes. They suggest properties, relationships, and additional areas of inquiry. Sometimes a model suggests areas of inquiry that are misleading, in which case the metaphor has been overextended. When the scientists looked for ether, they overextended their model.

As you might expect, some metaphors are better than others. A good metaphor is simple, relates well to other relevant metaphors, and explains much of the experimental evidence and other observed phenomena.

Consider the example of a heavy stone swinging back and forth on a string. Before Galileo, an Aristotelian looking at the swinging stone thought that a heavy object moved naturally from a higher position to a state of rest at a lower one. The Aristotelian would think that what the stone was really doing was falling with difficulty. When Galileo saw the swinging stone, he saw a pendulum. He thought that what the stone was really doing was repeating the same motion again and again, almost perfectly.

The suggestive powers of the two models are quite different. The Aristotelian who saw the swinging stone as an object falling would observe the stone's weight, the height to which it had been raised, and the time it took to come to rest. For Galileo's pendulum model, the prominent factors were different. Galileo observed the stone's weight, the radius of the pendulum's swing, the angular displacement, and the time per swing. Galileo discovered laws the Aristotelians could not discover because their model led them to look at different phenomena and ask different questions.

Metaphors contribute to a greater understanding of software-development issues in the same way that they contribute to a greater understanding of scientific questions. In his 1973 Turing Award lecture, Charles Bachman described the change from the prevailing earth-centered view of the universe to a sun-centered view. Ptolemy's earth-centered model had lasted without serious challenge for 1400 years. Then in 1543, Copernicus introduced a heliocentric theory, the idea that the sun rather than the earth was the center of the universe. This change in mental models led ultimately to the discovery of new planets, the reclassification of the moon as a satellite rather than a planet, and a different understanding of humankind's place in the universe.

> The value of metaphors should not be underestimated. Metaphors have the virtue of an expected behavior that is understood by all. Unnecessary communication and misunderstandings are reduced. Learning and education are quicker. In effect, metaphors are a way of internalizing and abstracting concepts allowing one's thinking to be on a higher plane and low-level mistakes to be avoided.
>
> *Fernando J. Corbató*

Bachman compared the Ptolemaic-to-Copernican change in astronomy to the change in computer programming in the early 1970s. When Bachman made the comparison in 1973, data processing was changing from a computer-centered view of information systems to a database-centered view. Bachman pointed out that the ancients of data processing wanted to view all data as a sequential stream of cards flowing through a computer (the computer-centered view). The change was to focus on a pool of data on which the computer happened to act (a database-oriented view).

Today it's difficult to imagine anyone's thinking that the sun moves around the earth. Similarly, it's difficult to imagine anyone's thinking that all data could be viewed as a sequential stream of cards. In both cases, once the old theory has been discarded, it seems incredible that anyone ever believed it at all. More fantastically, people who believed the old theory thought the new theory was just as ridiculous then as you think the old theory is now.

The earth-centered view of the universe hobbled astronomers who clung to it after a better theory was available. Similarly, the computer-centered view of the computing universe hobbled computer scientists who held on to it after the database-centered theory was available.

It's tempting to trivialize the power of metaphors. To each of the earlier examples, the natural response is to say, "Well, of course the right metaphor is more useful. The other metaphor was wrong!" Though that's a natural reaction, it's simplistic. The history of science isn't a series of switches from the "wrong" metaphor to the "right" one. It's a series of changes from "worse" metaphors to "better" ones, from less inclusive to more inclusive, from suggestive in one area to suggestive in another.

In fact, many models that have been replaced by better models are still useful. Engineers still solve most engineering problems by using Newtonian dynamics even though, theoretically, Newtonian dynamics have been supplanted by Einsteinian theory.

Software development is a younger field than most other sciences. It's not yet mature enough to have a set of standard metaphors. Consequently, it has a profusion of complementary and conflicting metaphors. Some are better than others. Some are worse. How well you understand the metaphors determines how well you understand software development.

2.2 How to Use Software Metaphors

KEY POINT

A software metaphor is more like a searchlight than a roadmap. It doesn't tell you where to find the answer; it tells you how to look for it. A metaphor serves more as a heuristic than it does as an algorithm.

An algorithm is a set of well-defined instructions for carrying out a particular task. An algorithm is predictable, deterministic, and not subject to chance. An algorithm tells you how to go from point A to point B with no detours, no sidetrips to points D, E, and F, and no stopping to smell the roses or have a cup of joe.

A heuristic is a technique that helps you look for an answer. Its results are subject to chance because a heuristic tells you only how to look, not what to find. It doesn't tell you how to get directly from point A to point B; it might not even know where point A and point B are. In effect, a heuristic is an algorithm in a clown suit. It's less predictable, it's more fun, and it comes without a 30-day money-back guarantee.

Here is an algorithm for driving to someone's house: Take highway 167 south to Sumner. Take the Bonney Lake exit and drive 2.4 miles up the hill. Turn left at the light by the gas station, and then take the first right. Turn into the driveway of the large tan house on the left, at 714 North Cedar.

CROSS-REFERENCE
For details on how to use heuristics in designing software, see "Design Is a Heuristic Process" in Section 7.5.

Here is a heuristic for getting to someone's house: Find the last letter we mailed you. Drive to the town in the return address. When you get to town, ask someone where our house is. Everyone knows us—someone will be glad to help you. If you can't find anyone, call us from a public phone, and we'll come get you.

The difference between an algorithm and a heuristic is subtle, and the two terms overlap somewhat. For the purposes of this book, the main difference between the two is the level of indirection from the solution. An algorithm gives you the instructions directly. A heuristic tells you how to discover the instructions for yourself, or at least where to look for them.

Having directions that told you exactly how to solve your programming problems would certainly make programming easier and the results more predictable. But programming science isn't yet that advanced and may never be. The most challenging part of programming is conceptualizing the problem, and many errors in programming are conceptual errors. Because each program is conceptually unique, it's difficult or impossible to create a general set of directions that lead to a solution in every case. Thus, knowing how to approach problems in general is at least as valuable as knowing specific solutions for specific problems.

How do you use software metaphors? Use them to give you insight into your programming problems and processes. Use them to help you think about your programming activities and to help you imagine better ways of doing things. You won't be able to look at a line of code and say that it violates one of the metaphors described in this chapter. Over time, though, the person who uses metaphors to illuminate the software-development process will be perceived as someone who has a better understanding of programming and produces better code faster than people who don't use them.

2.3 Common Software Metaphors

A confusing abundance of metaphors has grown up around software development. Fred Brooks says that writing software is like farming, hunting werewolves, or drowning with dinosaurs in a tar pit. Paul Heckel says it's like filming *Snow White and the Seven Dwarfs*. David Gries says it's a science. Donald Knuth says it's an art. Watts Humphrey says it's a process. Peter Freeman says it's a system. Harlan Mills says it's like solving mathematical problems, performing surgery, or butchering hogs. Mark Spinrad and Curt Abraham say it's like exploring the Wild West, bathing in cold streams, and eating beans around a campfire.

Software Penmanship: Writing Code

The most primitive metaphor for software development grows out of the expression "writing code." The writing metaphor suggests that developing a program is like writing a casual letter—you sit down with pen, ink, and paper and write it from start to finish. It doesn't require any formal planning, and you figure out what you want to say as you go.

Many ideas derive from the writing metaphor. Jon Bentley says you should be able to sit down by the fire with a glass of brandy, a good cigar, and your favorite hunting dog to enjoy a "literate program" the way you would a good novel. Brian Kernighan and P. J. Plauger named their programming-style book *The Elements of Programming Style* after the writing-style book *The Elements of Style*. Programmers often talk about "program readability."

In a few small cases, the letter-writing metaphor works adequately, but in the rest, it leaves the party early—it doesn't describe software development fully or adequately. Writing is usually a one-person activity, whereas a software project will most likely involve many people with many different responsibilities. When you finish writing a letter, you stuff it into an envelope and mail it. You can't change it anymore, and for all intents and purposes it's complete. Software isn't as difficult to change and is hardly ever fully complete. About 50 percent of the development effort on a typical software system comes after its initial release (Lientz and Swanson 1980). In writing, a high premium is placed on originality. In software construction, focusing on original work is often less effective than focusing on the reuse of code from previous projects. In short, the writing metaphor implies a software-development process that's too simple and rigid to be healthy.

HARD DATA

Plan to throw one away; you will, anyhow.

Fred Brooks

If you plan to throw one away, you will throw away two.

Craig Zerouni

Unfortunately, the letter-writing metaphor has been perpetuated by the most popular software book on the planet, Fred Brooks's *The Mythical Man-Month*. Brooks says, "Plan to throw one away; you will, anyhow." This conjures up an image of a pile of half-written drafts thrown into a wastebasket. Planning to throw one away might be practical when you're writing a polite how-do-you-do to your aunt, and it might have been state-of-the-art software-engineering practice in 1975, when Brooks wrote his book.

The letter-writing metaphor suggests that the software process relies on expensive trial and error rather than careful planning and design.

But extending the metaphor of "writing" software to a plan to throw one away is poor advice for software development in the 1990s, when a major system already costs as much as a 10-story office building or an ocean liner. It's easy to grab the brass ring if you can afford to sit on your favorite wooden pony for an unlimited number of spins around the carousel. The trick is to get it the first time around—or to take several chances when they're cheapest. Other metaphors better illuminate ways of attaining such goals.

Software Farming: Growing a System

In contrast to the rigid writing metaphor, some software developers say you should envision creating software as something like planting seeds and growing crops. You design a piece, code a piece, test a piece, and add it to the system a little bit at a time. By taking small steps, you minimize the trouble you can get into at any one time.

KEY POINT

FURTHER READING
For an illustration of a different farming metaphor, one that's applied to software maintenance, see the chapter "On the Origins of Designer Intuition" in *Rethinking Systems Analysis and Design* (Weinberg 1988).

Sometimes a good technique is described with a bad metaphor. In such cases, try to keep the technique and come up with a better metaphor. In this case, the incremental technique is valuable, but the farming metaphor is terrible.

The idea of doing a little bit at a time might bear some resemblance to the way crops grow, but the farming analogy is weak and uninformative, and it's easy to replace with the better metaphors described in the following sections. It's hard to extend the farming metaphor beyond the simple idea of doing things a little bit at a time. If you buy into the farming metaphor, you might find yourself talking about fertilizing the system plan, thinning the detailed design, increasing code yields through effective land management, and harvesting the code itself. You'll talk about rotating in a crop of assembler instead of barley, of letting the land rest for a year to increase the supply of nitrogen in the hard disk.

The weakness in the software-farming metaphor is its suggestion that you don't have any direct control over how the software develops. You plant the code seeds in the spring. *Farmer's Almanac* and the Great Pumpkin willing, you'll have a bumper crop of code in the fall.

It's hard to extend the farming metaphor to software development appropriately.

Software Oyster Farming: System Accretion

Sometimes people talk about growing software when they really mean software accretion. The two metaphors are closely related, but software accretion is the more insightful image. "Accretion," in case you don't have a dictionary handy, means any growth or increase in size by a gradual external addition or inclusion. Accretion describes the way an oyster makes a pearl, by gradually adding small amounts of calcium carbonate. In geology, "accretion" means a slow addition to land by the deposit of waterborne sediment. In legal terms, "accretion" means an increase of land along the shores of a body of water by the deposit of waterborne sediment.

CROSS-REFERENCE
For details on how to apply incremental strategies to system integration, see "Incremental Integration" in Section 27.2.

This doesn't mean that you have to learn how to make code out of waterborne sediment; it means that you have to learn how to add to your software systems a small amount at a time. Another word closely related to accretion is "incremental." Incremental designing, building, and testing are some of the most powerful software-development concepts available. The word "incremental" has never achieved the designer status of "structured" or "object-oriented," so no one has ever written a book on "incremental software engineering." That's too bad because the collection of techniques in such a book would be exceptionally potent.

In incremental development, you first make the simplest possible version of the system that will run. It doesn't have to accept realistic input, it doesn't have to perform realistic manipulations on data, it doesn't have to produce realistic output—it just has to be a skeleton strong enough to hold the real system as it's developed. It might call dummy routines for each of the basic functions you have identified. This basic beginning is like the oyster's beginning a pearl with a small grain of sand.

After you've formed the skeleton, little by little you lay on the muscle and skin. You change each of the dummy routines to a real routine. Instead of having your program pretend to accept input, you drop in code that accepts real input. Instead of having your program pretend to produce output, you drop in code that produces real output. You add a little bit of code at a time until you have a fully working system.

The anecdotal evidence in favor of this approach is impressive. Fred Brooks, who in 1975 advised building one to throw away, says that nothing in the past decade has so radically changed his own practice or its effectiveness (1987).

The strength of the incremental metaphor as a metaphor is that it doesn't overpromise. It's harder than the farming metaphor to extend inappropriately. The image of an oyster forming a pearl is a good way to visualize incremental development, or accretion.

Software Construction: Building Software

KEY POINT

The image of "building" software is more useful than that of "writing" or "growing" software, and it's compatible with the idea of software accretion. Building software implies many stages of planning, preparation, and execution. When you explore the metaphor, you find many other parallels.

Building a 4-foot tower requires a steady hand, a level surface, and 10 un-damaged beer cans. Building a tower 100 times that size doesn't merely re-quire 100 times as many beer cans. It requires a different kind of planning and construction altogether.

If you're building a simple structure—a doghouse, say—you can drive to the lumber store and buy some wood and nails. By the end of the afternoon, you'll have a new house for Fido. If you forget to provide for a door or make some other mistake, it's not a big problem; you can fix it or even start over from the beginning. All you've wasted is part of an afternoon. This loose ap-proach is appropriate for tiny software projects too. If you use the wrong design for 25 lines of code, you can start over completely without losing much.

The penalty for a mistake on a simple structure is only a little time and maybe some embarrassment.

If you're building a house, the building process is a lot more complicated, and so are the consequences of poor design. First you have to decide what kind of house you want to build—analogous in software development to problem definition. Then you and an architect have to come up with a general design and get it approved. This is similar to software architectural design. You draw detailed blueprints and hire a contractor. This is similar to detailed software design. You prepare the building site, lay a foundation, frame the house, put siding and a roof on it, and plumb and wire it. This is similar to software con-struction. When most of the house is done, the landscapers and interior designers come in to make the best of your land and the home you've built. This is similar to software optimization. Throughout the process, various in-spectors come to check the site, foundation, frame, wiring, and other inspect-ables. This is similar to software reviews and inspections.

Greater complexity and size imply greater consequences in both activities. In building a house, materials are somewhat expensive, but the main expense is labor. Ripping out a wall and moving it six inches is expensive not because you waste a lot of nails but because you have to pay the people for the extra time it takes to move the wall. You have to make the design as good as possible so that you don't waste time fixing mistakes that could have been avoided. In building a software product, materials are even less expensive, but labor costs just as much. Changing a report format is just as expensive as moving a wall in a house because the main cost component in both cases is people's time.

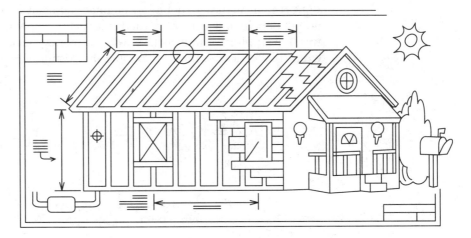

More complicated structures require more careful planning.

What other parallels do the two activities share? In building a house, you won't try to build things you can buy already built. You'll buy a washer and dryer, dishwasher, refrigerator, and freezer. Unless you're a mechanical wizard, you won't consider building them yourself. You'll also buy prefabricated cabinets, counters, windows, doors, and bathroom fixtures. If you're building a software system, you'll do the same thing. You'll make extensive use of high-level language features rather than writing your own operating-system-level code. You might also use prebuilt libraries of scientific, screen-manipulation, database-manipulation, and parsing routines. It generally doesn't make sense to code things you can buy ready made.

If you're building a fancy house with first-class furnishings, however, you might have your cabinets custom made. You might have a dishwasher, refrigerator, and freezer built in to look like the rest of your cabinets. You might have windows custom made in unusual shapes and sizes. This customization has parallels in software development. If you're building a first-class software product, you might build your own scientific functions for better speed or accuracy. You might build your own screen, database, and parsing routines to give your system a seamless, perfectly consistent look and feel.

The two activities share penalties too. Both processes have to go on according to a carefully planned sequence. If you build software in the wrong order, it's hard to code, hard to test, and hard to debug. It can take longer to complete, or the project can fall apart because everyone's work is too complex and therefore too confusing when it's all combined.

If you do a poor job building an office building, you endanger the people who work in the building. Likewise, if you write medical, avionics, air-traffic-control, manufacturing-control, or engineering-analysis software poorly, you can put people in danger. Physical danger is the worst but not the only problem. If your client stands to lose a lot of money because your program is wrong, that's bad too. Innocent people shouldn't be forced to pay for inferior software development.

Making changes in the software brings up another parallel with building construction. To move that wall six inches costs more if the wall is load-bearing than if it's merely a partition between rooms. Similarly, making structural changes in a program costs more than adding or deleting peripheral features.

Finally, the construction analogy holds up for extremely large software projects. Because the penalty for failure in an extremely large structure is severe, the structure has to be over-engineered. Builders make and inspect their plans carefully. They build in margins of safety; it's better to pay 10 percent more for stronger material than to have a skyscraper fall over. A great deal of attention is paid to timing. When the Empire State Building was built, each delivery truck had a 15-minute margin in which to make its delivery. If a truck wasn't in place at the right time, the whole project was delayed.

Likewise, for extremely large software projects, planning of a higher order is needed than for projects that are merely large. Capers Jones estimates, for example, that on a 750,000-line system, about 6000 pages of functional specs would be required (1977). It's unlikely that an individual would be able to understand the complete design for a project of this size—or even read it. Over-engineering is appropriate, and proper timing of component deliveries becomes crucial. We build software projects comparable in economic size to the Empire State Building, and technical and managerial controls of similar stature are needed. We have only begun to think about techniques for handling projects of such size.

The analogy could be extended in a variety of other directions, which is why the building-construction metaphor is so powerful. Many terms common in software development derive from the building metaphor: software architecture, scaffolding, construction, tearing code apart, plugging in a routine. You'll probably hear many more.

Applying Software Techniques: The Intellectual Toolbox

The methodology used
should be based on
choice of the latest
and best, and not
based on ignorance. It
should also be laced
liberally with the old
and dependable.

Harlan Mills

People who are effective at developing high-quality software have spent years accumulating dozens of techniques, tricks, and magic incantations. The techniques are not rules; they are analytical tools. A good craftsman knows the right tool for the job and knows how to use it correctly. Programmers do too. The more you learn about programming, the more you fill your mental toolbox with analytical tools and the knowledge of when to use them and how to use them correctly.

Regarding methods and techniques as tools is useful because it engenders a practical attitude toward them. You don't have to treat the latest object-oriented widget as a gift from heaven—you can treat it as a tool that's useful in some circumstances and not useful in others. If your only tool is a hammer, you see the whole world as a nail. Fortunately, no one is peddling $500-a-day seminars that tell you to buy into the hammer as a cure-all. No one asks you to give up your screwdriver, wrench, or vise grips.

CROSS-REFERENCE
For details on selecting and
combining methods in
design, see Section 7.5.

In software, people tell you to buy into certain software-development methods to the exclusion of other methods. That's unfortunate because if you buy into any single methodology 100 percent, you'll see the whole world in terms of that methodology. In some instances, you'll miss opportunities to use other methods better suited to your current problem. The toolbox metaphor helps to keep all the methods, techniques, and tips in perspective—ready for use when appropriate.

Combining Metaphors

Because metaphors are heuristic rather than algorithmic, they are not mutually exclusive. You can use both the accretion and the construction metaphors. You can use "writing" if you want to, and you can combine writing with farming, hunting for werewolves, or drowning in a tar pit with dinosaurs. Use whatever metaphor or combination of metaphors stimulates your own thinking.

Using metaphors is a fuzzy business. You have to extend them to benefit from the heuristic insights they provide. But if you extend them too far or in the wrong direction, they'll mislead you. Just as you can misuse any powerful tool, you can misuse metaphors, but their power makes them a valuable part of your intellectual toolbox.

Further Reading

Among general books on metaphors, models, and paradigms, the touchstone book is by Thomas Kuhn.

Kuhn, Thomas S. *The Structure of Scientific Revolutions*, 2d ed. Chicago: University of Chicago Press, 1970. Kuhn's book on how scientific theories emerge, evolve, and succumb to other theories in a Darwinian cycle set the philosophy of science on its ear when it was first published in 1962. It's clear and short, and it's loaded with interesting examples.

Barbour, Ian G. *Myths, Models, and Paradigms: A Comparative Study in Science and Religion.* New York: Harper & Row, 1974. Although the book contains a lot of discussion unrelated to the subject of software-development metaphors, Barbour's Chapter 3, "Models in Science," is a good survey of popular scientific models, kinds of models, and philosophical approaches to the use of models. Chapters 2 and 5, "Symbol and Myth" and "Complementary Models," further discuss the use of metaphors and models.

Floyd, Robert W. "The Paradigms of Programming." 1978 Turing Award Lecture. *Communications of the ACM*, August 1979, 455–60. This is a fascinating discussion of models in software development and applies Kuhn's ideas to the topic.

Key Points

- Metaphors are heuristics, not algorithms. As such, they tend to be a little sloppy.
- Metaphors help you understand the software-development process by relating it to other activities you already know about.
- Some metaphors are better than others.
- Treating software construction as similar to building construction suggests that careful preparation is needed and illuminates the difference between large and small projects.
- Thinking of software-development practices as tools in an intellectual toolbox suggests further that every programmer has many tools and that no single tool is right for every job. Choosing the right tool for each problem is one key to being an effective programmer.

3

Prerequisites to Construction

Contents

Related Topics

BEFORE BEGINNING WORK ON A HOUSE, a builder reviews the blueprints, checks that all permits have been obtained, and surveys the house's foundation. A builder prepares for building a skyscraper one way and for building a doghouse a different way. No matter what the project, the preparation is tailored to its needs and done conscientiously before construction begins.

This chapter describes the work that must be done to prepare for software construction. As with building construction, much of the success or failure of the project has already been determined before construction begins. If the foundation hasn't been laid well or the planning is inadequate, the best you can do during construction is to keep the project from failing. If you want to create a polished jewel, you have to start with a diamond in the rough. If you start with plans for a brick, the best you can create is a fancy brick.

Although this chapter lays the groundwork for successful software construction, it doesn't discuss construction directly. If you're feeling carnivorous or you're already well versed in the software-engineering life cycle, look for the construction meat beginning in Chapter 4.

3.1 Importance of Prerequisites

CROSS-REFERENCE
Paying attention to quality is also the best way to improve productivity. For details, see Section 23.5, "The General Principle of Software Quality."

A common denominator of programmers who build high-quality software is their use of high-quality processes. Such processes emphasize quality at the beginning, middle, and end of a project.

If you emphasize quality at the end of a project, you emphasize testing. Testing is what many people think of when they think of software quality assurance. Testing, however, is only one part of a complete quality-assurance strategy, and it's not the most influential part. Testing can't detect a flaw such as building the wrong product or building the right product in the wrong way. Such flaws must be worked out earlier than in testing—before construction begins.

KEY POINT

If you emphasize quality in the middle of the project, you emphasize construction practices. Such practices are the focus of most of this book.

If you emphasize quality at the beginning of the project, you plan for, require, and design a high-quality product. If you start the process with designs for a Fiat, you can test it all you want to, and it will never turn into a Rolls-Royce. You might build the best possible Fiat, but if you want a Rolls-Royce, you have to plan from the beginning to build one. In software development, you do such planning when you define the problem, when you specify the solution, and when you design the solution.

Since construction is in the middle of a project, by the time you get to construction, the earlier parts of the project have already laid the groundwork for success or failure. During construction, however, you should at least be able to determine how good your situation is and to back up if you see the black clouds of failure looming on the horizon. The rest of this chapter describes in detail why proper preparation is important and tells you how to determine whether you're really ready to begin construction.

Causes of Incomplete Preparation

You might think that all professional programmers know about the importance of preparation and check that the prerequisites have been satisfied before jumping into construction. Unfortunately, that isn't so.

Some programmers don't prepare because they can't resist the urge to begin coding as soon as possible. If you feed your horse at this trough, I have two suggestions. Suggestion 1: Read the argument in the next section. It may tell you a few things you haven't thought of. Suggestion 2: Pay attention to your problems. It takes only a few large programs to learn that you can avoid a lot of stress by planning ahead. Let your own experience be your guide.

Another reason programmers don't prepare is that managers are notoriously unsympathetic to programmers who spend time on construction prerequisites. People such as Ed Yourdon and Tom DeMarco have been banging the requirements and architecture drums for 15 years, and you'd expect that managers would have started to understand that software development is more than coding.

FURTHER READING
For many entertaining variations on this theme, read Gerald Weinberg's classic, *The Psychology of Computer Programming* (Weinberg 1971).

In the late 1980s, however, I was working on a Department of Defense project that was in its requirements-analysis phase when the Army general in charge of the project came for a visit. We told him that we were in the requirements stage and that we were mainly talking to our customer and writing documents. He insisted on seeing code anyway. We told him there was no code, but he walked around a work bay of 100 people, determined to catch someone programming. Frustrated by seeing so many people away from their desks or working on documents, the large, round man with the loud voice finally pointed to the engineer sitting next to me and bellowed, "What's he doing? He must be writing code!" In fact, the engineer was working on a document-formatting utility, but the general wanted to find code, thought it looked like code, and wanted the engineer to be working on code, so we told him it was code.

This phenomenon is known as the WISCA or WIMP syndrome: Why Isn't Sam Coding Anything? or Why Isn't Mary Programming?

If the manager of your project pretends to be a brigadier general and orders you to start coding right away, it's easy to say, "Yes, Sir!" (What's the harm? The old guy must know what he's talking about.) This is a bad response, and you have several better alternatives. First, you can flatly refuse to do work in the wrong order. If your relationship with your boss and your bank account are healthy enough for you to be able to do this, good luck.

Second, you can pretend to be coding when you're not. Put an old program listing on the corner of your desk. Then go right ahead and develop your requirements and architecture documents, with or without your boss's approval. You'll do the project faster and with higher-quality results. From your boss's perspective, ignorance is bliss.

Third, you can educate your boss in the nuances of technical projects. This is a good approach because it increases the number of enlightened bosses in the world. The next section presents an extended rationale for taking the time to do prerequisites before construction.

Finally, you can find another job. Good programmers are in short supply, and life is too short to work in an unenlightened programming shop when plenty of better alternatives are available.

Utterly Compelling and Foolproof Argument for Doing Prerequisites Before Construction

Suppose you've already been to the mountain of problem definition, walked a mile with the man of requirements analysis, shed your soiled garments at the fountain of architectural design, and bathed in the pure waters of prepared-ness. Then you know that before you implement a system, you need to under-stand what the system is supposed to do and how it's supposed to do it.

KEY POINT

Part of your job as a technical employee is to educate the nontechnical people around you about the development process. This section will help you deal with managers and bosses who have not yet seen the light. It's an extended argument for doing requirements and architecture right—before you begin coding, testing, and debugging. Learn the argument, and then sit down with your boss and have a heart-to-heart talk about the programming process.

Appeal to logic

One of the key ideas in effective programming is that preparation is impor-tant. It makes sense that before you start working on a big project, you should plan the project. Big projects require more planning; small projects require less. From a management point of view, planning means determining the amount of time, number of people, and number of computers the project will need. From a technical point of view, planning means understanding what you want to build so that you don't waste money building the wrong thing. Sometimes users aren't entirely sure what they want at first, so it might take more effort than seems ideal to find out what they really want. But that's cheaper than building the wrong thing, throwing it away, and starting over.

It's also important to think about how to build the system before you begin to build it. You don't want to spend a lot of time and money going down blind alleys when there's no need to, especially when that increases costs.

Appeal to analogy

Building a software system is like any other project that takes people and money. If you're building a house, you make architectural drawings and blue-prints before you begin pounding nails. You'll have the blueprints reviewed and approved before you pour any concrete. Having a technical plan counts just as much in software.

You don't start decorating the Christmas tree until you've put it in the stand. You don't start a fire until you've opened the flue. You don't go on a long trip with an empty tank of gas. You don't get dressed before you take a shower, and you don't put your shoes on before your socks. You have to do things in the right order in software too.

Programmers are at the end of the software food chain. The architect consumes the requirements analysis; the designer consumes the architecture; and the coder consumes the design.

Compare the software food chain to a real food chain. In an ecologically sound environment, seagulls eat fresh salmon. That's nourishing to them because the salmon ate fresh herring, and they in turn ate fresh waterbugs. The result is a healthy food chain. In programming, if you have healthy food at each stage in the food chain, the result is healthy code written by happy programmers.

In a polluted environment, the waterbugs have been swimming in nuclear waste. The herring are contaminated by PCBs, and the salmon that eat the herring swam through oil spills. The seagulls are, unfortunately, at the end of the food chain, so they don't eat just the oil in the bad salmon. They also eat the PCBs and the nuclear waste from the herring and the waterbugs. In programming, if your requirements are contaminated, they contaminate the architecture, and the architecture in turn contaminates construction. This leads to grumpy, malnourished programmers and radioactive, polluted software that's riddled with defects.

Appeal to data

Studies over the last 15 years have proven conclusively that it pays to do things right the first time. Unnecessary changes are expensive.

HARD DATA

Data from TRW shows that a change in the early stages of a project, in requirements or architecture, costs 50 to 200 times less than the same change later, in construction or maintenance (Boehm and Pappacio 1988).

Studies at IBM have shown the same thing. Researchers found that purging an error by the beginning of design, code, or unit test allows rework to be done 10 to 100 times less expensively than when it's done in the last part of the process, during unit test or functional test (Fagan 1976).

In general, the principle is to find an error as close as possible to the time at which it was introduced. The longer the defect stays in the software food chain, the more damage it causes further down the chain. Since requirements are done first, requirements defects have the potential to be in the system longer and to be more expensive. Defects inserted into the software upstream also tend to have broader effects than those inserted further downstream. That also makes early defects more expensive.

Robert Dunn compiled Table 3-1 on the next page, which shows the relative expense of fixing defects depending on when they're introduced and when they're found.

Table 3-1. Cost of Fixing Defects Based on When They're Introduced and When They're Detected

	Time Introduced		
Time Detected	Requirements	Design	Code
Analysis	1	—	—
Design	2	1	—
Passive tests	5	2	1
Structural tests	15	5	2
Functional tests	25	10	5

Source: *Software Defect Removal* (Dunn 1984).

The data in Table 3-1 shows that, for example, a requirements-analysis defect that costs $1000 to fix during requirements can cost $25,000 to fix during functional tests. This is a healthy incentive to fix your problems as early as you can. The graph below is a picture of the same phenomenon.

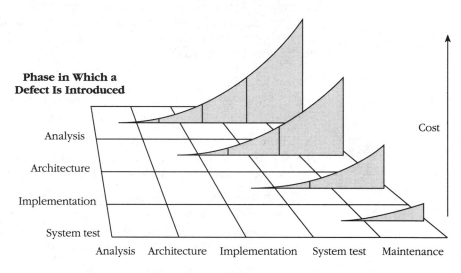

Phase in Which a Defect Is Introduced

Cost

Analysis

Architecture

Implementation

System test

Analysis   Architecture   Implementation   System test   Maintenance

Phase in Which a Defect Is Detected

The cost to fix a defect rises dramatically as the time from when it's introduced to when it's detected increases.

HARD DATA

If your boss isn't convinced by this data, point out that programmers who rush to coding generally take longer to finish their programs than programmers who plan first. A study at the Software Engineering Laboratory—a cooperative project of NASA, Computer Sciences Corporation, and the University of

Maryland—found that extensive computer use (edit, compile, link, test) is correlated with low productivity. Programmers who spent less time at their computers actually finished their projects faster. The implication is that heavy computer users didn't spend enough time on planning and design before coding and testing (Card, McGarry, and Page 1987; Card 1987).

Boss-readiness test

When you think your boss understands the importance of completing prerequisites before moving into construction, try the test below to be sure.

Which of these statements are self-fulfilling prophecies?

- We'd better start coding right away because we're going to have a lot of debugging to do.
- We haven't planned much time for testing because we're not going to find many defects.
- We've put so much thought into the requirements and architectural design that I can't think of any major problems we'll run into during coding or debugging.

All of these statements are self-fulfilling prophecies. Aim for the last one.

The rest of the chapter describes how to determine whether each prerequisite has been "prereq'd" or "prewrecked."

3.2 Problem-Definition Prerequisite

The first prerequisite you need to fulfill before beginning construction is a clear statement of the problem that the system is supposed to solve. Since this book is about construction, the purpose of this section isn't to tell you how to write a problem definition; it's to tell you how to recognize whether one has been written at all and whether the one that's written is good enough to be a foundation for construction.

A problem definition defines what the problem is without any reference to possible solutions. It's a simple statement, maybe one or two pages, and it should sound like a problem. The statement "We can't keep up with orders for the Gigatron" sounds like a problem and is a good problem definition. The statement "We need to optimize our automated data-entry system to keep up with orders for the Gigatron" is a poor problem definition. It doesn't sound like a problem; it sounds like a solution.

Problem definition comes before requirements analysis, which is a more detailed analysis of the problem.

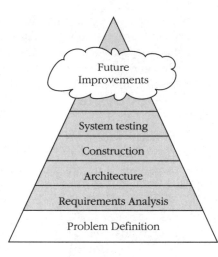

The problem definition lays the foundation for the rest of the programming process.

The problem definition should be in user language, and the problem should be described from a user's point of view. It usually should not be stated in technical computer terms. The best solution might not be a computer program. Suppose you need a report that shows your annual profit. You already have computerized reports that show quarterly profits. If you're locked into the programmer mind-set, you'll reason that adding an annual report to a system that already does quarterly reports should be easy. Then you'll pay a programmer to write and debug a time-consuming program that calculates annual profits. If you're not locked into the computer mind-set, you'll pay your secretary to create the annual figures by taking one minute to add up the quarterly figures on a pocket calculator.

The exception to this rule applies when the problem is with the computer: Compile times are too slow or the programming tools are buggy. Then it's appropriate to state the problem in computer or programmer terms.

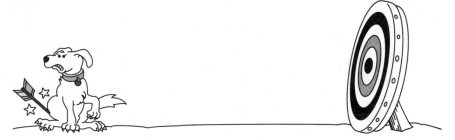

Without a good problem definition, you might put effort into solving the wrong problem. Be sure you know what you're aiming at before you shoot.

KEY POINT

The penalty for failing to define the problem is that you can waste a lot of time solving the wrong problem. This is a double-barreled penalty because you also don't solve the right problem.

3.3 Requirements Prerequisite

Requirements describe in detail what a software system is supposed to do, and they are the first step toward a solution. The requirements activity is also known as "requirements analysis," "requirements definition," "software requirements," "specification," "functional spec," "spec," and "analysis."

Why Have Formal Requirements?

An explicit set of requirements is important for several reasons.

Explicit requirements help to ensure that the user rather than the programmer drives the system's functionality. If the requirements are explicit, the user can review them and agree to them. If they're not, the programmer usually ends up making requirements decisions during programming. Explicit requirements keep you from guessing what the user wants.

Explicit requirements also help to avoid arguments. You decide on the scope of the system before you begin programming. If you have a disagreement with another programmer about what the program is supposed to do, you can resolve it by looking at the written requirements.

KEY POINT

Paying attention to requirements helps to minimize changes to a system after development begins. If you find a coding error during coding, you change a few lines of code and work goes on. If you find a requirements error during coding, you have to alter the design to meet the changed requirement. You might have to throw away part of the old design, and because it has to accommodate code that's already written, the new design will take longer than it would have in the first place. You also have to discard code and test cases affected by the requirement change and write new code and test cases. Even code that's otherwise unaffected must be retested so that you can be sure the changes in other areas haven't introduced any new errors.

HARD DATA

Data from IBM, GTE, and TRW indicates that on large projects an error in requirements detected during the architecture stage is typically 5 times as expensive to correct as it would be if it were detected during the requirements stage. If detected during coding, it's 10 times as expensive; during unit or system test, 20 times; during acceptance test, 50 times; and during maintenance, a whopping 100 times as expensive as it would be if it were detected during

Without good requirements analysis, you can have the right general problem but miss the mark on specific aspects of the problem.

the requirements phase (Boehm 1981). On smaller projects with lower administrative costs, the multiplier in the maintenance phase is closer to 20 than 100. In either case, it's not money you'd want to have taken out of your salary.

Specifying requirements adequately is a key to project success, perhaps even more important than effective construction techniques. Many good books have been written about how to specify requirements well. Consequently, the next few sections don't tell you how to do a good job of specifying requirements; they tell you how to determine whether the requirements have been done well and how to make the best of the requirements you have.

The Myth of Stable Requirements

Requirements are like water. They're easier to build on when they're frozen.

Anon.

Stable requirements are the holy grail of software development. With stable requirements, a project can proceed from architecture to design to coding to testing in a way that's orderly, predictable, and calm. This is software heaven! You have predictable expenses, and you never have to worry about a feature costing 100 times as much to implement as it would otherwise because your user didn't think of it until you were finished debugging.

It's fine to hope that once your customer has accepted a requirements document, no changes will be needed. On a typical project, however, the customer can't reliably describe what is needed before the code is written. The problem isn't that customers are a lower life-form. Just as the more you work with the project, the better you understand it, the more they work with it, the better they understand it. The development process helps customers better understand their own needs, and this is a major source of requirements changes

(Curtis, Krasner, and Iscoe 1988). A plan to follow the requirements rigidly is actually a plan not to respond to your customer.

HARD DATA

How much change is typical? On a typical sample of roughly one million instructions, a study at IBM found that the average project experiences a 25 percent change in requirements during development (Boehm 1981).

Maybe you think the Edsel was the greatest car ever made, belong to the Flat Earth Society, and vote for George McGovern every four years. If you do, go ahead and believe that requirements won't change on your projects. If, on the other hand, you've stopped believing in Santa Claus and the Tooth Fairy, or at least have stopped admitting it, you can take several steps to minimize the impact of requirements changes.

Handling Requirements Changes During Construction

KEY POINT

Here are several things you can do to make the best of changing requirements during the construction phase.

Use the requirements checklist at the end of the section to assess the quality of your requirements. If your requirements aren't good enough, stop work, back up, and make them right before you proceed. Sure, it feels like you're getting behind if you stop coding at this stage. But if you're driving from Chicago to Los Angeles, is it a waste of time to stop and look at a road map when you see signs for New York? No. If you're not heading in the right direction, stop and check your course.

Make sure everyone knows the cost of requirements changes. Clients get excited when they think of a new feature. In their excitement, their blood thins and runs to their medulla oblongata and they become giddy, forgetting all the meetings you had to discuss requirements, the signing ceremony, and the completed requirements document. The easiest way to handle such feature-intoxicated people is to say, "Gee, that sounds like a great idea. Since it's not in the requirements document, I'll work up a revised schedule and cost estimate so that you can decide whether you want to do it now or later." The words "schedule" and "cost" are more sobering than coffee and a cold shower, and many "must haves" will quickly turn into "nice to haves."

If your organization isn't sensitive to the importance of doing requirements first, point out that changes at requirements time are much cheaper than changes later. Use this chapter's "Utterly Compelling and Foolproof Argument for Doing Prerequisites Before Construction."

CROSS-REFERENCE
For details on handling
changes to design
and code, see Section
22.2, "Configuration
Management."

Set up a change-control procedure. If your client's excitement persists, consider establishing a formal change-control board to review such proposed changes. It's all right for customers to change their minds and to realize that they need more capabilities. The problem is their suggesting changes so frequently that you can't keep up. Having a built-in procedure for controlling changes makes everyone happy. You're happy because you know that you'll have to work with changes only at specific times. Your customers are happy because they know that you have a plan for handling their input.

CROSS-REFERENCE
For details on incremental
development approaches,
see Section 27.3, "Incre-
mental Integration
Strategies," and Section
27.4, "Evolutionary
Delivery."

Use development approaches that accommodate changes. Some development approaches maximize your ability to respond to changing requirements. A prototyping approach helps you explore a system's requirements before you send your forces in to build it. Evolutionary delivery is an approach that delivers the system in stages. You can build a little, get a little feedback from your users, adjust your design a little, make a few changes, and build a little more. The key is using short development cycles so that you can respond to your users quickly.

Dump the project. If the requirements are especially bad or volatile and none of the suggestions above are workable, cancel the project. Even if you can't really cancel the project, think about what it would be like to cancel it. Think about how much worse it would have to get before you would cancel it. If there's a case in which you would dump it, at least ask yourself how much difference there is between your case and that case.

CHECKLIST

Requirements

CROSS-REFERENCE
For details on the differences between formal and
informal projects (often
caused by differences in
project size), see Chapter
21, "How Program Size
Affects Construction."

The requirements checklist contains a list of questions to ask yourself about your project's requirements. This book doesn't tell you how to do a good requirements analysis, and the list won't tell you how to do one either. Use the list as a sanity check at construction time to determine how solid the ground that you're standing on is—where you are on the requirements Richter scale.

Not all of the checklist questions will apply to your project. If you're working on an informal project, you'll find some that you don't even need to think about. You'll find others that you need to think about but don't need to answer formally. If you're working on a large, formal project, however, you may need to consider every one.

(continued)

Requirements checklist, *continued*

REQUIREMENTS CONTENT

❏ Are all the inputs to the system specified, including their source, accuracy, range of values, and frequency?

❏ Are all the outputs from the system specified, including their destination, accuracy, range of values, frequency, and format?

❏ Are all the report formats specified?

❏ Are all the external hardware and software interfaces specified?

❏ Are all the communication interfaces specified, including handshaking, error-checking, and communication protocols?

❏ Is the expected response time, from the user's point of view, specified for all necessary operations?

❏ Are other timing considerations specified, such as processing time, data-transfer rate, and system throughput?

❏ Are all the tasks the user wants to perform specified?

❏ Are the data used in each task and the data resulting from each task specified?

❏ Is the level of security specified?

❏ Is the reliability specified, including the consequences of software failure, the vital information that needs to be protected from failure, and the strategy for error detection and recovery?

❏ Is maximum memory specified?

❏ Is the maximum storage specified?

❏ Is the maintainability of the system specified, including its ability to adapt to changes in the operating environment, in its interfaces with other software, in its accuracy, and in its performance?

❏ Are acceptable trade-offs between competing attributes specified— for example, between robustness and correctness?

❏ Is the definition of success included? Of failure?

REQUIREMENTS COMPLETENESS

❏ Where information isn't available before development begins, are the areas of incompleteness specified?

❏ Are the requirements complete in the sense that if the product satisfies every requirement, it will be acceptable?

(continued)

Requirements checklist, *continued*

❏ Are you uneasy about any part of the requirements? Are some parts impossible to implement and included just to please your customer or your boss?

REQUIREMENTS QUALITY

❏ Are the requirements written in user language? Do the users think so?

❏ Does each requirement avoid conflicts with other requirements?

❏ Do the requirements avoid specifying the design?

❏ Are the requirements at a fairly consistent level of detail? Should any requirement be specified in more detail? Should any requirement be specified in less detail?

❏ Are the requirements clear enough to be turned over to an independent group for implementation and still be understood?

❏ Is each item relevant to the problem and its solution? Can each item be traced to its origin in the problem environment?

❏ Is each requirement testable? Will it be possible for independent testing to determine whether each requirement has been satisfied?

❏ Are all possible changes to the requirements specified, including the likelihood of each change?

Further Reading on Requirements Specification

Here are a few books that give much more detail on specifying requirements.

DeMarco, Tom. *Structured Analysis and Systems Specification: Tools and Techniques.* Englewood Cliffs, N.J.: Prentice Hall, 1979. This is the classic on requirements specification.

Yourdon, Edward. *Modern Structured Analysis.* New York: Yourdon Press, 1989. This recent book contains a lot of information on textual and diagrammatic tools for specifying requirements.

Hatley, Derek J., and Imtiaz A. Pirbhai. *Strategies for Real-Time System Specification.* New York: Dorset House, 1988. This is a good alternative to either DeMarco's or Yourdon's book. It emphasizes real-time systems and extends the graphical notation used by DeMarco and Yourdon to real-time environments.

Shlaer, Sally, and Stephen Mellor. *Object Oriented Systems Analysis—Modeling the World in Data*. Englewood Cliffs, N.J.: Prentice Hall, 1988. This book discusses requirements analysis in an object-oriented framework.

IEEE Std 830-1984. *Guide for Software Requirements Specifications,* in IEEE 1991. This document is the IEEE-ANSI guide for writing software requirements specifications. It describes what should be included in the specification document and shows several alternative outlines for one.

Gibson, Elizabeth. "Objects—Born and Bred." *Byte,* October 1990: 245–54. This article is a concise introduction to object-oriented requirements analysis.

3.4 Architecture Prerequisite

CROSS-REFERENCE
For more information on
design, see Chapters 5
through 7.

Software architecture is the high-level part of software design, the frame that holds the more detailed parts of the design. Architecture is also known as "system architecture," "design," "high-level design," and "top-level design." Typically, the architecture is described in a single document referred to as the "architecture specification" or "top-level design."

Because this book is about construction, this section doesn't tell you how to develop a software architecture; it focuses on how to determine the quality of an existing architecture. Because architecture is one step closer to construction than requirements, however, the discussion of architecture is more detailed than the discussion of requirements.

KEY POINT

Why have architecture as a prerequisite? Because the quality of the architecture determines the conceptual integrity of the system. That in turn determines the ultimate quality of the system. Good architecture makes construction easy. Bad architecture makes construction almost impossible.

Without good software architecture, you may have the right problem but the wrong solution. It may be impossible to have a successful construction phase.

HARD DATA

Architectural changes are expensive to make during construction or later. The time needed to fix an error in a software architecture is, on average, less than that needed to fix a requirements error but more than that needed to fix a coding error (Basili and Perricone 1984). Architecture changes are like requirements changes: Whether the architectural changes arise from the need to fix errors or the need to make improvements, the earlier you can identify the changes, the better.

Typical Architectural Components

CROSS-REFERENCE
For details on lower-level program design, see Chapters 5 through 7.

Many components are common to good system architectures. If you're building the whole system yourself, your work on the top-level design, or architecture, will overlap your work on the detailed design. In such a case, you should at least think about each architectural component. If you're working on a system that was architected by someone else, you should be able to find the important components without a bloodhound, a deerstalker cap, and a magnifying glass. In either case, here are the architectural components to consider.

Program organization

If you can't explain something to a six-year-old, you really don't understand it yourself.

Albert Einstein

A system architecture first needs an overview that describes the system in broad terms. Without such an overview, you'll have a hard time building a coherent picture from a thousand details or even a dozen individual modules. If the system were a little 12-piece jigsaw puzzle, your two-year-old could solve it between spoonfuls of strained asparagus. A puzzle of 12 software modules is harder to put together, and if you can't put it together, you won't understand how a module you're developing contributes to the system.

In the architecture, you should find evidence that alternatives to the final organization were considered and find the reasons the organization used was chosen over the alternatives. It's frustrating to work on a module when it seems as if the module's role in the system has not been clearly conceived. By describing the organizational alternatives, the architecture provides the rationale for the system organization and shows that each module has been carefully considered. One review of design practices found that the design rationale is at least as important for maintenance as the design itself (Rombach 1990).

CROSS-REFERENCE
For details on creating high-quality modules, see Chapter 6, "Three out of Four Programmers Surveyed Prefer Modules."

The architecture should define the major modules in a program. In this case, the word "module" doesn't mean routine. Building-block-level routines aren't usually included in a top-level design. A module is a collection of routines that work together to perform a high-level function such as formatting output, interpreting commands, getting data from files, or accessing major data structures. Every feature listed in the requirements should be covered by at least one module. If a function is claimed by two or more modules, their claims should cooperate, not conflict.

CROSS-REFERENCE
Minimizing what each module knows about other modules is a key part of information hiding. For details, see Section 6.2, "Information Hiding."

What each module does should be well defined. A module should do one task and do it well and it should know as little as possible about the modules with which it interacts. By minimizing what each module knows about each other module, you localize information about the design in single modules.

The interface of each module should be well defined. The architecture should describe which other modules the module can call directly, which it can call indirectly, and which it shouldn't call at all. The architecture should specify the data the module passes to and receives from other modules.

Change strategy

CROSS-REFERENCE
For details on handling changes systematically, see Section 22.2, "Configuration Management."

Because building a software product is a learning process for both the programmers and the users, the product is likely to change throughout its development. Changes arise from volatile data structures and file formats, changed functionality, new features, and so on. The changes can be new capabilities likely to result from planned enhancements, or they can be capabilities that didn't make it into the first version of the system. Consequently, one of the major challenges facing a software architect is making the architecture flexible enough to accommodate likely changes.

Design bugs are often subtle and occur by evolution with early assumptions being forgotten as new features or uses are added to a system.
Fernando J. Corbató

The architecture should describe a strategy for handling changes clearly. The architecture should show that possible enhancements have been considered and that the enhancements most likely are also the easiest to implement. If changes are likely in input or output formats, style of user interaction, or processing requirements, the architecture should show that the changes have all been anticipated and that the effects of any single change will be limited to a small number of modules. The architecture's plan for changes can be as simple as one to put version numbers in data files, reserve fields for future use, or design files so that you can add new tables.

CROSS-REFERENCE
For a full explanation of delaying commitment, see Section 10.3, "Binding Time."

The architecture should indicate the strategies that are used to delay commitment. For example, the architecture might specify that a table-driven technique be used rather than hard-coded *if* tests. It might specify that data for the table is to be kept in an external file rather than coded inside the program, thus allowing changes in the program without recompiling.

Buy-vs.-build decisions

CROSS-REFERENCE
For a list of kinds of commercially available software libraries, see "Code Creation" in Section 20.3.

The most radical solution to building software is not to build it at all—to buy it instead. You can buy database managers, screen generators, report generators, and graphics environments. One of the greatest advantages of programming in an environment such as the Apple Macintosh or Microsoft Windows is the amount of functionality you get automatically: graphics routines, dialog-box managers, keyboard and mouse handlers, code that works automatically with any printer or monitor, and so on.

If the architecture isn't using off-the-shelf components, it should explain the ways in which it expects custom-built components to surpass ready-made libraries.

If the plan calls for using pre-existing software, the architecture should explain how the reused software will be made to conform to the other architectural goals—if it will be made to conform.

HARD DATA

Barry Boehm points out that in the long run, the biggest gains in productivity come from reuse of software (Boehm et al. 1984). Buying code reduces planning, detailed design, testing, and debugging effort. Capers Jones reported that increasing the amount of code you buy from 0 to 50 percent more than doubles your productivity (1986a).

Major data structures

CROSS-REFERENCE
For details on the importance of defining data structures, see Chapter 8, "Creating Data."

The architecture should describe the major files, tables, and data structures to be used. It should describe alternatives that were considered and justify the choices that were made. In *Software Maintenance Guidebook,* Glass and Noiseux argue that data structures affect maintenance so much that they should be chosen through formal studies of the trade-offs involved (1981). If the application maintains a list of customer IDs and the architects have chosen to implement the list of IDs as a sequential-access list, the document should explain why a sequential-access list is better than a random-access list, stack, or hash table. During construction, such information gives you insight into the minds of the architects. During maintenance, the same insight is an invaluable aid. Without it, you're watching a foreign movie with no subtitles.

> **The programmer's primary weapon in the never-ending battle against slow systems is to change the intramodular structure. Our first response should be to reorganize the modules' data structures.**
>
> *Fred Brooks*

Data structures shouldn't be accessible to more than one module, except through access routines that allow access to the data in controlled and abstract ways. This is explained in more detail in Section 6.2, "Information Hiding."

If the program uses a database, the architecture should specify the organization and contents of the database.

Finally, the law of conservation of data should be observed: Each piece of data that comes in should go out or be involved with some other data that does. If it doesn't go out, it doesn't need to come in.

Key algorithms

If the architecture depends on specific algorithms, it should describe or reference them. As for major data structures, the architecture should describe alternatives that were considered and indicate the reasons that certain algorithms were chosen. For example, if sorting is a big part of your system and the architects have specified that a heap sort be used, the architecture should specify why the heap-sort technique was chosen. It should explain why quick sort and insertion sort weren't chosen. If assumptions about the data have been made that lead to choosing a heap sort, the architecture should spell out the assumptions.

Major objects

CROSS-REFERENCE
For details on object-oriented design, see Section 7.3, "Object-Oriented Design."

In an object-oriented system, the architecture should specify the major objects to be implemented. It should identify the responsibilities of each major object and how the object interacts with other objects. It should include descriptions of the class hierarchies, of state transitions, and of object persistence.

The architecture should describe other objects that were considered and give reasons for preferring the organization that was chosen.

Generic functionality

In addition to the functionality required for the specific program, most programs need several kinds of generic functions that deserve a place in the software architecture.

CROSS-REFERENCE
For further reading on user-interface design, see "User-Interface Design" in Section 33.4.

User interface. Sometimes the user interface is specified at requirements time. If it isn't, it should be specified in the software architecture. The architecture should specify command structures, input forms, and menus. Careful architecture of the user interface makes the difference between a well-liked program and one that's never used.

The architecture should be modularized so that a new user interface can be substituted without affecting the processing and output parts of the program. For example, the architecture should make it fairly easy to lop off a group of interactive interface routines and plug in a group of batch interface routines. This ability is often useful, especially since batch interfaces are convenient for software testing at the unit or subsystem level.

The design of user interfaces deserves its own book-length discussion but is unfortunately outside the scope of this book.

Input/output. Input/output is another area that deserves attention in the architecture. The architecture should specify a look-ahead, look-behind, or just-in-time reading scheme. And it should describe the level at which I/O errors are detected: at the field, record, or file level.

Memory management. Memory management is another important area for the architecture to treat. The architecture should estimate the amount of memory used for nominal and extreme cases. For example, if you're writing a spreadsheet, the architecture should estimate the amount of memory required per cell. It should also estimate the memory required for the normal and largest expected spreadsheets. In a simple case, the estimates should show that memory management is well within the capabilities of the intended implementation environment. In a more complex case, the application might be required to perform its own memory management. If it is, the memory manager should be architected as carefully as any other part of the system.

String storage. Character-string storage deserves attention in the architecture for an interactive system. Most interactive systems contain dozens or hundreds of prompts, status displays, help messages, error messages, and so on. Memory used by the strings should be estimated. If the program is to be used commercially, the architecture should show that the typical string issues have been considered, including compressing the strings, maintaining the strings without changing code, and translating the strings into foreign languages with minimal impact on the code. The architecture can decide to use strings in line in the code where they're needed, keep the strings in a data structure and reference them with access routines, or store the strings in a resource file. The architecture should explain which option was chosen and why.

Error processing

HARD DATA

Error processing is turning out to be one of the thorniest problems of modern computer science, and you can't afford to deal with it haphazardly. Some people have estimated that as much as 90 percent of a program's code is written for exceptional, error-processing cases or housekeeping, implying that only 10 percent is written for nominal cases (Shaw in Bentley 1982). With so much code dedicated to handling errors, a strategy for handling them consistently should be spelled out in the architecture. Here are some questions to consider:

FURTHER READING
For a good discussion of the broader topic of exception handling, see the "Exception Handling" chapter in *Rationale for Design of the Ada Programming Language* (Ichbiah 1986).

- Is error processing corrective or merely detective? If corrective, the program can attempt to recover from errors. If it's merely detective, the program can continue processing as if nothing had happened, or it can quit. In either case, it should notify the user that it detected an error.

- Is error detection active or passive? The system can actively anticipate errors—for example, by checking user input for validity—or it can passively respond to them only when it can't avoid them—for example, when a combination of user input produces a numeric overflow. It can clear the way or clean up the mess. Again, in either case, the choice has user-interface implications.

- How does the program propagate errors? Once it detects an error, it can immediately discard the data that caused the error, it can treat the error as an error and enter an error-processing state, or it can wait until all processing is complete and notify the user that errors were detected (somewhere).

- What are the conventions for handling error messages? If the architecture doesn't specify a single, consistent strategy, the user interface will appear to be a confusing macaroni-and-dried-bean collage of different interfaces in different parts of the program. To avoid such an appearance, the architecture should establish conventions for error messages.

CROSS-REFERENCE
A consistent method of handling bad parameters passed to routines is another aspect of error-processing strategy that should be addressed architecturally. For examples, see "Garbage In Does Not Mean Garbage Out" in Section 5.6.

- Inside the program, at what level are errors handled? You can handle them at the point of detection, pass them off to error-handling routines, or pass them up to top-level routines.

- What is the level of responsibility of each module for validating its input data? Is each module responsible for validating its own data, or is there a group of modules responsible for validating the system's data? Can modules at any level assume that the data they're receiving is clean?

Robustness

Robustness is the ability of a system to continue to run after it detects an error. An architecture needs to address robustness in several ways.

Over-engineering. The architecture should clearly indicate what level of over-engineering is expected. Often an architecture specifies a more robust system than that specified by the requirements. One reason is that a system composed of many parts that are minimally robust might be less robust than is required overall. In software, the chain isn't as strong as its weakest link; it's as weak as all the weak links multiplied together.

Specifying a level of over-engineering is particularly important because many programmers over-engineer their modules automatically, out of a sense of professional pride. By setting expectations explicitly in the architecture, you can avoid the phenomenon in which some routines are exceptionally robust and others are barely adequate.

CROSS-REFERENCE
For details on assertions, see "Using Assertions" in Section 5.6.

Assertions. The architecture should also indicate the extent to which the program will use assertions. An assertion is an executable statement placed in the code that allows the code to check itself as it runs. When an assertion is true, that means everything is operating as expected. When it's false, that means it has detected an error in the code. For example, if the system assumes that a customer-information file will never have more than 5000 records, the program might contain an assertion that the number of records is less than or equal to 5000. As long as the number of records is less than or equal to 5000, the assertion will be silent. If it encounters more than 5000 records, however, it will loudly "assert" that it has found an error.

In order to put assertions into a program, you need to know the assumptions that went into designing the system—another reason architectural assumptions should be included in the architecture spec.

FURTHER READING
For a good introduction to fault tolerance, see the articles in the July 1990 issue of *Computer* (published by the IEEE Computer Society). In addition to providing a good introduction, the articles cite many key books and key articles on the topic. Another good source of information about fault tolerance is "Software Safety: Why, What, and How" (Leveson 1986).

Fault tolerance. The architecture should also indicate the kind of fault tolerance expected. Fault tolerance is a collection of techniques that increase a system's reliability by detecting errors, recovering from them if possible, and containing their bad effects if not.

For example, a system could make the computation of the square root of a number fault tolerant in any of several ways:

- The system might back up and try again when it detects a fault. If the first answer is wrong, it would back up to a point at which it knew everything was all right and continue from there.

- The system might have auxiliary code to use if it detects a fault in the primary code. In the example, if the first answer appears to be wrong, the system switches over to an alternative square-root routine and uses it instead.

- The system might use a voting algorithm. It might have three square-root routines that each use a different method. Each routine computes the square root, and then the system compares the results. Depending on the kind of fault tolerance built into the system, it then uses the mean, the median, or the mode of the three results.

- The system might replace the erroneous value with a phony value that it knows to have a benign effect on the rest of the system.

Other fault-tolerance approaches include having the system change to a state of partial operation or a state of degraded functionality when it detects an error. It can shut itself down or automatically restart itself. These examples are necessarily simplistic. Fault tolerance is a fascinating and complex subject—unfortunately, one that's outside the scope of this book.

Performance

FURTHER READING
For additional information on designing systems for performance, see Connie Smith's *Performance Engineering of Software Systems* (1990).

If performance is a concern, performance goals should be specified in the requirements. Performance goals can include both speed and memory use.

The architecture should provide estimates and explain why the architects believe the goals are achievable. If certain areas are at risk of failing to meet their goals, the architecture should say so. If certain areas require the use of specific algorithms or data structures to meet their performance goals, the architecture should say so. The architecture can also include space and time budgets for each module or object.

General architectural quality

A good architecture spec is characterized by discussions of the modules in the system, of the information that's hidden in each module, and of the rationales for including and excluding all possible design alternatives.

The architecture should be a polished conceptual whole with few ad hoc additions. The central thesis of the most popular software-engineering book ever, *The Mythical Man-Month,* is that the essential problem with large systems is maintaining their conceptual integrity (Brooks 1975). A good architecture should fit the problem. When you look at the architecture, you should be pleased by how natural and easy the solution seems. It shouldn't look as if the problem and the architecture have been forced together with duct tape.

You might know of ways in which the architecture was changed during its development. Each change should fit in cleanly with the overall concept. The architecture shouldn't look like a House appropriations bill complete with pork-barrel, boondoggle riders for each representative's home district.

The architecture's objectives should be clearly stated. A design for a system with a primary goal of modifiability will be different from one with a goal of uncompromised performance, even if both systems have the same function.

The architecture should describe the motivations for all major decisions. Be wary of "we've always done it that way" justifications. One story goes that Beth wanted to cook a pot roast according to an award-winning pot roast recipe handed down in her husband's family. Her husband, Abdul, said that his mother had taught him to sprinkle it with salt and pepper, cut both ends off, put it in the pan, cover it, and cook it. Beth asked, "Why do you cut both ends off?" Abdul said, "I don't know. I've always done it that way. Let me ask my mother." He called her, and she said, "I don't know. I've always done it that way. Let me ask your grandmother." She called his grandmother, who said, "I don't know why *you* do it that way. I did it that way because it was too big to fit in my pan."

Good software architecture is largely machine and language independent. Admittedly, you can't ignore the implementation environment. By being as independent of the environment as possible, however, you avoid the temptation to over-architect the system or to do a job that you can do better during construction. If the purpose of a program is to exercise a specific machine or language, this guideline doesn't apply.

The architecture should tread the line between under-specifying and over-specifying the system. No part of the architecture should receive more attention than it deserves, or be over-designed. Designers shouldn't pay attention to one part at the expense of another.

The architecture should explicitly identify risky areas. It should explain why they're risky and what steps have been taken to minimize the risk.

Finally, you shouldn't be uneasy about any parts of the architecture. It shouldn't contain anything just to please the boss. It shouldn't contain anything that's hard for you to understand. You're the one who'll implement it; if it doesn't make sense to you, how can you implement it?

CHECKLIST

Architecture

CROSS-REFERENCE
For details on how to adapt your development approach for programs of different sizes, see Chapter 21, "How Program Size Affects Construction."

Here's a list of issues that a good architecture should address. The list isn't intended to be a guide to architecture but to be a pragmatic way of evaluating the nutritional content of what you get at the programmer's end of the software food chain. Use this checklist as a starting point for your own checklist. As with the requirements checklist, if you're working on an informal project, you'll find some items that you don't even need to think about. If you're working on a larger project, most of the items will be useful.

- ❏ Is the overall organization of the program clear, including a good architectural overview and justification?
- ❏ Are modules well defined, including their functionality and their interfaces to other modules?
- ❏ Are all the functions listed in the requirements covered sensibly, by neither too many nor too few modules?
- ❏ Is the architecture designed to accommodate likely changes?
- ❏ Are necessary buy-vs.-build decisions included?
- ❏ Does the architecture describe how reused code will be made to conform to other architectural objectives?
- ❏ Are all the major data structures described and justified?
- ❏ Are the major data structures hidden behind access routines?
- ❏ Is the database organization and content specified?
- ❏ Are all key algorithms described and justified?
- ❏ Are all major objects described and justified?
- ❏ Is a strategy for handling user input described?
- ❏ Is a strategy for handling I/O described and justified?
- ❏ Are key aspects of the user interface defined?
- ❏ Is the user interface modularized so that changes in it won't affect the rest of the program?
- ❏ Are memory-use estimates and a strategy for memory management described and justified?

(continued)

Architecture checklist, *continued*

❏ Does the architecture set space and speed budgets for each module?

❏ Is a strategy for handling strings described, and are character-string–storage estimates provided?

❏ Is a coherent error-handling strategy provided?

❏ Are error messages managed as a set to present a clean user interface?

❏ Is a level of robustness specified?

❏ Is any part over- or under-architected? Are expectations in this area set out explicitly?

❏ Arc the major system goals clearly stated?

❏ Does the whole architecture hang together conceptually?

❏ Is the top-level design independent of the machine and language that will be used to implement it?

❏ Are the motivations for all major decisions provided?

❏ Are you, as a programmer who will implement the system, comfortable with the architecture?

3.5 Choice-of-Programming-Language Prerequisite

> **By relieving the brain of all unnecessary work, a good notation sets it free to concentrate on more advanced problems, and in effect increases the mental power of the race. Before the introduction of the Arabic notation, multiplication was difficult, and the division even of integers called into play the highest mathematical faculties. Probably nothing in the modern world would have more astonished a Greek mathematician than to learn that…a large proportion of the population of Western Europe could perform the operation of division for the largest numbers. This fact would have seemed to him a sheer impossibility…. Our modern power of easy reckoning with decimal fractions is the almost miraculous result of the gradual discovery of a perfect notation.**
>
> *Alfred North Whitehead*

The programming language in which the system will be implemented should be of great interest to you since you will be immersed in it from the beginning of construction to the end.

Studies have shown that the programming-language choice affects productivity and code quality in several ways.

HARD DATA

Programmers are more productive using a familiar language than an unfamiliar one. Data from TRW shows that programmers working in a language they've used for three years or more are about 30 percent more productive than programmers with equivalent experience who are new to a language (Boehm 1981). A study at IBM found that programmers who had extensive experience with a programming language were more than three times as productive as those with minimal experience (Walston and Felix 1977).

Programmers working with high-level languages achieve better productivity and quality than those working with lower-level languages. Languages such as Pascal and Ada have been credited with improving productivity, reliability, simplicity, and comprehensibility by a factor of 5 over low-level languages such as assembly and machine language (Brooks 1987). You save time when you don't need to have an awards ceremony every time a machine instruction does what it's supposed to. Moreover, higher-level languages are more expressive than lower-level languages. Each line of code says more. Table 3-2 shows typical ratios of source statements in several high-level languages to the equivalent code in assembly:

Table 3.2. Ratio of High-Level–Language Statements to Equivalent Assembly Code

Language	Ratio
Assembler	1 to 1
Ada	1 to 4.5
Quick/Turbo Basic	1 to 5
C	1 to 2.5
Fortran	1 to 3
Pascal	1 to 3.5

Source: *Applied Software Measurement* (Jones 1991).

Data from IBM points to another language characteristic that influences productivity: Developers working in interpreted languages tend to be more productive than those working in compiled languages (Jones 1986a). In languages that are available in both interpreted and compiled forms (such as many versions of Basic and C), you can productively develop programs in the interpreted form and then release them in the better-performing compiled form.

Some languages are better at expressing programming concepts than others. You can draw a parallel between natural languages such as English and programming languages such as Pascal and assembly. In the case of natural languages, the linguists Sapir and Whorf hypothesize a relationship between the expressive power of a language and the ability to think certain thoughts. The Sapir-Whorf hypothesis says that your ability to think a thought depends on knowing words capable of expressing the thought. If you don't know the words, you can't express the thought, and you might not even be able to formulate it (Whorf 1956).

Programmers may be similarly influenced by their languages. The words available in a programming language for expressing your programming thoughts certainly determine how you express your thoughts and might even determine what thoughts you can express.

Evidence of the effect of programming languages on programmers' thinking is common. A typical story goes like this: "We were writing a new system in Pascal, but most of our programmers didn't have much experience in Pascal. They came from Fortran backgrounds. They wrote code that compiled in Pascal, but they were really writing disguised Fortran. They stretched Pascal to use Fortran's bad features (such as *gotos* and global data) and ignored Pascal's rich set of control and data structures." This phenomenon has been reported throughout the industry (Hanson 1984, Yourdon 1986a).

Language Descriptions

FURTHER READING
For an even-handed introduction to fundamental language concepts, see *The Programming Language Landscape* (Ledgard and Marcotty 1986). The book doesn't provide extensive introduction to specific languages, but it is good supplementary reading for anyone whose knowledge of languages comes mainly from language-specific manuals and articles in popular magazines.

The development histories of some languages are interesting, as are their general capabilities. Here are descriptions of the languages used in the examples in this book.

Ada

Ada is a general-purpose, high-level programming language based on Pascal. It was developed under the aegis of the Department of Defense and is especially well suited to real-time and embedded systems. Ada emphasizes data abstraction and information hiding and forces you to differentiate between the public and private parts of each module.

"Ada" was chosen as the name of the language in honor of Ada Lovelace, a mathematician who is considered to have been the world's first programmer. Since 1986, Ada has been mandated for use in all DoD and NATO mission-critical, embedded systems.

Assembly language

Assembly language, or "assembler," is a kind of low-level language in which each statement corresponds to a single machine instruction. Because the statements use specific machine instructions, an assembly language is specific

47

to a particular processor—for example, the Intel 80x86 or the Motorola 680x0. Assembler is regarded as the second-generation language. Most programmers avoid it unless they're pushing the limits in execution speed or code size.

Basic

Basic is a high-level language developed by John Kemeny and Thomas Kurtz at Dartmouth College in the 1960s. The acronym BASIC stands for Beginner's All-purpose Symbolic Instruction Code, and Basic is used extensively to teach students computer programming. IBM popularized Basic on microcomputers by including a Basic interpreter with the IBM PC. Basic for microcomputers is now commonly available in both interpreted and compiled forms.

C

FURTHER READING
If you think C is the greatest language ever, take a look at "C in Education and Software Engineering" (Mody 1991). The article discusses conceptual gaps in C that commonly confuse introductory computer-science students and explains why experienced programmers make so many mistakes in C. It's an eye-opener.

C is a general-purpose, mid-level language that was originally associated with the UNIX operating system. C has some high-level language features, such as structured data, structured control flow, machine independence, and a rich set of operators. It has also been called a "portable assembly language" because it makes extensive use of pointers and addresses, has some low-level constructs such as bit manipulation, and is weakly typed.

C was developed in the 1970s by Dennis Ritchie at Bell Labs. It was originally designed for and used on the DEC PDP-11—whose operating system, C compiler, and UNIX application programs were all written in C. In 1988, an ANSI standard was issued to codify C, and it has become the de facto standard for microcomputer and workstation programming.

C++

C++, an object-oriented language similar to C, was developed by Bjarne Stroustrup at Bell Laboratories in the 1980s. In addition to being compatible with C, C++ provides classes, polymorphism, and function-name overloading, and it provides more robust type checking than C does.

Fortran

Fortran was the first high-level computer language, introducing the ideas of variables and high-level loops. "Fortran" stands for FORmula TRANslation. Fortran was originally developed in the 1950s by John Backus and has seen several significant revisions, including Fortran 77 in 1977, which added block structured IF-THEN-ELSE statements and character-string manipulations. Fortran 90 added user-defined data types, pointers, modules, and a richer set of operations on arrays. As of this writing (late 1992), the Fortran standard is so controversial that most language vendors have not fully implemented it. The discussions in this book confine themselves to Fortran 77. Fortran is used mainly in scientific and engineering applications.

Pascal

Pascal is a high-level language that was originally designed for teaching computer programming. Pascal features strict typing, structured control constructs, and structured data types. It was developed in the late 1960s by Niklaus Wirth and was popularized when Borland International introduced a low-cost microcomputer Pascal compiler in 1984.

Language-Selection Quick Reference

Table 3-3 provides a thumbnail sketch of languages suitable for various purposes. It can point you to languages you might be interested in learning more about. But don't use it as a substitute for a careful evaluation of a specific language for your particular project. The classifications are broad, so take them with a grain of salt, particularly if you know of specific exceptions.

Table 3-3. The Best and Worst Languages for Particular Kinds of Programs

Kind of Program	Best Languages	Worst Languages
Structured data	Ada, C/C++, Pascal	Assembler, Basic
Quick-and-dirty project	Basic	Pascal, Ada, assembler
Fast execution	Assembler, C	Interpreted languages such as many Basics
Mathematical calculation	Fortran	Pascal
Easy to maintain program	Pascal, Ada	C, Fortran
Dynamic memory use	Pascal, C	Basic
For environments with limited memory	Basic, assembler, C	Fortran
Real-time program	Ada, assembler, C	Basic, Fortran
String manipulation	Basic, Pascal	C

3.6 Programming Conventions

In high-quality software, you can see a relationship between the conceptual integrity of the architecture and its low-level implementation. The implementation must be consistent with the architecture that guides it and consistent internally. That's the point of implementation guidelines for variable names, routine names, formatting conventions, and commenting conventions.

In a complex program, architectural guidelines give the program structural balance and implementation guidelines provide low-level harmony, articulating each routine as a faithful part of a comprehensive design. Any large program requires a controlling structure that unifies its programming-language details. Part of the beauty of a large structure is the way in which its detailed parts bear out the implications of its architecture. Without a unifying discipline, your creation will be a jumble of poorly coordinated routines and sloppy variations in style.

What if you had a great design for a painting, but one part was classical, one impressionist, and one cubist? It wouldn't have conceptual integrity no matter how closely you followed its grand design. It would look like a collage. A program needs low-level integrity too.

KEY POINT

Before construction begins, spell out the programming conventions you'll use. They're at such a low level of detail that they're nearly impossible to retrofit into software after it's written. Details of such conventions are provided throughout the book.

3.7 Amount of Time to Spend on Prerequisites

The amount of time to spend on problem definition, requirements analysis, and software architecture varies according to the needs of your project. Generally, a well-run project devotes 20 to 30 percent of its schedule and effort to planning, requirements, and architecture. The 20 to 30 percent doesn't include time for detailed design—that's part of construction.

If requirements are unstable and you're working on a formal project, you'll probably have to work with a requirements analyst to resolve requirements problems. Allow time for your consultation with the requirements analyst and for the requirements analyst to re-interview customers before giving you a workable version of the requirements.

If requirements are unstable and you're working on an informal project, allow time for defining the requirements well enough that their volatility won't hurt construction.

CROSS-REFERENCE
For approaches to handling changing requirements, see "Handling Requirements Changes During Construction" in Section 3.3.

If the requirements are unstable on any project—formal or informal—treat requirements analysis as its own project. Estimate the time for the rest of the project after you've finished the requirements. This is a sensible approach since no one can reasonably expect you to estimate your schedule before you know what you're building. It's as if you were a contractor called to work on a house. Your customer says, "What will it cost to do the work?" You reasonably ask, "What do you want me to do?" Your customer says, "I can't tell you, but

50

how much will it cost?" You reasonably thank the customer for wasting your time and go home.

With a building, it's clear that it's unreasonable for clients to ask for a bid before telling you what you're going to build. Your clients wouldn't want you to show up with wood, hammer, and nails and start spending their money before the architect had finished the blueprints. People tend to understand software development less than they understand two-by-fours and Sheetrock, however, so the clients you work with might not immediately understand why you want to plan requirements analysis as a separate project. You might need to explain your reasoning to them.

When allocating time for software architecture, use an approach similar to the one for requirements analysis. If the software is a type that you haven't worked with before, allow more time for the uncertainty of designing in a new area. Ensure that the time you need to create a good architecture won't take away from the time you need for good work in other areas. If necessary, plan the architecture phase as a separate project too.

3.8 Adapting Prerequisites to Your Project

Prerequisites vary with the size and formality of the project. This chapter noted a few of the differences between large and small projects. You can adapt the prerequisites to your specific project by making them more or less formal as you see fit. For a complete discussion of different approaches to large and small projects (also known as the different approaches to formal and informal projects), see Chapter 21, "How Program Size Affects Construction."

Key Points

- If you want to develop high-quality software, attention to quality must be part of the software-development process from the beginning to the end. Attention to quality at the beginning has a greater influence on product quality than at the end.

- Part of a programmer's job is to educate bosses and coworkers about the software-development process, including the importance of adequate preparation before programming begins.

- If a good problem definition hasn't been specified, you might be solving the wrong problem during construction.

- If a good requirements analysis hasn't been done, you might have missed important details of the problem. Requirements changes cost 20 to 100 times as much in the stages following construction as they do earlier, so be sure the requirements are right before you start programming.

- If a good architectural design hasn't been done, you might be solving the right problem the wrong way during construction. The cost of architectural changes increases as more code is written for the wrong architecture, so be sure the architecture is right too.

- Establish programming conventions before you begin programming. It's nearly impossible to change code to match them later.

- If prerequisites can't be completed before construction begins, try to take an approach to construction that's based on the reality of a shaky foundation.

4

Steps in Building
a Routine

Contents

Related Topics

THIS CHAPTER EXAMINES THE STEPS you typically take to create a routine. Although you could view the whole book as an extended description of how to create a routine, this chapter puts the steps in context. The chapter focuses on programming in the small—on the specific steps for building an individual routine that are critical on projects of all sizes. The chapter also describes the PDL-to-code process, which reduces the work required during design and documentation and improves the quality of both.

If you're an expert programmer, you might just skim this chapter. Look at the summary of steps and review the PDL-to-code process. Few programmers exploit the full power of the process, and it offers many benefits.

4.1 Summary of Steps in Building a Routine

The many low-level details that go into building a routine don't need to be handled in any particular order, but the major activities—designing the routine, checking the design, coding the routine, and checking the code—are done in the order shown in Figure 4-1.

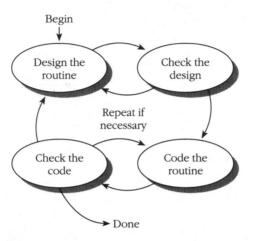

Figure 4-1. *These are the major activities that go into constructing a routine. They're usually performed in the order shown.*

4.2 PDL for Pros

FURTHER READING
If you want to read the original article on PDL, look for "PDL—A Tool for Software Design" (Caine and Gordon 1975). The description of PDL in this section differs substantially from the original conception of the language.

PDL (program design language) was originally developed by the company Caine, Farber & Gordon and has been modified substantially since they published their initial paper on it in 1975. Because PDL resembles English, it's natural to assume that any English-like description that collects your thoughts will have roughly the same effect as any other. In practice, you'll find that some styles of PDL are more useful than others. Here are guidelines for using PDL effectively:

- Use English-like statements that precisely describe specific operations.
- Avoid syntactic elements from the target programming language. PDL allows you to design at a slightly higher level than the code itself. When you use programming-language constructs, you sink to a lower level, eliminating the main benefit of design at a higher level, and you saddle yourself with unnecessary syntactic restrictions.

CROSS-REFERENCE
For details on commenting
at the level of intent, see
"Kinds of Comments" in
Section 19.4.

- Write PDL at the level of intent. Describe the meaning of the approach rather than how the the approach will be implemented in the target language.

- Write PDL at a low enough level that generating code from it will be nearly automatic. If the PDL is at too high a level, it can gloss over problematic details in the code. Refine the PDL in more and more detail until it seems as if it would be easier to simply write the code.

Once the PDL is written, you build the code around it and the PDL turns into programming-language comments. This eliminates most commenting effort. If the PDL follows the guidelines, the comments will be complete and meaningful.

Here's an example of a design in PDL that violates virtually all the principles just described:

CODING HORROR

Example of Bad PDL

```
increment resource number by 1
allocate a dlg struct using malloc
if malloc() returns NULL then return 1
invoke OSrsrc_init to initialize a resource for the operating system
*hRsrcPtr = resource number
return 0
```

What is the intent of this block of PDL? Because it's poorly written, it's hard to tell. This so-called PDL is bad because it includes coding details such as *hRsrcPtr* in specific C-language pointer notation, and *malloc()*, a specific C-language function. This PDL block focuses on how the code will be written rather than on the meaning of the design. It gets into coding details— whether the routine returns a *1* or a *0*. If you think about this PDL from the standpoint of whether it will turn into good comments, you'll begin to understand that it's not much help.

Here's a design for the same operation in a much-improved PDL:

Example of Good PDL

```
Keep track of current number of resources in use
If another resource is available
   Allocate a dialog box structure
   If a dialog box structure could be allocated
      Note that one more resource is in use
      Initialize the resource
      Store the resource number at the location provided by the caller
   Endif
Endif
Return TRUE if a new resource was created; else return FALSE
```

This PDL is better than the first because it's written entirely in English; it doesn't use any syntactic elements of the target language. In the first example, the PDL could have been implemented only in C. In the second example, the PDL doesn't restrict the choice of languages. The second block of PDL is also written at the level of intent. What does the second block of PDL mean? It is probably easier for you to understand than the first block.

Even though it's written in clear English, the second block of PDL is precise and detailed enough that it can easily be used as a basis for source-language code. When the PDL statements are converted to comments, they'll be a good explanation of the code's intent.

Here are the benefits you can expect from using this style of PDL:

- PDL makes reviews easier. You can review detailed designs without examining source code. PDL makes low-level design reviews easier and reduces the need to review the code itself.

- PDL supports the idea of iterative refinement. You start with a high-level architecture, refine the architecture to PDL, and then refine the PDL to source code. This successive refinement in small steps allows you to check your design as you drive it to lower levels of detail. The result is that you catch high-level errors at the highest level, mid-level errors at the middle level, and low-level errors at the lowest level—before any of them becomes a problem or contaminates work at more detailed levels.

FURTHER READING
For more information on the advantages of making changes at the least-value stage, see Andy Grove's *High Output Management* (Grove 1983).

- PDL makes changes easier. A few lines of PDL are easier to change than a page of code. Would you rather change a line on a blueprint or rip out a wall and nail in the two-by-fours somewhere else? The effects aren't as physically dramatic in software, but the principle of changing the product when it's most malleable is the same. One of the keys to the success of a project is to catch errors at the least-value stage, the stage at which the least has been invested. Much less has been invested at the PDL stage than after full coding, testing, and debugging, so it makes economic sense to catch the errors early.

- PDL minimizes commenting effort. In the typical coding scenario, you write the code and add comments afterward. In the PDL-to-code approach, the PDL statements become the comments, so it actually takes more work to remove the comments than to leave them in.

- PDL is easier to maintain than other forms of design documentation. With other approaches, design is separated from the code, and when one changes, the two fall out of agreement. With the PDL-to-code process, the PDL statements become comments in the code. As long as the inline comments are maintained, the PDL's documentation of the design will be accurate.

As a tool for detailed design, PDL is hard to beat. Programmers tend to prefer PDL to flowcharts. (Programmers tend to prefer everything to flowcharts.) One survey found that programmers prefer PDL for the way it eases implementation in a programming language, for its ability to help them detect insufficiently detailed designs, and for the ease of documentation and ease of modification it provides (Ramsey, Atwood, and Van Doren 1983). PDL isn't the only tool for detailed design, but PDL and the PDL-to-code process are useful tools to have in your programmer's toolbox. Try them. The next few sections show you how.

4.3   Design the Routine

CROSS-REFERENCE
For details on other aspects of design, see Chapters 5 through 7.

The first step in constructing a routine is to design it. Suppose that you want to write a routine to output an error message depending on an error code, and suppose that you call the routine *RecordErrorMessage()*. Here's the spec for *RecordErrorMessage()*:

> *RecordErrorMessage()* takes an error code as an input argument and outputs an error message corresponding to the code. It's responsible for handling invalid codes. If the program is operating interactively, *RecordErrorMessage()* prints the message to the user. If it's operating in batch mode, *RecordErrorMessage()* logs the message to a message file. After outputting the message, *RecordErrorMessage()* returns a status variable indicating whether it succeeded or failed.

The rest of the chapter uses this routine as a running example. The rest of this section describes how to design the routine. The activities involved in designing a routine are shown in Figure 4-2 on the next page.

CROSS-REFERENCE
For details on checking prerequisites, see Chapter 3, "Prerequisites to Construction."

Check the prerequisites. Before doing any work on the routine itself, check to see that the job of the routine is well defined and fits cleanly into the overall architecture. Check to be sure that the routine is actually called for, at the very least indirectly, by the project's requirements.

Define the problem the routine will solve. State the problem the routine will solve in enough detail to allow creation of the routine. If the architecture is sufficiently detailed, the job might already be done. The architecture should at least indicate the following:

CROSS-REFERENCE
For details on information hiding, see Section 6.2, "Information Hiding."

- The information the routine will hide
- Inputs to the routine
- Outputs from the routine, including any global variables affected
- How the routine will handle errors

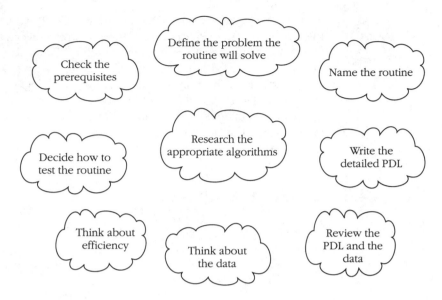

Figure 4-2. *You'll perform all of these steps as you design a routine but not necessarily in any particular order.*

Here's how these concerns are addressed in the *RecordErrorMessage()* example. The routine hides two facts: the error messages and the current processing method (interactive or batch). The input to the routine is an error code. Two kinds of output are called for: The first is the error message; the second is the status that *RecordErrorMessage()* returns to the calling routine.

Resolution of how the routine will handle errors doesn't follow directly from the problem statement. Suppose, for sake of the example, that the program's convention is to report errors at the point of detection. In that case, the routine must report any errors that it is the first to detect and will assume that others have already been reported. According to the spec, if it detects an error, it must also set the status-return variable to *Failure*.

CROSS-REFERENCE
For details on naming
routines, see Section 5.2,
"Good Routine Names."

Name the routine. Naming the routine might seem trivial, but good routine names are one sign of a superior program, and they're not easy to come up with. In general, a routine should have a clear, unambiguous name. If you have trouble creating a good name, that usually indicates that the purpose of the routine isn't clear. A vague, wishy-washy name is like a politician on the campaign trail. It sounds as if it's saying something, but when you take a hard look, you can't figure out what it means. If you can make the name clearer, do so. If the wishy-washy name results from a wishy-washy architecture, pay attention to the warning sign. Back up and improve the architecture.

In the example, *RecordErrorMessage()* is unambiguous. It is a good name.

Decide how to test the routine. As you're writing the routine, think about how you can test it. This is useful for you when you do unit testing and for the tester who tests your routine independently.

In the example, the input is simple, so you might plan to test *RecordError-Message()* with all valid error codes and a variety of invalid codes.

Think about efficiency. Depending on your situation, you can address efficiency in one of two ways. In the first situation, in the vast majority of systems, performance isn't critical. In such a case, see that the routine is well modularized and readable so that you can improve it later if you need to. If you have good modularization, you can replace a slow, high-level language routine with a better algorithm or a fast assembler routine and you won't affect any other routines.

CROSS-REFERENCE
For details on efficiency, see Chapter 28, "Code-Tuning Strategies," and Chapter 29, "Code-Tuning Techniques."

In the second situation, in the minority of systems, performance is critical and the architecture should indicate how much memory the routine is allowed to use and how fast it should be. Design your routine so that it will meet its space and speed goals. If either space or speed seems more critical, design so that you trade space for speed or vice versa. It's acceptable during initial construction of the routine to tune it enough to meet its space and speed budgets.

Aside from taking the approaches suggested for these two general situations, it's usually a waste of effort to work on efficiency at the level of individual routines. The big optimizations come from refining the top-level design, not the individual routines. You generally use micro-optimizations only when the top-level design turns out to be inadequate in some respect, and you won't know that until the whole program is done. Don't waste time scraping for incremental improvements until you know they're needed.

Research the algorithms and data structures. The single biggest way to improve both the quality of your code and your productivity is to reuse good code. Many algorithms have already been invented, tested, discussed in the trade literature, reviewed, and improved. Rather than spending your time inventing something when someone has already written a Ph.D. dissertation on it, take a few minutes to look through an algorithms book to see what's already available. If you use a predefined algorithm, be sure to adapt it correctly to your programming language.

Write the PDL. You might not have much in writing after you finish the preceding steps. The main purpose of the steps is to establish a mental orientation that's useful when you actually write the routine.

CROSS-REFERENCE
This discussion assumes that good design techniques are used to create the PDL version of the routine. For details on design, see Chapter 7, "High-Level Design in Construction."

With the preliminary steps completed, you can begin to write the routine as high-level PDL. Go ahead and use your programming editor or your integrated environment to write the PDL—the PDL will be used shortly as the basis for programming-language code.

Start with the general and work toward something more specific. The most general part of a routine is a header comment describing what the routine is supposed to do, so first write a concise statement of the purpose of the routine. Writing the statement will help you clarify your understanding of the routine. Trouble in writing the general comment is a warning that you need to understand the routine's role in the program better. In general, if it's hard to summarize the routine's role, you should probably assume that something is wrong. Here's an example of a concise header comment describing a routine:

Example of a Header Comment for a Routine

```
This routine outputs an error message based on an error code
supplied by the calling routine. The way it outputs the message
depends on the current processing state, which it retrieves
on its own. It returns a variable indicating success or failure.
```

After you've written the general comment, fill in high-level PDL for the routine. Here's the PDL for the example:

Example of PDL for a Routine

```
This routine outputs an error message based on an error code
supplied by the calling routine. The way it outputs the message
depends on the current processing state, which it retrieves
on its own. It returns a variable indicating success or failure.

set the default status
look up the message based on the error code
if the error code is valid
    determine the processing method
    if doing interactive processing
        print the error message interactively and declare success
    else doing batch processing
        if the batch message file opens properly
            log the error message to the batch file,
            close the file, and declare success
else the message code is not valid
    notify the user that an internal error has been detected
```

Note that the PDL is written at a fairly high level. It certainly isn't written in a programming language. It expresses in precise English what the routine needs to do.

CROSS-REFERENCE
For details on effective use of data, see Chapters 8 through 12.

Think about the data. You can design the routine's data at several different points in the process. In the example, the data is simple and data manipulation isn't a prominent part of the routine. If data manipulation is a prominent part of the routine, it's worthwhile to think about the major pieces of data before you think about the routine's logic. Definitions of key data structures are useful to have when you design the logic of a routine.

CROSS-REFERENCE
For details on review techniques, see Chapter 24, "Reviews."

Check the PDL. Once you've written the PDL and designed the data, take a minute to review the PDL you've written. Back away from it, and think about how you would explain it to someone else.

Ask someone else to look at it or listen to you explain it. You might think that it's silly to have someone look at 11 lines of PDL, but you'll be surprised. PDL can make your assumptions and high-level mistakes more obvious than programming-language code does. People are also more willing to review a few lines of PDL than they are to review 35 lines of C or Pascal.

Make sure you have an easy and comfortable understanding of what the routine does and how it does it. If you don't understand it conceptually, at the PDL level, what chance do you have of understanding it at the programming-language level? And if you don't understand it, who else will?

Iterate. Try as many ideas as you can in PDL before you start coding. Once you start coding, you get emotionally involved with your code and it becomes harder to throw away a bad design and start over.

The general idea is to refine the routine as PDL until the PDL statements become simple enough that you can fill in code below each statement and leave the original PDL as documentation. Some of the PDL from your first attempt might be high-level enough that you need to decompose it further. Be sure you do decompose it further. If you're not sure how to code something, keep working with the PDL until you are sure. Keep refining and decomposing the PDL until it seems like a waste of time to write it instead of the actual code.

4.4 Code the Routine

Once you've designed the routine, implement it. You can perform implementation steps in a nearly standard order, but feel free to vary them as you need to. Figure 4-3 on the next page shows the steps in implementing a routine.

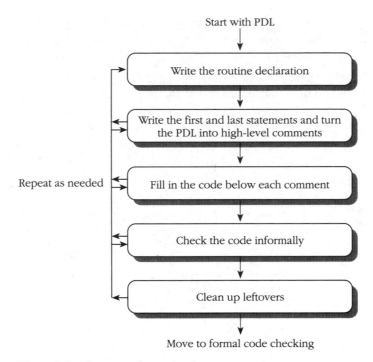

Start with PDL

Write the routine declaration

Write the first and last statements and turn the PDL into high-level comments

Repeat as needed → Fill in the code below each comment

Check the code informally

Clean up leftovers

Move to formal code checking

Figure 4-3. *The steps taken to implement a routine.*

Write the routine declaration. Write the routine interface statement—the procedure or function declaration in Pascal, function declaration in C, subroutine definition in Fortran, or whatever your language calls for. Turn the original header comment into a programming-language comment. Leave it in position above the PDL you've already written. Here are the example routine's interface statement and header in Pascal:

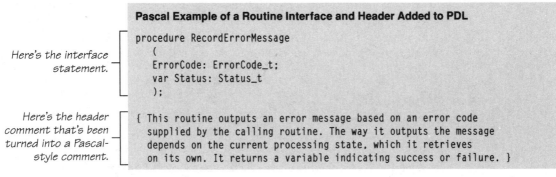

Pascal Example of a Routine Interface and Header Added to PDL

Here's the interface statement.
```
procedure RecordErrorMessage
   (
   ErrorCode: ErrorCode_t;
   var Status: Status_t
   );
```

Here's the header comment that's been turned into a Pascal-style comment.
```
{ This routine outputs an error message based on an error code
  supplied by the calling routine. The way it outputs the message
  depends on the current processing state, which it retrieves
  on its own. It returns a variable indicating success or failure. }
```

(continued)

```
set the default status
look up the message based on the error code
if the error code is valid
   determine the processing method
   if doing interactive processing
      print the error message interactively and declare success
   else doing batch processing
      if the batch message file opens properly
         log the error message to the batch file,
         close the file, and declare success
else the message code is not valid
   notify the user that an internal error has been detected
```

This is a good time to make notes about any interface assumptions. In this case, the interface variables *ErrorCode* and *Status* are straightforward and typed for their specific purposes; they don't contain any hidden assumptions.

Turn the PDL into high-level comments. Keep the ball rolling by writing the first and last statements—*begin* and *end* in Pascal, *{* and *}* in C. Then turn the PDL into comments. Here's how it would look in the example:

Pascal Example of Writing the First and Last Statements Around PDL

```
procedure RecordErrorMessage
   (
   ErrorCode: ErrorCode_t;
   var Status: Status_t
   );

{ This routine outputs an error message based on an error code
  supplied by the calling routine. The way it outputs the message
  depends on the current processing state, which it retrieves
  on its own. It returns a variable indicating success or failure. }

begin
   { set the default status }
   { look up the message based on the error code }
   { if the error code is valid }
      { determine the processing method }
      { if doing interactive processing }
         { print the error message interactively and declare success }
      { else doing batch processing }
         { if the batch message file opens properly }
            { log the error message to the batch file,
              close the file, and declare success }
   { else the message code is not valid }
      { notify the user that an internal error has been detected }
end; { RecordErrorMessage() }
```

The PDL statements from here down have been turned into Pascal comments.

You can also document the end of the routine.

At this point, the character of the routine is evident. The design work is complete, and you can sense how the routine works even without seeing any code. You should feel that converting the PDL to programming-language code will be mechanical, natural, and easy. If you don't, continue designing in PDL until the design feels solid.

Fill in the code below each comment. Fill in the code below each line of PDL comment. The process is a lot like writing a term paper. First you write an outline, and then you write a paragraph for each point in the outline. Each PDL comment describes a block or paragraph of code. Like the lengths of literary paragraphs, the lengths of code paragraphs vary according to the thought being expressed, and the quality of the paragraphs depends on the vividness and focus of the thoughts in them.

In the example, the first two PDL comments give rise to two lines of code:

Pascal Example of Expressing PDL Comments as Code

```
procedure RecordErrorMessage
    (
    ErrorCode: ErrorCode_t;
    var Status: Status_t
    );

{ This routine outputs an error message based on an error code
  supplied by the calling routine. The way it outputs the message
  depends on the current processing state, which it retrieves
  on its own. It returns a variable indicating success or failure. }

begin
    { set the default status }
    Status := Failure;

    { look up the message based on the error code }
    LookupErrorMessage( ErrorCode, ErrorMessage );

    { if the error code is valid }
        { determine the processing method }
        { if doing interactive processing }
            { print the error message interactively and declare success }
        { else doing batch processing }
            { if the batch message file opens properly }
                { log the error message to the batch file,
                  close the file, and declare success }
    { else the message code is not valid }
        { notify the user that an internal error has been detected }
end; { RecordErrorMessage() }
```

Here's the code that's been filled in.

Here's the new variable ErrorMessage.

This is a start on the code. The variable *ErrorMessage* is used, so it needs to be declared. If you were commenting after the fact, two lines of comments for two lines of code would nearly always be overkill. In this approach, however, it's the semantic content of the comments that's important, not how many lines of code they comment. The comments are already there, and they explain the intent of the code, so leave them in.

The code needs variable declarations, and the code below each of the remaining comments needs to be filled in. Here's the completed routine:

Pascal Example of a Complete Routine Created with the PDL-to-Code Process

```pascal
procedure RecordErrorMessage
    (
    ErrorCode: ErrorCode_t;
    var Status: Status_t
    );

{ This routine outputs an error message based on an error code
  supplied by the calling routine. The way it outputs the message
  depends on the current processing state, which it retrieves
  on its own. It returns a variable indicating success or failure. }

var
    ProcessingMethod: ProcessingMethod_t;
    ErrorMessage:     Message_t;
    FileStatus:       Status_t;

begin
    { set the default status }
    Status := Failure;

    { look up the message based on the error code }
    LookupErrorMessage( ErrorCode, ErrorMessage );

    { if the error code is valid }
    if ( ErrorMessage.ValidCode ) then begin

        { determine the processing method }
        ProcessingMethod := CurrentProcessingMethod;

        { if doing interactive processing }
        if ( ProcessingMethod = Interactive ) then begin

            { print the error message interactively and declare success }
            PrintInteractiveMessage( ErrorMessage.Text );
            Status := Success
        end
```

Here's where the variables were declared as they were needed.

The code for each comment has been filled in from here down.

(continued)

```
      { else doing batch processing }
      else if ( ProcessingMethod = Batch ) then begin

         { if the batch message file opens properly }
         FileStatus := OpenMessageFile;
         if ( FileStatus = Success ) then begin

            { log the error message to the batch file, close the file,
              and declare success }
            LogBatchMessage( ErrorMessage.Text );
            CloseMessageFile;
            Status := Success
         end { if }
      end { else }
   end

   { else the message code is not valid }
   else begin

      { notify the user that an internal error has been detected }
      PrintInteractiveMessage( 'Internal Error: Invalid error code',
         ' in RecordErrorMessage()' )
   end

end; { RecordErrorMessage() }
```

Each comment has given rise to one or more lines of code. Each block of code forms a complete thought based on the comment. The comments have been retained to provide a higher-level explanation of the code. All the variables that have been used have been declared at the top of the routine.

Now look again at the spec on page 57 and the initial PDL on page 60. The original 5-sentence spec expanded to 12 lines of PDL, which in turn expanded into a page-long routine. Even though the spec was detailed, creation of the routine required substantial design work in PDL and code. That low-level design is one reason why "coding" is a nontrivial task and why the subject of this book is important.

Check the code informally. Mentally test each block of code as you fill it in below its comment. Try to think of what it would take to break that block, and then prove to yourself that it won't happen.

Once you have an implementation of the routine, stop to check it for mistakes. You should already have checked it when you wrote it in PDL, but sometimes an important problem doesn't appear until the routine is implemented.

CROSS-REFERENCE
For details on checking
for errors in architecture
and requirements, see
Chapter 3, "Prerequisites to
Construction."

A problem might not appear until coding for several reasons. An error in the PDL might become more apparent in the detailed implementation logic. A design that looks elegant in PDL might become clumsy in the implementation language. Working with the detailed implementation might disclose an error in the architecture or the requirements analysis. Finally, the code might have an old-fashioned, mongrel coding error—nobody's perfect! For all these reasons, review the code before you move on.

Clean up the leftovers. When you've finished checking your code for problems, check it for the general characteristics described throughout this book. You can take several cleanup steps to make sure that the routine's quality is up to your standards:

- Check the routine's interface. Make sure that all input and output data is accounted for and that all parameters are used. For more details, see Section 5.7, "How to Use Routine Parameters."

- Check for general design quality. Make sure the routine does one thing and does it well, that it's loosely coupled to other routines, and that it's designed defensively. For details, see Chapter 5, "Characteristics of High-Quality Routines."

- Check the routine's data. Check for inaccurate variable names, unused data, undeclared data, and so on. For details, see the chapters on using data, Chapters 8 through 12.

- Check the routine's control structures. Check for off-by-one errors, infinite loops, and improper nesting. For details, see the chapters on using control structures, Chapters 13 through 17.

- Check the routine's layout. Make sure you've used white space to clarify the logical structure of the routine, expressions, and parameter lists. For details, see Chapter 18, "Layout and Style."

- Check the routine's documentation. Make sure the PDL that was translated into comments is still accurate. Check for algorithm descriptions, for documentation on interface assumptions and nonobvious dependencies, for justification of unclear coding practices, and so on. For details, see Chapter 19, "Self-Documenting Code."

Repeat steps as needed. If the quality of the routine is poor, back up to the PDL. High-quality programming is an iterative process, so don't hesitate to loop through the design and implementation activities again.

4.5 Check the Code Formally

KEY POINT

After designing and implementing the routine, the third big step in constructing it is checking to be sure that what you've constructed is correct. Didn't the informal checking and cleaning up of leftovers verify the correctness of the code? Yes, partially, but not completely, and any errors you miss at this stage won't be found until later testing. They're more expensive to find and correct then, so you should find all that you can at this stage.

CROSS-REFERENCE
For details on review techniques, see Chapter 24, "Reviews."

Mentally check the routine for errors. The first formal check of a routine is mental. The clean-up and informal-checking steps mentioned earlier are two kinds of mental checks. Another is executing each path mentally. Mentally executing a routine is difficult, and that difficulty is one reason to keep your routines small. Make sure that you check nominal paths and endpoints and all exception conditions. Do this both by yourself, which is called "desk checking," and with one or more peers, which is called a "peer review," a "walkthrough," or an "inspection," depending on how you do it.

One of the biggest differences between hobbyists and professional programmers is the difference that grows out of moving from superstition into understanding. The word "superstition" in this context doesn't refer to a program that gives you the creeps or generates extra errors when the moon is full. It means substituting feelings about the code for understanding. If you often find yourself suspecting that the compiler or the hardware made an error, you're still in the realm of superstition. Only about 5 percent of all errors are hardware, compiler, or operating-system errors (Brown and Sampson 1973, Ostrand and Weyuker 1984). Programmers who have moved into the realm of understanding always suspect their own work first because they know that they cause 95 percent of errors. Understand the role of each line of code and why it's needed. Nothing is ever right just because it seems to work. If you don't know why it works, it probably doesn't—you just don't know it yet.

HARD DATA

Bottom line: A working routine isn't enough. If you don't know why it works, study it, discuss it, and experiment with alternative designs until you do.

Compile the routine. After reviewing the routine, compile it. It might seem inefficient to wait this long to compile since the code was completed several pages ago. Admittedly, you might have saved some work by compiling the routine earlier and letting the computer check for undeclared variables, naming conflicts, and so on.

You'll benefit in several ways, however, by not compiling until late in the process. The main reason is that when you compile new code, an internal stopwatch starts ticking. After the first compile, you step up the pressure: Get it right with Just One More Compile. The "Just One More Compile" syndrome leads to hasty, error-prone changes that take more time in the long run. Avoid the rush to completion by not compiling until you've convinced yourself that the routine is right.

The point of this book is to show how to rise above the cycle of hacking something together and running it to see if it works. Compiling before you're sure your program works is often a symptom of the hacker mind-set. If you're not caught in the hacking-and-compiling cycle, compile when you feel it's appropriate to.

Here are some guidelines for getting the most out of compiling your routine:

- Set the compiler's warning level to the pickiest level possible. You can catch an amazing number of subtle errors simply by allowing the compiler to detect them.

- Eliminate the causes of all compiler errors and warnings. Pay attention to what the compiler tells you about your code. A lot of warnings often indicates low-quality code, and you should try to understand each warning you get. In practice, warnings you've seen again and again have one of two possible effects: You ignore them and they camouflage other, more important warnings, or they become annoying, like Chinese water torture. It's usually safer and less painful to rewrite the code to solve the underlying problem and eliminate the warnings.

Use the computer to check the routine for errors. Once the routine compiles, put it into the debugger and step through each line of code. Make sure each line executes as you expect it to. You can find many errors by following this simple practice.

CROSS-REFERENCE
For details, see Chapter 25, "Unit Testing." Also see "Building Scaffolding to Test Individual Routines" in Section 25.5.

After stepping through the code in the debugger, test it using the test cases you planned while you were developing the routine. You might have to develop scaffolding to support your test cases—code that is used to support routines while they're tested and isn't included in the final product. Scaffolding can be a test-harness routine that calls your routine with test data, or it can be stubs called by your routine.

CROSS-REFERENCE
For details, see Chapter 26, "Debugging."

Remove errors from the routine. Once an error has been detected, it has to be removed. If the routine you're developing is buggy at this point, chances are good that it will stay buggy. If you find that a routine is unusually buggy, start over. Don't patch it. Rewrite it. Patches usually indicate incomplete understanding and guarantee errors both now and later. Creating an entirely new design for a buggy routine pays off. Few things are more satisfying than rewriting a problematic routine and never finding another error in it.

CROSS-REFERENCE
The point of this list is to check whether you followed a good set of steps to create a routine. For a checklist that focuses on the quality of the routine itself, see the "High-Quality Routines" checklist in Chapter 5, page 113.

CHECKLIST

Constructing a Routine

- ❑ Have you checked that the prerequisites have been satisfied?
- ❑ Have you defined the problem that the routine will solve?
- ❑ Is the architecture clear enough to give your routine a good name?
- ❑ Have you thought about how to test the routine?
- ❑ Have you thought about efficiency mainly in terms of good modularization or in terms of meeting space and speed budgets?
- ❑ Have you checked reference books for helpful algorithms?
- ❑ Have you designed the routine using detailed PDL?
- ❑ Have you thought about the data, before the logic if necessary?
- ❑ Have you mentally checked the PDL? Is it easy to understand?
- ❑ Have you paid attention to warnings that would send you back to architecture (use of global data, operations that seem better suited to another routine, and so on)?
- ❑ Did you use the PDL-to-code process, using PDL as a basis for coding and converting the original PDL to comments?
- ❑ Did you translate the PDL to code accurately?
- ❑ Did you document assumptions as you made them?
- ❑ Have you chosen the best of several design attempts, rather than merely stopping after your first attempt?
- ❑ Do you thoroughly understand your code? Is it easy to understand?

Key Points

- Writing good PDL calls for using understandable English, avoiding features specific to a single programming language, and writing at the level of intent—describing what the design does rather than how it will do it.

- The PDL-to-code process is a useful tool for detailed design and makes coding easy. PDL translates directly into comments, ensuring that the comments are accurate and useful.

- You should check your work at each step and encourage others to check it too. That way, you'll catch mistakes at the least expensive level, when you've invested the least amount of effort.

5

Characteristics of High-Quality Routines

Contents

Related Topics

CHAPTER 4 DESCRIBED THE STEPS you take to build a routine. It focused on the construction process. This chapter zooms in on the routine itself, on the characteristics that make the difference between a good routine and a bad one.

If you'd rather read about high-level design issues before wading into the nitty-gritty details of individual routines, read the high-level design chapter, Chapter 7, first and come back to this chapter later. Since modules are also more abstract than individual routines, you might also prefer to read about high-quality modules in Chapter 6 before reading this chapter.

Before jumping into the details of high-quality routines, it will be useful to nail down two basic terms. What is a "routine"? A routine is an individual function or procedure invocable for a single purpose. Examples include a function in C, a function or a procedure in Pascal or Ada, a subprogram in Basic, and a subroutine in Fortran. For some uses, macros in C and sections of code called with *GOSUB* in Basic can also be thought of as routines. You can apply many of the techniques for creating a high-quality routine to these variants.

What is a "high-quality routine"? That's a harder question. Perhaps the easiest answer is to show what a high-quality routine is not. Here's an example of a low-quality routine:

CODING HORROR

Pascal Example of a Low-Quality Routine

```
Procedure HandleStuff( Var InputRec: CORP_DATA, CrntQtr: integer,
    EmpRec: EMP_DATA, Var EstimRevenue: Real, YTDRevenue: Real,
    ScreenX: integer, ScreenY: integer, Var NewColor: COLOR_TYPE,
    Var PrevColor: COLOR_TYPE, Var Status: STATUS_TYPE,
    ExpenseType: integer );

begin
for i:= 1 to 100 do begin
   InputRec.revenue[i] := 0;
   InputRec.expense[i] := CorpExpense[ CrntQtr, i ]
   end;
UpdateCorpDatabase( EmpRec );
EstimRevenue := YTDRevenue * 4.0 / real( CrntQtr );
NewColor := PrevColor;
Status := Success;
if ExpenseType = 1 then begin
                        for i := 1 to 12 do
                        Profit[i] := Revenue[i] - Expense.Type1[i]
                        end
else if ExpenseType = 2 then begin
                        Profit[i] := Revenue[i] - Expense.Type2[i]
                        end
else if ExpenseType = 3 then
   begin
   Profit[i] := Revenue[i] - Expense.Type3[i]
   end
end;
```

What's wrong with this routine? Here's a hint: You should be able to find at least 10 different problems with it. Once you've come up with your own list, look at the list below:

- The routine has a bad name. *HandleStuff()* tells you nothing about what the routine does.

- The routine isn't documented. (The subject of documentation extends beyond the boundaries of individual routines and is discussed in Chapter 19, "Self-Documenting Code.")

- The routine has a bad layout. The physical organization of the code on the page gives few hints about its logical organization. Layout strategies are used haphazardly, with different styles in different parts of the routine. Compare the styles where *ExpenseType = 2* and *ExpenseType = 3*. (Layout is discussed in Chapter 18, "Layout and Style.")

- The routine's input variable, *InputRec*, is changed. If it's an input variable, its value should not be modified. If the value of the variable is supposed to be modified, the variable should not be called *InputRec*.

- The routine reads and writes global variables. It reads from *CorpExpense* and writes to *Profit*. It should communicate with other routines more directly than by reading and writing global variables.

- The routine doesn't have a single purpose. It initializes some variables, writes to a database, does some calculations—none of which seem to be related to each other in any way. A routine should have a single, clearly defined purpose.

- The routine doesn't defend itself against bad data. If *CrntQtr* equals *0*, then the expression *YTDRevenue * 4.0 / real(CrntQtr)* causes a divide-by-zero error.

- The routine uses several magic numbers: *100, 4.0, 12, 2,* and *3*. Magic numbers are discussed in Section 11.1, "Numbers in General."

- The routine uses only two fields of the *CORP_DATA* type of parameter. If only two fields are used, the specific fields rather than the whole structured variable should be passed in.

- Some of the routine's parameters are unused. *ScreenX* and *ScreenY* are not referenced within the routine.

- One of the routine's parameters is mislabeled. *PrevColor* is labeled as a *Var* parameter even though it isn't assigned a value within the routine.

- The routine has too many parameters. The upper limit for an understandable number of parameters is about 7. This routine has 11. The parameters are laid out in such an intimidating way that most people wouldn't try to examine them closely or even count them.

- The routine's parameters are poorly ordered and are not documented. (Parameter ordering is discussed in this chapter. Documentation is discussed in Chapter 19.)

Aside from the computer itself, the routine is the single greatest invention in computer science. The routine makes programs easier to read and easier to understand than any other feature of any programming language. It's a crime to abuse this senior statesman of computer science with code like that shown in the example above.

The routine is also the greatest technique ever invented for saving space and improving performance. Imagine how much larger your code would be if you had to repeat the code for every call to a routine instead of branching to the routine. Imagine how hard it would be to make performance improvements in the same code used in a dozen places instead of making them all in one routine. The routine makes modern programming possible.

"OK," you say, "I already know that routines are great, and I program with them all the time. This discussion seems kind of remedial, so what do you want me to do about it?"

I want you to understand that there are many valid reasons to create a routine and that there are right ways and wrong ways to go about it. As an undergraduate computer-science student, I thought that the main reason to create a routine was to avoid duplicate code. The introductory textbook I used said that routines were good because the avoidance of duplication made a program easier to develop, debug, document, and maintain. Period. Aside from syntactic details about how to use parameters and local variables, that was the total extent of the textbook's explanation of the theory and practice of routines. It was not a good or complete explanation. The following sections describe why and how to create routines.

5.1   Valid Reasons to Create a Routine

Here's a list of valid reasons to create a routine. The reasons overlap somewhat, and they're not intended to make an orthogonal set.

KEY POINT

Reducing complexity. The single most important reason to create a routine is to reduce a program's complexity. Create a routine to hide information so that you won't need to think about it. Sure, you'll need to think about it when you write the routine. But after it's written, you should be able to forget the details and use the routine without any knowledge of its internal workings. Other reasons to create routines—minimizing code size, improving maintainability, and improving correctness—are also good reasons, but without the abstractive power of routines, complex programs would be impossible to manage intellectually.

One indication that a routine needs to be broken out of another routine is deep nesting of an inner loop or a conditional. Reduce the containing routine's complexity by pulling the nested part out and putting it into its own routine.

CROSS-REFERENCE
For a discussion of decomposition, see "Choosing Components to Modularize" in Section 7.2.

Avoiding duplicate code. Undoubtedly the most popular reason for creating a routine is to avoid duplicate code. Indeed, creation of similar code in two routines implies an error in decomposition. Pull the duplicate code from both routines, put a generic version of the common code into its own routine, and then let both call the part that was put into the new routine. With code in one place, you save the space that would have been used by duplicated code. Modifications will be easier because you'll need to modify the code in only one location. The code will be more reliable because you'll have to check only one place to ensure that the code is right. Modifications will be more reliable because you'll avoid making successive and slightly different modifications under the mistaken assumption that you've made identical ones.

CROSS-REFERENCE
For a discussion of areas that are likely to change, see "Areas likely to change" in Section 6.2.

Limiting effects of changes. Isolate areas that are likely to change so that the effects of changes are limited to the scope of a single routine or, at most, a few routines. Design so that areas that are most likely to change are the easiest to change. Areas likely to change include hardware dependencies, input/output, complex data structures, and business rules.

Hiding sequences. It's a good idea to hide the order in which events happen to be processed. For example, if the program typically gets data from the user and then gets auxiliary data from a file, neither the routine that gets the user data nor the routine that gets the file data should depend on the other routine's being performed first. If you commonly have two lines of code that read the top of a stack and decrement a *StackTop* variable, put them into a *PopStack()* routine. Design the system so that either could be performed first, and then create a routine to hide the information about which happens to be performed first.

CROSS-REFERENCE
For details on improving performance, see Chapter 28, "Code-Tuning Strategies," and Chapter 29, "Code-Tuning Techniques."

Improving performance. You can optimize the code in one place instead of several places. Having code in one place means that a single optimization benefits all the routines that use that routine, whether they use it directly or indirectly. Having code in one place makes it practical to recode the routine with a more efficient algorithm or a faster, more difficult language such as assembler.

CROSS-REFERENCE
For details on information hiding, see Section 6.2, "Information Hiding."

Making central points of control. It's a good idea to keep control for each task in one place. Control assumes many forms. Knowledge of the number of entries in a table is one form. Control of hardware devices—disks, tapes, printers, plotters, and so on—is another. Using one routine to read from a file and one routine to write to it is a form of centralized control. This is especially useful because if the file needs to be converted to an in-memory data structure, the changes affect only the access routines. Reading and modifying the contents of internal data structures with specialized routines is another form of centralized control.

The idea of centralized control is similar to information hiding, but it has unique heuristic power that makes it worth adding to your programming toolbox.

CROSS-REFERENCE
For details on hiding the implementation of data structures, see Section 12.3, "Abstract Data Types (ADTs)."

Hiding data structures. You can hide the implementation details of a data structure so that most of the program doesn't need to worry about the messy details of manipulating computer-science structures and can deal with the data in terms of how it's used in the problem domain. Routines that hide implementation details provide a valuable level of abstraction that reduces a program's complexity. They centralize data-structure operations in one place and reduce the chance of errors in working with the data structure. They make it easy to change the structure without changing most of the program.

Hiding global data. If you need to use global data, you can hide its implementation details as just described. Working with global data through access routines provides several benefits. You can change the structure of the data without changing your program. You can monitor accesses to the data. The discipline of using access routines also encourages you to think about whether the data is really global; it might be more accurate to treat it as data that's local to several routines in a single module or as part of an abstract data type.

Hiding pointer operations. Pointer operations tend to be hard to read and error prone. By isolating them in routines, you can concentrate on the intent of the operation rather than the mechanics of pointer manipulation. Also, if the operations are done in only one place, you can be more certain that the code is correct. If you find a better data structure than pointers, you can change the program without traumatizing the routines that would have used the pointers.

Promoting code reuse. Code put into modular routines can be reused in other programs more easily than the same code embedded in one larger routine. Even if a section of code is called from only one place in the program and is understandable as part of a larger routine, it makes sense to put it into its own routine if that piece of code might be used in another program.

Planning for a family of programs. If you expect a program to be modified, it's a good idea to isolate the parts that you expect to change by putting them into their own routines. You can then modify the routines without affecting the rest of the program, or you can put in completely new routines instead. Several years ago I managed a team that wrote a series of programs used by our clients to sell insurance. We had to tailor each program to the specific client's insurance rates, quote-report format, and so on. But many parts of the programs were similar: the routines that input information about potential customers, that stored information in a customer database, that looked up rates, that computed total rates for a group, and so on. The team modularized the program so that each part that varied from client to client was in its own module. The initial programming might have taken three months or so, but when we got a new client, we merely wrote a handful of new modules for the new client and dropped them into the rest of the code. Two or three days' work, and voilà! Custom software!

Making a section of code readable. Putting a section of code into a well-named routine is one of the best ways to document its function. Instead of reading a series of statements like

```
if ( Node <> NULL )
   while ( Node.Next <> NULL ) do
      Node = Node.Next
   LeafName = Node.Name
else
   LeafName = ""
```

you can read a statement like

```
LeafName = GetLeafName( Node )
```

The new routine is so short that nearly all it needs for documentation is a good name. Using a function call instead of six lines of code makes the routine that originally contained the code less complex and documents it automatically.

Improving portability. Use of routines isolates nonportable capabilities, explicitly identifying and isolating future portability work. Nonportable capabilities include nonstandard language features, hardware dependencies, operating-system dependencies, and so on.

Isolating complex operations. Complex operations—complicated algorithms, communications protocols, tricky boolean tests, operations on complex data, and so on—are prone to errors. If an error does occur, it will be easier to find if it isn't spread through the code but is contained in a routine. The error won't affect other code because only one routine will have to be fixed—other code won't be touched. If you find a better, simpler, or more reliable algorithm, it will be easier to replace the old algorithm if it has been isolated into a routine. During development, it will be easier to try several designs and use the one that works best.

Isolating use of nonstandard language functions. Most language implementations contain handy, nonstandard extensions. Using the extensions is a double-edged sword because they might not be available in a different environment, whether the different environment is different hardware, a different vendor's implementation of the language, or a new version of the language from the same vendor. If you use the extensions, build routines of your own that act as gateways to them. Then you can replace the vendor's nonstandard routines with custom-written ones if you need to.

CROSS-REFERENCE
For examples of putting
complicated tests into
boolean functions, see
"Making Complicated
Expressions Simple"
in Section 17.1.

Simplifying complicated boolean tests. Understanding complicated boolean tests in detail is rarely necessary for understanding program flow. Putting such a test into a function makes the code more readable because (1) the details of the test are out of the way and (2) a descriptive function name summarizes the purpose of the test.

Giving the test a function of its own emphasizes its significance. It encourages extra effort to make the details of the test readable inside its function. The result is that both the main flow of the code and the test itself become clearer.

For the sake of modularization? Absolutely not. With so many good reasons for putting code into a routine, this one is unnecessary. In fact, some jobs are performed better in a single large routine. (The best length for a routine is discussed in Section 5.5, "How Long Can a Routine Be?")

Operations That Seem Too Simple to Put into Routines

KEY POINT

One of the strongest mental blocks to creating effective routines is a reluctance to create a simple routine for a simple purpose. Constructing a whole routine to contain two or three lines of code might seem like overkill. But experience shows how helpful a good small routine can be.

Small routines offer several advantages. One is that they improve readability. I once had the following single line of code in about a dozen places in a program:

```
Points = DeviceUnits * ( POINTS_PER_INCH / DeviceUnitsPerInch() )
```

This is not the most complicated line of code you'll ever read. Most people would eventually figure out that it converts a measurement in device units to a measurement in points. They would see that each of the dozen lines did the same thing. It could have been clearer, however, so I created a well-named routine to do the conversion in one place:

```
DeviceUnitsToPoints( DeviceUnits Integer ): Integer;
begin
    DeviceUnitsToPoints = DeviceUnits *
                    ( POINTS_PER_INCH / DeviceUnitsPerInch()  )
end
```

When the routine was substituted for the inline code, the dozen lines of code all looked more or less like this one:

```
Points = DeviceUnitsToPoints( DeviceUnits )
```

which was more readable—even approaching self-documenting.

This example hints at another reason to put small operations into functions: Small operations tend to turn into larger operations. I didn't know it when I wrote the routine, but under certain conditions and when certain devices were active, *DeviceUnitsPerInch()* returned *0*. That meant I had to account for division by zero, which took three more lines of code:

```
DeviceUnitsToPoints( DeviceUnits: Integer ): Integer;
begin
   if ( DeviceUnitsPerInch() <> 0 ) then
      DeviceUnitsToPoints = DeviceUnits *
                             ( POINTS_PER_INCH / DeviceUnitsPerInch() )
   else
      DeviceUnitsToPoints = 0
end
```

If that original line of code had still been in a dozen places, the test would have been repeated a dozen times, for a total of 36 new lines of code. A simple routine reduced the 36 new lines to 3.

Summary of Reasons to Create a Routine

Here's a summary list of the valid reasons for creating a routine:

- Reducing complexity
- Avoiding duplicate code
- Limiting effects of changes
- Hiding sequences
- Improving performance
- Making central points of control
- Hiding data structures
- Hiding global data
- Hiding pointer operations
- Promoting code reuse
- Planning for a family of programs
- Making a section of code readable
- Improving portability
- Isolating complex operations
- Isolating use of nonstandard language functions
- Simplifying complicated boolean tests

5.2   Good Routine Names

CROSS-REFERENCE
For details on naming variables, see Chapter 9, "The Power of Data Names."

A good name for a routine clearly describes everything the routine does. Here are guidelines for creating effective routine names.

For a procedure name, use a strong verb followed by an object. A procedure with functional cohesion usually performs an operation on an object. The name should reflect what the procedure does, and an operation on an object implies a verb-plus-object name. *PrintReport()*, *CalcMonthlyRevenues()*, *CheckOrderInfo()*, and *RepaginateDocument()* are samples of good procedure names.

In object-oriented languages, you don't need to include the name of the object in the procedure name because the object itself is included in the call. You invoke routines with statements like *Report.Print()*, *OrderInfo.Check()*, and *MonthlyRevenues.Calc()*. Names like *Report.PrintReport()* are redundant.

CROSS-REFERENCE
For the distinction between procedures and functions, see Section 5.8, "Considerations in the Use of Functions," later in this chapter.

For a function name, use a description of the return value. A function returns a value, and the function should be named for the value it returns. For example, *cos()*, *NextCustomerId()*, *PrinterReady()*, and *CurrentPenColor()* are all good function names that indicate precisely what the functions return.

Avoid meaningless or wishy-washy verbs. Some verbs are elastic, stretched to cover just about any meaning. Routine names like *HandleCalculation()*, *PerformServices()*, *ProcessInput()*, and *DealWithOutput()* don't tell you what the routines do. At the most, these names tell you that the routines have something to do with calculations, services, input, and output. The exception would be when the verb "handle" was used in the specific technical sense of handling an event.

KEY POINT

Sometimes the only problem with a routine is that its name is wishy-washy; the routine itself might actually be well designed. If *HandleOutput()* is replaced with *FormatAndPrintOutput()*, you have a pretty good idea of what the routine does.

In other cases, the verb is vague because the operations performed by the routine are vague. The routine suffers from a weakness of purpose, and the weak name is a symptom. If that's the case, the best solution is to restructure the routine and any related routines so that they all have stronger purposes and stronger names that accurately describe them.

Describe everything the routine does. In the routine's name, describe all the outputs and side effects. If a routine computes report totals and sets a global variable that indicates all data is ready for printing, *ComputeReportTotals()* is not an adequate name for the routine. *ComputeReportTotalsAndSetPrinting-ReadyVar()* is an adequate name but is too long and silly. If you have routines with side effects, you'll have many long, silly names. The cure is not to use less-descriptive routine names; the cure is to program so that you cause things to happen directly rather than with side effects.

CROSS-REFERENCE
For details on creating good variable names, see Chapter 9, "The Power of Data Names."

Make names of routines as long as necessary. Research shows that the optimum average length for a variable name is 9 to 15 characters. Routines tend to be more complicated than variables, and good names for them tend to be longer. Michael Rees of the University of Southampton thinks that an average of 20 to 35 characters is a good nominal length (Rees 1982). An average length of 15 to 20 characters is probably more realistic, but clear names that happened to be longer would be fine.

Establish conventions for common operations. In some systems, it's important to distinguish among different kinds of operations. A naming convention is often the easiest and most reliable way of indicating these distinctions. In development of the OS/2 Presentation Manager, for example, the routine names had a *Get* prefix for destructive input and a *Query* prefix for non-destructive input. Thus, *GetInputChar()* returned the current input character and cleared the input buffer. *QueryInputChar()* also returned the current input character, but it left the input buffer intact.

5.3 Strong Cohesion

CROSS-REFERENCE
For a discussion of module cohesion, see Section 6.1, "Modularity: Cohesion and Coupling."

Cohesion refers to how closely the operations in a routine are related. Some programmers prefer the concept "strength": How strongly related are the operations in a routine? A function like *sin()* is perfectly cohesive because the whole routine is dedicated to performing one function. A function like *SinAndTan()* has lower cohesion because it tries to do more than one thing. The goal is to have each routine do one thing well and not do anything else.

HARD DATA

The payoff is higher reliability. One study of 450 Fortran routines found that 50 percent of the highly cohesive routines were fault free, whereas only 18 percent of routines with low cohesion were fault free (Card, Church, and Agresti 1986). Another study of 450 routines (not the same 450 routines, regardless of how unusual the coincidence is) found that routines with the highest coupling-to-strength ratios had 7 times as many errors as those with the lowest coupling-to-strength ratios and were 20 times as costly to fix (Selby and Basili 1991).

Discussions about cohesion typically refer to several levels of cohesion. Understanding the concepts is more important than remembering specific terms. Use the concepts as aids in thinking about how to make routines as cohesive as possible.

Acceptable Cohesion

CROSS-REFERENCE
The idea of cohesion is a part of structured design. For more information on structured design, see Section 7.2, "Structured Design."

The idea of cohesion was introduced in a paper by Wayne Stevens, Glenford Myers, and Larry Constantine (1974). Some of the ideas have evolved since then, and here are the levels of cohesion that are now generally considered to be acceptable:

Functional cohesion. Functional cohesion is the strongest and best kind of cohesion, occurring when a routine performs one and only one operation. Examples of highly cohesive routines include *sin()*, *GetCustomerName()*, *EraseFile()*, *CalcLoanPayment()*, and *GetIconLocation()*. Of course, this evaluation of their cohesiveness assumes that the routines do what their names say they do. If they do anything else, they are less cohesive and poorly named.

Sequential cohesion. Sequential cohesion occurs when a routine contains operations that must be performed in a specific order, that share data from step to step, and that don't make up a complete function when done together. Suppose that a program has five operations: Open File, Read File, Perform Calculations, Output Results, and Close File. Suppose they are organized into two routines, *DoStep1()* to do the Open File, Read File, and Perform Calculations operations, and *DoStep2()* to do the Output Results and Close File operations. Both *DoStep1()* and *DoStep2()* have sequential cohesion because breaking up the operations that way doesn't create independent functions.

If, instead, a routine called *GetFileData()* did the Open File and Read File operations, that routine would have functional cohesion. If the operations work together to perform a single function, they constitute a routine with functional cohesion. In practice, if you can come up with a strong verb-plus-object name for a routine, the cohesion is probably functional rather than sequential. It's hard to create a respectable name for a routine with sequential cohesion, so a wishy-washy name like *DoStep1()* is a hint to redesign and try for functional cohesion.

Communicational cohesion. Communicational cohesion occurs when operations in a routine make use of the same data and aren't related in any other way. For example, *GetNameAndChangePhoneNumber()* would have communicational cohesion if the name and phone number were both in, say, a customer record. The routine does two things rather than just one, so it doesn't have functional cohesion. The name and phone number are both in the customer record, and they don't need to be dealt with in any particular order, so the routine doesn't have sequential cohesion.

This level of cohesion is still acceptable. On a practical level, a system could frequently need to get a name and change a phone number at the same time. A system composed of routines like this would be pretty eccentric but would still be clean enough that it would be maintainable. On an aesthetic level, it would be far from the ideal routine, which does one thing and does it well.

Temporal cohesion. Temporal cohesion occurs when operations are combined into a routine because they are all done at the same time. Typical examples would be *Startup()*, *CompleteNewEmployee()*, and *Shutdown()*. Some programmers consider temporal cohesion to be unacceptable because it's sometimes associated with bad programming practices such as having a hodgepodge of code in a *Startup()* routine.

FURTHER READING
For a critical view of temporal cohesion, see *Structured Design* (Yourdon and Constantine 1979) or *The Practical Guide to Structured Systems Design* (Page-Jones 1988).

To avoid this problem, think of temporal routines as organizers of other events. The *Startup()* routine, for example, might read a configuration file, initialize a scratch file, set up a memory manager, and show an initial screen. To make it most effective, have the temporally cohesive routine call other routines to perform specific activities rather than performing the operations directly itself. That way, it will be clear that the point of the routine is to orchestrate activities rather than to do them directly.

Unacceptable Cohesion

The remaining kinds of cohesion are generally unacceptable. They result in code that's poorly organized, hard to debug, and hard to modify. If a routine has bad cohesion, it's better to put effort into a good rewrite than into a pinpoint diagnosis of the problem. Knowing what to avoid can be useful, however, so here are the unacceptable kinds of cohesion:

Procedural cohesion. Procedural cohesion occurs when operations in a routine are done in a specified order. Unlike in sequential cohesion, the sequential operations in procedural cohesion don't share the same data. For example, if your users like reports to be printed in a certain order, you might have a routine that prints a revenue report, an expense report, a list of employee phone numbers, and invitations to the company picnic. This kind of routine is difficult to name specifically, and its vague routine name would be a tip-off.

CROSS REFERENCE
Module packaging is discussed in more detail in Chapter 6, "Three out of Four Programmers Surveyed Prefer Modules."

Logical cohesion. Logical cohesion occurs when several operations are stuffed into the same routine and one of the operations is selected by a control flag that's passed in. It's called logical cohesion because the control flow or "logic" of the routine is the only thing that ties the operations together—they're all in a big *if* statement or *case* statement together. It isn't because the operations are logically related in any other sense.

One example would be an *InputAll()* routine that input customer names, employee time-card information, or inventory data depending on a flag passed to the routine. Other examples would be *ComputeAll()*, *EditAll()*, *PrintAll()*, and *SaveAll()*. The main problem with such routines is that you shouldn't need to pass in a flag to control another routine's processing. Instead of having a routine that does one of three distinct operations, depending on a flag passed to it, it's cleaner to have three routines, each of which does one distinct operation. If the operations use some of the same code or share data, the code should be put into a lower-level routine and the routines should be packaged into a module.

It's usually all right, however, to create a logically cohesive routine if its code consists solely of a series of *if* or *case* statements and calls to other routines. In such a case, if the routine's only function is to dispatch commands and it doesn't do any of the processing itself, that's usually a good design. The technical term for this kind of routine is "transaction center." A transaction center is often used as an event-handler routine in message-based environments such as the Apple Macintosh and Microsoft Windows.

Coincidental cohesion. Coincidental cohesion occurs when the operations in a routine have no discernable relationship to each other. Other good names are "no cohesion" or "chaotic cohesion." The low-quality Pascal routine at the beginning of the chapter had coincidental cohesion.

None of these terms are magical or sacred. Learn the ideas rather than the terminology. It's nearly always possible to write routines with functional cohesion, so focus your attention on functional cohesion for maximum benefit.

Examples of Cohesion

Here are examples of the several kinds of cohesion, both good and bad:

Example of functional cohesion. A routine calculates an employee's age, given a birth date. The routine does one thing and one thing only, so it has functional cohesion.

Example of sequential cohesion. A routine calculates an employee's age and time to retirement, given a birth date. If the routine calculates the age and then uses that result to calculate the employee's time to retirement, it has sequential cohesion. If the routine calculates the age and then calculates the time to retirement in a completely separate computation that happens to use the same birth-date data, it has only communicational cohesion.

Deciding what kind of weak cohesion the routine has, however, is less important than determining how to make it better. How would you make the routine functionally cohesive? You'd create separate routines to compute an employee's age given a birth date, and time to retirement given a birth date. The time-to-retirement routine could call the age routine. They'd both have functional cohesion. Other routines could call either routine or both.

Example of communicational cohesion. A routine prints a summary report and when it's done, reinitializes the summary data passed in to it. The routine has communicational cohesion because the two operations are related only by the fact that they use the same data.

More important than identifying the routine as one with communicational cohesion is deciding how to make it functionally cohesive. The summary data should be reinitialized close to where it's created, which shouldn't be in the report-printing routine. Split the operations into individual routines. The first prints the report. The second reinitializes the data, close to the code that creates or modifies the data. Call both routines from the higher-level routine that originally called the communicationally cohesive routine.

Example of logical cohesion. A routine prints a quarterly expense report, a monthly expense report, or a daily expense report, depending on the value of a control flag that's passed in. The routine has logical cohesion because its internal logic is controlled by the flag that's passed in. The routine certainly doesn't do one thing and do it well.

How do you make this routine functionally cohesive? Create three routines: one that prints a quarterly expense report, one that prints a monthly expense report, and one that prints a daily expense report. Modify the original routine so that it calls one of the new routines, depending on the value of the control flag that's passed in. The calling routine, containing no code of its own except the code that calls the appropriate routine, now has functional cohesion. Each of the three routines called also has functional cohesion.

Incidentally, the routine that does nothing but call the appropriate printing routine is another example of a transaction center. It's good to name a transaction center something like *DispatchReportPrinting()*—something with "Dispatch" or "Control" in the name—so that it's clear that the transaction center doesn't do anything on its own and that it's not supposed to.

Another example of logical cohesion. A routine prints an expense report, enters a new employee name, or backs up a database, depending on the value of a control flag that's passed in. The routine has logical cohesion only—although the cohesion in this example seems more like *illogical* cohesion.

To achieve functional cohesion, break up the separate functions into separate routines. The operations are so unrelated that the code that calls the routine probably needs to be reorganized too. Once you have separate routines to call, reorganizing the calling code is easier.

Example of procedural cohesion. A routine gets an employee name, then an address, and then a phone number. The order of these operations is important only because it matches the order in which the user is asked for the data on the input screen. Another routine gets the rest of the employee data. The routine has procedural cohesion because it puts a set of operations in a specified order and the operations don't need to be combined for any other reason.

The more important question of how to achieve functional cohesion is answered in the usual way. Put the separate operations into their own routines. Make sure that the calling routine has a single, complete job: *GetEmployeeData()* rather than *GetFirstPartOfEmployeeData()*. You'll probably need to modify the routines that get the rest of the data too. It's common to modify two or more original routines before you achieve functional cohesion in any of them.

Example of functional and temporal cohesion. A routine performs all the processing necessary to complete a transaction—getting a confirmation from the user, saving a record to a database, clearing data fields, and incrementing counters. The routine has functional cohesion. It does one job, completing a transaction, and that's all it does. It would also be accurate to describe the routine as having temporal cohesion, but if you can classify a routine at more than one level of cohesion, it's considered to have the strongest level of cohesion at which it can be classified.

This example raises the issue of choosing a name that describes the routine at the right level of abstraction. You could decide to name the routine *ConfirmEntryAndAdjustData()*, which would imply that the routine had only coincidental cohesion. If you named it *CompleteTransaction()*, however, it would be clear that it had a single purpose and clear that it had functional cohesion.

Example of procedural, temporal, or possibly logical cohesion. A routine performs the first five steps in a complicated mathematical operation and returns the intermediate results of the five steps to the calling routine. Since it takes several hours to do the first five steps, the routine stores the intermediate results in a file in case the system crashes. Then the routine checks the disk to see whether it has enough space to store the final results of the calculations and returns the disk status to the calling routine along with the intermediate results.

This routine probably has procedural cohesion, but you could argue persuasively for temporal or even logical cohesion. The real issue isn't precisely identifying the routine's brand of imperfect cohesion. It's improving the routine's cohesion.

The original routine is a strange collection of activities that's far from being functionally cohesive. At a minimum, the calling routine should call not one but several separate routines to (1) do the first five steps in the calculation, (2) store the intermediate results in a file, and (3) determine available disk space. If the calling routine is named, say, *ComputeExtravagantNumber()*, it shouldn't be writing the intermediate result to disk, and it absolutely should not be checking disk space for some later activity. It should just compute the number. A good reorganization is bound to affect routines at least one or two levels above it. A better design of the job would look like the diagram in Figure 5-1.

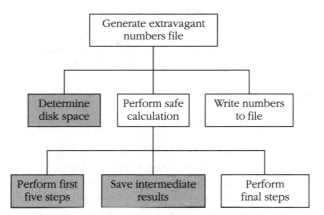

Figure 5-1. *An example of decomposition to achieve functional cohesion.*

The activities covered by the original routine are shown in shaded boxes. They should be at different levels in the organization, which is why so much reorganization is required to put them into more appropriate routines. It's not unusual to need several functionally cohesive routines to rescue one routine with poor cohesion.

5.4 Loose Coupling

CROSS-REFERENCE
The idea of coupling is a part of structured design. For more information on structured design, see Section 7.2, "Structured Design."

The degree of coupling refers to the strength of a connection between two routines. Coupling is a complement to cohesion. Cohesion describes how strongly the internal contents of a routine are related to each other. Coupling describes how strongly a routine is related to other routines. The goal is to create routines with internal integrity (strong cohesion) and small, direct, visible, and flexible relations to other routines (loose coupling).

Good coupling between routines is loose enough that one routine can easily be called by other routines. Model railroad cars are coupled by opposing hooks that latch when pushed together. Connecting two cars is easy—you just push the cars together. Imagine how much more difficult it would be if you had to screw things together, or connect a set of wires, or if you could connect only certain kinds of cars to certain other kinds of cars. The coupling of model railroad cars works because it's as simple as possible. In software, make the connections among routines as simple as possible.

Try to create routines that depend little on other routines. Make them detached, as business associates are, rather than attached, as Siamese twins are. A function like *sin()* is loosely coupled because everything it needs to know is passed in to it with one value representing an angle in degrees. A function such as *InitVars(var 1, var2, var3, ..., varN)* is more tightly coupled because the calling routine virtually knows what is happening inside it. Two routines that depend on each other's use of the same global data are even more tightly coupled.

Coupling Criteria

FURTHER READING
These criteria are adapted from *Structured Design* (Yourdon and Constantine 1979) and *The Practical Guide to Structured Systems Design* (Page-Jones 1988).

Here are several criteria to use in evaluating coupling between routines:

Size. Size refers to the number of connections between routines. With coupling, small is beautiful because it's less work to connect other routines to a routine with a smaller interface. A routine that takes one parameter is more loosely coupled to routines that call it than a routine that takes six parameters. A routine that takes an integer parameter is more loosely coupled to the routines that call it than one that takes a 10-element array or a structured variable. A routine that uses one global variable is more loosely connected to other routines in a program than a routine that uses twelve.

Intimacy. Intimacy refers to the directness of the connection between two routines. The more intimate the connection, the better. The most intimate connection between routines is a parameter in a parameter list. The routines communicate directly. The parameter is like a kiss on the lips between the routines. A less intimate connection is found between routines that work with the same piece of global data. They communicate less directly. Global data is like a love letter between routines—it might go where you want it to, or it might get lost in the mail. The least intimate connection is found between routines that work with the same database records or files. They both need the data but are too shy to acknowledge each other. A shared data file is like passing a note in class that says "Do you like me? Check ☐yes or ☐no."

Visibility. Visibility refers to the prominence of the connection between two routines. Programming is not like being in the CIA; you don't get credit for being sneaky. It's more like advertising; you get lots of credit for making your connections as blatant as possible. Passing data in a parameter list is making an obvious connection and is therefore good. Modifying global data so that another routine can use it is making a sneaky connection and is therefore bad. Documenting the global-data connection makes it more obvious and is slightly better.

Flexibility. Flexibility refers to how easily you can change the connections between routines. Ideally, you want something more like the snap-in modular connector on your phone than like bare wire and a soldering gun. Flexibility is partly a product of the other coupling characteristics, but it's a little different too. For example, suppose you have a routine that looks up the first supervisor an employee ever had, given a hiring date and a hiring department. Name the routine *LookupFirstSupervisor()*. Suppose you also have in another routine a structured variable called *EmpRec* that includes the hiring date and the hiring department, among other things, and that the second routine passes the variable to *LookupFirstSupervisor()*.

From the point of view of the other criteria, the two routines would look pretty loosely coupled. The *EmpRec* connection between the first and second routines is a smack on the lips, in public, and there's only one connection. Now suppose that you need to call the *LookupFirstSupervisor()* routine from a third routine that doesn't have an *EmpRec* but does have a hiring date and a hiring department. Suddenly *LookupFirstSupervisor()* looks less friendly, unwilling to associate with the new routine.

For the third routine to call *LookupFirstSupervisor()*, it has to know about the *EmpRec* data structure. It could dummy up an *EmpRec* variable with only two fields, but that would require internal knowledge of *LookupFirstSupervisor()*, namely that those are the only fields it uses. Such a solution would be a kludge, and an ugly one. The second option would be to modify *Lookup-FirstSupervisor()* so that it would take hiring date and hiring department instead of *EmpRec*. In either case, the original routine turns out to be a lot less flexible than it seemed to be at first.

The happy ending to the story is that an unfriendly routine can make friends if it's willing to be flexible—in this case, by changing to take hiring date and hiring department specifically instead of *EmpRec*.

In short, the more easily other routines can call a routine, the more loosely coupled it is, and that's good because it's more flexible and maintainable. In creating a system structure, break up the program along the lines of minimal interconnectedness. If a program were a piece of wood, you would try to split it with the grain.

Levels of Coupling

The traditional names for the levels of coupling are unintuitive, so the following descriptions of the classes of coupling use good, mnemonic names along with the confusing traditional names. Examples of good and bad coupling follow the coupling descriptions.

Simple-data coupling. Two routines are simple-data–coupled if all the data passed between them is nonstructured and it's all passed through a parameter list. This is often called "normal coupling" and is the best kind.

Data-structure coupling. Two routines are data-structure–coupled if the data passed between them is structured and is passed through a parameter list.

This is sometimes called "stamp coupling" (for reasons that have always been opaque to me) and is fine if used properly. Its main difference from simple-data coupling is that structured data is involved.

Control coupling. Two routines are control-coupled if one routine passes data to the other that tells the second routine what to do. Control coupling is as undesirable as the logical cohesion it's associated with. It generally requires that the calling routine know about the internal workings of the called routine.

CROSS-REFERENCE
Coupling with global data is distinct from coupling with module data. For details on module-data coupling, see "Module data mistaken for global data" in Section 6.2 and discussions throughout Chapter 6.

Global-data coupling. Two routines are global-data–coupled if they make use of the same global data. This is also called "common coupling" or "global coupling." If use of the data is read-only, the practice is tolerable. Generally, however, global-data coupling is undesirable because the connection between routines is neither intimate nor visible. The connection is so easy to miss that you could refer to it as information hiding's evil cousin—"information losing."

Pathological coupling. Two routines are pathologically coupled if one uses the code inside another or if one alters the local data used inside another. This is also called "content coupling." This kind of coupling is unacceptable because it fails all the criteria of size, intimacy, visibility, and flexibility. One routine's executing another routine's code makes a large connection between the two routines. Although it's a close connection, the connection between the two routines is not intimate. Altering another routine's data is more like stabbing it in the back. The connection is invisible from the point of view of the routine being stabbed. And the connection is not flexible; it depends on one routine's having detailed knowledge of the internal affairs of another. Most structured languages have scoping rules that prevent pathological coupling. It's still possible in Basic and assembler, however, so if you're working in either of those languages, watch out!

Each of these kinds of coupling is shown in Figure 5-2.

Examples of Coupling

Here are examples of the kinds of coupling, both good and bad:

Example of simple-data coupling. One routine passes a variable containing an angle in degrees to a *tan()* routine.

Another example of simple-data coupling. One routine passes five variables to another routine, including a name, an address, a phone number, a birth date, and a social security number.

Example of acceptable data-structure coupling. One routine passes an *EmpRec* variable to another routine. *EmpRec* is a structured variable that includes a

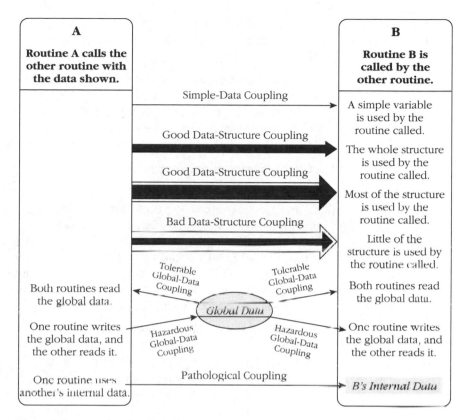

Figure 5-2. *Some kinds of coupling.*

name, an address, a phone number, a birth date, and a social security number.
The called routine uses all five fields.

Example of unacceptable data-structure coupling. One routine passes the
same *EmpRec* variable to another routine. The called routine uses only the
birth date and phone number. This is data-structure coupling also, but it's not
a good use of it. Passing the birth date and phone number as simple variables
would make the connection more flexible and the real connection of the two
specific fields more visible.

CROSS-REFERENCE
For details on creating good
routine parameter lists, see
Section 5.7, "How to Use
Routine Parameters."
Example of questionable data-structure coupling. One routine passes an
OfficeRec variable to another routine. *OfficeRec* has 27 fields, and the called
routine uses 16 of them. This is data-structure coupling. But is it good data-
structure coupling? It's a close call. Passing *OfficeRec* makes it obvious that the
connection is large; passing 16 individual parameters would just be an awkward way of showing the same thing. If the called routine used only 6 or 7 of
OfficeRec's fields, it would be a good idea to pass them individually.

If it made sense to structure *OfficeRec*'s data more, so that the 16 fields used by the called routine were contained in a substructure or two, that would be the cleanest solution.

Example of simple-data or possibly data-structure coupling. A routine passes an *EraseFile()* routine a string containing the name of the file to erase. This is probably simple-data coupling. You might argue that it's data-structure coupling because a string is a data structure. I say, "You say tom-AY-to, I say tom-AH-to." Both are fine, and the distinction isn't important.

Example of control coupling. One routine passes a flag to another that tells it whether to print a monthly report, a quarterly report, or an annual report.

Example of unacceptable global-data coupling. A routine modifies an entry in a table stored as a global variable. The table is indexed by employee ID. The routine then calls another routine and passes it the employee ID as a parameter. The called routine uses the employee ID to read the global-data table. This is a classic example of global-data coupling. (Although merely passing the employee ID would constitute simple-data coupling, the first routine's modification of the table entry earns the coupling the worst rating.)

CROSS-REFERENCE
For guidelines on using global data safely, see Section 10.6, "Global Variables."

Example of acceptable global-data coupling. One routine passes an employee ID to another routine. Both routines use the employee ID to read the corresponding employee name from a global table. Neither routine changes any global data. This is often described as global-data coupling, but it's more like simple-data coupling or "tolerable global-data coupling." Unlike the routines in the example in which one routine modifies data used by another, these routines aren't connected to each other by the global data. With respect to each other, their read-only use of the same global data is benign. There is a world of difference between two routines conspiring to hide a connection by using global data (as in the previous example) and two routines coincidentally reading a value from the same global table.

Example of pathological coupling. An assembler routine knows the address of a table declared as a local variable inside another routine. It uses the address to modify the table directly. The address is not passed between the routines as a parameter.

Another example of pathological coupling. A Basic routine uses a *GOSUB* to execute a piece of code within another routine.

KEY POINT

The whole point of good coupling is that an effective routine provides an additional level of abstraction—once you write it, you can take it for granted. It reduces overall program complexity and allows you to focus on one thing at a time. If using a routine requires you to focus on more than one thing at once—knowledge of its internal workings, modification to global data, uncertain functionality—the abstractive power is lost and the value of the routine is reduced or eliminated. Routines are primarily an intellectual tool for reducing complexity. If they're not making your job simpler, they're not doing their job.

5.5 How Long Can a Routine Be?

On their way to America, the Pilgrims argued about the best maximum length for a routine. After arguing about it for the entire trip, they arrived at Plymouth Rock and started to draft the Mayflower Compact. They still hadn't settled the maximum-length question, and since they couldn't disembark until they'd signed the compact, they gave up and didn't include it. The result has been an interminable debate ever since about how long a routine can be.

The theoretical best maximum length is often described as one or two pages of program listing, 66 to 132 lines. In this spirit, in the 1970s IBM limited routines to 50 lines, and TRW limited them to two pages (McCabe 1976). The evidence in favor of short routines, however, is very thin, and the evidence in favor of longer routines is compelling. Consider the following:

HARD DATA

- A study by Basili and Perricone found that routine size was inversely correlated with errors; as the size of routines increased (up to 200 lines of code), the number of errors per line of code decreased (1984).

- Another study found that routine size was not correlated with errors, even though structural complexity and amount of data were correlated with errors (Shen et al. 1985).

- A 1986 study found that small routines (32 lines of code or fewer) were not correlated with lower cost or fault rate (Card, Church, and Agresti 1986; Card and Glass 1990). The evidence suggested that larger routines (65 lines of code or more) were cheaper to develop per line of code.

- An empirical study of 450 routines found that small routines (those with fewer than 143 source statements, including comments) had 23 percent more errors per line of code than larger routines (Selby and Basili 1991).

- A study of upper-level computer-science students found that students' comprehension of a program that was super-modularized into routines about 10 lines long was no better than their comprehension of a program that had no routines at all (Conte, Dunsmore, and Shen 1986). When the program was broken into routines of moderate length (about 25 lines), however, students scored 65 percent better on a test of comprehension.

- A recent study found that code needed to be changed least when routines averaged 100 to 150 lines of code (Lind and Vairavan 1989).

Where does all this leave the question of routine length? Well, if you're a manager, don't tell your programmers to keep their routines to one page—the studies cited and your programmers' experience will tell them you're full of hooey. Second, if you think it makes sense to make a certain routine 100, 150, or 200 lines long, it's probably all right to do so. Current evidence says that routines of such length are no more error prone than shorter routines and are likely to be cheaper to develop.

HARD DATA

If you want to write routines longer than about 200 lines, be careful. (A line is a noncomment, nonblank line of source code.) None of the studies that reported decreased cost, decreased error rates, or both with larger routines distinguished among sizes larger than 200 lines, and you're bound to run into an upper limit of understandability as you pass 200 lines of code. In a study of the code for IBM's OS/360 operating system and other systems, the most error-prone routines were those that were larger than 500 lines of code. Beyond 500 lines, the error rate tended to be proportional to the size of the routine (Jones 1986a). Moreover, an empirical study of a 148,000-line program found that routines with fewer than 143 source statements were 2.4 times less expensive to fix than larger routines (Selby and Basili 1991).

5.6 Defensive Programming

KEY POINT

Defensive programming doesn't mean being defensive about your programming—"It does so work!" The idea is based on defensive driving. In defensive driving, you adopt the mind-set that you're never sure what the other drivers are going to do. That way, you make sure that if they do something dangerous you won't be hurt. You take responsibility for protecting yourself even when it might be the other driver's fault. In defensive programming, the main idea is that if a routine is passed bad data, it won't be hurt, even if the bad data is another routine's fault. More generally, it's the recognition that programs will have problems and modifications, and that a smart programmer will develop code accordingly.

Defensive programming is useful as an adjunct to the other techniques for quality improvement described in this book. The best form of defensive coding is not installing errors in the first place. Using iterative design, writing PDL before code, and having low-level design inspections are all activities that help to prevent installing defects. They should thus be given a higher priority than defensive programming. Fortunately, you can use defensive programming in combination with the other techniques.

Mike Siegel/The Seattle Times

Part of the Interstate-90 floating bridge in Seattle sank during a storm because the flotation tanks were left uncovered, they filled with water, and the bridge became too heavy to float. During construction, protecting yourself against the small stuff matters more than you might think.

Using Assertions

An assertion is a function or macro that complains loudly if an assumption isn't true. Use assertions to document assumptions made in the code and to flush out unexpected conditions. An assertion function usually takes two arguments: a boolean expression that describes the assumption that's supposed to be true and a message to print if it's not. Here's what a Pascal assertion would look like if the variable *Denominator* were expected to be nonzero:

Pascal Example of an Assertion

```
Assert( Denominator <> 0, 'Denominator is unexpectedly equal to 0.' );
```

This assertion asserts that *Denominator* is not equal to *0*. The first argument, *Denominator <> 0*, is a boolean expression that evaluates to *True* or *False*. The second argument is a message to print if the first argument is *False*—that is, if the assertion is false.

Even if you don't want your users to see assertion messages in production code, assertions are handy during development and maintenance. During development, assertions flush out contradictory assumptions, unexpected conditions, bad values passed to routines, and so on. During maintenance, they indicate whether modifications have damaged other parts of the code.

Assertion procedures are easy to write. Here's one in Pascal:

Pascal Example of an Assertion Procedure

```pascal
Procedure Assert
   (
   Assertion:  boolean;
   Message:    string
   );
begin
if ( not Assertion )
   begin
   writeln( Message );
   writeln( 'Stopping the program.' );
   halt( FATAL_ERROR )
   end
end;
```

The halt() statement terminates the program. It isn't part of standard Pascal, but most implementations of Pascal have something similar.

Once you've written a procedure like this, you can call it with statements like the first one above.

Here are some guidelines for using assertions:

Use a preprocessor macro for assertions, if you have a preprocessor. Using a preprocessor for assertions makes it easy to use assertions during development and to take them out of production code.

Avoid putting executable code in assertions. Putting code in an assertion raises the possibility that the compiler will eliminate the code when you turn off the assertions. Suppose you have an assertion like this:

CROSS-REFERENCE
You could view this as one of many problems associated with putting multiple statements on one line. For more examples, see "Using Only One Statement per Line" in Section 18.5.

Pascal Example of a Dangerous Use of an Assertion

```pascal
Assert( FileOpen( InputFile ) <> nil, 'Couldn"t open input file' );
```

The problem with this code is that if you don't compile the assertions, you don't compile the code that performs the file open. Put executable statements on their own lines, assign the results to status variables, and test the status variables instead. Here's an example of a safe use of an assertion:

Pascal Example of a Safe Use of an Assertion

```pascal
FileStatus := FileOpen( InputFile );
Assert( FileStatus <> nil, 'Couldn"t open input file' );
```

Garbage In Does Not Mean Garbage Out

A good program never puts out garbage, regardless of what it takes in. A good program uses "garbage in, nothing out"; "garbage in, error message out"; or "no garbage allowed in" instead. By today's standards, "garbage in, garbage out" is the mark of a sloppy program.

Check the values of all data input from external sources. When getting data from a file or a user, check to be sure that the data falls in the allowable range. Make sure that numeric values are within tolerances and that strings are short enough to handle. Comment assumptions about acceptable input ranges in the code.

CROSS-REFERENCE
If you program using pointers, it's an especially good idea to check any that are passed as input parameters. For details on the kinds of checks you can make on pointers, see Section 11.9, "Pointers."

Check the values of all routine input parameters. Checking the values of routine input parameters is essentially the same as checking data that comes from an external source, except that the data comes from another routine instead of from a file or a user.

Here's an example of a routine that checks its input parameters:

This statement calls a routine, Assert(), that prints the message and stops the program if the logical expression isn't true.

```
C Example of Using an Assertion to Check an Input Parameter
float tan
    (
    float OppositeLength,
    float AdjacentLength
    )
    {
    /* compute tangent of an angle */

    Assert( AdjacentLength != 0, "AdjacentLength detected to be 0." );

    return( OppositeLength / AdjacentLength );
    }
```

Decide how to handle bad parameters. Once you've detected an invalid parameter, what do you do with it? Depending on the situation, you might want to return an error code, return a neutral value, substitute the next piece of valid data and continue as planned, return the same answer as the previous time, use the closest legal value, call an error-processing routine, log a warning message to a file, print an error message, or shut down. You have so many options that you need to be careful not to handle invalid parameters in randomly different ways in different parts of the program. Deciding on a general approach to bad parameters is an architectural decision and should be addressed at the architectural level.

Exception Handling

CROSS-REFERENCE
For more details on handling unanticipated cases, see "Tips for Using *case* Statements" in Section 14.2.

Use exception handling to draw attention to unexpected cases. Exceptional cases should be handled in a way that makes them obvious during development and recoverable when production code is running. For example, suppose you have a *case* statement that interprets five kinds of events, and you expect to have only five kinds of events. During development, the default case should be used to generate a warning that says "Hey! There's another case here! Fix the program!" During production, however, the default case should do something more graceful, like writing a message to an error-log file. Try to design the program so that you can flip from development mode to production mode without too much trouble.

Anticipating Changes

Change is a fact of life with every program. New versions of old programs require more changes to the existing code base than new code does. But even during development of the first version of a program, you'll add unanticipated features that require changes. Error corrections also introduce changes. Develop the program so that likely changes can be accommodated without an act of Congress. The more likely the change, the less trauma it should cause the program. Hiding the areas in which you anticipate changes is one of the most powerful techniques for minimizing the impact of changes.

CROSS-REFERENCE
For details on information hiding, see Section 6.2, "Information Hiding."

Planning to Remove Debugging Aids

Debugging aids are assertions, memory checksums, print statements, and a variety of other coding practices that can help in debugging. If you're writing code for your own use, it might be fine to leave all the debugging code in the program. If you're writing code for commercial use, the performance penalty in size and speed is often prohibitive. If that's the case, plan to avoid shuffling debugging code in and out of a program. Here are several ways to do that.

CROSS-REFERENCE
For details on version control, see Section 22.2, "Configuration Management."

Use version control. Version-control tools can build different versions of a program from the same source files. In development mode, you can set the version-control tool to include all the debug code. In production mode, you can set it to exclude any debug code you don't want in the commercial version.

Use a built-in preprocessor. If your programming environment has a preprocessor—as C does, for example—you can include or exclude debug code at the flick of a compiler switch. You can use the preprocessor directly or by writing a macro that works with preprocessor definitions. Here's an example of writing code using the preprocessor directly:

C Example of Using the Preprocessor Directly to Control Debug Code

To include the debug- ───
ging code, use #define
to define the symbol
DEBUG. To exclude
the debugging code,
don't define DEBUG.

```
#define DEBUG
...

#if defined( DEBUG )
/* debugging code */
...

#endif
```

This theme has several variations. Rather than just defining *DEBUG*, you can assign it a value and then test for the value rather than testing whether it's defined. That way you can differentiate between different levels of debug code. You might have some debug code that you want in your program all the time, so you surround that by a statement like *#if DEBUG > 0*. Other debug code might be for specific purposes only, so you can surround it by a statement like *#if DEBUG == POINTER_ERROR*. In other places, you might want to set debug levels, so you could have statements like *#if DEBUG > LEVEL_A*

If you don't like having *#if defined()*s spread throughout your code, you can write a preprocessor macro to accomplish the same task. Here's an example:

C Example of Using a Preprocessor Macro to Control Debug Code

```
#define DEBUG

#if defined( DEBUG )
#define DebugCode( code_fragment )   { code_fragment }
#else
#define DebugCode( code_fragment )
#endif
...

DebugCode
   (
   statement 1;
   statement 2;
   ...
   statement n;
   );
...
```

This code is included
or excluded depending
on whether DEBUG
has been defined.

As in the first example of using the preprocessor, this technique can be altered in a variety of ways that make it more sophisticated than completely including all debug code or completely excluding all of it.

CROSS-REFERENCE
For more information on
preprocessors and direction
to sources of information
on writing one of your own,
see "Macro preprocessors"
in Section 20.3.

Write your own preprocessor. If a language doesn't include a preprocessor, it's fairly easy to write one for including and excluding debug code. Establish a convention for designating debug code and write your precompiler to follow that convention. For example, in Pascal you could write a precompiler to respond to the keywords {#BEGIN DEBUG} and {#END DEBUG}. Write a script or batch file to call the preprocessor, and then compile the processed code. You'll save time in the long run, and you won't mistakenly compile the un-preprocessed code.

CROSS-REFERENCE
For details on stubs, see
"Building Scaffolding to
Test Individual Routines"
in Section 25.5.

Use debugging stubs. In many instances, you can call a routine to do debugging checks. During development, the routine might perform several operations before control returns to the caller. For production code, you can replace the complicated routine with a stub routine that merely returns control immediately to the caller or performs only a couple of quick operations before returning control. This approach incurs only a small performance penalty, and it's a quicker solution than writing your own preprocessor. Keep both the development and production versions of the routines so that you can switch back and forth during future development and production.

You might start with a routine designed to check pointers that are passed to it:

Pascal Example of a Routine that Uses a Debugging Stub

```
Procedure DoSomething
    (
    Pointer: POINTER_TYPE;
    ...
    );
begin

{ check parameters passed in }
CheckPointer( Pointer );
...

end;
```

This line calls the routine to check the pointer.

During development, the *CheckPointer()* routine would perform full checking on the pointer. It would be slow but effective. It could look like this:

Pascal Example of a Routine for Checking Pointers During Development

```
Procedure CheckPointer( Pointer: POINTER_TYPE );
begin
    { perform check 1--maybe check that it's not nil }
    { perform check 2--maybe check that its dogtag is legitimate }
    { perform check 3--maybe check that what it points to isn't corrupted }
```

This routine checks any pointer that's passed to it. It can be used during development to perform as many checks as you can bear.

(continued)

```
    ...
    { perform check n--... }
end;
```

When the code is ready for production, you might not want all the overhead associated with this pointer checking. You could swap out the routine above and swap in this routine:

Pascal Example of a Routine for Checking Pointers During Production

This routine just —
returns immediately
to the caller.

```
Procedure CheckPointer( Pointer: POINTER_TYPE );
begin
{ no code; just return to caller }
end;
```

This is not an exhaustive survey of all the ways you can plan to remove debugging aids, but it should be enough to give you an idea for some things that will work in your environment.

Introducing Debugging Aids Early

The earlier you introduce debugging aids, the more they'll help. Typically, you won't go to the effort of writing a debugging aid until after you've been bitten by a problem several times. If you write the aid after the first time, however, or use one from a previous project, it will help throughout the project.

Firewalling to Contain the Damage Caused by Errors

Firewalling is a damage-containment strategy. A firewall in a building keeps a fire from spreading, isolating it in one place. The reason is similar to that for having isolated compartments in the hull of a ship. If the ship runs into an iceberg and pops open the hull, that compartment is shut off and the rest of the ship isn't affected.

Information hiding helps to firewall a program. The less you know about the internal workings of another routine, the fewer assumptions you make about how the routine operates. The fewer the assumptions you make, the less the chance that one of them is wrong.

Loose coupling also helps to firewall a program. The looser the connection between two routines, the less the chance that an error in one routine will affect the other. If the connection is tighter, if one routine borrows code from inside another, chances are high that an error in one routine will affect the other.

A final way to firewall is to designate certain interfaces as boundaries to "safe" areas. Check data crossing the boundaries of a safe area for validity and respond sensibly if the data isn't valid. Another way of thinking of this approach is as an operating-room technique. Data is sterilized before it's allowed to enter the operating room. Anything that's in the operating room is assumed to be safe. The key design decision is deciding what to put in the operating room, what to keep out, and where to put the doors—which routines are considered to be inside the safety zone, which are outside, and which sanitize the data. The easiest way to do this is usually by sanitizing external data as it arrives, but data often needs to be sanitized at more than one level, so multiple levels of sterilization are sometimes required.

Routines That Assume Data Is Safe:	Routines That Check Their Data:
PrintBeginPage()	PointsToDeviceUnits()
PrintEndPage()	DeviceUnitsToPoints()
PrintBeginDoc()	SetFontSize()
PrintEndDoc()	SetUnderlinePosition()
SetFontName()	SetStrikeoutPosition()
SetCursorHeight()	SetItalicAngle()
SetCursorPosition()	
ShowCursor()	
TimestampOutput()	

Distinguish between routines that assume their data is safe and routines that check the data they receive.

Checking Function Return Values

If you call a function and have the option of ignoring a function's return value (for example, in C, where you don't even have to acknowledge that a function returns a value), don't! Test the value. If you don't expect it ever to produce an error, check it anyway. The whole point of defensive programming is guarding against unexpected errors.

This guideline holds true for system functions as well as your own. Unless you've set an architectural guideline of not checking system calls for errors, check for error codes after each call. If you detect an error, include the error number and the description of the error from *perror()* in C or the equivalent in other languages.

Determining How Much Defensive Programming to Leave in Production Code

One of the paradoxes of defensive programming is that during development, you'd like an error to be noticeable—you'd rather have it be obnoxious than risk overlooking it. But during production, you'd rather have the error be as unobtrusive as possible, to have the program recover or fail gracefully. Here are some guidelines for deciding which defensive programming tools to leave in your production code and which to leave out:

Leave in code that checks for important errors. Decide which areas of the program can afford to have undetected errors and which areas cannot. For example, if you were writing a spreadsheet program, you could afford to have undetected errors in the screen-update area of the program because the main penalty for an error is only a messy screen. You could not afford to have undetected errors in the calculation engine because the errors might result in subtly incorrect results in someone's spreadsheet. Most users would rather suffer a messy screen than incorrect tax calculations and an audit by the IRS.

Remove code that checks for trivial errors. If an error has truly trivial consequences, remove code that checks for it. In the previous example, you might remove the code that checks the spreadsheet screen update. "Remove" doesn't mean physically remove the code. It means use version control, pre-compiler switches, or some other technique to compile the program without that particular code. If space isn't a problem, you could leave in the error-checking code but have it log messages to an error-log file unobtrusively.

Remove code that results in hard crashes. During development, when your program detects an error, you'd like the error to be as noticeable as possible so that you can fix it. Often, the best way to accomplish such a goal is to have the program print a debugging message and crash when it detects an error. This is useful even for minor errors.

During production, your users need a chance to save their work before the program crashes and are probably willing to tolerate a few anomalies in exchange for keeping the program going long enough for them to do that. Users don't appreciate anything that results in the loss of their work, regardless of how much it helps debugging and ultimately improves the quality of the program. If your program contains debugging code that could cause a loss of data, take it out of the production version.

Leave in code that helps the program crash gracefully. The opposite is also true. If your program contains debugging code that detects potentially fatal errors, users appreciate having a chance to save their work before the error becomes terminal. The word processor I'm using has a "SAVE" light that

103

comes on right before the program runs out of memory. I've learned not to keep working when the light comes on but to save immediately and exit. When I restart the program, everything is fine. Theoretically, the program shouldn't run out of memory, and it shouldn't have more memory available when I restart it with the same document and the same machine. The fact that it runs out of memory is a defect. But the programmers were thoughtful enough to leave the debugging aid in the program, and I appreciate having the warning rather than losing my work.

See that the messages you leave in are friendly. If you leave internal error messages in the program, verify that they're in language that's friendly to the user. In one of my early programs, I got a call from a user who reported that she'd gotten a message that read "You've got a bad pointer allocation, Dog Breath!" Fortunately for me, she had a sense of humor. A common and effective approach is to notify the user of an "internal error" and list a phone number the user can call to report it.

Being Defensive About Defensive Programming

> Too much of anything is bad, but too much whiskey is just enough.
>
> *Mark Twain*

Too much defensive programming creates problems of its own. If you check data passed as parameters in every conceivable way in every conceivable place, your program will be fat and slow. What's worse, the additional code needed for defensive programming adds complexity to the software. Code installed for defensive programming is not immune to defects, and you're just as likely to find a defect in defensive-programming code as in any other code— more likely, if you write the code casually. Think about where you need to be defensive, and set your defensive-programming priorities accordingly.

5.7 How to Use Routine Parameters

HARD DATA

Interfaces between routines are some of the most error-prone areas of a program. One study by Basili and Perricone (1984) found that 39 percent of all errors were internal interface errors—errors in communication between routines. Here are a few guidelines for minimizing interface problems:

Make sure actual parameters match formal parameters. Formal parameters, also known as dummy parameters, are the variables declared in a routine definition. Actual parameters are the variables or constants used in the actual routine calls.

A common mistake is to put the wrong type of variable in a routine call—for example, using an integer when a floating point is needed. (This is a problem only in weakly typed languages like C when you're not using full compiler warnings and in assembler. Strongly typed languages such as Pascal don't have this problem.) When arguments are input only, this is seldom a problem; usually the compiler converts the actual type to the formal type before passing it to the routine. If it is a problem, usually your compiler gives you a warning. But in some cases, particularly when the argument is used for both input and output, you can get stung by passing the wrong type of argument.

Develop the habit of checking types of arguments in parameter lists and heeding compiler warnings about mismatched parameter types. In C, use ANSI function prototypes for all your functions so that the compiler will check all function arguments automatically and warn you of mismatches.

CROSS-REFERENCE
For details on documenting routine parameters, see "Commenting Routines" in Section 19.5. For details on formatting parameters, see Section 18.7, "Laying Out Routines."

Put parameters in input-modify-output order. Instead of ordering parameters randomly or alphabetically, list the parameters that are input-only first, input-and-output second, and output-only third. This ordering implies the sequence of operations happening within the routine—inputting data, changing it, and sending back a result. Here are examples of parameter lists in Ada:

Ada Example of Parameters in Input-Modify-Output Order

```
procedure InvertMatrix
   (
   OriginalMatrix:  in MATRIX;
   ResultMatrix:    out MATRIX
   );
...

procedure ChangeStringCase
   (
   DesiredCase:      in STRING_CASE;
   MixedCaseString:  in out USER_STRING
   );
...

procedure PrintPageNumber
   (
   PageNumber: in INTEGER;
   Status:     out STATUS_TYPE
   );
```

This ordering convention conflicts with the C-language convention of putting the modified parameter first. The input-modify-output convention makes more sense to me, but if you consistently order parameters in some way, you still do the readers of your code a service.

If several routines use similar parameters, put the similar parameters in a consistent order. The order of routine parameters can be a mnemonic, and inconsistent order can make parameters hard to remember. For example, in C, the *fprintf()* function is the same as the *printf()* function except that it adds a file as the first argument. A similar function, *fputs()*, is the same as *puts()* except that it adds a file as the last argument. This is an aggravating, pointless difference that makes the parameters of these functions harder to remember than they need to be.

On the other hand, the function *strncpy()* in C takes the arguments target string, source string, and maximum number of bytes, in that order, and the function *memcpy()* takes the same arguments in the same order. The similarity between the two functions helps in remembering the parameters in either function.

In Microsoft Windows programming, most of the Windows routines take a "handle" as their first parameter. The convention is easy to remember and makes each routine's argument list easier to remember.

HARD DATA

Use all the parameters. If you pass a parameter to a routine, use it. If you aren't using it, remove the parameter from the routine interface. Unused parameters are correlated with an increased error rate. In one study, 46 percent of routines with no unused variables had no errors. Only 17 to 29 percent of routines with more than one unreferenced variable had no errors (Card, Church, and Agresti 1986).

This rule to remove unused parameters has two exceptions. First, if you're using function pointers in C or procedure variables in Pascal, you'll have several routines with identical parameter lists. Some of the routines might not use all the parameters. That's OK. Second, if you're compiling part of your program conditionally, you might compile out parts of a routine that use a certain parameter. Be nervous about this practice, but if you're convinced it works, that's OK too. In general, if you have a good reason not to use a parameter, go ahead and leave it in place. If you don't have a good reason, make the effort to clean up the code.

Put *Status* or *Error* variables last. By convention, status variables and variables that indicate an error has occurred go last in the parameter list. They are incidental to the main purpose of the routine, and they are output-only parameters, so it's a sensible convention.

Don't use routine parameters as working variables. It's dangerous to use the parameters passed to a routine as working variables. Use local variables instead. For example, in the Pascal fragment below, the variable *InputVal* is improperly used to store intermediate results of a computation.

Pascal Example of Improper Use of Input Parameters

```pascal
procedure Sample
   (
        InputVal:   Integer;
   VAR OutputVal:   Integer
   );
begin
   InputVal  := InputVal * CurrentMultiplier( InputVal );
   InputVal  := InputVal + CurrentAdder( InputVal );
   ...
   OutputVal := InputVal
end;
```

At this point, InputVal no longer contains the value that was input.

InputVal in this code fragment is misleading because by the time execution reaches the last line, *InputVal* no longer contains the input value; it contains a computed value based in part on the input value, and it is therefore misnamed. If you later need to modify the routine to use the original input value in some other place, you'll probably use *InputVal* and assume that it contains the original input value when it actually doesn't.

How do you solve the problem? Can you solve it by renaming *InputVal*? Probably not. You could name it something like *WorkingVal*, but that's an incomplete solution because the name fails to indicate that the variable's original value comes from outside the routine. You could name it something ridiculous like *InputValThatBecomesAWorkingVal*, or give up completely and name it *X* or *Val*, but all these approaches are weak.

A better approach is to avoid current and future problems by using working variables explicitly. The following code fragment demonstrates the technique:

Pascal Example of Good Use of Input Parameters

```pascal
procedure Sample
   (
        InputVal:   Integer;
   VAR OutputVal:   Integer
   );
var
   WorkingVal: Integer;
begin
   WorkingVal := InputVal;
   WorkingVal := WorkingVal * CurrentMultiplier( WorkingVal );
   WorkingVal := WorkingVal + CurrentAdder( WorkingVal );
   ...

   ...
   OutputVal := WorkingVal
end;
```

If you need to use the original value of Input-Val here or somewhere else, it's still available.

Introducing the new variable *WorkingVal* clarifies the role of *InputVal* and eliminates the chance of erroneously using *InputVal* at the wrong time. In Ada, this practice can be enforced by the compiler. If you designate a parameter as *in,* you're not allowed to modify its value within a function. Don't take this reasoning as a justification for literally naming a variable *WorkingVal.* In general, *WorkingVal* is a terrible name for a variable, and the name is used in this example only to make the variable's role clear.

In Fortran, using working variables is a particularly good practice. When a variable in the parameter list of the calling routine is modified in the called routine, it's also modified in the calling routine. In any language, assigning the input value to a working variable emphasizes where the value comes from. It eliminates the possibility that a variable from the parameter list will be modified accidentally.

CROSS-REFERENCE
For details on considerations in using global variables, see Section 10.6, "Global Variables."

The same technique should be used to preserve the value of a global variable. If you need to compute a new value for a global variable, assign the global variable the final value at the end of the computation rather than using it to hold the result of intermediate calculations.

CROSS-REFERENCE
For details on documentation, see Chapter 19, "Self-Documenting Code."

Document interface assumptions about parameters. If you assume the data being passed to your routine has certain characteristics, document the assumptions as you make them. It's not a waste of effort to document your assumptions both in the routine itself and in the place where the routine is called. Don't wait until you've written the routine to go back and write the comments—you won't remember all your assumptions. Even better than commenting your assumptions, use assertions to put them into code.

What kinds of interface assumptions about parameters should you document?

- Whether parameters are input-only, modified, or output-only
- Units of numeric parameters (inches, feet, meters, and so on)
- Meanings of status codes and error values if enumerated types aren't used
- Ranges of expected values
- Specific values that should never appear

HARD DATA

Limit the number of a routine's parameters to about seven. Seven is a magic number for people's comprehension. Psychological research has found that people generally cannot keep track of more than about seven chunks of information at once (Miller 1956). This discovery has been applied to an enormous number of disciplines, and it seems safe to conjecture that most people can't keep track of more than about seven routine parameters at once.

In practice, how much you can limit the number of parameters depends on how your language handles complex data structures. If you program in a modern language that supports structured data, you can pass a composite data structure containing 13 fields and think of it as one mental "chunk" of data. If you program in a more primitive language, you might need to pass all 13 fields individually.

If you find yourself consistently passing more than a few arguments, the coupling among your routines is too tight. Design the routine or group of routines to reduce the coupling. If you are passing the same data to many different routines, group the routines into a module and treat the frequently used data as module data.

CROSS-REFERENCE
For details on module data, see "Module data mistaken for global data" in Section 6.2.

Consider an input, modify, and output naming convention for parameters. If you find that it's important to distinguish among input, modify, and output parameters, establish a naming convention that identifies them. You could prefix them with $i\_$, $m\_$, and $o\_$. If you're feeling verbose, you could prefix them with *INPUT*, *MODIFY*, and *OUTPUT*.

Pass only the parts of structured variables that the routine needs. As discussed earlier, in Section 5.4 on coupling, it's better to pass only the specific fields of a structure that the called routine uses unless it uses almost all of them. The whole routine is easier to use somewhere else if you've specified a precise interface. A precise interface decreases inter-routine coupling and makes the routine more flexible.

CROSS-REFERENCE
For details on abstract data types, see Section 12.3, "Abstract Data Types (ADTs)."

The precise-interface rule has an exception when you're working with abstract data types (ADTs). The data type might require that you keep track of a structured variable, but it's good practice with an abstract data type that you not look inside the structure. If that's the case, design the abstract-data-type routines so that they take the whole record as a parameter. This allows you to treat the record as an object outside the ADT routines and keeps the record at the same level of abstraction as the ADT routines. If you open the structure by working with individual fields, you lose the level of abstraction that the ADT provides.

Don't assume anything about the parameter-passing mechanism. Some hard-core nanosecond scrapers worry about the overhead associated with passing parameters and bypass the high-level language's parameter-passing mechanism. This is dangerous and makes code nonportable. Parameters are commonly passed on a system stack, but that's hardly the only parameter-passing mechanism that languages use. Even with stack-based mechanisms, the parameters themselves can be passed in different orders and each parameter's bytes can be ordered differently. If you fiddle with parameters directly, you virtually guarantee that your program won't run on a different machine.

5.8 Considerations in the Use of Functions

Modern languages such as C, Pascal, and Ada support both functions and procedures. A function is a routine that returns a value; a procedure is a routine that does not.

When to Use a Function and When to Use a Procedure

Purists argue that a function should return only one value, just as a mathematical function does. This means that a function would take only input parameters and return its only value through the function itself. The function would always be named for the value it returned, as *sin()*, *CustomerID()*, and *ScreenHeight()* are. A procedure, on the other hand, could take input, modify, and output parameters—as many of each as it wanted to.

A common programming practice is to have a function that operates as a procedure and returns a status value. Logically, it works as a procedure, but because it returns a value, it's officially a function. For example, you might have a procedure called *FormatOutput()* used in statements like this one:

```
if ( FormatOutput( Input, Formatting, Output ) = Success ) then ...
```

In this example, *FormatOutput()* operates as a procedure in that it has an output parameter, *Output*, but it is technically a function because the routine itself returns a value. Is this a valid way to use a function? In defense of this approach, you could maintain that the function return value has nothing to do with the main purpose of the routine, formatting output, or with the routine name, *FormatOutput()*; in that sense it operates more as a procedure does even if it is technically a function. The use of the return value to indicate the success or failure of the procedure is not confusing if the technique is used consistently.

The alternative is to create a procedure that has a status variable as an explicit parameter, which promotes code like this fragment:

```
FormatOutput( Input, Formatting, Output, Status )
if ( Status = Success ) then ...
```

I prefer the second style of coding, not because I'm hard-nosed about the difference between functions and procedures but because it makes a clear separation between the routine call and the test of the status value. To combine the call and the test into one line of code increases the density of the statement and correspondingly its complexity. The following use of a function is fine too:

```
Status = FormatOutput( Input, Formatting, Output )
if ( Status = Success ) then ...
```

A Unique Risk with Functions

Using a function creates the risk that the function will return its value improperly. This usually happens when the function has several possible paths and one of the paths avoids setting a return value. When creating a function, mentally execute each path to be sure that the function returns a value under all possible circumstances.

5.9 Macro Routines

CROSS-REFERENCE
Even if your language doesn't have a macro pre-processor, you can build your own. For details, see Section 20.5, "Building Your Own Programming Tools."

Routines created with preprocessor macros call for a few unique considerations. The following rules and examples pertain to using the preprocessor in C. If you're using a different language or preprocessor, adapt the rules to your situation.

Enclose macro expressions in parentheses. Because macros and their arguments are expanded into code, be careful that they expand the way you want them to. One common problem lies in creating a macro like this one:

C Example of a Macro That Doesn't Expand Properly

```
#define product( a, b ) a*b
```

This macro has a problem. If you pass it nonatomic values for *a* or *b*, it won't do the multiplication properly. If you use the expression *product(x+1, y+2)*, it expands to *x+1 * y+2*, which, because of the precedence of the multiplication and addition operators, is not what you want. A better but still not perfect version of the macro looks like this:

C Example of a Macro That Still Doesn't Expand Properly

```
#define product( a, b ) (a)*(b)
```

This is close, but still no cigar. If you use *product()* in an expression that has operators with higher precedence than multiplication, the *(a)*(b)* will be torn apart. To prevent that, enclose the whole expression in parentheses:

C Example of a Macro That Works

```
#define product( a, b ) ((a)*(b))
```

111

Surround multiple-statement macros with curly braces. A macro can have multiple statements, which is a problem if you treat it as if it were a single statement. Here's an example of a macro that's headed for trouble:

C Example of a Macro with Multiple Statements That Doesn't Work

```
#define LookupEntry( Key, Index ) \
    Index = (Key - 10) / 5; \
    Index = min( Index, MAX_INDEX ); \
    Index = max( Index, MIN_INDEX );
...

for ( EntryCount = 0; EntryCount < NumEntries; EntryCount++ )
    LookupEntry( EntryCount, TableIndex[ EntryCount ] );
```

This macro is headed for trouble because it doesn't work as a regular function would. As it's shown, the only part of the macro that's executed in the *for* loop is the first line of the macro:

```
Index = (Key - 10) / 5;
```

To avoid this problem, surround the macro with curly braces, as shown here:

C Example of a Macro with Multiple Statements That Works

```
#define LookupEntry( Key, Index ) \
    { \
    Index = (Key - 10) / 5; \
    Index = min( Index, MAX_INDEX ); \
    Index = max( Index, MIN_INDEX ); \
    }
```

Name macros that expand to code like routines so that they can be replaced by routines if necessary. The C-language convention for naming macros is to use all capital letters. If the macro can be replaced by a routine, however, name it using the naming convention for routines instead. That way you can replace macros with routines and vice versa without changing anything but the routine involved.

Following this recommendation entails some risk. If you commonly use *++* and *−−* as side effects (as part of other statements), you'll get burned when you use macros that you think are routines. That might cause you to avoid this recommendation. But considering the other problems with side effects, you'll do better to follow this recommendation and avoid side effects instead.

CROSS-REFERENCE
This is a checklist of considerations about the quality of the routine. For a list of the steps used to build a routine, see the checklist "Constructing a Routine" in Chapter 4, page 70.

CHECKLIST

High-Quality Routines

BIG-PICTURE ISSUES

❑ Is the reason for creating the routine sufficient?

❑ Have all parts of the routine that would benefit from being put into routines of their own been put into routines of their own?

❑ Is the routine's name a strong, clear verb-plus-object name for a procedure or a description of the return value for a function?

❑ Does the routine's name describe everything the routine does?

❑ Does the routine have strong, functional cohesion—doing one and only one thing and doing it well?

❑ Do the routines have loose coupling—is one routine's connection to other routines small, intimate, visible, and flexible?

❑ Is the length of the routine determined naturally by its function and logic, rather than by an artificial coding standard?

DEFENSIVE-PROGRAMMING ISSUES

❑ Are assertions used to document assumptions?

❑ Does the routine protect itself from bad input data?

❑ Does the routine handle exceptions gracefully?

❑ Is the routine designed to handle changes gracefully?

❑ Have debugging aids been installed in such a way that they can be activated or deactivated without a great deal of fuss?

❑ Have information hiding, loose coupling, and data checks been used to firewall errors so that they won't affect code outside the routine?

❑ Does the routine check function return values?

❑ Is the defensive code that's left in the production code designed to help the user rather than the programmer?

PARAMETER-PASSING ISSUES

❑ Do the formal and actual parameters match?

❑ Are the routine's parameters in a sensible order, including matching the order of parameters in similar routines?

❑ Are interface assumptions documented?

(continued)

113

High-Quality Routines checklist, *continued*

❏ Does the routine have seven or fewer parameters?

❏ Are only the parts of a structured variable that are needed, rather than the whole variable, passed to the routine?

❏ Is each input parameter used?

❏ Is each output parameter used?

❏ If the routine is a function, does it return a value under all possible circumstances?

Key Points

- The most important reason to create a routine is to improve the intellectual manageability of a program, and you can create a routine for many other good reasons. Saving space is a minor reason; improved correctness, reliability, and modifiability are better reasons.

- The point of strong cohesion and loose coupling is that they provide for higher levels of abstraction—you can take the operation of a cohesive, loosely coupled routine for granted, which allows you to focus completely on other tasks.

- Sometimes the operation that most benefits from being put into a routine of its own is a simple one.

- The name of a routine is an indication of its quality. If the name is bad and it's accurate, the routine might be poorly designed. If the name is bad and it's inaccurate, it's not telling you what the program does. Either way, a bad name means that the program needs to be changed.

- Defensive-programming techniques make errors easier to find, easier to fix, and less damaging to production code.

6

Three out of Four Programmers Surveyed Prefer Modules

Contents

Related Topics

"YOU'VE GOT YOUR ROUTINE IN MY MODULE."

"No, you've got your module around my routine."

The distinction between routines and modules is one that some people don't make very carefully, but you should understand the difference so that you can use modules to their full advantage.

"Routine" and "module" are flexible words that have different meanings in different contexts. In this book's context, a routine is a function or procedure invocable for a single purpose, as described in Chapter 5.

KEY POINT

A module is a collection of data and the routines that act on the data. A module might also be a collection of routines that provides a cohesive set of services even if no common data is involved. Examples of modules include a source file in C, a package in Ada, and a unit in some versions of Pascal. If your language doesn't support modules directly, you can still get many of their benefits by emulating them with disciplined programming practices.

6.1 Modularity: Cohesion and Coupling

"Modularity" has one foot in routine design, one foot in module design. The basic idea is powerful and worth exploring.

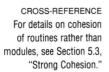

HARD DATA

In the *Software Maintenance Guidebook,* Glass and Noiseux argue that modularity contributes far more to maintainability than structure does and is the most important factor in preventing corrective maintenance (1981). In *Software Maintenance Management,* Lientz and Swanson cite a study finding that 89 percent of code users reported improved maintainability with modular programming (1980). On a test of comprehension, Shneiderman and Mayer found that programmers scored 15 percent higher on a modular program than on a nonmodular one (1979).

The modularity goal for individual routines is to make each routine like a "black box": You know what goes in, and you know what comes out, but you don't know what happens inside. A black box has such a simple interface and such well-defined functionality that for any specific input you can accurately predict the corresponding output. If your routines are like black boxes, they're perfectly modular, perform well-defined functions, and have simple interfaces.

The goal of perfect modularity is often hard to achieve with individual routines, however, and that's where modules come in. A group of routines often needs to share a set of common data. In such cases, the individual routines aren't perfectly modular because they share data with other routines. As individual routines, they thus don't have simple interfaces. As a group, however, the routines can present a simple interface to the rest of the world, and as a group, the routines can be perfectly modular.

Module Cohesion

CROSS-REFERENCE
For details on cohesion of routines rather than modules, see Section 5.3, "Strong Cohesion."

The criterion for module cohesion is as simple as the criterion for the cohesion of an individual routine. A module should offer a group of services that clearly belong together.

You might have a module that implements a cruise-control simulator. It would contain data describing the car's current cruise-control setting and current speed. It would offer services to set the speed, resume the former speed, and deactivate. Internally, it might have additional routines and data to support these services, but routines outside the module wouldn't need to know anything about them. The module would have great cohesion because every routine in it would work toward implementing the cruise-control simulator.

Or you might have a module of trigonometry functions. The module might include *sin()*, *cos()*, *tan()*, *arcsin()*, *arccos()*, and *arctan()*, a cohesive set of routines. If the routines were standard trig functions, they wouldn't need to share any data, but the routines would be related, so the module would still have great cohesion.

An incohesive module would be one that contained a collection of miscellaneous functions. Suppose that a module contains routines to implement a stack: *init_stack()*, *push()*, and *pop()*; that it contains routines to format report data; and that it defines all the global data used in a program. It's hard to see any connection among the stack and report routines or the module's data, so the module wouldn't be cohesive. The routines should be reorganized into more-focused modules.

The evaluations of module cohesion in these examples are based on each module's package of data and services. This cohesion is at the level of the module as a whole. The routines inside the module aren't necessarily cohesive just because the overall module is. The routines inside the module need to be designed so that they're individually cohesive too. For guidelines on that, see Section 5.3, "Strong Cohesion."

Module Coupling

CROSS-REFERENCE
For details on coupling
of routines rather than
modules, see Section 5.4,
"Loose Coupling."

The criterion for a module's coupling to the rest of the program is similar to the criterion for the coupling of an individual routine. A module should offer a collection of services designed so that the rest of the program can interact with it cleanly.

In the cruise-control example, the module offered the services *SetSpeed()*, *GetCurrentSettings()*, *ResumeFormerSpeed()*, and *Deactivate()*. This is a complete set of services that allows the rest of the program to interact with the module entirely through its official, public interface.

If a module offers an incomplete set of services, other routines might be forced to read or write its internal data directly. That opens up the module, making it a glass box instead of a black box, and virtually eliminates the module's "modularity." Larry Constantine, the principal developer of structured design, points out that a module's services should be "fully factored" so that its clients can tailor the services to their own needs (Constantine 1990a).

In designing a module for maximum cohesion and minimal coupling, you'll find that you have to balance trade-offs between criteria for designing modules and criteria for designing individual routines. One guideline for reducing coupling between individual routines is to minimize the use of global data.

Part of the reason for creating a module, however, is so that routines can share data; you want to make data accessible to all the routines in a module without passing it through their parameter lists.

CROSS-REFERENCE
For more details on the differences between module data and global data, see "Module data mistaken for global data" in the next section.

Module data is like global data in that more than one routine can access it. It's unlike global data in that it's not accessible to all the routines in a program; it's accessible only to the routines in a single module. Consequently, one of the most important decisions in designing a module is deciding which routines require direct access to module data. If a routine can access the data just as well through the module's service routines and if it doesn't have another compelling reason to stay in the module, kick it out.

6.2 Information Hiding

If you've been reading the cross-references throughout the book, you've probably noticed about 400 references to information hiding. With that many references, it had better be important.

It is.

KEY POINT

The idea of information hiding comes into play at all levels of design, from the use of named constants instead of literals, to routine design, to module and program design. Because the idea is often best applied at the module level, it's discussed at length in this chapter.

HARD DATA

Information hiding is one of the few theoretical techniques that has indisputably proven its value in practice (Boehm 1987a). Large programs that use information hiding have been found to be easier to modify—by a factor of 4—than programs that don't (Korson and Vaishnavi 1986). Moreover, information hiding is part of the foundation of both structured design and object-oriented design. In structured design, the notion of black boxes comes from information hiding. In object-oriented design, information hiding gives rise to the notions of encapsulation and abstraction.

Secrets and the Right to Privacy

CROSS-REFERENCE
For a description of encapsulation in object-oriented design, see "Key Ideas" in Section 7.3.

The key concept in information hiding is the idea of "secrets." Each module is characterized by design or implementation decisions that it hides from all other modules. The secret might be an area that's likely to change, the format of a file, the way a data structure is implemented, or an area that needs to be walled off from the rest of the program so that errors in it cause as little damage as possible. The module's job is to keep this information hidden and to protect its own right to privacy. Another term for information hiding is "encapsulation," which expresses the idea of a package that has an outside that's distinct from its inside.

Regardless of what you call it, information hiding is a way of designing routines and, more important, modules. When you hide secrets, you design a collection of routines that access a common data set. Minor changes to a system might affect several routines, but they should affect only one module.

One key task in designing a module is deciding which features should be known outside the module and which should remain secret. A module might use 25 routines and expose only 5 of them, using the other 20 internally. A module might use several data structures and expose no information about them. It might or might not provide routines that give data-structure information to the rest of the program. This aspect of module design is also known as "visibility" since it has to do with which features of the module are "visible," "exposed," or "exported" outside the module.

The interface to a module should reveal as little as possible about its inner workings. A module is a lot like an iceberg: Seven-eighths is under water, and you can see only the one-eighth that's above the surface.

A good module interface is like the tip of an iceberg, leaving most of the module unexposed.

Designing the module interface is an iterative process just like any other aspect of design. If the interface isn't right the first time, try a few more times until it stabilizes. If it doesn't stabilize, it needs to be redesigned.

Various diagramming techniques are available for representing modules. The key aspect of a module diagram is that it differentiates between services that are available within a module and services that are exposed to the outside world. The kind of diagram generally known as a "module diagram" was originally developed by Grady Booch for use in conjunction with Ada development. Figure 6-1 shows an adaptation:

Module (Package) Body

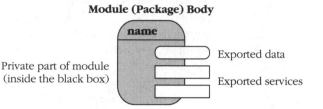

Private part of module
(inside the black box)

Exported data

Exported services

Figure 6-1. *A module diagram differentiates between the public and private parts of a module. The public parts are shown as the rounded and rectangular bars coming out of the bigger rectangle. The private part is shown as a "black box."*

Information hiding doesn't necessarily imply a system shape: A system might have a hierarchical structure, or it might have a network structure like the one sketched in Figure 6-2.

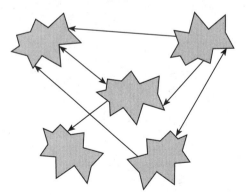

Figure 6-2. *Some systems are shaped like networks rather than hierarchies.*

In a network structure, you simply specify which modules can communicate with which other modules and how the specific communication occurs, and then you make the connections. As Figure 6-3 shows, the module diagram works in the network configuration too.

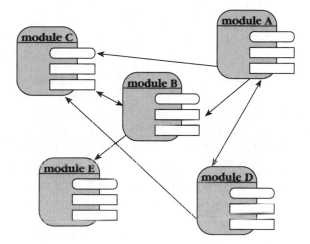

Figure 6-3. *Network-shaped systems are represented naturally with a notation that includes the idea of information hiding.*

Example of Information Hiding

A few years ago I wrote a medium-sized (20K lines of code) system that made extensive use of a linked-list structure. The problem area was made up of data nodes, each of which was connected to subordinate, superordinate, and peer nodes. I chose to use a linked-list data structure, so throughout the code, I had statements like

```
node = node.next
```

and

```
phone = node.data.phone
```

These statements directly manipulated the linked-list data structure. Although the linked list modeled the problem naturally, taking that approach turned out to be an inefficient use of memory. I wanted to replace the memory pointers with integer array indexes, which would have halved the memory used and created opportunities for performance optimizations in other areas.

CROSS-REFERENCE
A way to handle complex changes like this is to use a multi-file search-and-replace tool that handles regular expressions. For details on such tools, see "Editing" in Section 20.2.

I couldn't make the change easily because I had hard-coded statements like the ones above throughout the program, and I wasn't going to wade through 20,000 lines of code looking for them. If, instead, I had created a module with access routines like

```
node  = NearestNeighbor( node )
phone = EmergencyContact( node )
```

I would have had to change the code in only one place—in the access routines.

Exactly how much memory would I have gained? How much speed would I have gained or lost? I don't know. But if I had hidden the details of the data structure and used access routines, I could easily have found out, and I could have tried several other approaches too. I could have selected the best alternative from a group of alternatives rather than using the one I was stuck with because I had exposed the details of the data structure to the whole program.

CROSS-REFERENCE
When information hiding is applied to data structures, as it is in this example, you can treat the data as an abstract data type. For more details, see Section 12.3, "Abstract Data Types (ADTs)."

The second big reason, after ease of modification, to hide details of complex data structures is that hiding the details clarifies the intent of your code. In the example above, experienced programmers would have no problem reading

```
node = node.next
```

Clearly, the statement refers to a linked-list structure, but it tells you little else. On the other hand, an access routine such as *node = NearestNeighbor(node)* describes what the linked list represents, which is useful. And that makes you realize that a name such as *node* leaves room for improvement. (What does *node* have to do with neighbors?) Computer-sciencey statements such as *node = node.next* are so completely removed from the real-world problem that you wouldn't even think about improving them to convey information about the real-world problem.

The final big reason to hide complex data structures is reliability. If you access data structures through specialized routines, you can build in safeguards that would be awkward to build in everywhere that the routines reference a variable. For example, if you have a linked list and you want to get the next element in the list, being careful not to run past the end of the list, you could code something like

```
if ( node.next <> null ) then
   node = node.next
```

Depending on the specific circumstances, if you wanted to be really careful, you could code something like

```
if ( node <> null ) then
   if ( node.next <> null ) then
      node = node.next
```

If you have a lot of *node = node.next* code spread throughout your program, you might make the test in some places, skip it in others. But if the operation is isolated in a routine call,

```
node = NearestNeighbor( node )
```

you make the test once, in the routine, and it works for the whole program. Moreover, sometimes, even if you intend to make the test everywhere *node* is used, it's easy to forget the test in a few places. If the linked-list manipulation is isolated in a routine, however, it's not possible to forget the tests. They are done automatically.

Another advantage of hiding a data structure's implementation details is easier debugging. Suppose you know that the *node* variable is getting bad values somewhere, and you don't know where. If the code that accesses *node* is spread throughout your program, good luck in ever finding the source of the bad data. But if it's isolated in a single routine, you can add a debugging test to check *node* in that one place, every time it's accessed.

A last advantage pertaining to reliability is that access routines provide a way of making all accesses to data follow a parallel organization: Either manipulate a data structure directly or use access routines—don't do both. Of course, within the module responsible for the data structure, the accesses are direct, and lack of parallelism at that level is unavoidable. The goal is to avoid airing dirty laundry in public, which is accomplished by hiding the ugly secrets of direct data manipulation in access routines.

Common Kinds of Secrets

You'll deal with many kinds of secrets specific to the project you're working on, but you'll deal with a few general classes of secrets again and again:

- Areas likely to change
- Complex data
- Complex logic
- Operations at the programming-language level

Each of these classes of secrets is discussed in more detail below.

Areas likely to change

Accommodating changes is one of the most challenging aspects of good program design. The goal is to isolate unstable areas so that the effect of a change will be limited to one module. Here are the steps you should follow in preparing for such perturbations.

FURTHER READING
These steps are adapted
from "Designing Software
for Ease of Extension and
Contraction" (Parnas 1979).

1. Identify items that seem likely to change. If the requirements have been done well, they include a list of potential changes and the likelihood of each change. In such a case, identifying the likely changes is easy. If the requirements don't cover potential changes, see the discussion that follows of areas that are likely to change in any project.

2. Separate items that are likely to change. Compartmentalize each volatile component identified in step 1 into its own module, or into a module with other volatile components that are likely to change at the same time.

3. Isolate items that seem likely to change. Design the intermodule interfaces to be insensitive to the potential changes. Design the interfaces so that changes are limited to the inside of the module and the outside remains unaffected. Any other module using the changed module should be unaware that the change has occurred. The module's interface should protect its secrets.

Here are a few areas that are likely to change:

Hardware dependencies. For screens, printers, and plotters, be aware of possible changes in dimensions, resolution, number of colors, available fonts, memory, control codes, and graphics capabilities. Other hardware dependencies include interfaces with disks, tapes, communications ports, sound facilities, and so on.

Input and output. At a slightly higher level of design than raw hardware interfaces, input/output is a volatile area. If your application creates its own data files, the file format will probably change as your application becomes more sophisticated. User-level input and output formats will also change—the positioning of fields on the page, the number of fields on each page, the sequence of fields, and so on. In general, it's a good idea to examine all external interfaces for possible changes.

Nonstandard language features. If you use nonstandard extensions to your programming language, hide those extensions in a module of their own so that you can replace them with your own code when you move to a different environment. Likewise, if you use library routines that aren't available in all environments, hide the actual library routines behind an interface that works just as well in another environment.

Difficult design and implementation areas. It's a good idea to hide difficult design and implementation areas because they might be done poorly and you might need to do them again. Compartmentalize them and minimize the impact their bad design or implementation might have on the rest of the system.

Status variables. Status variables indicate the state of a program and tend to be changed more frequently than most other data. In a typical scenario, you might originally define an error-status variable as a boolean variable and decide later that it would be better implemented as an enumerated type with the values *NoError, WarningError*, and *FatalError*.

You can add at least two levels of flexibility and readability to your use of status variables:

CROSS-REFERENCE
For details on simulating enumerated types using integers, see "If Your Language Doesn't Have Enumerated Types" in Section 11.6.

- Don't use a boolean variable as a status variable. Use an enumerated type instead. It's common to add a new state to a status variable, and adding a new type to an enumerated type requires a mere recompilation rather than a major revision of every line of code that checks the variable.

- Use access routines rather than checking the variable directly. By checking the access routine rather than the variable, you allow for the possibility of more sophisticated state detection. For example, if you wanted to check combinations of an error-state variable and a current-function-state variable, it would be easy to do if the test were hidden in a routine and hard to do if it were a complicated test hard-coded throughout the program.

Data-size constraints. When you declare an array of size *15*, you're exposing information to the world that the world does not need to see. Defend your right to privacy! Information hiding isn't always as complicated as a collection of functions packaged into a module. Sometimes it's as simple as using a constant such as *MAX_EMPLOYEES* to hide a *15*.

Business rules. Business rules are the laws, regulations, policies, and procedures that you encode into a computer system. If you're writing a payroll system, you might encode rules from the IRS about the number of allowable withholdings and the estimated tax rate. Additional rules for a payroll system might come from a union contract specifying overtime rates, vacation and holiday pay, and so on. If you're writing a program to quote auto insurance rates, rules might come from state regulations on required liability coverages, actuarial rate tables, or underwriting restrictions.

Such rules tend to be the source of frequent changes in data-processing systems. Congress changes the tax structure, or an insurance company changes its rate tables. If you follow the principle of information hiding, logic based on these rules won't be strewn throughout your program. The logic will stay hidden in a single dark corner of the system until it needs to be changed.

Anticipating changes. When thinking about potential changes to a system, design the system so that the effect or scope of the change is proportional to the chance that the change will occur. If a change is likely, make sure that the system can accommodate it easily. Only extremely unlikely changes should be allowed to have drastic consequences for more than one module in a system.

FURTHER READING
This point is adapted from
"Designing Software for
Ease of Extension and Con-
traction" (Parnas 1979).

A good technique for identifying areas likely to change is first to identify the minimal subset of the program that might be of use to the user. The subset makes up the core of the system and is unlikely to change. Next, define minimal increments to the system. They can be so small that they seem trivial. These areas of potential improvement constitute potential changes to the system; design these areas using the principles of information hiding. By identifying the core first, you can see which components are really add-ons and then extrapolate and hide improvements from there.

Complex data

CROSS-REFERENCE
Additional techniques for
hiding complex data are
presented in Section 12.3,
"Abstract Data Types
(ADTs)."

All complex data is likely to change; if it's complicated and you use it much, you'll discover better ways to implement it after you've worked with it at the implementation level and are well into coding. If you use information-hiding principles to hide the implementation of the data, you can change to a better implementation with little fuss. If not, every time you work with the data, you'll think of how you want to change the implementation and how much easier it would be to change if you'd used information hiding.

The extent to which you'll hide complex data depends somewhat on the size of the program you're writing. If you have a small program of a few hundred lines of code and want to manipulate a variable directly, go ahead. It might hurt the program, but then again, it might not. Consider the small program's future before committing yourself to the maintenance headache of direct data manipulation. If you're working on a larger program or using global data, consider using access routines as a matter of course.

Complex logic

CROSS-REFERENCE
Techniques for hiding
complex boolean tests
are discussed in "Making
Complicated Expressions
Simple" in Section 17.1.

Hiding complex logic improves program readability. The complex logic isn't always the most important aspect of a routine, and hiding it makes the main activity of the routine clearer. Complex logic is about as likely to change as complex data, so it's a good idea to insulate the rest of the program from the effects of such changes. In some instances, you can hide the kind of logic used—for example, you can code certain tests as a big *if* statement, *case* statement, or table lookup. No code other than the code that performs the logic needs to know the ugly details. If the rest of the code just needs to know the result, just give it the result.

Operations at the programming-language level

The more you make the program read like a solution to the real-world problem and the less like a collection of programming-language constructs, the better your program will be. Hide the information about computer-science entities. For example, the statement

```
EmployeeID = EmployeeID + 1
CurrentEmployee = EmployeeList[ EmployeeID ]
```

is not bad programming, but it represents the problem in computer-science terms. Instead, deal with the operation at a higher level of abstraction:

```
CurrentEmployee = NextAvailableEmployee()
```

or possibly

```
CurrentEmployee = NextAvailableEmployee( EmployeeList, EmployeeID )
```

By adding a routine that hides the computer-science interpretation of what's happening, you deal with the problem at a higher level of abstraction. This makes your intent clearer and makes the code easier to understand, work with, and modify.

Suppose you use a linked list to implement a scheduling queue. The functions *HighestPriorityEvent()*, *LowestPriorityEvent()*, and *NextEvent()* are abstract functions that would hide the implementation details. The functions *FrontOfQueue()*, *BackOfQueue()*, and *NextInQueue()* don't hide much because they refer to the implementation—exposing secrets that should be hidden.

Generally, design one level of routines that deal with data at the level of programming-language statements. Hide direct data manipulations inside that group of routines. The rest of your program can then work at the more abstract level of the problem area, as the abstract functions above do.

Barriers to Information Hiding

FURTHER READING
Parts of this section are adapted from "Designing Software for Ease of Extension and Contraction" (Parnas 1979).

Most of the barriers to information hiding are mental blocks built up from the habitual use of other techniques. In some instances, information hiding is truly impossible. Certain practices that seem to create barriers to information hiding, however, might only be excuses.

Excessive distribution of information

One common barrier to information hiding is an excessive distribution of information throughout a system. You might have hard-coded the literal *100* throughout a system. Using *100* as a literal decentralizes references to it. It's better to hide the information in one place, in a constant *MaxEmployees* perhaps, whose value is changed in only one place.

Another example of excessive information distribution is threading interaction with human users throughout a system. If the mode of interaction changes—say, from a command-line to a forms-driven interface—virtually all the code will have to be modified. It's better to concentrate user interaction in a single module you can change without affecting the whole system.

Yet another example would be a global data structure—perhaps an array of employee data with 1000 elements maximum that's accessed throughout a program. If the program uses the global data directly, information about the data structure's implementation—such as the fact that it's an array and has a maximum of 1000 elements—will be spread throughout the program. If the program uses the data structure only through access routines, only the access routines will know the implementation details.

Circular dependencies

A more subtle barrier to information hiding is circular dependencies, as when a routine in module *A* calls a routine in module *B*, and a routine in module *B* calls a routine in module *A*. Avoid such dependency loops. They make it hard to test a system because you can't test either module *A* or module *B* until at least part of the other is ready. If the program will be overlaid, module *A* and module *B* will always need to be in memory at the same time to prevent thrashing. Eliminating circularities is nearly always possible by identifying the parts of modules *A* and *B* used by the other module, factoring those parts into new modules *A'* and *B'*, and calling *A'* and *B'* with whatever is left of modules *A* and *B*.

Module data mistaken for global data

If you're a conscientious programmer, one of the barriers to effective information hiding might be thinking of module data as global data and avoiding it because you want to avoid the problems associated with global data. As was mentioned in Section 6.1, "Modularity: Cohesion and Coupling," the two kinds of data are different. Accessible only to the routines in a single module, module data entails far fewer risks than global data.

CROSS-REFERENCE
For several examples of cases in which you need to use module data to program effectively, see Section 12.3, "Abstract Data Types (ADTs)."

If you don't use module data, you don't realize all of the power that comes from creating modules. A module can't be truly responsible for a collection of data and operations on the data if other routines pass it the data that only it can manipulate. For instance, an earlier example advised providing a level of abstraction by having an assignment such as

```
CurrentEmployee = NextAvailableEmployee()
```

or possibly

```
CurrentEmployee = NextAvailableEmployee( EmployeeList, EmployeeID )
```

The difference between the two assignments is that in the first case, *NextAvailableEmployee()* owns the information about the employee list and about which entry is the current entry in the list. In the second example, *NextAvailableEmployee()* is only borrowing the information from the routine that passes it in. In order to provide a full level of abstraction when you use *NextAvailableEmployee()*, you shouldn't need to worry about the data it needs. Make it take responsibility for its own problems!

KEY POINT

Global data is generally subject to two problems: (1) Routines operate on global data without knowing that other routines are operating on it; and (2) routines are aware that other routines are operating on the global data, but they don't know exactly what they're doing to it. Module data isn't subject to either of these problems. Direct access to the data is restricted to a few routines packaged into a single module. The routines are aware that other routines operate on the data, and they know exactly which other routines they are. If you're still not convinced, try it. You'll be happy with the results.

Perceived performance penalties

CROSS-REFERENCE
Code-level performance optimizations are discussed in Chapter 28, "Code-Tuning Strategies," and Chapter 29, "Code-Tuning Techniques."

A final barrier to information hiding can be an attempt to avoid performance penalties at both the architectural and the coding levels. You don't need to worry at either level. At the architectural level, the worry is unnecessary because architecting a system for information hiding doesn't conflict with architecting it for performance. If you keep both information hiding and performance in mind, you can achieve both objectives.

The more common worry is at the coding level. The concern is that accessing data structures indirectly incurs run-time performance penalties for additional levels of routine calls and so on. This concern is premature. Until you can measure the system's performance and pinpoint the bottlenecks, the best way to prepare for code-level performance work is to create a highly modular design. When you detect hot spots later, you can optimize individual routines without affecting the rest of the system.

Further Reading

I'm not aware of any comprehensive treatment of information hiding. Most software-engineering textbooks discuss it briefly, frequently in the context of object-oriented techniques. The three Parnas papers listed below are the seminal presentations of the idea and are probably still the best resources on information hiding.

Parnas, David L. "On the Criteria to Be Used in Decomposing Systems into Modules." *Communications of the ACM* 5, no. 12 (December 1972): 1053–58.

Parnas, David L. "Designing Software for Ease of Extension and Contraction." *IEEE Transactions on Software Engineering* SE-5, no. 2 (March 1979): 128–38.

Parnas, David L., Paul C. Clements, and D. M. Weiss. "The Modular Structure of Complex Systems." *IEEE Transactions on Software Engineering* SE-11, no. 3 (March 1985): 259–66.

Freeman, Peter, and Anthony I. Wasserman, eds. *Tutorial on Software Design Techniques*, 4th ed. Silver Spring, Md.: IEEE Computer Society Press, 1983. This collection includes the first two Parnas papers above and about 45 others.

6.3 Good Reasons to Create a Module

Even if you aren't using modules much yet, you probably have an intuitive idea of the kinds of routines and data you can collect in a module. In a sense, modules are poor folks' objects. They're collections of data and operations on data, and they support the object-oriented concepts of abstraction and encapsulation. They don't support inheritance, so they don't fully support object-oriented programming. The term that has emerged to describe this limited kind of object orientation is "object-based" programming (Booch 1991).

Here are some good areas in which to create modules:

User interface. Create a module to isolate user-interface components so that the user interface can evolve without damaging the rest of the program. In many cases, a user-interface module uses several subordinate modules for menu operations, window management, the help system, and so forth.

Hardware dependencies. Isolate hardware dependencies in their own module or modules. Examples of hardware dependencies include interfaces to screens, printers, keyboards, mice, disk drives, and communications devices. Isolating such dependencies helps when you move the program to a new hardware environment. It also helps initially when you're developing a program for volatile hardware. You can write software that simulates interaction with specific hardware, have the hardware-interface routines use the simulator as long as the hardware is unstable or unavailable, and then unplug the hardware-interface routines from the simulator and plug the routines into the hardware when it's ready to use.

Input and output. Encapsulate input/output operations to protect the rest of the program from volatile file and report formats. Having a module for input/output also makes a program easier to adapt to other input/output devices.

System dependencies. Package operating-system dependencies into a module for the same reason you package hardware dependencies. If you're developing a program for Microsoft Windows, for example, why limit yourself to the Windows environment? Isolate the Windows calls in a Windows-interface module. If you later want to move your program to a Macintosh or the OS/2 Presentation Manager, all you'll have to rewrite is the interface module.

Data management. Hide data management in its own module. Have routines inside the module worry about messy implementation-language details. Have routines outside the module work with the data in abstract terms, terms that are as close to the real-world problem as possible. Referring to this data-management module as a single module is probably misleading. You'll normally need individual modules to handle each major abstract data type.

CROSS-REFERENCE
For details on abstract data types, see Section 12.3, "Abstract Data Types (ADTs)."

Real-world objects and abstract data types. Create a module for each real-world object that your program models. Put the data needed for the object into the module, and then build service routines that model the behavior of the object. This is known as creating an abstract data type.

Reusable code. Modularize parts of the program that you plan to reuse in other programs. One of the huge advantages of creating modules is that reuse is more practical with them than with functionally oriented programs. NASA's Software Engineering Laboratory studied ten projects that pursued reuse aggressively (McGarry, Waligora, and McDermott 1989). In both the object-based and the functionally oriented approaches, the initial projects weren't able to take much of their code from previous projects because previous projects hadn't established a sufficient code base. Subsequently, the projects that used functional design were able to take about 35 percent of their code from previous projects. Projects that used an object-based approach were able to take more than 70 percent of their code from previous projects. If you can avoid writing 70 percent of your code by planning ahead, do it!

HARD DATA

Related operations that are likely to change. Build a partition around groups of related operations that are likely to change. This is a damage-containment policy that prevents changes in specific areas from affecting the rest of the program. Section 6.2 on information hiding described several common sources of change.

Related operations. Finally, put related operations together. In most cases, you'll be able to find a stronger organizing principle than grouping routines and data that seem related. In cases in which you can't hide information, share data, or plan for flexibility, you can still package sets of operations into sensible groups such as trig functions, statistical functions, string-manipulation routines, bit-manipulation routines, graphics routines, and so on. Who knows—if you group related operations carefully, you might even be able to reuse them on your next project.

6.4 Implementing Modules in Any Language

Some languages provide direct support for modularity. Others need to be supplemented with programming standards.

Language Support Needed for Modularity

A module consists of data, data types, operations on data, and a distinction between public and private operations. To support modularity, a language needs to support multiple modules. Without multiple modules, any other requirement is moot.

Data needs to be accessible and hideable at three levels: local, module, and global. Most languages support local data and global data. Language support for module data, data accessible to some but not all routines, is required if some data is to be private to a collection of routines in a module.

The demand for data type accessibility and hideability in modules is similar to the requirement for data. Some types should be hidden within a specific module; others should be made available to other modules. The module needs to be able to control which other modules know about its types.

The demands on module-level routines are similar. Some routines should be accessible only within a specific module, and the module should be able to control whether routines are public or private. Outside the module, no other modules or routines should know that the private routines exist. If the module is designed well, other modules and routines shouldn't have any reason to care about the existence of the private routines.

Language-Support Summary

The following table summarizes the support of several languages for constructs necessary to provide information hiding:

Language	Multiple Modules	Data			Data Types			Routines	
		Local	Module	Global	Local	Module	Global	Private	Module/Global
Ada	•	•	•	•	•	•	•	•	•
C	•	•	•	•	•	†	•	•	•
C++	•	•	•	•	•	•	•	•	•
Fortran 77	†	•	†	•	—	—	—	—	•
Generic Basic	—	—	—	•	—	—	—	—	•
Generic Pascal	—	•	—	•	•	—	•	—	•
Turbo Pascal	•	•	•	•	•	•	•	•	•
QuickBasic	•	•	•	•	•	—	—	—	•

† Possible if the language is used with discipline; the capability is not entirely dependent on programming standards.

Generic Basic and generic Pascal don't support multiple modules, so they don't get to first base in supporting modularity. Fortran and QuickBasic don't have the control over data types required to support modularity. Only Ada, C, C++, and Turbo Pascal allow their modules to restrict access to specified routines so that the routines are truly private.

KEY POINT

In short, unless you're using Ada, C, C++, or Turbo Pascal, you'll have to supplement your language's capabilities with naming and other conventions to simulate the use of modules. The following sections take a look at the languages that support modularity directly and tell you how to simulate modularity in other languages.

Ada and Modula-2 support

Ada supports modularity through the notion of "packages." If you program in Ada, you already know how to create packages. Modula-2 supports it through the notion of modules. Even though Modula-2 isn't featured in this book, its support for modularity is so direct that an example of a Modula-2 implementation of a module for an event queue is shown below:

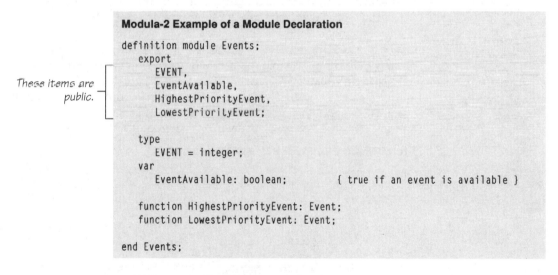

These items are public.

```
Modula-2 Example of a Module Declaration

definition module Events;
   export
      EVENT,
      EventAvailable,
      HighestPriorityEvent,
      LowestPriorityEvent;

   type
      EVENT = integer;
   var
      EventAvailable: boolean;        { true if an event is available }

   function HighestPriorityEvent: Event;
   function LowestPriorityEvent: Event;

end Events;
```

Object-oriented language support

Object-oriented languages such as C++ also support modularity directly. Modularity is at the core of object-oriented programming. Here's how an event-queue module (object) looks in C++.

C++ Example of a Module (Object) Declaration

```
class Buffer
  {
  public:

  typedef int EVENT;

  BOOL EventAvailable;              /* true if an event is available */

  EVENT HighestPriorityEvent( void );
  EVENT LowestPriorityEvent( void );

  private:
  ...
  };
```

Pascal support

Some versions of Pascal, notably versions 4 and later of Turbo Pascal, support modularization through the notion of units. A "unit" is a data file that can contain data types, data, and routines. A unit has an interface section that declares the data and the routines that can be used outside the module. The rest of the data and routines are available only inside the unit. Data can also be declared to be available to all functions or procedures within a file and only within that file. That gives Turbo Pascal the local, module, and global levels of data accessibility necessary to support modularity. Here's how the event-queue module would look in Turbo Pascal version 5:

Turbo Pascal Example of a Module Declaration

```
unit Events;

INTERFACE

   type
      EVENT = integer;
   var
      EventAvailable: boolean;          { true if an event is available }

   function HighestPriorityEvent: Event;
   function LowestPriorityEvent: Event;

IMPLEMENTATION
...

end. { unit Events }
```

Routines and data in this part of the file are hidden from routines in other files unless they are declared in the INTERFACE section above. ——

Implementations of Pascal that adhere to the generic Pascal standard don't support modularity directly, but you can supplement them to achieve modularity, as discussed later.

C support

C also supports modules, although many C programmers aren't accustomed to using modules in C. Each C source file can contain both data and functions. You can declare the data and functions to be *static,* which makes them available only inside the source file. If they're not declared *static,* they're available outside the source file. When each source file is thought of as a module, C fully supports modularity.

Because a source file isn't exactly the same as a module, you'll need to create two header files for each source file—one that acts as a public, module header file and one that acts as a private, source-file header file. In the source file's public header file, put only the public data and function declarations. Here's an example:

C Example of a Public, Module Header File

This file contains only the publicly available type, data, and function declarations.

```
/*   File: Event.h
     Contains public declarations for the "Event" module. */

typedef int EVENT;

extern BOOL EventAvailable;     /* true if an event is available */

EVENT HighestPriorityEvent( void );
EVENT LowestPriorityEvent( void );
```

In the source file's private header file, put all the private data and function declarations used internally by the routine. *#include* the header file only in the source file that makes up a module; don't allow other files to *#include* it. Here's an example:

C Example of a Private, Source-File Header File

```
/*   File: _Event.h
     Contains private declarations for the "Event" module. */
```

Here are the private types, data, and functions.

```
/* private declarations */
...
```

Use *#include* for both header files in the *.c* source file. In other modules that use the public routines from the *Event* module, *#include* only the public, module header file.

If you need more than one source file to make a single module, you might need a private header file for each source file, but you should create only one public, module header file for the group of files that make up the module. It's all right for the source files within the module to *#include* private header files from the other source files in the same module.

Fortran support

Fortran 90 provides full support for modules. Fortran 77, used with discipline, provides limited support for modules. It has a mechanism for constructing a group of routines that have exclusive access to data. The mechanism is multiple entry points. Although indiscreet use of multiple entry points begs for problems, careful use provides a way to give a group of routines access to common data without making the data public.

You can declare variables as local, global, or *COMMON*. Such distinctions are another means of providing restricted access to data among routines. Define a set of routines that make up a module. The routines won't constitute a module in any sense that the Fortran compiler recognizes, but they will in a logical sense. Have each routine in the module use a named *COMMON* to access the variables it has permission to manipulate directly. Don't allow routines outside the module to use that particular named *COMMON*. Programming standards to make up for language deficiencies are discussed next.

Faking Modularity

What about modularity in generic Basic, generic Pascal, and other languages that don't support modules directly or indirectly? The germ of the answer was mentioned earlier: Use programming standards as a substitute for direct language support. Even if your compiler doesn't enforce good programming practices, you can adopt coding standards that do. The following discussions suggest standards for each of the required aspects of modularity.

Packaging data and routines into modules

Packaging can be simple or complicated depending on whether your language allows you to use multiple source files or requires that all code be in one source file. If it allows you to use multiple source files, put all the data and code used by a single module into a single source file. If you have 10 modules, create 10 source files. If your environment requires everything to be in one file, separate the file into sections for each module. Clearly identify the beginning and end of each module section with comments.

Keeping a module's internal routines private

If your language doesn't support restrictions on the visibility of internal routines, all routines are publicly available to all other routines. Use coding standards to emphasize your intention that only the routines designated as public be used publicly, regardless of what the compiler allows. Here's what to do:

Identify public and private routines prominently in comments where they're declared. Clearly identify the module with which each routine is associated. If someone has to look up the routine declaration in order to use the routine, make sure it's marked noticeably as public or private.

Require that no routines use internal routines from other modules. Use comments to associate all routines with the modules they belong to.

CROSS-REFERENCE
For details on naming conventions, see Section 9.3, "The Power of Naming Conventions," and the sections following it.

Adopt a naming convention that indicates whether routines are internal or external. You could have the names of all internal routines begin with an underscore (_). This convention wouldn't differentiate between the internal routines of one module and the internal routines of another, but most people should be able to determine whether the internal routine is from their own module. If it isn't, it's obviously from some other module.

Adopt a naming convention that indicates the source of the routine and whether it's internal or external. Details of the specific convention you adopt depend a lot on how much flexibility your language gives you in creating routine names. For example, an internal routine from the *DataRetrieval* module might start with a *dr_* prefix. An internal *UserInterface* routine might start with a *ui_* prefix. External routines from the same modules might start with *DR_* and *UI_* prefixes. If you're limited to a few characters (for example, only six characters in ANSI Fortran 77), naming-convention characters will cost dearly and you'll have to develop a standard with that restriction in mind.

Keeping a module's internal data private

The guidelines for keeping module-level data private are about the same as those for keeping module-level routines private. In general, adopt coding standards that make it clear that only specific data is to be used outside the module, regardless of what the compiler allows. Here are the steps to take:

First, use comments to document whether data is public or private. Clearly identify the module with which each piece of data is associated.

Second, require that no routines use private, module-level data from other modules, even if the compiler treats the data as global.

Third, adopt a naming convention that calls attention to the distinction between public and private data. For consistency's sake, handle this convention similarly to the naming convention for routines.

Fourth, adopt a naming convention that indicates which module owns the data and whether the data is internal or external. Handle this similarly to the routine convention.

CHECKLIST

Module Quality

❏ Does the module have a central purpose?

❏ Is the module organized around a common set of data?

❏ Does the module offer a cohesive set of services?

❏ Are the module's services complete enough that other modules don't have to meddle with its internal data?

❏ Is the module independent of other modules? Is it loosely coupled?

❏ Does the module hide implementation details from other modules?

❏ Are the module's interfaces abstract enough that you don't have to think about how its services are implemented? Can you treat the module as a black box?

❏ Have you thought about subdividing the module into component modules, and have you subdivided it as much as you can?

❏ If you're working in a language that doesn't fully support modules, have you implemented programming conventions to support them?

Key Points

- The difference between a routine and a module is important, regardless of what you call either one. Think of design in terms of both routines and modules.

- Module data is similar to global data in that it's used by more than one routine. It's different from global data in that the number of routines that use it is strictly limited and you know exactly which routines they are. Consequently, you can use module data without the risks associated with global data.

- Information hiding is always appropriate. It results in reliable, easily modifiable systems. It is also at the core of popular design methods.

- You create modules for many of the same reasons you create routines. The module is a more powerful concept than the routine because it can offer more than one service. Consequently, it's a higher-level design tool than the routine.

- You can implement modules in any language. If your language doesn't support them directly, you can supplement your language with programming conventions to help you achieve a kind of modularity.

7

High-Level Design
in Construction

Contents

Related Topics

SOME PEOPLE MIGHT ARGUE THAT high-level design isn't really an implementation activity, but on small projects, many activities are thought of as implementation, often including design. On some larger projects, a formal architecture might address only the top level of system decomposition and much design work might intentionally be left for construction. On other large projects, the design might be intended to be detailed enough for coding to be fairly mechanical, but design is rarely that complete—the coder usually designs part of the program, officially or otherwise.

High-level design is a huge topic. For that reason, and because high-level design is only partially related to the focus of this book, only a few aspects of it are considered in this chapter. A large part of good routine or module design is determined by the system architecture, so be sure that the architecture prerequisite discussed in Section 3.4 has been satisfied. Even more design work is done at the level of individual routines and modules, described in Chapters 4, 5, and 6.

If you're already familiar with structured design and object-oriented design, you might want to read the introduction in the next section, skip to the comparison of the two techniques in Section 7.4, and then read the discussion of round-trip design in Section 7.5.

7.1 Introduction to Software Design

The phrase "software design" means the conception, invention, or contrivance of a scheme for turning a specification for a computer program into an operational program. Design is the activity that links requirements specification to coding and debugging. It's a heuristic process rather than a deterministic one, requiring creativity and insight. A big part of the design process is appropriate only for the specific project at hand.

CROSS-REFERENCE
The difference between heuristic and deterministic processes is described in Chapter 2, "Metaphors for a Richer Understanding of Programming."

Design on Large and Small Projects

On large, formal projects, design is often distinct from other activities such as requirements analysis and coding. It might even be performed by different people. A large project might have several stages of design—software architecture, high-level module design, and detailed implementation design. The guidelines that contribute to a good design at the architectural level are useful on a smaller scale during coding. If only a general or top-level design has been done, the guidelines might be useful on a large scale during coding. Regardless of the reasons, design work rarely stops when the official design stage is over.

CROSS-REFERENCE
For details on the different levels of formality required on large and small projects, see Chapter 21, "How Program Size Affects Construction."

On small, informal projects, a lot of design is done while the programmer sits in front of the keyboard. "Design" might be just writing a routine in Program Design Language (PDL) before writing it in programming-language code. It might be drawing diagrams of a few routines before coding them. Regardless of how it's done, small projects benefit from careful design just as larger projects do, and making design activity explicit maximizes the benefit you receive from it.

Levels of Design

Design is needed at several different levels of detail in a software system. Some of the techniques apply at all levels, and some apply at only one or two. Here are the levels:

Level 1: Division into subsystems

The main product of design at this level is the identification of all major subsystems. The subsystems can be big—database interface, user interface, command interpreter, report formatter, and so on. The major design activity at this level is deciding how to partition the program into major components and defining the interfaces between the components. Division at this level is typically needed on any project that takes longer than a few days. In Figure 7-1, design at this level is shown by the three main groupings and their interconnections.

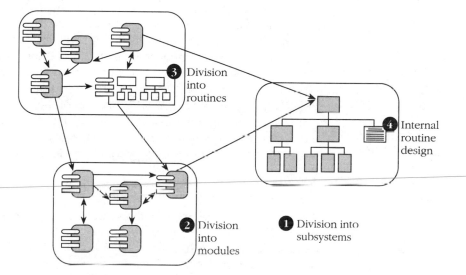

Figure 7-1. *The levels of design in a program. The three major groupings come from the division of the program into subsystems (1). The subsystems are further divided into modules (2), and some of the modules are divided into routines (3). The inside of each routine is also designed (4).*

Specific meanings for the terms "routine" and "module" have been introduced in previous chapters. The term "subprogram" is used several times in this chapter and refers generically to any part of a program that's smaller than the whole program, including modules and routines.

Level 2: Division into modules

CROSS-REFERENCE
For details on characteristics of high-quality modules, see Chapter 6, "Three out of Four Programmers Surveyed Prefer Modules."

Design at this level includes identifying all modules in the system. In large systems, the subsystems identified at the program-partitioning level might be too big to translate directly into modules. For example, a database-interface subsystem might be complicated enough to require dozens of routines to implement. If that were the case, the subsystem would be further partitioned into modules at this level of design: perhaps into data-storage, data-retrieval, and query-interpreter modules. If the resulting modules were too complicated, they'd be partitioned too. In the design of many programs, subsystems identified at Level 1 turn directly into modules at Level 2, and the two levels of design aren't distinct.

Details of the ways in which each module interacts with the rest of the system are also specified as the modules are specified. For example, access functions to data owned by a module would be defined. Overall, the major design activity at this level is making sure that all the subsystems have been decomposed to a level of detail fine enough that you can implement their parts as individual modules.

Like division of a program into subsystems, the division of subsystems into modules is typically needed on any project that takes longer than a few days. If the project is large, the division is clearly distinct from the program partitioning of Level 1. If the project is small, Levels 1 and 2 might be done at the same time. In Figure 7-1, decomposition into modules is shown inside each of the three main groups. As the illustration indicates, different methods of design might be used within different parts of the system; the design of the relationships among some modules might be based on the idea of a network or might be object oriented, as shown in the two subsystems on the left; the design of others might be more hierarchical, as shown in the subsystem on the right.

Level 3: Division into routines

Design at this level includes dividing each module into the services offered by the module. Once each routine has been identified, its function is also specified at this level. Because the module interacts with the rest of the system through its service routines, specific syntactic details of how the module interacts with the system are specified at this design level. For example, the exact syntax of how to invoke the query interpreter would be defined.

This level of decomposition and design is needed on any project that takes more than a few hours. It doesn't need to be done formally, but it at least needs to be done mentally. In Figure 7-1, division into routines is shown inside one of the modules in the upper left grouping. When you take the cover off the black box, as has been done in the module marked with a *3*, you can see that the services offered by the module are composed of hierarchically organized routines. This doesn't mean that hierarchical groups of routines lurk inside every black box—just that they lurk inside some. Other organizations of routines might have a less hierarchical structure.

Level 4: Internal routine design

CROSS-REFERENCE
For details on creating high-quality routines, see Chapter 5, "Characteristics of High-Quality Routines."

Design at the routine level consists of laying out the detailed functionality of the individual routines. Internal routine design is typically left to the individual programmer working on an individual routine. The design consists of activities such as writing PDL, looking up algorithms in reference books,

In other words—and
this is the rock-solid
principle on which
the whole of the Cor-
poration's Galaxywide
success is founded—
their fundamental
design flaws are
completely hidden
by their superficial
design flaws.

Douglas Adams

deciding how to organize the paragraphs of code in a routine, and writing programming-language code. This level of design is always needed on projects of any size and is always done, consciously or unconsciously, soundly or poorly, by every programmer. Computer programs can't be written without this level of design. The diagram in Figure 7-1 indicates the level at which this occurs in the routine marked with a *4.*

Design During Construction

The discussion of levels of design has been necessary to set the stage for the design discussion in the rest of the chapter. People mean a lot of different things when they talk about design, and it's such a big subject that it's important to know which part of the subject you're reading about. Here's how each level of design is discussed in this book—this time from the lowest level of decomposition to the highest:

Internal routine design

Internal routine design is discussed explicitly in Chapter 4, "Steps in Building a Routine." Internal routine design is discussed further in Chapter 5, "Characteristics of High-Quality Routines." The sections in Chapter 5 on data and control deal with design at the level of individual programming-language statements and blocks of code within routines. Routine design is discussed implicitly throughout the rest of the chapters.

We try to solve the
problem by rushing
through the design
process so that
enough time is left at
the end of the project
to uncover the errors
that were made be-
cause we rushed
through the design
process.

Glenford Myers

Division into routines

In the world of structured methodology, "design" refers to designing the structure of a program rather than the internals of individual routines. Program structure is a topic worthy of a book-length discussion, and most of this chapter is a summary of techniques for structuring simple collections of routines, collections that you would often design during implementation.

Division into modules

In the world of object-oriented programming, "design" refers to designing the different modules in a system. Module specification is a big topic, as worthy of book-length discussion as structured design, and is discussed here and in Chapter 6, "Three out of Four Programmers Surveyed Prefer Modules."

Division into subsystems

For small- to medium-sized programs (up to about 10,000 lines of code), techniques for module and routine specification hint at design techniques for entire programs. Larger programs require unique design approaches that can't be covered well in a book about implementation like this one. In many circumstances, on smaller projects, design work is done at the keyboard and is therefore an implementation activity, whether or not it should have been done earlier. The book dips into module and routine design because they are activities that border on implementation. Any other discussion of program partitioning is, unfortunately, outside the scope of this book. References to many good books on the topic are provided in the "Further Reading" sections throughout the chapter.

7.2 Structured Design

CROSS-REFERENCE
For details on how structured design compares to other design methods and on when to use it, see Section 7.4, "Comments on Popular Methodologies," later in this chapter.

The notion of structured design was first introduced in the paper "Structured Design," published in the *IBM Systems Journal* in 1974. The idea was fully expanded in a later book, *Structured Design: Fundamentals of a Discipline of Computer Program and Systems Design,* by Ed Yourdon and Larry Constantine (1979). Constantine was one of the authors of the original paper. The term "top-down design" refers to an informal kind of structured design, and "stepwise refinement" and "decomposition" are similar peas in the same pod. Structured design works hand in hand with the other structured methodologies.

Structured design is made up of these parts:

CROSS-REFERENCE
Information hiding, cohesion, and coupling are also usually associated with structured design. For details on information hiding, see Section 6.2, "Information Hiding." For details on cohesion and coupling, see Sections 5.3 and 5.4.

- System organization. Systems are organized into black boxes, routines that have well-defined, narrow interfaces and whose implementation details are hidden from other routines.
- Strategies for developing designs.
- Criteria for evaluating designs.
- A clear statement of the problem to guide the solution to the problem.
- Graphical and verbal tools for expressing designs, including structure charts and PDL.

The following sections describe these characteristics of structured design in more detail.

Choosing Components to Modularize

The preceding chapters provided criteria for evaluating whether routines and modules are sufficiently cohesive and provided checklists for determining the quality of routines and modules. They did not provide any guidelines for coming up with the routines and modules in the first place. This section describes how to identify the subprograms initially.

Top-down decomposition

CROSS-REFERENCE
Top-down implementation is entirely different from top-down decomposition and is discussed in Chapter 27, "System Integration." Top-down testing is yet another subject and is discussed in Chapter 25, "Unit Testing."

A popular technique for decomposing a program into routines is top-down decomposition, also called top-down design or stepwise refinement. It's characterized by moving from a general statement of what the program does to detailed statements about specific tasks that are performed. Starting at the most general level possible usually means starting at the "main" routine in a program, which is typically drawn at the top of a structure chart.

Here are some things to keep in mind as you do top-down decomposition:

- Design the top levels first.
- Steer clear of language-specific details. You shouldn't be able to tell from the design what language you're going to implement the program in—or you should be able to change the implementation language midstream without much turmoil.
- Postpone working out the details to the lower levels of design (much as in information hiding).
- Formalize each level.
- Verify each level.
- Move to the next lower level to make the next set of refinements.

FURTHER READING
For an early discussion of these concepts, see "Program Development by Stepwise Refinement" (Wirth 1971).

The guiding principle behind top-down decomposition is the idea that the human brain can concentrate on only a certain amount of detail at a time. If you start with one general routine and decompose it into more specific routines step by step, your brain isn't forced to deal with too many details at once. This approach is often called "divide and conquer." It works best for hierarchical systems like the one shown in Figure 7-2 on the next page.

The divide-and-conquer process is iterative in a couple of senses. First, it's iterative because you usually don't stop after one level of decomposition. You keep going for several levels. Second, it's iterative because you don't usually settle for your first attempt. You decompose a program one way and see what happens. Then you start over and decompose it another way and see whether that works better. After several attempts, you'll have a good idea of what works and why.

How far do you decompose a program? Continue decomposing until it seems as if it would be easier to code the next level than to decompose it. Work until you become somewhat impatient at how obvious and easy the design seems. At that point, you're done. You're closer to the problem when you design its solution than anyone else ever will be, and you understand it better than anyone else ever will, so make sure its solution is easy to understand. If the solution is even slightly tricky for you now, it'll be a bear for anyone who works on it later.

Bottom-up composition

CROSS-REFERENCE
Bottom-up implementation
is an entirely different
subject and is discussed in
"Bottom-Up Integration" in
Section 27.3.

Sometimes the top-down approach is so abstract that it's hard to get started. If you need to work with something more concrete, try the bottom-up design approach, also illustrated in Figure 7-2. Ask yourself, "What do I know this system needs to do?" Undoubtedly, you can answer that question. You might identify a few low-level capabilities the system needs to have. For example, you might know that a system needs to format reports, compute report totals, center report headings, print characters to the screen in a variety of colors, sum a list of expenses, and so on. After you identify several low-level capabilities, you'll usually start to feel comfortable enough to look at the top again.

Here are some things to keep in mind as you do bottom-up composition:

- Ask yourself what you know the system needs to do.
- Identify low-level capabilities from that question.
- Identify common aspects of low-level components and group them.
- Continue with the next level up, or go back to the top and try again to work down.

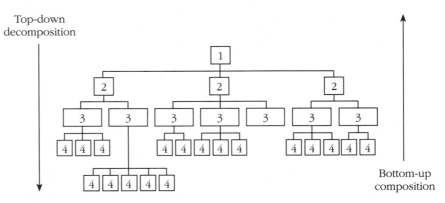

Figure 7-2. *Working from the general to the specific, top-down decomposition best applies to hierarchical systems that are easily decomposed. Bottom-up composition works from the specific to the general.*

Top down vs. bottom up

The key difference between top-down and bottom-up strategies is that one is a decomposition strategy and the other is a composition strategy. One starts from the general problem and breaks it into manageable pieces; the other starts with manageable pieces and combines them to create a general solution. Both approaches have strengths and weaknesses that you'll want to consider as you apply them to your design problems.

The strength of top-down design is that it's easy. People are good at breaking something big into smaller components, and programmers are especially good at it. If the problem is naturally modeled hierarchically, a top-down decomposition follows the structure of the problem nicely.

Another strength of top-down design is that you can defer implementation details. Since systems are often perturbed by changes in implementation details (for example, changes in a file structure or a report format), it's useful to have those details hidden in routines at the bottom of the hierarchy rather than playing prominent roles at the top.

Top-down design also has several weaknesses that come into play mainly in functional decomposition. One is that the top function of a system might be hard to identify. One of the most important decisions you make about a system is how to do the first level of decomposition, and in top-down design you're asked to make that decision at the beginning of the design process, when you have the least information. Another weakness is that many systems aren't naturally hierarchical, so they don't decompose neatly. Perhaps the most serious weakness is that top-down, functional design requires a system to be characterized by a single function at the top, a dubious requirement for many modern event-driven systems.

One strength of the bottom-up approach is that it typically results in early identification of useful utility routines, which results in a compact design. If similar systems have already been built, the bottom-up approach allows you to start the design of the new system by looking at pieces of the old system and asking, "What can I reuse?"

A weakness of the bottom-up composition approach is that it's hard to use exclusively. Most people are better at taking one big concept and breaking it into smaller concepts than they are at taking small concepts and making one big one. It's like the old assemble-it-yourself problem: I thought I was done, so why does the box still have parts in it? Fortunately, you don't have to use the bottom-up composition approach exclusively.

Another weakness of the bottom-up design strategy is that sometimes you find that you can't build a program from the pieces you've started with. You can't build an airplane from bricks, and you might have to work at the top before you know what kinds of pieces you need at the bottom.

Fortunately, top-down and bottom-up design aren't competing strategies—they're mutually beneficial. Design is a heuristic process, which means that no solution is guaranteed to work every time; design always contains an element of trial and error. Try a variety of approaches until you find a good one. Work from the top awhile, and then work from the bottom awhile.

Design is also an iterative process, so what you learn from looking at the bottom of the system on iteration n might help you do a better top-down decomposition on iteration $n+1$.

Further Reading

This description of structured design has been necessarily superficial. In particular, the graphical notations are much richer than what has been shown here. Fortunately, you won't need to rely on this brief summary; you can read any of several good books on the topic.

Yourdon, Edward, and Larry L. Constantine. *Structured Design: Fundamentals of a Discipline of Computer Program and Systems Design.* Englewood Cliffs, N.J.: Yourdon Press, 1979. This book is the classic text on structured design co-authored by one of the authors (Constantine) of the original structured-design paper. It's written with obvious care. It contains full discussions of coupling, cohesion, graphical notations, and other relevant concepts. Although some people have characterized it as "technically difficult," a motivated reader won't have any trouble.

Myers, Glenford J. *Composite/Structured Design.* New York: Van Nostrand Reinhold, 1978. This book is one of the original texts on structured design, written by another of the authors of the original paper on structured design. It's short and to the point and probably less technical than the Yourdon and Constantine book.

Page-Jones, Meilir. *The Practical Guide to Structured Systems Design.* Englewood Cliffs, N.J.: Yourdon Press, 1988. This book is a popular textbook presentation of the same basic content as the Yourdon and Constantine book. It's intended to be readable and humorous without sacrificing technical content. The author isn't as funny as he tries to be, but the technical content is sound, and no one has asked me to be on "The Tonight Show" either. This is a good book to start with.

Freeman, Peter, and Anthony I. Wasserman, eds. *Tutorial on Software Design Techniques*, 4th ed. Silver Spring, Md.: IEEE Computer Society Press, 1983. This book is an IEEE tutorial, allegedly about design but actually about requirements, user interface, architecture, design, and review methodologies. Its 40 papers by various authors are threaded together with comments by the editors. The papers make up a good collection and include the original structured-design paper.

Stevens, W., G. Myers, and L. Constantine. "Structured Design," *IBM Systems Journal* 13, no. 2 (May 1974): 115–39. This article is the original paper on structured design. The books make better presentations of the concepts, but the paper is interesting for its historical value.

7.3 Object-Oriented Design

Ask not first what the system does; ask WHAT it does it to!
Bertrand Meyer

Object-oriented design is characterized by the identification of real-world and abstract objects that are then represented by programming-language objects. The process is one of identifying objects and classes of objects, identifying the operations on the objects and classes, and then building a system from those objects, classes, and operations. Object-oriented design is a way of designing objects, or modules, in a program. To a much lesser extent, it's also a way of designing individual routines.

Although some advocates of object-oriented design measure computing history as B.O.O.M. (before object-oriented methods) and A.O.O.M. (after object-oriented methods), object-oriented design doesn't have to conflict with other design methods. Specifically, object-oriented design isn't incompatible with the low-level structuring provided by structured programming—just with the high-level structuring. At higher levels, the object-oriented approach adds clusters, classes, and inheritance to simple functional hierarchies. Exploring and standardizing these high-level composition ideas will be the next big step in programming.

The discussion of object-oriented design in this section is necessarily light. Object-oriented design works at a higher level of abstraction than structured design, and this book focuses on techniques that work at lower levels of abstraction—mostly at the levels of the individual statement, the routine, and the handful of routines. Object-oriented design is also still a relatively new, theoretical approach to design. It hasn't yet accumulated the body of experience that would support a completely practical explanation. Still, it seems promising, so the following subsections describe the high points.

Key Ideas

Object-oriented design is based on the proposition that the more closely a program models the real-world problem it represents, the better the program will be. In many cases, the data definitions on a project are more stable than the functionality is, so building a design based on the data, as object-oriented design does, is a more stable approach. Object-oriented design uses several ideas that are important to modern programming.

Abstraction

FURTHER READING
You can find much more
detail on these ideas in
*Object Oriented Design:
With Applications*
(Booch 1991, Chapter 2).

The principal benefit of abstraction is that it it allows you to ignore irrelevant details and concentrate on relevant characteristics. Most real-world objects are already abstractions of some kind. A house is an abstraction of wood, brick, nails, glass, plaster, shingles, insulation, and a particular way of organizing them. Wood is, in turn, an abstraction of a specific arrangement of tough, fibrous plant cells, which is in turn an abstraction of a collection of certain kinds of molecules.

In building a house, you'd be stopped dead if you had to deal with wood, nails, and insulation at the molecular level of abstraction. Likewise, when you build a software system, you can be stopped dead if you work at too molecular a level. With object-oriented design, you try to create levels of abstraction that let you manipulate pieces of the problem in ways similar to the ways you would manipulate real-world pieces of the problem, rather than manipulating programming-language entities.

Object-oriented design is especially good at abstraction because it uses bigger intellectual building blocks than do functional approaches such as structured design. In structured design, the unit of abstraction is a *function*. In object-oriented design, the unit of abstraction is an *object*. Since an object includes both functions and the data that's affected by them, it's possible to work with chunks of a problem that are bigger than functions. Such an ability increases the level of abstraction at which you can think about a problem and means you can think about more of it at once without blowing a mental fuse.

Encapsulation

Encapsulation picks up where abstraction leaves off. Abstraction says, "You are allowed to look at an object at a high level of detail." Encapsulation says, "You aren't allowed to look at an object at any other level of detail." This is the information hiding described in Section 6.2 all over again. You know everything about a module that it wants you to know and nothing else.

To continue the housing-materials analogy: Encapsulation is a way of saying that you can look at the outside of the house, and you might even be able to see a little through the windows, but you can't go inside. With older languages, any information hiding counts on voluntary compliance: The yard might have a "No Trespassing" sign, but the doors are unlocked and the windows are open. With Ada and object-oriented languages, a programmer can make respect for the information hiding mandatory: The doors are locked, the windows are barred, and the alarm system is active. What you see is what you get—it's all you get!

Modularity

Modularity in object-oriented design means about the same thing it does in structured design. Groups of related services and data are bundled into modules that, ideally, are highly cohesive and loosely coupled. As in information hiding, the goal is to define an interface to the module that stands unchanged in the face of changes to the module's interior.

Hierarchy and inheritance

In designing a software system, you'll often find objects that are much like other objects, except for a few differences. In an accounting system, for instance, you might have both full-time and part-time employees. Most of the data associated with both kinds of employees is the same, but some is different. In object-oriented programming, you can define a general type of employee and then define full-time employees as general employees, except for a few differences, and part-time employees also as general employees, except for a few differences. When an operation on an employee doesn't depend on the type of employee, the operation is handled as if the employee were just a general employee. When the operation depends on whether the employee is full-time or part-time, the operation is handled differently.

Defining similarities and differences among such objects is called "inheritance" because the specific part-time and full-time employees inherit characteristics from the general-employee type.

CROSS-REFERENCE
Objects and classes are closely related to abstract data types. For details, see Section 12.3, "Abstract Data Types (ADTs)," and especially the subsection "ADTs and Information Hiding, Modules, and Objects."

The benefit of the inheritance strategy is that it works synergistically with the notion of abstraction. Abstraction deals with objects at different levels of detail. Recall the tree that was a collection of certain kinds of molecules at one level; a collection of tough, fibrous plant cells at the next; and a piece of wood at the highest level. Wood has certain properties (for example, you can cut it with a saw or glue it with wood glue), and two-by-fours or cedar shingles have the general properties of wood as well as some specific properties of their own.

In object-oriented programming, inheritance simplifies programming because you write a general routine to handle anything that depends on wood's general properties and then write specific routines to handle specific operations on specific kinds of wood. Some operations, such as *GetSize()*, might apply regardless of the level of abstraction. The ability of a language to support an operation like *GetSize()* without knowing until run time whether the object it operates on is a collection of plant cells, a piece of wood, or a two-by-four is called "polymorphism." Object-oriented languages such as C++ and Eiffel support inheritance and polymorphism automatically. Object-based languages such as Ada and procedural languages such as C and Pascal do not.

Objects and classes

A final key concept in object-oriented design is the differentiation of objects and classes. An object is any specific entity that exists in your program at run time. A class is any abstract entity represented by the program. A class is the static thing you look at in the program listing. An object is the dynamic thing with specific values and attributes you see when you run the program. For example, you could declare a class *Person* that had attributes of name, age, gender, and so on. At run time you would have the objects *Nancy*, *Hank*, *Diane*, *Tony*, *Tammy*, and so on—that is, specific instances of the class. If you're familiar with database terms, it's the same as the distinction between "schema" and "instance." The rest of this section uses the terms informally, and generally refers to both entities as "objects."

Steps in Object-Oriented Design

FURTHER READING
These steps are explained in much more detail in *Software Engineering with Ada* (Booch 1987) and *Object Oriented Design: With Applications* (Booch 1991).

The steps in object-oriented design are

- Identify the objects and their attributes, which are probably data.
- Determine what can be done to each object.
- Determine what each object can do to other objects.
- Determine the parts of each object that will be visible to other objects—which parts will be public and which will be private.
- Define each object's public interface.

These steps aren't necessarily performed in order, and they're often repeated. Iteration is as important to object-oriented design as it is to any other design approach. Each of these steps is summarized below.

Identify the objects and their attributes. Computer programs are usually based on real-world entities. For example, you could base a time-billing system on real-world employees, clients, time cards, and bills. Figure 7-3 shows an object-oriented view of such a billing system.

Objects in a graphical user interface system would include windows, dialog boxes, buttons, fonts, and drawing tools. Further examination of the problem domain might produce better choices for software objects than a one-to-one mapping to real-world objects, but the real-world objects are always a good place to start.

Identifying the objects' attributes is no more complicated than identifying the objects themselves. Each object has characteristics that are relevant to the computer program. For example, in the time-billing system, an employee object has a name, a title, and a billing rate. A client object has a name, a billing address, an account balance, and a retainer amount. A bill object has a billing amount, a client name, a date, a project code, and so on.

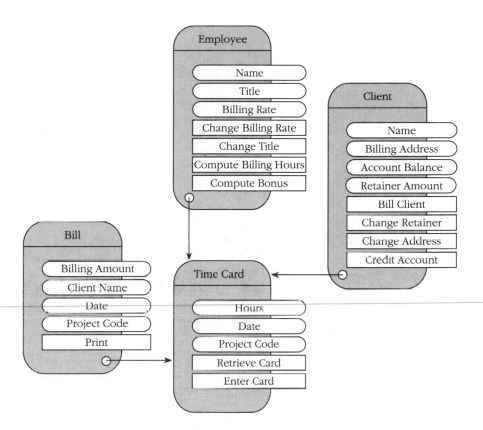

Figure 7-3. *This billing system is composed of four major objects. The objects have been simplified for this example. The graphical notation for the objects is similar to the module notation introduced in Chapter 6, "Three out of Four Programmers Surveyed Prefer Modules."*

Determine what can be done to each object. A variety of operations can be performed on each object. In the billing system, an employee object could have a change in title or billing rate, and it could be asked to provide the number of billing hours for a given period or the employee's bonus. A client object can be billed, have its retainer amount or address changed, or have its account credited.

Determine what each object can do to other objects. This step is just what it sounds like. What can an employee in the time-billing system do to the other objects? Not much. About all an employee can do is enter time-card information. A bill can retrieve time-card information. Other interactions would be more evident in a more complicated system.

CROSS-REFERENCE
For details on modules and
information hiding, see
Section 6.2, "Information
Hiding."

Determine the parts of each object that will be visible to other objects. One of the key design decisions is identifying the parts of an object that should be made public and those that should be kept private. This decision has to be made for both data and services.

In the diagram of the billing system, only the public parts of each object are shown. The private parts are hidden inside the black boxes. The Client and Employee objects look complicated because they have seven or eight visible features each. This complicated appearance is a weakness of the diagrammatic technique that worsens as the number of features increases—a well-designed object often has many additional visible features.

Define each object's interface. As a final step in the design of an object, define the formal, syntactic, programming-language-level interfaces to each object. This includes services offered by the object as well as inheritance relations among object classes. Typically, this would include function or procedure declarations. For example, the interface to the time-card object might look like this:

```
C++ Example of an Interface to a Time Card
class TimeCard
    {
    public:

    int Enter
        (
        EMPLOYEE_ID    Employee,
        DATE           Date,
        CLIENT_ID      Client,
        PROJECT        ProjectCode,
        int            Hours
        );

    int Retrieve
        (
        int&           Hours,
        DATE&          Date,
        CLIENT_ID&     Client,
        PROJECT        ProjectCode,
        EMPLOYEE_ID    Employee
        );

    protected:
    ...
    };
```

When you finish going through the steps to achieve a top-level object-oriented system organization, you'll iterate in two ways. You'll iterate on the top-level system organization to get a better object-class organization. You'll also iterate on each of the objects you've defined, driving the design to a more detailed level.

Components of a Typical Object-Oriented Design

FURTHER READING
These descriptions are adapted from *Object-Oriented Design* (Coad and Yourdon 1991).

An object-oriented system typically has at least four categories of objects. If you don't have something from each of these categories, you're probably missing something:

- Problem-domain component. This component refers directly to the problem domain. In the billing-system example, the problem domain includes the real-world objects like employees, clients, time cards, and bills.

- User-interface component. This component refers to the part of the system responsible for human interaction. It includes data-entry forms, windows, dialog boxes, buttons, and so on. As mentioned in Section 6.2, it's a good idea to hide the user-interface part of the system so that it can accommodate changes easily.

- Task-management component. This component includes objects from the computer itself. It includes real-time task managers, hardware interfaces, communications protocols, and so on.

- Data-management component. This component includes objects for maintaining persistent data. It includes databases and files and all the storage, retrieval, and maintenance services associated with them.

Further Reading

Booch, Grady. *Object Oriented Design: With Applications.* Redwood City, Calif.: Benjamin/Cummings, 1991. This book is about exactly what it says it's about: object-oriented design with applications. It discusses the theoretical and practical foundations of object-oriented design for about 200 pages and then spends 250 more pages on object-oriented application development in Smalltalk, Object Pascal, C++, Common Lisp Object System, and Ada. No one has been a more active advocate of object-oriented design than Grady Booch, and his dedication shows in this fine volume.

Meyer, Bertrand. *Object-Oriented Software Construction.* New York: Prentice Hall, 1988. Meyer is one of the hardest of the hard-core object-oriented programming advocates, and this book contains a forceful advocacy of pure object-oriented programming—including inheritance, multiple inheritance, and polymorphism. It contains a lively criticism of traditional, structured techniques as well as of hybrid approaches such as the one suggested later in this chapter.

Coad, Peter, and Edward Yourdon. *Object-Oriented Design*. Englewood Cliffs, N.J.: Yourdon Press, 1991. This is another popular book about object-oriented design. It's a fraction of the size of Booch's or Meyer's book and contains an even smaller fraction of content. Some readers might find it an easier introduction to object-oriented design than the thoughtful treatments in the other sources.

Communications of the ACM 33, no. 9 (September 1990). This issue of *CACM* is devoted to object-oriented design and is an excellent survey of the field as of late 1990.

Beck, Kent. "Think Like An Object." *Unix Review* 9, no. 10 (October 1991): 39–43. This article introduces a new low-end design tool: 3x5 cards. On each card, designers write a class name, responsibilities of the class, and collaborators (other classes that cooperate with the class). A design group then works with the cards until they're satisfied that they've created a good design. Beck argues that 3x5 cards are cheap, unintimidating, and portable and that they encourage group interaction. The article itself is short, sweet, and practical.

Hecht, Alan. "Cute Object-oriented Acronyms Considered FOOlish." *Software Engineering Notes,* January 1990, 48. This charming article helps relieve the frustration you might feel from the profusion of double-O acronyms in object-oriented programming.

7.4 Comments on Popular Methodologies

If you look carefully at the popular methodologies—including structured design and object-oriented design—you'll see that each consists of two main elements:

- Criteria for decomposing a system into subprograms
- Verbal or graphical notation for expressing the decomposition

Some methodologies contain a third element:

- Arm-twisting to prevent your using other methods

Restricting the meaning of the term "design" to the first two elements implies that the hard part of design is decomposing a program into smaller subprograms and further implies that the implementation of the subprograms isn't challenging enough to be worthy of discussion.

It's true that a good system decomposition is valuable. It's not true that the need for good design stops as soon as a sound structure has been identified. A great deal of design work still needs to be done within individual modules and routines after they've been identified.

The third element that accompanies some design methodologies, the idea that any design methodology should be used exclusively, is particularly harmful. No methodology can account for all the creativity and insight required to design a system. Imposing an exclusive design methodology on the design activity stifles important thought processes.

CROSS-REFERENCE
For more on programming and religion, see Section 32.8, "Thou Shalt Rend Software and Religion Asunder."

All too often, choice of a design methodology is a religious issue—you go to a revival meeting and hear sermons from some of the prophets of structured objectness and then return to your shrine to write a few holy programs on clay tablets. After such a conversion, you aren't allowed to stray into the pagan territory of other methodologies. This fanaticism violates the constitutional separation of church and software engineering.

If you were a construction worker, you wouldn't try to use the same approach on every project. You might pour concrete during the week and build a treehouse on the weekend. You wouldn't try to build a treehouse out of cement, and you wouldn't put a "No Grownups Allowed" sign on a new skyscraper. You would vary your approach to suit the problem. Take a page from the construction industry in your choice of programming methodologies. Choose the one appropriate to the problem. The advisability of a secular approach to design has been confirmed by several studies that have found that each design approach has a particular strength and that none works best in all cases (Peters and Tripp 1977, Mannino 1987, Kelly 1987, Loy 1990).

An objection to the methods themselves is the tangle of terminology they've generated. To know structured design by the book, for example, you must learn at least the following terms: afferent stream and module; efferent stream and module; normal, stamp, control, common, global, content, and pathological coupling; functional, sequential, communicational, procedural, temporal, logical, and coincidental cohesion; fan-in and fan-out; tramp data; transaction center, transaction analysis, and transaction module; transform center, transform analysis, and transform module; system morphology; and even *Benützerfreundlichkeit* (seriously!). Not every methodology applies to Merriam-Webster for its own chapter in the dictionary, but buzzword supernovas are too common, and they're tiresome.

Structured design, design with the goal of information hiding, and object-oriented design foster different ways of looking at problems. Figure 7-4 on the next page compares the ways in which they are typically used.

One reason the structured people and the object-oriented people have trouble talking with each other is that they forget that they're talking about different levels of design and therefore different subjects. Edna Structured Design might say, "I think this system should be decomposed into 50 routines." Gladys Object-Oriented Design might say, "I think this system should be divided into 7 objects." When you look closely, the 7 objects might contain a total of 50 routines, and Edna's routines might map to Gladys's one-to-one.

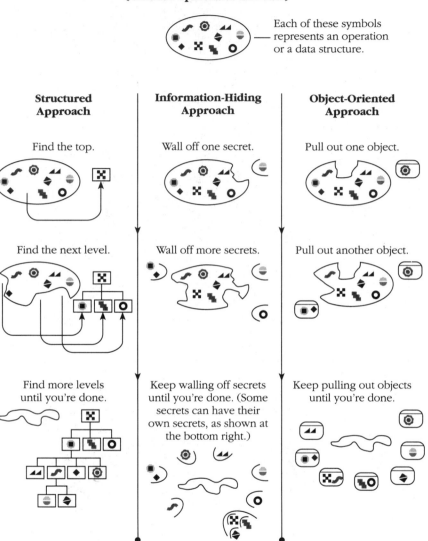

The Problem Area
(includes operations and data)

Each of these symbols represents an operation or a data structure.

Structured Approach	Information-Hiding Approach	Object-Oriented Approach
Find the top.	Wall off one secret.	Pull out one object.
Find the next level.	Wall off more secrets.	Pull out another object.
Find more levels until you're done.	Keep walling off secrets until you're done. (Some secrets can have their own secrets, as shown at the bottom right.)	Keep pulling out objects until you're done.

Figure 7-4. *Different design methodologies lead to different ways of looking at a problem, which in turn lead to different ways of solving it. Each of the approaches is right for certain kinds of programs.*

When to Use Structured Design

Structured design is mainly a way of breaking a program into routines. It emphasizes functionality and doesn't stress data. An example of a functionally oriented problem domain would be a system that reads data in batch mode, performs predictable processes on the data in a predictable order, and writes the data.

Structured design doesn't include the notion of packaging routines into groups that work well together or of designing routine internals, except as the internals affect the entire system. Consequently, structured design is particularly appropriate for systems that have a lot of independent functions that don't interact much. It also works well for small programs of a few hundred lines of code—systems that are too simple to justify the overhead of setting up classes and objects and attributes.

Larry Constantine, the principal author of the original paper on structured design and co-author of the seminal book on structured design, published an article titled "Objects, Functions, and Program Extensibility" that explains how to combine structured design with object-oriented approaches (Constantine 1990b). If data is likely to change, the object-oriented approach is appropriate because it isolates the data likely to change into individual objects (modules). If functionality is likely to change, the object-oriented approach is not so appropriate because functionality is spread throughout many objects (modules). If the functionality is more likely to change than the data, you are better off using the functional decomposition of structured design.

When to Use Information Hiding

CROSS-REFERENCE
For details on information hiding, see Section 6.2, "Information Hiding."

Use information hiding as much as possible, regardless of the problem domain. It has no known hazards. The FDA has not found that it causes cancer or promotes tooth decay. It's effective in the design of routines, modules, and objects, so use it liberally.

When to Use Object-Oriented Design

One of the big differences between structured design and object-oriented design is that object-oriented design works well at a higher level of abstraction than structured design does. This makes sense historically because the massively complex systems that programmers were building when structured design was developed were nowhere near as massively complex as the systems are today.

Object-oriented design is mainly a way of designing *modules*—collections of data and operations on the data. It's great for decomposing a system from the highest level.

At the point at which you've identified the object interfaces and you start designing the code to support them, you usually switch to structured design. If you're working in an object-oriented language, it's hard to say you're not still doing object-oriented design because you're still working in terms of methods or messages or other object-oriented constructs. If you're working in a more traditional procedural language, it's easier to say that you're doing plain old structured design, which is appropriate at that point.

Object-oriented design is applicable to any system that acts as objects in the real world do. Examples of such systems include highly interactive programs that use windows, dialog boxes, buttons, and so on; object-oriented databases (by definition); and event-driven systems that require specific responses to randomly ordered events.

Much of the research being done on object-oriented techniques is focused on successful implementation of systems from 100,000 to over a million lines of code. Structured techniques have too often failed on such large projects, and object-oriented techniques seem to be a better solution. However, the older techniques are still useful on any but the largest projects, and the superiority of object-oriented design for smaller problems has yet to be proven.

7.5 Round-Trip Design

KEY POINT

It's possible to combine the major design approaches, making the most of their strengths and minimizing their weaknesses. Each of the design approaches is a tool in the programmer's toolbox, and different design tools are appropriate for different jobs. You'll benefit from exploiting the heuristic power of any or all of the approaches.

The following subsections describe some of the reasons that software design is hard, how to make it easier, and how to combine structured design, object-oriented design, and other design approaches.

What's a Round Trip?

You might have had an experience in which you learned so much from writing a program that you wished you could write it again, knowing what you learned from writing it. The same phenomenon applies to design, but in design the cycles are shorter and the effects downstream are bigger, so you can afford to whirl through the design loop a few times.

KEY POINT

The term "round-trip design" captures the idea that design is an iterative process: You don't usually go from point A just to point B; you go from point A to point B and back to point A. The term is inspired by a similar term in *Object Oriented Design: With Applications* (Booch 1991).

As you cycle through candidate designs and try different approaches, you'll look at both high-level and low-level views. The big picture you get from working with high-level issues will help you to put the low-level details in perspective. The details you get from working with low-level issues will provide a foundation in solid reality for the high-level decisions. The tug and pull between top-level and bottom-level considerations is a healthy dynamic; it creates a stressed structure that is more stable than one built wholly from the top down or the bottom up.

Many programmers—many people, for that matter—have trouble ranging between high-level and low-level considerations. Switching from one view of a system to another is mentally strenuous, but it's essential to effective design. For entertaining exercises to enhance your mental flexibility, read *Conceptual Blockbusting* (Adams 1980), described in the "Further Reading" section at the end of the chapter.

Design Is a Sloppy Process

J. P. Morgan said that every person has two reasons for doing things: the one that sounds good and the real reason. In design, the finished product usually looks well organized and clean, as if the designers had never taken a wrong turn. The process used to develop the design is rarely as tidy as the end result.

FURTHER READING
For a fuller exploration of this viewpoint, see "A Rational Design Process: How and Why to Fake It" (Parnas and Clements 1986).

Design is a sloppy process. It's sloppy because the right answer is often hard to distinguish from the wrong one. If you send three people away to design the same program, they might easily return with three vastly different designs, each of which is perfectly acceptable. It's sloppy because you take many false steps and go down many blind alleys—you make a lot of mistakes. Design is also sloppy because it's hard to know when your design is "good enough." When are you done? Since design is open-ended, the answer to that question is usually "When you're out of time."

Design Is a Wicked Problem

Horst Rittel and Melvin Webber defined a "wicked" problem as one that could be clearly defined only by solving it, or by solving part of it (1973). This paradox implies, essentially, that you have to "solve" the problem once in order to clearly define it and then solve it again to create a solution that works. This process is almost motherhood and apple pie in software development.

In my part of the world, a dramatic example of such a wicked problem was the design of the original Tacoma Narrows bridge. At the time the bridge was built, the main consideration in designing a bridge was that it be strong

The picture of the software designer deriving his design in a rational, error-free way from a statement of requirements is quite unrealistic. No system has ever been developed in that way, and probably none ever will. Even the small program developments shown in textbooks and papers are unreal. They have been revised and polished until the author has shown us what he wishes he had done, not what actually did happen.

David Parnas and Paul Clements

The Tacoma Narrows bridge—an example of a wicked problem.

enough to support its planned load. In the case of the Tacoma Narrows bridge, wind created an unexpected, side-to-side harmonic ripple. One blustery day in 1940, the ripple grew uncontrollably until the bridge collapsed.

This is a good example of a wicked problem because until the bridge collapsed, its engineers didn't know that aerodynamics needed to be considered to such an extent. Only by building the bridge (solving the problem) could they learn about the additional consideration in the problem that allowed them to build another bridge that still stands.

One of the main differences between programs you develop in school and those you develop as a professional is that the design problems solved by school programs are rarely, if ever, wicked. Programming assignments in school are devised to move you in a beeline from beginning to end. You'd probably want to lynch a teacher who gave you a programming assignment, then changed the assignment as soon as you finished the design, and then changed it again just as you were about to turn in the completed program. But that very process is an everyday reality in professional programming.

Design Is a Heuristic Process

A key to effective design is recognizing that it's a heuristic process. Design always involves some trial and error. The round-trip design concept accounts for the fact that design is heuristic by treating all design methodologies as tools in an intellectual toolbox. One tool works well on one job or on one phase or aspect of a job; other tools work well on others. No tool is right for everything, and it's useful to have several tools at your disposal.

> **When in doubt, use brute force.**
>
> *Butler Lampson*

One powerful heuristic tool is brute force. Don't underestimate it. A brute-force solution that works is better than an elegant solution that doesn't work. It can take a long time to get an elegant solution to work. In describing the history of searching algorithms, for example, Donald Knuth pointed out that even though the first description of a binary search algorithm was published in 1946, it took another 16 years for someone to publish an algorithm that correctly searched lists of all sizes (1973b).

Diagrams are another powerful heuristic tool. A picture is worth 1000 words—kind of. You actually want to leave out most of the 1000 words because one point of using a picture is that a picture can represent the problem at a higher level of abstraction. Sometimes you want to deal with the problem in detail, but other times you want to be able to work with it at a more general level.

> **More alarming, the same programmer is quite capable of doing the same task himself in two or three ways, sometimes unconsciously, but quite often simply for a change, or to provide elegant variation, or to find a way that will take less core or time.**
>
> *A. R. Brown and W. A. Sampson*

An additional aspect of the heuristic power of round-trip design is that you can leave some details unresolved during early design cycles. You don't have to decide everything at once. Remember that a point needs to be decided, but recognize that you don't yet have enough information to resolve that specific issue. Why fight your way through the last 10 percent of the design when it will drop into place easily the next time through? Why make bad decisions based on limited experience with the design when you can make good decisions based on more experience with it later? Some people are uncomfortable if they don't come to closure after a design cycle, but after you have created a few designs without resolving issues prematurely, it will seem natural to leave issues unresolved until you have more information (Zahniser 1992).

One of the most effective guidelines is not to get stuck on a single approach. If writing the program in PDL isn't working, make a picture. Write it in English. Write a short test program. Try a completely different approach. Think of a brute-force solution. Keep outlining and sketching with your pencil, and your brain will follow. If all else fails, walk away from the problem. Literally go for a walk, or think about something else before returning to the problem. If you've given it your best and are getting nowhere, putting it out of your mind for a time often produces results more quickly than sheer persistence can.

Finally, approaches to design in software can learn from approaches to design in other fields. One of the original books on heuristics in problem solving was G. Polya's *How to Solve It* (1957). Polya's generalized problem-solving approach focuses on problem solving in mathematics. Table 7-1 is a summary of his approach, adapted from a similar summary in his book (emphases his).

Table 7-1. How to Solve It

1. Understanding the Problem. You have to *understand* the problem.

What is the unknown? What are the data? What is the condition? Is it possible to satisfy the condition? Is the condition sufficient to determine the unknown? Or is it insufficient? Or redundant? Or contradictory?

Draw a figure. Introduce suitable notation. Separate the various parts of the condition. Can you write them down?

2. Devising a Plan. Find the connection between the data and the unknown. You might be obliged to consider auxiliary problems if you can't find an intermediate connection. You should eventually come up with a *plan* of the solution.

Have you seen the problem before? Or have you seen the same problem in a slightly different form? *Do you know a related problem?* Do you know a theorem that could be useful?

Look at the unknown! And try to think of a familiar problem having the same or a similar unknown. *Here is a problem related to yours and solved before. Can you use it?* Can you use its result? Can you use its method? Should you introduce some auxiliary element in order to make its use possible?

Can you restate the problem? Can you restate it still differently? Go back to definitions.

If you cannot solve the proposed problem, try to solve some related problem first. Can you imagine a more accessible related problem? A more general problem? A more special problem? An analogous problem? Can you solve a part of the problem? Keep only a part of the condition, drop the other part; how far is the unknown then determined, how can it vary? Can you derive something useful from the data? Can you think of other data appropriate for determining the unknown? Can you change the unknown or the data, or both if necessary, so that the new unknown and the new data are nearer to each other?

Did you use all the data? Did you use the whole condition? Have you taken into account all essential notions involved in the problem?

3. Carrying out the Plan. *Carry out* your plan.

Carrying out your plan of the solution, *check each step*. Can you see clearly that the step is correct? Can you prove that it is correct?

4. Looking Back. *Examine* the solution.

Can you *check the result?* Can you check the argument? Can you derive the result differently? Can you see it at a glance?

Can you use the result, or the method, for some other problem?

Source: *How to Solve It* (Polya 1957).

Desirable Design Characteristics

A high-quality design has several general characteristics. If you could achieve all these goals, your design would be considered very good indeed. Some goals contradict other goals, but that's the challenge of design—creating a good set of trade-offs from competing objectives. Some characteristics of design quality are also characteristics of the program: reliability, performance, and so on. Others are internal characteristics of the design.

CROSS-REFERENCE
These characteristics are related to general software-quality attributes. For details on general attributes, see Section 23.1, "Characteristics of Software Quality."

Here's a list of internal design characteristics:

Intellectual manageability. Intellectual manageability is a primary goal in any system. It's essential to the overall system integrity and affects how easily programmers can build a system initially as well as maintain it later.

Low complexity. Low complexity is part of intellectual manageability and is important for the same reasons.

Ease of maintenance. Ease of maintenance means designing for the maintenance programmer. Continually imagine the questions a maintenance programmer would ask about the code you are writing. Think of the maintenance programmer as your audience, and then design the system to be self-explanatory.

Minimal connectedness. Minimal connectedness means designing so that you hold connections among subprograms to a minimum. Use the principles of strong cohesion, loose coupling, and information hiding to design systems with as few interconnections as possible. Minimal connectedness minimizes work during integration, testing, and maintenance.

Extensibility. Extensibility means that you can enhance a system without causing violence to the underlying structure. You can change a piece of a system without affecting other pieces. The most likely changes cause the system the least trauma.

Reusability. Reusability means designing the system so that you can reuse pieces of it in other systems.

High fan-in. High fan-in means sharing a high number of routines that call a given routine. High fan-in implies that a system has been designed to make good use of utility routines at the lower levels in the system.

Low-to-medium fan-out. Low-to-medium fan-out means having a given routine call a low-to-medium number of other routines. High fan-out (more than about seven) indicates that a routine controls a large number of other routines and may therefore be hard to understand. Medium fan-out implies that a routine has delegated tasks to a small number of other routines and that the routine is therefore easy to understand. Low fan-out (fewer than about four) would seem to imply that a routine doesn't delegate enough of its activities, but empirical evidence indicates otherwise. One study found that 42 percent of routines that called one other routine had no errors, 32 percent of routines that called two through seven other routines had no errors, and only 12 percent of routines that called more than seven routines had no errors (Card, Church, and Agresti 1986). This result led one of the authors of the study to conclude that a fan-out of zero, one, or two is optimum (Card and Glass 1990).

HARD DATA

Portability. Portability means designing the system so that you can easily move it to another environment.

Leanness. Leanness means designing the system so that it has no extra parts. Voltaire said that a book is finished not when nothing more can be added but when nothing more can be taken away. In software, this is especially true because extra code has to be developed, reviewed, tested, maintained, understood, and considered when the other code is modified, and future versions of the software must remain backward-compatible with the extra code. The fatal question is "It's easy, so what can it hurt to put it in?"

CROSS-REFERENCE
For more information on stratifying your design, see "Separating a Program into Levels of Abstraction" in Section 32.5.

Stratified design. Stratified design means trying to keep the levels of decomposition stratified so that you can view the system at any single level and get a consistent view of the system. Design the system so that you can view it at one level without dipping into other levels. You'll often run into cases in which some routines or modules are able to function at more than one level, but that makes for a messy system and is better avoided.

If you're writing a modern system that has to use a lot of older, poorly designed code, for example, write a layer of the new system that's responsible for interfacing with the old code. Design the layer so that it hides the poor quality of the old code, presenting a consistent set of services to the newer layers. Then have the rest of the system call those routines rather than the old code. The beneficial effects of stratified design in such a case are (1) it compartmentalizes the messiness of dealing with the bad code and (2) if you ever get to jettison the old routines, you won't need to modify any new code except the interface layer.

Standard techniques. Standard techniques are desirable. The more a system relies on exotic pieces, the more intimidating it is for someone trying to understand it the first time. Try to give the whole system a familiar feeling by using standardized, common approaches.

Further Reading

The other sections of this chapter contain pointers to further reading on the specific topics of structured design, information hiding, and object-oriented design. Here are a few books on general design topics.

Software design

Peters, Lawrence J. *Handbook of Software Design: Methods and Techniques.* New York: Yourdon Press, 1981. This design cookbook includes overviews of several different design methods and graphical design notations. It describes how to create your own approach by using parts of other design approaches. It's slightly dated but gives a more balanced coverage than most one-size-fits-all design books, and that makes it refreshing.

Parnas, David L., and Paul C. Clements. "A Rational Design Process: How and Why to Fake It." *IEEE Transactions on Software Engineering* SE-12, no. 2 (February 1986): 251–57. This classic article describes the gap between how programs are really designed and how you sometimes wish they were designed. The main point is that no one ever really goes through a rational, orderly design process but that aiming for it makes for better designs in the end.

IEEE Std 1016-1987. Recommended Practice for Software Design Descriptions in IEEE 1991. This document contains the IEEE-ANSI standard for software-design descriptions. It describes what should be included in a software-design document.

Alternative software-design methods

Jackson, Michael A. *Principles of Program Design.* New York: Academic Press, 1975. Jackson is an evangelist for data-view design, and this is the book in which he explains the full data-view design methodology. It's not used much in the United States, but it's popular in Europe—maybe because Jackson is British. This book is easy to understand, well written, and humorous—very readable.

King, David. *Creating Effective Software: Computer Program Design Using the Jackson Methodology.* New York: Yourdon Press, 1988. This is an alternative description of Jackson's data-view design method and is even easier to read than Jackson's book.

Webster, Dallas E. "Mapping the Design Information Representation Terrain." *IEEE Computer,* December 1988: 8–23. This survey of existing design and requirements-analysis methods is heavily theoretical, but if you want to get a sense of the full sweep of available design methods and you're not intimidated by a little terminology, it's a good place to look.

Design in general

Adams, James L. *Conceptual Blockbusting: A Guide to Better Ideas,* 2d ed. New York: Norton, 1980. Although not specifically about software design, this book was written to teach design to engineering students at Stanford. Even if you never design anything, the book is a fascinating discussion of creative thought processes. It includes many exercises in the kinds of thinking required for effective design. It also contains a well-annotated bibliography on design and creative thinking. If you like problem solving, you'll like this book.

Polya, G. *How to Solve It: A New Aspect of Mathematical Method,* 2d ed. Princeton, N.J.: Princeton University Press, 1957. This discussion of heuristics and problem solving focuses on mathematics but is applicable to software development. Polya's book was the first written about the use of heuristics in mathematical problem solving. It draws a clear distinction between the messy heuristics used to discover solutions and the tidier techniques used to present them once they've been discovered. It's not easy reading, but if you're interested in heuristics, you'll eventually read it whether you want to or not. Polya's book makes it clear that problem solving isn't a deterministic activity and that adherence to any single methodology is like walking with your feet in chains. Microsoft gives this book to all its new programmers.

Simon, Herbert. *The Sciences of the Artificial.* Cambridge, Mass.: MIT Press, 1969. This fascinating book draws a distinction between sciences that deal with the natural world (biology, geology, and so on) and sciences that deal with the artificial world created by humans (business, architecture, and computer science). It then discusses the characteristics of the sciences of the artificial, emphasizing the science of design. It has an academic tone and is well worth reading for anyone intent on a career in software development or any other "artificial" field.

CHECKLIST

High-Level Design

This checklist describes generic considerations you can use to evaluate the quality of a design. The list complements the architecture checklist in Section 3.4. This list is concerned primarily with the quality of a design; the list in Section 3.4 is concerned with the contents of an architecture or a design. Some elements on the two lists overlap.

(continued)

High-Level Design checklist, *continued*

❏ Have you used round-trip design, selecting the best of several attempts rather than the first attempt?

❏ Is the design of each subprogram consistent with the design of related subprograms?

❏ Does the design adequately address issues that were identified and deferred at the architectural level?

❏ Are you satisfied with the way the program has been decomposed into modules or objects?

❏ Are you satisified with the way the modules have been decomposed into routines?

❏ Are subprogram boundaries well defined?

❏ Are subprograms designed for minimal interaction with each other?

❏ Does the design make sense both from the top down and from the bottom up?

❏ Does the design differentiate between the problem-domain component, the user-interface component, the task-management component, and the data-management component?

❏ Is the design intellectually manageable?

❏ Does the design have low complexity?

❏ Will the program be easy to maintain?

❏ Does the design hold connections among subprograms to a minimum?

❏ Does the design anticipate future extensions to the program?

❏ Are subprograms designed so that you can use them in other systems?

❏ Do low-level routines have high fan-in?

❏ Do most routines have low-to-medium fan-out?

❏ Will the design be easy to port to another environment?

❏ Is the design lean? Are all of its parts strictly necessary?

❏ Is the design stratified into layers?

❏ Does the design use standard techniques and avoid exotic, hard-to-understand elements?

Key Points

- Design is heuristic. Dogmatic adherence to any single methodology hurts creativity and hurts your programs. A little tenaciousness in using a design methodology is probably beneficial in that it forces you to understand the methodology fully. Make sure, however, that you're being tenacious and not stubborn.

- Good design is iterative; the more design possibilities you try, the better your final design will be.

- Structured design is especially appropriate for small collections of routines and for problems in which functionality is more likely to change than data.

- Object-oriented design is appropriate for combinations of routines and data, and it is generally appropriate at a higher level than structured design. It is especially appropriate for problems in which the data is more likely to change than the functionality.

- Design methods are tools. How well you use the tools determines the ultimate quality of your program. You can make a good program with poor design methods, and you can make a bad program with good design methods. Nonetheless, choosing the right tool for the job makes it easier to build high-quality software.

- Lots of useful, interesting information on design is available outside this book. The perspectives presented here are just the tip of the iceberg.

8

Creating Data

Contents

Related Topics

IN THIS CHAPTER CONSIDERATION TURNS FROM the high-level discussion of routine, module, and program design to a more detailed discussion of the nuts and bolts of data-implementation issues.

CROSS-REFERENCE
For details on data considerations in the phases preceding construction, see "Major data structures" in Section 3.4.

The amount of influence good data structures can exercise during construction is somewhat determined by the amount of influence they have had on the earlier work leading up to construction. Much of the power of good data structures manifests itself during requirements analysis and architecture. For maximum advantage, consider defining major data structures then.

The influence of data structures is also determined by construction practices. It's normal and desirable for construction to fill in small gaps in the requirements and architecture. It would be inefficient to draw blueprints to such a microscopic level that no inconsistencies or deficiencies remained. The rest of this chapter describes the first step in effectively filling the gaps—creating the data to do it.

If you're an expert programmer, some of the information in this chapter will be old news to you. You might just skim the headings and examples for tips you haven't seen before.

8.1 Data Literacy

KEY POINT

The first step in creating effective data structures is knowing which data structures to create. A good repertoire of data structures is a key part of a programmer's toolkit. A tutorial in data structures is beyond the scope of this book, but take the "Data-Structure Literacy Test" below to determine how much more you might need to learn about them.

The Data-Structure Literacy Test

Put a *1* next to each term that looks familiar. If you think you know what a term means but aren't sure, give yourself a *0.5*. Add the points when you're done, and interpret your score according to the descriptions in the next section.

_____	abstract data type	_____	literal
_____	array	_____	local variable
_____	B-tree	_____	lookup table
_____	bitmap	_____	pointer
_____	boolean variable	_____	queue
_____	character variable	_____	record
_____	named constant	_____	retroactive synapse
_____	double precision	_____	set
_____	elongated stream	_____	stack
_____	enumerated type	_____	string
_____	floating point	_____	structured variable
_____	hash table	_____	tree
_____	heap	_____	trie
_____	index	_____	union
_____	integer	_____	value chain
_____	linked list	_____	variant record
		_____	**Total Score**

Here is how you can interpret the scores (loosely):

0–14   You are a beginning programmer, probably in your first year of computer science in school or teaching yourself your first programming language. You can learn a lot by reading one of the books listed below. Many of the descriptions of techniques in this part of the book are addressed to advanced programmers, and you'll get more out of them after you've read one of these books.

15–19   You are an intermediate programmer or an experienced programmer who has forgotten a lot. Although many of the concepts will be familiar to you, you too can benefit from reading one of the books listed below.

20–24   You are an expert programmer. You probably already have the books listed below on your shelf.

25–29   You know more about data structures than I do! Consider writing your own computer book. (Send me a copy.)

30–32   You are a pompous fraud. The terms "elongated stream," "retroactive synapse," and "value chain" don't refer to data structures—I made them up. Please read the intellectual-honesty section in Chapter 31!

These books are good sources of information about data structures:

Aho, Alfred V., John E. Hopcroft, and Jeffrey D. Ullman. *Data Structures and Algorithms*. Reading, Mass.: Addison-Wesley, 1983.

Reingold, Edward M., and Wilfred J. Hansen. *Data Structures*. Boston: Little, Brown, 1983.

Wirth, Niklaus. *Algorithms and Data Structures*. Englewood Cliffs, N.J.: Prentice Hall, 1986

8.2 Reasons to Create Your Own Types

KEY POINT

Programmer-defined variable types are one of the most powerful capabilities a language can give you to clarify your understanding of a program. They protect your program against unforeseen changes and make it easier to read. If you're using C, Pascal, or another language that allows user-defined types, take advantage of them! If you're using Fortran, generic Basic, or a language that doesn't allow user-defined types, read on. You might end up wanting to switch to a new language.

To appreciate the power of type creation, suppose you're writing a program to convert coordinates in an x, y, z system to latitude, longitude, and elevation. You think that double-precision floating-point numbers might be needed but would prefer to write a program with single-precision floating-point numbers until you're absolutely sure. You can create a new type specifically for coordinates by using a *typedef* statement in C, a *type* declaration in Pascal, or the equivalent in another language. Here's how you'd set up the type definition in C:

CROSS-REFERENCE
The _t suffix indicates that *Coordinate_t* is a type name rather than a variable name. For details on this and other naming conventions, see Section 9.3, "The Power of Naming Conventions," and the sections that follow it.

C Example of Creating a Type

```
typedef float Coordinate_t;  /* for coordinate variables */
```

This type definition declares a new type, *Coordinate_t*, that's functionally the same as the type *float*. To use the new type, you declare variables with it just as you would with a predefined type such as *float*. Here's an example:

C Example of Using the Type You've Created

```
Routine1(...)
   {
   Coordinate_t latitude;    /* latitude in degrees */
   Coordinate_t longitude;   /* longitude in degrees */
   Coordinate_t elevation;   /* elevation in meters from earth center */
   ...
   }
...

Routine2(...)
   {
   Coordinate_t x;  /* x coordinate in meters */
   Coordinate_t y;  /* y coordinate in meters */
   Coordinate_t z;  /* z coordinate in meters */
   ...
   }
```

In this code, the variables *latitude, longitude, elevation, x, y,* and *z* are all declared to be of type *Coordinate_t.*

Now suppose that the program changes and you find that you need to use double-precision variables for coordinates after all. Because you defined a type specifically for coordinate data, all you have to change is the type definition. And you have to change it in only one place: in the *typedef* statement. Here's the changed type definition:

C Example of Changed Type Definition

The original float has changed to double.

```
typedef double Coordinate_t;  /* for coordinate variables */
```

Here's a second example—this one in Pascal. Suppose you're creating a payroll system in which employee names are a maximum of 30 characters long. Your users have told you that no one *ever* has a name longer than 30 characters. Do you hard-code the number *30* throughout your program? If you do, you trust your users a lot more than I trust mine! A better approach is to define a type for employee names:

Pascal Example of Creating a Type for Employee Names

```
Type
    EmployeeName_t = array[ 1..30 ] of char;
```

When a string or an array is involved, it's usually wise to define a named constant that indicates the length of the string or array and then use the named constant in the type definition. You'll find many places in your program in which to use the constant—this is just the first place in which you'll use it. Here's how it looks:

Pascal Example of Better Type Creation

Here's the declaration of the named constant. —

Here's where the named constant is used. —

```
Const
    NameLength_c = 30;
    ...
Type
    EmployeeName_t = array[ 1..NameLength_c ] of char;
```

A more powerful example would combine the idea of creating your own types with the idea of information hiding. In some cases, the information you want to hide is information about the type of the data.

The coordinates example in C is about halfway to information hiding. If you always use *Coordinate_t* rather than *float* or *double*, you effectively hide the type of the data. In C or Pascal, this is about all the information hiding the language does for you. For the rest, you or subsequent users of your code have to have the discipline not to look up the definition of *Coordinate_t*. Both C and Pascal give you figurative, rather than literal, information-hiding ability.

Other languages such as Ada and C++ go a step further and support literal information hiding. Here's how the *Coordinate_t* code fragment would look in an Ada package that declares it:

This statement declares Coordinate_t as private to the package. —

Ada Example of Hiding Details of a Type Inside a Package

```
package Transformation is
    type Coordinate_t is private;
    ...
```

175

Here's how *Coordinate_t* looks in another package, one that uses it:

Ada Example of Using a Type from Another Package

```
with Transformation;
...
procedure Routine1(...) ...
    latitude:  Coordinate_t;
    longitude: Coordinate_t;
begin
    -- statements using latitude and longitude
    ...
end Routine1;
```

Notice that the *Coordinate_t* type is declared as *private* in the package specification. That means that the only part of the program that knows the definition of the *Coordinate_t* type is the private part of the *Transformation* package. In a development environment with a group of programmers, you could distribute only the package specification, which would make it harder for a programmer working on another package to look up the underlying type of *Coordinate_t*. The information would be literally hidden.

These examples have illustrated several reasons to create your own types:

- To make modifications easier. It's little work to create a new type, and it gives you a lot of flexibility.

- To avoid excessive information distribution. Hard typing spreads data-typing details around your program instead of centralizing them in one place. This is an example of the information-hiding principle of centralization discussed in Section 6.2.

- To increase reliability. In Pascal and Ada you can define types such as *Age_t = 1..99*. The compiler then generates run-time checks to verify that any variable of type *Age_t* is always within the range *1..99*.

- To make up for language weaknesses. If your language doesn't have the predefined type you want, you can create it yourself. For example, C doesn't have a boolean or logical type. This deficiency is easy to compensate for by creating the type yourself:

```
typedef int Boolean_t;
```

8.3   Guidelines for Creating Your Own Types

Here are a few guidelines to keep in mind as you create your own "user-defined" types:

Create types with functionally oriented names. Avoid type names that refer to the kind of computer data underlying the type. Use type names that refer to the parts of the real-world problem that the new type represents. In the examples above, the definitions created well-named types for coordinates and names—real-world entities. Similarly, you could create types for currency, payment codes, ages, and so on—aspects of real-world problems.

Be wary of creating type names that refer to predefined types. Type names like *BigInteger* or *LongString* refer to computer data rather than the real-world problem. The big advantage of creating your own type is that it provides a layer of insulation between your program and the implementation language. Type names that refer to the underlying programming-language types poke holes in the insulation. They don't give you much advantage over using a predefined type. Problem-oriented names, on the other hand, buy you easy modifiability and data declarations that are self-documenting.

Avoid predefined types. If there is any possibility that a type might change, avoid using predefined types anywhere but in *typedef* or *type* definitions. It's easy to create new types that are functionally oriented, and it's hard to change data in a program that uses hard-wired types. Moreover, use of functionally oriented type declarations partially documents the variables declared with them. A declaration like *Coordinate_t x* tells you a lot more about *x* than a declaration like *float x*. Use your own types as much as you can.

Don't redefine a predefined type. Changing the definition of a standard type can create confusion. For example, if your language has a predefined type *Integer*, don't create your own type called *Integer*. Readers of your code might forget that you've redefined the type and assume that the *Integer* they see is the *Integer* they're used to seeing.

Define substitute types for portability. In contrast to the advice that you not change the definition of a standard type, you might want to define substitutes for the standard types so that on different hardware platforms you can make the variables represent exactly the same entities. For example, you can define a type *INT* and use it instead of *int*, or a type *LONG* instead of *long*. Originally, the only difference between the two types would be their capitalization. But when you moved the program to a new hardware platform, you could redefine the capitalized versions so that they could match the data types on the original hardware.

If your language isn't case sensitive, you'll have to differentiate the names by some means other than capitalization.

CROSS-REFERENCE
For details on creating more complex types, see Chapter 12, "Complex Data Types."

Create types using other types. You can build up complex types based on simple types you've already created. Such record variables or structures extend the flexibility you've achieved with the initial type creation.

8.4 Making Variable Declarations Easy

CROSS-REFERENCE
For details on layout of
variable declarations, see
"Laying Out Data Declara-
tions" in Section 18.5. For
details on documenting
them, see "Commenting
Data Declarations" in
Section 19.5.

This section describes what you can do to streamline the task of declaring variables. To be sure, this is a small task, and you may think it's too small to deserve its own section in this book. Nevertheless, you spend a lot of time creating variables, and developing the right habits can save time and frustration over the life of a project.

Use a Template for Variable Declarations

Keep a variable-declaration template in a file by itself. When you need to declare a new variable, hit a couple of keys to pull the template into your file. Then edit the lines to create the variable. The template looks like this:

C Example of a Variable-Declaration Template

```
extern    *          *;       /* */
static    *          *;       /* */
          *          *;       /* */
```

This particular template has several advantages. First, you can easily select the line that's most similar to the line you want to create and then delete the others. Second, the asterisks (*) serve as placeholders and make it easy to jump to a spot to edit the line. Third, the asterisks guarantee a syntax error if you forget to change them. Fourth, using a template promotes stylistic consistency in your declarations. Finally, the empty comment reminds you to comment the variable as you declare it—making it easy to document a program as you go along.

Don't feel that you have to adopt the exact style of declaration shown in the example. Feel free to develop your own style. Choose a style that reduces the work of declaring variables, makes your code more readable, and makes debugging easier. One of my friends gives herself a reason to document her variables. Her name is Chris, and her template file looks like this:

Pascal Example of a Variable-Declaration Template

```
    *              *              { Chris is a jerk! }
```

Implicit Declarations

Some languages have implicit variable declarations. For example, if you use a variable in Basic or Fortran without declaring it, the compiler declares it for you automatically.

Implicit declaration is one of the most hazardous features available in any language.

If you program in Fortran or Basic, you know how frustrating it is to try to figure out why *ACCTNO* doesn't have the right value and then notice that *ACCTNUM* is the variable that's reinitialized to *0*. This kind of mistake is an easy one to make if your language doesn't require you to declare variables.

KEY POINT

If you're programming in a language that requires you to declare variables, you have to make two mistakes before your program will bite you. First you have to put both *ACCTNUM* and *ACCTNO* into the body of the routine. Then you have to declare both variables in the declaration section of the routine. This is a harder mistake to make and virtually eliminates the synonymous-variables problem. Languages that require you to declare data explicitly force you to use data more carefully, which is one of their primary advantages. What do you do if you program in a language with implicit declarations? Here are some suggestions:

Turn off implicit declarations. Some compilers allow you to disable implicit declarations. For example, in Fortran you would use an *IMPLICIT NONE* statement. *IMPLICIT NONE* isn't part of ANSI Fortran 77 but is a common extension to the language.

Declare all variables. As you type in a new variable, declare it, even though the compiler doesn't require you to. This won't catch all the errors, but it will catch some of them.

CROSS-REFERENCE
For details on the standardization of abbreviations, see "General Abbreviation Guidelines" in Section 9.6.

Use naming conventions. Establish a naming convention for common suffixes such as *NUM* and *NO* so that you don't use two variables when you mean to use one.

Check variable names. Use the cross-reference list generated by your compiler or another utility program. Many compilers list all the variables in a routine, allowing you to spot both *ACCTNUM* and *ACCTNO*. They also point out variables that you've declared and not used.

8.5 Guidelines for Initializing Data

KEY POINT

Improper data initialization is one of the most fertile sources of error in computer programming. Developing effective techniques for avoiding initialization problems can save a lot of debugging time.

The problems with improper initialization stem from a variable's containing an initial value that you do not expect it to contain. This can happen for any of the several reasons described on the next page.

179

CROSS-REFERENCE
For a testing approach based on data initialization and use patterns, see "Data-Flow Testing" in Section 25.3.

- The variable has never been assigned a value. Its value is whatever bits happened to be in its area of memory when the program started.

- The value in the variable is outdated. The variable was assigned a value at some point, but the value is no longer valid.

- Part of the variable has been assigned a value and part has not. If you're using pointer variables, a common mistake is to allocate memory for the pointer and then forget to initialize the variable the pointer points to. The effect is the same as the effect of never having assigned a value to the variable.

This theme has several variations. You can initialize part of a structure but not all of it. You can forget to allocate memory and then initialize the "variable" the uninitialized pointer points to. This means that you are really selecting a random portion of computer memory and assigning it some value. It might be memory that contains data. It might be memory that contains code. It might be the operating system. The symptom of the pointer problem can manifest itself in completely surprising ways that are different each time—that's what makes debugging pointer errors harder than debugging other errors.

Here are guidelines for avoiding initialization problems:

CROSS-REFERENCE
Checking input parameters is a form of defensive programming. For details on defensive programming, see Section 5.6, "Defensive Programming."

Check input parameters for validity. Another valuable form of initialization is checking input parameters for validity. Before you assign input values to anything, make sure the values are reasonable.

Initialize each variable close to where it's used. Some programmers like to initialize all their variables in a block at the top of a routine:

CODING HORROR

Basic Example of Bad Initialization

```
' initialize all variables
Idx   = 0
Total = 0
Done  = False

...

' lots of code using Idx and Total

...

' code using Done
while not Done
    ...
```

Other programmers prefer to initialize their variables as close as possible to where they're first used:

Basic Example of Good Initialization

```
Idx = 0
' code using Idx
...
```

Total is initialized —
```
Total = 0
' code using Total
...
```
close to where
it's used.

Done is also initialized —
```
Done = False
' code using Done
while not Done
    ...
```
close to where
it's used.

The second example is superior to the first for several reasons. By the time execution of the first example gets to the code that uses *Done*, *Done* could have been modified. If that's not the case when you first write the program, later modifications might make it so. Another problem with the first approach is that throwing all the initializations together creates the impression that all the variables are used throughout the whole routine—when in fact *Done* is used only at the end. Finally, as the program is modified (as it will be, if only by debugging), loops might be built around the code that uses *Done*, and *Done* will need to be reinitialized. The code in the second example will require little modification in such a case. The code in the first example is more prone to producing an annoying initialization error.

CROSS-REFERENCE
For more details on keeping related actions together, see Section 13.2, "Statements Whose Order Doesn't Matter."

This is an example of the Principle of Proximity: Keep related actions together. The same principle applies to keeping comments close to the code they describe, to keeping loop setup code close to the loop, to grouping statements in straight-line code, and to many other areas.

Pay special attention to counters and accumulators. The variables i, j, k, *Sum,* and *Total* are often counters or accumulators. A common error is forgetting to reset a counter or an accumulator before the next time it's used.

Check the need for reinitialization. Ask yourself whether the variable will ever need to be reinitialized—either because a loop in the routine uses the variable many times or because the variable retains its value between calls to the routine and needs to be reset between calls. If it needs to be reinitialized, make sure that the initialization statement is inside the part of the code that's repeated.

Initialize named constants once; initialize variables with executable code. If you're using variables to emulate named constants, it's OK to write code that initializes them once, at the beginning of the program. To do this, write a *DATA* statement in Fortran, or initialize them in a *Startup()* routine in other languages.

Initialize true variables in executable code close to where they're used. One of the most common program modifications is to change a routine that was originally called once so that you call it multiple times. Variables that are initialized in *DATA* statements or a *Startup()* routine aren't reinitialized the second time through the routine.

Initialize each variable as it's declared. Although not a substitute for initializing variables close to where they're used, initializing variables as they're declared is an inexpensive form of defensive programming. If you make a habit of it, it's a good insurance policy against initialization errors. The example below ensures that *student_name* will be reinitialized each time you call the routine that contains it.

C Example of Initialization at Declaration Time

```
char   student_name[ NAME_LENGTH+1 ] = {'\0'};   /* full name of student */
```

Take advantage of your compiler's warning messages. Many compilers warn you that you're using an uninitialized variable.

Use the compiler setting that automatically initializes all variables. If your compiler supports such an option, having the compiler set to automatically initialize all variables is an easy variation on the theme of relying on your compiler. Relying on specific compiler settings, however, can cause problems when you move the code to another machine and another compiler. Make sure you document your use of the compiler setting; assumptions that rely on specific compiler settings are hard to uncover otherwise.

Use a memory-access checker to check for bad pointers. In some operating systems, the operating-system code checks for invalid pointer references. In others, you're on your own. You don't have to stay on your own, however, because you can buy memory-access checkers that check your program's pointer operations.

Initialize working memory at the beginning of your program. Initializing working memory to a known value helps to expose initialization problems. You can take any of several approaches:

- You can use a preprogram memory filler to fill the memory with a predictable value. The value *0* is good for some purposes because it ensures that uninitialized pointers point to low memory, making it relatively easy to detect them when they're used. On the Intel 80x86 processors, hex 0CCh is a good value to use because it's the machine code for a breakpoint interrupt; if you are running code in a debugger and try to execute your data rather than your code, you'll be awash in breakpoints. Another virtue of the value 0CCh is that it's easy to recognize in memory dumps—and it's rarely used for legitimate reasons.

- If you're using a memory filler, you can change the value you use to fill the memory once in awhile. Shaking up the program sometimes uncovers problems that stay hidden if the environmental background never changes.

- You can have your program initialize its working memory at startup time. Whereas the purpose of using a preprogram memory filler is to expose defects, the purpose of this technique is to hide them. By filling working memory with the same value every time, you guarantee that your program won't be affected by random variations in the startup memory.

CHECKLIST

Data Creation

CREATING TYPES

CROSS-REFERENCE
For a checklist of issues in naming variables, see the "Naming Data" checklist in Chapter 9, page 212.

❏ Does the program use a different type for each kind of data that might change?

❏ Are type names oriented toward the real-world entities the types represent rather than toward programming-language types?

❏ Are the type names descriptive enough to help document data declarations?

❏ Have you avoided redefining predefined types?

DECLARING DATA

❏ Have you used a template to streamline data declarations and promote stylistic consistency?

❏ If your language uses implicit declarations, have you compensated for the problems they cause?

INITIALIZATION

❏ Does each routine check input parameters for validity?

❏ Does the code initialize variables close to where they're used?

❏ Are counters and accumulators initialized properly and, if necessary, reinitialized each time they are used?

❏ Are variables reinitialized properly in code that's executed repeatedly?

❏ Does the code compile with no warnings from the compiler?

Key Points

- You need a full repertoire of data structures in your programming tool-box to approach each problem in the most appropriate way.
- Creating your own types makes your programs easier to modify and more self-documenting.
- Data initialization is prone to errors, so use the initialization techniques described in this chapter to avoid the problems caused by unexpected initial values.

9

The Power
of Data Names

Contents

Related Topics

THIS CHAPTER DESCRIBES HOW TO CHOOSE good names for data. As important as this topic is to effective programming, I have never read a discussion that covered more than two or three of the dozens of considerations that go into creating good names. Many programming texts devote a few paragraphs to choosing abbreviations, spout a few platitudes, and expect you to fend for yourself. I intend to be guilty of the opposite, to inundate you with more information about good names than you will ever be able to use!

9.1 Considerations in Choosing Good Names

You can't give a variable a name the way you give a dog a name—because it's cute or it has a good sound. Unlike the dog and its name, which are different entities, a variable and a variable's name are essentially the same thing.

Consequently, the goodness or badness of a variable is largely determined by its name. Choose variable names with care.

Here's an example of code that uses bad variable names:

CODING HORROR

C Example of Poor Variable Names

```c
X   = X - XX;
XXX = Aretha + SalesTax( Aretha );
X   = X + LateFee( X1, X ) + XXX;
X   = X + Interest( X1, X );
```

What's happening in this piece of code? What do *X1*, *XX*, and *XXX* mean? What does *Aretha* mean? Suppose someone told you that the code computed a total customer bill based on an outstanding balance and a new set of purchases. Which variable would you use to print the customer's bill for just the new set of purchases?

Here's a different version of the same code that makes these questions easier to answer:

C Example of Good Variable Names

```c
Balance      = Balance - LastPayment;
MonthlyTotal = NewPurchases + SalesTax( NewPurchases );
Balance      = Balance + LateFee( CustomerID, Balance ) + MonthlyTotal;
Balance      = Balance + Interest( CustomerID, Balance );
```

In view of the contrast between these two pieces of code, a good variable name is readable, memorable, and appropriate. You can use several general rules of thumb to achieve these goals.

The Most Important Naming Consideration

KEY POINT

The most important consideration in naming a variable is that the name fully and accurately describe the entity the variable represents. An effective technique for coming up with a good name is to state in words what the variable represents. Often that statement itself is the best variable name. It's easy to read because it doesn't contain cryptic abbreviations, and it's unambiguous. Because it's a full description of the entity, it won't be confused with something else. And it's easy to remember because the name is similar to the concept.

For a variable that represents the number of people on the U.S. Olympic team, you would create the name *NumberOfPeopleOnTheUSOlympicTeam*.

A variable that represents the number of seats in the Calgary Saddle Dome would be *NumberOfSeatsInTheSaddleDome*. A variable that represents the maximum number of points scored by a country's team in any modern Olympics would be *MaximumNumberOfPointsSince1896*. A variable that contains the current interest rate is better named *Rate* or *InterestRate* than *r* or *x*. You get the idea.

Note two characteristics of these names. First, they're easy to decipher. In fact, they don't need to be deciphered at all because you can simply read them. But second, some of the names are long—too long to be practical. I'll get to the question of variable-name length shortly.

Here are several examples of variable names, good and bad:

CROSS-REFERENCE
The name *nChecks* uses the Hungarian naming convention described later in this chapter.

Purpose of Variable	Good Names, Good Descriptors	Bad Names, Poor Descriptors
Running total of checks written to date	*RunningTotal, CheckTotal, nChecks*	*Written, CT, Checks, CHKTTL, X, X1, X2*
Velocity of a bullet train	*Velocity, TrainVelocity, VelocityInMPH*	*VELT, V, TV, X, X1, X2, Train*
Current date	*CurrentDate, CrntDate*	*CD, Current, C, X, X1, X2, Date*
Lines per page	*LinesPerPage*	*LPP, Lines, I, X, X1, X2*

CurrentDate and *CrntDate* are good names because they fully and accurately describe the idea of "current date." In fact, they use the obvious words. Programmers sometimes overlook using the ordinary words, which is often the easiest solution. *CD* and *C* are poor names because they're too short and not at all descriptive. *Current* is poor because it doesn't tell you what is current. *Date* is almost a good name, but it's a poor name in the final analysis because the date involved isn't just any date, but the current date. *Date* by itself gives no such indication. *X, X1*, and *X2* are poor names because they're always poor names—*X* traditionally represents an unknown quantity; if you don't want your variables to be unknown quantities, think of better names.

Problem-Orientation

A good mnemonic name generally speaks to the problem rather than the solution. A good name tends to express the *what* more than the *how*. In general, if a name refers to some aspect of computing rather than to the problem, it's a *how* rather than a *what*. Avoid such a name in favor of a name that refers to the problem itself.

A record of employee data could be called *InputRec* or *EmployeeData*. *Input-Rec* is a computer term that refers to computing ideas—input and record. *EmployeeData* refers to the problem domain rather than the computing universe. Similarly, for a bit field indicating printer status, *BitFlag* is a more computerish name than *PrinterReady*. In an accounting application, *CalcVal* is more computerish than *Sum*.

Optimum Name Length

The optimum length for a name seems to be somewhere between the lengths of *X* and *MaximumNumberOfPointsSince1896*. Names that are too short don't convey enough meaning. The problem with names like *X1* and *X2* is that even if you can discover what *X* is, you won't know anything about the relationship between *X1* and *X2*. Names that are too long are hard to type and can obscure the visual structure of a program.

HARD DATA

Gorla, Benander, and Benander found that the effort required to debug a COBOL program was minimized when variables had names that averaged 10 to 16 characters (1990). Programs with names averaging 8 to 20 characters were almost as easy to debug. The guideline doesn't mean that you should try to make all of your variable names 9 to 15 or 10 to 16 characters long. It does mean that if you look over your code and see many names that are shorter, you should check to be sure that the names are as clear as they need to be.

You'll probably come out ahead by taking the Goldilocks-and-the-Three-Bears approach to naming variables:

Too long:	*NumberOfPeopleOnTheUSOlympicTeam*
	NumberOfSeatsInTheSaddleDome
	MaximumNumberOfPointsSince1896
Too short:	*N, NP, NTM*
	N, NS, NSISD
	M, MP, Max, Points
Just right:	*NumTeamMembers, TeamMbrCount, cTeamMbrs*
	NumSeatsInDome, SeatCount, cSeats
	MaxTeamPoints, RecordPoints, cPoints

The Effect of Scope on Variable Names

CROSS-REFERENCE
Scope is discussed in more detail in Section 10.1, "Scope."

Are short variable names always bad? No, not always. When you give a variable a short name like *i*, the length itself says something about the variable—namely, that the variable is a scratch value with a limited scope of operation.

A programmer reading such a variable should be able to assume that its value isn't used outside a few lines of code. When you name a variable *i*, you're saying, "This variable is a run-of-the-mill loop counter or array index and doesn't have any significance outside these few lines of code."

HARD DATA

A study by W. J. Hansen found that longer names are better for rarely used variables or global variables and shorter names are better for local variables or loop variables (Shneiderman 1980). Short names are subject to many problems, however, and some careful programmers avoid them altogether as a matter of defensive-programming policy.

Computed-Value Qualifiers in Variable Names

Many programs have variables that contain computed values: totals, averages, maximums, and so on. If you modify a name with a qualifier like *Ttl, Sum, Avg, Max, Min, Rec, Str,* or *Ptr,* put the modifier at the end of the name.

This practice offers several advantages. First, the most significant part of the variable name, the part that gives the variable most of its meaning, is at the front, so it's most prominent and gets read first. Second, by establishing this convention, you avoid the confusion you might create if you were to use both *TtlRevenue* and *RevenueTtl* in the same program. The names are semantically equivalent, and the convention would prevent their being used as if they were different. Third, a set of names like *RevenueTtl, ExpenseTtl, RevenueAvg,* and *ExpenseAvg* has a pleasing symmetry. A set of names like *TtlRevenue, ExpenseTtl, RevenueAvg,* and *AvgExpense* doesn't appeal to a sense of order. Finally, the consistency improves readability and eases maintenance.

An exception to the rule that computed values go at the end of the name is the customary position of the *Num* qualifier. Placed at the beginning of a variable name, *Num* refers to a total. *NumSales* is the total number of sales. Placed at the end of the variable name, *Num* refers to an index. *SaleNum* is the number of the current sale. The *s* at the end of *NumSales* is another tip-off about the difference in meaning. But, because using *Num* so often creates confusion, it's probably best to sidestep the whole issue by using *Count* to refer to a total number of sales and *Index* to refer to a specific sale. Thus, *SalesCount* is the total number of sales and *SalesIndex* refers to a specific sale.

Common Opposites in Variable Names

Use opposites precisely. Using naming conventions for opposites helps consistency, which helps readability. Pairs like *first/last* are commonly understood. Pairs like *first/end* are less common and tend to be confusing. Here are some common opposites:

add/remove	begin/end	create/destroy
insert/delete	first/last	get/release
increment/decrement	put/get	up/down
lock/unlock	min/max	next/previous
old/new	open/close	show/hide
source/destination	source/target	start/stop

9.2 Naming Specific Types of Data

In addition to the general considerations in naming data, special considerations come up in the naming of specific kinds of data. This section describes considerations specifically for loop variables, status variables, temporary variables, boolean variables, enumerated types, and named constants.

Naming Loop Indexes

CROSS-REFERENCE
For details on loops, see Chapter 15, "Controlling Loops."

Guidelines for naming variables in loops have arisen because loops are such a common feature of computer programming.

Loop control variables in simple loops may have simple names. *i*, *j*, and *k* are customary:

Pascal Example of a Simple Loop Variable Name

```
for i := FirstItem to LastItem do
   Data[ i ] := 0;
```

If the variable is to be used outside the loop, it should be given a more meaningful name than *i*, *j*, or *k*. For example, if you are reading records from a file and need to remember how many records you've read, a more meaningful name like *RecordCount* would be appropriate:

Pascal Example of a Good Descriptive Loop Variable Name

```pascal
RecordCount := 0;
while not eof( InputFile ) do
   begin
   RecordCount := RecordCount + 1;
   ReadLn( Score[ RecordCount ] )
   end;

{ lines using RecordCount }
...
```

If the loop is longer than a few lines, it's easy to forget what *i* is supposed to stand for, and you're better off giving the loop index a more meaningful name. Because code is so often changed, expanded, and copied into other programs, many experienced programmers avoid names like *i* altogether.

One common reason loops grow longer is that they're nested. If you have several nested loops, assign longer names to the loop variables to improve readability.

Pascal Example of Good Loop Names in a Nested Loop

```pascal
for TeamIndex := 1 to TeamCount do begin
   for EventIndex := 1 to EventCount[ TeamIndex ] do
      Score[ TeamIndex, EventIndex ] := 0
end;
```

Carefully chosen names for loop-index variables avoid the common problem of index cross talk: saying *i* when you mean *j* and *j* when you mean *i*. They also make array accesses clearer. *Score[TeamIndex, EvenIndex]* is more informative than *Score[i, j]*. In short, think of better names than *i*, *j*, and *k*. If you have to use them, don't use them for anything other than loop indexes—the convention is too well established, and breaking it to use them in other ways is confusing.

Naming Status Variables

Status variables describe the state of your program. The rest of this section gives some guidelines for naming them.

Think of a better name than _flag_ for status variables. It's better to think of flags as status variables. A flag should never have _flag_ in its name because that doesn't give you any clue about what the flag does. For clarity, flags should be assigned values and their values should be tested with enumerated types, named constants, or global variables that act as named constants. Here are some examples of flags with bad names:

CODING HORROR

C Examples of Cryptic Flags

```
if ( Flag ) ...
if ( StatusFlag & 0x0F ) ...
if ( PrintFlag == 16 ) ...
if ( ComputeFlag == 0 ) ...

Flag        = 0x1;
StatusFlag  = 0x80;
PrintFlag   = 16;
ComputeFlag = 0;
```

Statements like _StatusFlag = 0x80_ give you no clue about what the code does unless you wrote the code or have documentation that tells you both what _StatusFlag_ is and what _0x80_ represents. Here are equivalent code examples that are clearer:

C Examples of Better Use of Status Variables

```
if ( DataReady ) ...
if ( CharacterType & PRINTABLE_CHAR ) ...
if ( ReportType == AnnualRpt ) ...
if ( RecalcNeeded == TRUE ) ...

DataReady     = TRUE;
CharacterType = CONTROL_CHARACTER;
ReportType    = AnnualRpt;
RecalcNeeded  = FALSE;
```

Clearly, _CharacterType = CONTROL_CHARACTER_, from the second code example, is more meaningful than _StatusFlag = 0x80_, from the first. Likewise, the conditional _if (ReportType == AnnualRpt)_ is clearer than _if (PrintFlag == 16)_. The second example shows that you can use this approach with enumerated types as well as predefined named constants. Here's how you could use named constants and enumerated types to set up the values used in the example:

```
Declaring Status Variables in C

/* values for DataReady and RecalcNeeded */

#define TRUE  1
#define FALSE 0

/* values for CharacterType */

#define LETTER            0x01
#define DIGIT             0x02
#define PUNCTUATION       0x04
#define LINE_DRAW         0x08
#define PRINTABLE_CHAR    (LETTER | DIGIT | PUNCTUATION | LINE_DRAW)

#define CONTROL_CHARACTER 0x80

/* values for ReportType */

typedef enum { DailyRpt, MonthlyRpt, QuarterlyRpt,
               AnnualRpt, AllRpts } REPORT_TYPE T;
```

When you find yourself "figuring out" a section of code, consider renaming the variables. It's OK to figure out murder mysteries, but you shouldn't need to figure out code. You should be able to read it.

Naming Temporary Variables

Temporary variables are used to hold intermediate results of calculations, as temporary placeholders, and to hold housekeeping values. They're usually called *Temp*, *X*, or some other vague and nondescriptive name. In general, temporary variables are a sign that the programmer does not yet fully understand the problem. Moreover, because the variables are officially given a "temporary" status, programmers tend to treat them more casually than other variables, increasing the chance of errors.

Be leery of "temporary" variables. It's often necessary to preserve values temporarily. But in one way or another, most of the variables in your program are temporary. Calling a few of them temporary may indicate that you aren't sure of their real purposes. Consider the first example on the next page.

C Example of an Uninformative "Temporary" Variable Name

```
/* Compute roots of a quadratic equation.
   This assumes that (b^2-4*a*c) is positive. */

Temp    = sqrt( b^2 - 4*a*c );
root[0] = ( -b + Temp ) / ( 2 * a );
root[1] = ( -b - Temp ) / ( 2 * a );
```

It's fine to store the value of the expression $sqrt(b^2 - 4*a*c)$ in a variable, especially since it's used in two places later. But the name *Temp* doesn't tell you anything about what the variable does. A better approach is shown in this example:

C Example with a "Temporary" Variable Name Replaced with a Real Variable

```
/* Compute roots of a quadratic equation.
   This assumes that (b^2-4*a*c) is positive. */

Discriminant = sqrt( b^2 - 4*a*c );
root[0]      = ( -b + Discriminant ) / ( 2 * a );
root[1]      = ( -b - Discriminant ) / ( 2 * a );
```

This is essentially the same code, but it's improved with the use of an accurate, descriptive variable name.

Naming Boolean Variables

Here are a few guidelines to use in naming boolean variables:

Keep typical boolean names in mind. Here are some particularly useful boolean variable names:

Done. Use *Done* to indicate whether something is done. The variable can indicate whether a loop is done or a routine is done. Set *Done* to *False* before something is done, and set it to *True* when something is completed.

Error. Use *Error* to indicate that an error has occurred. Set the variable to *False* when no error has occurred and to *True* when an error has occurred.

Found. Use *Found* to indicate whether a value has been found. Set *Found* to *False* when the value has not been found and to *True* once the value has been found. Use *Found* when searching an array for a value, a file for an employee ID, a list of paychecks for a certain paycheck amount, and so on.

Success. Use *Success* to indicate whether an operation has been successful. Set the variable to *False* when an operation has failed and to *True* when an operation has succeeded. If you can, replace *Success* with a more specific name that describes precisely what it means to be successful. If the program is successful when processing is complete, you might use *ProcessingComplete* instead. If the program is successful when a value is found, you might use *Found* instead.

Give boolean variables names that imply *True* or *False*. Names like *Done* and *Success* are good boolean names because the state is either *True* or *False*; something is done or it isn't; it's a success or it isn't. Names like *Status* and *SourceFile*, on the other hand, are poor boolean names because they're not obviously *True* or *False*. What does it mean if *Status* is *True*? Does it mean that something has a status? Everything has a status. Does *True* mean that the status of something is OK? Or does *False* mean that nothing has gone wrong? With a name like *Status*, you can't tell.

For better results, replace *Status* with a name like *Error* or *StatusOK*, and replace *SourceFile* with *SourceFileAvailable* or *SourceFileFound*, or whatever the variable represents.

Some programmers like to put *Is* in front of their boolean names. Then the variable name becomes a question: *IsDone? IsError? IsFound? IsSuccess?* Answering the question with *True* or *False* provides the value of the variable. A benefit of this approach is that it won't work with vague names: *IsStatus?* makes no sense at all.

Use positive boolean variable names. Negative names like *NotFound*, *NotDone*, and *NotSuccessful* are difficult to read when they are negated—for example,

```
if not NotFound
```

Such a name should be replaced by *Found*, *Done*, or *Successful* and then negated with an operator as appropriate. If what you're looking for is found, you have *Found* instead of *not NotFound*.

Naming Enumerated Types

CROSS-REFERENCE
For details on using enumerated types, see Section 11.6, "Enumerated Types."

When you use an enumerated type, you can ensure that it's clear that members of the type all belong to the same group by using a group prefix or suffix. Here's an example in Ada:

Ada Example of Using a Naming Convention for Enumerated Types

```
type COLOR is ( COLOR_RED, COLOR_GREEN, COLOR_BLUE );
type PLANET is ( PLANET_EARTH, PLANET_MARS, PLANET_VENUS );
```

195

Naming Constants

CROSS-REFERENCE
For details on using named
constants, see Section 11.7,
"Named Constants."

When naming constants, name the abstract entity the constant represents rather than the number the constant refers to. *FIVE* is a bad name for a constant (regardless of whether the value it represents is *5.0*). *CYCLES_NEEDED* is a good name. *CYCLES_NEEDED* can equal *5.0* or *6.0*. *FIVE = 6.0* would be ridiculous. By the same token, *BAKERS_DOZEN* is a poor constant name; *MAX_DONUTS* is a good constant name.

9.3 The Power of Naming Conventions

Some programmers resist standards and conventions—and with good reason. Some standards and conventions are rigid and ineffective—destructive to creativity and program quality. This is unfortunate since effective standards are some of the most powerful tools at your disposal. This section discusses why, when, and how you should create your own standards for naming variables.

Why Have Conventions?

Conventions offer several specific benefits:

- They let you take more for granted. By making one global decision rather than many local ones, you can concentrate on the more important characteristics of the code.

- They help you transfer knowledge across projects. Similarities in names give you an easier and more confident understanding of what unfamiliar variables are supposed to do.

- They help you learn code more quickly on a new project. Rather than learning that Anita's code looks like this, Julia's like that, and Kristin's like something else, you can work with a more consistent set of code.

- They reduce name proliferation. Without naming conventions, you can easily call the same thing by two different names. For example, you might call total points both *PointTtl* and *TtlPoints*. This might not be confusing to you when you write the code, but it can be enormously confusing to a new programmer who reads it later.

- They compensate for language weaknesses. You can use conventions to emulate named constants and enumerated types. The conventions can differentiate among local, module, and global data and can incorporate type information for types that aren't supported by the compiler.

- They emphasize relationships among related items. If you use structured data, the compiler takes care of this automatically. If your language doesn't support structured data, you can supplement it with a naming convention. Names like *Addr*, *Phone*, and *Name* don't indicate that the variables are related. But suppose you decide that all employee-data variables should begin with an *Emp* prefix. *EmpAddr*, *EmpPhone*, and *EmpName* leave no doubt that the variables are related. You make up for the weakness of the language by creating pseudostructured data.

KEY POINT

The key is that any convention at all is often better than no convention. The convention may be arbitrary. The power of naming conventions doesn't come from the specific convention chosen but from the fact that a convention exists, adding structure to the code and giving you fewer things to worry about.

When You Should Have a Naming Convention

There are no hard-and-fast rules for when you should establish a naming convention, but here are a few cases in which conventions are worthwhile:

- When multiple programmers are working on a project
- When you plan to turn a program over to another programmer for modifications and maintenance (which is nearly always)
- When your programs are reviewed by other programmers in your organization
- When your program is so large that you can't hold the whole thing in your brain at once and must think about it in pieces
- When you have a lot of unusual terms that are common on a project and want to have standard terms or abbreviations to use in coding

KEY POINT

You always benefit from having some kind of naming convention. The considerations above should help you determine the extent of the convention to use on a particular project.

CROSS-REFERENCE
For details on the differences in formality in small and large projects, see Chapter 21, "How Program Size Affects Construction."

Degrees of Formality

Different conventions have different degrees of formality. An informal convention might be as simple as the rule "Use meaningful names." Slightly more formal conventions are described in the next section. A still more formal convention is the Hungarian convention, described in Section 9.5. In general, the degree of formality you need is dependent on the number of people working on a program, the size of the program, and the program's expected life span. On small projects, a strict convention might be unnecessary overhead. On larger projects in which several people are involved, either initially or over the program's life span, formal conventions are an indispensable aid to readability.

9.4   Informal Naming Conventions

Most projects use relatively informal naming conventions such as the ones laid out in this section.

Guidelines for a Language-Independent Convention

Here are some guidelines for creating a language-independent convention:

KEY POINT

Identify global variables. One common programming problem is misuse of global variables. If you give all global variable names a *g_* prefix, for example, a programmer seeing the variable *g_RunningTotal* will know it's a global variable and treat it as such.

Identify module variables. Identify a variable that is used by several routines within a module. Make it clear that the variable isn't a local variable and that it isn't a global variable either. For example, you can identify module variables with an *m_* prefix. In C, you can create module-level data by declaring *static* variables outside the scope of any individual routines. Such variables are available to all the routines in the file but not to routines outside the file.

Identify type definitions. Naming conventions for types serve two purposes: They explicitly identify a name as a type name, and they avoid naming clashes with variables. To meet those considerations, a prefix or suffix is a good approach. In Pascal, you can use a lowercase *_t* suffix for a type name—for example, *Color_t* or *Menu_t*. C is a little more difficult. The customary approach is to use all uppercase letters for a type name—for example, *COLOR* and *MENU*—but this creates the possibility of confusion with named preprocessor constants. The convention of appending a *_t* has already been established with the standard *size_t* type, so keep the upper case and append a *_T*, making the type names *COLOR_T* and *MENU_T.*

Identify named constants. Named constants need to be identified so that you can tell whether you're assigning a variable a value from another variable (whose value might change) or from a named constant. In Pascal and Basic you have the additional possibility that the value might be from a function. Those languages don't require function names to use parentheses, whereas in C even a function with no parameters uses parentheses.

One approach to naming constants is to use a suffix like *_c* for constant names. In Pascal, that would give you names like *MaxRecs_c* or *MaxLinesPer-Page_c*. In C, you can follow the uppercase convention and append a *_C* if you think it makes the existence of the named constant clearer.

Identify enumerated types. Enumerated types need to be identified for the same reasons that named constants do: to make it easy to tell that the name is for an enumerated type as opposed to a variable, named constant, or function. The standard approach applies; you can use an $\_e$ or $\_E$ suffix.

Identify input-only parameters in languages that don't enforce them. Sometimes input parameters are accidentally modified. In languages such as C and Pascal, you must indicate explicitly that you want a modified value to be returned to the calling routine. This is indicated with the *VAR* qualifier in Pascal, * in C, or the *out* qualifier in Ada. In other languages, such as Fortran, if you modify an input variable, it is returned whether you like it or not. If you establish a naming convention in which input-only parameters are given an *IP* prefix, you'll know that an error has occurred when you see anything with an *IP* prefix on the left side of an equal sign. If you see *IPMAX = IPMAX + 1* you'll know it's a goof because the *IP* prefix indicates that the variable isn't supposed to be modified.

Format names to enhance readability. Two common techniques for increasing readability are using capitalization and spacing characters to separate words. For example, *GYMNASTICSPOINTTOTAL* is less readable than *GymnasticsPointTotal* or *gymnastics_point_total*. C, Pascal, Ada, and other languages allow for mixed uppercase and lowercase characters. C, Pascal, and other languages allow the use of the underscore (_) separator.

Try not to mix these techniques; that makes code hard to read. If you make an honest attempt to use any of these readability techniques consistently, however, it will improve your code. People have managed to have zealous, blistering debates over fine points such as whether the first character in a name should be capitalized (*TotalPoints* vs. *totalPoints*), but as long as you're consistent, it won't make much difference.

Guidelines for Language-Specific Conventions

Follow the naming conventions of the language you're using. You can find books for most languages that describe style guidelines. Guidelines for C, Pascal, and Fortran are provided in the sections below.

C Conventions

Several naming conventions apply specifically to the C programming language. You may use these conventions in C, or you may adapt them to other languages.

FURTHER READING
The classic book on C
programming style is *C
Programming Guidelines*
(Plum 1984).

- *c* and *ch* are character variables.
- *i* and *j* are integer indexes.
- *n* is a number of something.
- *p* is a pointer.

- *s* is a string.
- Preprocessor macros are typed in *ALL_CAPS*. This is usually extended to include *typedef*s as well.
- Variable and routine names are in *all_lower_case*.
- The underscore (_) character is used as a separator: *lower_case* is more readable than *lowercase*.

These are the conventions for generic, UNIX-style C programming, but C conventions are different in different environments. In Microsoft Windows, C programmers tend to use a form of the Hungarian naming convention and mixed uppercase and lowercase letters for variable names. On the Macintosh, C programmers tend to use Pascal-like names for routines because the Macintosh toolbox and operating-system routines were designed for a Pascal interface.

Pascal Conventions

FURTHER READING
A good book on Pascal style is *Oh! Pascal!* (Cooper and Clancy 1985).

Pascal has a few specific conventions. You may use these in Pascal, or you may adapt them to some other language.

- *i*, *j*, and *k* are integer indexes.
- Variable and routine names are typed in mixed uppercase and lowercase letters—for example, *MixedUpperAndLowerCase*.

Fortran Conventions

FURTHER READING
The classic book on Fortran programming style is *The Elements of Programming Style*, 2d ed. (Kernighan and Plauger 1978).

Fortran has several naming conventions built into the language. You may use them in Fortran, but most of the world would appreciate your not spreading these conventions to other languages.

- Variable names beginning with the letters *I* through *N* are integers.
- *I*, *J*, and *K* are never anything but loop indexes.
- *X*, *Y*, and *Z* are floating-point numbers.

Sample Naming Conventions

The naming-convention guidelines can look complicated when they're strung across several pages. They don't need to be terribly complex, however, and you can adapt them to your needs. Variable names include three kinds of information:

- The contents of the variable (what it represents)
- The data type of the variable (integer, float, and so on)

- The variable's place in the structure of the program—for example, the name of the module that defines the variable or a prefix indicating that the variable is a global

Here are examples of naming conventions for Pascal and C that have been adapted from the guidelines presented earlier. These specific conventions aren't necessarily recommended, but they give you an idea of what an informal naming convention includes.

FURTHER READING
For another informal naming convention, see "A Guide to Natural Naming" (Keller 1990).

Sample Naming Convention for Pascal

LocalVariable	Local variables are in mixed uppercase and lowercase. The name should be independent of the underlying data type and should refer to whatever the variable represents.
RoutineName()	Routines are in mixed uppercase and lowercase (Good routine names are discussed in Section 5.2.)
m_ModuleVariable	Variables that are available to all routines within a module, but only within a module, are prefixed with an *m_*.
g_GlobalVariable	Global variables are prefixed with a *g_*.
Constant_c	Named constants are suffixed with a *_c*.
Type_t	Types are suffixed with a *_t*.
Base_EnumeratedType	Enumerated types are prefixed with a mnemonic for their base type—for example, *Color_Red, Color_Blue*.

Sample Naming Convention for C

GlobalRoutineName()	Public routines are in mixed uppercase and lowercase.
_FileRoutineName()	Routines that are private to a single module (file) are prefixed with an underscore.
LocalVariable	Local variables are in mixed uppercase and lowercase. The name should be independent of the underlying data type and should refer to whatever the variable represents.
_FileStaticVariable	Module (file) variables are prefixed with an underscore.
GLOBAL_GlobalVariable	Global variables are prefixed with a mnemonic of the module (file) that defines the variables in all uppercase—for example, *SCR_Dimensions*.

(continued)

Sample Naming Convention for C, *continued*

LOCAL_CONSTANT	Named constants that are private to a single routine or module (file) are in all uppercase.
GLOBAL_*CONSTANT*	Global named constants are in all uppercase and are prefixed with a mnemonic of the module (file) that defines the named constant in all uppercase—for example, *SCR_MAXROWS*.
TYPE	Type definitions are in all uppercase.
LOCAL_MACRO()	Macro definitions that are private to a single routine or module (file) are in all uppercase.
GLOBAL_*MACRO()*	Global macro definitions are in all uppercase and are prefixed with a mnemonic of the module (file) that defines the macro in all uppercase—for example, *SCR_LOCATION()*.

9.5 The Hungarian Naming Convention

FURTHER READING
For further details on the Hungarian naming convention, see "The Hungarian Revolution" (Simonyi and Heller 1991).

The Hungarian naming convention is a set of detailed guidelines for naming variables and routines (not Hungarians). The convention is widely used with the C programming language, especially in Microsoft Windows programming. The term "Hungarian" refers both to the fact that names that follow the convention look like words in a foreign language and to the fact that the creator of the convention, Charles Simonyi, is originally from Hungary.

Hungarian names are composed of three parts: the base type, one or more prefixes, and a qualifier. The examples below apply the Hungarian convention to the C language, and you can easily adapt it to any other language.

Base Types

CROSS-REFERENCE
For more information on abstract data types, see Section 12.3, "Abstract Data Types (ADTs)."

The base type is the data type of the variable being named. A base-type name generally doesn't refer to any of the predefined data types offered by the programming language. The base type is usually a more abstract data type. Base-type names might refer to entities such as windows, screen regions, and fonts. You can have only one base type in a Hungarian name.

Base types are described with short codes that you create for a specific program and then standardize on for use in that program. The codes are mnemonics such as *wn* for windows and *scr* for screen regions. Here's a sample list of base types that you might use in a program for a word processor:

Base Type	Meaning
wn	Window
scr	Screen region
fon	Font
ch	Character (a character not in the C sense, but in the sense of the data structure a word-processing program would use to represent a character in a document)
pa	Paragraph

When you use Hungarian base types, you also define data types that use the same abbreviations as the base types. Thus, if you had the base types in the table above, you'd see data declarations like these:

```
WN    wnMain;
SCR   scrUserWorkspace;
CH    chCursorPosition;
```

Prefixes

Prefixes go a step beyond the base type and describe the use of a variable. Unlike base types, prefixes are somewhat standard. Table 9-1 shows a list of standard Hungarian prefixes.

Table 9-1. Prefixes for Hungarian Variable Names

Prefix	Meaning
a	Array
c	Count (as in the number of records, characters, and so on)
d	Difference between two variables of the same type
e	Element of an array
g	Global variable
h	Handle
i	Index into an array
m	Module-level variable
p (lp, np)	Pointer (long pointer, near pointer—for Intel machines)

Prefixes are in lowercase and are placed before the base type in a variable name. You can combine them with base types and with each other as you need to. For example, an array of windows is named by using an *a* to show that it's an array and a *wn* to show that it's a window: *awn*. An index into an array of windows is designated by *iwn*, and a handle to a window is *hwn*; *cwn* is the count, or the number, of windows; *cfon* is the number of fonts.

Qualifiers

The final component of a Hungarian name is the qualifier. The qualifier is the descriptive part of the name that would probably make up the entire name if you weren't using Hungarian. In the examples given earlier—*wnMain*, *scrUserWorkspace*, and *chCursorPosition*—the components *Main*, *User-Workspace*, and *CursorPosition* are the qualifiers. The rules for creating meaningful variable names that were given earlier in the chapter apply to qualifiers.

In addition to qualifiers you create, Hungarian has standard qualifiers used to regularize the treatment of concepts that are often muddled otherwise. Table 9-2 shows the standard qualifiers.

Table 9-2. Standard Qualifiers for Hungarian Variable Names

Qualifier	Meaning
Min	The absolute first element in an array or other kind of list.
First	The first element that needs to be dealt with in an array. *First* is similar to *Min* but relative to the current operation rather than to the array itself.
Last	The last element that needs to be dealt with in an array. *Last* is the counterpart of *First*.
Lim	The upper limit of elements that need to be dealt with in an array. *Lim* is not a valid index. Like *Last*, *Lim* is used as a counterpart of *First*. Unlike *Last*, *Lim* represents a noninclusive upper bound on the array; *Last* represents a final, legal element. Generally, *Lim* equals *Last + 1*.
Max	The absolute last element in an array or other kind of list. *Max* refers to the array itself rather than to operations on the array.

Qualifiers can and should be combined with prefixes and base types. For example, *paReformat* is a paragraph to reformat. *apaReformat* is an array of paragraphs to reformat. *ipaReformat* is an index into an array of paragraphs to reformat. *cpaReformat* would be a count of paragraphs to reformat. A *for* loop to reformat paragraphs looks like this:

```
C Example of a Loop in Hungarian
for (
    ipaReformat = ipaFirstReformat;
    ipaReformat <= ipaLastReformat;
    ipaReformat++
    ) ...
```

The same loop could be rewritten to use *ipaLimReformat* instead of *ipaLast-Reformat*. In that case, because of the difference between *Lim* and *Last,* the test for loop termination would use < instead of <=, as in

```
ipaReformat < ipaLimReformat
```

instead of

```
ipaReformat <= ipaLastReformat
```

Examples of Hungarian Names

Here are examples of variables named with the Hungarian convention. The examples use the word-processor base types described earlier.

Variable Name	Meaning
ch	A character variable (a character not in the C sense, but in the sense of the data structure a word-processing program would use to represent a character in a document).
achDelete	An array of characters to delete.
ich	An index into an array of characters.
ichMin	An index to the absolute first character in an array.
ichFirst	An index to the first character in an array that's needed for a particular operation.
echDelete	An element from a character array, such as the result of *echDelete = achDelete[ichFirst].*
pachInsert	A pointer to an array of characters to insert.
ppach	A pointer to a pointer to an array of characters.
cchInsert	A count of the number of characters to insert.
cscrMenu	A count of the number of screen regions used as menus.
hscrMenu	A handle to a screen region used as a menu.
mhscrUserInput	A module-level handle to a screen region for user input. (All the routines within a particular module can access the variable.)
ghscrMessages	A global handle to a screen region for messages.

Note: Some of these names don't have qualifiers. Although omitting qualifiers is a typical practice, it's not recommended. Use qualifiers as much as you can.

Advantages of Hungarian

KEY POINT

Hungarian gives you the general advantages of having a naming convention as well as several other advantages. Because so many names are standard, there are fewer names to remember in any single program or routine. The Hungarian convention is broad enough to be applied across multiple projects.

Hungarian adds precision to several areas of naming that tend to be imprecise. The precise distinctions between *Min*, *First*, *Last*, and *Max* are particularly helpful.

Hungarian allows you to check types accurately when you're using abstract data types that your compiler can't check: *cpaReformat[i]* is probably wrong because *cpaReformat* isn't an array. *apaReformat[i]* is probably right because *apaReformat* is an array.

Hungarian serves to document types in a weakly typed language or environment. For example, in Windows programming, the environment forces you to do a lot of type casts, which foils the compiler's ability to do strict type checking. Having a convention makes up for a weakness in the environment.

Finally, the Hungarian convention makes names more compact. For example, you can use *cMedals* for the count of medals rather than *TotalMedals*. You can use *pNewScore* to name a pointer to a new score rather than *NewScorePtr*.

Disadvantages of Hungarian

Some of the versions of Hungarian that are in wide circulation virtually ignore the use of abstract data types as base types. Instead, they set up base types based on programming-language integers, long integers, floating-point numbers, and strings. The result is a convention of little value, one that forces programmers to worry about manual type checking instead of letting the compiler check the types more rapidly and accurately.

A second problem with that form of Hungarian is that it combines data *meaning* with data *representation*. When you declare a variable to be an integer, you shouldn't have to change the variable's name if you change it to a long integer. Yet that's exactly what programming-language Hungarian types force you to do.

A final criticism of Hungarian in general is that it encourages lazy, uninformative variable names. Programmers who name a handle to a window *hwnd* often neglect to describe the kind of window they're referring to. Is it the user-input window? A dialog box? A menu? A help screen? *hwndMenu* is more informative than *hwnd*. Trading the semantics of the variable for a precise description of its type is a poor trade-off. Fortunately, you can have precise typing and full semantics if you use Hungarian and remember to add qualifiers.

9.6   Creating Short Names That Are Readable

KEY POINT

In some ways, the desire to use short variable names is a historical remnant of an earlier age of computing. Older languages like assembler, Basic, and Fortran limited variable names to two to eight characters and forced programmers to create short names. In modern languages like C, Pascal, and Ada, you can create names of virtually any length; you have almost no reason to shorten meaningful names.

If circumstances do require you to create short names, note that some methods of shortening names are better than others. You can create good short variable names by eliminating needless words, using short synonyms, and using other abbreviation techniques. You can use any of several abbreviation strategies. It's a good idea to be familiar with multiple techniques for abbreviating because no single technique works well in all cases.

General Abbreviation Guidelines

Here are several guidelines for creating abbreviations. Some of them contradict others, so don't try to use them all at the same time.

- Use standard abbreviations (the ones in common use, which are listed in a dictionary).
- Remove all nonleading vowels. (*Computer* becomes *Cmptr*, and *Screen* becomes *Scrn*. *Apple* becomes *Appl*, and *Integer* becomes *Intgr*).
- Use the first letter or first few letters of each word.
- Truncate after the first, second, or third (whichever is appropriate) letter of each word.
- Keep the first and last letters of each word.
- Use every significant word in the name, up to a maximum of three words.
- Remove useless suffixes—*ing*, *ed*, and so on.
- Keep the most noticeable sound in each syllable.
- Iterate through these techniques until you abbreviate each variable name to between 8 to 20 characters, or the number of characters to which your language limits variable names.

Phonetic Abbreviations

Some people advocate creating abbreviations based on the sound of the words rather than their spelling. Thus *skating* becomes *sk8ing*, *highlight* becomes *hilite*, *before* becomes *b4*, *execute* becomes *xqt*, and so on. This seems too much like asking people to figure out personalized license plates to me, and I don't recommend it. As an exercise, figure out what these names mean:

ILV2SK8   XMEQWK   S2DTM8O   NXTC   TRMN8R

Comments on Abbreviations

You can fall into several traps when creating abbreviations. Here are some rules for avoiding pitfalls:

Don't abbreviate by removing one character from a word. Typing one character is little extra work, and the one-character savings hardly justifies the loss in readability. It's like the calendars that have "Jun" and "Jul." You have to be in a big hurry to spell June as "Jun." With most one-letter deletions, it's hard to remember whether you removed the character. Either remove more than one character or spell out the word.

Abbreviate consistently. Always use the same abbreviation. For example, use *Num* everywhere or *No* everywhere, but don't use both. Similarly, don't abbreviate a word in some names and not in others. For instance, don't use the full word *Number* in some places and the abbreviation *Num* in others.

Create names that you can pronounce. Use *XPos* rather than *XPstn* and *CurTotal* rather than *CrntTtl*. A good test is to ask whether you can read your code over the phone. If you can't, come up with names that are easier to say.

Avoid combinations that result in mispronunciation. To refer to the end of *B*, favor *ENDB* over *BEND*. If you use a good separation technique, you won't need this guideline since *B-END*, *BEnd*, or *b_end* won't be mispronounced.

Use a thesaurus to resolve naming collisions. One problem in creating short names is naming collisions—names that abbreviate to the same thing. For example, if you're limited to three characters and you need to use *fired* and *full revenue disbursal* in the same area of a program, you might inadvertently abbreviate both to *frd*.

One easy way to avoid naming collisions is to use a different word with the same meaning, so a thesaurus is handy. In this example, *dismissed* might be substituted for *fired* and *complete revenue disbursal* might be substituted for *full revenue disbursal*. The three-letter abbreviations become *dsm* and *crd*, eliminating the naming collision.

Document short names with translation tables. In languages that allow only very short names, include a translation table to provide a reminder of the mnemonic content of the variables. Include the table as comments at the beginning of a block of code. Here's an example in Fortran:

```
Fortran Example of a Good Translation Table

C  ***********************************************************************
C     Translation Table
C
C     Variable       Meaning
C     --------       -------
C     XPOS           X-Coordinate Position (in meters)
C     YPOS           Y-Coordinate Position (in meters)
C     NDSCMP         Needs Computing (=0 if no computation is needed;
C                                     -1 if computation is needed)
C     PTGTTL         Point Grand Total
C     PTVLMX         Point Value Maximum
C     PSCRMX         Possible Score Maximum
C  ***********************************************************************
```

Remember that names matter more to the reader of the code than to the writer. Read code of your own that you haven't seen for at least six months and notice where you have to work to understand what the names mean. Resolve to change the practices that cause confusion.

9.7 Kinds of Names to Avoid

Here are some kinds of variable names to avoid:

Avoid misleading names or abbreviations. Be sure that a name is unambiguous. For example, *FALSE* is usually the opposite of *TRUE* and would be a bad abbreviation for "Fig and Almond Season."

Avoid names with similar meanings. If you can switch the names of two variables without hurting the program, you need to rename both variables. For example, *Input* and *InVal*, *RecNum* and *NumRecs*, and *FileNum* and *FileIdx* are so semantically similar that if you use them in the same piece of code you'll easily confuse them and install some subtle, hard-to-find errors.

CROSS-REFERENCE
The technical term for differences like this is "psychological distance." For details, see "How 'Psychological Distance' Can Help" in Section 26.4.

Avoid variables with different meanings but similar names. If you have two variables with similar names and different meanings, try to rename one of them or change your abbreviations. Avoid names like *ClientRecs* and *ClientReps*. They're only one letter different from each other, and the letter is hard to notice. Have at least two-letter differences between names, or put the differences at the beginning or at the end. *ClientRecords* and *ClientReports* are better than the original names.

Avoid names that sound similar, such as *wrap* and *rap*. Homonyms get in the way when you try to discuss your code with others.

Avoid numerals in names. If the numerals in a name are really significant, use an array instead of separate variables. If an array is inappropriate, numerals are even more inappropriate. For example, avoid *File1* and *File2*, or *Total1* and *Total2*. You can almost always think of a better way to differentiate between two variables than by tacking a *1* or a *2* onto the end of the name. I can't say *never* use numerals, but you should be desperate before you do.

Avoid misspelled words in names. It's hard enough to remember how words are supposed to be spelled. To require people to remember "correct" misspellings is simply too much to ask. For example, misspelling *highlight* as *hilite* to save three characters makes it devilishly difficult for a reader to remember how *highlight* was misspelled. Was it *highlite? Hilite? Hilight? Hilit? Jai-a-lai-t?* Who knows?

Avoid words that are commonly misspelled in English. *Absense, acummulate, acsend, calender, concieve, defferred, definate, independance, occassionally, prefered, reciept, superseed*, and many others are common misspellings in English. Most English handbooks contain a list of commonly misspelled words. Avoid using such words in your variable names.

Don't differentiate variable names solely by capitalization. If you're programming in a case-sensitive language such as C, you may be tempted to use *Frd* for *fired*, *FRD* for *final review duty*, and *frd* for *full revenue disbursal*. Avoid this practice. Although the names are unique, the association of each with a particular meaning is arbitrary and confusing. *frd* could just as easily be associated with *final review duty* and *FRD* with *full revenue disbursal*, and no logical rule will help you or anyone else to remember which is which.

Avoid the names of standard library routines and predefined variables. All programming-language guides contain lists of the language's reserved and predefined names. Read the list occasionally to make sure you're not stepping on the toes of the language you're using. For example, the following code fragment is legal in PL/I, but you would be a certifiable idiot to use it:

```
if if = then then
   then = else;
else else = if;
```

Don't use names that are totally unrelated to what the variables represent.
Sprinkling names such as *Margaret* and *Cookie* throughout your program virtually guarantees that no one else will be able to understand it. Avoid your boyfriend's name, wife's name, favorite beer's name, or other clever (aka silly) names for variables, unless the program is really about your boyfriend, wife, or favorite beer. Even then, you would be wise to recognize that each of these might change, and that therefore the generic names *BoyFriend*, *Wife*, and *FavoriteBeer* are superior!

Avoid names containing hard-to-read characters. Be aware that some characters look so similar that it's hard to tell them apart. If the only difference between two names is one of these characters, you might have a hard time telling the names apart. For example, try to circle the name that doesn't belong in each of the following sets:

Which one of these is not like the others?

EyeChart1	EyeChartI	EyeChart1
TTLCONFUSION	TTLCONFUSION	TTLCONFUSION
Hard2Read	HardZRead	Hard2Read
GRANDTOTAL	GRANDTOTAL	6RANDTOTAL
Ttl5	TtlS	TtlS

Pairs that are hard to distinguish include (1 and l), (1 and I), (. and ,), (0 and O), (2 and Z), (; and :), (S and 5), and (G and 6).

Key Points

- Good variable names are a key element of program readability. Specific kinds of variables such as loop indexes and status variables require specific considerations.
- Naming conventions distinguish among local, module, and global data. They distinguish among type names, named constants, enumerated types, and variables.
- Regardless of the kind of project you're working on, you should adopt a variable naming convention. The kind of convention you adopt depends on the size of your program and the number of people working on it.
- The Hungarian convention is an especially powerful variable-naming tool for large programs and large projects.
- Abbreviations are hardly ever needed with modern programming languages.

CROSS-REFERENCE
For considerations in creating data, see the checklist "Data Creation" in Chapter 8, page 183.

CHECKLIST

Naming Data

GENERAL NAMING CONSIDERATIONS

❏ Does the name fully and accurately describe what the variable represents?

❏ Does the name refer to the real-world problem rather than to the programming-language solution?

❏ Is the name long enough that you don't have to puzzle it out?

❏ Are computed-value qualifiers, if any, at the end of the name?

❏ Does the name use *Count* or *Index* instead of *Num*?

NAMING SPECIFIC KINDS OF DATA

❏ Are loop index names meaningful (something other than *i*, *j*, or *k* if the loop is more than one or two lines long or is nested)?

❏ Have all "temporary" variables been renamed to something more meaningful?

❏ Are boolean variables named so that their meanings when they're *True* are clear?

❏ Do enumerated-type names include a prefix or suffix that indicates the category—for example, *Color* for *ColorRed*, *ColorGreen*, *ColorBlue*, and so on?

❏ Are named constants named for the abstract entities they represent rather than the numbers they refer to?

NAMING CONVENTIONS

❏ Does the convention distinguish among local, module, and global data?

❏ Does the convention distinguish among type names, named constants, enumerated types, and variables?

❏ Does the convention identify input-only parameters to routines in languages that don't enforce them?

❏ Is the convention as compatible as possible with standard conventions for the language?

❏ Are names formatted for readability?

(continued)

Naming Data checklist, *continued*

SHORT NAMES

❏ Does the code use long names (unless it's necessary to use short ones)?

❏ Does the code avoid abbreviations that save only one character?

❏ Are all words abbreviated consistently?

❏ Are the names pronounceable?

❏ Are names that could be mispronounced avoided?

❏ Are short names documented in translation tables?

COMMON NAMING PROBLEMS: HAVE YOU AVOIDED...

❏ ...names that are misleading?

❏ ...names with similar meanings?

❏ ...names that are different by only one or two characters?

❏ ...names that sound similar?

❏ ...names that use numerals?

❏ ...names intentionally misspelled to make them shorter?

❏ ...names that are commonly misspelled in English?

❏ ...names that conflict with standard library-routine names or with predefined variable names?

❏ ...totally arbitrary names?

❏ ...hard-to-read characters?

10

General Issues
in Using Variables

Contents

Related Topics

WITH ALL THE ATTENTION THE PRECEDING chapter paid to data names, you might have gotten the impression that once your variables are well named you're home free. On the contrary! Naming's just the beginning. The way you use variables is also important.

The information in this chapter should be particularly valuable to you if you're an experienced programmer. It's easy to start using hazardous practices before you're fully aware of your alternatives and then to continue to use them out of habit even after you've learned ways to avoid them. An experienced programmer might find the discussions on using each variable for one purpose in Section 10.5 and on using global variables in Section 10.6 particularly interesting.

10.1 Scope

"Scope" is a way of thinking about a variable's celebrity status: How famous is it? Scope, or visibility, refers to the extent to which your variables are known and can be referenced throughout a program. A variable with limited or small scope is known in only a small area of a program—a loop index used in only one small loop, for instance. A variable with large scope is known in many places in a program—a table of employee information that's used throughout a program, for instance.

Different languages handle scope in different ways. In some implementations of Basic, all variables are global. You therefore don't have any control over the scope of a variable, and this is one of Basic's chief weaknesses. In C, a variable can be visible to a block (a section of code enclosed in curly brackets), a routine, a source file, or the whole program. In Ada, a variable's scope can be visible to a block, a subprogram, a package, a task, a unit, or the whole program.

Here are some guidelines that apply to scope:

Minimize scope. Your approach to minimizing visibility probably depends on how you view the issues of "convenience" and "intellectual manageability." Some programmers make many of their variables global because global status makes variables convenient to access and the programmers don't have to fool around with parameter lists and module-scoping rules. In their minds, the convenience of being able to access variables at any time outweighs the risks involved.

CROSS-REFERENCE
The idea of minimizing scope is related to the idea of information hiding. For details, see Section 6.2, "Information Hiding."

Other programmers prefer to keep their variables as local as possible because local scope helps intellectual manageability. The more information you can hide, the less you have to keep in mind at any one time. The less you have to keep in mind, the smaller the chance that you'll make an error because you forgot one of the many details you needed to remember.

KEY POINT

The difference between the "convenience" philosophy and the "intellectual manageability" philosophy boils down to a difference in emphasis between writing programs and reading them. Maximizing scope might indeed make programs easy to write, but a program in which any routine can use any variable at any time is harder to understand than a program that uses modularized routines. In such a program, you can't understand only one routine; you have to understand all the other routines with which that routine shares global data. Such programs are hard to read, hard to debug, and hard to modify.

CROSS-REFERENCE
For details on using access routines, see "Using Access Routines Instead of Global Data" in Section 10.6, later in this chapter.

Consequently, you should declare each variable to be visible to the smallest segment of code that needs to see it. If you can confine the variable's scope to a single routine, great. If you can't confine the scope to one routine, restrict the visibility to the routines in a single module. If you can't restrict the variable's scope to the module that's most responsible for the variable, create access routines to share the variable's data with other modules. You'll find that you rarely if ever need to use global data.

Keep references to a variable together. Some researchers have suggested that the closer together you put references to a variable, the fewer mental demands you place on the person reading your code (Elshoff 1976). The idea has a great deal of intuitive appeal—you focus on fewer variables at a time. The idea of proximity gives rise to corollary guidelines.

CROSS-REFERENCE
For details on initializing variables close to where they're used, see Section 8.5, "Guidelines for Initializing Data."

Initialize variables used in a loop immediately before the loop rather than back at the beginning of the routine containing the loop. Doing this improves the chance that when you modify the loop, you'll remember to make corresponding modifications to the loop initialization. Later, when you modify the program and put another loop around the initial loop, the initialization will work on each pass through the new loop rather than on only the first pass.

Don't assign a value to a variable until just before the value is used. You might have experienced the frustration of trying to figure out where a variable was assigned its value. The more you can do to clarify where a variable receives its value, the better.

CROSS-REFERENCE
For more details on keeping related statements together, see Section 13.2, "Statements Whose Order Doesn't Matter."

The following examples show a routine for summarizing daily receipts and illustrate how to put references to variables together so that they're easier to locate. The first example illustrates the violation of this principle:

C Example of Using Two Sets of Variables in a Confusing Way

```
void SummarizeData( ... )
    {
    ...
    GetOldData( OldData, &NumOldData );
    GetNewData( NewData, &NumNewData );
    TtlOldData = Sum( OldData, NumOldData );
    TtlNewData = Sum( NewData, NumNewData );
    PrintOldDataSummary( OldData, TtlOldData, NumOldData );
    PrintNewDataSummary( NewData, TtlNewData, NumNewData );
    SaveOldDataSummary( TtlOldData, NumOldData );
    SaveNewDataSummary( TtlNewData, NumNewData );
    ...
    }
```

Statements using two sets of variables

Note that, in the example above, you have to keep track of *OldData*, *NewData*, *NumOldData*, *NumNewData*, *TtlOldData*, and *TtlNewData* all at once—six variables for just this short fragment. The example below shows how to reduce that number to only three elements.

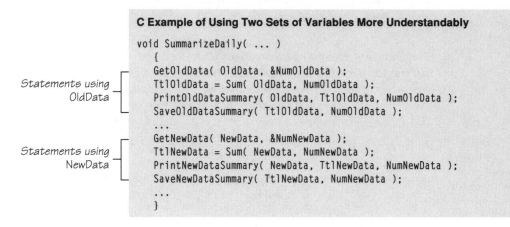

C Example of Using Two Sets of Variables More Understandably

```
void SummarizeDaily( ... )
  {
  GetOldData( OldData, &NumOldData );
  TtlOldData = Sum( OldData, NumOldData );
  PrintOldDataSummary( OldData, TtlOldData, NumOldData );
  SaveOldDataSummary( TtlOldData, NumOldData );
  ...
  GetNewData( NewData, &NumNewData );
  TtlNewData = Sum( NewData, NumNewData );
  PrintNewDataSummary( NewData, TtlNewData, NumNewData );
  SaveNewDataSummary( TtlNewData, NumNewData );
  ...
  }
```

Statements using OldData

Statements using NewData

When the code is broken up as shown above, the two blocks are each shorter than the original block and individually contain fewer variables. They're easier to understand, and if you need to break this code out into separate routines, the shorter blocks with fewer variables make better-defined routines.

10.2 Persistence

"Persistence" is another word for the life span of a piece of data. Persistence takes several forms. Some variables persist

- for the life of a particular block of code or routine. *auto* variables in C and local variables in Pascal are examples of this kind of persistence.

- as long as you allow them to. In Pascal, variables created with *new()* persist until you *dispose()* of them. In C, variables created with *malloc()* persist until you *free()* them.

- for the life of a program. Global variables in most languages fit this description. *static* variables in C and "typed constants" in Turbo Pascal meet this description. (Typed constants are a nonstandard extension to the Pascal language.)

- forever. These variables might include values that you store in a database between executions of a program. For example, if you have an interactive program in which users can customize the color of the screen, you can store their colors in a file and then read them back each time the program is loaded. Few languages currently have built-in support for this kind of persistence.

The main problem with persistence arises when you assume that a variable has a longer persistence than it really does. The variable is like that jug of milk in your refrigerator. It's supposed to last a week. Sometimes it lasts a month, and sometimes it turns sour after five days. A variable can be just as unpredictable. If you try to use the value of a variable after its normal life span is over, will it have retained its value? Sometimes the value in the variable is sour, and you know that you've got an error. Other times, the computer leaves the old value in the variable, letting you imagine that you have used it correctly.

Here are a few steps you can take to avoid this kind of problem:

CROSS-REFERENCE
Debug code is easy to in-
clude in access routines
and is discussed more in
"Advantages of access routines" in Section 10.6, later
in this chapter.

- Use debug code in your program to check critical variables for reasonable values. If the values aren't reasonable, print a warning that tells you to look for improper initialization.

- Write code that assumes data isn't persistent. For example, if a variable has a certain value when you exit a routine, don't assume it has the same value the next time you enter the routine. This doesn't apply if you're using language-specific features that guarantee the value will remain the same, such as *static* in C.

- Develop the habit of initializing all data right before it's used. If you see data that's used without a nearby initialization, be suspicious!

10.3 Binding Time

FURTHER READING
For another view of binding
time, see "Delaying Commitment" (Thimbleby 1988).

An initialization topic with far-reaching implications for program mainte-nance and modifiability is "binding time"—the time at which the variable and its value are bound together. Are they bound together when the routine is written? When it is compiled? When it is loaded? When the program is run?

It can be to your advantage to use the latest binding time possible. In general, the later you make the binding time, the more flexibility you build into your code. The next example shows binding at the earliest possible time, when the code is written.

C Example of a Variable That's Bound at Code Time

```
TestID = 47;
```

The value *47* is bound to the variable *TestID* at the time the code is written because *47* is a literal value, hard-coded into the program. Hard-coding like this is nearly always a bad idea because if this *47* changes, it can get out of synch with *47*s used elsewhere in the code that must be the same value as this one.

Here's an example of binding at a slightly later time, when the code is compiled:

C Example of a Variable That's Bound at Compile Time

```
#define MAX_ID 47
...
TestID = MAX_ID;
```

MAX_ID is a macro, or named constant, an expression for which the compiler substitutes a value at compile time. This is nearly always better than hard-coding, if your language supports it. It increases readability because *MAX_ID* tells you more about what is being represented than *47* does. It makes changing the maximum ID value easier because one change accounts for all occurrences. And it doesn't incur a run-time performance penalty.

Here's an example of binding at the latest time, at run time:

C Example of a Variable That's Bound at Run Time

```
TestID = MaxID;
```

MaxID is a variable that's given a value somewhere else. This is also more readable and flexible than hard-coding a value. Here's another example of binding at run time:

C Example of a Variable That's Bound at Run Time

```
TestID = ReadFileForMaxID();
```

ReadFileForMaxID() is a routine that reads a value from a file while a program is executing. This example assumes that the value was placed in the file sometime before execution began. The code is more readable and flexible than it would be if a value were hard-coded. You don't need to change the program to change the *TestID*; you simply change the contents of the file read by *ReadFileForMaxID()*. This approach is commonly used for interactive applications in which a user can customize the application environment. Customizations are saved in a file and read when the program begins execution.

Here's a final kind of run-time binding:

C Example of a Variable That's Bound at Run Time

```
TestID = GetMaxIDFromUser();
```

GetMaxIDFromUser() is a routine that gets a value from the user interactively. This code is far more readable and flexible than a hard-coded value. You don't need to change the program to change *TestID*; the user simply enters a different number when prompted.

As you can see from these run-time examples, different variables can be bound to their values at different times even when they all are bound at run time. The variable in the last example could bind at any time during program execution—it depends on when the user is asked for the value.

10.4 Relationship Between Data Structures and Control Structures

Several researchers have tried to develop a general relationship between data and control structures. One of the most successful has been the British computer scientist Michael Jackson. Jackson's technique involves mapping data structures to control structures in a systematic way (1975). His approach is well developed and is in widespread use in Europe. This book doesn't have the space to describe the details of Jackson's powerful theory, but it can sketch the regular relationship between data and control flow the theory is based on.

In data-structured design, you start by thinking of a stream of data flowing from the input into the output. Writing the program consists of modifying the input stream so that it turns into the output. Modifying the data is easier when you understand the connection between kinds of data and kinds of control structures.

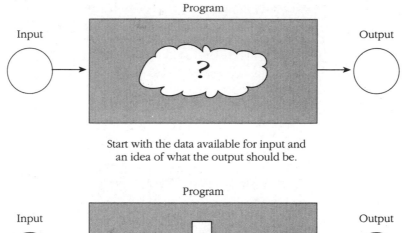

Start with the data available for input and
an idea of what the output should be.

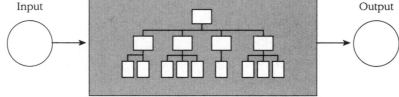

Then define the program so that it
changes the input into the output.

Jackson draws connections between three types of data and corresponding control structures.

CROSS-REFERENCE
For details on sequences,
see Chapter 13, "Organizing
Straight-Line Code."

Sequential data translates to sequential statements in a program. Sequences consist of clusters of data used together in a certain order. If you have five statements in a row that handle five different values, they are sequential statements. If you read an employee's name, social security number, address, phone number, and age from a file, you'd have sequential statements in your program to read sequential data from the file.

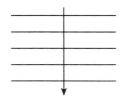

Sequential data is data that's handled in a defined order.

CROSS-REFERENCE
For details on conditionals,
see Chapter 14, "Using
Conditionals."

Selective data translates to *if* and *case* statements in a program. In general, selective data is a collection in which one of several pieces of data is present at any particular time—one of the elements is selected. The corresponding program statements must do the actual selection, and they consist of *If-Then-Else* or *Case* statements. If you had an employee payroll program, you might process employees differently depending on whether they were paid hourly or salaried. Again, patterns in the code match patterns in the data.

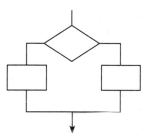

Selective data allows you to use one piece or the other, but not both.

CROSS-REFERENCE
For details on loops,
see Chapter 15,
"Controlling Loops."

Iterative data translates to *for*, *repeat*, and *while* looping structures in a program. Iterative data is the same type of data repeated several times. Typically, iterative data is stored as records in a file or in arrays. You might have a list of social security numbers that you read from a file. The iterative data would match the iterative code loop used to read the data.

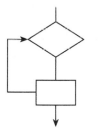

Iterative data is repeated.

Your real data can be combinations of the sequential, selective, and iterative types of data. You can combine the simple building blocks to describe more complicated data structures.

10.5   Using Each Variable for Exactly One Purpose

KEY POINT

It's possible to use variables for more than one purpose in several subtle ways. You're better off without this kind of subtlety.

Use each variable for one purpose only. It's sometimes tempting to use one variable in two different places for two different activities. Usually, the variable is named inappropriately for one of its uses, or a "temporary" variable is used in both cases (with the usual unhelpful name *X* or *Temp*). Here's an example that shows a temporary variable that's used for two purposes:

CODING HORROR

C Example of Using One Variable for Two Purposes—Bad Practice

```
/* Compute roots of a quadratic equation.
   This code assumes that (b*b-4*a*c) is positive. */

Temp    = sqrt( b*b - 4*a*c );
root[0] = ( -b + Temp ) / ( 2 * a );
root[1] = ( -b - Temp ) / ( 2 * a );

...
/* swap the roots */

Temp    = root[0];
root[0] = root[1];
root[1] = Temp;
```

CROSS-REFERENCE
Routine parameters should also be used for one purpose only. For details on using routine parameters, see Section 5.7, "How to Use Routine Parameters."

Question: What is the relationship between *Temp* in the first few lines and *Temp* in the last few? Answer: The two *Temp*s have no relationship. Using the same variable in both instances makes it seem as though they're related when they're not. Creating unique variables for each purpose makes your code more readable. Here's an improvement on the example above:

C Example of Using Two Variables for Two Purposes—Good Practice

```
/* Compute roots of a quadratic equation.
   This code assumes that (b^2-4*a*c) is positive. */

Discriminant = sqrt( b*b - 4*a*c );
root[0]      = ( -b + Discriminant ) / ( 2 * a );
root[1]      = ( -b - Discriminant ) / ( 2 * a );

...
/* swap the roots */

OldRoot = root[0];
root[0] = root[1];
root[1] = OldRoot;
```

Avoid variables with hidden meanings. Another way in which a variable can be used for more than one purpose is to have different values for the variable mean different things. The value in the variable *PageCount* might represent the number of pages printed, unless it equals −1, in which case it indicates that an error has occurred. The variable *CustomerID* might represent a customer number, unless its value is greater than *500,000*, in which case you subtract *500,000* to get the number of a delinquent account. The variable *BytesWritten* might be the number of bytes written to an output file, unless its value is negative, in which case it indicates the number of the disk drive used for the output.

FURTHER READING
For more information on hybrid coupling, see *The Practical Guide to Structured Systems Design* (Page-Jones 1988), Section 5.2.3.

Avoid variables with these kinds of hidden meanings. The technical name for this kind of abuse is "hybrid coupling." The variable is stretched over two jobs, meaning that the variable is the wrong type for one of the jobs. In the *PageCount* example above, *PageCount* normally indicates the number of pages and is an integer. When *PageCount* is −1, it indicates that an error has occurred and that the integer is moonlighting as a boolean.

Even if the double use is clear to you, it won't be to someone else. The extra clarity you'll achieve by using two variables to hold two kinds of information will amaze you. And no one will begrudge you the extra storage.

Make sure that all declared variables are used. The opposite of using a variable for more than one purpose is not using it at all. A study by Card, Church, and Agresti found that unreferenced variables were correlated with higher fault rates (1986). Get in the habit of checking to be sure that all variables that are declared are used. Some compilers and utilities (such as lint) report unused variables as a warning.

HARD DATA

10.6 Global Variables

CROSS-REFERENCE
For details on the differences between global data and module data, see "Module data mistaken for global data" in Section 6.2.

Global variables are accessible anywhere in a program. The term is also sometimes used sloppily to refer to variables with a broader scope than local variables—such as module variables that are accessible anywhere within a single file. But accessibility anywhere within a single file does not by itself mean that a variable is global.

Most experienced programmers have concluded that using global data is riskier than using local data. Most experienced programmers have also concluded that access to data from several routines is pretty doggone useful. In spite of all the hoopla about the dangers of global variables, research into the hazards of using them has not been conclusive. Card, Church, and Agresti found that the use of global variables was not correlated with an increased number of errors (1986).

KEY POINT

Even if global variables don't always produce errors, however, they're hardly ever the best way to program. The rest of this section fully explores the issues involved.

Common Problems with Global Data

If you use global variables indiscriminately or you feel that not being able to use them is restrictive, you probably haven't caught on to the full value of information hiding and modularity yet. Modularity and information hiding might not be revealed truths, but they go a long way toward making large programs understandable and maintainable. Once you get the message, you'll want to write routines and modules with as little connection as possible to global variables and the outside world.

People cite many problems in using global data, but the problems come down to a few major issues.

Inadvertent changes to global data. You might change the value of a global variable in one place and mistakenly think that it has remained unchanged somewhere else. Such a problem is known as a side effect. For example, in the following code fragment, *TheAnswer* is a global variable:

TheAnswer is a global variable.

GetOtherAnswer changes TheAnswer.

AverageAnswer is wrong.

Pascal Example of a Side-Effect Problem

```
TheAnswer    := GetTheAnswer;
OtherAnswer  := GetOtherAnswer;
AverageAnswer := (TheAnswer + OtherAnswer) / 2;
```

You might assume that the call to *GetOtherAnswer* doesn't change the value of *TheAnswer*; if it does, the average in the third line will be wrong. And in fact, *GetOtherAnswer* does change the value of *TheAnswer*, so the program has an error to be fixed.

Bizarre and exciting aliasing problems with global data. "Aliasing" refers to calling the same variable by two or more different names. This happens when a global variable is passed to a routine and then used by the routine both as a global variable and as a parameter. Here's a routine that uses a global variable:

CODING HORROR

Pascal Example of a Routine That's Ripe for an Aliasing Problem

```
procedure WriteGlobal( VAR InputVar: Integer );
begin
   GlobalVar := InputVar + 1;
   Writeln( 'Input Variable:  ', InputVar );
   Writeln( 'Global Variable: ', GlobalVar )
end;
```

Here's the code that calls the routine with the global variable as an argument:

**Pascal Example of Calling the Routine with an Argument,
Which Exposes the Aliasing Problem**

```
WriteGlobal( GlobalVar );
```

Since *WriteGlobal()* adds *1* to *InputVar* to get *GlobalVar,* you'd expect *Input-Var* to be one more than *GlobalVar.* But here's the surprising result:

The Result of the Aliasing Problem

```
Input Variable:  2
Global Variable: 2
```

The subtlety here is that *GlobalVar* and *InputVar* are actually the same variable! Since *GlobalVar* is passed into *WriteGlobal()* by the calling routine, it's referenced or "aliased" by two different names. The effect of the *Writeln()* lines is thus quite different from the one intended: They print the same variable twice, even though they identify it by two different names.

KEY POINT

Re-entrant code problems with global data. Code that can be entered by more than one thread of control is becoming increasingly common. Such code is used in programs for Microsoft Windows, the Apple Macintosh, and OS/2 Presentation Manager and also in recursive routines. Re-entrant code creates the possibility that global data will be shared not only among routines, but among different copies of the same program. In such an environment, you have to make sure that global data keeps its meaning even when multiple copies of a program are running. This is a significant problem, and you can avoid it by using techniques suggested later in this section.

Code reuse hindered by global data. In order to use code from one program in another program, you have to be able to pull it out of the first program and plug it into the second. Ideally, you'd be able to lift out a single routine or module, plug it into another program, and continue merrily on your way.

Global data complicates the picture. If the module you want to reuse reads or writes global data, you can't just plug it into the new program. You have to modify the new program or the old module so that they're compatible. If you take the high road, you'll modify the old module so that it doesn't use global data. If you do that, the next time you need to reuse the module you'll be able to plug it in with no extra fuss. If you take the low road, you'll modify the new program to create the global data that the old module needs to use. This is like a virus; not only does the global data affect the original program, but it also spreads to new programs that use any of the old program's modules.

Modularity and intellectual manageability damaged by global data. The essence of creating programs that are larger than a few hundred lines of code is managing complexity. The only way you can intellectually manage a large program is to break it into pieces so that you only have to think about one part at a time. Modularization is the most powerful tool at your disposal for breaking a program into pieces.

Global data pokes holes in your ability to modularize. If you use global data, can you concentrate on one routine at a time? No. You have to concentrate on one routine and every other routine that uses the same global data. Although global data doesn't completely destroy a program's modularity, it weakens it, and that's reason enough to try to find better solutions to your problems.

Reasons to Use Global Data

Global variables are useful in several situations:

Preservation of global values. Sometimes you have data that applies conceptually to your whole program. This might be a variable that reflects the state of a program—for example, interactive vs. batch mode, or normal vs. error-recovery mode. Or it might be information that's needed throughout a program—for example, a data table that every routine in the program uses.

CROSS-REFERENCE
For more details on named constants, see Section 11.7, "Named Constants."

Substitution for named constants. Although C, Pascal, and most modern languages support named constants, some languages still don't. You can use global variables as a substitute for named constants when your language doesn't support them. For example, you can replace the literal values *1* and *0* with the global variables *TRUE* and *FALSE* set to *1* and *0*, or replace *66* as the number of lines per page with *LinesPerPage = 66*. It's easier to change code later when this approach is used, and the code tends to be easier to read.

Streamlining use of extremely common data. Sometimes you have so many references to a variable that it appears in the parameter list of every routine you write. Rather than including it in every parameter list, you can make it a global variable. In cases in which a variable seems to be accessed everywhere, however, it rarely is. Usually it's accessed by a limited set of routines you can package into a module with the data they work on. More on this later.

Eliminating tramp data. Sometimes you pass data to a routine merely so that it can pass the data to another routine. When the routine in the middle of the call chain doesn't use the data, the data is called "tramp data." Global variables eliminate tramp data.

How to Reduce the Risks of Using Global Data

You might think of following the guidelines in this section as getting shots so that you can drink the water when you travel to a foreign country: They're kind of painful, but they improve the odds of staying healthy.

Begin by making each variable local and make variables global only as you need to. Make all variables local to individual routines initially. If you find they're needed elsewhere, make them module variables before you go so far as to make them global. If you finally find that you have to make them global, do it, but only when you're sure you have to. If you start by making a variable global, you'll never make it local, whereas if you start by making it local, you might never need to make it global.

Distinguish between global and module variables. Some variables are truly global in that they are accessed throughout a whole program. Others are really module variables, used heavily only within a certain set of routines. It's OK to access a module variable any way you want to within the set of routines that use it heavily. If other routines need to use it, provide the variable's value by means of an access routine. Don't access module values as if they were global variables even if your programming language allows you to. This advice is tantamount to saying "Modularize! Modularize! Modularize!"

CROSS-REFERENCE
For details on naming conventions for global variables, see "Guidelines for a Language-Independent Convention" in Section 9.4 as well as the rest of Chapter 9.

Develop a naming convention that makes global variables obvious. You can avoid some mistakes just by making it obvious that you're working with global data. If you're using global variables for more than one purpose (for example, as variables and as substitutes for named constants), make sure your naming convention differentiates among the types of uses.

Create a well-annotated list of all your global variables. Once your naming convention indicates that a variable is global, it's helpful to indicate what the variable does. A list of global variables is one of the most useful tools that someone working with your program can have (Glass 1982).

If you're using Fortran, use labeled *COMMON* only. Don't use blank *COMMON*. Blank *COMMON* gives every routine access to every variable. Use named *COMMON* to specify in detail the routines that can access specific

HARD DATA

COMMON data. This is one way to simulate module data in Fortran. This approach was found to be effective in a study at TRW (Glass 1982).

Use locking to control access to global variables. Similar to concurrency control in a multi-user database environment, locking requires that before the value of a global variable can be used or updated, the variable must be "checked out." After the variable is used, it's checked back in. During the time it's in use (checked out), if some other part of the program tries to check it out, the lock/ unlock routine prints an error message.

CROSS-REFERENCE
For details on planning for differences between developmental and production versions of a program, see "Planning to Remove Debugging Aids" and "Determining How Much Defensive Programming to Leave in Production Code" in Section 5.6.

Locking is most useful in the development stage. When the program is put into production, the code is modified to do something more graceful than printing error messages. An advantage of having access routines for global data is that you can implement locking and unlocking more easily than in programs that use global data indiscriminately.

Don't pretend you're not using global data by putting all your data into a monster variable and passing it everywhere. Putting everything into one huge structure might satisfy the letter of the law by avoiding global variables. But it's pure overhead, producing none of the benefits of true modularity. If you use global data, do it openly. Don't try to disguise it with obese data structures.

Using Access Routines Instead of Global Data

KEY POINT

Anything you can do with global data, you can do better with access routines. Access routines are at the base of abstract data types and information hiding. Even if you don't want to use a full-blown abstract data type, you can still use access routines to centralize control over your data and to protect yourself against changes.

CROSS-REFERENCE
Using access routines to access "global" data is related to the idea of abstract data types. For details, see Section 12.3, "Abstract Data Types (ADTs)."

Advantages of access routines

Here are several advantages of using access routines:

- You get centralized control over the data. If you discover a more appropriate implementation of the data structure later, you don't have to change the code everywhere the data is referenced. Changes don't ripple through your whole program. They stay inside the access routines.

CROSS-REFERENCE
For more details on firewalling, see "Firewalling to Contain the Damage Caused by Errors" in Section 5.6.

- You can ensure that all references to the variable are firewalled. If you allow yourself to push elements onto the stack with statements like *stack.array[stack.top] = new_element*, you can easily forget to check for stack overflow and make a serious mistake. If you use access routines— for example, *push_stack(new_element)*—you can write the check for stack overflow into the *push_stack()* routine; the check will be done automatically every time the routine is called, and you can forget about it.

CROSS-REFERENCE
For details on information hiding, see Section 6.2, "Information Hiding."

- You get the general benefits of information hiding automatically. Access routines are an example of information hiding, even if you don't design them for that reason. You can change the interior of an access routine without changing the rest of the program. Access routines allow you to redecorate the interior of your house and leave the exterior unchanged so that your friends still recognize it.

- Access routines are easy to convert to abstract data types. One advantage of access routines is that you can create a level of abstraction that's harder to do when you're working with global data directly. For example, instead of writing code that says *if LineCount > MaxLines*, an access routine allows you to write code that says *if PageFull()*. It's a small gain, but consistent attention to such details makes the difference between beautifully crafted software and code that's just hacked together.

How to use access routines

Here's the short version of the theory and practice of access routines: Hide data in a module. Write routines that let you look at the data and change it. Require routines outside the data's module to use the access routines rather than working directly with the data. As an example, suppose you have a status variable. You can have two access routines: *GetStatus()* and *SetStatus()*, each of which does what it sounds like it does.

Here are a few detailed guidelines for using access routines:

CROSS-REFERENCE
Some changes affect data and some affect functionality. For details on the differences between them, see Section 7.4, "Comments on Popular Methodologies."

Require all routines to go through the access routines for the data. Conceal a data structure behind access routines. You'll usually need a routine to report the variable's value and another routine to assign it a new value. Aside from a few service routines that access the data directly, all other routines reach the data through the access-routine interface.

Don't just throw all your global data into the same barrel. If you throw all your global data into a big pile and write access routines for it, you eliminate the problems of global data but you miss out on some of the advantages of information hiding and abstract data types. As long as you're writing access routines, take a moment to think about which module each global variable belongs in and then package the data and its access routines with the other routines in that module.

Build a level of abstraction into your access routines. Building access routines at the level of the meaning of the data rather than at the computer-science implementation level buys you insurance against changes.

Compare the following pairs of statements:

Direct Use of Complex Data	Use of Complex Data Through Access Routines
node = node.next	*node = NearestNeighbor(node)*
node = node.next	*node = NextEmployee(node)*
node = node.next	*node = NextRateLevel(node)*
Event = EventQueue[QueueFront]	*Event = HighestPriorityEvent()*
Event = EventQueue[QueueBack]	*Event = LowestPriorityEvent()*

In the first three examples, the point is that an abstract access routine tells you a lot more than a generic data structure. If you use the data structure directly, you do too much at once: You show both what the data structure itself is doing (moving to the next link in a linked list) and what's being done with respect to the entity it represents (getting a neighbor, next employee, or rate level). This is a big burden to put on a simple data-structure assignment. Hiding the information behind abstract access routines lets the code speak for itself and makes the code read at the level of the problem domain, rather than at the level of implementation details.

Keep all accesses to the data at the same level of abstraction. If you use an access routine to do one thing to a data structure, you should use an access routine to do everything else to it too. If you read from the data structure with an access routine, write to it with an access routine. If you call *init_stack()* to initialize a stack and *push_stack()* to push an item onto the stack, you've created a consistent view of the data. If you then write *value = array[stack.top]* to get an entry from the stack, you've created an inconsistent view of the data. The inconsistency makes it harder for others to understand the code. Create a *pop_stack()* routine instead of writing *value = array[stack.top]*.

CROSS-REFERENCE
Using access routines for an event queue creates an abstract data type. For details on abstract data types, see Section 12.3, "Abstract Data Types (ADTs)."

In the example pairs of statements in the table above, the two event-queue operations occurred in parallel. Inserting an event into the queue would be trickier than either of the two operations in the table, requiring several lines of code to find the place to insert the event, adjust existing events to make room for the new event, and adjust the front or back of the queue. Removing an event from the queue would be just as complicated. During coding, the complex operations would be put into routines and the others would be left as direct data manipulations. This would create an ugly, nonparallel use of the data structure. Compare the following pairs of statements:

Nonparallel Use of Complex Data	Parallel Use of Complex Data
Event = EventQueue[QueueFront]	*Event = HighestPriorityEvent()*
Event = EventQueue[QueueBack]	*Event = LowestPriorityEvent()*
AddEvent(Event)	*AddEvent(Event)*
EventCount = EventCount – 1	*RemoveEvent(Event)*

Note that these guidelines apply to large programs with many modules and routines. You might find less use for access routines in smaller programs. Nevertheless, access routines have shown themselves to be a productive way of avoiding the problems of global data and adding flexibility to the code.

CROSS-REFERENCE
For a checklist that applies
to specific types of data
rather than general issues,
see the checklist "Funda-
mental Data" in Chapter 11,
page 263. For considera-
tions in creating data, see
the checklist "Data Creation"
in Chapter 8, page 183. For
issues in naming variables,
see the checklist "Naming
Data" in Chapter 9,
page 212.

CHECKLIST

General Considerations in Using Data

GENERAL DATA

❑ Do all variables have the smallest scope possible?

❑ Are references to variables close together?

❑ Do control structures correspond to the data structures?

❑ Does each variable have one and only one purpose?

❑ Is each variable's meaning explicit, with no hidden meanings?

❑ Are all the declared variables being used?

GLOBAL DATA

❑ Are all variables local unless they absolutely need to be global?

❑ Do variable naming conventions differentiate among local, module, and global data?

❑ Are all global variables documented?

❑ Is the code free of pseudoglobal data—big data structures containing a mishmash of data that's passed to every routine?

❑ Are access routines used instead of global data?

❑ Are access routines and data organized into modules rather than lumped together?

❑ Do access routines provide a level of abstraction beyond the underlying computer-science implementations?

❑ Are all related access routines at the same level of abstraction?

Key Points

- Minimize the scope of each variable. Keep references to it close together. Keep it local or modular. Try to avoid global data.

- Use each variable for one and only one purpose.

- Avoid global variables, not because they're dangerous (even though they are) but because you can replace them with something better.

- If you can't avoid global variables, work with them through access routines. Access routines give you everything that global variables give you, and more.

11

Fundamental Data Types

Contents

Related Topics

THE FUNDAMENTAL DATA TYPES ARE THE BASIC building blocks for all other data types. This chapter contains tips for using integers, floating-point numbers, character data, boolean variables, enumerated types, constants, arrays, and pointers. Data structures, or data types that are combinations of one or more simple types, are discussed in the next chapter.

This chapter covers basic troubleshooting for the fundamental types of data. If you've got your fundamental-data bases covered, skip to the end of the chapter, review the checklist of problems to avoid, and move on.

11.1 Numbers in General

Here are several guidelines for making your use of numbers less error prone:

CROSS-REFERENCE
For more details on using named constants instead of magic numbers, see Section 11.7, "Named Constants," later in this chapter.

Avoid "magic numbers." Magic numbers are literal numbers such as *100* or *47524* that appear in the middle of a program without explanation. If you program in a language that supports named constants, use them instead. If you can't use named constants, use global variables when it's feasible to.

Avoiding magic numbers yields three advantages:

- Changes can be made more reliably. If you use named constants, you won't overlook one of the *100*s, or change a *100* that refers to something else.

- Changes can be made more easily. When the maximum number of entries changes from 100 to 200, if you're using magic numbers you have to find all the *100*s and change them to *200*s. If you use *100+1* or *100−1*, you'll also have to find all the *101*s and *99*s and change them to *201*s and *199*s. If you're using a named constant, you simply change the definition of the constant from *100* to *200* in one place.

- Your code is more readable. Sure, in the expression

```
for i := 1 to 100
```

you can guess that *100* refers to the maximum number of entries. But the expression

```
for i := 1 to MaxEntries
```

leaves no doubt. Even if you're certain that a number will never change, you get a readability benefit if you use a named constant.

Use hard-coded *0*s and *1*s if you need to. The values *0* and *1* are used to increment, decrement, and start loops at the first element of an array. The *0* in

```
for i := 0 to CONSTANT
```

is OK, and the *1* in

```
Total := Total + 1
```

is OK. A good rule of thumb is that the only literals that should occur in the body of a program are *0* and *1*. Any other literals should be replaced with something more descriptive.

Anticipate divide-by-zero errors. Each time you use the division symbol (/ in most languages), think about whether it's possible for the denominator of the expression to be *0*. If the possibility exists, write code to prevent a divide-by-zero error.

Make type conversions obvious. Make sure that someone reading your code will be aware of it when a conversion between different data types occurs. In Pascal you could say

```
x = a + float( i )
```

and in C you could say

```
x = a + (float) i
```

This practice also helps to ensure that the conversion is the one you want to occur—different compilers do different conversions, so you're taking your chances otherwise.

CROSS-REFERENCE
For a variation on this example, see "Avoid equality comparisons" in Section 11.3.

Avoid mixed-type comparisons. If x is a floating-point number and i is an integer, the test

```
if ( i = x ) then ...
```

is almost guaranteed not to work. By the time the compiler figures out which type it wants to use for the comparison, converts one of the types to the other, does a bunch of rounding, and determines the answer, you'll be lucky if your program runs at all. Do the conversion manually so that the compiler can compare two numbers of the same type and you know exactly what's being compared.

KEY POINT

Heed your compiler's warnings. Many modern compilers tell you when you have different numeric types in the same expression. Pay attention! Every programmer has been asked at one time or another to help someone track down a pesky error, only to find that the compiler had warned about the error all along. Top programmers fix their code to eliminate all compiler warnings. It's easier to let the compiler do the work than to do it yourself.

11.2 Integers

Here are a few considerations to bear in mind when using integers:

Check for integer division. When you're using integers, 7/10 does not equal 0.7. It usually equals 0. This applies equally to intermediate results. In the real world 10 * (7/10) = (10*7) / 10 = 7. Not so in the world of integer arithmetic. 10 * (7/10) equals 0 because the integer division (7/10) equals 0. The easiest way to remedy this problem is to reorder the expression so that the divisions are done last: (10*7) / 10.

Check for integer overflow. When doing integer multiplication or addition, you need to be aware of the largest possible integer. The largest possible unsigned integer is often 65,535, or $2^{16}-1$. The problem comes up when you multiply two numbers that produce a number bigger than the maximum integer. For example, if you multiply 250 * 300, the right answer is 75,000. But if the maximum integer is 65,535, the answer you'll get is probably 9464 because of integer overflow (75,000 − 65,536 = 9464). Here are the ranges of common integer types:

Integer Type	Range
Signed 8-bit	−128 through 127
Unsigned 8-bit	0 through 255
Signed 16-bit	−32,768 through 32,767
Unsigned 16-bit	0 through 65,535
Signed 32-bit	−2,147,483,648 through 2,147,483,647
Unsigned 32-bit	0 through 4,294,967,295

The easiest way to prevent integer overflow is to think through each of the terms in your arithmetic expression and try to imagine the largest value each can assume. For example, if in the integer expression $M = J * K$, the largest expected value for J is *200* and the largest expected value for K is *25*, the largest value you can expect for M is *200 * 25 = 5000*. This is OK since the largest integer is 65,535. On the other hand, if the largest expected value for J is *200* and the largest expected value for K is *1000*, the largest value you can expect for M is *200 * 1000 = 200,000*. This is not OK since 200,000 is larger than 65,535. In this case, you would have to use long integers or floating-point numbers to accommodate the largest expected value of M.

Also consider future extensions to the program. If M will never be bigger than *5000*, that's great. But if you expect M to grow steadily for several years, take that into account.

Check for overflow in intermediate results. The number at the end of the equation isn't the only number you have to worry about. Suppose you have the following code:

```
Pascal Example of Overflow of Intermediate Results
var
   TermA:   integer;
   TermB:   integer;
   Product: integer;

begin
   TermA := 1000;
   TermB := 1000;
   Product := (TermA * TermB) div 1000;
   writeln( '(', TermA, ' * ', TermB, ') div 1000 = ', Product );
```

If you think the *Product* assignment is the same as *(1000*1000) / 1000*, you might expect to get the answer *1000*. But the code has to compute the intermediate result of *1000*1000* before it can divide by the final *1000*, and that means it needs a number as big as *1,000,000*. Guess what? Here's the result:

```
(1000 * 1000) div 1000 = 16
```

If your integers go to only 32,767, the intermediate result is too large for the integer data type. In this case, the intermediate result that should be *1,000,000* is *16,960*, so when you divide by *1000*, you get *16*, rather than *1000*.

You can handle overflow in intermediate results the same way you handle integer overflow, by switching to a long-integer or floating-point type.

11.3 Floating-Point Numbers

KEY POINT

The main consideration in using floating-point numbers is that many fractional decimal numbers can't be represented precisely using the 1s and 0s available on a digital computer. Nonterminating decimals like ⅓ or ⅐ can usually be represented to only 7 or 15 digits of accuracy. In my version of Pascal, a 4-byte floating-point representation of ⅓ equals 0.33333343267440796. It's accurate to 7 digits. This is precise enough for most purposes, but imprecise enough to trick you sometimes.

Here are a few specific guidelines for using floating-point numbers:

Avoid additions and subtractions on numbers that have greatly different magnitudes. With a 4-byte floating-point variable, 1,000,000.00 + 0.01 probably produces an answer of 1,000,000.00 because 4 bytes don't give you enough significant digits to encompass the range between 1,000,000 and 0.01. Likewise, 5,000,000.02 − 5,000,000.01 is probably 0.0.

CROSS-REFERENCE
For algorithms books that describe ways to solve these problems, see Section 33.1, "The Library of a Software Professional."

Solutions? If you have to add a sequence of numbers that contains huge differences like this, sort the numbers first, and then add them starting with the smallest values. Likewise, if you need to sum an infinite series, start with the smallest term—essentially, sum the terms backwards. This doesn't eliminate round-off problems, but it minimizes them. Many algorithms books have suggestions for dealing with cases like this.

1 is equal to 2 for sufficiently large values of 1.

Anonymous

Avoid equality comparisons. Floating-point numbers that should be equal are not always equal. The main problem is that two different paths to the same number don't always lead to the same number. For example, 0.1 added 10 times rarely equals 1.0. The first example on the next page shows two variables, *Nominal* and *Sum*, that should be equal but aren't.

Pascal Example of a Bad Comparison of Floating-Point Numbers

The variable Nominal *is a 4-byte real.*

```
var
   Nominal: single;
   Sum:     single;
   i:       integer;
begin
   Nominal := 1.0;
```

*Sum is computed as 10*1.0. It should be 1.0.*

```
   Sum := 0;
   for i := 1 to 10 do
      Sum := Sum + 0.1;
```

Here's the bad comparison.

```
   if ( Nominal = Sum ) then
      Writeln( 'Numbers are the same.' )
   else
      Writeln( 'Numbers are different.' );
end;
```

As you can probably guess, the output from this program is

```
Numbers are different.
```

Thus, it's a good idea to find an alternative to using an equality comparison. One effective approach is to determine a range of accuracy that is acceptable and then use a boolean function to determine whether the values are close enough. Typically, you would write an *Equals()* function that returns *True* if the values are close enough and *False* otherwise. In Pascal, such a function would look like this:

CROSS-REFERENCE
This example is proof of the maxim that there's an exception to every rule. Variables in this realistic example have digits in their names. For the rule *against* using digits in variable names, see Section 9.7, "Kinds of Names to Avoid."

Pascal Example of a Routine to Compare Floating-Point Numbers

```
const
   AcceptableDelta = 0.00001;

function Equals( Term1: single; Term2: single ): boolean;
begin
   if ( abs( Term1 - Term2 ) < AcceptableDelta ) then
      Equals := True
   else
      Equals := False;
end;
```

If the code in the "bad comparison of floating-point numbers" example were converted so that this routine could be used for comparisons, the new comparison would look like this:

```
if ( Equals( Nominal, Sum ) ) then ...
```

The output from the program when it uses this test is

```
Numbers are the same.
```

Depending on the demands of your application, it might be inappropriate to use a hard-coded value for *AcceptableDelta*. You might need to compute *AcceptableDelta* based on the size of the two numbers being compared.

Anticipate rounding errors. Rounding-error problems are no different from the problem of numbers with greatly different magnitudes. The same issue is involved, and many of the same techniques help to solve rounding problems. In addition, here are common specific solutions to rounding problems:

First, change to a variable type that has greater precision. If you're using single-precision reals, change to double-precision reals, and so on.

Second, change to binary coded decimal (BCD) variables. The BCD scheme is slower and takes up more storage space but prevents many rounding errors. This is particularly valuable if the variables you're using represent dollars and cents or other quantities that must balance precisely.

Third, change from floating-point to integer variables. This is a roll-your-own approach to BCD variables. You will probably have to use long integers to get the precision you want. This technique requires you to keep track of the fractional part of your numbers yourself. Suppose you were originally keeping track of dollars using floating point with cents expressed as fractional parts of dollars. This is a normal way to handle dollars and cents. When you switch to integers, you have to keep track of cents using integers and of dollars using multiples of 100 cents. In other words, you multiply dollars by 100 and keep the cents in the 0-to-99 range of the variable. This might seem absurd at first glance, but it's an effective solution in terms of both speed and accuracy.

You can make the change from floating point to integer easier by writing a set of conversion routines to (1) extract dollars from a variable containing dollars and cents, (2) extract cents from a variable containing dollars and cents, and (3) combine a dollars variable and a cents variable into a dollars-and-cents variable. These conversion routines give you a handy place to check for integer overflow as well.

11.4   Characters and Strings

CROSS-REFERENCE
Issues for using magic characters and strings are similar to those for magic numbers, discussed in Section 11.1, "Numbers in General."

Here are some tips for using strings. The first applies to strings in all languages.

Avoid magic characters and strings. Magic characters are literal characters (such as *'A'*) and magic strings are literal strings (such as *"Gigamatic Accounting Program"*) that appear throughout a program. If you program in a language that supports the use of named constants, use them instead. Otherwise, use global variables. Several reasons for avoiding literal strings follow.

- For commonly occurring strings like the name of your program, command names, report titles, and so on, you might at some point need to change the string's contents. For example, *"Gigamatic Accounting Program"* might change to *"New and Improved! Gigamatic Accounting Program"* for a later version.

- International markets are becoming increasingly important, and it's easier to translate strings that are grouped in a string resource file than it is to translate them *in situ* throughout a program.

- String literals tend to take up a lot of space. They're used for menus, messages, help screens, entry forms, and so on. If you have too many, they grow beyond control and cause memory problems. Solutions to string-space problems are easier to implement if the strings are relatively independent of the source code.

- Character and string literals are cryptic. Comments or named constants clarify your intentions. In the example below, what '\027' is, isn't clear. The use of the *ESCAPE* constant makes the meaning more obvious.

C Examples of Comparisons Using Strings

```
Bad! —    if ( input_char == '\027' ) ...
Better! — if ( input_char == ESCAPE ) ...
```

Watch for off-by-one errors. Because substrings can be indexed much as arrays are, watch for off-by-one errors that read or write past the end of a string.

Strings in C

In most languages, it's hard to get into much trouble with character and string data. Unfortunately, it's easy in C, so the rest of the suggestions focus on C.

Be aware of the difference between string pointers and character arrays. The problem with string pointers and character arrays arises because of the way C handles strings. Be alert to the difference between them in two ways:

- Be suspicious of any expression containing a string that involves an equals sign. String operations in C are nearly always done with *strcmp()*, *strcpy()*, *strlen()*, and related routines. Equals signs often imply some kind of pointer error. In C, assignments do not copy string literals to a string variable. Suppose you have a statement like

```
StringPtr = "Some Text String";
```

In this case, *"Some Text String"* is a pointer to a literal text string and the assignment merely sets the pointer *StringPtr* to point to the text string. The assignment does not copy the contents to *StringPtr.*

CROSS-REFERENCE
For details on Hungarian names, see Section 9.5, "The Hungarian Naming Convention."

- Use a naming convention to indicate whether the variables are arrays of characters or pointers to strings. The Hungarian naming convention described in Chapter 9 is helpful here: Names of pointers to strings are prefixed with *psz*, and arrays of characters with *ach*. Although they're not always wrong, you should regard expressions involving both *psz* and *ach* prefixes with suspicion.

Declare strings to have length *CONSTANT+1*. In C, off-by-one errors with strings are easy to make because it's easy to forget that a string of length *n* requires *n + 1* bytes of storage and to forget to leave room for the null terminator (the byte set to 0 at the end of the string). An easy and effective way to avoid such problems is to use named constants to declare all strings. A key to this approach is that you use the named constant the same way every time: Declare the string to be length *CONSTANT+1*, and then use *CONSTANT* to refer to the length of a string in the rest of the code. Here's an example:

C Example of Good String Declarations

```
/* Declare the string to have length of "constant+1".
   Every other place in the program, "constant" rather
   than "constant+1" is used. */
```

The string is declared to be of length NAME_LENGTH + 1.

```
char string[ NAME_LENGTH + 1 ] = {0};  /* string of length NAME_LENGTH */

...

/* Example 1: Set the string to all 'A's using the constant,
   NAME_LENGTH, as the number of 'A's that can be copied.
   Note that NAME_LENGTH rather than NAME_LENGTH + 1 is used. */
```

Operations on the string use NAME_LENGTH here...

```
for ( i = 0; i < NAME_LENGTH; i++ )
    string[ i ] = 'A';

...

/* Example 2: Copy another string into the first string using
   the constant as the maximum length that can be copied. */
```

... and here.

```
strncpy( string, some_other_string, NAME_LENGTH );
```

If you don't have a convention to handle this, you'll sometimes declare the string to be of length *NAME_LENGTH* and have operations on it work with *NAME_LENGTH–1*; at other times you'll declare the string to be of length *NAME_LENGTH+1* and have operations on it work with length *NAME_LENGTH*. Every time you use a string, you'll have to remember which way you declared it.

When you use strings the same way every time, you don't have to remember how you dealt with each string individually and you eliminate mistakes caused by forgetting the specifics of an individual string. Having a convention minimizes mental overload and programming errors.

CROSS-REFERENCE
For more details on initializing data, see Section 8.5, "Guidelines for Initializing Data."

Initialize strings to null to avoid endless strings. C determines the end of a string by finding a null terminator, a byte set to 0 at the end of the string. No matter how long you think the string is, C doesn't find the end of the string until it finds a 0 byte. If you forget to put a null at the end of the string, your string operations might not act the way you expect them to.

You can avoid endless strings in two ways. First, initialize arrays of characters to *0* when you declare them, as shown below:

C Example of a Good Declaration of a Character Array
```
char EventName[ MAX_NAME_LENGTH + 1 ] = {0};
```

Second, when you allocate strings dynamically, initialize them to *0* by using *calloc()* instead of *malloc()*. *calloc()* allocates memory and initializes it to *0*. *malloc()* allocates memory without initializing it, so you get potluck when you use memory allocated by *malloc()*.

CROSS-REFERENCE
For more discussion of arrays, read Section 11.8, "Arrays," later in this chapter.

Use arrays of characters instead of pointers in C. If memory isn't a constraint—and often it is not—declare all your string variables as arrays of characters. This helps to avoid pointer problems, and the compiler will give you more warnings when you do something wrong.

Use *strncpy()* instead of *strcpy()* to avoid endless strings. String routines in C come in safe versions and dangerous versions. The more dangerous routines such as *strcpy()* and *strcmp()* keep going until they run into a NULL terminator. Their safer companions, *strncpy()* and *strncmp()*, take a parameter for maximum length, so that even if the strings go on forever, your function calls won't.

11.5 Boolean Variables

It's hard to misuse logical or boolean variables, and using them thoughtfully makes your program clearer.

CROSS-REFERENCE
For details on using comments to document your program, see Chapter 19, "Self-Documenting Code."

Use boolean variables to document your program. Instead of merely testing a boolean expression, you can assign the expression to a variable that makes the implication of the test unmistakable. For example, in the fragment below, it's not clear whether the purpose of the *if* test is to check for completion, for an error condition, or for something else:

CROSS-REFERENCE
For an example of using a boolean function to document your program, see "Making Complicated Expressions Simple" in Section 17.1.

C Example of Boolean Test in Which the Purpose Is Unclear
```
if ( (ElementIdx < 0) || (MAX_ELEMENTS < ElementIdx) ||
    ElementIdx == LastElementIdx )
    {
    ...
    }
```

In the next fragment, the use of boolean variables makes the purpose of the *if* test crystal clear:

C Example of Boolean Test in Which the Purpose Is Clear
```
Finished     = ( (ElementIdx < 0) || (MAX_ELEMENTS < ElementIdx) );
RepeatedEntry = ( ElementIdx == LastElementIdx );

if ( Finished || RepeatedEntry )
    {
    ...
    }
```

Use boolean variables to simplify complicated tests. Often when you have to code a complicated test, it takes several tries to get it right. When you later try to modify the test, it can be hard to understand what the test was doing in the first place. Logical variables can simplify the test. In the example above, the program is really testing for two conditions: whether the routine is finished and whether it's working on a repeated entry. By creating the boolean variables *Finished* and *RepeatedEntry*, you make the *if* test simpler—easier to read, less error prone, and easier to modify.

Here's another example of a complicated test:

Pascal Example of a Complicated Test
```
If ( ( eof( InputFile ) and (Not InputError)) and
    ((MinAcceptableElmts < ElmtCount) and (ElmtCount <= MaxElmts)) ) then
    begin
    { do something or other }
    ...
    end;
```

The test in the example is fairly complicated but not uncommonly so. It places a heavy mental burden on the reader. My guess is that you won't even try to understand the *if* test but will look at it and say, "I'll figure it out later if I really need to." Pay attention to that thought because that's exactly the same thing other people do when they read your code and it contains tests like this.

Here's a rewrite of the code with boolean variables added to simplify the test:

Pascal Example of a Simplified Test

Here's the
simple test.

```
AllDataRead      := eof( InputFile ) and (Not InputError);
LegalElementCount := (MinAcceptableElmts < ElmtCount) and
                     (ElmtCount <= MaxElmts);
If ( AllDataRead and LegalElementCount ) then
   begin
   { do something or other }
   ...
   end;
```

This second version is simpler. My guess is that you'll read the boolean condition in the *if* test without any difficulty.

Create your own boolean type, if necessary. Some languages, such as Pascal, have a predefined boolean type. Others, such as C, do not. In languages such as C, you can define your own boolean type. In C, you'd do it this way:

C Example of Defining the *BOOLEAN* Type

```
typedef int BOOLEAN;    /* define the boolean type */
```

Declaring variables to be *BOOLEAN* rather than *int* makes their intended use more obvious and your program a little more self-documenting.

11.6 Enumerated Types

An enumerated type is a type of data that allows each member of a class of objects to be described in English. Enumerated types are available in Ada, C, and Pascal and are generally used when you know all the possible values of a variable and want to express them in words. Here are several examples of enumerated types in Ada:

Ada Example of Enumerated Types

```
type COLOR is
   (
   COLOR_INVALID,
   COLOR_RED,
   COLOR_GREEN,
   COLOR_BLUE
   );
```

(continued)

```
type COUNTRY is
   (
   COUNTRY_INVALID,
   COUNTRY_US,
   COUNTRY_ENGLAND,
   COUNTRY_FRANCE,
   COUNTRY_CHINA,
   COUNTRY_JAPAN
   );

type OUTPUT is
   (
   OUTPUT_INVALID,
   OUTPUT_SCREEN,
   OUTPUT_PRINTER,
   OUTPUT_FILE
   );
```

Enumerated types are a powerful alternative to shopworn schemes in which you explicitly say, "1 stands for red, 2 stands for green, 3 stands for blue,..." This ability suggests several guidelines for using enumerated types.

Use enumerated types for readability. Instead of writing statements like

```
if ChosenColor = 1
```

you can write more readable expressions like

```
if ChosenColor = COLOR_RED
```

Anytime you see a numeric literal, ask whether it makes sense to replace it with an enumerated type.

Use enumerated types for reliability. In Pascal and Ada, an enumerated type lets the compiler perform more thorough type checking than it can with integer values and constants. With named constants, the compiler has no way of knowing that the only legal values are *COLOR_RED*, *COLOR_GREEN*, and *COLOR_BLUE*. The compiler won't object to statements like *Color = COUNTRY_ENGLAND* or *Output = COLOR_RED*. If you use an enumerated type, declaring a variable as *COLOR*, the compiler will allow the variable to be assigned only the values *COLOR_RED*, *COLOR_GREEN*, and *COLOR_BLUE*.

Use enumerated types for modifiability. Enumerated types make your code easy to modify. If you discover a flaw in your "1 stands for red, 2 stands for green, 3 stands for blue" scheme, you have to go through your code and change all the *1s*, *2s*, *3s*, and so on. If you use an enumerated type, you can continue adding elements to the list just by putting them into the type definition and recompiling.

Use enumerated types as an alternative to boolean variables. Often, a boolean variable isn't rich enough to express the meanings it needs to. For example, suppose you have a routine return *True* if it has successfully performed its task and *False* otherwise. Later you might find that you really have two kinds of *False*. The first kind means that the task failed, and the effects are limited to the routine itself; the second kind means that the task failed and caused a fatal error that will need to be propagated to the rest of the program. In this case, an enumerated type with the values *Success*, *Warning*, and *FatalError* would be more useful than a boolean with the values *True* and *False*. This scheme can easily be expanded to handle additional distinctions in the kinds of success or failure.

Check for invalid values. When you test an enumerated type in an *if* or *case* statement, check for invalid values. Use the *else* clause in a *case* statement to trap invalid values:

Good Pascal Example of Checking for Invalid Values in an Enumerated Type

```
case( ScreenColor )
   ColorRed:   ...
   ColorGreen: ...
   ColorBlue:  ...
   else
      PrintErrorMsg( 'Internal Error 752: Invalid color.' )
end; { case }
```

Here's the test for the invalid value.

Reserve the first entry in an enumerated type as invalid. When you declare an enumerated type, reserve the first value as an invalid value. Examples of this were shown earlier in the Ada declarations of *COLOR, COUNTRY,* and *OUTPUT* types. Many compilers assign the first element in an enumerated type to the value *0*. Declaring the element that's mapped to *0* to be invalid helps to catch variables that were not properly initialized since they are more likely to be *0* than any other invalid value.

If Your Language Doesn't Have Enumerated Types

If your language doesn't have enumerated types, you can simulate them with preprocessor macros or global variables. For example, here are declarations you could use in Basic:

Basic Example of Simulating Enumerated Types

```
' set up COLOR enumerated type

ETColorInvalid = 0
ETColorRed     = 1
```

(continued)

```
ETColorGreen   = 2
ETColorBlue    = 3

' set up COUNTRY enumerated type

ETCountryInvalid = 0
ETCountryUS      = 1
ETCountryEngland = 2
ETCountryFrance  = 3
ETCountryChina   = 4
ETCountryJapan   = 5

' set up ANSWER enumerated type

ETAnswerInvalid = 0
ETAnswerYes     = 1
ETAnswerNo      = 2
ETAnswerMaybe   = 3
```

Now, rather than using numeric literals, you can use the variables as you've defined them and improve the readability of your code.

CROSS-REFERENCE
For details on naming conventions for this purpose and others, see Section 9.3, "The Power of Naming Conventions."

Incidentally, this is another occasion for using a naming convention. In the example, the *ET* prefix indicates that the variables are used to simulate an enumerated type. Using the naming convention clearly indicates that the variables are not to be assigned values after they have been initialized. It also reduces the possibility of name clashes later if you need to use a name similar to the name of one of the enumerated-type values.

11.7 Named Constants

A named constant is like a variable except that you can't change the constant's value once you've assigned it. Named constants enable you to refer to fixed quantities such as the maximum number of employees by a name rather than a number—*MaximumEmployees* rather than *1000*, for instance.

Using a named constant is a way of "parameterizing" your program—putting an aspect of your program that might change into a parameter that you can change in one place rather than having to make changes throughout the program. If you have ever declared an array to be as big as you think it will ever need to be and then run out of space because it wasn't big enough, you can appreciate the virtue of named constants. When an array size changes, you change only the definition of the constant you used to declare the array. This "single-point control" goes a long way toward making software truly "soft"—easy to work with and change.

Use named constants in data declarations. Using named constants helps program readability and maintainability in data declarations and in statements that need to know the size of the data they are working with. In the example below, you use *PhoneLength_c* to describe the length of employee phone numbers rather than the literal *7.*

PhoneLength_c is declared as a constant here. ——

It's used here. ——

It's used here too. ——

Good Pascal Example of Using a Named Constant in a Data Declaration

```
Const
    PhoneLength_c = 7;

Type
    EmployeePhone_t = array[ 1..PhoneLength_c ] of char;

...
{ make sure all characters in phone number are digits }

for i := 1 to PhoneLength_c do
    if PhoneNumber[ i ] < '0' or PhoneNumber[ i ] > '9' then
        { do some error processing }
    ...
```

This is a simple example, but you can probably imagine a program in which the information about the phone-number length is needed in many places.

At the time you create the program, the employees all live in one city, so you need only seven digits for their phone numbers. As the company expands and employees move to different cities and states, you'll need longer phone numbers. If you have parameterized, you can make the change in only one place: in the definition of the named constant *PhoneLength_c.*

As you might expect, the use of named constants has been shown to greatly aid program maintenance. As a general rule, any technique that centralizes control over things that might change is a good technique for reducing maintenance efforts (Glass and Noiseux 1981).

FURTHER READING
For more details on the value of single-point control, see pages 57–60 of *Software Conflict* (Glass 1991).

CROSS-REFERENCE
For details on simulating enumerated types, see "If Your Language Doesn't Have Enumerated Types" in Section 11.6, earlier in this chapter.

Avoid literals. Use named constants instead. Be a fanatic about rooting out literals in your code. Use a text editor to search for *2, 3, 4, 5, 6, 7, 8, 9, ",* and *'* to make sure you haven't used them accidentally.

Simulate named constants with global variables. If your language doesn't support named constants, you can create your own. By using an approach similar to the approach suggested in the earlier Basic example in which enumerated types were simulated, you can gain many of the advantages of named constants even if your language doesn't support them directly.

Use named constants consistently. It's dangerous to use a named constant in one place and a literal in another to represent the same entity. Some programming practices beg for errors; this one is like calling an 800 number and having errors delivered to your door. If the value of the named constant needs to be changed, you'll change it and think you've made all the necessary changes. You'll overlook the hard-coded literals, your program will develop mysterious defects, and fixing them will be a lot harder than picking up the phone and yelling for help.

11.8 Arrays

Arrays are the simplest and most common type of structured data. In some languages, arrays are the only type of structured data. An array contains a group of items that are all of the same type and that are directly accessed through the use of an array index. Here are some tips on using arrays.

KEY POINT

Make sure that all array indexes are within the bounds of the array. In one way or another, all problems with arrays are caused by the fact that array elements can be accessed randomly. The most common problem arises when a program tries to access an array element that's out of bounds. In some languages, this produces an error; in others, it simply produces bizarre and unexpected results.

Think of arrays as sequential structures. Some of the brightest people in computer science have suggested that arrays never be accessed randomly, but only sequentially (Mills and Linger 1986). Their argument is that random accesses in arrays are similar to random *gotos* in a program: Such accesses tend to be undisciplined, error prone, and hard to prove correct. Instead of arrays, they suggest using sets, stacks, and queues, whose elements are accessed sequentially.

HARD DATA

Future languages may have these structures built in; today's programmers have to write access routines to implement sets, stacks, and queues. In a small experiment, Mills and Linger found that designs created this way resulted in fewer variables and fewer variable references. The designs were relatively efficient and led to highly reliable software.

CROSS-REFERENCE
Issues in using arrays and loops are similar and related. For details on loops, see Chapter 15, "Controlling Loops."

Check the end points of arrays. Just as it's helpful to think through the end points in a loop structure, you can catch a lot of errors by checking the end points of arrays. Ask yourself whether the code correctly accesses the first element of the array or mistakenly accesses the element before or after the first element. What about the last element? Will the code make an off-by-one error? Finally, ask yourself whether the code correctly accesses the middle elements of the array.

If an array is multidimensional, make sure its subscripts are used in the correct order. It's easy to say *Array[i, j]* when you mean *Array[j, i]*, so take the time to double-check that the indexes are in the right order. Consider using more meaningful names than *i* and *j* in cases in which their roles aren't immediately clear.

Watch out for index cross talk. If you're using nested loops, it's easy to write *Array[j]* when you mean *Array[i]*. Switching loop indexes is called "index cross talk." Check for this problem. Better yet, use more meaningful index names than *i* and *j* and make it harder to commit cross-talk mistakes in the first place.

Throw in an extra element at the end of an array. Off-by-one errors are common with arrays. If your array access is off by one and you write beyond the end of an array, you can cause a serious error. When you declare the array to be one bigger than the size you think you'll need, you give yourself a cushion and soften the consequences of an off-by-one error.

This is admittedly a sloppy way to program, and you should consider what you're saying about yourself before you do it. But if you decide that it's the least of your evils, it can be an effective safeguard.

In C, use the *ARRAY_LENGTH()* macro to work with arrays. You can build extra flexibility into your work with arrays by defining an *ARRAY_LENGTH()* macro that looks like this:

C Example of Defining an *ARRAY_LENGTH()* Macro

```
#define ARRAY_LENGTH( x )   (sizeof(x)/sizeof(x[0]))
```

When you use operations on an array, instead of using a named constant for the upper bound of the array size, use the *ARRAY_LENGTH()* macro. Here's an example:

C Example of Using the *ARRAY_LENGTH()* Macro for Array Operations

```
ConsistencyRatios[] =
   {  0.0,  0.0, 0.58, 0.90, 1.12,
      1.24, 1.32, 1.41, 1.45, 1.49,
      1.51, 1.48, 1.56, 1.57, 1.59 };
...
```
Here's where the —
macro is used.
```
for ( RatioIdx = 0; RatioIdx < ARRAY_LENGTH( ConsistencyRatios );
   RatioIdx++ )
   ...
```

This technique is particularly useful for dimensionless arrays such as the one in the example. If you add or subtract entries, you don't have to remember to change a named constant that describes the array's size. Of course, the technique works with dimensioned arrays too, but if you use this approach, you don't always need to set up an extra named constant for the array definition.

11.9 Pointers

Pointers are one of the most error-prone areas of modern programming. Using pointers is inherently complicated, and using them correctly requires that you have an excellent understanding of your compiler's memory-management scheme.

Paradigm for Understanding Pointers

Conceptually, every pointer consists of two parts: a location in memory and a knowledge of how to interpret the contents of that location.

Location in memory

The location in memory is an address, often expressed in hexadecimal notation. An address on a segmented Intel processor would be a combination of a segment and an offset, such as 02BF:0010. An address on a Motorola processor would be a straight 32-bit value, such as 0001EA40. The pointer itself contains only this address. To use the data the pointer points to, you have to go to that address and interpret the contents of memory at that location. If you were to look at the memory in that location, it would be just a collection of bits. It has to be interpreted to be meaningful.

Knowledge of how to interpret the contents

The knowledge of how to interpret the contents of a location in memory is provided by the base type of the pointer. If a pointer points to an integer, what that really means is that the compiler interprets the memory location given by the pointer as an integer. Of course, you can have an integer pointer, a string pointer, and a floating-point pointer all pointing to the same memory location. But only one of the pointers interprets the contents at that location correctly.

In thinking about pointers, it's helpful to remember that memory doesn't have any inherent interpretation associated with it. It is only through use of a specific type of pointer that the bits in a particular location are interpreted as meaningful data.

Figure 11-1 on the next page shows several views of the same location in memory, interpreted in several different ways.

0A	61	62	63	64	65	66	67	68	69	6A

Viewed as   Raw memory contents used for further examples (in hex)
Interpreted as   No interpretation possible without associated pointer variable

0A	61	62	63	64	65	66	67	68	69	6A

Viewed as   String[10] (in Pascal format with length byte first)
Interpreted as   abcdefghij

0A	61	62	63	64	65	66	67	68	69	6A

Viewed as   2-byte integer
Interpreted as   24842

0A	61	62	63	64	65	66	67	68	69	6A

Viewed as   4-byte floating point
Interpreted as   4.17595656202980E+0021

0A	61	62	63	64	65	66	67	68	69	6A

Viewed as   4-byte integer
Interpreted as   1667391754

0A	61	62	63	64	65	66	67	68	69	6A

Viewed as   char
Interpreted as   linefeed character (ASCII hex 0A or decimal 10)

Figure 11-1. *The amount of memory used by each data type is shown by double lines.*

FURTHER READING
One of the best ways to understand how pointers work is to read a book on building a compiler. A good choice is *Principles of Compiler Design* (Aho and Ullman 1977).

In each of the cases in Figure 11-1, the pointer points to the location containing the hex value *0A*. The number of bytes used beyond the *0A* depends on how the memory is interpreted. The way memory contents are used also depends on how the memory is interpreted. (It also depends on what processor you're using, so keep that in mind if you try to duplicate these results on your PC-CRAY.) The same raw memory contents can be interpreted as a string, an integer, a floating point, or anything else—it all depends on the base type of the pointer that points to the memory.

General Tips on Pointers

With many types of defects, locating the error is the easiest part of correcting the error. Correcting it is the hard part. Pointer errors are different. A pointer error is usually the result of a pointer's pointing somewhere it shouldn't. When you assign a value to a bad pointer variable, you write data into an area of memory you shouldn't. This is called memory corruption. Sometimes memory corruption produces horrible, fiery system crashes; sometimes it alters the results of a calculation in another part of the program; sometimes it causes your program to skip routines unpredictably; sometimes it doesn't do anything at all. In the last case, the pointer error is a ticking time bomb, waiting to ruin your program five minutes before you show it to your most important customer. In short, symptoms of pointer errors tend to be unrelated to causes of pointer errors. Thus, most of the work in correcting a pointer error is locating the cause.

KEY POINT

Working with pointers successfully requires a two-pronged strategy. First, avoid installing pointer errors in the first place. Pointer errors are so difficult to find that extra preventive measures are justified. Second, detect pointer errors as soon after they are coded as possible. Symptoms of pointer errors are so erratic that extra measures to make the symptoms more predictable are justified. Here's how to achieve these key goals:

CROSS-REFERENCE
You can make pointer operations even safer and more meaningful by creating an abstract data type based on the underlying data that the pointer represents. For details, see Section 12.3, "Abstract Data Types (ADTs)."

Isolate pointer operations in routines. Suppose you use a linked list in several places in a program. Rather than traversing the list manually each place it's used, write access routines such as *NextLink()*, *PreviousLink()*, *InsertLink()*, and *DeleteLink()*. By minimizing the number of places in which pointers are accessed, you minimize the possibility of making careless mistakes that spread throughout your program and take forever to find. Because the code is then relatively independent of data-implementation details, you also improve the chance that you can reuse it in other programs. Writing functions for pointer allocation is another way to centralize control over your data.

Check pointers before using them. Before you use a pointer in a critical part of your program, make sure the memory location it points to is reasonable. For example, if you expect memory locations to be between *StartData* and *EndData*, you should view a pointer that points before *StartData* or after *EndData* suspiciously. You'll have to determine what the values of *StartData* and *EndData* are in your environment. You can set this up to work automatically if you use pointers through access routines rather than manipulating them directly.

Check the variable referenced by the pointer before using it. Sometimes you can perform reasonableness checks on the value the pointer points to. For example, if you are supposed to be pointing to an integer value between 0 and 1000, you should be suspicious of values over 1000. If you are pointing to a C-style string, you might be suspicious of strings with lengths greater than 100. This can also be done automatically if you work with pointers through access routines.

CROSS-REFERENCE
For details on using
tag fields, see the full
discussion below.

Use tag fields to check for corrupted memory. A "tag field" or "dog tag" is a field you add to a structure solely for the purpose of error checking. When you allocate a variable, put a value that should remain unchanged into its tag field. When you use the structure, check the tag field's value. If the tag field doesn't have the expected value, the data has been corrupted.

Of course, you don't have to check the tag field each time you use the variable. You could just check the tag field before you dispose of the variable. A corrupted tag would then tell you that sometime during the life of that variable its contents were corrupted. The more often you check the tag field, however, the closer to the root of the problem you will detect the corruption.

Add explicit redundancies. An alternative to using a tag field is to use certain fields twice. If the data in the redundant fields doesn't match, you know memory has been corrupted. This can result in a lot of overhead if you manipulate pointers directly. If you isolate pointer operations in routines, however, it adds duplicate code in only a few places.

Set pointers to NULL or NIL after freeing or disposing of them. A common type of pointer error is the "dangling pointer," use of a pointer that has been *Dispose()*d or *Free()*d. One reason pointer errors are hard to detect is that sometimes the error doesn't produce any symptoms. By setting pointers to NULL after freeing them, you don't change the fact that you can read data pointed to by a dangling pointer. But you do ensure that writing data to a dangling pointer produces an error. It will probably be an ugly, nasty, disaster of an error, but at least you'll find it instead of someone else finding it. As with many other operations, you can do this automatically if you use access routines.

Use extra pointer variables for clarity. By all means, don't skimp on pointer variables. The point is made elsewhere that a variable shouldn't be used for more than one purpose. This is especially true for pointer variables. It's hard enough to figure out what someone is doing with a linked list without having to figure out why one *GenericLink* variable is used over and over again or what *Pointer->Next->Last->Next* is pointing at. Consider this code fragment:

C Example of Traditional Node-Insertion Code

```
void insert_link
    (
    NODE * CrntNode,
    NODE * InsertNode
    )
    {
```

(continued)

```
/* insert "InsertNode" after "CrntNode" */

InsertNode->Next     = CrntNode->Next;
InsertNode->Previous = CrntNode;

if ( CrntNode->Next != NULL )
   {
   CrntNode->Next->Previous = InsertNode;
   }
CrntNode->Next = InsertNode;
}
```

This line is needlessly difficult.

This is traditional code for inserting a node in a linked list, and it's needlessly hard to understand. Inserting a new node involves three objects: the current node, the node currently following the current node, and the node to be inserted between them. The code fragment explicitly acknowledges only two objects—*InsertNode* and *CrntNode*. It forces you to figure out and remember that *CrntNode->Next* is also involved. If you tried to diagram what is happening without the node originally following *CrntNode*, you would get something like this:

A better diagram would identify all three objects. It would look like this:

Here's code that explicitly references all three of the objects involved:

```
C Example of More Readable Node-Insertion Code
void insert_link
   (
   NODE * StartNode,
   NODE * NewMiddleNode
   )
   {
   NODE * FollowingNode;

   /* insert "NewMiddleNode" between "StartNode" and "FollowingNode" */

   FollowingNode           = StartNode->Next;
   NewMiddleNode->Next     = FollowingNode;
   NewMiddleNode->Previous = StartNode;
```

(continued)

```
    if ( FollowingNode != NULL )
      {
      FollowingNode->Previous = NewMiddleNode;
      }
    StartNode->Next = NewMiddleNode;
    }
```

This code fragment has an extra line of code, but without the first fragment's *CrntNode->Next->Previous*, it's easier to follow.

Simplify complicated pointer expressions. Complicated pointer expressions are hard to read. If your code contains expressions like *p.q.r.s^.data* or *p->q->r->s.data*, think about the person who has to read the expression. Here's a particularly egregious example:

CODING HORROR

C Example of a Pointer Expression That's Hard to Understand

```
for ( RateIdx = 0; RateIdx < Num; RateIdx++ )
   {
   NetRate[ RateIdx ] =
      BaseRate[ RateIdx ] * Rates->Discounts->Factors->Net;
   }
```

Complicated expressions like the pointer expression in this example make for code that has to be figured out rather than read. If your code contains a complicated expression, assign it to a well-named variable to clarify the intent of the operation. Here's an improved version of the example:

C Example of Simplifying a Complicated Pointer Expression

```
QuantityDiscount = Rates->Discounts->Factors->Net;
for ( i = 0; i < Num; i++ )
   {
   NetRate[ i ] = BaseRate[ i ] * QuantityDiscount;
   }
```

With this simplification, not only do you get a gain in readability, but you might also get a boost in performance from simplifying the pointer operation inside the loop. As usual, you'd have to measure the performance benefit before you bet any folding money on it.

Write routines to keep track of pointer allocations. One of the best ways to ruin a program is to *free()* or *dispose()* a pointer after it has already been *free()*d or *dispose()*d. Unfortunately, few languages detect this kind of problem.

If your language won't support you, you can support yourself. Keep a list of the pointers you have allocated and check whether a pointer is in the list before you dispose of it. For example, in C you could use these two routines:

CROSS-REFERENCE
Although the routines
safe_calloc() and
safe_free() are useful
during debugging, they
should be replaced with
stubs in production code.
For details on planning
to remove code used for
debugging, see "Planning
to Remove Debugging
Aids" in Section 5.6.

- *safe_calloc()*. This routine accepts the same parameters as C's *calloc()* routine. It calls *calloc()* to allocate the pointer, adds the new pointer to a list of allocated pointers, and returns the newly allocated pointer to the calling routine. An ancillary benefit of this approach is that you can also check for a NULL return from *calloc()* (aka an "out-of-memory" error) in this one place only, which simplifies error processing in other parts of your program.

- *safe_free()*. This routine accepts the same parameters as C's *free()* routine. It checks to see whether the pointer passed to it is in the list of allocated pointers. If it is in the list, the pointer *safe_free()* calls C's *free()* routine to deallocate the pointer and removes the pointer from the list. If it isn't, *safe_free()* prints a diagnostic message and stops the program.

You can easily adapt this scheme to Pascal and other languages.

Allocate a few bytes more than you need in *safe_calloc()*, and set that field as a dog tag. When you *safe_free()* the pointer, check the tag field for corruption. After the check, corrupt the field so that if you accidentally try to free the same pointer again, you'll detect the corruption. For example, let's say that you need to allocate 100 bytes:

1. *calloc()* 104 bytes, 4 bytes more than requested.

104 bytes

2. Set the last 4 bytes to a dog-tag value, and then return a pointer to the allocated memory.

⌐ Set pointer to here.

	tag

3. When the time comes to free the pointer in *safe_free()*, check the tag.

⌐ pointer passed to *safe_free()*

| | tag | ←— Check this tag.

4. If the tag is OK, set it to *0* or some other value that you and your program recognize as an invalid tag value. You don't want the value to be mistaken for a valid tag after the memory has been freed. Set the data to *0, 0xCC,* or some other nonrandom value for the same reason.

5. Finally, free the pointer.

```
free the whole 104 bytes
```

You can use this approach in concert with the reasonableness check suggested earlier—checking that the pointers are between *StartData* and *End-Data*. To be sure that a pointer points to a reasonable location, rather than checking for a probable range of memory, check to see that the pointer is in the list of allocated pointers.

CROSS-REFERENCE
Diagrams such as this can become part of the external documentation of your program. For details on good documentation practices, see Chapter 19, "Self-Documenting Code."

Draw a picture. Code descriptions of pointers can get confusing. It usually helps to draw a picture. For example, a picture of the linked-list insertion problem might look like the one shown in Figure 11-2.

Initial Linkage

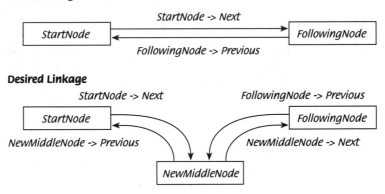

Desired Linkage

Figure 11-2. *A picture that illustrates relinking pointers.*

Free pointers in linked lists in the right order. A common problem in working with dynamically allocated linked lists is freeing the first pointer in the list first and then not being able to get to the next pointer in the list. To avoid this problem, make sure that you have a pointer to the next element in a list before you free the current one.

Write a routine to output pointer addresses. If you're working on a machine with a segmented architecture such as the Intel 80x86 series, your language probably doesn't support formatted output of pointer addresses. This makes printing diagnostic messages difficult. An easy solution is to write a routine that takes a pointer as an argument and returns a string version of a pointer,

"03af:bf8a" or something similar. Then use this routine in calls to *print,* *writeln()*, *printf()*, or whatever standard output facility your language uses.

Allocate a reserve parachute of memory. If your program uses dynamic memory, you need to avoid the problem of suddenly running out of memory, leaving your user and your user's data lost in RAM space. One way to give your program a margin of error is to pre-allocate a memory parachute. Determine how much memory your program needs to save work, clean up, and exit gracefully. Allocate that amount of memory at the beginning of the program as a reserve parachute, and leave it alone. When you run out of memory, free the reserve parachute, clean up, and shut down.

Use a nonpointer technique. Pointers are harder than average to understand, they're error prone, and they tend to require machine-dependent, unportable code. If you can think of an alternative to using a pointer that works reasonably well, save yourself a few headaches and use it instead.

C-Pointer Pointers

Here are a few tips on using pointers that apply specifically to the C language.

Use explicit pointer types rather than the default type. C lets you use *char* or *void* pointers for any type of variable. As long as the pointer points, the language doesn't really care what it points at. If you use explicit types for your pointers, however, the compiler can give you warnings about mismatched pointer types and inappropriate dereferences. If you don't, it can't. Use the specific pointer type whenever you can.

The corollary to this rule is to use explicit type casting when you have to make a type conversion. For example, in the fragment below, it's clear that a variable of type *NODE_PTR* is being allocated:

C Example of Explicit Type Casting

```
NodePtr = (NODE_PTR) calloc( 1, sizeof( NODE ) );
```

Avoid type casting. Avoiding type casting doesn't have anything to do with going to acting school or getting out of always playing "the heavy." It has to do with avoiding squeezing a variable of one type into the space for a variable of another type. Type casting turns off your compiler's ability to check for type mismatches and therefore creates a hole in your defensive-programming armor. A program that requires many type casts probably has some architectural gaps that need to be revisited. Redesign if that's possible; otherwise, try to avoid type casts as much as you can.

Follow the asterisk rule for parameter passing. You can pass an argument back from a routine in C only if you have an asterisk (*) in front of the argument in the assignment statement. Many C programmers have difficulty determining when C allows a value to be passed back to a calling routine. It's easy to remember that, as long as you have an asterisk in front of the parameter when you assign it a value, the value is passed back to the calling routine. Regardless of how many asterisks you stack up in the declaration, you must have at least one in the assignment statement if you want to pass back a value. For example, in the following fragment, the value assigned to *parameter* isn't passed back to the calling routine because the assignment statement doesn't use an asterisk:

C Example of Parameter Passing That Won't Work

```
void TryToPassBackAValue( int * parameter )
   {
   parameter = SOME_VALUE;
   }
```

In the next fragment, the value assigned to *parameter* is passed back because *parameter* has an asterisk in front of it:

C Example of Parameter Passing That Will Work

```
void TryToPassBackAValue( int * parameter )
   {
   *parameter = SOME_VALUE;
   }
```

Use *sizeof()* to determine the size of a variable in a memory allocation. It's easier to use *sizeof()* than to look up the size in a manual, and *sizeof()* works for structures you create yourself, which aren't in the manual. *sizeof()* doesn't carry a performance penalty since it's calculated at compile time. It's portable—recompiling in a different environment automatically changes the value calculated by *sizeof()*. And it requires little maintenance since you can change types you have defined and allocations will be adjusted automatically.

CROSS-REFERENCE
For a checklist that applies to general data issues rather than to issues with specific types of data, see the checklist "General Considerations in Using Data" in Chapter 10, page 233. For a checklist on issues in creating data, see the checklist "Data Creation" in Chapter 8, page 183. For a checklist of considerations in naming variables, see the checklist "Naming Data" in Chapter 9, page 212.

CHECKLIST

Fundamental Data

NUMBERS IN GENERAL

❏ Does the code avoid magic numbers?

❏ Does the code anticipate divide-by-zero errors?

❏ Are type conversions obvious?

❏ If variables with two different types are used in the same expression, will the expression be evaluated as you intend it to be?

❏ Does the code avoid mixed-type comparisons?

❏ Does the program compile with no warnings?

INTEGERS

❏ Do expressions that use integer division work the way they're meant to?

❏ Do integer expressions avoid integer-overflow problems?

FLOATING-POINT NUMBERS

❏ Does the code avoid additions and subtractions on numbers with greatly different magnitudes?

❏ Does the code systematically prevent rounding errors?

❏ Does the code avoid comparing floating-point numbers for equality?

CHARACTERS AND STRINGS

❏ Does the code avoid magic characters and strings?

❏ Are references to strings free of off-by-one errors?

❏ Does C code treat string pointers and character arrays differently?

❏ Does C code follow the convention of declaring strings to be length *constant+1*?

❏ Does C code use arrays of characters rather than pointers, when appropriate?

❏ Does C code initialize strings to NULLs to avoid endless strings?

❏ Does C code use *strncpy()* rather than *strcpy()*? And *strncat()* and *strncmp()*?

(continued)

Fundamental Data checklist, *continued*

BOOLEAN VARIABLES

❏ Does the program use additional boolean variables to document conditional tests?

❏ Does the program use additional boolean variables to simplify conditional tests?

ENUMERATED TYPES

❏ Does the program use enumerated types instead of named constants for their improved readability, reliability, and modifiability?

❏ Does the program use enumerated types instead of boolean variables for improved readability and flexibility?

❏ Do tests using enumerated types test for invalid values?

❏ Is the first entry in an enumerated type reserved for "invalid"?

NAMED CONSTANTS

❏ Does the program use named constants in data declarations?

❏ Have named constants been used consistently—not named constants in some places, literals in others?

ARRAYS

❏ Are all array indexes within the bounds of the array?

❏ Are array references free of off-by-one errors?

❏ Are all subscripts on multidimensional arrays in the correct order?

❏ In nested loops, is the correct variable used as the array subscript, avoiding loop-index cross talk?

POINTERS

❏ Are pointer operations isolated in functions?

❏ Are pointer references valid, or could the pointer be dangling?

❏ Does the code check pointers for validity before using them?

❏ Is the variable that the pointer references checked for validity before it's used?

❏ Are pointers set to NULL or NIL after they're freed?

❏ Does the code use all the pointer variables needed for the sake of readability?

(continued)

Fundamental Data checklist, *continued*

❑ Are pointers in linked lists freed in the right order?

❑ Does the program allocate a reserve parachute of memory so that it can shut down gracefully if it runs out of memory?

❑ Are pointers used only as a last resort, when no other method is available?

Key Point

- Working with specific data types means remembering many individual rules for each type. Use the checklist to make sure that you've considered the common problems.

12

Complex Data Types

Contents

Related Topics

THIS CHAPTER DISCUSSES TYPES OF DATA that you create on your own. The fundamental data types covered in Chapter 11, "Fundamental Data Types," are indispensable. When you use them as building blocks to create higher-level structures, you truly begin to unlock the power of effective data use.

If you're familiar with advanced data structures, you already know some of the information in this chapter: Skip Section 12.1; skim the "Flexible-Message-Format Example" beginning on page 276; and skim Section 12.3 for a view of abstract data types that you won't find in data-structures textbooks.

12.1 Records and Structures

The term "structured data" refers to data that's built up from other types. Because arrays are a special case, they are treated separately in Chapter 11. This section deals with user-created structured data—"records" in Pascal and Ada, "structs" in C. Here are some reasons for using structured data:

Use structured data to clarify data relationships. Structured data bundles groups of related items together. Sometimes the hardest part of figuring out a program is figuring out which data goes with which other data. It's like going to a small town and asking who's related to whom. You come to find out that everybody's kind of related to everybody else, but not really, and you never get a good answer.

If the data has been carefully structured, figuring out what goes with what is much easier. Here's an example of data that hasn't been structured:

Pascal Example of Misleading, Unstructured Variables

```
Name       := InputName;
Address    := InputAddress;
Phone      := InputPhone;
Title      := InputTitle;
Department := InputDepartment;
Bonus      := InputBonus;
```

Because this data is unstructured, it looks as if all the assignment statements belong together. Actually, *Name*, *Address*, and *Phone* are variables associated with individual employees and *Title*, *Department*, and *Bonus* are variables associated with a supervisor. The code fragment provides no hint that there are two kinds of data at work. In the code fragment below, the use of structured data makes the relationships clearer:

Pascal Example of More Informative, Structured Variables

```
Employee.Name    := InputName;
Employee.Address := InputAddress;
Employee.Phone   := InputPhone;

Supervisor.Title      := InputTitle;
Supervisor.Department := InputDepartment;
Supervisor.Bonus      := InputBonus;
```

In the code that uses structured variables, it's clear that some of the data is associated with an employee, other data with a supervisor.

Use structured data to simplify operations on blocks of data. You can combine related elements into a data structure and perform operations on the structure. It's easier to operate on the structure than to perform the same operation on each of the elements. It's also more reliable, and it takes fewer lines of code.

Suppose you have a group of data items that belong together—for instance, data about an employee in a personnel database. If the data isn't combined into a structure, merely copying the group of data can involve a lot of statements. Here's an example in Basic:

Basic Example of Copying a Group of Data Items

```
NewName      = OldName
NewAddress   = OldAddress
NewPhone     = OldPhone
NewSSN       = OldSSN
NewSex       = OldSex
NewSalary    = OldSalary
```

Every time you want to transfer information about an employee, you have to have this whole group of statements. If you ever add a new piece of employee information—for example, *NumWithholdings*—you have to find every place at which you have a block of assignments and add an assignment for *New-NumWithholdings = OldNumWithholdings*.

Imagine how horrible swapping data between two employees would be. You don't have to use your imagination—here it is:

CODING HORROR

Basic Example of Swapping Two Groups of Data the Hard Way

```
' swap new and old employee data

PrevOldName      = OldName
PrevOldAddress   = OldAddress
PrevOldPhone     = OldPhone
PrevOldSSN       = OldSSN
PrevOldSex       = OldSex
PrevOldSalary    = OldSalary

OldName      = NewName
OldAddress   = NewAddress
OldPhone     = NewPhone
OldSSN       = NewSSN
OldSex       = NewSex
OldSalary    = NewSalary

NewName      = PrevOldName
NewAddress   = PrevOldAddress
NewPhone     = PrevOldPhone
NewSSN       = PrevOldSSN
NewSex       = PrevOldSex
NewSalary    = PrevOldSalary
```

An easier way to approach the problem is to declare a structured variable. An example of the technique is shown at the top of the next page using Microsoft QuickBasic. This example uses a feature that isn't part of standard Basic: the *TYPE...END TYPE* statement.

Basic Example of Declaring Structured Data

```
TYPE tEmployee
    Name      AS STRING
    Address   AS STRING
    Phone     AS STRING
    SSN       AS STRING
    Sex       AS STRING
    Salary    AS LONG
END TYPE

DIM NewEmployee     AS tEmployee
DIM OldEmployee     AS tEmployee
DIM PrevOldEmployee AS tEmployee
```

Now you can switch all the elements in the old and new employee records with three statements:

Basic Example of an Easier Way to Swap Two Groups of Data

```
PrevOldEmployee = OldEmployee
OldEmployee     = NewEmployee
NewEmployee     = PrevOldEmployee
```

If you want to add a field such as *NumWithholdings*, you simply add it to the type declaration. Neither the three statements above nor any similar statements throughout the program need to be modified. All standard versions of Pascal and C have similar capabilities.

CROSS-REFERENCE
For details on how much data to share between routines, see Section 5.4, "Loose Coupling."

Use structured data to simplify parameter lists. You can simplify routine parameter lists by using structured variables. The technique is similar to the one just shown. Rather than passing each of the elements needed individually, you can group related elements into a data structure and pass the whole enchilada as a group structure. Here's an example of the hard way to pass a group of related parameters:

Basic Example of a Clumsy Routine Call with Unstructured Data

```
CALL HardWayRoutine( Name, Address, Phone, SSN, Sex, Salary )
```

Here's an example of the easy way to call a routine by using a structured variable that contains the elements of the first parameter list:

Basic Example of an Elegant Routine Call with Structured Data

```
CALL EasyWayRoutine( EmployeeRec )
```

If you want to add *NumWithholdings* to the first kind of call, you have to wade through your code and change every call to *HardWayRoutine()*. If you add a *NumWithholdings* element to *EmployeeRec*, you don't have to change the parameters to *EasyWayRoutine()* at all.

CROSS-REFERENCE
For details on the hazards
of passing too much data,
see Section 5.4, "Loose
Coupling."

You can carry this technique to extremes, putting all the variables in your program into one big, juicy variable and then passing it everywhere. Careful programmers avoid bundling data any more than is logically necessary. Furthermore, careful programmers avoid passing a data structure as a parameter when only one or two fields from the structure are needed—they pass the specific fields needed instead. This is an aspect of information hiding: Some information is hidden *in* routines; some is hidden *from* routines. Information is passed around on a need-to-know basis.

CROSS-REFERENCE
In some cases, you might
want to keep the details of
a record a secret. In such
cases, the record is con-
sidered to be "closed."
For more information on
open and closed records,
see "Mixing Levels of
Abstraction (Don't!)" in
Section 12.3.

Use structured data to reduce maintenance. Because you group related data when you use structured data types, changing a data structure requires fewer changes throughout a program. This is especially true in sections of code that aren't logically related to the change in the data structure. Since changes tend to produce errors, fewer changes mean fewer errors. If your *EmployeeRec* structure has a *Title* field and you decide to delete it, you don't need to change any of the parameter lists or assignment statements that use the whole record. Of course, you have to change any code that deals specifically with employee titles, but that is conceptually related to deleting the *Title* field and is hard to overlook.

The big advantage of having structured the data comes in sections of code that bear no logical relation to the *Title* field. Sometimes programs have statements that refer conceptually to a collection of data rather than to individual components. In such cases, individual components such as the *Title* field are referenced merely because they are part of the collection. Such sections of code don't have any logical reason to work with the *Title* field specifically, and those sections are easy to overlook when you change *Title*. If you use structured data, it's all right to overlook such sections because the code refers to the collection of related data rather than to each component individually.

12.2 Table-Driven Methods

Tables in general are useful data structures that are covered in virtually all data-structure textbooks. Table-driven methods use tables for a particular purpose and are covered here.

Programmers often talk about "table-driven" methods, but textbooks never tell you what a "table-driven" method is. A table-driven method is a scheme that allows you to look up information in a table rather than using logic statements (*if* and *case*) to figure it out. Virtually anything you can select with logic statements, you can select with tables instead. In simple cases, logic statements are easier and more direct. As the logic chain becomes more complex, however, tables become increasingly attractive.

For example, if you wanted to classify characters into letters, punctuation marks, and digits, you might use a complicated chain of logic like this one:

Pascal Example of Using Complicated Logic to Classify a Character

```pascal
if ( ('a' <= InputChar) and (InputChar <= 'z') ) or
   ( ('A' <= InputChar) and (InputChar <= 'Z') ) then begin
   CharType := Letter
end
else if ( InputChar = ' ' ) or ( InputChar = ',' ) or
   ( InputChar = '.' ) or ( InputChar = '!' ) or ( InputChar = '(' ) or
   ( InputChar = ')' ) or ( InputChar = ':' ) or ( InputChar = ';' ) or
   ( InputChar = '?' ) or ( InputChar = '-' ) then begin
   CharType := Punctuation
end
else if ( '0' <= InputChar and InputChar <= '9' ) then begin
   CharType := Digit
end;
```

If you used a lookup table instead, you'd store the type of each character in an array that's accessed by type of character. The complicated code fragment above would be replaced by this:

KEY POINT

Pascal Example of Using a Lookup Table to Classify a Character

```pascal
CharType := CharTypeTable[ InputChar ];
```

This fragment assumes that the *CharTypeTable* array has been set up earlier. You put your program's knowledge in its data rather than in its logic—in the table instead of in the *if* tests. Used in appropriate circumstances such as the one above, table-driven code is simpler than complicated logic, easier to modify, and more efficient.

General Issues with Table-Driven Methods

When you use table-driven methods, you have to address two issues:

First you have to address the question of how to look up entries in the table. You can use some data to access a table directly. If you need to classify data by month, for example, keying into a month table is straightforward. You can use an array with indexes 1 through 12.

Other data is too awkward to be used to look up a table entry directly. If you need to classify data by social security number, for example, you can't use the social security number to key into the table directly unless you can afford to store 999-99-9999 entries in your table. You're forced to use a more complicated approach. Here's a list of ways to look up an entry in a table:

- Direct access
- Indexed access
- Stair-step access

Each of these kinds of accesses is described in more detail in later subsections.

The second issue you have to address if you're using a table-driven method is what you should store in the table. In some cases, the result of a table lookup is data. If that's the case, you can store the data in the table. In other cases, the result of a table lookup is an action. In such a case, you can store a code that describes the action or, in some languages, you can store a reference to the routine that implements the action. In either of these cases, tables become more complicated.

Direct Access

Like all lookup tables, direct-access tables replace more complicated logical control structures. They are "direct access" because you don't have to jump through any complicated hoops to find the information you want in the table. As Figure 12-1 suggests, you can pick out the entry you want directly.

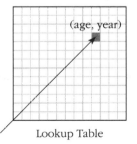

Figure 12-1. *Direct access.*

Days-in-Month Example

Suppose you need a function to return the number of days per month (forgetting about leap year, for the sake of argument). A clumsy way to do it, of course, is to write a large *if* statement.

Basic Example of a Clumsy Way to Determine the Number of Days in a Month

```
IF Month =  1 THEN Days = 31
ELSEIF Month =  2 THEN Days = 28
ELSEIF Month =  3 THEN Days = 31
ELSEIF Month =  4 THEN Days = 30
ELSEIF Month =  5 THEN Days = 31
ELSEIF Month =  6 THEN Days = 30
ELSEIF Month =  7 THEN Days = 31
ELSEIF Month =  8 THEN Days = 31
ELSEIF Month =  9 THEN Days = 30
ELSEIF Month = 10 THEN Days = 31
ELSEIF Month = 11 THEN Days = 30
ELSEIF Month = 12 THEN Days = 31
ENDIF
```

An easier, more modifiable, and more efficient way to perform the same function is to put the data in a table. In Basic, you'd first set up the table:

Basic Example of an Elegant Way to Determine the Number of Days in a Month

```
' INITIALIZE TABLE OF "Days Per Month" DATA
'
DATA 31, 28, 31, 30, 31, 30, 31, 31, 30, 31, 30, 31
DIM DaysPerMonth(12)
FOR I = 1 TO 12
   READ DaysPerMonth(I)
NEXT I
```

Now, instead of the long *if* statement shown above, you can just use a simple array access to find out the number of days in a month:

Basic Example of an Elegant Way to Determine the Number of Days in a Month (continued)

```
Days = DaysPerMonth( Month )
```

If you wanted to account for leap year in the table-lookup version, the code would still be simple:

Basic Example of an Elegant Way to Determine the Number of Days in a Month (continued)

```
Days = DaysPerMonth( Month, IsLeapYear )
```

Needless to say, in the *if*-statement version, the long string of *if*s would grow even more complicated if leap year were considered.

Determining the number of days per month is a convenient example because you can use the *Month* variable to look up an entry in the table. You can often use the data that would have controlled a lot of *if* statements to access a table directly.

Insurance-Rates Example

Suppose you're writing a program to compute medical-insurance rates, and you have rates that vary by age, sex, marital status, and whether a person smokes. If you had to write a logical control structure for the rates, you'd get something like this:

CODING HORROR

Pascal Example of a Clumsy Way to Determine an Insurance Rate

```
if ( Sex = Female ) then begin
   if ( MaritalStatus = Single ) then begin
      if ( SmokingStatus = NonSmoking ) then begin
         if ( Age < 18 ) then
            Rate = 40.00
         else if ( Age = 18 ) then
            Rate = 42.50
         else if ( Age = 19 ) then
            Rate = 45.00
         ...
         else if ( Age > 65 ) then
            Rate = 150.00
      end
      else begin { Smoking Status = Smoking }
         if ( Age < 18 ) then
            Rate = 44.00
         else if ( Age = 18 ) then
            Rate = 47.00
         else if ( Age = 19 ) then
            Rate = 50.00
         ...
         else if ( Age > 65 ) then
            Rate = 200.00
      end
   else { Marital Status = Married }
   ...
end; { if Sex ... }
```

The abbreviated version of the logic structure should be enough to give you an idea of how complicated this kind of thing can get. It doesn't show married females, any males, or most of the ages between 18 and 65. You can imagine how complicated it would get when you programmed the whole rate table.

You might say, "Yeah, but why did you do a test for each age? Why don't you just put the rates in arrays for each age?" That's a good question, and one obvious improvement would be to put the rates into separate arrays for each age.

A better solution, however, is to put the rates into arrays for all the factors, not just age. Here's how you would declare the array in Pascal:

> **Pascal Example of Declaring Data to Set Up an Insurance-Rates Table**
>
> ```
> type
>     Smoking_t = ( Smoking, NonSmoking );
>     Sex_t     = ( Male, Female );
>     Marital_t = ( Single, Married );
>     Age_t        = 1..100;
>
> var
>     RateTable = array[ Smoking_t, Sex_t, Marital_t, Age_t ];
> ```

The Age_t type has subtly different semantics than Age did in the original logic and is discussed in more detail later in this chapter.

One of the great features of using enumerated types in Pascal is that you can declare an array with parameters like *Smoking_t* and the compiler will automatically figure out that there are two kinds of smoking status and that the array should thus have two elements.

CROSS-REFERENCE
One advantage of a table-driven approach is that you can put the table's data in a file and read it at run time. That allows you to change something like an insurance-rates table without changing the program itself. For more on the idea, see Section 10.3, "Binding Time."

Once you declare the array, you have to figure out some way of putting data into it. You can use assignment statements, read the data from a disk file, compute the data, or do whatever is appropriate. After you've set up the data, you've got it made when you need to calculate a rate. The complicated logic shown earlier is replaced with a simple statement like this one:

> **Pascal Example of an Elegant Way to Determine an Insurance Rate**
>
> ```
> Rate := RateTable[ SmokingStatus, Sex, MaritalStatus, Age ];
> ```

This approach has the general advantages of replacing complicated logic with a table lookup. The table lookup is more readable and easier to change, takes up less space, and executes faster.

Flexible-Message-Format Example

You can use a table to describe logic that's too dynamic to represent in code. With the character-classification example, the days-in-the-month example, and the insurance-rates example, you at least knew that you could write a long string of *if* statements if you needed to. In some cases, however, the data is too complicated to describe with hard-coded *if* statements.

If you think you've got the idea of how direct-access tables work, you might want to skip the next example. It's a little more complicated than the earlier examples, though, and it further demonstrates the power of table-driven approaches.

Suppose you're writing a routine to print messages that are stored in a file. The file usually has about 500 messages, and each file has about 20 kinds of messages. The messages originally come from a buoy and give water temperature, the buoy's location, and so on.

Each of the messages has several fields, and each message starts with a header that has an ID to let you know which of the 20 or so kinds of messages you're dealing with. Figure 12-2 illustrates how the messages are stored.

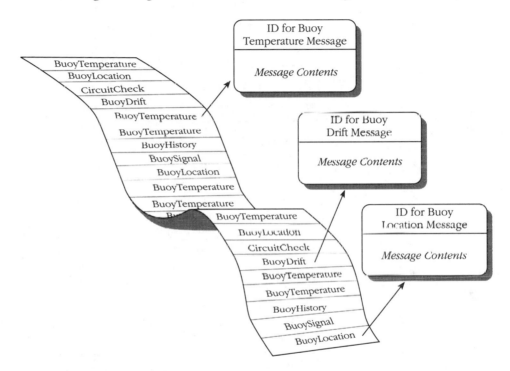

Figure 12-2. *Messages are stored in no particular order, and each one is identified with a message ID.*

The format of the messages is volatile, determined by your customer, and you don't have enough control over your customer to stabilize it. Figure 12-3 on the next page shows what a few of the messages look like in detail.

If you used a logic-based approach, you'd probably read each message, check the ID, and then call a routine that's designed to read, interpret, and print each kind of message. If you had 20 kinds of messages, you'd have 20 routines. You'd also have who-knows-how-many lower-level routines to support them. For example, you'd have a *PrintBuoyTemperatureMessage()* routine to print the buoy temperature message.

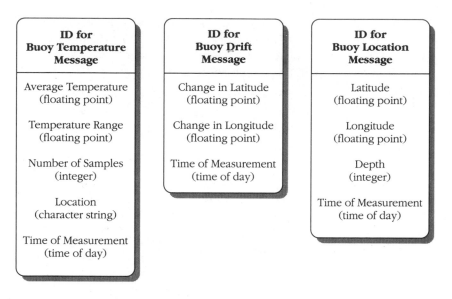

**ID for
Buoy Temperature
Message**

Average Temperature
(floating point)

Temperature Range
(floating point)

Number of Samples
(integer)

Location
(character string)

Time of Measurement
(time of day)

**ID for
Buoy Drift
Message**

Change in Latitude
(floating point)

Change in Longitude
(floating point)

Time of Measurement
(time of day)

**ID for
Buoy Location
Message**

Latitude
(floating point)

Longitude
(floating point)

Depth
(integer)

Time of Measurement
(time of day)

Figure 12-3. *Aside from the Message ID, each kind of message has its own format.*

Each time the format of any message changed, you'd have to change the logic in the routine that printed that message. In the detailed message above, if the average-temperature field changed from a floating point to something else, you'd have to change the logic of *PrintBuoyTemperatureMessage()*. (If the buoy changed from a "floating point" to something else, you'd have to get a new buoy!)

With a table-driven approach, you can describe the format of each message in a table rather than hard-coding it in program logic. This makes it easier to code originally and easier to change. It also generates less code. To use this approach, you start by listing the kinds of messages and the types of fields. In Pascal, you could define the types of all the possible fields this way:

Pascal Example of Defining Message Data Types

```
var
    FieldTypes = ( FloatingPoint, Integer, CharString,
                   TimeOfDay, SingleFlag, BitField );
```

Rather than hard-coding printing routines for each of the 20 kinds of messages, you can create a handful of routines that print each of the primary data types—*FloatingPoint, Integer, CharString,* and so on. You can describe the contents of each kind of message in a table (including the name of each field) and then decode each message based on the description in the table. A table entry to describe one kind of message might look like this:

Pascal Example of Defining a Message Table Entry

```
Message[ Type1 ].NumFields        := 5;
Message[ Type1 ].MessageName      := 'Buoy Temperature Message';

Message[ Type1 ].FieldType[ 1 ]   := FloatingPoint;
Message[ Type1 ].FieldLabel[ 1 ]  := 'Average Temperature';

Message[ Type1 ].FieldType[ 2 ]   := FloatingPoint;
Message[ Type1 ].FieldLabel[ 2 ]  := 'Temperature Range';

Message[ Type1 ].FieldType[ 3 ]   := Integer;
Message[ Type1 ].FieldLabel[ 3 ]  := 'Number of Samples';

Message[ Type1 ].FieldType[ 4 ]   := CharString;
Message[ Type1 ].FieldLabel[ 4 ]  := 'Location';

Message[ Type1 ].FieldType[ 5 ]   := TimeOfDay;
Message[ Type1 ].FieldLabel[ 5 ]  := 'Time of Measurement';
```

Now, instead of having all the information embedded in a program's logic, you have it embedded in data. Data tends to be more flexible than logic. It's easy to change when a message format changes. If you have to add a new kind of message, you can just add another element to the *Message* array.

The code that reads the messages is simpler too. In the logic-based approach, the message-reading routine consists of a loop to read each message, decode the ID, and then call one of 20 routines based on the message ID. Here's the pseudocode for the logic-based approach:

CROSS-REFERENCE
This low-level pseudocode is used for a different purpose than the PDL you use for routine design. For details on designing a routine in PDL, see Section 4.2, "PDL for Pros."

```
While more messages to read
   Read a message header
   Decode the message ID from the message header
   If the message header is type 1 then
      Print a type 1 message
   Else if the message header is type 2 then
      Print a type 2 message
   ...
   Else if the message header is type 19 then
      Print a type 19 message
   Else if the message header is type 20 then
      Print a type 20 message
```

The pseudocode is abbreviated because you can get the idea without seeing all 20 cases. In the logic below this level, each of the 20 kinds of messages has its own routine for printing its message. Each routine could also be expressed in pseudocode. Here's the pseudocode (on the next page) for the routine to print the buoy temperature message.

```
Print 'Buoy Temperature Message'

Read a floating-point value
Print 'Average Temperature'
Print the floating-point value

Read a floating-point value
Print 'Temperature Range'
Print the floating-point value

Read an integer value
Print 'Number of Samples'
Print the integer value

Read a character string
Print 'Location'
Print the character string

Read a time of day
Print 'Time of Measurement'
Print the time of day
```

This is the code for just one kind of message. Each of the other 19 kinds of messages would have similar code.

The table-driven approach is more economical than this one. The message-reading routine consists of a loop that reads each message header, decodes the ID, looks up the message description in the *Message* array, and then calls the same routine every time to decode the message. Here's the pseudocode for the top-level loop in the table-driven approach:

The first three lines here are the same as in the logic-based approach.

```
While more messages to read
    Read a message header
    Decode the message ID from the message header
    Look up the message description in the message-description table
    Read the message fields and print them based on the message description
```

Unlike the pseudocode for the logic-based approach, the pseudocode in this case isn't abbreviated because the logic is so much less complicated. In the logic below this level, you'll find one routine that's capable of interpreting a message description from the *Message* array and printing a message. That routine is more general than any of the logic-based message-printing routines but not much more complicated, and it will be one routine instead of 20:

```
While more fields to print
    Get the field type from the message description
    Depending on the type of the field
        case of floating point =>
            read a floating-point value
            print the field label
            print the floating-point value
```

(continued)

```
case of integer =>
   read an integer value
   print the field label
   print the integer value

case of character string =>
   read a character string
   print the field label
   print the character string

case of time of day =>
   read a time of day
   print the field label
   print the time of day

case of single flag =>
   read a single flag
   print the field label
   print the single flag

case of bit field =>
   read a bit field
   print the field label
   print the bit field
```

Admittedly, this routine with its six cases is longer than the single routine needed to print the buoy temperature message. But this is the only routine you need. You don't need 19 other routines for the 19 other kinds of messages. This routine handles the six field types and takes care of all the kinds of messages.

This routine also shows the most complicated way of implementing this kind of table lookup because it uses a *case* statement. Many languages allow references to routines to be stored in tables, just as data can be. If that's true of the language you're using, you don't need a *case* statement; you can store routines in the table and call them based on the field type.

Here's how to set up the code for a table of procedures in Pascal. First you have to create a Pascal "procedure type," a kind of variable that holds a reference to a procedure. Here's how the type for this example would look:

Pascal Example of Setting Up a Procedure Type

```
type
   HandleFieldProc = procedure
      (
           FieldDescription:  String;
      var FileStatus:         FileStatusType
      );
```

This code fragment declares a procedure type for procedures that have a string parameter and a *FileStatusType* parameter.

The second step is to declare an array to hold the procedure references. The array is the lookup table, and here's how it looks:

Pascal Example of Setting Up a Table to Hold Procedure References

```
var
    ReadAndPrintFieldByType: array[ FieldTypes ] of HandleFieldProc;
```

The final step required to set up the table of procedures is to assign the names of specific procedures to the *ReadAndPrintFieldByType* array. Here's how those assignments would look:

Pascal Example of Setting Up Procedure References in a Table

```
ReadAndPrintFieldByType[ FloatingPoint ] := ReadAndPrintFloatingPoint;
ReadAndPrintFieldByType[ Integer ]       := ReadAndPrintInteger;
ReadAndPrintFieldByType[ CharString ]    := ReadAndPrintCharString;
ReadAndPrintFieldByType[ TimeOfDay ]     := ReadAndPrintTimeOfDay;
ReadAndPrintFieldByType[ SingleFlag ]    := ReadAndPrintSingleFlag;
ReadAndPrintFieldByType[ BitField ]      := ReadAndPrintBitField;
```

This code fragment assumes that *ReadAndPrintFloatingPoint* and the other identifiers on the right side of the assignment statements are names of procedures of type *HandleFieldProc*. Assigning the procedures to array elements in the array made up of procedure variables means that you can call one of the procedures by referencing an array element instead of by using the procedure name directly.

Once the table of procedures is set up, you can handle a field in the message simply by accessing the table of field handlers and calling one of the procedures in the table. The code looks like this:

Pascal Example of Looking Up Procedures in a Table

This stuff is just housekeeping for each field in a message.

This is the table lookup that calls a procedure depending on the type of the field—just by looking it up in a table.

```
MessageIdx := 1;
while ( MessageIdx <= NumFieldsInMessage ) and ( FileStatus = OK ) do
    begin
    FieldType := FieldDescription[ MessageIdx ].FieldType;
    FieldName := FieldDescription[ MessageIdx ].FieldName;
    ReadAndPrintFieldByType[ FieldType ]( FieldName, FileStatus )
    end;
```

Remember the original 27 lines of pseudocode containing the *case* statement? If you replace the *case* statement with a table of routines, this is all the code you'd need to provide the same functionality. Incredibly, it's also all the code needed to replace all 20 of the individual routines in the logic-based approach. You can use a similar approach in C and in other languages that allow procedure variables. It's much less error prone, more maintainable, and more efficient—a dramatic illustration of the power of table-driven approaches.

Fudging Lookup Keys

In each of the three previous examples, you could use the data to key into the table directly. That is, you could use *MessageID* as a key without alteration, as you could use *Month* in the days-per-month example and *Sex, MaritalStatus,* and *SmokingStatus* in the insurance-rates example.

You'd always like to key into a table directly because it's simple and fast. Sometimes, however, the data isn't cooperative. In the insurance-rates example, *Age* wasn't well behaved. The original logic had one rate for people under 18, individual rates for ages 18 through 65, and one rate for people over 65. This meant that for ages 0 through 17 and 66 and over, you couldn't use the age to key directly into a table that stored only one set of rates for several ages.

This leads to the topic of fudging table-lookup keys. You can fudge keys in several ways:

Duplicate information to make the key work directly. One straightforward way to make *Age* work as a key into the rates table is to duplicate the under-18 rates for each of the ages 0 through 17 and then use the age to key directly into the table. You can do the same thing for ages 66 and over. The benefits of this approach are that the table structure itself is straightforward and the table accesses are straightforward. If you needed to add age-specific rates for ages 17 and below, you could just change the table. The drawbacks are that the duplication would waste space for redundant information and increase the possibility of errors in the table—if only because the table would contain more data.

Transform the key to make it work directly. A second way to make *Age* work as a direct key is to apply a function to *Age* so that it works well. In this case, the function would have to change all ages 0 through 17 to one key, say *17*, and all ages above 66 to another key, say *66*. This particular range is well behaved enough that you could just use *min()* and *max()* functions to make the transformation. For example, you could use the expression

```
max( min( 66, Age ), 17 )
```

to create a table key that ranges from 17 to 66.

Creating the transformation function requires that you recognize a pattern in the data you want to use as a key, and that's not always as simple as using the *min()* and *max()* functions. Suppose that in this example the rates were for five-year age bands instead of one-year bands. Unless you wanted to duplicate all your data five times, you'd have to come up with a function that divided *Age* by 5 properly and used the *min()* and *max()* functions.

Isolate the key-transformation in its own function. Anytime you have to fudge data to make it work as a table key, put the operation that changes the data to a key into its own function. A function eliminates the possibility of using different transformations in different places. It makes modifications easier when the transformation changes. A good name for the function, like *GetKeyFromAge()*, also clarifies and documents the purpose of the mathematical machinations.

Package the function with the module that contains the table definition and other table-related routines. If it's close to the table data, when the table changes, it's easy to remember to change the transformation function.

Indexed Access

Sometimes a simple mathematical transformation isn't powerful enough to make the jump from data like *Age* to a table key. Some such cases are suited to the use of an indexed access scheme.

When you use indexes, you use the primary data to look up a key in an index table and then you use the value from the index table to look up the main data you're interested in.

Suppose you run a warehouse and have an inventory of about 100 items. Suppose further that each item has a four-digit part number that ranges from 0000 through 9999. In this case, if you want to use the part number to key directly into a table that describes some aspect of each item, you set up an index array with 10,000 entries (from 0 through 9999). The array is empty except for the 100 entries that correspond to part numbers of the 100 items in your warehouse. As Figure 12-4 shows, those entries point to an item-description table that has far fewer than 10,000 entries.

Indexed access schemes offer two main advantages. First, if each of the entries in the main lookup table is large, it takes a lot less space to create an index array with a lot of wasted space than it does to create a main lookup table with a lot of wasted space. For example, suppose that the main table takes 100 bytes per entry and that the index array takes 2 bytes per entry. Suppose that the main table has 100 entries and that the data used to access it has 10,000 possible values. In such a case, the choice is between having an index structure with 10,000 entries or a main data structure with 10,000 entries. If you use an index structure, your total memory use is 30,000 bytes. If you forgo the index structure and waste space in the main table, your total memory use is 1,000,000 bytes.

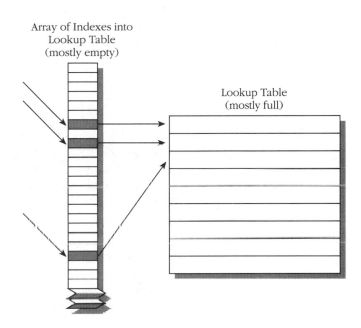

Figure 12-4. *Indexed access.*

The second advantage, even if you don't save space by using an index, is that it's sometimes cheaper to manipulate entries in an index than entries in a main table. For example, if you have a table with employee names, hiring dates, and salaries, you can create one index that accesses the table by employee name, another that accesses the table by hiring date, and a third that accesses the table by salary.

A final advantage of an index-access scheme is the general table-lookup advantage of maintainability. Data encoded in tables is easier to maintain than data embedded in code. To maximize the flexibility, put the index-access code in its own routine and call the routine when you need to get a table key from a part number. When it's time to change the table, you might decide to switch the index-accessing scheme or to switch to another table-lookup scheme altogether. The access scheme will be easier to change if you don't spread index accesses throughout your program.

Stair-Step Access

Yet another kind of table access is the stair-step method. This access method isn't as direct as an index structure, but it doesn't waste as much data space.

The general idea of stair-step structures, illustrated in Figure 12-5 on page 288, is that entries in a table are valid for ranges of data rather than for distinct data points. For example, if you're writing a grading program, the "B" entry range might be from 77.5 percent to 90 percent. Here's a range of grades you might have to program someday:

≥ 90.0%	A
< 90.0%	B
< 77.5%	C
< 65.0%	D
< 50.0%	F

This is an ugly range for a table lookup because you can't use a simple data-transformation function to key into the letters *A* through *F.* An index scheme would be awkward because the numbers are floating point. You might consider converting the floating-point numbers to integers, and in this case that would be a valid design option, but for the sake of illustration, this example will stick with floating point.

To use the stair-step method, you put the upper end of each range into a table and then write a loop to check a score against the upper end of each range. When you find the point at which the score first exceeds the top of a range, you know what the grade is. With the stair-step technique, you have to be careful to handle the endpoints of the ranges properly. Here's the code in Basic that assigns grades to a group of students based on this example:

Basic Example of a Stair-Step Table Lookup

```
' set up data for grading table

RangeLimit( 1 ) = 50.0
Grade( 1 )      = 'F'
RangeLimit( 2 ) = 65.0
Grade( 2 )      = 'D'
RangeLimit( 3 ) = 77.5
Grade( 3 )      = 'C'
RangeLimit( 4 ) = 90.0
Grade( 4 )      = 'B'
RangeLimit( 5 ) = 100.0
Grade( 5 )      = 'A'

MaxGradeLevel   = 5
...

' assign a grade to a student based on the student's score

GradeLevel = 1
StudentGrade = "A"
```

This is the top of the range. (annotation pointing to `RangeLimit( 5 ) = 100.0`)

(continued)

```
while ( StudentGrade = "A" and GradeLevel < MaxGradeLevel )
   if ( StudentScore < RangeLimit( GradeLevel ) ) then
      StudentGrade = Grade( GradeLevel )
   end if
   GradeLevel = GradeLevel + 1
wend
```

Although this is a simple example, you can easily generalize it to handle multiple students, multiple grading schemes (for example, different grades for different point levels on different assignments), and changes in the grading scheme.

The advantage of this approach over other table-driven methods is that it works well with irregular data. The grading example is simple in that, although grades are assigned at irregular intervals, the numbers are "round," ending with 5s and 0s. The stair-step approach is equally well suited to data that doesn't end neatly with 5s and 0s. You can use the stair-step approach in statistics work for probability distributions with numbers like this:

0.458747	$0.00
0.547651	$254.32
0.627764	$514.77
0.778883	$747.82
0.893211	$1,042.65
0.957665	$5,887.55
0.976544	$12,836.98
0.987889	$27,234.12
...	

Ugly numbers like these defy any attempt to come up with a function to neatly transform them into table keys. The stair-step approach is the answer.

This approach also enjoys the general advantages of table-driven approaches. It is flexible and modifiable. If the grading ranges in the grading example were to change, the program could easily be adapted by modifying the entries in the *RangeLimit* array. You could easily generalize the grade-assignment part of the program so that it would accept a table of grades and corresponding cut-off scores. The grade-assignment part of the program wouldn't have to use scores expressed as percentages; it could use raw points rather than percentages, and the program wouldn't have to change much.

Here are a few subtleties to consider as you use the stair-step technique:

Watch the endpoints. Make sure you've covered the case at the top end of each stair-step range. Run the stair-step search so that it finds items that map to any range other than the uppermost range, and then have the rest fall into

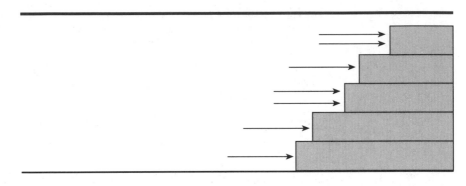

Figure 12-5. *The stair-step approach categorizes each entry by determining the level at which it hits a "staircase." The "step" it hits determines its category.*

the uppermost range. Sometimes this requires creating an artificial value for the top of the uppermost range.

Be careful too about mistaking < for <=. Make sure that the loop terminates properly with values that fall into the top ranges and that the range boundaries are handled correctly.

Consider using a binary search rather than a sequential search. In the grading example, the loop that assigns the grade searches sequentially through the list of grading limits. If you had a larger list, the cost of the sequential search might become prohibitive. If it does, you can replace it with a quasi-binary search. It's a "quasi" binary search because the point of most binary searches is to find a value. In this case, you don't expect to find the value; you expect to find the right category for the value. The binary-search algorithm must correctly determine where the value should go. Remember also to treat the endpoint as a special case.

Consider using indexed access instead of the stair-step technique. An index-access scheme such as the ones described in the preceding section might be a good alternative to a stair-step technique. The searching required in the stair-step method can add up, and if execution speed is a concern, you might be willing to trade the space an extra index structure takes up for the time advantage you get with a more direct access method.

Obviously, this alternative isn't a good choice in all cases. In the grading example, you could probably use it; if you had only 100 discrete percentage points, the memory cost of setting up an index array wouldn't be prohibitive. If, on the other hand, you had the probability data mentioned above, you couldn't set up an indexing scheme because you can't key into entries with numbers like *0.458747* and *0.547651.*

In some cases, any of the several options might work. The point of design is choosing one of the several good options for your case. Don't worry too much about choosing the best one. As Butler Lampson, a senior engineer at Digital Equipment Corporation, says, it's better to strive for a good solution and avoid disaster rather than trying to find the best solution (Lampson 1984).

Put the stair-step table lookup into its own routine. When you create a transformation function that changes a value like *StudentGrade* into a table key, put it into its own routine.

Other Examples of Table Lookups

A few other examples of table lookups appear in other sections of the book. They're used in the course of making other points, and the contexts don't emphasize the table lookups per se. Here's where you'll find them:

- Looking up rates in an insurance table: Section 15.3, "Creating Loops Easily—from the Inside Out"
- Cost of paging during a table lookup: Section 28.3, "Kinds of Fat and Molasses"
- Combinations of boolean values (A or B or C): "Substitute Table Lookups for Complicated Expressions" in Section 29.2
- Precomputing values in a loan repayment table: Section 29.4, "Expressions"

12.3 Abstract Data Types (ADTs)

CROSS-REFERENCE
Abstract data types are usually implemented as modules. Both ADTs and modules are combinations of data and operations on the data. For details on modules, see Chapter 6, "Three out of Four Programmers Surveyed Prefer Modules."

An abstract data type is a collection of data and operations that work on that data. The operations both describe the data to the rest of the program and allow the rest of the program to change the data. The word "data" in "abstract data type" is used loosely. An ADT might be a graphics window with all the operations that affect it; a file and file operations; or even an insurance-rates table and the operations on it.

Traditionally, programming books wax mathematical when they arrive at the topic of abstract data types. They tend to make statements like "One can think of an abstract data type as a mathematical model with a collection of operations defined on it." Then they provide some boring examples of how to write access routines for a stack, a queue, or a list. Such books make it seem as if you'd never actually use an abstract data type except as a sleep aid.

Such dry explanations of abstract data types completely miss the point. Abstract data types are exciting because you can use them to manipulate real-world entities rather than computer-science entities. Instead of inserting a node into a linked list, you can add a cell to a spreadsheet, a new type of window to a list of window types, or another passenger car to a bullet-train simulation. Don't underestimate the power of being able to work in the problem domain rather than the computer-science domain. This isn't to say that you shouldn't use abstract data types to implement stacks, queues, and lists; you should. It is to say that ADTs have much more power than is usually acknowledged.

Example of the Need for an Abstract Data Type

To get things started, here's an example of a case in which an ADT would be useful. We'll get to the theoretical details after we have an example to talk about.

Suppose you're writing a program to control text output to the screen using a variety of typefaces, point sizes, and font attributes (such as bold and italic). Part of the program manipulates the text's fonts. If you use an ADT, you'll have a group of font routines bundled with the data—the typeface names, point sizes, and font attributes—they operate on. The collection of font routines and data is an ADT.

If you're not using ADTs, you'll take an ad hoc approach to manipulating fonts. For example, if you need to change to a 12-point font size, you'll have code like this:

```
CurrentFont.Size = 12
```

If you change sizes in several places in the program, you'll have similar lines spread throughout your program.

If you need to set a font to bold, you might have code like this:

```
CurrentFont.Attribute = CurrentFont.Attribute or 02h
```

If you're lucky, you'll have something cleaner than that, but this is about the best you'll get with an ad hoc approach:

```
CurrentFont.Bold = True
```

If you program this way, you're likely to have similar lines in several places in your program.

Finally, if you set the face name, you'll have lines like this:

```
CurrentFont.Typeface = TIMES_ROMAN
```

Benefits of Using Abstract Data Types (ADTs)

The problem isn't that the ad hoc approach is bad programming practice. It's that you can replace the approach with a better programming practice that produces these benefits:

You can hide implementation details. Hiding information about the font data structure means that if the data structure changes, you can change it in one place without affecting the whole program. For example, unless you hid the implementation details in an ADT, changing the data structure from the first representation of bold to the second would entail changing your program in every place in which bold was set rather than in just one place. Hiding the information also protects the rest of the program if you decide to store data in external storage rather than in memory or to rewrite all the font-manipulation routines in another language.

Changes don't affect the whole program. If fonts need to become richer and support more operations (such as switching to small caps, superscripts, strikethrough, and so on), you can change the program in one place. The change won't affect the rest of the program.

It's easier to improve performance. If you need to improve font performance, you can recode a few well-defined routines rather than wading through an entire program.

The program is more obviously correct. You can replace the more tedious task of verifying that statements like *CurrentFont.Attribute = Current-Font.Attribute or 02h* are correct with the easier task of verifying that calls to *SetCurrentFontToBold( )* are correct. With the first statement, you can have the wrong structure name, the wrong field name, the wrong logical operation (a logical *and* instead of *or*), or the wrong value for the attribute (*20h* instead of *02h*). In the second case, the only thing that could possibly be wrong with the call to *SetCurrentFontToBold( )* is that it's a call to the wrong routine name, so it's easier to see that it's correct.

The program becomes more self-documenting. You can improve statements like *CurrentFont.Attribute or 02h* by replacing *02h* with *BOLD* or whatever *02h* represents, but that doesn't compare to the readability of a routine call such as *SetCurrentFontToBold()*.

HARD DATA

Woodfield, Dunsmore, and Shen conducted a study in which graduate and senior undergraduate computer-science students answered questions about two programs—one that was divided into eight routines along functional lines and one that was divided into eight abstract-data-type routines (1981). Students using the abstract-data-type program scored over 30 percent higher than students using the functional version.

You don't have to pass data all over your program. In the examples just presented, you have to change *CurrentFont* directly or pass it to every routine that works with fonts. If you use an abstract data type, you don't have to pass *CurrentFont* all over the program and you don't have to turn it into global data either. The ADT has a structure that contains *CurrentFont*'s data. The data is directly accessed only by routines that are part of the ADT. Routines that aren't part of the ADT don't have to worry about the data.

You're able to work with real-world entities rather than with computer-science structures. You can define operations dealing with fonts so that most of the program operates solely in terms of fonts rather than in terms of array accesses, record definitions, and *BOLD* as a true or false boolean.

In this case, to define an abstract data type, you'd define a few routines to control fonts—perhaps these:

```
SetCurrentFontSize( Size )
SetCurrentFontToBold()
SetCurrentFontToItalic()
SetCurrentFontToRegular()
SetCurrentFontTypeFace( FaceName )
```

KEY POINT

The code inside these routines would probably be short—it would probably be similar to the code you saw in the ad hoc approach to the font problem earlier. The difference would be that you would have isolated font operations in a set of routines. That would provide a better level of abstraction for the rest of your program to work with fonts, and it would give you a layer of protection against changes in font operations. Putting direct data manipulations behind access routines is like having an air lock in a submarine. You can go out, and you can go in, but the air stays inside and the water stays outside.

More Examples of ADTs

Here are a few more examples of ADTs:

Suppose you're writing software that controls the cooling system for a nuclear reactor. You can treat the cooling system as an abstract data type by defining the following operations for it:

```
GetReactorTemperature()
SetCirculationRate( Rate )
OpenValve( ValveNumber )
CloseValve( ValveNumber )
```

The specific environment would determine the code written to implement each of these operations. The rest of the program could deal with the cooling system through these functions and wouldn't have to worry about internal details of data-structure implementation, data-structure limitations, changes, and so on.

Here are more examples of abstract data types and likely operations on them:

Cruise Control
Set speed
Get current settings
Resume former speed
Deactivate

Set of Help Screens
Add help topic
Remove help topic
Set current help topic
Display help screen
Remove help display
Display help index
Back up to previous
   screen

List
Initialize list
Insert item in list
Remove item from list
Read next item from list

Light
Turn on
Turn off

Blender
Turn on
Turn off
Set speed
Start "Insta-Pulverize"
Stop "Insta-Pulverize"

Menu
Start new menu
Delete menu
Add menu item
Remove menu item
Activate menu item
Deactivate menu item
Display menu
Hide menu
Get menu choice

Pointer
Get pointer to new memory
Dispose of memory from
   existing pointer
Change amount of
   memory allocated

Fuel Tank
Fill tank
Drain tank
Get tank capacity
Get tank status

Stack
Initialize stack
Push item onto stack
Pop item from stack
Read top of stack

File
Open file
Read file
Write file
Set current location
Close file

Elevator
Move up one floor
Move down one floor
Move to specific floor
Report current floor
Return to home floor

You can derive several guidelines from a study of these examples:

Build typical computer-science data structures as ADTs. Most discussions of ADTs focus on representing typical computer-science data structures as ADTs. As you can see from the examples, you can represent stacks, lists, and pointers, as well as virtually any other typical data structures, as ADTs.

The question you need to ask is What does this stack, list, or pointer represent? If a stack represents a set of employees, treat the ADT as employees rather than a stack. If a list represents a set of billing records, treat it as billing records rather than a list. If a pointer represents a cell in a spreadsheet, treat it as a cell rather than a pointer. Treat yourself to the highest possible level of abstraction.

Treat common objects such as files as ADTs. Most languages include a few abstract data types that you're probably familiar with but might not think of as ADTs. File operations are a good example. While writing to disk, the operating system spares you the grief of positioning the read/write head at a specific physical address, allocating a new disk sector when you exhaust an old one, and checking for binary error codes. The operating system provides a first level of abstraction and the ADTs for that level. High-level languages provide a second level of abstraction and ADTs for that higher level. A high-level language protects you from the messy details of generating operating-system calls and manipulating data buffers. It allows you to treat a chunk of disk space as a "file."

You can layer ADTs similarly. If you want to use an ADT at one level that offers data-structure level operations (like pushing and popping a stack), that's fine. You can create another level on top of that one that works at the level of the real-world problem.

Treat even simple items as ADTs. You don't have to have a formidable data structure to justify using an abstract data type. One of the ADTs in the example lists is a light that supports only two operations—turning it on and turning it off. You might think that it would be a waste to isolate simple "on" and "off" operations in routines of their own, but even simple operations can benefit from the use of ADTs. Putting the light and its operations into an ADT makes the code more self-documenting and easier to change, confines the potential consequences of changes to the *TurnLightOn()* and *TurnLightOff()* routines, and reduces the amount of data you have to pass around.

Provide services in pairs with their opposites. Most operations have corresponding, equal, and opposite operations. If you have an operation that turns a light on, you'll probably need one to turn it off. If you have an operation to add an item to a list, you'll probably need one to delete an item from the list. If you have an operation to activate a menu item, you'll probably need one to deactivate an item. When you design an ADT, check each service to determine whether you need its complement. Don't create an opposite gratuitously, but do check to see whether you need one.

Refer to an ADT independently of the medium it's stored on. Suppose you have an insurance-rates table that's so big that it's always stored on disk. You might be tempted to refer to it as a "rate *file*" and create access routines such as *ReadRateFile()*. When you refer to it as a file, however, you're exposing more information about the data than you need to. If you ever change the program so that the table is in memory instead of on disk, the code that refers to it as a file will be incorrect, misleading, and confusing. Try to make the names of access routines independent of how the data is stored, and refer to the abstract data type, like the insurance-rates table, instead. That would give your access routine a name like *ReadRateTable()* instead of *ReadRateField()*.

Handling Multiple Instances of Data with ADTs

Once you've defined the base operations for an ADT, you might find that you need to work with more than one piece of data of that type. For example, if you're working with fonts, you might want to keep track of multiple fonts. In

ADT terms, each font you want to keep track of would be an "instance." One solution is to write a separate set of ADT operations for each font instance you want to keep track of. A better solution is to design the single ADT so that it works with multiple font instances. That usually means including services to create and delete instances and designing the other services so that they can work with multiple instances.

The font ADT originally offered these services:

```
SetCurrentFontSize( Size )
SetCurrentFontToBold()
SetCurrentFontToItalic()
SetCurrentFontToRegular()
SetCurrentFontTypeFace( FaceName )
```

If you want to work with more than one font at a time, you'll need to add services to create and delete font instances—maybe these:

```
CreateFont( FontID )
DeleteFont( FontID )
SetCurrentFont( FontID )
```

The notion of a *FontID* has been added as a way to keep track of multiple fonts as they're created and used. For other operations, you can choose from among three ways to handle the ADT interface:

Use font instances implicitly. Design a new service to call to make a specific font instance the current one—something like *SetCurrentFont(FontID)*. Setting the current font makes all other services use the current font when they're called. If you use this approach, you don't need *FontID* as a parameter to the other services.

Explicitly identify instances each time you use ADT services. In this case, you don't have the notion of a "current font." Routines that use the ADT's services don't have to keep track of font data, but they do have to use a font ID. This requires adding *FontID* as a parameter to each routine.

Explicitly provide the data used by the ADT services. In this approach, you declare the data that the ADT uses within each routine that uses an ADT service. In other words, you create a *Font* data structure that you pass to each of the ADT service routines. You must design the ADT service routines so that they use the *Font* data that's passed to them each time they're called. You don't need a font ID if you use this approach because you keep track of the font data itself. (Even though the data is available directly from the *Font* data structure, you should access it only with the ADT service routines. This is called keeping the record "closed" and is discussed more later in this section.)

The advantage of this approach is that the ADT service routines don't have to look up font information based on a font ID. The disadvantage is that it's dangerous for the rest of the program because the data is directly available to be fooled with.

Inside the abstract data type, you'll have a wealth of options for handling multiple instances, but outside, this sums up the choices.

Mixing Levels of Abstraction (Don't!)

If you directly access the data structure only within the service routines for the ADT and use the ADT service routines everywhere else, you'll have a consistent level of abstraction. If you don't, you'll have an inconsistent level of abstraction, and you'll defeat one of the principal benefits of using ADTs. The practical consequence of inconsistent abstraction is that modifications are more error prone. You create the false impression that changing an access routine catches all the accesses to the data.

To extend an earlier analogy: If the ADT's service routines work as an air lock that keeps water from getting into a submarine, inconsistent use of service routines are leaky panels in the routine. The leaky panels might not let water in as quickly as an open air lock, but if you give them enough time, they'll still sink the ship. In practice, this is what happens when you mix levels of abstraction. As the program is modified, the mixed levels of abstraction make the program harder and harder to understand, and it gradually degrades until it becomes unmaintainable.

Open and Closed Records

Along with the idea of mixing levels of abstraction comes the idea of "open" and "closed" records. A record, or structure, is considered to be open in a routine if the routine uses any of its fields directly. It's closed in the routine if none of its fields are used directly—that is, if it's used only as a complete structure. As mentioned earlier, you can use closed records as one way of handling multiple instances of an ADT. The fact that a record's available doesn't mean that you have to open it. Keep the record closed except within the confines of the ADT's service routines.

As you consider the three ways to handle multiple fonts, note that the temptation to open records is a good reason to prefer the *FontID* approach to the *Font*-record approach.

ADTs and Information Hiding, Modules, and Objects

Abstract data types and information hiding are related concepts. If you want to make an abstract data type, you hide its implementation details. That's the road that leads from abstract data types to information hiding. If you want to practice information hiding, you look for secrets you can hide. One of the most obvious secrets is the implementation details of an abstract data type. That's the road leading from information hiding to abstract data types.

The abstract-data-type concept is also related to the module idea. In languages that support modules directly, you can implement each abstract data type in its own module. A module is a collection of data and operations on that data just as an ADT is a collection of data and operations on that data.

CROSS-REFERENCE
For more on object-oriented design, see Section 7.3, "Object-Oriented Design."

The ADT concept is closely related to the concept of objects too. "Object" is a loosely defined term, but it generally refers to a collection of data and operations on the data. In that limited sense, all objects are abstract data types. The idea of an "object," however, also makes use of the ideas of inheritance and polymorphism. One way of thinking of an object is as an abstract data type plus inheritance and polymorphism. Abstract data types are part of the notion of an object, not the whole idea.

Language Support for ADTs

Some languages provide better support for ADTs than others. Ada provides excellent support. For the font example, Ada would allow you to package all the font service routines into a single package. You could declare a few service routines to be public and have other routines that you used only within the package. You could restrict the definition of *Font* so that routines using ADT services wouldn't be allowed to operate on *Font*'s innards. They could declare *Font* data, but they wouldn't be able to operate on specific fields and would have no knowledge of how *Font* was structured.

In other languages—Pascal, C, Basic, and Fortran—you can package an ADT within a single source file, export some routines, and keep other routines private to varying degrees. C works well for ADTs because it always supports multiple source files (modules) and private routines. The ADT capabilities of the other languages depend on the capabilities of specific implementations. In other words, in other languages, your work won't necessarily be portable.

Regardless of how effectively you can hide routines in a given language, hiding data is problematic in all these languages. To extend the font example: If you declare a *Font* variable outside a service routine, you can operate on its innards anywhere that you can reference the variable. It is always an open record—which, unfortunately, often means it will be a broken record. The languages don't enforce closed records. Only discipline, programming standards, and painful memories of the sins of past indulgences will keep your records closed.

Key Points

- Properly structured data helps to make programs less complicated, easier to understand, and easier to maintain.

- Tables provide an alternative to complicated logic structures. If you find that you're confused by a program's logic, ask yourself whether you could simplify by using a lookup table.

- Abstract data types are a valuable tool for reducing complexity. They allow you to write your program in layers and to write the top layer in terms of the problem domain rather than in terms of computer-science, programming-language details.

13

Organizing Straight-Line Code

Contents

13.1 Statements That Must Be in a Specific Order
13.2 Statements Whose Order Doesn't Matter

Related Topics

General control topics: Chapter 17
Code with conditionals: Chapter 14
Code with loops: Chapter 15

THIS CHAPTER TURNS FROM a data-centered view of programming to a control-centered view. It introduces the simplest kind of control flow — putting statements and blocks of statements in sequential order.

Although organizing straight-line code is a relatively simple task, some subtleties of organization influence code quality, correctness, readability, and maintainability.

13.1 Statements That Must Be in a Specific Order

The easiest sequential statements to order are those in which the order counts. Here's an example:

Pascal Example of Statements in Which Order Counts

```
ReadData( Data );
CalculateResultsFromData( Data, Results );
PrintResults( Results );
```

Unless something mysterious is happening in this code fragment, the statements must be executed in the order shown. The data must be read before the results can be calculated, and the results must be calculated before they can be printed.

The underlying concept in this example is that of dependencies. The third statement depends on the second, the second on the first. In this example, the fact that one statement depends on another is obvious from the routine names. In the code fragment below, the dependencies are less obvious:

C Example of Statements in Which Order Counts, but Not Obviously

```
ComputeMonthlyRevenues( Revenues );
ComputeQuarterlyRevenues( Revenues );
ComputeAnnualRevenues( Revenues );
```

In this case, the quarterly revenue calculation assumes that the monthly revenues have already been calculated. A familiarity with accounting—or even common sense—might tell you that quarterly revenues have to be calculated before annual revenues. There is a dependency, but it's not obvious merely from reading the code. In the code fragment below, the dependencies aren't obvious—they're literally hidden:

Basic Example of Statements in Which Order Dependencies Are Hidden

```
CALL ComputeMarketingExpenses
CALL ComputeMISExpenses
CALL ComputeAccountingExpenses
CALL PrintExpenseSummary
```

Because the routine calls don't have any parameters, you might be able to guess that each of these routines accesses module or global data. Suppose that *ComputeMarketingExpenses()* initializes the global variable that all the other routines put their data into. In such a case, it needs to be called before the other routines, but you couldn't possibly determine that by reading the code in the example.

KEY POINT

When statements have dependencies that require you to put them in a certain order, take steps to make the dependencies clear. Here are some simple guidelines for ordering statements:

Organize code so that dependencies are obvious. In the Basic example presented above, *ComputeMarketingExpenses()* shouldn't initialize the global variable. The routine names suggest that *ComputeMarketingExpenses()* is

CROSS-REFERENCE
Some of the confusion surrounding the code in this
example arises from its use
of a global variable. For
details on using global data
effectively, see Section
10.6, "Global Variables."

similar to *ComputeMISExpenses()* and *ComputeAccountingExpenses()* except
that it works with marketing data rather than with MIS or accounting data.
Having *ComputeMarketingExpenses()* initialize the global variable is an arbitrary practice you should avoid. Why should initialization be done in that routine instead of one of the other two? Unless you can think of a good reason,
you should write another routine, *InitializeExpenseData()*, to initialize the
global variable. The routine's name is a clear indication that it should be called
before the other expense routines.

Name routines so that dependencies are obvious. In the example above,
ComputeMarketingExpenses() is misnamed because it does more than compute marketing expenses; it also initalizes global data. If you're opposed to
creating an additional routine to initialize the data, at least give *Compute-
MarketingExpenses()* a name that describes all the functions it performs. In
this case, *ComputeMarketingExpensesAndInitGlobalData()* would be an adequate name. You might say it's a terrible name because it's so long, but the
name describes what the routine does and is not terrible. The routine itself is
terrible.

CROSS-REFERENCE
For details on using rou-
tines and their parameters,
see Chapter 5, "Characteristics of High-Quality
Routines."

Use routine parameters to make dependencies obvious. In the example
above, since no data is passed between routines, you don't know whether any
of the routines use the same data. By rewriting the code so that data is passed
between the routines, you set up a clue that the execution order is important.
Here's how the code would look:

Basic Example of Data That Indicates an Order Dependency

```
CALL InitializeExpenseData( ExpenseData )
CALL ComputeMarketingExpenses( ExpenseData )
CALL ComputeMISExpenses( ExpenseData )
CALL ComputeAccountingExpenses( ExpenseData )
CALL PrintExpenseSummary( ExpenseData )
```

Because all the routines use *ExpenseData*, you have a hint that they might be
working on the same data and that the order of the statements might be important. The opposite is also true: Data can also indicate that execution order
isn't important. Here's an example:

Basic Example of Data That Doesn't Indicate an Order Dependency

```
CALL ComputeMarketingExpenses( MarketingData )
CALL ComputeMISExpenses( MISData )
CALL ComputeAccountingExpenses( AccountingData )
CALL PrintExpenseSummary( MarketingData, MISData, AccountingData )
```

Since the routines in the first three lines don't have any data in common, the code implies that the order in which they're called doesn't matter. Because the routine in the fourth line uses data from each of the first three routines, you can assume that it needs to be executed after the first three routines.

KEY POINT

Document unclear dependencies. Try first to write code without order dependencies. Try second to write code that makes dependencies obvious. If you're still concerned that an order dependency isn't explicit enough, document it. Documenting unclear dependencies is one aspect of documenting coding assumptions, which is critical to writing maintainable, modifiable code. In the Basic example, comments along these lines would be helpful:

Basic Example of Statements in Which Order Dependencies Are Hidden but Clarified with Comments

```
' Compute expense data. Each of the routines accesses the
' global data structure ExpenseData. ComputeMarketingExpenses
' should be called first because it initializes ExpenseData.
' PrintExpenseSummary should be called last because it uses
' data calculated by the other routines.

CALL ComputeMarketingExpenses
CALL ComputeMISExpenses
CALL ComputeAccountingExpenses
CALL PrintExpenseSummary
```

The code in this example doesn't use the techniques for making order dependencies obvious. It's better to rely on such techniques rather than on comments, but if you're maintaining tightly controlled code or you can't improve the code itself for some other reason, use documentation to compensate for code weaknesses.

13.2 Statements Whose Order Doesn't Matter

You might encounter cases in which it seems as if the order of a few statements or a few blocks of code doesn't matter at all. One statement doesn't depend on, or logically follow, another statement. But ordering affects readability, performance, and maintainability, and in the absence of execution-order dependencies, you can use secondary criteria to determine the order of statements or blocks of code. The guiding principle is the Principle of Proximity: *Keep related actions together.*

Making Code Read from Top to Bottom

FURTHER READING
You'll find this and other good advice in Kernighan and Plauger's *The Elements of Programming Style* (1978).

As a general principle, make the program read from top to bottom rather than jumping around. Experts agree that top-to-bottom order contributes most to readability. Simply making the control flow from top to bottom at run time isn't enough. If someone who is reading your code has to search the whole program to find needed information, you should reorganize the code. Here's an example:

C Example of Bad Code That Jumps Around

```
InitMarketingData( MarketingData );
InitMISData( MISData );
InitAccountingData( AccountingData );

ComputeQuarterlyAccountingData( AccountingData );
ComputeQuarterlyMISData( MISData );
ComputeQuarterlyMarketingData( MarketingData );

ComputeAnnualMISData( MISData );
ComputeAnnualMarketingData( MarketingData );
ComputeAnnualAccountingData( AccountingData );

PrintMISData( MISData );
PrintAccountingData( AccountingData );
PrintMarketingData( MarketingData );
```

Suppose that you want to determine how *MarketingData* is calculated. You have to start at the last line and track all references to *MarketingData* back to the first line. *MarketingData* is used in only two other places, but you have to keep in mind how *MarketingData* is used everywhere between the first and last references to it. In other words, you have to look at and think about every line of code in this fragment to figure out how *MarketingData* is calculated. Here's the same code with better organization:

C Example of Good, Sequential Code That Reads from Top to Bottom

```
InitMarketingData( MarketingData );
ComputeQuarterlyMarketingData( MarketingData );
ComputeAnnualMarketingData( MarketingData );
PrintMarketingData( MarketingData );

InitMISData( MISData );
ComputeQuarterlyMISData( MISData );
ComputeAnnualMISData( MISData );
PrintMISData( MISData );
```

(continued)

```
InitAccountingData( AccountingData );
ComputeQuarterlyAccountingData( AccountingData );
ComputeAnnualAccountingData( AccountingData );
PrintAccountingData( AccountingData );
```

CROSS-REFERENCE
A more technical definition
of "live" variables is given
in the section after the next.

This code is better in several ways. References to each variable are "localized"; they're kept close together. Values are assigned to variables close to where they're used. The number of lines of code in which the variables are "live" is small. And perhaps most important, the code now looks as if it could be broken into separate routines for marketing, MIS, and accounting data. The first code fragment gave no hint that such a decomposition was possible.

Localizing References to Variables

The code between references to a variable is a "window of vulnerability." In the window, new code might be added, inadvertently altering the variable, or someone reading the code might forget the value the variable is supposed to contain. It's always a good idea to localize references to variables by keeping them close together, as in the example above.

The idea of localizing references to a variable is pretty self-evident, but it's an idea that lends itself to formal measurement. One method of measuring how close together the references to a variable are is to compute the "span" of a variable. Here's an example:

Pascal Example of Variable Span

```
a := 0;
b := 0;
c := 0;
a := b + c;
```

In this case, two lines come between the first reference to a and the second, so a has a span of two. One line comes between the two references to b, so b has a span of one, and c has a span of zero. Here's another example:

Pascal Example of Spans of One and Zero

```
a := 0;
b := 0;
c := 0;
b := a + 1;
b := b / c;
```

FURTHER READING
For more information on
variable span, see *Software
Engineering Metrics and
Models* (Conte, Dunsmore,
and Shen 1986).

In this case, there is one line between the first reference to *b* and the second, for a span of one. There are no lines between the second reference to *b* and the third, for a span of zero.

The average span is computed by averaging the individual spans; in *b*'s case, (1+0)/2 equals an average span of 0.5. When you keep references to variables close together, you enable the person reading your code to focus on one section at a time. If the references are far apart, you force the reader to jump around in the program. Thus the main advantage of keeping references to variables together is that it improves program readability.

Keeping Variables Live for As Short a Time As Possible

A concept that's related to variable span is variable "live time," the total number of statements over which a variable is live. A variable's life begins at the first statement in which it's referenced; its life ends at the last statement in which it's referenced.

Unlike span, live time isn't affected by how many times the variable is used between the first and last times it's referenced. If the variable is first referenced on line 1 and last referenced on line 25, it has a live time of 25 statements. If those are the only two lines in which it's used, it has an average span of 23 statements. If the variable were used on every line from line 1 through line 25, it would have an average span of 0 statements, but it would still have a live time of 25 statements. Figure 13-1 on the next page illustrates both span and live time.

As with span, the goal with respect to live time is to keep the number low, to keep a variable live for as short a time as possible. And as with span, the basic advantage of maintaining a low number is that it reduces the window of vulnerability. You reduce the chance of incorrectly or inadvertently altering a variable between the places in which you intend to alter it.

A second advantage of keeping the live time short is that it gives you an accurate picture of your code. If a variable is assigned a value in line 10 and not used again until line 45, the very space between the two references implies that the variable is used between lines 10 and 45. If the variable is assigned a value in line 44 and used in line 45, no other uses of the variable are implied, and you can concentrate on a smaller section of code when you're thinking about that variable.

A short live time also reduces the chance of initialization errors. As you modify a program, straight-line code tends to turn into loops and you tend to forget initializations that were made far away from the loop. By keeping the initialization code and the loop code closer together, you reduce the chance that modifications will introduce initialization errors.

Finally, a short live time makes your code more readable. The fewer lines of code a reader has to keep in mind at once, the easier your code is to understand. Likewise, the shorter the live time, the less code you have to keep on your screen when you want to see all the references to a variable during editing and debugging.

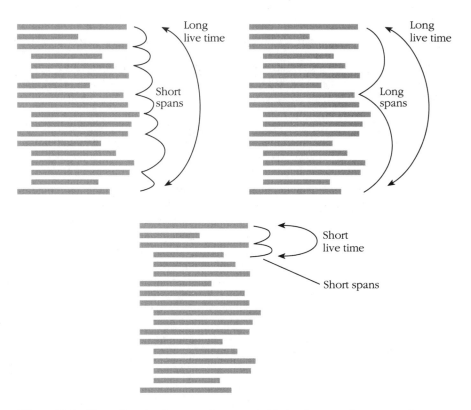

Figure 13-1. *"Long live time" means that a variable is alive over the course of many statements. "Short live time" means it's alive for only a few statements. "Span" refers to how close together the references to a variable are.*

Measuring the live time of a variable

You can formalize the concept of live time by counting the number of lines between the first and last references to a variable (including both the first and last lines). Here's an example with live times that are too long:

Pascal Example of Variables with Excessively Long Live Times

```
1    { initialize all variables }
2
3    RecordIndex := 0
4    Total       := 0
5    Done        := False
     ...
27   while ( RecordIndex < RecordCount ) do
28      begin
29         RecordIndex := RecordIndex + 1;
           ...

65   while not Done
        begin
        ...
70      if ( Total > ProjectedTotal )
71         Done := True;
```

Last reference to RecordIndex — line 28

Last reference to Total — line 70

Last reference to Done — line 71

Here are the live times for the variables in this example:

RecordIndex	(line 29 − line 3 + 1) = 27
Total	(line 70 − line 4 + 1) = 67
Done	(line 71 − line 5 + 1) = 67

Average Live Time   (27 + 67 + 67) / 3 ≈ 54

The example has been rewritten below so that the variable references are closer together:

Pascal Example of Variables with Good, Short Live Times

```
     ...
26   RecordIndex := 0
27   while ( RecordIndex < RecordCount ) do
28      begin
29         RecordIndex := RecordIndex + 1;
           ...

63   Total := 0
64   Done  := False
65   while not Done
        begin
        ...
70      if ( Total > ProjectedTotal )
71         Done := True;
```

Initialization of RecordIndex is moved down from line 3. — lines 26

Initializations of Total and Done are moved down from lines 4 and 5. — lines 63, 64

Here are the live times for the variables in this example:

RecordIndex	(line 29 − line 26 + 1) = 4
Total	(line 70 − line 63 + 1) = 8
Done	(line 71 − line 64 + 1) = 8
Average Live Time	(4 + 8 + 8) / 3 ≈ 7

FURTHER READING
For more information on "live" variables, see *Software Engineering Metrics and Models* (Conte, Dunsmore, and Shen 1986).

Intuitively, the second example seems better than the first because the initializations for the variables are performed closer to where the variables are used. The measured difference in average live time between the two examples is significant: An average of 54 vs. an average of 7 provides good quantitative support for the intuitive preference for the second piece of code.

Earlier in this section, the code fragment containing the *InitMarketingData()* routine was rearranged so that references to variables were closer together. That improved both the average span and the average live time of the code. How much? You can figure that out.

Does a hard number separate a good live time from a bad one? A good span from a bad one? Researchers haven't yet produced that quantitative data, but it's safe to assume that minimizing both span and live time is a good idea.

If you try to apply the ideas of span and live time to global variables, you'll find that global variables have enormous spans and live times—another good reason to avoid global variables.

Grouping Related Statements

CROSS-REFERENCE
If you follow the PDL-to-code process, your code will automatically be grouped into related statements. For details on the process, see Section 4.2, "PDL for Pros."

Put related statements together. They can be related because they operate on the same data, perform similar tasks, or depend on each other's being performed in order.

An easy way to test whether related statements are grouped well is to print out a listing of your routine and then draw boxes around the related statements. If the statements are ordered well, you'll get a picture like that shown in Figure 13-2, in which the boxes don't overlap.

If statements aren't ordered well—usually as a result of using *gotos*—you'll get a picture something like the one shown in Figure 13-3, in which the boxes do overlap. If you find that your boxes overlap, reorganize your code so that related statements are grouped better.

Figure 13-2. *If the code is well organized into groups, boxes drawn around related sections don't overlap. They might be nested.*

Figure 13-3. *If the code is organized poorly, boxes drawn around related sections overlap. It's hard to write this kind of code without using* gotos.

Once you've grouped related statements, you might find that they're strongly related and have no meaningful relationship to the statements that precede or follow them. In such a case, you might want to put the strongly related statements into their own routine.

——CHECKLIST——

Organizing Straight-Line Code

❏ Does the code make dependencies among statements obvious?

❏ Do the names of routines make dependencies obvious?

❏ Do parameters to routines make dependencies obvious?

❏ Do comments describe any dependencies that would otherwise be unclear?

❏ Does the code read from top to bottom?

❏ Are references to variables as close together as possible—both from each reference to a variable to the next and in total live time?

❏ Are related statements grouped together?

❏ Have relatively independent groups of statements been moved into their own routines?

Key Points

- The strongest principle for organizing straight-line code is order dependencies.

- Dependencies should be made obvious through the use of good routine names, parameter lists, and comments.

- If code doesn't have order dependencies, you should keep related statements as close together as possible—especially statements that work with the same variables.

14

Using Conditionals

Contents

Related Topics

A CONDITIONAL IS A STATEMENT that controls the execution of other statements; execution of the other statements is "conditioned" on statements such as *if*, *else*, *case*, and *switch*. Although it makes sense logically to refer to loop controls such as *while* and *for* as conditionals too, by convention they've been treated separately. Chapter 15, on loops, will examine *while* and *for* statements.

14.1 *if* Statements

Depending on the language you're using, you might be able to use any of several kinds of *if* statements. The simplest is the plain *if* or *if-then* statement. The *if-then-else* is a little more complex, and chains of *if-then-else-if* are the most complex.

If your language doesn't support structured *if-then-else* statements, you can emulate them using the techniques described in Section 17.6, "Emulating Structured Constructs with *goto*s." The suggestions in this chapter apply to the emulations as well as to the built-in statements.

Plain *if-then* Statements

Follow these guidelines when writing *if* statements:

KEY POINT

Write the nominal path through the code first; then write the exceptions.
Write your code so that the normal path through the code is clear. Make sure
that the exceptions don't obscure the normal path of execution. This is important for both readability and performance.

Make sure that you branch correctly on equality. Using > instead of >= or <
instead of <= is analogous to making an off-by-one error in accessing an array
or computing a loop index. In a loop, think through the endpoints to avoid an
off-by-one error. In a conditional statement, think through the equals case to
avoid an off-by-one error.

Put the normal case after the *if* rather than after the *else*. Put the case you
normally expect to process first. This is in line with the general principle of
putting code that results from a decision as close as possible to the decision.
Here's a code example that does a lot of error processing, haphazardly checking for errors along the way:

Basic Example of Code That Processes a Lot of Errors Haphazardly

```
                   OpenFile( InputFile, Status )
                   if Status = Error then
error case ────        ErrorType = FileOpenError
                   else
nominal case ────      ReadFile( InputFile, FileData, Status )
                       if Status = Success then
nominal case ────          SummarizeFileData( FileData, SummaryData, Status )
                           if Status = Error then
error case ────                ErrorType = DataSummaryError
                           else
nominal case ────              PrintSummary( SummaryData )
                               SaveSummaryData( SummaryData, Status )
                               if Status = Error then
error case ────                    ErrorType = SummarySaveError
                               else
nominal case ────                  UpdateAllAccounts
                                   EraseUndoFile
                                   ErrorType = None
                               end if
                           end if
                       else
error case ────            ErrorType = FileReadError
                       end if
                   end if
```

This code is hard to follow because the nominal cases and the error cases are all mixed together. It's hard to find the path that is normally taken through the code. In addition, because the error conditions are sometimes processed in the *if* clause rather than the *else* clause, it's hard to figure out which *if* test the normal case goes with. In the rewritten code below, the normal path is consistently coded first, and all the exceptions are coded last. This makes it easier to find and read the nominal case.

Basic Example of Code That Processes a Lot of Errors Systematically

```
                     OpenFile( InputFile, Status )
                     if Status <> Error then
                        ReadFile( InputFile, FileData, Status )
nominal case ———        if Status = Success then
nominal case ———           SummarizeFileData( FileData, SummaryData, Status )
                           if Status <> Error then
                              PrintSummary( SummaryData )
nominal case ———              SaveSummaryData( SummaryData, Status )
                              if Status <> Error then
                                 UpdateAllAccounts
nominal case ———                 EraseUndoFile
                                 ErrorType = None
                              else
                                 ErrorType = SummarySaveError
error case ———                end if
                           else
                              ErrorType = DataSummaryError
error case ———             end if
                        else
                           ErrorType = FileReadError
error case ———          end if
                     else
                        ErrorType = FileOpenError
error case ———       end if
```

In the revised example, you can read the main flow of the *if* tests to find the normal case. The revision puts the focus on reading the main flow rather than on wading through the exceptions. The code is easier to read overall. The stack of error conditions at the bottom of the nest is a sign of well-written error-processing code.

Follow the *if* clause with a meaningful statement. Sometimes you see code like the next example, in which the *if* clause is null.

C Example of a Null *if* Clause

```
if ( SomeTest )
    ;
else
    {
    /* do something */
    ...
    }
```

CROSS-REFERENCE
One key to writing an effective *if* statement is writing the right boolean expression to control it. For details on using boolean expressions effectively, see Section 17.1, "Boolean Expressions."

Most experienced programmers would avoid code like this if only to avoid the work of coding the extra null line and the *else* line. It looks silly and is easily improved by negating the predicate in the *if* statement, moving the code from the *else* clause to the *if* clause, and eliminating the *else* clause. Here's how the code would look after such a change:

C Example of a Converted Null *if* Clause

```
if ( ! SomeTest )
    {
    /* do something */
    ...
    }
```

HARD DATA

Consider the *else* clause. If you think you need a plain *if* statement, consider whether you don't actually need an *if-then-else* statement. In a General Motors analysis of code written in PL/I, only 17 percent of *if* statements had an *else* clause. Further analysis of the code showed that 50 to 80 percent should have had one (Elshoff 1976).

One option is to code the *else* clause—with a null statement if necessary—to show that the *else* case has been considered (Van Tassel 1978, Myers 1976). Coding null *else*s just to show that that case has been considered might be overkill, but at the very least, take the *else* case into account. When you have an *if* test without an *else*, unless the reason is obvious, use comments to explain why the *else* clause isn't necessary. Here's an example:

Pascal Example of a Helpful, Commented *else* Clause

```
{ if color is valid }

if ( Min.Color <= Color and Color <= Max.Color )
    begin
    { do something }
    ...
    end;
{ else color is invalid }
    { screen not written to -- safely ignore command }
```

Test the *else* clause for correctness. When testing your code, you might think that the main clause, the *if*, is all that needs to be tested. If it's possible to test the *else* clause, however, be sure to do that.

Check for reversal of the *if* and *else* clauses. A common mistake in programming *if-then*s is to flip-flop the code that's supposed to follow the *if* clause and the code that's supposed to follow the *else* clause or to get the logic of the *if* test backward. Check your code for this common error.

Chains of *if-then-else* Statements

In languages that don't support *case* statements—or that support them only partially—you will often find yourself writing chains of *if-then-else* tests. For example, the code to categorize a character might use a chain like this one:

CROSS-REFERENCE
For more details on simplifying complicated expressions, see Section 17.1, "Boolean Expressions."

C Example of Using an *if-then-else* Chain to Categorize a Character

```
if ( InputChar < SPACE )
   CharType = ControlChar;
else if ( InputChar == ' ' || InputChar == ',' || InputChar == '.' ||
          InputChar == '!' || InputChar == '(' || InputChar == ')' ||
          InputChar == ':' || InputChar == ';' || InputChar == '?' ||
          InputChar == '-' )
   CharType = Punctuation;
else if ( '0' <= InputChar && InputChar <= '9' )
   CharType = Digit;
else if ( ('a' <= InputChar && InputChar <= 'z') ||
          ('A' <= InputChar && InputChar <= 'Z') )
   CharType = Letter;
```

Here are some guidelines to follow when writing such *if-then-else* chains:

Simplify complicated tests with boolean function calls. One reason the code above is hard to read is that the tests that categorize the character are complicated. To improve readability, you can replace them with calls to boolean functions. Here's how the code above looks when the tests are replaced with boolean functions:

C Example of an *if-then-else* Chain That Uses Boolean Function Calls

```
if ( IsControl( InputChar ) )
   CharType = ControlChar;
else if ( IsPunctuation( InputChar ) )
   CharType = Punctuation;
else if ( IsDigit( InputChar ) )
   CharType = Digit;
else if ( IsLetter( InputChar ) )
   CharType = Letter;
```

Put the most common cases first. By putting the most common cases first, you minimize the amount of exception-handling code someone has to read to find the usual cases. You improve efficiency because you minimize the number of tests the code does to find the most common cases. In the example above, letters would be more common than punctuation but the test for punctuation is made first. Here's the code revised so that it tests for letters first:

C Example of Testing the Most Common Case First

This test, ⎯
the most common,
is now done first.

```
if ( IsLetter( InputChar ) )
    CharType = Letter;
else if ( IsPunctuation( InputChar ) )
    CharType = Punctuation;
else if ( IsDigit( InputChar ) )
    CharType = Digit;
else if ( IsControl( InputChar ) )
    CharType = ControlChar;
```

This test, ⎯
the least common,
is now done last.

Make sure that all cases are covered. Code a final *else* clause with an error message to catch cases you didn't plan for. This error message is intended for you rather than for the user, so word it appropriately. Here's how you can modify the character-classification example to perform an "other cases" test:

CROSS-REFERENCE
This is also a good example of how you can use a chain of *if-then-else* tests instead of deeply nested code. For details on this technique, see Section 17.4, "Taming Dangerously Deep Nesting."

C Example of Using the Default Case to Trap Errors

```
if ( IsLetter( InputChar ) )
    CharType = Letter;
else if ( IsPunctuation( InputChar ) )
    CharType = Punctuation;
else if ( IsDigit( InputChar ) )
    CharType = Digit;
else if ( IsControl( InputChar ) )
    CharType = ControlChar;
else
    PrintMsg( "Internal Error: Unexpected type of character detected." );
```

Replace *if-then-else* chains with other constructs if your language supports them. A few languages—Ada, for example—support *case* statements that are sophisticated enough to replace most *if-then-else* chains. Use them. They are easier to code and easier to read than *if-then-else* chains. Here's how the code for classifying character types would be written using a *case* statement in Ada:

Ada Example of Using a *case* Statement Instead of an *if-then-else* Chain

```
case InputChar is
   when 'a'..'z' | 'A'..'Z' =>
      CharType := Letter;
   when ' ' | ',' | '.' | '!' | '(' | ')' | ':' | ';' | '?' | '-' =>
      CharType := Punctuation;
   when '0'..'9' =>
      CharType := Digit;
   when nul..us =>
      CharType := ControlChar;
   others =>
      PUT_LINE( "Internal Error: Unexpected type of character detected." );
end case;
```

14.2   *case* Statements

The *case* or *switch* statement is a construct that varies a great deal from language to language. Many versions of Basic don't support *case* at all. C supports *case* only for ordinal types taken one value at a time. Pascal supports *case* only for ordinal types, including ranges of data. Ada supports *case* for ordinal types and has powerful shorthand notations for expressing ranges and combinations of values.

Large *case* statements are common in programming for the Apple Macintosh and Microsoft Windows environments. The *case* statement is being used with increasing frequency as highly interactive, event-driven programs become more common. The following sections present guidelines for using *case* statements effectively.

Choosing the Most Effective Ordering of Cases

You can choose from among a variety of ways to organize the cases in a *case* statement. If you have a small *case* statement with three options and three corresponding lines of code, the order you use doesn't matter much. If you have a long *case* statement—for example, a *case* statement in an event-driven program—order is significant. Here are some ordering possibilities:

Order cases alphabetically or numerically. If cases are equally important, putting them in A-B-C order improves readability. A specific case is easy to pick out of the group.

Put the normal case first. If you have one normal case and several exceptions, put the normal case first. Indicate with comments that it's the normal case and that the others are exceptions.

Order cases by frequency. Put the most frequently executed cases first and the least frequently executed last. This approach has two advantages. First, human readers can find the most common cases easily. Readers scanning the list for a specific case are likely to be interested in one of the most common cases. Putting the common ones at the top of the code makes the search quicker. Second, machine execution is faster. Each case represents a test that the machine performs at run time. If you have 12 cases and the last one is the one that needs to be executed, the machine executes the equivalent of 12 *if* tests before it finds the right one. By putting the common cases first, you reduce the number of tests the machine must perform and thus improve the efficiency of your code.

Tips for Using *case* Statements

Here are several tips for using *case* statements:

Keep the actions of each case simple. Keep the code associated with each case short. Short code following each case helps make the structure of the *case* statement clear. If the actions performed for a case are complicated, write a routine and call the routine from the case rather than putting the code into the case itself.

Don't make up phony variables in order to be able to use the *case* statement. A *case* statement should be used for simple data that's easily categorized. If your data isn't simple, use chains of *if-then-else*s instead. Phony variables are confusing, and you should avoid them. Here's an example of what not to do:

CODING HORROR

Pascal Example of Creating a Phony *case* Variable—Bad Practice

```
Action := UserCommand[ 1 ];
case Action of
   'c':  Copy;
   'd':  DeleteCharacter;
   'f':  Format;
   'h':  Help;
   ...
   else  PrintErrorMsg( 'Error: Invalid command.' );
end; { case }
```

The variable that controls the *case* statement is *Action*. In this case, *Action* is created by peeling off the first character of the *UserCommand* string, a string that was entered by the user.

CROSS-REFERENCE
In contrast to this advice,
sometimes you can improve
readability by assigning a
complicated expression to
a well-named boolean
variable. For details, see
"Making Expressions
Simple" in Section 17.1.

This troublemaking code is from the wrong side of town and invites problems. In general, when you manufacture a variable to use in a *case* statement, the real data might not map onto the *case* statement the way you want it to. In this example, if the user types "copy," the *case* statement peels off the first "c" and correctly calls the *Copy()* routine. On the other hand, if the user types "cement overshoes," "clambake," or "cellulite," the *case* statement also peels off the "c" and calls *Copy()*. The test for an erroneous command in the *case* statement's *else* clause won't work very well because it will miss only erroneous first letters rather than erroneous commands.

This code should use a chain of *if-then-else-if* tests to check the whole string rather than making up a phony variable. A virtuous rewrite of the code looks like this:

Pascal Example of Using *If-then-elses* Instead of a Phony *case* Variable— Good Practice

```
if ( UserCommand = 'copy' ) then
    Copy
else if ( UserCommand = 'delete' ) then
    DeleteCharacter
else if ( UserCommand = 'format' ) then
    Format
else if ( UserCommand = 'help' ) then
    Help
...
else
    PrintErrorMsg( 'Error: Invalid command.' );
```

Use the default clause only to detect legitimate defaults. You might sometimes have only one case remaining and decide to code that case as the default clause. Though sometimes tempting, that's dumb. You lose the automatic documentation provided by *case*-statement labels, and you lose the ability to detect errors with the default clause.

Such *case* statements break down under modification. If you use a legitimate default, adding a new case is trivial—you just add the case and the corresponding code. If you use a phony default, the modification is more difficult. You have to add the new case, possibly making it the new default, and then change the case previously used as the default so that it's a legitimate case. Use a legimate default in the first place.

Use the default clause to detect errors. If the default clause in a *case* statement isn't being used for other processing and isn't supposed to occur, put a diagnostic message in it. An example follows, on the next page.

Pascal Example of Using the Default Case to Detect Errors—Good Practice

```
case Letter of
   'a':  PrintArchives;
   'p':  { no action required, but case was considered }
         ;
   'q':  PrintQuarterlyReport;
   's':  PrintSummary;
   else  PrintErrorMsg( 'Internal Error 905: Call customer assistance.' );
end; { case }
```

Messages like this are useful in both debugging and production code. Most users prefer a message like "Internal Error: Please call customer support" to a system crash—or worse, subtly incorrect results that look right until the user's boss checks them.

If the default clause is used for some purpose other than error detection, the implication is that every case selector is correct. Double-check to be sure that every value that could possibly enter the *case* statement would be legitimate. If you come up with some that wouldn't be legitimate, rewrite the statements so that the default clause will check for errors.

In C, avoid dropping through the end of a case. C is the only common high-level language that doesn't automatically break out of each case. Instead, you have to code the end of each case explicitly. If you don't code the end of a case, the program drops through the end and executes the code for the next case. This can lead to some particularly egregious coding practices, including the following horrible example:

CODING HORROR

CROSS-REFERENCE
This code's formatting makes it look better than it is. For details on how to use formatting to make good code look good and bad code look bad, see "Endline Layout" in Section 18.3 and the rest of Chapter 18.

C Example of Abusing the *case* Statement

```
switch ( InputVar )
   {
   case( 'A' ): if ( test )
                   {
                   /* statement 1 */
                   /* statement 2 */
   case( 'B' ):    /* statement 3 */
                   /* statement 4 */
                   ...
                   } /* if ( test ) */
                ...
                break;
   ...
   }
```

This practice is bad because it intermingles control constructs. Nested control constructs are hard enough to understand; overlapping constructs are all but impossible. Modifications of case *'A'* or case *'B'* will be harder than brain surgery, and it's likely that the cases will need to be cleaned up before any modifications will work. You might as well do it right the first time. In general, it's a good idea to avoid dropping through the end of a *case* statement.

In C, clearly and unmistakably identify flow-throughs at the end of a *case* statement. If you intentionally write code to drop through the end of a case, comment the place at which it happens and explain why it needs to be coded that way.

CHECKLIST

Conditionals

IF-THEN STATEMENTS

❑ Is the nominal path through the code clear?

❑ Do *if-then* tests branch correctly on equality?

❑ Is the *else* clause present and documented?

❑ Is the *else* clause correct?

❑ Are the *if* and *else* clauses used correctly—not reversed?

❑ Does the normal case follow the *if* rather than the *else*?

IF-THEN-ELSE-IF CHAINS

❑ Are complicated tests encapsulated in boolean function calls?

❑ Are the most common cases tested first?

❑ Are all cases covered?

❑ Is the *if-then-else-if* chain the best implementation—better than a *case* statement?

CASE STATEMENTS

❑ Are cases ordered meaningfully?

❑ Are the actions for each case simple—calling other routines if necessary?

❑ Does the *case* statement test a real variable, not a phony one that's made up solely to use and abuse the *case* statement?

❑ Is the use of the default clause legitimate?

❑ Is the default clause used to detect and report unexpected cases?

❑ In C, does the end of each case have a *break*?

Key Points

- Pay attention to the order of *if*s and *else*s, especially if they process a lot of errors. Make sure the nominal case is clear.
- Order *if-then-else* chains and cases in *case* statements for maximum readability.
- Use the default clause in a *case* statement or the last *else* in a chain of *if-then-else*s to trap errors.
- All control constructs are not created equal. Choose the control construct that's most appropriate for each section of code.

15

Controlling Loops

Contents

15.1 Selecting the Kind of Loop
15.2 Controlling the Loop
15.3 Creating Loops Easily—from the Inside Out
15.4 Correspondence Between Loops and Arrays

Related Topics

General control topics: Chapter 17
Straight-line code: Chapter 13
Code with conditionals: Chapter 14

"LOOP" IS AN INFORMAL TERM that refers to any kind of iterative control structure—any structure that causes a program to repeatedly execute a block of code. Common loop types are *FOR-NEXT* in Basic, *DO* in Fortran, *while-do* and *for* in Pascal, *while* and *for* in C, and *loop* in Ada. Using loops is one of the most complex aspects of programming in a procedural language; knowing how and when to use each kind of loop is a decisive factor in constructing high-quality software.

15.1 Selecting the Kind of Loop

In most languages, you'll use several kinds of loops.

- The counted loop is performed a specific number of times, perhaps one time for each employee.

- The continuously evaluated loop doesn't know ahead of time how many times it will be executed and tests whether it has finished on each iteration. It runs while money remains, until the user selects quit, or until it encounters an error.

- The endless loop executes forever once it has started. It's the kind you find in embedded systems such as pacemakers, microwave ovens, and cruise controls.

The kinds of loops are differentiated first by flexibility—whether the loop executes a specified number of times or whether it tests for completion on each iteration.

The kinds of loops are also differentiated by the location of the test for completion. You can put the test at the beginning, the middle, or the end of the loop. This characteristic tells you whether the loop executes at least once. If the loop is tested at the beginning, its body isn't necessarily executed. If the loop is tested at the end, its body is executed at least once. If the loop is tested in the middle, the part of the loop that precedes the test is executed at least once, but the part of the loop that follows the test isn't necessarily executed at all.

Flexibility and the location of the test determine the kind of loop to choose as a control structure. Table 15-1 shows the kinds of loops in several languages and describes each loop's flexibility and test location.

Table 15-1. The Kinds of Loops

Language	Kind of Loop	Flexibility	Test Location
Ada	*for*	rigid	beginning
	while	flexible	beginning
	loop-with-*exit*	flexible	usually the middle
	loop	n/a	none (used for embedded systems)
Basic	*FOR-NEXT*	rigid	beginning
	WHILE-WEND	flexible	beginning
	DO-LOOP	flexible	beginning or end
C	*do-while*	flexible	end
	for	flexible	beginning
	while	flexible	beginning
Fortran	*DO*	rigid	beginning
Pascal	*for*	rigid	beginning
	repeat-until	flexible	end
	while	flexible	beginning

When to Use a *while* Loop

Novice programmers sometimes think that a *while* loop is continuously evaluated and that it terminates the instant the *while* condition becomes false, regardless of which statement in the loop is being executed (Curtis et al. 1986). Although it's not quite that flexible, a *while* loop is a flexible loop choice. If you don't know ahead of time exactly how many times you'll want the loop to iterate, use a *while* loop. Contrary to what some novices think, the test for the loop exit is performed only once each time through the loop, and the main issue with respect to *while* loops is deciding whether to test at the beginning or the end of the loop.

Loop with test at the beginning

For a loop that tests at the beginning, you can use a *while* loop in C, Basic, Pascal, and Ada, and you can emulate a *while* loop in Fortran, assembler, and other languages.

A loop that is tested at its beginning is the preferred kind of *while* loop. Some researchers advocate always using this kind unless it's impossible to do so (Plum 1984, Jackson 1975). The value of following such a recommendation is that you minimize the kinds of control structures the reader of your code has to understand. If you use one kind of loop primarily, a reader develops a sensitivity to your style of coding it. If you use several kinds of loops, you place higher demands on your reader and yourself—forcing the reader to become familiar with more styles and yourself to be consistent in several styles.

Loop with test at the end

You might occasionally have a situation in which you want a flexible loop but the loop needs to execute at least one time. In such a case, you can use a *while* loop that is tested at its end. You can use *do-while* in C, *repeat-until* in Pascal, *DO-LOOP-WHILE* in Basic, or an appropriately constructed *loop*-with-*exit* in Ada. You can emulate end-tested loops in Fortran, assembler, and other languages.

This is another area in which you can do readers of your code a favor. One strength of C's looping structure is that the *while* loop and the *do-while* loop use the same test. The only difference between the two kinds of loops is that *while* tests at the beginning and *do-while* tests at the end. Pascal's *while* loop and *repeat-until* loop have two differences. As in C, the *while* loop tests at the beginning and the *repeat-until* loop tests at the end. The quirkier difference is that the *repeat-until* condition is logically backward from the equivalent *while* condition. If the *while* condition were *while not done*, the *repeat-until* condition would be *repeat until done*. This difference is more confusing than the difference in test location, and it's a good reason to use the test-at-the-beginning *while* loop as much as possible.

When to Use a loop-with-exit Loop

A loop-with-exit loop is a loop in which the exit condition appears in the middle of the loop rather than at the beginning or at the end. The *loop-with-exit* loop is available explicitly in Ada, and you can emulate it with the structured constructs *while* and *break* in C or with *goto*s in other languages.

Normal loop-with-exit loops

A loop-with-exit loop usually consists of the loop beginning, the loop body including an exit condition, and the loop end, as in this Ada example:

Ada Example of a Generic *loop-with-exit* Loop

```
loop
   ...
   exit when ( some exit condition );
   ...
end loop;
```

Statements — `...`
More statements — `exit when ( some exit condition );`

The typical use of a loop-with-exit loop is for the case in which testing at the beginning or at the end of the loop requires coding a loop-and-a-half. Here's a C example of a case that warrants a loop-with-exit loop but doesn't use one:

C Example of Duplicated Code That Will Break Down Under Maintenance (A Place to Use a loop-with-exit Loop)

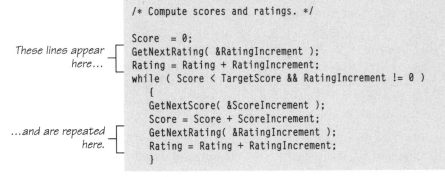

```
/* Compute scores and ratings. */

Score = 0;
GetNextRating( &RatingIncrement );
Rating = Rating + RatingIncrement;
while ( Score < TargetScore && RatingIncrement != 0 )
   {
   GetNextScore( &ScoreIncrement );
   Score = Score + ScoreIncrement;
   GetNextRating( &RatingIncrement );
   Rating = Rating + RatingIncrement;
   }
```

These lines appear here... ⎡ `GetNextRating( &RatingIncrement );` / `Rating = Rating + RatingIncrement;`

...and are repeated here. ⎡ `GetNextRating( &RatingIncrement );` / `Rating = Rating + RatingIncrement;`

The two lines of code at the top of this example are repeated in the last two lines of code of the *while* loop. During modification, you can easily forget to keep the two sets of lines parallel. Another programmer modifying the code probably won't even realize that the two sets of lines are supposed to be modified in parallel. Either way, the result will be errors arising from incomplete modifications. Here's how you can rewrite the code more clearly:

CROSS-REFERENCE
The *FOREVER* macro used at the top of this loop is equivalent to *for(;;)* and is described later in this chapter.

C Example of a loop-with-exit Loop That's Easier to Maintain

```
/* Compute scores and ratings. The loop uses a FOREVER macro
   and a break statement to emulate a loop-with-exit loop. */

Score = 0;
FOREVER
   {
   GetNextRating( &RatingIncrement );
   Rating = Rating + RatingIncrement;

   if ( ! (Score < TargetScore && RatingIncrement != 0) )
      break;

   GetNextScore( &ScoreIncrement );
   Score = Score  + ScoreIncrement;
   }
```

*This is the loop-exit ——
condition.*

Here's how the same code is written in Ada:

Ada Example of a *loop*-with-*exit* Loop

```
-- Compute scores and ratings

Score := 0;
loop
   GetNextRating( RatingIncrement );
   Rating := Rating + RatingIncrement;

   exit when ( not ( Score < TargetScore and RatingIncrement /= 0 ) );

   GetNextScore( ScoreIncrement );
   Score := Score + ScoreIncrement;
end loop;
```

Here are a couple of fine points to consider when you use this kind of loop:

CROSS-REFERENCE
Details on exit conditions are presented later in the chapter. For details on using comments with loops, see "Commenting Control Structures" in Section 19.5.

- Put all the exit conditions in one place. Spreading them around practically guarantees that one exit condition or another will be overlooked during debugging, modification, or testing.

- Use comments for clarification. If you use the loop-with-exit loop technique in a language that doesn't support it directly—in virtually any language other than Ada—use comments to make what you're doing clear.

The loop-with-exit loop is a one-entry, one-exit, structured control construct, and it is the preferred kind of loop control in Ada programming (Software Productivity Consortium 1989). It has been shown to be easier to understand

HARD DATA

than other kinds of loops. A study of student programmers compared this kind of loop with those that exited at either the top or the bottom (Soloway, Bonar, and Ehrlich 1983). Students scored 25 percent higher on a test of comprehension when loop-with-exit loops were used, and the authors of the study concluded that the loop-with-exit structure more closely models the way people think about iterative control than other loop structures do.

The loop-with-exit loop isn't widely used yet. The jury is still locked in a smoky room arguing about whether it's a good practice. Until the jury is in, the loop-with-exit is a good technique to have in your programmer's toolbox—as long as you use it carefully.

Abnormal loop-with-exit loops

Another kind of loop-with-exit loop that's used to avoid a loop-and-a-half is shown here:

CODING HORROR

C Example of Entering the Middle of a Loop with a *goto*—Bad Practice

```
goto Start;
while ( expression )
    {
    /* do something */
    ...

    Start:

    /* do something else */
    ...
    }
```

At first glance, this seems to be similar to the previous loop-with-exit examples. It's used in situations in which /* *do something* */ doesn't need to be executed at the first pass through the loop but /* *do something else* */ does. It's a one-in, one-out control construct: The only way into the loop is through the *goto* at the top; the only way out of the loop is through the *while* test. This approach has two problems: It uses a *goto,* and it's unusual enough to be confusing.

CROSS-REFERENCE
For details on emulating structured constructs with *goto*s, see Section 17.6, "Emulating Structured Constructs with *goto*s."

In C, you can accomplish the same effect without using a *goto,* as demonstrated in the following example. If the language you're using doesn't support a *break* or *leave* command, you can emulate one with a *goto.*

C Example of Code Rewritten Without a *goto*—Better Practice

```
FOREVER
  {
  /* do something else */
  ...

  if ( ! ( expression ) )
     break;

  /* do something */
  ...
  }
```

The blocks before and after the break have been switched.

When to Use a *for* Loop

A *for* loop is a good choice when you need a loop that executes a specified number of times. You can use *for* in C, Pascal, Basic, and Ada or *DO* in Fortran.

Use *for* loops for simple activities that don't require internal loop controls. The point of a *for* loop is that you set it up at the top of the loop and then forget about it. You don't have to do anything inside the loop to control it. If you have a condition under which execution has to jump out of a loop, use a *while* loop instead.

Likewise, don't explicitly change the index value of a *for* loop to force it to terminate. Use a *while* loop instead. The *for* loop is for simple uses. Most complicated looping tasks are better handled by a *while* loop.

15.2 Controlling the Loop

What can go wrong with a loop? Any answer would have to include at the very least incorrect or omitted loop initialization, omitted initialization of accumulators or other variables related to the loop, improper nesting, incorrect termination of the loop, forgetting to increment a loop variable or incrementing the variable incorrectly, and indexing an array element from a loop index incorrectly.

KEY POINT

You can forestall these problems by observing two practices. First, minimize the number of factors that affect the loop. Simplify! Simplify! Simplify! Second, treat the inside of the loop as if it were a routine—keep as much of the control as possible outside the loop. Explicitly state the conditions under which the body of the loop is to be executed. Don't make the reader look inside the loop to understand the loop control. Think of a loop as a black box: The surrounding program knows the control conditions but not the contents.

CROSS-REFERENCE
If you use the *FOREVER-break* technique described earlier, the exit condition is inside the black box. Even if you use only one exit condition, you lose the benefit of treating the loop as a black box.

C Example of Treating a Loop as a Black Box

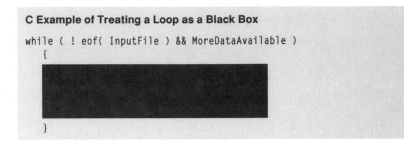

```
while ( ! eof( InputFile ) && MoreDataAvailable )
   {

   }
```

What are the conditions under which this loop terminates? Clearly, all you know is that either *eof(InputFile)* becomes true or *MoreDataAvailable* becomes false.

Entering the Loop

Here are several guidelines for entering a loop:

Enter the loop from one location only. A variety of loop-control structures allows you to test at the beginning, middle, or end of a loop. These structures are rich enough to allow you to enter the loop from the top every time. You don't need to enter at multiple locations.

Put initialization code directly before the loop. The Principle of Proximity advocates putting related statements together. If related statements are strewn across a routine, it's easy to overlook them during modification and to make the modifications incorrectly. If related statements are kept together, it's easier to avoid errors during modification.

Keep loop-initialization statements with the loop they're related to. If you don't, you're more likely to cause errors when you generalize the loop into a bigger loop and forget to modify the initialization code. The same kind of error can occur when you move or copy the loop code into a different routine without moving or copying its initialization code. Putting initializations away from the loop—in the data-declaration section or in a housekeeping section at the top of the routine that contains the loop—invites initialization troubles.

In C, use the *FOREVER* macro for infinite loops and event loops. You might have a loop that runs without terminating—for example, a loop in firmware such as a pacemaker or a microwave oven. Or you might have a loop that terminates only in response to an event—an "event loop." You could code an infinite loop in several ways, but the following macro is the standard way to code one in C:

C Example of an Infinite Loop

```
#define FOREVER    for (;;)
...
FOREVER
   {
   ...
   }
```

Here's the infinite ——
loop.

In Pascal, use the *while (True)* construct for infinite loops and event loops. If you want the loop to terminate under some condition, you'll have to use *goto* or *exit* to leave the loop in Pascal. In this case, one *goto* or one *exit* would be a defensible structured programming construct because it would allow the loop to have exactly one exit, supporting the one-in, one-out requirement of structured programming. Here's the standard way to set up an infinite loop in Pascal:

Pascal Example of an Infinite Loop

```
while ( True )
   begin
   { infinite loop }
   ...
   end;
```

This technique and the one suggested for C are the standard ways to implement infinite loops and event loops. Faking an infinite loop with a statement like *for i := 1 to 9999* is making a poor substitution because using loop limits muddies the intent of the loop—maybe *9999* is a legitimate value. Such a fake infinite loop can also break down under maintenance.

In C, prefer *for* loops when they're appropriate. The C *for* loop is one of the language's powerful constructs. Not only is it flexible, but it packages loop-control code in one place, which makes for readable loops. One mistake programmers commonly make when modifying software is changing the loop-initialization code at the top of a loop but forgetting to change related code at the bottom. In a C *for* loop, all the relevant code is together at the top of the loop, which makes correct modifications easier. If you can use the *for* loop appropriately in C instead of another kind of loop, do it.

Don't use a *for* loop when a *while* loop is more appropriate. A common abuse of C's flexible *for* loop is haphazardly cramming the contents of a *while* loop into a *for* loop header. The following example shows a *while* loop crammed into a *for* loop header.

C Example of a *while* Loop Abusively Crammed into a *for* Loop Header

```
/* read all the records from a file */

for ( rewind( InFile ), RecCount = 0; ! feof( InFile ); RecCount++ )
    {
    fgets( InputRec[ RecCount ], MAX_CHARS, InFile );
    }
```

The advantage of C's *for* loop over *for* loops in other languages is that it's more flexible about the kinds of initialization and termination information it can use. The weakness inherent in such flexibility is that you can put statements into the loop header that have nothing to do with controlling the loop.

Reserve the *for* loop header for loop-control statements—statements that initialize the loop, terminate it, or move it toward termination. In the example above, the *fgets()* statement in the body of the loop moves the loop toward termination, but the *RecCount* statements don't; they're housekeeping statements that don't control the loop's progress. Putting the *RecCount* statements in the loop header and leaving the *fgets()* statement out is misleading; it creates the false impression that *RecCount* controls the loop.

If you want to use the *for* loop rather than the *while* loop in this case, put the loop-control statements in the loop header and leave everything else out. Here's the right way to use the loop header:

C Example of Logical if Unconventional Use of a *for* Loop Header

```
RecCount = 0;
for ( rewind( InFile );
      ! feof( InFile );
      fgets( InputRec[ RecCount-1 ], MAX_CHARS, InFile ))
    {
    RecCount++;
    }
```

The contents of the loop header in this example are all related to control of the loop. The *rewind()* statement initializes the loop; the *feof()* statement tests whether the loop has finished; and the *fgets()* statement moves the loop toward termination. The statements that affect *RecCount* don't directly move the loop toward termination and are appropriately not included in the loop header. The *while* loop is probably still more appropriate for this job, but at least this code uses the loop header logically. For the record, here's how the code looks when it uses a *while* loop:

C Example of Appropriate Use of a *while* Loop

```c
/* read all the records from a file */

rewind( InFile );
RecCount = 0;
while ( ! feof( InFile ) )
   {
   fgets( InputRec[ RecCount ], MAX_CHARS, InFile );
   RecCount++;
   }
```

Processing the Middle of the Loop

Here are several guidelines for handling the middle of a loop:

Use *begin* and *end* or *{* and *}* to enclose the statements in a loop. Use code brackets every time if you have a tendency to forget them. They don't cost anything in space or speed at run time, and they don't hurt readability. If they give you extra assurance that your program works, use them.

Avoid empty loops. In C, it's possible to create an empty loop, one in which the work the loop is doing is coded on the same line as the test that checks whether the work is finished. Here's an example:

C Example of an Empty Loop

```c
while ( (InputChar = getch()) != '\n' )
   ;
```

In this example, the loop is empty because the *while* expression includes two things: the work of the loop—*InputChar = getch()*—and a test for whether the loop should terminate—*InputChar != '\n'*. The loop would be clearer if it were recoded so that the work it does is evident to the reader. Here's how the revised loop would look:

C Example of an Empty Loop Converted to an Occupied Loop

```c
do
   InputChar = getch();
while ( InputChar != '\n' );
```

The new code takes up three full lines rather than one line and a semicolon, which is appropriate since it does the work of three lines rather than that of one line and a semicolon.

Keep loop-housekeeping chores at either the beginning or the end of the loop. "Housekeeping" chores are expressions like $i := i + 1$, expressions whose main purpose isn't to do the work of the loop but to control the loop. Here's an example in which the housekeeping is done at the end of the loop:

Pascal Example of Housekeeping Statements at the End of a Loop

```
StringIdx := 1;
TtlLength := 0;
while not eof( InputFile ) do
   begin

   { do the work of the loop }

   ReadString( InputFile, StringIdx, Str );
   ...

   { prepare for next pass through the loop--housekeeping }

   StringIdx := StringIdx + 1;
   TtlLength := TtlLength + Length( Str )

   end;
```

Here are the housekeeping statements.

As a general rule, the variables you initialize before the loop are the variables you'll manipulate in the housekeeping part of the loop.

Make each loop perform only one function. The mere fact that a loop can be used to do two things at once isn't sufficient justification for doing them together. Loops should be like routines in that each one should do only one thing and do it well. If it seems inefficient to use two loops where one would suffice, write the code as two loops, comment that they could be combined for efficiency, and then wait until benchmarks show that the section of the program poses a performance problem before changing the two loops into one.

Exiting the Loop

Here are several guidelines for handling the end of a loop:

Assure yourself that the loop ends. This is fundamental. Mentally simulate the execution of the loop until you are confident that, in all circumstances, it ends. Think through the nominal case, the endpoints, and each of the exceptional cases.

Make loop-termination conditions obvious. If you use a *for* loop and don't fool around with the loop index and don't use a *goto* or *break* to get out of the loop, the termination condition will be obvious. Likewise, if you use a *while* or *repeat-until* loop and put all the control in the *while* or *repeat-until* clause, the termination condition will be obvious. The key is putting the control in one place.

Don't monkey with the loop index of a *for* loop to make the loop terminate.
Some programmers jimmy the value of a *for* loop index to make the loop terminate early. Here's an example:

CODING HORROR

Here's the monkeying. ——

Pascal Example of Monkeying with a Loop Index

```
for i := 1 to 100 do
   begin
   { some code }
   ...
   if ( ... ) then
      i = 101

   { more code }
   ...
   end;
```

The intent in this example is to terminate the loop under some condition by setting *i* to *101*, a value that's larger than the end of the *for* loop's range of *1* through *100*. Virtually all good programmers avoid this practice; it's the sign of an amateur. When you set up a *for* loop, the loop counter is off limits. If you need more control over the loop's exit condition, use a *while* loop to provide more control over the loop's termination.

Avoid code that depends on the loop index's final value. It's bad form to use the value of the loop index upon termination. The terminal value of the loop index varies from language to language and implementation to implementation. The value is different when the loop terminates normally and when it terminates abnormally. Even if you happen to know what the final value is without stopping to think about it, the next person to read the code will probably have to think about it. It's better form and more self-documenting if you assign the final value to a variable at the appropriate point inside the loop.

Here's an example of code that misuses the index's final value:

C Example of Code That Misuses a Loop Index's Terminal Value

```
for ( i = 0; i < MaxRecords; i++ )
   {
   if ( Entry[ i ] == TestValue )
      {
      break;
      }
   }
```

(continued)

```
if ( i < MaxRecords )
   return( TRUE );
else
   return( FALSE );
```

In this fragment, the test for *i < MaxRecords* makes it look as if the loop is supposed to loop through all the values in *Entry[]* and return *TRUE* if it finds the one equal to *TestValue*, *FALSE* otherwise. It's hard to remember whether the index gets incremented past the end of the loop, so it's easy to make an off-by-one error. You're better off writing code that doesn't depend on the index's final value. Here's how to rewrite the code:

C Example of Code That Doesn't Misuse a Loop Index's Terminal Value

```
Found = FALSE;
for ( i = 0; i < MaxRecords; i++ )
   {
   if ( Entry[ i ] == TestValue )
      {
      Found = TRUE;
      break;
      }
   }
return( Found );
```

This second code fragment uses an extra variable, and as is often the case when an extra boolean variable is used, the resulting code is clearer. Incidentally, using a loop index after a loop is such a significant problem that the designers of Ada decided to make *for* loop indexes invalid outside their loops; trying to use one outside its *for* loop generates an error at compile time.

Consider using safety counters. If you have a program in which an error would be catastrophic, you can use safety counters to ensure that all loops end. Here's a Pascal loop that could profitably use a safety counter:

Pascal Example of a Loop That Could Use a Safety Counter

```
repeat
   Node := Node^.Next;
   ...

until ( Node^.Next = Nil );
```

Here's the same code with the safety counters added:

```pascal
Pascal Example of Using a Safety Counter
SafetyCounter := 0;
repeat
   Node := Node^.Next;
   ...

   SafetyCounter := SafetyCounter + 1;
   if ( SafetyCounter >= SAFETY_LIMIT )
      begin
      PrintErrorMsg( "Internal Error: Safety-Counter Violation." );
      exit ( Error )
      end;
   ...

until ( Node^.Next = Nil );
```

Here's the safety-counter code.

Introduced into the code one at a time, safety counters might lead to additional errors. If safety counters aren't used in every loop, you could forget during modification to maintain safety-counter code when you modify loops in parts of the program that do use them. If safety counters are instituted as a projectwide standard, you learn to expect them, and safety-counter code is no more prone to produce errors later than any other code is.

Using *break* and *continue*

The *break* statement is an auxiliary control construct that enables a program to exit from a loop prematurely. It causes a loop to terminate through the normal exit channel; the program resumes execution at the first statement following the loop. In this discussion, *break* is a generic term for *break* in C, *exit* in Pascal, and similar constructs, including those simulated with *goto*s in languages that don't support *break* directly.

The *continue* statement is similar to *break* in that it's an auxiliary loop-control statement. Rather than causing a loop exit, however, *continue* causes the program to skip the loop body and continue executing at the beginning of the next iteration of the loop. A *continue* statement is shorthand for an *if-then* clause that would prevent the rest of the loop from being executed.

Use *break* and *continue* only with caution. Use of *break* eliminates the possibility of treating a loop as a black box. Limiting yourself to only one statement to control a loop's exit condition is a powerful way to simplify your loops. Using a *break* forces the person reading your code to look inside the loop for an understanding of the loop control. That makes the loop more difficult to understand.

Use *break* only after you have considered the alternatives. To paraphrase the nineteenth-century Danish philosopher Søren Kierkegaard, you don't know with certainty whether *continue* and *break* are virtuous or evil constructs. Some computer scientists argue that they are a legitimate technique in structured programming; some argue that they are not. Because you don't know in general whether *continue* and *break* are right or wrong, use them, but only with a fear that you might be wrong. It really is a simple proposition: If you can't defend a *break* or a *continue*, don't use it.

Consider using *break* statements rather than boolean flags in a *while* loop. In some cases, adding boolean flags to a *while* loop to emulate exits from the body of the loop makes the loop hard to read. Sometimes you can remove several levels of indentation inside a loop just by using a *break* instead of a series of *if* tests. Putting multiple *break* conditions into separate statements and placing them near the code that produces the *break* can reduce nesting and make the loop more readable.

Be wary of a loop with a lot of *break*s scattered through it. A loop's containing a lot of *break*s can indicate unclear thinking about the structure of the loop or its role in the surrounding code. A proliferation of *break*s raises the possibility that the loop could be more clearly expressed as a series of loops rather than as one loop with many exits. Multiple *break*s don't necessarily indicate an error, but their existence in a loop is a warning sign, a canary in a coal mine that's not singing as loud as it should be.

If you use a *goto* to emulate a *break*, go to the statement immediately following the loop. It might be tempting to go farther than the first statement past the loop. That is a dangerous practice because it makes the *goto* less predictable. You're on shaky ground breaking out of a loop and on even shakier ground using the *goto* to do it. Don't compound the problem by using the *goto* in any way other than to emulate a structured *break*.

Use *continue* for tests at the top of a loop. A good use of *continue* is for moving execution past the body of the loop after testing a condition at the top. For example, if the loop reads records, discards records of one kind, and processes records of another kind, you could put a test like this one at the top of the loop:

Pseudocode Example of a Relatively Safe Use of *continue*

```
while ( not eof( File ) ) do
   read( Record, File )
   if ( Record.type <> TargetType ) then
      continue

   { process record of TargetType }
   ...

end while
```

Using *continue* in this way lets you avoid an *if* test that would effectively indent the entire body of the loop. If, on the other hand, the *continue* occurs toward the middle or end of the loop, use an *if-then* instead.

Checking Endpoints

A single loop usually has three cases of interest: the first case, an arbitrarily selected middle case, and the last case. When you create a loop, mentally run through the first, middle, and last cases to make sure that the loop doesn't have any off-by-one errors. If you have any special cases that are different from the first or last case, check those too. If the loop contains complex computations, get out your calculator and manually check the calculations.

KEY POINT

Willingness to perform this kind of check is a key difference between efficient and inefficient programmers. Efficient programmers do the work of mental simulations and hand calculations because they know that such measures help them find errors.

Inefficient programmers tend to experiment randomly until they find a combination that seems to work. If a loop isn't working the way it's supposed to, the inefficient programmer changes the < sign to a <= sign. If that fails, the inefficient programmer changes the loop index by adding or subtracting 1. Eventually the programmer using this approach might stumble onto the right combination or simply replace the original error with a more subtle one. Even if this random process results in a correct program, it doesn't result in the programmer's knowing why the program is correct.

You can expect several benefits from mental simulations and hand calculations. The mental discipline results in fewer errors during initial coding, in more rapid detection of errors during debugging, and in a better overall understanding of the program. The mental exercise means that you understand how your code works rather than guessing about it.

Using Loop Variables

Here are some guidelines for using loop variables:

CROSS-REFERENCE
For details on naming
loop variables, see
"Naming Loop Indexes"
in Section 9.2.

Use ordinal or enumerated types for limits on both arrays and loops.
Generally, loop counters should be integer values. Floating-point values don't
increment well. For example, you could add 1.0 to 42,897.0 and get 42,897.0 instead of 42,898.0. If this incremented value were a loop counter, you'd have an
infinite loop.

KEY POINT

Use meaningful variable names to make nested loops readable. Arrays are
often indexed with the same variables that are used for loop indexes. If you
have a one-dimensional array, you might be able to get away with using i, j, or
k to index it. But if you have an array with two or more dimensions, you
should use meaningful index names to clarify what you're doing. Meaningful
array-index names clarify both the purpose of the loop and the part of the array you intend to access.

Here's code that doesn't put this principle to work, using the meaningless
names i, j, and k instead:

CODING HORROR

Pascal Example of Bad Loop Variable Names

```pascal
for i := 1 to NumPayCodes do
   for j := 1 to 12 do
      for k := 1 to NumDivisions do
         Sum := Sum + Transaction[ j, i, k ];
```

What do you think the array indexes in *Transaction* mean? Do i, j, and k tell
you anything about the contents of *Transaction*? If you had the declaration of
Transaction, could you easily determine whether the indexes were in the
right order? Here's the same loop with more readable loop variable names:

Pascal Example of Good Loop Variable Names

```pascal
for PayCodeIdx := 1 to NumPayCodes do
   for Month := 1 to 12 do
      for DivisionIdx := 1 to NumDivisions do
         Sum := Sum + Transaction[ Month, PayCodeIdx, DivisionIdx ];
```

What do you think the array indexes in *Transaction* mean this time? In this
case, the answer is easier to come by because the variable names *PayCodeIdx*,
Month, and *DivisionIdx* tell you a lot more than i, j, and k did. The computer
can read the two versions of the loop equally easily. People can read the second version more easily than the first, however, and the second version is better since your primary audience is made up of humans, not computers.

Use meaningful names to avoid loop-index cross talk. Habitual use of i, j, and k can give rise to index cross talk—using the same index name for two different purposes. Here's an example:

i is used first here...

...and again here.

```
C Example of Index Cross Talk
for ( i = 0;  i < NumPayCodes; i++ )
   {
   /* lots of code */
   ...
   for ( j = 0; j < 12; j++ )
      {
      /* lots of code */
      ...
      for ( i = 0; i < NumDivisions; i++ )
         {
         Sum += Transaction[ j ][ i ][ k ];
         }
      }
   }
```

The use of i is so habitual that it's used twice in the same nesting structure. The second *for* loop controlled by i conflicts with the first, and that's index cross talk. Using more meaningful names than i, j, and k would have prevented the problem. In general, if the body of a loop has more than a couple of lines, if it might grow, or if it's in a group of nested loops, avoid i, j, and k.

How Long Should a Loop Be?

Loop length can be measured in lines of code or depth of nesting. Here are some guidelines:

Make your loops short enough to view all at once. If you usually look at loops on 66-line paper, that puts a 66-line restriction on you. If you usually look at loops on a 25-line monitor, that puts a 25-line restriction on you. Experts have suggested a loop-length limit of one printed page, or 66 lines. When you begin to appreciate the principle of writing simple code, however, you'll rarely write loops longer than 15 or 20 lines.

CROSS-REFERENCE
For details on simplifying nesting, see Section 17.4, "Taming Dangerously Deep Nesting."

Limit nesting to three levels. Studies have shown that the ability of programmers to comprehend a loop deteriorates significantly beyond three levels of nesting (Yourdon 1986a). If you're going beyond that number of levels, make the loop shorter (conceptually) by breaking part of it into a routine or simplifying the control structure.

Make long loops especially clear. Length adds complexity. If you write a short loop, you can use riskier control structures such as *break* and *continue*,

341

multiple exits, complicated termination conditions, and so on. If you write a longer loop and feel any concern for your reader, you'll give the loop a single exit and make the exit condition unmistakably clear.

15.3 Creating Loops Easily—from the Inside Out

If you sometimes have trouble coding a complex loop—which most programmers do—you can use a simple technique to get it right the first time.

Here's the general process. Start with one case. Code that case with literals. Then indent it, put a loop around it, and replace the literals with loop indexes or computed expressions. Put another loop around that, if necessary, and replace more literals. Continue the process as long as you have to. When you finish, add all the necessary initializations. Since you start at the simple case and work outward to generalize it, you might think of this as coding from the inside out.

CROSS-REFERENCE
This process is similar to the PDL-to-code process described in Section 4.2, "PDL for Pros."

Suppose you're writing a program for an insurance company. It has life-insurance rates that vary according to a person's age and sex. Your job is to write a routine that computes the total life-insurance premium for a group. You need a loop that takes the rate for each person in a list and adds it to a total. Here's how you'd do it.

First, in comments, write the steps the body of the loop needs to perform. It's easier to write down what needs to be done when you're not thinking about details of syntax, loop indexes, array indexes, and so on.

Step 1: Creating a Loop from the Inside Out

```
{ get rate from table }
{ add rate to total }
```

Second, convert the comments in the body of the loop to code, as much as you can without actually writing the whole loop. In this case, get the rate for one person and add it to the overall total. Use concrete, specific data rather than abstractions.

Step 2: Creating a Loop from the Inside Out

Table doesn't have any —
indexes yet.
```
Rate    := Table[ ];
TtlRate := TtlRate + Rate;
```

The example assumes that *Table* is an array that holds the rate data. You don't have to worry about the array indexes at first. *Rate* is the variable that holds the rate data selected from the rate table. Likewise, *TtlRate* is a variable that holds the total of the rates.

Next, put in indexes for the *Table* array.

Step 3: Creating a Loop from the Inside Out

```
Rate := Table[ Census.Age, Census.Sex ];
TtlRate := TtlRate + Rate;
```

The array is accessed by age and sex, so *Census.Age* and *Census.Sex* are used to index the array. The example assumes that *Census* is a structured variable that holds information about people in the group to be rated.

The next step is to build a loop around the existing statements. Since the loop is supposed to compute the rates for each person in a group, the loop should be indexed by person.

Step 4: Creating a Loop from the Inside Out

```
for Person := FirstPerson to LastPerson do
   begin
   Rate    := Table[ Census.Age, Census.Sex ];
   TtlRate := TtlRate + Rate
   end;
```

All you have to do here is put the *for* loop around the existing code and then indent the existing code and put it inside a *begin-end* pair. Finally, check to make sure that the variables that depend on the *Person* loop index have been generalized. In this case, the *Census* variable varies with *Person*, so it should be generalized appropriately.

Step 5: Creating a Loop from the Inside Out

```
for Person := FirstPerson to LastPerson do
   begin
   Rate    := Table[ Census[ Person ].Age, Census[ Person ].Sex ];
   TtlRate := TtlRate + Rate
   end;
```

Finally, write any initializations that are needed. In this case, the *TtlRate* variable needs to be initialized. The final code appears on the next page.

Final Step: Creating a Loop from the Inside Out

```
TtlRate := 0;
for Person := FirstPerson to LastPerson do
   begin
   Rate    := Table[ Census[ Person ].Age, Census[ Person ].Sex ];
   TtlRate := TtlRate + Rate
   end;
```

If you had to put another loop around the *Person* loop, you would proceed in the same way. You don't need to follow the steps rigidly. The idea is to start with something concrete, worry about only one thing at a time, and build up the loop from simple components. Take small, understandable steps as you make the loop more general and complex. That way, you minimize the amount of code you have to concentrate on at any one time and therefore minimize the chance of error.

15.4 Correspondence Between Loops and Arrays

CROSS-REFERENCE
For further discussion of the correspondence between loops and arrays, see Section 10.4, "Relationship Between Data Structures and Control Structures."

Loops and arrays are often related. In many instances, a loop is created to perform an array manipulation, and loop counters correspond one-to-one with array indexes. For example, the Pascal *for* loop indexes below correspond to the array indexes:

Pascal Example of an Array Multiplication

```
for Row := 1 to MaxRows do
   for Column := 1 to MaxCols do
      Product[ Row, Column ] := a[ Row, Column ] * b[ Row, Column ];
```

In Pascal, a loop is necessary for this array operation. But it's worth noting that looping structures and arrays aren't inherently connected. Some languages, especially APL and Fortran 90, provide powerful array operations that eliminate the need for loops like the one above. Here's an APL code fragment that performs the same operation:

APL Example of an Array Multiplication

```
Product <- a x b
```

The APL is simpler and less error prone. It uses only 3 operands, whereas the Pascal fragment uses 15. It doesn't have loop variables, array indexes, or control structures to code incorrectly.

One point of this example is that you do some programming to solve a problem and some to solve it in a particular language. The language you use to solve a problem substantially affects your solution.

CHECKLIST

Loops

❏ Is the loop entered from the top?

❏ Is initialization code directly before the loop?

❏ If the loop is an infinite loop or an event loop, is it constructed cleanly rather than using a kludge such as *for i := 1 to 9999*?

❏ If the loop is a C *for* loop, is the loop header reserved for loop-control code?

❏ Does the loop use *begin* and *end* or their equivalent to prevent problems arising from improper modifications?

❏ Does the loop have something in it? Is it nonempty?

❏ Are housekeeping chores grouped, at either the beginning or the end of the loop?

❏ Does the loop perform one and only one function—as a well-defined routine does?

❏ Does the loop end under all possible conditions?

❏ Is the loop's termination condition obvious?

❏ If the loop is a *for* loop, does the code inside it avoid monkeying with the loop index?

❏ Is a variable used to save important loop-index values rather than using the loop index outside the loop?

❏ Does the loop use safety counters—if you've instituted a safety-counter standard?

❏ Is the loop index an ordinal type or an enumerated type?

❏ Does the loop index have a meaningful name?

❏ Does the loop avoid index cross talk?

❏ Is the loop short enough to view all at once?

❏ Is the loop nested to three levels or less?

❏ If the loop is long, is it especially clear?

Key Points

- Loops are complicated. Keeping them simple helps readers of your code.
- Techniques for keeping loops simple include avoiding exotic kinds of loops, minimizing nesting, making entries and exits clear, and keeping housekeeping code in one place.
- Loop indexes are subjected to a great deal of abuse. Name them clearly and use them for only one purpose.
- Think the loop through carefully to verify that it operates normally under each case and terminates under all possible conditions.

16

Unusual Control Structures

Contents

Related Topics

SEVERAL CONTROL CONSTRUCTS MAKE UP a twilight zone of structured programming--not quite structured, but not quite unstructured either. These facilities aren't available in all languages but are useful in those languages that do offer them.

16.1   *goto*

Computer scientists are zealous in their beliefs, and when the discussion turns to *gotos*, they get out their jousting poles, armor, and maces, mount their horses, and charge through the gates of Camelot to the holy wars.

No one quarrels with using *gotos* to emulate structured constructs in languages that don't support structured control constructs directly. The debate is about using *gotos* in languages that support structured constructs, in which *gotos* are theoretically not needed. Here's a summary of the points on each side.

The Argument Against *goto*s

The general argument against *goto*s is that code without *goto*s is higher-quality code. The famous letter that sparked the original controversy was Edsger Dijkstra's "Go To Statement Considered Harmful" in the March 1968 *Communications of the ACM*. Dijkstra observed that the quality of code was inversely proportional to the number of *goto*s the programmer used. In subsequent work, Dijkstra has argued that code that doesn't contain *goto*s can more easily be proven correct.

Code containing *goto*s is hard to format. Indentation should be used to show logical structure, and *goto*s have an effect on logical structure. Using indentation to show the logical structure of a *goto* and its target, however, is difficult or impossible.

Use of *goto*s defeats compiler optimizations. Some optimizations depend on a program's flow of control residing within a few statements. An unconditional *goto* makes the flow harder to analyze and reduces the ability of the compiler to optimize the code. Thus, even if introducing a *goto* produces an efficiency at the source-language level, it may well reduce overall efficiency by thwarting compiler optimizations.

Proponents of *goto*s sometimes argue that they make code faster or smaller. But code containing *goto*s is rarely the fastest or smallest possible. Donald Knuth's marvelous article "Structured Programming with go to Statements" gives several examples of cases in which using *goto*s makes for slower and larger code (1974).

In practice, the use of *goto*s leads to the violation of structured-programming principles. Even if *goto*s aren't confusing when used carefully, once *goto*s are introduced, they spread through the code like termites through a rotting house. If any *goto*s are allowed, the bad creep in with the good, so it's better not to allow any of them.

Overall, experience in the two decades since the publication of Dijkstra's letter has shown the folly of producing *goto*-laden code. In a survey of the literature, Ben Shneiderman concluded that the evidence supports Dijkstra's view that we're better off without the *goto* (1980).

The Argument for *goto*s

The argument for the *goto* is characterized by an advocacy of its careful use in specific circumstances rather than its indiscriminate use. Most arguments against *goto*s speak against indiscriminate use. The *goto* controversy erupted when Fortran was the most popular language. Fortran had no presentable loop structures, and in the absence of good advice on programming structured loops with *goto*s, programmers wrote a lot of spaghetti code. Such code was undoubtedly correlated with the production of low-quality programs but has little to do with the careful use of a *goto* to make up for a gap in a structured language's capabilities.

A well-placed *goto* can eliminate the need for duplicate code. Duplicate code leads to problems if the two sets of code are modified differently. Duplicate code increases the size of source and executable files. The bad effects of the *goto* are outweighed in such a case by the risks of duplicate code.

CROSS-REFERENCE
For details on using *goto*s
in code that allocates
resources, see "Error Processing and *goto*s" in this
section.

The *goto* is useful in a routine that allocates resources, performs operations on those resources, and then deallocates the resources. With a *goto*, you can clean up in one section of code. The *goto* reduces the likelihood of your forgetting to deallocate the resources in each place you detect an error.

In some cases, the *goto* can result in faster and smaller code. Knuth's 1974 article cited a few cases in which the *goto* produced a legitimate gain.

Good programming doesn't mean eliminating *goto*s. Methodical decomposition, refinement, and selection of control structures automatically lead to *goto*-free programs in most cases. Achieving *goto*less code is not the aim, but the outcome, and putting the focus on avoiding *goto*s isn't helpful.

> **The evidence suggests only that deliberately chaotic control structure degrades [programmer] performance. These experiments provide virtually no evidence for the beneficial effect of any specific method of structuring control flow.**
> *B. A. Sheil*

Two decades' worth of research with *goto*s has failed to demonstrate their harmfulness. In a survey of the literature, B. A. Sheil concluded that unrealistic test conditions, poor data analysis, and inconclusive results failed to support the claim of Shneiderman and others that the number of bugs in code was proportional to the number of *goto*s (1981). Sheil didn't go so far as to conclude that using *goto*s is a good idea—rather that experimental evidence against them was not conclusive.

Finally, the *goto* was incorporated into the Ada language, the most carefully engineered programming language in history. Ada was developed long after the arguments on both sides of the *goto* debate had been fully developed, and after considering all sides of the issue, Ada's engineers decided to include the *goto*.

The Phony *goto* Debate

A primary feature of most *goto* discussions is a shallow approach to the question. The arguer on the "*goto*s are evil" side usually presents a trivial code fragment that uses *goto*s and then shows how easy it is to rewrite the fragment without *goto*s. This proves mainly that it's easy to write trivial code without *goto*s.

The arguer on the "I can't live without *goto*s" side usually presents a case in which eliminating a *goto* results in an extra comparison or the duplication of a line of code. This proves mainly that there's a case in which using a *goto* results in one less comparison—rarely a significant gain on today's computers.

Most textbooks don't help. They often provide a trivial example of rewriting some code without a *goto* as if that covered the subject. Here's a disguised example of a trivial piece of code from such a textbook:

Pascal Example of Code That's Supposed to Be Easy to Rewrite Without *goto*s

```pascal
repeat
   GetData( InputFile, Data );
   if eof( InputFile ) then
      goto LOOP_EXIT;
   DoSomething( Data );
until ( Data = -1 );
LOOP_EXIT:
```

The book quickly replaces this code with *goto*less code:

Pascal Example of Supposedly Equivalent Code, Rewritten Without *goto*s

```pascal
GetData( InputFile, Data );
while ( not eof( InputFile ) and ( Data <> -1 ) do
   begin
   DoSomething( Data );
   GetData( InputFile, Data )
   end;
```

This so-called "trivial" example contains an error. In the case in which *Data* equals −1, the translated code detects the −1 and exits the loop before executing *DoSomething()*. The original code executes *DoSomething()* before the −1 is detected. The programming book trying to show how easy it is to code using only structured programming techniques translated its own example incorrectly. But the author of that book shouldn't feel too bad; other books make similar mistakes. Even the pros have difficulty achieving *goto*less nirvana.

Here's a faithful translation of the code with no *goto*s:

Pascal Example of Truly Equivalent Code, Rewritten Without *goto*s

```pascal
repeat
   GetData( InputFile, Data );
   if ( not eof( InputFile )) then
      DoSomething( Data );
until ( Data = -1 or eof( InputFile ) );
```

Even with a correct translation of the code, the example is still phony because it shows a trivial use of the *goto*. Such cases are not the ones for which thoughtful programmers choose a *goto* as their preferred form of control.

It would be hard at this late date to add anything worthwhile to the theoretical *goto* debate. What's not usually addressed, however, is the situation in which a programmer fully aware of the *goto*less alternatives chooses to use a *goto* to enhance readability and maintainability.

The following sections present cases in which some experienced programmers have argued for using *goto*s. The discussions provide examples of code with *goto*s and code rewritten without *goto*s and evaluate the trade-offs between the versions.

Error Processing and *goto*s

Writing highly interactive code calls for paying a lot of attention to error processing and cleaning up resources when errors occur. Here's a code example that purges a group of files. The routine first gets a group of files to be purged, and then it finds each file, opens it, overwrites it, and erases it. The routine checks for errors at each step:

Pascal Code with *goto*s That Processes Errors and Cleans Up Resources

```
PROCEDURE PurgeFiles( var ErrorState: ERROR_CODE );

{ This routine purges a group of files. }

var
   FileIndex:        Integer;
   FileHandle:       FILEHANDLE_T;
   FileList:         FILELIST_T;
   NumFilesToPurge:  Integer;

label
   END_PROC;

begin
   MakePurgeFileList( FileList, NumFilesToPurge );

   ErrorState := Success;
   FileIndex  := 0;
   while ( FileIndex < NumFilesToPurge ) do
      begin
      FileIndex := FileIndex + 1;
```

(continued)

```
                        if not FindFile( FileList[ FileIndex ], FileHandle ) then
                           begin
                           ErrorState := FileFindError;
Here's a goto. ──────       goto END_PROC
                           end;

                        if not OpenFile( FileHandle ) then
                           begin
                           ErrorState := FileOpenError;
Here's a goto. ──────       goto END_PROC
                           end;

                        if not OverwriteFile( FileHandle ) then
                           begin
                           ErrorState := FileOverwriteError;
Here's a goto. ──────       goto END_PROC
                           end;

                        if Erase( FileHandle ) then
                           begin
                           ErrorState := FileEraseError;
Here's a goto. ──────       goto END_PROC
                           end

                     end; { while }

Here's the goto label. ──  END_PROC:

                     DeletePurgeFileList( FileList, NumFilesToPurge )

                  end; { PurgeFiles }
```

This routine is typical of circumstances in which experienced programmers decide to use a *goto*. Similar cases come up when a routine needs to allocate and clean up resources like memory or handles to fonts, windows, brushes, and printers. The alternative to *goto*s in those cases is usually duplicating code to clean up the resources. In such cases, a programmer might balance the evil of the *goto* against the headache of duplicate-code maintenance and decide that the *goto* is the lesser evil.

You can rewrite the routine above in a couple of ways that avoid *goto*s, and both ways involve trade-offs. Here are the possible rewrite strategies:

Rewrite with nested *if* statements. To rewrite with nested *if* statements, nest the *if* statements so that each is executed only if the previous test succeeds. This is the standard, textbook, structured-programming approach to eliminating *goto*s. Here's a rewrite of the routine using the standard approach:

CROSS-REFERENCE
C programmers might point
out that this routine could
easily be rewritten with
break and no *goto*s. For
details on *break*, see "Using
break and *continue*" in
Section 15.2.

Pascal Code That Avoids *goto*s by Using Nested *if*s

```
PROCEDURE PurgeFiles( var ErrorState: ERROR_CODE );

{ This routine purges a group of files. }

var
    FileIndex:        Integer;
    FileHandle:       FILEHANDLE_T;
    FileList:         FILELIST_T;
    NumFilesToPurge:  Integer;

begin
    MakePurgeFileList( FileList, NumFilesToPurge );

    ErrorState  := Success;
    FileIndex   := 0;
    while ( FileIndex < NumFilesToPurge and ErrorState = Success ) do
        begin
        FileIndex := FileIndex + 1;

        if FindFile( FileList[ FileIndex ], FileHandle ) then
            begin
            if OpenFile( FileHandle ) then
                begin
                if OverwriteFile( FileHandle ) then
                    begin
                    if not Erase( FileHandle ) then
                        begin
                        ErrorState := FileEraseError
                        end
                    end
                else { couldn't overwrite file }
                    begin
                    ErrorState := FileOverwriteError
                    end
                end
            else { couldn't open file }
                begin
                ErrorState := FileOpenError
                end
            end
        else { couldn't find file }
            begin
            ErrorState := FileFindError
            end

        end; { while }

    DeletePurgeFileList( FileList, NumFilesToPurge )

end; { PurgeFiles }
```

The while test has been changed to add a test for ErrorState.

This line is 23 lines away from the if statement that invokes it.

353

For people used to programming without *goto*s, this code might be easier to read than the *goto* version, and if you use it, you won't have to face an inquisition from the *goto* goon squad.

CROSS-REFERENCE
For more details on indentation and other coding layout issues, see Chapter 18, "Layout and Style." For details on nesting levels, see Section 17.4, "Taming Dangerously Deep Nesting."

The main disadvantage of this nested-*if* approach is that the nesting level is deep. Very deep. To understand the code, you have to keep the whole set of nested *if*s in your mind at once. Moreover, the distance between the error-processing code and the code that invokes it is too great: The code that sets *ErrorState* to *FileFindError*, for example, is 23 lines from the *if* statement that invokes it.

With the *goto* version, no statement is more than 4 lines from the condition that invokes it. And you don't have to keep the whole structure in your mind at once. You can essentially ignore any preceding conditions that were successful and focus on the next operation. In this case, the *goto* version is more readable and more maintainable than the nested-*if* version.

Rewrite with a status variable. To rewrite with a status variable (also called a state variable), create a variable that indicates whether the routine is in an error state. In this case, the routine already uses the *ErrorState* status variable, so you can use that.

Pascal Code That Avoids *goto*s by Using a Status Variable

```
PROCEDURE PurgeFiles( var ErrorState: ERROR_CODE );

{ This routine purges a group of files. }

var
    FileIndex:        Integer;
    FileHandle:       FILEHANDLE_T;
    FileList:         FILELIST_T;
    NumFilesToPurge:  Integer;

begin
    MakePurgeFileList( FileList, NumFilesToPurge );

    ErrorState := Success;
    FileIndex  := 0;
    while ( FileIndex < NumFilesToPurge ) and ( ErrorState = Success ) do
        begin
        FileIndex := FileIndex + 1;

        if not FindFile( FileList[ FileIndex ], FileHandle ) then
            begin
            ErrorState := FileFindError
            end;
```

The while test has been changed to add a test for ErrorState.

(continued)

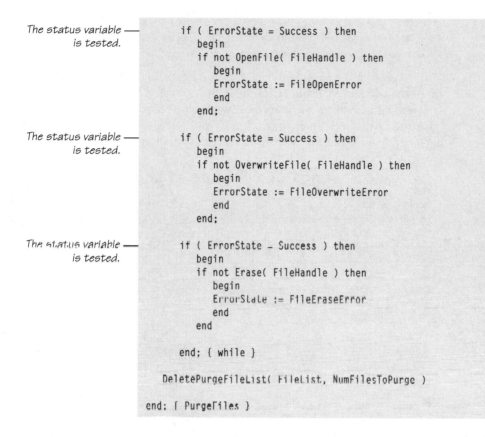

The status variable is tested.

```
if ( ErrorState = Success ) then
   begin
   if not OpenFile( FileHandle ) then
      begin
      ErrorState := FileOpenError
      end
   end;
```

The status variable is tested.

```
if ( ErrorState = Success ) then
   begin
   if not OverwriteFile( FileHandle ) then
      begin
      ErrorState := FileOverwriteError
      end
   end;
```

The status variable is tested.

```
if ( ErrorState = Success ) then
   begin
   if not Erase( FileHandle ) then
      begin
      ErrorState := FileEraseError
      end
   end

   end; { while }

   DeletePurgeFileList( FileList, NumFilesToPurge )

end; { PurgeFiles }
```

The advantage of the status-variable approach is that it avoids the deeply nested *if-then-else* structures of the first rewrite and is thus easier to understand. It also places the action following the *if-then-else* test closer to the test than the nested-*if* approach did and completely avoids *else* clauses.

Understanding the nested-*if* version requires some mental gymnastics. The status-variable version is easier to understand because it closely models the way people think about the problem. You find the file. If everything is OK, you open the file. If everything is still OK, you overwrite the file. If everything is still OK,...

The disadvantage of this approach is that using status variables isn't as common a practice as it should be. Document their use fully, or some programmers might not understand what you're up to. In this example, the use of well-named enumerated types helps significantly.

Comparison of the approaches

Each of the three methods has something to be said for it. The *goto* approach avoids deep nesting and unnecessary tests but of course has *goto*s. The nested-*if* approach avoids *goto*s but is deeply nested and gives an exaggerated picture of the logical complexity of the routine. The status-variable approach avoids *goto*s and deep nesting but introduces extra tests.

The status-variable approach is slightly preferable to the first two because it's more readable and it models the problem better, but that doesn't make it the best approach in all circumstances. Any of these techniques works well when applied consistently to all the code in a project. Consider all the trade-offs, and then make a projectwide decision about which method to favor.

*goto*s and Sharing Code in an *else* Clause

One challenging situation in which some programmers would use a *goto* is the case in which you have two conditional tests and an *else* clause and want to execute code in one of the conditions and in the *else* clause. Here's an example of a case that could drive someone to *goto*:

CODING HORROR

C Example of Sharing Code in an *else* Clause with a *goto*

```c
if ( StatusOK )
   {
   if ( DataAvail )
      {
      ImportantVar = x;
      goto MID_LOOP;
      }
   }
else
   {
   ImportantVar = GetVal();

   MID_LOOP:

   /* lots of code */
   ...
   }
```

This is a good example because it's logically tortuous—it's nearly impossible to read as it stands, and it's hard to rewrite correctly without a *goto*. If you think you can easily rewrite it without *goto*s, ask someone to review your code! Several expert programmers have rewritten it incorrectly.

You can rewrite the code in several ways. You can duplicate code, put the common code into a routine and call it from two places, or retest the conditions. In most languages, the rewrite won't be as fast as the original, but it will be almost as fast. Unless the code is in a really hot loop, rewrite it without thinking about efficiency.

The best rewrite would be to put the /* *lots of code* */ part into its own routine. Then you can call the routine from the places you would otherwise have used as origins or destinations of *goto*s and preserve the original structure of the conditional. Here's how it looks:

C Example of Sharing Code in an *else* Clause by Putting Common Code into a Routine

```c
if ( StatusOK )
   {
   if ( DataAvail )
      {
      ImportantVar = x;
      DoLotsOfCode( ImportantVar );
      }
   }
else
   {
   ImportantVar = GetVal();
   DoLotsOfCode( ImportantVar );
   }
```

Normally, writing a new routine (or a macro in C) is the best approach. Sometimes, however, it's not practical to put duplicated code into its own routine. In this case you can work around the impractical solution by restructuring the conditional so that you keep the code in the same routine rather than putting it into a new routine. Here's how it looks:

C Example of Sharing Code in an *else* Clause Without a *goto*

```c
if ( (StatusOK && DataAvail) || ! StatusOK )
   {
   if ( StatusOK && DataAvail )
      ImportantVar = x;
   else
      ImportantVar = GetVal();

   /* lots of code */
   ...
   }
```

CROSS-REFERENCE
Another approach to this problem is to use a decision table. For details, see Section 12.2, "Table-Driven Methods."

This is a faithful and mechanical translation of the logic in the *goto* version. It tests *StatusOK* two extra times and *DataAvail* one, but the code is equivalent. If retesting the conditionals bothers you, notice that the value of *StatusOK* doesn't need to be tested twice in the first *if* test. You can also drop the test for *DataAvail* in the second *if* test.

Summary of Guidelines for Using *goto*s

KEY POINT

Use of *goto*s is a matter of religion. My dogma is that in modern languages, you can easily replace nine out of ten *goto*s with equivalent structured constructs. In these simple cases, you should replace *goto*s out of habit. In the hard cases, you can still exorcise the *goto* in nine out of ten cases: You can break the code into smaller routines; use nested *if*s; test and retest a status variable; or restructure a conditional. Eliminating the *goto* is harder in these cases, but it's good mental exercise and the techniques discussed in this section give you the tools to do it.

In the remaining one case out of 100 in which a *goto* is a legitimate solution to the problem, document it clearly and use it. If you have your rain boots on, it's not worth walking around the block to avoid a mud puddle. But keep your mind open to *goto*less approaches suggested by other programmers. They might see something you don't.

Here's a summary of guidelines for using *goto*s:

- Use *goto*s to emulate structured control constructs in languages that don't support them directly. When you do, emulate them exactly. Don't abuse the extra flexibility the *goto* gives you.

- Don't use the *goto* when an equivalent structured construct is available.

CROSS-REFERENCE
For details on improving efficiency, see Chapter 28, "Code-Tuning Strategies," and Chapter 29, "Code-Tuning Techniques."

- Measure the performance of any *goto* used to improve efficiency. In most cases, you can recode without *goto*s for improved readability and no loss in efficiency. If your case is the exception, document the efficiency improvement so that *goto*less evangelists won't remove the *goto* when they see it.

- Limit yourself to one *goto* label per routine unless you're emulating structured constructs.

CROSS-REFERENCE
For details on emulating structured constructs with *goto*s, see Section 17.6, "Emulating Structured Constructs with *goto*s."

- Limit yourself to *goto*s that go forward, not backward, unless you're emulating structured constructs.

- Make sure all *goto* labels are used. Unused labels might be an indication of missing code, namely the code that goes to the labels. If the labels aren't used, delete them.

- Make sure a *goto* doesn't create unreachable code.

- If you're a manager, adopt the perspective that a battle over a single *goto* isn't worth the loss of the war. If the programmer is aware of the alternatives and is willing to argue, the *goto* is probably OK.

Further Reading

These articles contain the whole *goto* debate. It erupts from time to time in most workplaces, textbooks, and magazines, but you won't hear anything that wasn't fully explored 20 years ago.

Dijkstra, Edsger. "Go To Statement Considered Harmful." *Communications of the ACM* 11, no. 3 (March 1968): 147–48. This is the famous letter in which Dijkstra put the match to the paper and ignited a controversy that shows no signs of abating.

Wulf, W. A. "A Case Against the GOTO." *Proceedings of the 25th National ACM Conference*, August 1972: 791–97. This paper was another argument against the indiscriminate use of *goto*s. Wulf argued that if programming languages provided adequate control structures, *goto*s would become largely unnecessary. Since 1972, when the paper was written, languages such as Pascal, C, and Ada have proven Wulf correct.

Knuth, Donald. "Structured Programming with go to Statements." 1974. In *Classics in Software Engineering*, edited by Edward Yourdon. Englewood Cliffs, N. J.: Yourdon Press, 1979. This long paper isn't entirely about *goto*s, but it includes a horde of code examples that are made more efficient by eliminating *goto*s and another horde of code examples that are made more efficient by adding *goto*s.

Rubin, Frank. " 'GOTO Considered Harmful' Considered Harmful." *Communications of the ACM* 30, no. 3 (March 1987): 195–96. In this rather hot-headed letter to the editor, Rubin asserts that *goto*less programming has cost businesses "hundreds of millions of dollars." He then offers a short code fragment that uses a *goto* and argues that it's superior to *goto*less alternatives.

> The response that Rubin's letter generated was more interesting than the letter itself. For five months, *Communications of the ACM* published letters that offered different versions of Rubin's original seven-line program. The letters were evenly divided between those defending *goto*s and those castigating them. Readers suggested roughly 17 different rewrites, and the rewritten code fully covered the spectrum of approaches to avoiding *goto*s. The editor of *CACM* noted that the letter had generated more response by far than any other issue ever considered in the pages of *CACM*.
>
> For the follow-up letters, see
> *Communications of the ACM* 30, no. 5 (May 1987): 351–55.
> *Communications of the ACM* 30, no. 6 (June 1987): 475–78.
> *Communications of the ACM* 30, no. 7 (July 1987): 632–34.
> *Communications of the ACM* 30, no. 8 (August 1987): 659–62.
> *Communications of the ACM* 30, no. 12 (December 1987): 997, 1085.

16.2 *return*

The *return* and *exit* statements are control constructs that enable a program to exit from a routine at will. They cause the routine to terminate through the normal exit channel, returning control to the calling routine. The word *return* is used here as a generic term for *return*, *exit*, and similar constructs. Here are guidelines for using the *return* statement:

Minimize the number of *return*s in each routine. It's harder to understand a routine if, reading it at the bottom, you're unaware of the possibility that it *return*ed somewhere above.

KEY POINT

Use a *return* when it enhances readability. In certain routines, once you know the answer, you want to return it to the calling routine immediately. If the routine is defined in such a way that it doesn't require any cleanup, not returning immediately means that you have to write more code.

The following is a good example of a case in which returning from multiple places in a routine makes sense:

```
C Example of a Good Multiple Return from a Routine
int Compare
   (
   int Value1,
   int Value2
   )
{
if ( Value1 < Value2 )
   return( LessThan );
else if ( Value1 > Value2 )
   return( GreaterThan );
else
   return( Equal );
}
```

16.3 Recursion

In recursion, a routine solves a small part of a problem itself, divides the problem into smaller pieces, and then calls itself to solve each of the smaller pieces. Recursion is usually called into play when a small part of the problem is easy to solve and a large part is easy to decompose into smaller pieces.

Recursion isn't useful very often, but when used judiciously it produces exceptionally elegant solutions. Here's an example in which a sorting algorithm makes excellent use of recursion:

Pascal Example of a Sorting Algorithm That Uses Recursion

```
Procedure QuickSort
   (
   FirstIdx:  integer;
   LastIdx:   integer;
   Names:     NAME_ARRAY
   );
var
   MidPoint: integer;
begin
   if ( LastIdx > FirstIdx ) then
      begin
      Partition( FirstIdx, LastIdx, Names, MidPoint );
      QuickSort( FirstIdx, MidPoint-1, Names );
      QuickSort( MidPoint+1, LastIdx, Names )
      end
end;
```

Here are the recursive calls.

In this case, the sorting algorithm chops up an array and then calls itself to sort each half of the array. When it calls itself with a subarray that's too small to sort (*LastIdx <= FirstIdx*), it stops calling itself.

In general, recursion leads to small code and slow execution and chews up stack space. For a small group of problems, recursion can produce simple, elegant solutions. For a slightly larger group of problems, it can produce simple, elegant, hard-to-understand solutions. For most problems, it produces massively complicated solutions—in those cases, simple iteration is usually more understandable. Use recursion selectively.

Example of Recursion

Suppose you have a data structure that represents a maze. A maze is basically a grid, and at each point on the grid you might be able to turn left, turn right, move up, or move down. You'll often be able to move in more than one direction.

How do you write a program to find its way through the maze? If you use recursion, the answer is fairly straightforward. You start at the beginning and then try all possible paths until you find your way out of the maze. The first time you visit a point, you try to move left. If you can't move left, you try to go up or down, and if you can't go up or down, you try to go right. You don't have to worry about getting lost because you drop a few bread crumbs on each spot as you visit it, and you don't visit the same spot twice.

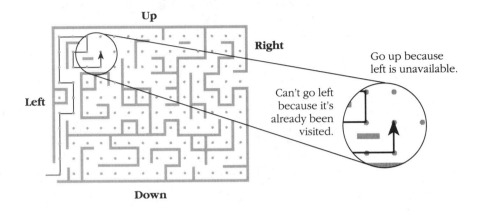

Here's how the recursive code looks:

C Example of Moving Through a Maze Recursively

```
BOOLEAN function FindPathThroughMaze
   (
   MAZE_T  Maze,
   POINT   Position
   )
{
/* if the position has already been tried, don't try it again */
if ( AlreadyTried( Maze, Position ) )
   return( FALSE );

/* if this position is the exit, declare success */
if ( ThisIsTheExit( Maze, Position ) )
   return( TRUE );

/* remember that this position has been tried */
RememberPosition( Maze, Position );

/* check the paths to the left, up, down, and to the right; if
   any path is successful, stop looking */
if ( MoveLeft( Maze, Position, &NewPosition ) )
   if ( FindPathThroughMaze( Maze, NewPosition ) )
      return( TRUE );
```

(continued)

```
if ( MoveUp( Maze, Position, &NewPosition ) )
   if ( FindPathThroughMaze( Maze, NewPosition ) )
      return( TRUE );

if ( MoveDown( Maze, Position, &NewPosition ) )
   if ( FindPathThroughMaze( Maze, NewPosition ) )
      return( TRUE );

if ( MoveRight( Maze, Position, &NewPosition ) )
   if ( FindPathThroughMaze( Maze, NewPosition ) )
      return( TRUE );

return( FALSE );
}
```

The first line of code checks to see whether the position has already been tried. One key aim in writing a recursive routine is the prevention of infinite recursion. In this case, if you don't check for having tried a point, you might keep trying it infinitely.

The second statement checks to see whether the position is the exit from the maze. If *ThisIsTheExit()* returns *TRUE*, the routine itself returns *TRUE*.

The third statement remembers that the position has been visited. This prevents the infinite recursion that would result from a circular path.

The remaining lines in the routine try to find a path to the left, up, down, and to the right. The code stops the recursion if the routine ever returns *TRUE*, that is, when the routine finds a path through the maze.

The logic used in this routine is fairly straightforward. Most people experience some initial discomfort using recursion because it's self-referential. In this case, however, an alternative solution would be much more complicated and recursion works well.

Tips for Using Recursion

Here are some tips for using recursion:

Make sure the recursion stops. Check the routine to make sure that it includes a nonrecursive path. That usually means that the routine has a test that stops further recursion when it's not needed. In the maze example, the tests for *AlreadyTried()* and *ThisIsTheExit()* ensure that the recursion stops.

Use safety counters to prevent infinite recursion. If you're using recursion in a situation that doesn't allow a simple test such as the one just described, use a safety counter to prevent infinite recursion. The safety counter has to be a variable that's not re-created each time you call the routine. Use a module-level variable or pass the safety counter as a parameter. Here's an example:

Pascal Example of Using a Safety Counter to Prevent Infinite Recursion

The recursive routine must be able to change the value of SafetyCounter, so in Pascal it's a var parameter.

```
procedure RecursiveProc( var SafetyCounter: integer );
begin
    if ( SafetyCounter > SAFETY_LIMIT ) then
        exit;
    SafetyCounter := SafetyCounter + 1;
    ...
end;
```

In this case, if the routine exceeds the safety limit, it stops recursing.

Limit recursion to one routine. Cyclic recursion (A calls B calls C calls A) is dangerous because it's hard to detect. Mentally managing recursion in one routine is tough enough; understanding recursion that spans routines is too much. If you have cyclic recursion, you can usually redesign the routines so that the recursion is restricted to a single routine. If you can't and you still think that recursion is the best approach, use safety counters as a recursive insurance policy.

Keep an eye on the stack. With recursion, you have no guarantees about how much stack space your program uses and it's hard to predict in advance how the program will behave at run time. You can take a couple of steps to control its run-time behavior, however.

First, if you use a safety counter, one of the considerations in setting a limit for it should be how much stack you're willing to allocate to the recursive routine. Set the safety limit low enough to prevent a stack overflow.

Second, you can estimate the memory used by a recursive routine. Before you execute your program, fill memory with a recognizable value: *0s* and *0xCC* are good values. Put the program through its paces, and then walk through memory with a debugger to see how much of the stack the program used. Look for the point at which the *0s* or the *0xCC* values are undisturbed, and use that point in your estimation of the amount of stack your program uses.

Don't use recursion for factorials or fibonacci numbers. One problem with computer-science textbooks is that they present silly examples of recursion. The typical examples are computing a factorial or computing a fibonacci sequence. Recursion is a powerful tool, and it's really dumb to use it in either of those cases. If a programmer who worked for me used recursion to compute a factorial, I'd hire someone else. Here's the recursive version of the factorial routine:

CODING HORROR

Pascal Example of an Inappropriate Solution: Using Recursion to Compute a Factorial

```pascal
Function Factorial( Number: integer ): integer;
begin
    if ( Number = 1 ) then
        Factorial := 1
    else
        Factorial := Number * Factorial( Number - 1 );
end;
```

In addition to being slow and making the use of run-time memory unpredictable, the recursive version of this routine is harder to understand than the iterative version. Here's the iterative version:

Pascal Example of an Appropriate Solution: Using Iteration to Compute a Factorial

```pascal
Function Factorial( Number: integer ): integer;
var
    IntermediateResult: integer;
    Factor:             integer;
begin
    IntermediateResult := 1;
    for Factor := 2 to Number do
        IntermediateResult := IntermediateResult * Factor;
    Factorial := IntermediateResult
end;
```

You can draw three lessons from this example. First, computer-science textbooks aren't doing the world any favors with their examples of recursion. Second, and more important, recursion is a much more powerful tool than its confusing use in computing factorials or fibonacci numbers would suggest. Third, and most important, you should consider alternatives to recursion before using it. You can do anything with stacks and iteration that you can do with recursion. Sometimes one approach works better; sometimes the other does. Consider both before you choose either one.

CHECKLIST

Unusual Control Structures

goto

❏ Are *goto*s used only as a last resort, and then only to make code more readable and maintainable?

❏ If a *goto* is used for the sake of efficiency, has the gain in efficiency been measured and documented?

❏ Are *goto*s limited to one label per routine?

❏ Do all *goto*s go forward, not backward?

❏ Are all *goto* labels used?

return

❏ Does each routine use the minimum number of *return*s possible?

❏ Do *return*s enhance readability?

RECURSION

❏ Does the recursive routine include code to stop the recursion?

❏ Does the routine use a safety counter to guarantee that the routine stops?

❏ Is recursion limited to one routine?

❏ Is the routine's depth of recursion within the limits imposed by the size of the program's stack?

❏ Is recursion the best way to implement the routine? Is it better than simple iteration?

Key Points

- In a few cases, *goto*s are the best way to write code that's readable and maintainable. Such cases, however, are rarer than you might think. Use *goto*s only as a last resort.

- Multiple *return*s can enhance a routine's readability and maintainability, and they help prevent deeply nested logic. They should, nevertheless, be used carefully.

- Recursion provides elegant solutions to a small set of problems. Use it carefully too.

17

General Control Issues

Contents

Related Topics

NO DISCUSSION OF CONTROL WOULD BE COMPLETE unless it went into several general issues that crop up when you think about control constructs. Most of the information in this chapter is detailed and pragmatic. If you're reading for the theory of control structures rather than for the gritty details, concentrate on the definition of structured programming in Section 17.5 and on the exploration of the relationship between control structures and complexity in Section 17.7.

17.1 Boolean Expressions

Except for the simplest control structure, the one that calls for the execution of statements in sequence, all control structures depend on the evaluation of boolean expressions.

Using *True* and *False* for Boolean Tests

Use the identifiers *True* and *False* in boolean expressions rather than using flags like *0* and *1*. Languages like Pascal that have a boolean data type supply predefined identifiers for true and false. They make it easy—they don't even allow you to assign values other than *True* or *False* to boolean variables. Languages that don't have a boolean data type require you to have more discipline to make boolean expressions readable. Here's an example of the problem:

CODING HORROR

Basic Example of Using Ambiguous Flags for Boolean Values

```
1200 IF PRINTERROR = 0 GOSUB 2000          ' initialize printer
1210 IF PRINTERROR = 1 GOSUB 3000          ' notify user of error
1230 '
1240 IF REPORTSELECTED = 1 GOSUB 4000      ' print report
1250 IF SUMMARYSELECTED = 1 GOSUB 5000     ' print summary
1260 '
1270 IF PRINTERROR = 0 GOSUB 6000          ' clean up successful printing
```

If using flags like *0* and *1* is common practice, what's wrong with it? It's not clear from reading the code whether the *GOSUB*s are executed when the tests are true or when they're false. Nothing in the code fragment itself tells you whether *1* represents true and *0* false or whether the opposite is true. It's not even clear that the values *1* and *0* are being used to represent true and false. For example, in the *IF REPORTSELECTED = 1* line, the *1* could easily represent the first report, a *2* the second, a *3* the third; nothing in the code tells you that *1* represents either true or false. It's also easy to write *0* when you mean *1* and vice versa.

CROSS-REFERENCE
For details on using pre-processor macros or global variables to simulate enumerated types, see "If Your Language Doesn't Have Enumerated Types" in Section 11.6.

Use terms named *True* and *False* for tests with boolean expressions. If your language doesn't support such terms directly, create them using preprocessor macros or global variables. The code example is rewritten below using global variables for *True* and *False*:

Basic Example of Using Global Variables (*TRUE* and *FALSE*) for Boolean Values

```
100 TRUE  = 1
110 FALSE = 0
...
1200 IF PRINTERROR = FALSE GOSUB 2000       ' initialize printer
1210 IF PRINTERROR = TRUE GOSUB 3000        ' notify user of error
1230 '
1240 IF REPORTSELECTED = FIRST GOSUB 4000   ' print report
1250 IF SUMMARYSELECTED = TRUE GOSUB 5000   ' print summary
1260 '
1270 IF PRINTERROR = FALSE GOSUB 6000       ' clean up successful printing
```

Use of the variables named *TRUE* and *FALSE* makes the intent clearer. You don't have to remember what *1* and *0* represent, and you won't accidentally reverse them. Moreover, in the rewritten code, it's now clear that some of the *1*s and *0*s in the original Basic example weren't being used as boolean flags. The *IF REPORTSELECTED = 1* line was not a boolean test at all; it tested whether the first report had been selected.

This approach tells the reader that you're making a boolean test; it's harder to write *True* when you mean *False* than it is to write *1* when you mean *0*, and you avoid spreading the magic numbers *0* and *1* throughout your code. Here are some tips on defining *True* and *False* in boolean tests:

In C, use the *1==1* trick to define *TRUE* and *FALSE*. In C, sometimes it's hard to remember whether *TRUE* equals *1* and *FALSE* equals *0* or vice versa. You could remember that testing for *FALSE* is the same as testing for a null terminator or another zero value. Otherwise, an easy way to avoid the problem is to define *TRUE* and *FALSE* as follows:

C Example of Easy-to-Remember Boolean Definitions

```
#define TRUE  (1==1)
#define FALSE (!TRUE)
```

CROSS-REFERENCE
For details, see Section
11.5, "Boolean Variables."

Compare boolean values to *False* implicitly. If your language supports boolean variables, you can write clearer tests by treating the expressions as boolean expressions. For example, write

```
while ( not Done ) ...
while ( a = b ) ...
```

rather than

```
while ( Done = False ) ...
while ( (a = b) = True ) ...
```

Using implicit comparisons reduces the number of terms that someone reading your code has to keep in mind, and the resulting expressions read more like conversational English.

If your language doesn't support boolean variables and you have to emulate them, you might not be able to use this technique because emulations of *True* and *False* can't always be tested with statements like *while (not Done)*.

Making Complicated Expressions Simple

You can take several steps to simplify complicated expressions.

CROSS-REFERENCE
Examples of simplifying
complicated tests are given
in Section 14.1, "*if* Statements," and Section 11.5,
"Boolean Variables."

Break complicated tests into partial tests with new boolean variables. Rather than creating a monstrous test with half a dozen terms, assign intermediate values to terms that allow you to perform a simpler test.

Move complicated expressions into boolean functions. If a test is repeated often or distracts from the main flow of the program, move the code for the test into a function and test the value of the function. For example, here's a complicated test:

Pascal Example of a Complicated Test

```
if ( ( eof( InputFile ) and (Not InputError) ) and
     ( (MIN_ACCEPTABLE_ELEMENTS_C < CountElementsRead) and
       (CountElementsRead <= MAX_ELEMENTS_C) ) or
     ( Not ErrorProcessing )
   ) then

   { do something or other }
   ...
```

This is an ugly test to have to read through if you're not interested in the test itself. By putting it into a boolean function, you can isolate the test and allow the reader to forget about it unless it's important. Here's how you could put the *if* test into a function:

Pascal Example of a Complicated Test Moved into a Boolean Function

```
Function FileReadError
   (
   var FILE    InputFile;
       Boolean InputError;
       Integer CountElementsRead
   ): Boolean;

begin
if ( ( eof( InputFile ) and (Not InputError) ) and
     ( (MIN_ACCEPTABLE_ELEMENTS_C < CountElementsRead) and
       (CountElementsRead <= MAX_ELEMENTS_C) ) or
     ( Not ErrorProcessing )
   ) then
   FileReadError := False
else
   FileReadError := True;
end;
```

This example assumes that *ErrorProcessing* is a boolean function that indicates the current processing status. Now, when you read through the main flow of the code, you don't have to read the complicated test:

Pascal Example of the Main Flow of the Code Without the Complicated Test

```
if ( not FileReadError( InputFile, InputError, CountElementsRead ) ) then

   { do something or other }
   ...
```

KEY POINT

If you use the test only once, you might not think it's worthwhile to put it into a routine. But putting the test into a well-named routine improves readability and makes it easier for you to see what your code is doing, and that is a sufficient reason to do it.

Use decision tables to replace complicated conditions. Sometimes you have a complicated test involving several variables. It can be helpful to use a decision table to perform the test rather than using *ifs* or *cases*. A decision-table lookup is easier to code initially, having only a couple of lines of code and no tricky control structures. This minimization of complexity minimizes the opportunity for mistakes. If your data changes, you can change a decision table without changing the code; you only need to update the contents of the data structure.

CROSS-REFERENCE
For details on using tables as substitutes for complicated logic, see Section 12.2, "Table-Driven Methods."

Forming Boolean Expressions Positively

Not a few people don't have not any trouble understanding a nonshort string of nonpositives—that is, most people have trouble understanding a lot of negatives. You can do several things to avoid complicated negative boolean expressions in your programs.

In *if* statements, convert negatives to positives and flip-flop the code in the *if* and *else* clauses. Here's an example of a negatively expressed test:

Pascal Example of a Confusing Negative Boolean Test

Here's the ⎯ *negative not.*

```
if ( not StatusOK ) begin
   { do something }
   ...
end
else begin
   { do something else }
   ...
end;
```

You can change this to the following positively expressed test:

The test in this line
has been reversed. —
The code in this block —
has been switched...

...with the code in —
this block.

Pascal Example of a Clearer Positive Boolean Test

```
if ( StatusOK ) begin
   { do something else }
   ...
end
else begin
   { do something }
   ...
end;
```

CROSS-REFERENCE
The recommendation to
frame boolean expressions
positively sometimes con-
tradicts the recommenda-
tion to code the nominal
case after the *if* rather than
the *else*. (See Section 14.1,
"*if* Statements.") In such a
case, you have to think
about the benefits of each
approach and decide which
is better for your situation.

The second code fragment is logically the same as the first but is easier to read because the negative expression has been changed to a positive.

Alternatively, you could choose a different variable name, one that would reverse the truth value of the test. In the example, you could replace *StatusOK* with *ErrorDetected*, which would be true when *StatusOK* was false.

Apply DeMorgan's Theorems to simplify boolean tests with negatives. DeMorgan's Theorems let you exploit the logical relationship between an expression and a version of the expression that means the same thing because it's doubly negated. For example, you might have a code fragment that contains the following test:

Pascal Example of a Negative Test

```
if ( not DisplayOK or not PrinterOK ) then ...
```

This is logically equivalent to the following:

Pascal Example After Applying DeMorgan's Theorem

```
if ( not ( DisplayOK and PrinterOK ) ) then ...
```

Here you don't have to flip-flop *if* and *else* clauses; the expressions in the last two code fragments are logically equivalent. To apply DeMorgan's Theorems to the logical operator *and* or the logical operator *or* and a pair of operands, you negate each of the operands, switch the *and*s and *or*s, and negate the entire expression. Table 17-1 summarizes the possible transformations under DeMorgan's Theorems:

**Table 17-1. Transformations of Logical Expressions
Under DeMorgan's Theorems**

Initial Expression	Equivalent Expression
not A and not B	not (A or B)
not A and B	not (A or not B)
A and not B	not (not A or B)
A and B	not (not A or not B)
not A or not B*	not (A and B)
not A or B	not (A and not B)
A or not B	not (not A and B)
A or B	not (not A and not B)

* This is the expression used in the example.

Using Parentheses to Clarify Boolean Expressions

CROSS REFERENCE
For an example of using
parentheses to clarify
other kinds of expressions,
see "Parentheses"
in Section 18.2.

If you have a complicated boolean expression, rather than relying on the language's evaluation order, parenthesize to make your meaning clear. Using parentheses makes less of a demand on your reader, who might not understand the subtleties of how your language evaluates boolean expressions. If you're smart, you won't depend on your own or your reader's in-depth memorization of evaluation precedence—especially when you have to switch among two or more languages. Using parentheses isn't like sending a telegram: You're not charged for each character—the extra characters are free.

Here's an expression with too few parentheses:

C Example of an Expression Containing Too Few Parentheses
```
if ( a < b == c == d ) ...
```

This is a confusing expression to begin with, and it's even more confusing because it's not clear whether the coder means to test $(a < b) == (c == d)$ or $((a < b) == c) == d$. The following version of the expression is still a little confusing, but the parentheses help:

C Example of an Expression Better Parenthesized
```
if ( (a < b) == (c == d) ) ...
```

In this case, the parentheses help readability and the program's correctness—the compiler wouldn't have interpreted the first code fragment this way. When in doubt, parenthesize.

CROSS-REFERENCE
Many programmer-oriented text editors have commands that match parentheses, brackets, and braces. For details on programming editors, see "Editing" in Section 20.2.

Use a simple counting technique to balance parentheses. If you have trouble telling whether parentheses balance, here's a simple counting trick that helps. Start by saying "zero." Move along the expression, left to right. When you encounter an opening parenthesis, say "one." Each time you encounter another opening parenthesis, increase the number you say. Each time you encounter a closing parenthesis, decrease the number you say. If, at the end of the expression, you're back to 0, your parentheses are balanced.

```
Pascal Example of Balanced Parentheses

Read this. ── if ( ( ( A < B ) = ( C = D ) ) and not Done ) ...
                  | | |         |   |         | |             |
Say this.  ── 0   1 2 3         2   3         2 1             0
```

In this example, you ended with a 0, so the parentheses are balanced. In the next example, the parentheses aren't balanced:

```
Pascal Example of Unbalanced Parentheses

Read this. ── if ( ( A < B ) = ( C = D ) ) and not Done ) ...
                  | |         |   |         | |             |
Say this.  ── 0   1 2         1   2         1 0            −1
```

The 0 in the middle of the line is a tip-off that a parenthesis is missing before that point. You shouldn't get a 0 until the last parenthesis of the expression.

Knowing How Boolean Expressions Are Evaluated

Many languages have an implied form of control that comes into play in the evaluation of boolean expressions. Compilers for some languages evaluate each term in a boolean expression before combining the terms and evaluating the whole expression. Compilers for other languages have "short-circuit" or "lazy" evaluation, evaluating only the pieces necessary. This is particularly significant when, depending on the results of the first test, you might not want the second test to be executed. For example, suppose you're checking the elements of an array and you have the following test:

CROSS-REFERENCE
The pseudocode used here doesn't follow the guidelines for using PDL in Section 4.2. In this case, pseudocode is used to avoid tripping over details of how the tests are performed in a specific language.

Pseudocode Example of an Erroneous Test

```
while ( i <= MaxElements and item[ i ] <> 0 ) do ...
```

If this whole expression is evaluated, you'll get an error on the last pass through the loop. The variable i equals *MaxElements+1*, so the expression *item[i]* is equivalent to *item[MaxElements+1]*, which is an array-index error. You might argue that it doesn't matter since you're only looking at the value, not changing it. That's true in real-mode operating systems like the Macintosh's and MS-DOS. But in operating systems that have a protected mode, like Microsoft Windows and OS/2, you can get a protection violation. The same holds true in languages that perform run-time bounds checking, like Pascal and Basic.

In pseudocode, you could restructure the test so that the error doesn't occur:

Pseudocode Example of a Correctly Restructured Test

```
while ( i <- MaxElements ) do
    if ( item[ i ] <> 0 ) then
        ...
```

This is correct because *item[i]* isn't evaluated unless i is less than or equal to *MaxElements*.

Many modern languages provide facilities that prevent this kind of error from happening in the first place. For example, C and Pascal use short-circuit evaluation: If the first operand of the *and* is false, the second isn't evaluated because the whole expression would be false anyway. In other words, in C and Pascal, the only part of

```
if SomethingFalse and SomeCondition ...
```

that's evaluated is *if SomethingFalse*. Evaluation stops as soon as *SomethingFalse* is identified as false.

Evaluation is similarly short-circuited with the *or* operator. In C and Pascal, the only part of

```
if SomethingTrue or SomeCondition ...
```

that is evaluated is *if SomethingTrue*. The evaluation stops as soon as *SomethingTrue* is identified as true. As a result of this method of evaluation, the statement on the next page is a fine, legal statement.

> **Pascal Example of a Test That Works Because of Short-Circuit Evaluation**
>
> ```
> if ( ( Denominator <> 0 ) and ( Item / Denominator > MinVal ) ) do ...
> ```

If this full expression were evaluated when *Denominator* equaled *0*, the division in the second operand would produce a divide-by-zero error. But since the second part isn't evaluated unless the first part is true, it is never evaluated when *Denominator* equals *0*, so no divide-by-zero error occurs.

On the other hand, since the *and* is evaluated left to right, the following logically equivalent statement doesn't work:

> **Pascal Example of a Test That Short-Circuit Evaluation Doesn't Rescue**
>
> ```
> if ( ( Item / Denominator < MinVal ) and ( Denominator <> 0 ) ) do ...
> ```

In this case, *Item / Denominator* is evaluated before *Denominator <> 0*. Consequently, this code commits the divide-by-zero error.

Different languages use different kinds of evaluation, and language implementers tend to take liberties with expression evaluation, so check the manual for the specific version of the language you're using to find out what kind of evaluation your language uses. Better yet, since a reader of your code might not be as sharp as you are, use nested tests to clarify your intentions instead of depending on evaluation order and short-circuit evaluation.

Writing Numeric Expressions in Number-Line Order

Organize numeric tests so that they follow the points on a numberline. In general, structure your numeric tests so that you have comparisons like

```
MinElmts <= i and i <= MaxElmts
i < MinElmts or MaxElmts < i
```

The idea is to order the elements left to right, from smallest to largest. In the first line, *MinElmts* and *MaxElmts* are the two endpoints, so they go at the ends. The variable *i* is supposed to be between them, so it goes in the middle. In the second example, you're testing whether *i* is outside the range, so *i* goes on the outside of the test at either end and *MinElmts* and *MaxElmts* go on the inside. This approach maps easily to a visual image of the comparison:

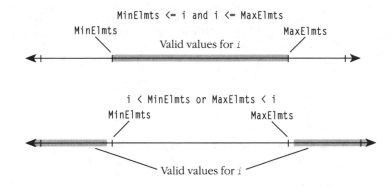

If you're testing *i* against *MinElmts* only, the position of *i* varies depending on where *i* is when the test is successful. If *i* is supposed to be smaller, you'll have a test like

```
while ( i < MinElmts ) ...
```

But if *i* is supposed to be larger, you'll have a test like

```
while ( MinElmts < i ) ...
```

This approach is clearer than tests like

```
i > MinElmts and i < MaxElmts
```

which give the reader no help in visualizing what is being tested.

Guidelines for Comparisons to *0* in C

C uses *0* for several purposes. It's a numeric value. It's a null terminator in a string. It's the lowest address a pointer can have. It's *False* in logical expressions. Because it's used for so many purposes, you should write code that highlights the specific way *0* is used.

Compare logical variables implicitly. As mentioned earlier, it's appropriate to write logical expressions such as

```
while ( ! Done ) ...
```

This implicit comparison to *0* is appropriate because the comparison is in a logical expression.

Compare numbers to *0*. Although it's appropriate to compare logical expressions implicitly, you should compare numeric expressions explicitly. For numbers, write

```
while ( Balance != 0 ) ...
```

rather than

```
while ( Balance ) ...
```

Compare characters to the null terminator ('*0*'). Characters, like numbers, aren't logical expressions. Thus, for characters, write

```
while ( *CharPtr != '\0' ) ...
```

rather than

```
while ( *CharPtr ) ...
```

This recommendation goes against the common C convention for handling character data (as in the second example), but it reinforces the idea that the expression is working with character data rather than logical data. Some C conventions aren't based on maximizing readability or maintainability, and this is an example of one.

Compare pointers to NULL. For pointers, write

```
while ( BufferPtr != NULL ) ...
```

rather than

```
while ( BufferPtr ) ...
```

Like the recommendation for characters, this one goes against the established C convention, but the gain in readability justifies it.

Common Problems with Boolean Expressions

C poses some special problems with boolean expressions. In C, interchanging bitwise operators with logical operators is a common gotcha. It's easy to use *|* instead of *||* or *&* instead of *&&*. If you have such a problem, create macros for boolean *and* and *or*, and use *AND* and *OR* instead of *&&* and *||*. Similarly, using = when you mean == is an easy mistake to make. If you get stung often by this one, create a macro for assignment or logical equals. Usually an *EQUALS* macro for logical equals (==) is sufficient.

17.2   Compound Statements (Blocks)

A "compound statement" or "block" is a collection of statements that are treated as a single statement for purposes of controlling the flow of a program. Compound statements are created by writing *begin* and *end* or *{* and *}* around a group of statements. Sometimes they are implied by the keywords of a command, such as *FOR* and *NEXT* in Basic or any control structure in Ada. Here are some guidelines for using compound statements effectively:

CROSS-REFERENCE
Many programmer-oriented text editors have commands that match braces, brackets, and parentheses. For details, see "Editing" in Section 20.2.

Write pairs of braces or *begin*-and-*end* pairs together. Fill in the middle after you write both the opening and closing parts of a block. People often complain about how hard it is to match pairs of braces or *begin*-and-*end* pairs, and that's a completely unnecessary problem. If you follow this guideline, you will never have trouble matching such pairs again.

Write this first:
```
for i := 0 to MaxLines do
```

Write this next:
```
for i := 0 to MaxLines do
    begin
    end;
```

Write this last:
```
for i := 0 to MaxLines do
    begin
    { whatever goes in here }
    ...
    end;
```

This applies to all blocking structures, to *FOR-NEXT*, *WHILE-WEND*, and *IF-THEN-ELSE* combinations in Basic, and to Fortran *do* loops and loop labels.

Use pairs of braces or *begin*-and-*end* pairs to clarify conditionals. Conditionals are hard enough to read without having to determine which statements go with the *if* test. If the code is at all ambiguous, use block statements to clarify your intentions.

17.3   Null Statements

In C, it's possible to have a null statement, a statement consisting entirely of a semicolon. An example is shown on the next page.

C Example of a Traditional Null Statement

```
while ( (c = getch()) != '\n' )
    ;
```

The *while* in C requires that a statement follow, but it can be a null statement. The semicolon on a line by itself is a null statement. Here are guidelines for handling null statements in C:

CROSS-REFERENCE
The best way to handle null statements is probably to avoid them. For details, see "Avoid empty loops" in Section 15.2.

Call attention to null statements. Null statements are uncommon, so make them obvious. One way is to give the semicolon of a null statement a line of its own. Indent it, just as you would any other statement. This is the approach shown in the previous example. Alternatively, you can use a set of empty braces to emphasize the null statement. Here are two examples:

C Examples of a Null Statement That's Emphasized

This is one way —
to show the null
statement.

```
while ( (c = getch()) != '\n' ) {};
```

This is another way —
to show it.

```
while ( (c = getch()) != '\n' )
    {
    ;
    }
```

Create a preprocessor *null()* macro for null statements. The statement doesn't do anything but make indisputably clear the fact that nothing is supposed to be done. This is similar to marking blank document pages with the statement "This page intentionally left blank." The page isn't really blank, but you know nothing else is supposed to be on it.

Here's how you can make your own null statement in C:

C Example of a Null Statement That's Emphasized with a *null()* Macro

```
#define null()
...
while ( ( c = getch() ) != '\n' )
    null();
```

In addition to using the *null()* macro in empty *while* and *for* loops, you can use it for unimportant choices of a *switch* statement; including *null()* makes it clear that the case was considered and nothing is supposed to be done. This guideline applies equally to Pascal, in which you can simulate *null()* with a routine, and to Ada, which has a built-in *null()*.

Note that this *null()* macro is different from the traditional preprocessor macro *NULL* that's used for a null pointer. The value of the pointer *NULL* depends on your hardware but is usually *0*, or *0L*, or something like that. It's never simply empty, as the *null()* macro defined here is.

17.4 Taming Dangerously Deep Nesting

HARD DATA

KEY POINT

Excessive indentation, or "nesting," has been pilloried in computing literature for 15 years and is still one of the chief culprits in confusing code. Studies by Noam Chomsky and Gerald Weinberg suggest that few people can understand more than three levels of nested *if*s (Yourdon 1986a), and many researchers recommend avoiding nesting to more than three or four levels (Myers 1976, Marca 1981, and Ledgard and Tauer 1987a).

It's not hard to avoid deep nesting. If you have deep nesting, you can redesign the tests performed in the *if* and *else* clauses or you can break code into simpler routines. The following sections present several ways to reduce the nesting depth.

CROSS-REFERENCE
Retesting part of the condition to reduce complexity is similar to retesting a status variable. That technique is demonstrated in "Error Processing and *goto*s" in Section 16.1.

Simplify a nested *if* by retesting part of the condition. If the nesting gets too deep, you can decrease the number of nesting levels by retesting some of the conditions. Here's a code example with nesting that's deep enough to warrant restructuring:

```
C Example of Badly, Deeply, Nested Code
if ( Error == None )
   {
   /* lots of code */
   ...
   if ( PrinterRoutine != NULL )
      {
      /* lots of code */
      ...
      if ( SetupPage() )
         {
         /* lots of code */
         ...
         if ( AllocMem( &PrintData ) )
            {
            /* lots of code */
            ...
            } /* if AllocMem() */
         } /* if SetupPage() */
      } /* if PrinterRoutine */
   } /* if Error */
```

This example is contrived to show nesting levels. The */* lots of code */ parts are intended to suggest that the routine has enough code to stretch across several screens or across the page boundary of a printed code listing. Here's the code revised to use retesting rather than nesting:

C Example of Code Mercifully Unnested by Retesting

```c
if ( Error == None )
   {
   /* lots of code */
   ...
   if ( PrinterRoutine != NULL )
      {
      /* lots of code */
      ...
      }
   }

if ( Error == None && PrinterRoutine != NULL && SetupPage() )
   {
   /* lots of code */
   ...
   if ( AllocMem( &PrintData ) )
      {
      /* lots of code */
      ...
      }
   }
```

This is a particularly realistic example because it shows that you can't reduce the nesting level for free; you have to put up with a more complicated test in return for the reduced level of nesting. A reduction from four levels to two is a big improvement in readability, however, and is worth considering.

Convert a nested *if* to a set of *if-then-else*s. If you think about a nested *if* test critically, you might discover that you can reorganize it so that it uses *if-then-else*s rather than nested *if*s. Suppose you have a bushy decision tree like this:

Pascal Example of an Overgrown Decision Tree

```pascal
if ( Qty > 10 ) then
   if ( Qty > 100 ) then
      if ( Qty > 1000 ) then
         Discount := 0.10
```

(continued)

382

```
      else
          Discount := 0.05
    else
        Discount := 0.025
else
    Discount := 0.0;
```

This test is poorly organized for several reasons, one of which is that the tests are redundant. When you test whether *Qty* is greater than *1000*, you don't also need to test whether it's greater than *100* and greater than *10*. Consequently, you can reorganize the code:

Pascal Example of a Nested *if* Converted to a Set of *if-then-else*s

```
if ( Qty > 1000 ) then
    Discount := 0.10
else if ( Qty > 100 ) then
    Discount := 0.05
else if ( Qty > 10 ) then
    Discount := 0.025
else
    Discount := 0;
```

This solution is easier than some because the numbers increase neatly. Here's how you could rework the nested *if* if the numbers weren't so tidy:

Pascal Example of a Nested *if* Converted to a Set of *if-then-else*s When the Numbers Are "Messy"

```
if ( Qty > 1000 ) then
    Discount := 0.10
else if ( Qty > 100 and Qty <= 1000 ) then
    Discount := 0.05
else if ( Qty > 10 and Qty <= 100 ) then
    Discount := 0.025
else if ( Qty <= 10 )
    Discount := 0;
```

The main difference between this code and the previous code is that the expressions in the *else-if* clauses don't rely on previous tests. This code doesn't need the *else* clauses to work, and the tests actually could be performed in any order. The code could consist of four *if*s and no *else*s. The only reason the *else* version is preferable is that it avoids repeating tests unnecessarily.

Convert a nested *if* to a *case* statement. You can recode some kinds of tests, particularly those with integers, to use a *case* statement rather than chains of *if*s and *else*s. You can't use this technique in some languages, but it's a powerful technique for those in which you can. Here's how to recode the example in Pascal:

Pascal Example of Converting a Nested *if* to a *case* Statement

```
case Qty of
   0..10:     Discount := 0.0;
   11..100:   Discount := 0.025;
   101..1000: Discount := 0.05;
   else       Discount := 0.10;
end; { case }
```

This example reads like a book. When you compare it to the two examples of multiple indentations a few pages earlier, it seems like a particularly clean solution.

Factor deeply nested code into its own routine. If deep nesting occurs inside a loop, you can often improve the situation by putting the inside of the loop into its own routine. This is especially effective if the nesting is a result of both conditionals and iterations. Leave the *if-then-else* branches in the main loop to show the decision branching, and then move the statements within the branches to their own routines. Here's an example of code that needs to be improved by such a modification:

C Example of Nested Code That Needs to Be Broken into Routines

```
while ( ! feof( TransFile ) )
   {
   /* read transaction record */

   ReadTransRec( TransFile, TransRec );

   /* process transaction depending on type of transaction */

   if ( TransRec.TransType == Deposit )
      {
      /* process a deposit */

      if ( TransRec.AccountType == Checking )
         {
```

(continued)

```
            if ( TransRec.AcctSubType == Business )
               MakeBusinessCheckDep( TransRec.AcctNum, TransRec.Amount );
            else if ( TransRec.AcctSubType == Personal )
               MakePersonalCheckDep( TransRec.AcctNum, TransRec.Amount );
            else if ( TransRec.AcctSubType == School )
               MakeSchoolCheckDep( TransRec.AcctNum, TransRec.Amount );
            }
         else if ( TransRec.AccountType == Savings )
            MakeSavingsDep( TransRec.AcctNum, TransRec.Amount );
         else if ( TransRec.AccountType == DebitCard )
            MakeDebitCardDep( TransRec.AcctNum, TransRec.Amount );
         else if ( TransRec.AccountType == MoneyMarket )
            MakeMoneyMarketDep( TransRec.AcctNum, TransRec.Amount );
         else if ( TransRec.AccountType == CD )
            MakeCDDep( TransRec.AcctNum, TransRec.Amount );
         }
      else if ( TransRec.TransType == Withdrawal )
         {
         /* process a withdrawal */

         if ( TransRec.AccountType == Checking )
            MakeCheckingWithdrawal( TransRec.AcctNum, TransRec.Amount );
         else if ( TransRec.AccountType == Savings )
            MakeSavingsWithdrawal( TransRec.AcctNum, TransRec.Amount );
         else if ( TransRec.AccountType == DebitCard )
            MakeDebitCardWithdrawal( TransRec.AcctNum, TransRec.Amount );
         }
      else if ( TransRec.TransType == Transfer )
         {
         MakeFundsTransfer( TransRec.SrcAcctType, TransRec.TgtAcctType,
            TransRec.AcctNum, TransRec.Amount );
         }
      else
         {
         /* process unknown kind of transaction */

         LogTransError( "Unknown Transaction Type", TransRec );
         }
      }
```

Here's the Transfer transaction type.

Although it's complicated, this isn't the worst code you'll ever see. It's nested to only four levels, it's commented, it's logically indented, and the functional decomposition is adequate, especially for the *Transfer* transaction type. In spite of its adequacy, however, you can improve it by breaking the contents of the inner *if* tests into their own routines.

CROSS-REFERENCE
This kind of functional decomposition is especially easy if you initially built the routine using the steps described in Chapter 4, "Steps in Building a Routine." Guidelines for functional decomposition are given in "Choosing Components to Modularize" in Section 7.2.

C Example of Good, Nested Code After Decomposition into Routines

```c
while ( ! feof( TransFile ) )
   {
   /* read transaction record */

   ReadTransRec( TransFile, TransRec );

   /* process transaction depending on type of transaction */

   if ( TransRec.TransType == Deposit )
      {
      ProcessDeposit( TransRec.AccountType, TransRec.AcctSubType,
         TransRec.AcctNum, TransRec.Amount );
      }
   else if ( TransRec.TransType == Withdrawal )
      {
      ProcessWithdrawal( TransRec.AccountType, TransRec.AcctNum,
         TransRec.Amount );
      }
   else if ( TransRec.TransType == Transfer )
      {
      MakeFundsTransfer( TransRec.SrcAcctType, TransRec.TgtAcctType,
         TransRec.AcctNum, TransRec.Amount );
      }
   else
      {
      /* process unknown transaction type */

      LogTransError( "Unknown Transaction Type", TransRec );
      }
   }
```

CROSS-REFERENCE
For details on the general advantages of modularization, see Chapter 6, "Three out of Four Programmers Surveyed Prefer Modules."

The code in the new routines has simply been lifted out of the original routine and formed into new routines. (The new routines aren't shown here.) The new code has several advantages. First, two-level nesting makes the structure simpler and easier to understand. Second, you can read, modify, and debug the shorter *while* loop on one screen—it doesn't need to be broken across screen or printed-page boundaries. Third, putting the functionality of *ProcessDeposit()* and *ProcessWithdrawal()* into routines accrues all the other general advantages of modularization. Fourth, it's now easy to see that the code could be broken into a *switch-case* statement, which would make it even easier to read, as shown below:

C Example of Good, Nested Code After Decomposition and Use of a
switch-case Statement

```c
while ( ! feof( TransFile ) )
   {
   /* read transaction record */

   ReadTransRec( TransFile, TransRec );

   /* process transaction depending on type of transaction */

   switch ( TransRec.TransType )
      {
      case ( Deposit ):
         ProcessDeposit( TransRec.AccountType, TransRec.AcctSubType,
            TransRec.AcctNum, TransRec.Amount );
         break;

      case ( Withdrawal ):
         ProcessWithdrawal( TransRec.AccountType, TransRec.AcctNum,
            TransRec.Amount );
         break;

      case ( Transfer ):
         MakeFundsTransfer( TransRec.SrcAcctType, TransRec.TgtAcctType,
            TransRec.AcctNum, TransRec.Amount );
         break;

      default:
         /* process unknown transaction type */

         LogTransError( "Unknown Transaction Type", TransRec );
         break;
      }
   }
```

Redesign deeply nested code. In general, complicated code is a sign that you don't understand your program well enough to make it simple. Deep nesting is a warning sign that indicates a need to break out a routine or redesign the part of the code that's complicated. It doesn't mean you have to modify the routine, but you should have a good reason if you don't.

17.5 The Power of Structured Programming

FURTHER READING
The term "structured programming" originated in a landmark paper, "Structured Programming," presented by Edsger Dijkstra at the 1969 NATO conference on software engineering (Dijkstra 1969). A definitive description of the practice is the subject of *Structured Programming* (Dahl, Dijkstra, and Hoare 1972).

What does "structured programming" mean? The core of structured programming is the simple idea that a program should use only one-in, one-out control constructs (also called single-entry, single-exit control constructs). A one-in, one-out control construct is a block of code that has only one place it can start and only one place it can end. It has no other entries or exits.

Benefits of Structured Programming

Why does this book devote an entire section to the 20-year-old topic of structured programming? Doesn't everyone use it?

No. Not everyone uses structured programming, and many of the people who think they're using it aren't. Gerald Weinberg visited about 100 programming shops and interviewed thousands of programmers. He reports that only about 5 percent of code is thoroughly structured; 20 percent is structured enough to be an improvement over the average code of 1969; 50 percent shows evidence of an attempt to follow structuring rules but with little success; and 25 percent shows no evidence of influence by any programming ideas of the past 20 years (Weinberg 1988).

HARD DATA

Some programmers are skeptical about the value of structured programming. They mistakenly believe that structured programming is expensive and time-consuming, produces slow programs, and hurts programmer motivation and productivity (Glass 1982). Other reports confirm the resistance to structured programming (Elshoff 1976; Lientz and Swanson 1980; Parnas, Clements, and Weiss 1985).

HARD DATA

In spite of the negative perception, the evidence on the effectiveness of structured programming is overwhelming. A review of experimental data found that structured code always exhibits a gain in productivity (Brooks 1981). In projects with severe constraints or complexity, the productivity gain was strongest, ranging from 200 to 600 percent. A study at General Motors found that time and training for structured techniques had almost paid for itself within six months (Elshoff 1977).

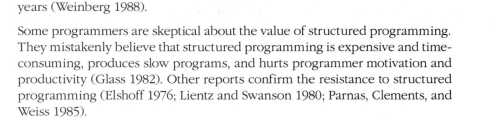

HARD DATA

In addition to improving productivity, structured programming improves readability. In an experiment in which 36 professional programmers tried to understand programs written in both structured and unstructured Fortran, the mean comprehension score for the structured programs was 56 percent and for the nonstructured programs was 42 percent (Sheppard et al. 1978). This is a 33 percent improvement in comprehension with structured programming. Similar results were reported in "Improving Computer Program Readability to Aid Modification" (Elshoff and Marcotty 1982).

A structured program progresses in an orderly, disciplined way, rather than jumping around unpredictably. You can read it from top to bottom, and it executes in much the same way. Less disciplined approaches result in source code that provides a less meaningful, less readable picture of how a program executes in the machine. Less readability means less understanding and, ultimately, lower program quality.

The Three Components of Structured Programming

The term "structured" has been a popular buzzword for many years and has been applied to every software-development activity, including structured analysis, structured design, and structured goofing off. The various structured methodologies aren't joined by any common thread except that they were all created at a time when the word "structured" gave them extra cachet.

Consequently, some people have misperceptions about structured programming and the term has been abused in several ways. First, structured programming isn't a method of indentation. It doesn't have anything to do with program layout. Second, structured programming isn't top-down design. It applies only at the detailed coding level. Third, structured programming isn't any time-saving technique whatsoever that makes a buck for someone conducting a seminar. Incidentally, all of the points above hold true for "object-oriented," the name of a valuable concept that promises to be the abused phrase of the 1990s.

The next few sections describe the three constructs that constitute the legitimate core of structured programming.

Sequence

CROSS-REFERENCE
For details on using sequences, see Chapter 13, "Organizing Straight-Line Code."

A sequence is a set of statements executed in order. Typical sequential statements include assignments and calls to routines. Here are two examples:

Pascal Examples of Sequential Code

```
{ a sequence of assignment statements }

a := 1;
b := 2;
c := 3;

{ a sequence of calls to routines }

Writeln( a );
Writeln( b );
Writeln( c );
```

Selection

CROSS-REFERENCE
For details on using selections, see Chapter 14, "Using Conditionals."

A selection is a control structure that causes statements to be executed selectively. The *if-then-else* statement is a common example. Either the *if-then* clause or the *else* clause is executed, but not both. One of the clauses is "selected" for execution.

A *case* statement is another example of selection control. The *case* statements in Pascal and Ada and the *switch* statement in C are all examples of *case*. In each instance, one of several cases is selected for execution. Conceptually, *if* statements and *case* statements are similar. If your language doesn't support *case* statements, you can emulate them with *if* statements. Here are two examples of selection:

Pascal Examples of Selection

```
{ selection in an if statement }

if ( a = 0 ) then
   { do something }
else
   { do something else }

{ selection in a case statement }

case ( Shape ) of
    Square:      DrawSquare;
    Circle:      DrawCircle;
    Pentagon:    DrawPentagon;
    DoubleHelix: DrawDoubleHelix;
end;
```

Iteration

CROSS-REFERENCE
For details on using iterations, see Chapter 15, "Controlling Loops."

An iteration is a control structure that causes a group of statements to be executed multiple times. An iteration is commonly referred to as a "loop." Kinds of iterations include *FOR-NEXT* in Basic, *DO* in Fortran, and *while* and *for* in Pascal and C. Once you kick the *goto* habit, iteration is the trickiest control structure. The code fragment below shows examples of iteration in Ada:

Ada Examples of Iteration

```
-- example of iteration using a for loop

for INDEX in FIRST..LAST loop
   DO_SOMETHING( INDEX );
end loop;
```

(continued)

```
-- example of iteration using a while loop

INDEX := FIRST;
while ( INDEX <= LAST ) loop
   DO_SOMETHING( INDEX );
   INDEX := INDEX + 1;
end loop;

-- example of iteration using a loop-with-exit loop

INDEX := FIRST;
loop
   exit when INDEX > LAST;
   DO_SOMETHING( INDEX );
   INDEX := INDEX + 1;
end loop;
```

17.6 Emulating Structured Constructs with *gotos*

If you program in assembler, Fortran, generic Basic, or another language that doesn't support structured control constructs directly, you're probably asking, "How does structured programming apply to me?" Well, just as critics of *gotos* often point out that you can replace every control construct with one or more of the three structured constructs, you can replace the three structured constructs with one or more *gotos*. The general recommendation to avoid *gotos* is meaningless if your language offers no other means of controlling the flow of a program. In such a case, you can restrict your use of *gotos* to emulations of the three structured programming constructs.

Emulating an *if-then-else* Statement

CROSS-REFERENCE
You can buy or write a pre-processor to add structured constructs to a language that doesn't have them. Writing your own tools is one key to making the best of an archaic programming environment. For details, see Section 20.5, "Building Your Own Programming Tools."

If you want to write an *if-then-else* test using *gotos*, first write the test and the *if-then-else* structure in comments, as shown below. The example is in Fortran, but it can easily be adapted to assembler, Basic, or any other language you're using.

Fortran Example of Writing an *if-then-else* Test as Comments

```
C      if ( A < B ) then
C      else
C      endif
```

Second, fill in code around the comments. As a standard practice, you'll need to negate the condition written in the comments and branch on the rewritten condition's being true—the original condition's being false. To negate the original condition, put parentheses around it and put the *.NOT.* operator in front of the parenthesized expression. The *if* part of the statement uses a *goto* to jump to the *else* part of the statement. Here's the result:

This statement is the negated version of the structured statement in the comment immediately preceding it.

Fortran Example of Filling In an *if-then-else* Test

```
C      if ( A < B ) then
       IF ( .NOT. ( A .LT. B ) ) GOTO 1100
          CODE TO PERFORM IF THE ORIGINAL CONDITION IN COMMENTS IS TRUE
          ...
          GOTO 1200
C      else
1100      CONTINUE
          CODE TO PERFORM IF THE ORIGINAL CONDITION IN COMMENTS IS FALSE
          ...
1200   CONTINUE
C      endif
```

Notice that the *if, else,* and *endif* comments are indented with the code that implements them. This is done so that the logical structure of the code isn't visually disturbed by the comments.

Here's the same code fragment in Basic:

Basic Example of Emulating an *if-then-else* Test with *goto*s

```
1000 'if ( A < B ) then
1010 IF ( NOT ( A < B ) ) THEN GOTO 1100
1020    CODE TO PERFORM IF THE ORIGINAL CONDITION IN COMMENTS IS TRUE
        ...
1090    GOTO 1200
1100 'else
1110    CODE TO PERFORM IF THE ORIGINAL CONDITION IN COMMENTS IS FALSE
        ...
1200 'endif
```

You can use the same technique in any other language that features *goto*s.

Emulating a *case* Statement

Conceptually, when you emulate a *case* statement with *goto*s you're writing a big chain of *if-then-else* clauses that all happen to have a common termination point after the last clause. It's a good idea to write the comments first and then fill in the code, as was shown for the *if-then* statement. Here's the completed *case* statement in Fortran:

Fortran Example of Filling In a *case* Statement

```
C     case ( LETTER )
C         'A':
          IF ( LETTER .NE. 'A' ) GOTO 1100
              DO SOMETHING FOR CASE 'A'
              GOTO 1900
C         'E':
1100      IF ( LETTER .NE. 'E' ) GOTO 1200
              DO SOMETHING FOR CASE 'E'
              GOTO 1900
C         'F':
1200      IF ( LETTER .NE. 'F' ) GOTO 1300
              DO SOMETHING FOR CASE 'F'
              GOTO 1900
C         else
1300      CONTINUE
              CALL ERROR( "Internal error: Call customer assistance." )
1900  CONTINUE
C     end case
```

In this example, each case is tested with an *if*. Each test that fails uses a *goto* to move to the next test. The *else* clause uses a *CONTINUE* statement for the *goto* label (line 1300 in the example). The last line of code in each case uses a *goto* to move to the end of the *case* structure (line 1900 in the example). Thus, only one case is executed. You can use the same technique in Basic and assembler.

Emulating a *while* Loop

The *while* loop is the most common looping structure if you practice structured programming. If you want to write a *while* loop that tests at the beginning of the loop, follow this example:

Fortran Example of a *while* Loop Emulated with *gotos*

```
C     loop initialization
      I = 0
C     while ( I < MAXI and X > 0.5 ) do
1000  IF ( .NOT. ( I .LT. MAXI .AND. X .GT. 0.5 ) ) GOTO 1010
C         DO SOMETHING
C         ...
          GOTO 1000
1010  CONTINUE
C     end while
```

The salient points here are about the same as those for the *case* statement discussed above. Note that loop initialization is explicitly present as a reminder that some initialization is often needed and that the *while* condition is negated as the *for* condition was earlier.

General Comments About Emulating Control Constructs

KEY POINT

Emulating structured control constructs with *goto*s helps you program *into* a language rather than *in* it. As David Gries pointed out, the choice of a language does not have to determine how you think about programming (1981). Understanding the distinction between programming into a language and programming in one is critical to understanding this book. Most of the important programming principles depend not on specific languages but on the way you use them.

If your language lacks structured constructs or is prone to other kinds of problems, try to compensate for them. Invent your own coding conventions, standards, library routines, and other augmentations.

By emulating structured-programming constructs, you can rise above the limited control constructs of assembler, generic Basic, or Fortran and program in a programming language of your own creation. Later you can translate the program from that language into whatever pale, real language you happen to be using.

17.7 Control Structures and Complexity

One reason so much attention has been paid to control structures is that they are a big contributor to overall program complexity. Poor use of control structures increases complexity; good use decreases it.

Make things as simple as possible— but no simpler.
Albert Einstein

One measure of "programming complexity" is the number of mental objects you have to keep in mind simultaneously in order to understand a program. This mental juggling act is one of the most difficult aspects of programming and is the reason programming requires more concentration than other activities. It's the reason programmers get upset about "quick interruptions"— such interruptions are tantamount to asking a juggler to keep three balls in the air and hold your groceries at the same time.

KEY POINT

Intuitively, the complexity of a program would seem to largely determine the amount of effort required to understand it. Tom McCabe published an influential paper arguing that a program's complexity is defined by its control flow (1976). Other researchers have identified factors other than McCabe's complexity metric (such as the number of variables used in a routine), but they agree that control flow is at least one of the largest contributors to complexity, if not the largest.

How Important Is Complexity?

Computer-science researchers have been aware of the importance of complexity for at least two decades. Twenty years ago, Edsger Dijkstra cautioned against the hazards of complexity: "The competent programmer is fully aware of the strictly limited size of his own skull; therefore he approaches the programming task in full humility" (1972). This does not imply that you should increase the capacity of your skull to deal with enormous complexity. It implies that you can never deal with enormous complexity and must take steps to reduce it wherever possible.

HARD DATA

Control-flow complexity is important because it has been correlated with low reliability and frequent errors (McCabe 1976, Shen et al. 1985). William T. Ward reported a significant gain in software reliability resulting from using McCabe's complexity metric at Hewlett-Packard (1989b). McCabe's metric was used on one 77,000-line program to identify problem areas. The program had a post-release defect rate of 0.31 defects per thousand lines of code. A 125,000-line program had a post-release defect rate of 0.02 defects per thousand lines of code. Ward reported that because of their lower complexity both programs had substantially fewer defects than other programs at Hewlett-Packard.

General Guidelines for Reducing Complexity

You can better deal with complexity in one of two ways. First, you can improve your own mental juggling abilities by doing mental exercises. But programming itself is usually enough exercise, and people seem to have trouble juggling more than about five to nine mental entities (Miller 1956). The potential for improvement is small. Second, you can decrease the complexity of your programs and the amount of concentration required to understand them.

FURTHER READING
The approach described here is based on Tom McCabe's influential paper "A Complexity Measure" (1976).

How to measure complexity

You probably have an intuitive feel for what makes a routine more or less complex. Researchers have tried to formalize their intuitive feelings and have come up with several ways of measuring complexity. Perhaps the most influential of the numeric techniques is Tom McCabe's, in which complexity is measured by counting the number of "decision points" in a routine. Table 17-2 describes a method for counting decision points.

Table 17-2. Techniques for Counting the Decision Points in a Routine

1. Start with 1 for the straight path through the routine.
2. Add 1 for each of the following keywords, or their equivalents:
   if   while   repeat   for   and   or
3. Add 1 for each case in a *case* statement.

Here's an example:

```
if ( ( (Status = Success) and Done ) or
    ( not Done and ( NumLines >= MaxLines ) ) ) then ...
```

In this fragment, you count 1 to start; 2 for the *if*; 3 for the *and*; 4 for the *or*; and 5 for the *and*. Thus, this fragment contains a total of five decision points.

What to do with your complexity measurement

After you have counted the decision points, you can use the number to analyze your routine's complexity. If the score is

0–5	The routine is probably fine.
6–10	Start to think about ways to simplify the routine.
10+	Break part of the routine into a second routine and call it from the first routine.

Moving part of a routine into another routine doesn't reduce the overall complexity of the program; it just moves the decision points around. But it reduces the amount of complexity you have to deal with at any one time. Since the important goal is to minimize the number of items you have to juggle mentally, reducing the complexity of a given routine is worthwhile.

The maximum of 10 decision points isn't an absolute limit. Use the number of decision points as a warning flag that indicates a routine might need to be redesigned. Don't use it as an inflexible rule. A *case* statement with many cases could be more than 10 elements long, and it would be foolish to break it up. Such *case* statements are common in event-driven programs such as those written for Microsoft Windows or the Apple Macintosh. In such programs, a long *case* statement might be the least complex way to organize the code.

Other Kinds of Complexity

FURTHER READING
For an excellent discussion of complexity metrics, see *Software Engineering Metrics and Models* (Conte, Dunsmore, and Shen 1986).

The McCabe measure of complexity isn't the only sound measure, but it's the measure most discussed in computing literature, and it's especially helpful when you're thinking about control flow. Other measures include the amount of data used, the number of nesting levels in control constructs, the number of lines of code, the number of lines between successive references to variables, and the amount of input and output. Some researchers have developed composite metrics based on combinations of these simpler ones.

CHECKLIST

Control-Structure Issues

❑ Do expressions use *True* and *False* rather than *1* and *0*?

❑ Are boolean values compared to *False* implicitly?

❑ Have expressions been simplified by the addition of new boolean variables and the use of boolean functions and decision tables?

❑ Are boolean expressions stated positively?

❑ In C, are numbers, characters, and pointers compared to *0* explicitly?

❑ Do *begin*-and-*end* pairs balance?

❑ Are *begin*-and-*end* pairs used everywhere they're needed for clarity?

❑ Are null statements obvious?

❑ Have nested statements been simplified by retesting part of the conditional, converting to *if-then-else* or *case* statements, or moving nested code into its own routine?

❑ If a routine has a decision count of more than 10, is there a good reason for not redesigning it?

Key Points

- Making boolean expressions simple and readable contributes substantially to the quality of your code.

- Deep nesting makes a routine hard to understand. Fortunately, you can avoid it relatively easily.

- Structured programming is the simple idea that you can build any program out of a combination of sequences, selections, and iterations. Following this simple idea improves productivity and code quality.

- If you don't have structured constructs in your language, you can emulate them. You should program *into* a language rather than *in* it, anyway.

- Minimizing complexity is a key to writing high-quality code.

18

Layout and Style

Contents

Related Topics

THIS CHAPTER TURNS TO AN AESTHETIC ASPECT of computer programming—the layout of program source code. The visual and intellectual enjoyment of well-formatted code is a pleasure that few nonprogrammers can appreciate. But programmers who take pride in their work derive great artistic satisfaction from polishing the visual structure of their code.

The techniques in this chapter don't affect execution speed, memory use, or other aspects of a program that are visible from outside the program. They affect how easy it is to understand the code, review it, and revise it months after you write it. They also affect how easy it is for others to read, understand, and modify once you're out of the picture.

This chapter is full of the picky details that people refer to when they talk about "attention to detail." Over the life of a project, attention to such details makes a difference in the initial quality and the ultimate maintainability of the code you write. Such details are too integral to the coding process to be changed effectively later. If they're to be done at all, they must be done during initial construction. If you're working on a team project, have your team read this chapter and agree on a team style before you begin coding.

You might not agree with everything you read here. But the point is less to win your agreement than to persuade you to consider the issues involved in formatting style. If you have high blood pressure, move on to the next chapter. It's less controversial.

18.1 Layout Fundamentals

This section explains the theory of good layout. The rest of the chapter explains the practice.

Layout Extremes

Consider the routine shown in Listing 18-1:

Listing 18-1. *Pascal layout example #1.*

CODING HORROR

```
procedure InsertionSort( Var Data: SortArray_t; FirstElmt: Integer;
LastElmt: Integer ); { Use the insertion sort technique to sort the
"Data" array in ascending order. This routine assumes that Data
[ FirstElmt ] is not the FirstElmt element in Data and that Data
[ FirstElmt-1 ] can be accessed. } Const SortMin = ''; Var SortBoundary:
Integer; { upper end of sorted range } InsertPos: Integer; { position
to insert element } InsertVal: SortElmt_t; { value to insert }
LowerBoundary: SortElmt_t; { first value below range to sort } begin
{ Replace element at lower boundary with an element guaranteed to be first
in a sorted list } LowerBoundary := Data[ FirstElmt-1 ]; Data
[ FirstElmt-1 ] := SortMin; { The elements in positions FirstElmt through
SortBoundary-1 are always sorted. In each pass through the loop,
SortBoundary is increased, and the element at the position of the new
SortBoundary probably isn't in its sorted place in the array, so it's
inserted into the proper place somewhere between FirstElmt and
SortBoundary. } for SortBoundary := FirstElmt+1 to LastElmt do begin
InsertVal := Data [ SortBoundary ]; InsertPos := SortBoundary; while
InsertVal < Data [ InsertPos-1 ] do begin Data[ InsertPos ]
:= Data[ InsertPos-1 ]; InsertPos := InsertPos-1; end; Data
[ InsertPos ] := InsertVal; end; { Replace original lower-boundary
element } Data[ FirstElmt-1 ] := LowerBoundary; end; { InsertionSort }
```

The routine is syntactically correct. It's thoroughly commented and has good variable names and clear logic. If you don't believe that, read it and find a mistake! What the routine doesn't have is good layout. This is an extreme example, headed toward "negative infinity" on the number line of bad-to-good layout. Listing 18-2 is a less extreme example:

Listing 18-2. *Pascal layout example #2.*

CODING HORROR

```pascal
procedure InsertionSort( Var Data: SortArray_t; FirstElmt: Integer;
LastElmt: Integer );
{ Use the insertion sort technique to sort the "Data" array in ascending
order. This routine assumes that Data[ FirstElmt ] is not the
first element in Data and that Data[ FirstElmt-1 ] can be accessed. }
Const
SortMin = '';
Var
SortBoundary: Integer; { upper end of sorted range }
InsertPos: Integer; { position to insert element }
InsertVal: SortElmt_t; { value to insert }
LowerBoundary: SortElmt_t; { first value below range to sort }
begin
{ Replace element at lower boundary with an element
guaranteed to be first in a sorted list }
LowerBoundary := Data[ FirstElmt-1 ];
Data[ FirstElmt-1 ] := SortMin;
{ The elements in positions FirstElmt through SortBoundary-1 are
always sorted. In each pass through the loop, SortBoundary
is increased, and the element at the position of the
new SortBoundary probably isn't in its sorted place in the
array, so it's inserted into the proper place somewhere
between FirstElmt and SortBoundary. }
for SortBoundary := FirstElmt+1 to LastElmt do
begin
InsertVal := Data[ SortBoundary ];
InsertPos := SortBoundary;
while InsertVal < Data[ InsertPos-1 ] do
begin
Data[ InsertPos ] := Data[ InsertPos-1 ];
InsertPos := InsertPos-1;
end;
Data[ InsertPos ] := InsertVal;
end;
{ Replace original lower-boundary element }
Data[ FirstElmt-1 ] := LowerBoundary;
end; { InsertionSort }
```

This code is the same as Listing 18-1's. Although most people would agree that the code's layout is much better than the first example's, the code is still not very readable. The layout is still crowded and offers no clue to the routine's logical organization. It's at about 0 on the number line of bad-to-good layout. The first example was contrived, but the second one isn't at all uncommon. I've seen programs several thousand lines long with layout at least as bad as this; with no documentation and bad variable names, overall readability was worse than in this example. This code is formatted for the computer. There's no evidence that the author expected the code to be read by humans. Listing 18-3 on the next page is an improvement.

Listing 18-3. *Pascal layout example #3.*

```
procedure InsertionSort
   (
   Var Data:       SortArray_t;
       FirstElmt:  Integer;
       LastElmt:   Integer
   );

{ Use the insertion sort technique to sort the "Data" array in ascending
  order. This routine assumes that Data[ FirstElmt ] is not the
  first element in Data and that Data[ FirstElmt-1 ] can be accessed. }

Const
   SortMin = '';

Var
   SortBoundary: Integer;            { upper end of sorted range }
   InsertPos:    Integer;            { position to insert element }
   InsertVal:    SortElmt_t;         { value to insert }
   LowerBoundary: SortElmt_t;        { first value below range to sort }

begin
   { Replace element at lower boundary with an element
     guaranteed to be first in a sorted list }
   LowerBoundary      := Data[ FirstElmt-1 ];
   Data[ FirstElmt-1 ] := SortMin;

   { The elements in positions FirstElmt through SortBoundary-1 are
     always sorted. In each pass through the loop, SortBoundary
     is increased, and the element at the position of the
     new SortBoundary probably isn't in its sorted place in the
     array, so it's inserted into the proper place somewhere
     between FirstElmt and SortBoundary. }
   for SortBoundary := FirstElmt+1 to LastElmt do
      begin
      InsertVal := Data[ SortBoundary ];
      InsertPos := SortBoundary;
      while InsertVal < Data[ InsertPos-1 ] do
         begin
         Data[ InsertPos ] := Data[ InsertPos-1 ];
         InsertPos         := InsertPos-1;
         end;
      Data[ InsertPos ] := InsertVal;
      end;

   { Replace original lower-boundary element }
   Data[ FirstElmt-1 ] := LowerBoundary;
end; { InsertionSort }
```

This layout of the routine is a strong positive on the number line of bad-to-good layout. The routine is now laid out according to principles that are explained throughout this chapter. The routine has become much more readable, and the effort that has been put into documentation and good variable names is now evident. The variable names were just as good in the earlier examples, but the layout was so poor that they weren't helpful.

The only difference between this example and the first two is the use of white space—the code and comments are exactly the same. White space is of use only to human readers—your computer could interpret any of the three fragments with equal ease. Don't feel bad if you can't do as well as your computer!

FURTHER READING
For details on the typographic approach to formatting source code, see *Human Factors and Typography for More Readable Programs* (Baecker and Marcus 1990).

Still another formatting example is shown in Figure 18-1 on the next page. It's based on a source-code format developed by Ronald M. Baecker and Aaron Marcus (1990). In addition to using white space as the previous example did, it uses shading, different typefaces, and other typographic techniques. Baecker and Marcus have developed a tool that automatically prints normal source code in a way similar to that shown in Figure 18-1. Although the tool isn't yet commercially available, this sample is a glimpse of the source-code layout support that tools will offer within the next few years.

The Fundamental Theorem of Formatting

The Fundamental Theorem of Formatting is that good visual layout shows the logical structure of a program.

KEY POINT

Making the code look pretty is worth something, but it's worth less than showing the code's structure. If one technique shows the structure better and another looks better, use the one that shows the structure better. This chapter presents numerous examples of formatting styles that look good but misrepresent the code's logical organization. In practice, prioritizing logical representation usually doesn't create ugly code—unless the logic of the code is ugly. Techniques that make good code look good and bad code look bad are more useful than techniques that make all code look good.

Human and Computer Interpretations of a Program

Layout is a useful clue to the structure of a program. Whereas the computer might care exclusively about *begin* and *end*, a human reader is apt to draw clues from the visual presentation of the code. Consider the code fragment in Listing 18-4 on page 405, in which the indentation scheme makes it look to a human as if three statements are executed each time the loop is executed.

Use the insertion sort technique to sort the "Data" array in ascending order. This routine assumes that Data[FirstElmt] is not the first element in Data and that Data[FirstElmt-1] can be accessed.

procedure
InsertionSort (

```
Var     Data:        SORTARRAY_T;
        FirstElmt:   Integer;
        LastElmt:    Integer )
```

const

```
SORTMIN = '';
```

var

upper end of sorted range	SortBoundary: *Integer;*
position at which to insert	InsertPos: *Integer;*
value to insert	InsertVal: SORTELMT_T;
first value below range to sort	LowerBoundary: SORTELMT_T;

begin

Replace element at lower boundary with an element guaranteed to be first in a sorted list.

```
LowerBoundary      := Data[ FirstElmt - 1 ];
Data[ FirstElmt - 1 ]   := SORTMIN;
```

The elements in positions FirstElmt to SortBoundary-1 are always sorted. In each pass through the loop, SortBoundary is increased, and the element at the position of the new SortBoundary probably isn't in its sorted place in the array, so it's inserted into the proper place somewhere between FirstElmt and SortBoundary.

```
for SortBoundary := FirstElmt + 1 to LastElmt do begin
    InsertVal := Data[ SortBoundary ];
    InsertPos := SortBoundary;
    while InsertVal < Data[ InsertPos - 1 ] do begin
        Data[ InsertPos ]   := Data[ InsertPos - 1 ];
        InsertPos           := InsertPos - 1;
    end;
    Data[ InsertPos ] := InsertVal;
end;
```

Replace original lower-boundary element.

```
Data[ FirstElmt - 1 ] := LowerBoundary;
end;
```

Figure 18-1. *Source-code formatting that exploits typographic features.*

Listing 18-4. *C example of layout that tells different stories to humans and computers.*

```
/* swap left and right elements for whole array */

for ( i = 0; i < MAX_ELMTS; i++ )
   LeftElmt  = Left[ i ];
   Left[ i ] = Right[ i ];
   Right[ i ] = LeftElmt;
```

If the code has no enclosing braces, the compiler will execute the first statement *MAX_ELMTS* times and the second and third statements one time each. The indentation makes it clear to you and me that the author of the code wanted all three statements to be executed together and intended to put braces around them. That won't be clear to the compiler.

Listing 18-5 is another example:

Listing 18-5. *Another C example of layout that tells different stories to humans and computers.*

```
x = 3+4 * 2+7;
```

A human reader of this code would be inclined to interpret the statement to mean that x is assigned the value *(3+4) * (2+7)*, or *63*. The computer will ignore the white space and obey the rules of precedence, interpreting the expression as *3 + (4*2) + 7*, or *18*. The point is that a good layout scheme would make the visual structure of a program match the logical structure, or tell the same story to the human that it tells to the computer.

How Much Is Good Layout Worth?

> **Our studies support the claim that knowledge of programming plans and rules of programming discourse can have a significant impact on program comprehension. In their book called *[The] Elements of [Programming] Style*, Kernighan and Plauger also identify what we would call discourse rules. Our empirical results put teeth into these rules: It is not merely a matter of aesthetics that programs should be written in a particular style. Rather there is a psychological basis for writing programs in a conventional manner: programmers have strong expectations that other programmers will follow these discourse rules. If the rules are violated, then the utility afforded by the expectations that programmers have built up over time is effectively nullified. The results from the experiments with novice and advanced student programmers and with professional programmers described in this paper provide clear support for these claims.**

> *Elliot Soloway and Kate Ehrlich*

CROSS-REFERENCE
Good layout is one key to
readability. For details on
the value of readability,
see Section 32.3, "Write
Programs for People First,
Computers Second."

In layout, perhaps more than in any other aspect of programming, the difference between communicating with the computer and communicating with human readers comes into play. The smaller part of the job of programming is writing a program so that the computer can read it; the larger part is writing it so that other humans can read it.

In their classic paper "Perception in Chess," Chase and Simon reported on a study that compared the abilities of experts and novices to remember the positions of pieces in chess (1973). When pieces were arranged on the board as they might be during a game, the experts' memories were far superior to the novices'. When the pieces were arranged randomly, there was little difference between the memories of the experts and the novices. The traditional interpretation of this result is that an expert's memory is not inherently better than a novice's but that the expert has a knowledge structure that helps him or her remember particular kinds of information. When new information corresponds to the knowledge structure—in this case, the sensible placement of chess pieces—the expert can remember it easily. When new information doesn't correspond to a knowledge structure—the chess pieces are randomly positioned—the expert can't remember it any better than the novice.

A few years later, Ben Shneiderman duplicated Chase and Simon's results in the computer-programming arena and reported his results in a paper called "Exploratory Experiments in Programmer Behavior" (1976). Shneiderman found that when program statements were arranged in a sensible order, experts were able to remember them better than novices. When statements were shuffled, the experts' superiority was reduced. Shneiderman's results have been confirmed in other studies (McKeithen et al. 1981, Soloway and Ehrlich 1984). The basic concept has also been confirmed in the games Go and bridge and in electronics, music, and physics (McKeithen et al. 1981).

KEY POINT

These studies suggest that structure helps experts to perceive, comprehend, and remember important features of programs. Given the variety of styles of layout and the tenacity with which programmers cling to their own styles, even when they're vastly different from other styles, it's easy to believe that the details of a specific method of structuring a program are much less important than the fact that the program is structured at all.

Layout as Religion

The importance to comprehension and memory of structuring one's environment in a familiar way has led some researchers to hypothesize that layout might harm an expert's ability to read a program if the layout is different from the scheme the expert uses (Sheil 1981, Soloway and Ehrlich 1984). That possibility, compounded by the fact that layout is an aesthetic as well as a logical exercise, means that debates about program formatting often sound more like religious wars than philosophical discussions.

At a coarse level, it's clear that some forms of layout are better than others. The successively better layouts of the same code at the beginning of the chapter made that evident. This book won't steer clear of the finer points of layout just because they're controversial. Good programmers should be open-minded about their layout practices and accept practices proven to be better than the ones they're used to, even if adjusting to a new method results in some initial discomfort.

Objectives of Good Layout

*The results point out the fragility of programming expertise: advanced programmers have **strong** expectations about what programs should look like, and when those expectations are violated—in seemingly innocuous ways— their performance drops drastically.*

Elliot Soloway and Kate Ehrlich

Many decisions about layout details are a matter of subjective aesthetics— often, you can accomplish the same goal in many ways. You can make debates about subjective issues less subjective if you explicitly specify the criteria for your preferences. Explicitly, then, a good layout scheme should

Accurately represent the logical structure of the code. That's the Fundamental Theorem of Formatting again—the primary purpose of good layout is to show the logical structure of the code. Typically, programmers use indentation and other white space to show the logical structure.

Consistently represent the logical structure of the code. Some styles of layout have rules with so many exceptions that it's hard to follow the rules consistently. A good style applies to most cases.

Improve readability. An indentation strategy that's logical but that makes the code harder to read is useless. A layout scheme that calls for spaces only where they are required by the compiler is logical but not readable. A good layout scheme makes code easier to read.

Withstand modifications. The best layout schemes hold up well under code modification. Modifying one line of code shouldn't require modifying several others.

In addition to these criteria, minimizing the number of lines of code needed to implement a simple statement or block is also sometimes considered.

How to put the layout objectives to use

KEY POINT

You can use the criteria for a good layout scheme to ground a discussion of layout so that the subjective reasons for preferring one style over another are brought into the open.

Weighting the criteria in different ways might lead to different conclusions. For example, if you feel strongly that minimizing the number of lines used on the screen is important—perhaps because you have a small computer screen—you might criticize one style because it uses two more lines for a routine parameter list than another.

18.2 Layout Techniques

You can achieve good layout by using a few layout tools in several different ways. This section describes each of them.

White Space

Usewhitespacetoenhancereadability. White space, including spaces, tabs, line breaks, and blank lines, is the main tool available to you for showing a program's structure.

CROSS-REFERENCE
Some researchers have explored the similarity between the structure of a book and the structure of a program. For information, see "The Book Paradigm for program documentation" in Section 19.5.

You wouldn't think of writing a book with no spaces between words, no paragraph breaks, and no divisions into chapters. Such a book might be readable cover to cover, but it would be virtually impossible to skim it for a line of thought or to find an important passage. Perhaps more important, the book's layout wouldn't show the reader how the author intended to organize the information. The author's organization is an important clue to the topic's logical organization.

Breaking a book into chapters, paragraphs, and sentences shows a reader how to mentally organize a topic. If the organization isn't evident, the reader has to provide the organization, which puts a much greater burden on the reader and adds the possibility that the reader may never figure out how the topic is organized.

The information contained in a program is denser than the information contained in most books. Whereas you might read and understand a page of a book in a minute or two, most programmers can't read and understand a naked program listing at anything close to that rate. A program should give more organizational clues than a book, not fewer.

Grouping. From the other side of the looking glass, white space is grouping, making sure that related statements are grouped together.

In writing, thoughts are grouped into paragraphs. A well-written paragraph contains only sentences that relate to a particular thought. It shouldn't contain extraneous sentences. Similarly, a paragraph of code should contain statements that accomplish a single task and that are related to each other.

Blank lines. Just as it's important to group related statements, it's important to separate unrelated statements from each other. The start of a new paragraph in English is identified with indentation or a blank line. The start of a new paragraph of code should be identified with a blank line.

Using blank lines is a way to indicate how a program is organized. You can use them to divide groups of related statements into paragraphs, to separate routines from one another, and to highlight comments.

HARD DATA

Although this particular statistic may be hard to put to work, a study by Gorla, Benander, and Benander found that the optimal number of blank lines in a program is about 8 to 16 percent. Above 16 percent, debug time increases dramatically (1990).

Alignment. Align elements that belong together, such as equals signs in groups of related assignments. Visual alignment reinforces the idea that a group of statements belong together. If they don't belong together, don't align them.

Indentation. Use indentation to show the logical structure of a program. As a rule, you should indent statements under the statement to which they are logically subordinate.

HARD DATA

Indentation has been shown to be correlated with increased programmer comprehension. The article "Program Indentation and Comprehensibility" reported that several studies found correlations between indentation and improved comprehension (Miaria et al. 1983). Subjects scored 20 to 30 percent higher on a test of comprehension when programs had a two-to-four-spaces indentation scheme than they did when programs had no indentation at all.

HARD DATA

The same study found that it was important to neither under-emphasize nor over-emphasize a program's logical structure. The lowest comprehension scores were achieved on programs that were not indented at all. The second lowest were achieved on programs that used six-space indentation. The study concluded that two-to-four-space indentation was optimal. Interestingly, many subjects in the experiment felt that the six-space indentation was easier

409

to use than the smaller indentations, even though their scores were lower. That's probably because six-space indentation looks pleasing. But regardless of how pretty it looks, six-space indentation turns out to be less readable. This is an example of a collision between aesthetic appeal and readability.

Parentheses

Use more parentheses than you think you need. Use parentheses to clarify expressions that involve more than two terms. They may not be needed, but they add clarity and they don't cost you anything. For example, how are the following expressions evaluated?

C Version:	12 + 4 % 3 * 7 / 8
Pascal Version:	12 + 4 mod 3 * 7 div 8
Basic Version:	12 + 4 mod 3 * 7 \ 8

The key question is, did you have to think about how the expressions are evaluated? Can you be confident in your answer without checking some references? Even experienced programmers don't answer confidently, and that's why you should use parentheses whenever there is any doubt about how an expression is evaluated.

18.3 Layout Styles

CROSS-REFERENCE
An alternative to requiring all programmers to code in the same style is simply to require them to run their code through the reformatting program before they add it to a group project. For details on pretty printers, see "Editing" in Section 20.2.

Most layout issues have to do with laying out blocks, the groups of statements below control statements. A block is enclosed between keywords: *begin* and *end* in Pascal; *{* and *}* in C; and *if-then-endif* in the versions of Basic that support block structures. For simplicity, much of this discussion uses *begin* and *end* generically, assuming that you can figure out how the discussion applies to braces in C or other blocking mechanisms in other languages. The following sections describe four general styles of layout:

- Pure blocks
- Endline layout
- Emulating pure blocks
- *begin* and *end* as block boundaries

Pure Blocks

Much of the layout controversy stems from the inherent awkwardness of the more popular programming languages. A well-designed language has clear block structures that lend themselves to a natural indentation style. In Ada, for example, each control construct has its own terminator, and you can't use a control construct without using the terminator. Code is blocked naturally. Some examples in Ada are shown in Listing 18-6, Listing 18-7, and Listing 18-8:

Listing 18-6. *Ada example of a pure* if *block.*

```
if PixelColor = RedColor then
    statement1;
    statement2;
    ...
end if;
```

Listing 18-7. *Ada example of a pure* while *block.*

```
while PixelColor = RedColor loop
    statement1;
    statement2;
    ...
end loop;
```

Listing 18-8. *Ada example of a pure* case *block.*

```
case PixelColor of
    when RedColor =>
        statement1;
        statement2;
        ...
    when GreenColor =>
        statement1;
        statement2;
        ...
    when others =>
        statement1;
        statement2;
        ...
end case;
```

A control construct in Ada always has a beginning statement—*if-then, while-loop*, and *case-of* in the examples—and it always has a corresponding *end* statement. Indenting the inside of the structure isn't a controversial practice, and the options for aligning the other keywords are somewhat limited. Listing 18-9 is an abstract representation of how this kind of formatting works:

Listing 18-9. *Abstract example of the pure-block layout style.*

411

In this example, statement A begins the control construct and statement D ends the control construct. The alignment between the two provides solid visual closure.

The controversy about formatting control structures arises in part from the fact that some languages don't *require* block structures. You can have an *if-then* followed by a single statement and not have a formal block. You have to add a *begin-end* pair or opening and closing braces to create a block rather than getting one automatically with each control construct. Uncoupling *begin* and *end* from the control structure as some languages do leads to questions about where to put the *begin* and *end*. Consequently, many indentation problems are problems only because you have to compensate for poorly designed language structures. Various ways to compensate are described in the following sections.

Endline Layout

If you're not programming in Ada, you can't use pure-block layout. You're forced to adopt a layout strategy based on the reality of *begin* and *end* keywords. One strategy is "endline layout," which refers to a large group of layout strategies in which the code is indented almost to the end of the line. The endline indentation is used to align a block with the keyword that began it, to make a routine's subsequent parameters line up under its first parameter, and to line up cases in a *case* statement. Listing 18-10 is an abstract example:

Listing 18-10. *Abstract example of the endline layout style.*

In this example, statement A begins the control construct and statement D ends it. Statements B, C, and D are aligned under the keyword that began the block in statement A. The uniform indentation of B, C, and D shows that they're grouped together. Listing 18-11 is a less abstract example of code formatted using this strategy:

Listing 18-11. *Pascal example of endline layout of a* while *block.*

```
while PixelColor = RedColor do begin
                          statement1;
                          statement2;
                          ...
                          end;
```

In the example, the *begin* is placed at the end of the line rather than under the corresponding keyword. Some people prefer to put *begin* under the keyword, but choosing between those two fine points is the least of this style's problems.

The endline layout style works acceptably in a few cases. Listing 18-12 is an example in which it works:

Listing 18-12. *A rare Pascal example in which endline layout works acceptably.*

The else keyword is aligned with the then keyword above it. —

```
if ( SoldCount > 1000 ) then begin
                             Markdown := 0.10;
                             Profit   := 0.05
                             end
                   else Markdown := 0.05
```

In this case, the block following the *then* is aligned with the *begin* at the end of the line, and the *else* clause is aligned with the *then* keyword. The visual effect is a clear logical structure.

If you look critically at the earlier *case*-statement example, you can probably predict the unraveling of this style. If the conditional expression becomes complicated, the style will give useless or misleading clues about the logical structure. Listing 18-13 is an example of how the style breaks down when it's used with a more complicated conditional:

Listing 18-13. *A more typical Pascal example, in which endline layout breaks down.*

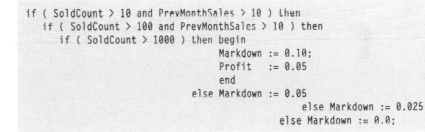

CODING HORROR

```
if ( SoldCount > 10 and PrevMonthSales > 10 ) then
   if ( SoldCount > 100 and PrevMonthSales > 10 ) then
      if ( SoldCount > 1000 ) then begin
                                   Markdown := 0.10;
                                   Profit   := 0.05
                                   end
                         else Markdown := 0.05
                                        else Markdown := 0.025
                                   else Markdown := 0.0;
```

What's happening with the *else* clauses at the end of the example? They're consistently indented under the corresponding keywords, but it's hard to argue that their indentations clarify the logical structure. And if the code were modified so that the length of the first line changed, the endline style would require that the indentation of corresponding statements be changed. This poses a maintenance problem that other styles don't.

In short, avoid endline layout because it's inaccurate, it's hard to apply consistently, and it's hard to maintain. You'll see other problems with endline layout throughout the chapter.

Emulating Pure Blocks

A better alternative to using endline layout in languages that don't have pure blocks is to view the *begin* and *end* keywords as extensions of the control construct they're used with. Then it's sensible to try to emulate the Ada formatting in your language. Listing 18-14 is an abstract view of the visual structure you're trying to emulate:

Listing 18-14. *Abstract example of the pure-block layout style.*

In this style, the control structure opens the block in statement A and finishes the block in statement D. This implies that the *begin* should be at the end of statement A and the *end* should be statement D. In the abstract, to emulate pure blocks, you'd have to do something like Listing 18-15:

Listing 18-15. *Abstract example of emulating the pure-block style.*

Some examples of how the style looks in Pascal are shown in Listing 18-16, Listing 18-17, and Listing 18-18:

Listing 18-16. *Pascal example of emulating a pure* if *block.*

```
if PixelColor = RedColor then begin
   statement1;
   statement2;
   ...
end;
```

Listing 18-17. *Pascal example of emulating a pure* while *block.*

```
while PixelColor = RedColor do begin
   statement1;
   statement2;
   ...
end;
```

Listing 18-18. *Pascal example of emulating a pure* case *block.*

```
case PixelColor of
   RedColor: begin
      statement1;
      statement2;
      ...
   end;
   GreenColor: begin
      statement1;
      statement2;
      ...
   end
   else begin
      statement1;
      statement2;
      ...
   end
end;
```

This style of alignment works pretty well. It looks good, you can apply it consistently, and it's maintainable. It supports the Fundamental Theorem of Formatting in that it helps to show the logical structure of the code. It's a reasonable style choice. An interesting sidenote on this style is that even though it's relatively uncommon in Pascal, it's extremely common in C.

begin-end Block Boundaries

A substitute for a pure block structure is to view *begin-end* pairs as block boundaries. If you take that approach, you view the *begin* and the *end* as statements that follow the control construct rather than as fragments that are part of it.

Graphically, this is the ideal, just as it was with the pure-block emulation shown again in Listing 18-19:

Listing 18-19. *Abstract example of the pure-block layout style.*

But in this style, to treat the *begin* and the *end* as parts of the block structure rather than the control statement, you have to put the *begin* at the beginning of the block (rather than at the end of the control statement) and the *end* at the end of the block (rather than terminating the control statement). In the abstract, you'll have to do something like Listing 18-20 on the next page.

Listing 18-20. *Abstract example of using* begin *and* end *as block boundaries.*

Some examples of how using *begin* and *end* as block boundaries looks in Pascal are shown in Listing 18-21, Listing 18-22, and Listing 18-23:

Listing 18-21. *Pascal example of using* begin *and* end *as block boundaries in an* if *block.*

```
if PixelColor = RedColor then
    begin
    statement1;
    statement2;
    ...
    end;
```

Listing 18-22. *Pascal example of using* begin *and* end *as block boundaries in a* while *block.*

```
while PixelColor = RedColor do
    begin
    statement1;
    statement2;
    ...
    end;
```

This alignment style works well. It supports the Fundamental Theorem of Formatting by exposing the code's underlying logical structure. You can apply it consistently in all instances, and it doesn't give rise to the maintenance problems endline layout does.

Which Style Is Best?

It's easier to answer the question of which style is worst. Endline layout is worst. It can't be applied consistently and it's difficult to maintain.

If you're working in Ada, use pure-block indentation.

KEY POINT

If you're working in C or Pascal, choose either pure-block emulation or *begin-end* block boundaries. The only study that has compared the two styles found no statistically significant difference between the two as far as understandability is concerned (Hansen and Yim 1987). Choose the one you like.

Listing 18-23. *Pascal example of using* begin *and* end *as block boundaries in a* case *block.*

```
case PixelColor of
   RedColor:
      begin
      statement1;
      statement2;
      ...
      end;
   GreenColor:
      begin
      statement1;
      statement2;
      ...
      end
   else
      begin
      statement1;
      statement2;
      ...
      end
end;
```

Neither of the styles is foolproof, and each requires an occasional "reasonable and obvious" compromise. You might prefer one or the other for aesthetic reasons. This book uses both styles in its code examples, so you can see many more illustrations of how each style works just by skimming through the examples. Once you've chosen a style, you reap the most benefits of good layout when you apply it consistently.

18.4 Laying Out Control Structures

CROSS-REFERENCE
For details on documenting control structures, see "Commenting Control Structures" in Section 19.5. For a discussion of other aspects of control structures, see Chapters 13 through 17.

The layout of some program elements is primarily a matter of aesthetics. Layout of control structures, however, affects readability and comprehensibility and is therefore a practical priority.

Fine Points of Formatting Control-Structure Blocks

Working with control-structure blocks requires attention to some fine details. Here are some guidelines:

Avoid unindented *begin-end* pairs. In the style shown in Listing 18-24 on the next page, the *begin-end* pair is aligned with the control structure, and the statements that *begin* and *end* enclose are indented under *begin*.

Listing 18-24. *Pascal example of unindented* begin-end *pairs.*

The begin is aligned with the for.

The statements are indented under begin.

The end is aligned with the for.

```
for i := 1 to MaxLines do
begin
    ReadLine( i );
    ProcessLine( i );
end;
```

Although this approach looks fine, it violates the Fundamental Theorem of Formatting; it doesn't show the logical structure of the code. Used this way, the *begin* and *end* aren't part of the control construct, but they aren't part of the statement(s) after it either.

Listing 18-25 is an abstract view of this approach:

Listing 18-25. *Abstract example of misleading indentation.*

In this example, is statement B subordinate to statement A? It doesn't look like part of statement A, and it doesn't look as if it's subordinate to it either. If you have used this approach, change to one of the two layout styles described earlier, and your formatting will be more consistent.

Avoid double indentation with *begin* and *end*. A corollary to the rule against nonindented *begin-end* pairs is the rule against doubly indented *begin-end* pairs. In this style, shown in Listing 18-26, *begin* and *end* are indented and the statements they enclose are indented again:

Listing 18-26. *Pascal example of inappropriate double indentation of* begin-end *block.*

The statements below the begin are indented as if they were subordinate to it.

```
for i := 1 to MaxLines do
    begin
        ReadLine( i );
        ProcessLine( i );
    end;
```

This is another example of a style that looks fine but violates the Fundamental Theorem of Formatting. One study showed no difference in comprehension between programs that are singly indented and programs that are doubly indented (Miaria et al. 1983), but this style doesn't accurately show the logical structure of the program; *ReadLine()* and *ProcessLine()* are shown as if they are logically subordinate to the *begin-end* pair, and they aren't.

The approach also exaggerates the complexity of a program's logical structure. Which of the structures shown in Listing 18-27 and Listing 18-28 looks more complicated?

Listing 18-27. *Abstract Structure 1.*

Listing 18-28. *Abstract Structure 2.*

Both are abstract representations of the structure of the *for* loop. Abstract Structure 1 looks more complicated even though it represents the same code as Abstract Structure 2. If you were to nest statements to two or three levels, double indentation would give you four or six levels of indentation. The layout that resulted would look more complicated than the actual code would be. Avoid the problem by using pure-block emulation or by using *begin* and *end* as block boundaries and aligning *begin* and *end* with the statements they enclose.

Other Considerations

Although indentation of blocks is the major issue in formatting control structures, you'll run into a few other kinds of issues. Here are some more guidelines:

Use blank lines between paragraphs. Some blocks of code aren't demarcated with *begin-end* pairs. A logical block—a group of statements that belong together—should be treated the way paragraphs in English are. Separate them from each other with blank lines. Listing 18-29 on the next page shows an example of paragraphs that should be separated.

CROSS-REFERENCE
If you use the PDL-to-code process, your blocks of code will be separated automatically. For details, see Section 4.2, "PDL for Pros."

This code looks all right, but blank lines would improve it in two ways. First, when you have a group of statements that don't have to be executed in any particular order, it's tempting to lump them all together this way. You don't need to further refine the statement order for the computer, but human readers appreciate more clues about which statements need to be performed in a specific order and which statements are just along for the ride. The

Listing 18-29. *C example of code that should be grouped and separated.*

```
Cursor.Start          = StartingScanLine;
Cursor.End            = EndingScanLine;
Window.Title          = EditWindow.Title;
Window.Dimensions     = EditWindow.Dimensions;
Window.ForegroundColor = UserPreferences.ForegroundColor;
Cursor.BlinkRate      = EditMode.BlinkRate;
Window.BackgroundColor = UserPreferences.BackgroundColor;
SaveCursor( Cursor );
SetCursor( Cursor );
```

discipline of putting blank lines throughout a program makes you think harder about which statements really belong together. The revised fragment in Listing 18-30 shows how this collection should really be organized:

Listing 18-30. *C example of code that is appropriately grouped and separated.*

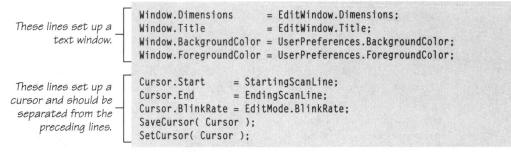

These lines set up a text window.

```
Window.Dimensions     = EditWindow.Dimensions;
Window.Title          = EditWindow.Title;
Window.BackgroundColor = UserPreferences.BackgroundColor;
Window.ForegroundColor = UserPreferences.ForegroundColor;
```

These lines set up a cursor and should be separated from the preceding lines.

```
Cursor.Start      = StartingScanLine;
Cursor.End        = EndingScanLine;
Cursor.BlinkRate  = EditMode.BlinkRate;
SaveCursor( Cursor );
SetCursor( Cursor );
```

The reorganized code shows that two things are happening. In the first example, the lack of statement organization and blank lines, and the old aligned-equals-signs trick, make the statements look more related than they are.

The second way in which using blank lines tends to improve code is that it opens up natural spaces for comments. In the code above, a comment above each block would nicely supplement the improved layout.

Format single-statement blocks consistently. A single-statement block is a single statement following a control structure, such as one statement following an *if* test. In such a case, *begin* and *end* aren't needed for correct compilation and you have the three style options shown in Listing 18-31.

There are arguments in favor of each of these approaches. Style 1 follows the indentation scheme used with blocks, so it's consistent with other approaches. Style 2 (either 2a or 2b) is also consistent, and the *begin-end* pair reduces the chance that you'll add statements after the *if* test and forget to add

Listing 18-31. *Pascal example of style options for single-statement blocks.*

```
Style 1 ── if ( expression ) then
              one-statement;

Style 2a ── if ( expression ) then begin
              one-statement;
           end;

Style 2b ── if ( expression ) then
              begin
              one-statement;
              end;

Style 3 ── if ( expression ) then one-statement;
```

begin and *end*. This would be a particularly subtle error because the indentation would tell you that everything is OK, but the indentation wouldn't be interpreted the same way by the compiler. Style 3's main advantage over Style 2 is that it's easier to type. Its advantage over Style 1 is that if it's copied to another place in the program, it's more likely to be copied correctly. Its disadvantage is that in a line-oriented debugger, the debugger treats the line as one line and the debugger doesn't show you whether it executes the statement after the *if* test.

I've used Style 1 and have been the victim of incorrect modification many times. I don't like the exception to the indentation strategy caused by Style 3, so I avoid it altogether. On a group project, I favor either variation of Style 2 for its consistency and safe modifiability. Regardless of the style you choose, use it consistently and use the same style for *if* tests and all loops.

For complicated expressions, put separate conditions on separate lines. Put each part of a complicated expression on its own line. Listing 18-32 shows an expression that's formatted without any attention to readability:

Listing 18-32. *Pascal example of an essentially unformatted (and unreadable) complicated expression.*

```
if (( '0' <= InChar and InChar <= '9' ) or ( 'a' <= InChar and
   InChar <= 'z' ) or ( 'A' <= InChar and InChar <= 'Z' )) then
   ...
```

This is an example of formatting for the computer instead of for human readers. By breaking the expression into several lines, as in Listing 18-33 on the next page, you can improve readability.

Listing 18-33. *Pascal example of a readable complicated expression.*

```
if ( ( '0' <= InChar and InChar <= '9' ) or
    ( 'a' <= InChar and InChar <= 'z' ) or
    ( 'A' <= InChar and InChar <= 'Z' ) ) then
   ...
```

CROSS-REFERENCE
Another technique for making complicated expressions readable is to put them into boolean functions. For details on putting complicated expressions into boolean functions and other readability techniques, see Section 17.1, "Boolean Expressions."

The second fragment uses several formatting techniques—alignment, indentation, making each incomplete line obvious—and the result is a readable expression. Moreover, the intent of the test is clear. If the expression contained a minor error, such as using a *z* instead of a *Z*, it would be obvious in code formatted this way, whereas the error wouldn't be clear with less careful formatting.

CROSS-REFERENCE
For details on the use of *goto*s, see Section 16.1, "*goto*s."

Avoid *goto*s. The original reason to avoid *goto*s was that they made it difficult to prove that a program was correct. That's a nice argument for all the people who want to prove their programs correct, which is practically no one. The more pressing problem for most programmers is that *goto*s make code hard to format. Do you indent all the code between the *goto* and the label it goes to? What if you have several *goto*s to the same label? Do you indent each new one under the previous one? Here's some advice for formatting *goto*s:

- Avoid *goto*s. This sidesteps the formatting problem altogether.
- Use a name in all caps for the label the code goes to. This makes the label obvious.
- Put the statement containing the *goto* on a line by itself. This makes the *goto* obvious.
- Put the label the *goto* goes to on a line by itself. Surround it with blank lines. This makes the label obvious. Indent the line containing the label the same number of spaces as the surrounding code. This keeps the logical view of the program intact.

Listing 18-34 shows these *goto* layout conventions at work.

The Pascal example in Listing 18-34 is relatively long so that you can see a case in which an expert programmer might conscientiously decide that a *goto* is the best design choice. In such a case, the formatting shown is the best you can do.

CROSS-REFERENCE
For details on using *case* statements, see Section 14.2, "*case* Statements."

No endline exception for *case* statements. One of the hazards of endline layout comes up in the formatting of *case* statements. A popular style of formatting *case*s is to indent them to the right of the description of each case, as shown in Listing 18-35 on page 424. The big problem with this style is that it's a maintenance headache.

Listing 18-34. *Pascal example of making the best of a bad situation (using* goto*).*

```
PROCEDURE PurgeFiles( var ErrorCode: ERROR_CODE );

var
    FileIdx:          Integer;
    FileHandle:       FILEHANDLE_T;
    FileList:         FILELIST_T;
    NumFilesToPurge:  Integer;

label
    END_PROC;

begin
    GrabScreen;
    GrabHelp( PURGE_FILES );
    MakePurgeFileList( FileList, NumFilesToPurge );

    ErrorCode := Success;
    FileIdx   := 0;
    while ( FileIdx < NumFilesToPurge ) do begin
        FileIdx := FileIdx + 1;
        if not FindFile( FileList[ FileIdx ], FileHandle ) then begin
            ErrorCode := FileFindError;
            goto END_PROC;
        end;

        if not OpenFile( FileHandle ) then begin
            ErrorCode := FileOpenError;
            goto END_PROC;
        end;

        if not OverwriteFile( FileHandle ) then begin
            ErrorCode := FileOverwriteError;
            goto END_PROC;
        end;

        if Erase( FileHandle ) then begin
            ErrorCode := FileEraseError;
            goto END_PROC;
        end;

    end; { while }

    END_PROC:

    DeletePurgeFileList( FileList, NumFilesToPurge );
    ReleaseHelp;
    ReleaseScreen;

end; { PurgeFiles }
```

Here's a goto. —— (at `goto END_PROC;` after FileFindError)

Here's a goto. —— (at `goto END_PROC;` after FileOpenError)

Here's a goto. —— (at `goto END_PROC;` after FileOverwriteError)

Here's a goto. —— (at `goto END_PROC;` after FileEraseError)

Here's the goto label. —— *The intent of the capitalization and layout is to make the label hard to miss.* (at `END_PROC:`)

Listing 18-35. *Pascal example of hard-to-maintain endline layout of a* case *statement.*

```
case BallColor of
    Blue:               Rollout( Ball );
    Orange:             SpinOnFinger( Ball );
    FluorescentGreen:   Spike( Ball );
    White:              KnockCoverOff( Ball );
    WhiteAndBlue:       begin
                        if ( MainColor = White ) then
                            begin
                            KnockCoverOff( Ball )
                            end
                        else if ( MainColor = Blue ) then
                            begin
                            RollOut( Ball )
                            end
                        end
    else                FatalError( "Unrecognized kind of ball.")
end; { case }
```

If you add a case with a longer name than any of the existing names, you have to shift out all the cases and the code that goes with them. The large initial indentation makes it awkward to accommodate any more logic, as shown in the *WhiteAndBlue* case. The solution is to switch to your standard indentation increment. If you indent statements in a loop three spaces, indent cases in a *case* statement the same number of spaces, as in Listing 18-36:

Listing 18-36. *Pascal example of good standard indentation of a* case *statement.*

```
case BallColor of
    Blue:
        Rollout( Ball );
    Orange:
        SpinOnFinger( Ball );
    FluorescentGreen:
        Spike( Ball );
    White:
        KnockCoverOff( Ball );
    WhiteAndBlue:
        begin
        if ( MainColor = White ) then
            begin
            KnockCoverOff( Ball )
            end
        else if ( MainColor = Blue ) then
            begin
            RollOut( Ball )
            end
        end
    else
        FatalError( "Unrecognized kind of ball.")
end; { case }
```

This is an instance in which most people probably prefer the looks of the first example. For the ability to accommodate longer lines, consistency, and maintainability, however, the second approach wins hands down.

If you have a *case* statement in which all the cases are exactly parallel and all the actions are short, you could consider putting the case and action on the same line. In most instances, however, you'll live to regret it. The formatting is a pain initially and breaks under modification, and it's hard to keep the structure of all the cases parallel as some of the short actions become longer ones.

18.5 Laying Out Individual Statements

CROSS-REFERENCE
For details on documenting individual statements, see "Commenting Individual Lines" in Section 19.5.

This section explains many ways to improve individual statements in a program.

Statement Length

A common rule is to limit statement line length to 80 characters. Here are the reasons:

- Lines longer than 80 characters are hard to read.
- The 80-character limitation discourages deep nesting.
- Lines longer than 80 characters often won't fit on 8.5" x 11" paper.
- Paper larger than 8.5" x 11" is hard to file.

With larger screens, narrow typefaces, laser printers, and landscape mode, the arguments for the 80-character limit aren't as compelling as they used to be. A single 90-character-long line is usually more readable than one that has been broken in two just to avoid spilling over the 80th column. With modern technology, it's probably all right to exceed 80 columns occasionally.

Using Spaces for Clarity

Add white space within a statement for the sake of readability:

Use spaces to make logical expressions readable. The expression

```
while(PathName[StartPath+Pos]<>';') and
    ((StartPath+Pos)<=length(PathName)) do
```

is about as readable as Idareyoutoreadthis.

As a rule, you should separate identifiers from other identifiers with spaces. If you use this rule, the *while* expression looks like this:

```
while ( PathName[ StartPath+Pos ] <> ';' ) and
    (( StartPath + Pos ) <= length( PathName )) do
```

Some software artists might recommend enhancing this particular expression with additional spaces to emphasize its logical structure, this way:

```
while (  PathName[ StartPath + Pos ] <> ';'  ) and
    (  ( StartPath + Pos ) <= length( PathName )  ) do
```

This is fine, although the first use of spaces was sufficient to ensure readability. Extra spaces hardly ever hurt, however, so be generous with them.

Use spaces to make array references readable. The expression

```
GrossRate[Census[GroupID].Sex,Census[GroupID].AgeGroup]
```

is no more readable than the earlier dense *while* expression. Use spaces around each index in the array to make the indexes readable. If you use this rule, the expression looks like this:

```
GrossRate[ Census[ GroupID ].Sex, Census[ GroupID ].AgeGroup ]
```

Use spaces to make routine arguments readable. What is the fourth argument to the following routine?

```
ReadEmployeeData(MaxEmps,EmpData,InputFile,EmpCount,InputError);
```

Now, what is the fourth argument to the following routine?

```
GetCensus( InputFile, EmpCount, EmpData, MaxEmps, InputError );
```

Which one was easier to find? This is a realistic, worthwhile question because argument positions are significant in all major procedural languages. It's common to have a routine specification on one half of your screen and the call to the routine on the other half, and to compare each formal parameter with each actual parameter.

Aligning Groups of Related Assignments

Align the equals signs for groups of assignments that are supposed to be done together. Listing 18-37 is an example of poor alignment:

Listing 18-37. *Basic example of poor alignment.*

```
EmployeeName = InputName
EmployeeSalary = InputSalary
EmployeeBirthdate = InputBirthdate
```

Listing 18-38 is an example of better alignment:

Listing 18-38. *Basic example of good alignment.*

```
EmployeeName      = InputName
EmployeeSalary    = InputSalary
EmployeeBirthdate = InputBirthdate
```

Aside from the fact that it looks neater, what is better about the formatting of the second fragment? How do you justify the extra bytes it takes to store all those spaces? How do you justify the extra work of lining up the equals signs?

The main justification is that these statements belong together and the alignment scheme shows that they belong together. If the statements weren't related, it wouldn't be wise to align them. Listing 18-39 shows an example of misleading alignment:

Listing 18-39. *Basic example of misleading alignment.*

```
EmployeeName    = InputName
EmployeeAddress = InputAddress
EmployeePhone   = InputPhone
BossTitle       = Title
BossDept        = Department
```

This code is misleading because it looks as if these statements all perform one operation. In fact, the code is doing two jobs, one with employee data and one with boss data. The formatting should differentiate between the two activities, probably with independent alignment and a blank line between them. It should look like Listing 18-40:

Listing 18-40. *Basic example of accurate alignment.*

```
EmployeeName    = InputName
EmployeeAddress = InputAddress
EmployeePhone   = InputPhone

BossTitle = Title
BossDept  = Department
```

Formatting Continuation Lines

One of the most vexing problems of program layout is deciding what to do with the part of a statement that spills over to the next line. Do you indent it by the normal indentation amount? Do you align it under the keyword? What about assignments?

Here's a sensible, consistent approach that's particularly useful in Pascal, C, C++, Ada, and other languages that encourage long variable names.

Make the incompleteness of a statement obvi . Sometimes a statement must be broken across lines, either because it's longer than programming standards allow or because it's too absurdly long to put on one line. Make it obvious that the part of the statement on the first line is only part of a statement. The easiest way to do that is to break up the statement so that the part on the first line is blatantly incorrect syntactically if it stands alone. Some examples are shown in Listing 18-41:

Listing 18-41. *Pascal examples of obviously incomplete statements.*

The and signals that the statement isn't complete.
```
while ( PathName[ StartPath + Pos ] <> ';' ) and
    ( ( StartPath + Pos ) <= length( PathName ) ) do
...
```

The plus sign (+) signals that the statement isn't complete.
```
TotalBill := TotalBill + CustomerPurchases[ CustomerID ] +
            SalesTax( CustomerPurchases[ CustomerID ] );
...
```

The comma (,) signals that the statement isn't complete.
```
DrawLine( Window.North, Window.South, Window.East, Window.West,
    CurrentWidth, CurrentAttribute );
...
```

In addition to telling the reader that the statement isn't complete on the first line, the break helps prevent incorrect modifications. If the continuation of the statement were deleted, the first line wouldn't look as if you had merely forgotten a parenthesis or semicolon—it would clearly need something more.

Keep closely related elements together. When you break a line, keep things together that belong together—array references, arguments to a routine, and so on. The example shown in Listing 18-42 is poor form:

Listing 18-42. *Pascal example of breaking a line poorly.*

CODING HORROR

```
CustomerBill := PrevBalance( PaymentHistory[ CustomerID ] ) + LateCharge(
            PaymentHistory[ CustomerID ] );
```

Admittedly, this line break follows the guideline of making the incompleteness of the statement obvious, but it does so in a way that makes the statement unnecessarily hard to read. You might find a case in which the break is necessary, but in this case it isn't. It's better to keep the array references all on one line. Listing 18-43 shows better formatting:

Listing 18-43. *Pascal example of breaking a line well.*

```
CustomerBill := PrevBalance( PaymentHistory[ CustomerID ] ) +
                LateCharge( PaymentHistory[ CustomerID ] );
```

Indent routine-call continuation lines the standard amount. If you normally indent three spaces for statements in a loop or a conditional, indent the continuation lines for a routine by three spaces. Some examples are shown in Listing 18-44:

Listing 18-44. *Pascal examples of indenting routine-call continuation lines using the standard indentation increment.*

```
DrawLine( Window.North, Window.South, Window.East, Window.West,
   CurrentWidth, CurrentAttribute );
SetFontAttributes( Font.FaceName, Font.Size, Font.Bold, Font.Italic,
   Font.SyntheticAttribute[ FontID ].Underline,
   Font.SyntheticAttribute[ FontID ].Strikeout );
```

One alternative to this approach is to line up the continuation lines under the first argument to the routine, as shown in Listing 18-45:

Listing 18-45. *Pascal examples of indenting a routine-call continuation line to emphasize routine names.*

```
DrawLine( Window.North, Window.South, Window.East, Window.West,
          CurrentWidth, CurrentAttribute );
SetFontAttributes( Font.FaceName, Font.Size, Font.Bold, Font.Italic,
                   Font.SyntheticAttribute[ FontID ].Underline,
                   Font.SyntheticAttribute[ FontID ].Strikeout );
```

From an aesthetic point of view, this looks a little ragged compared to the first approach. It does, however, make the routine name easier to pick out, so which you choose to do is really a personal preference.

Make it easy to find the end of a continuation line. One problem with the approach shown above is that you can't easily find the end of each line. Another alternative is to put each argument on a line of its own and indicate the end of the group with a closing parenthesis. Listing 18-46 on the next page shows how it looks.

This approach takes up a lot of real estate. If the arguments to a routine are long structures or pointer names, however, as the last two are, using one argument per line improves readability substantially. The *);* at the end of the block

Listing 18-46. *Pascal examples of formatting routine-call continuation lines one argument to a line.*

```
DrawLine
   (
   Window.North,
   Window.South,
   Window.East,
   Window.West,
   CurrentWidth,
   CurrentAttribute
   );

SetFontAttributes
   (
   Font.FaceName,
   Font.Size,
   Font.Bold,
   Font.Italic,
   Font.SyntheticAttribute[ FontID ].Underline,
   Font.SyntheticAttribute[ FontID ].Strikeout
   );
```

makes the end of the call clear. In practice, usually only a few routines need to be broken into multiple lines. You can handle others on one line. Any of the three options for formatting multiple-line routine calls works all right if you use it consistently.

Indent control-statement continuation lines the standard amount. If you run out of room for a *for* loop, a *while* loop, or an *if* statement, indent the continuation line by the same amount of space that you indent statements in a loop or after an *if* statement. Two examples are shown in Listing 18-47:

Listing 18-47. *Pascal examples of indenting control-statement continuation lines.*

This continuation line is indented the standard number of spaces...

...as is this one.

```
while ( PathName[ StartPath + Pos ] <> ';' ) and
    ( ( StartPath + Pos ) <= length( PathName ) ) do
    begin
    ...
    end;

for RecNum := ( Employee.Rec.Start + Employee.Rec.Offset ) to
    ( Employee.Rec.Start + Employee.Rec.Offset + Employee.NumRecs ) do
    begin
    ...
    end;
```

Because C doesn't format in quite the same way, a similar version of the code in C is shown in Listing 18-48:

Listing 18-48. *C examples of indenting control-statement continuation lines.*

```
while ( PathName[ StartPath + Pos ] != ';' ) &&
   ( ( StartPath + Pos ) <= length( PathName ) )
   {
   ...
   }

for ( RecNum = Employee.Rec.Start + Employee.Rec.Offset;
   RecNum <= Employee.Rec.Start + Employee.Rec.Offset + Employee.NumRecs;
   RecNum++ )
   {
   ...
   }
```

CROSS-REFERENCE
Sometimes the best solution to a complicated test is to put it into a boolean function. For examples, see "Making Complicated Expressions Simple" in Section 17.1.

This meets the criteria set earlier in the chapter. The continuation part of the statement is done logically—it's always indented underneath the statement it continues. The indentation can be done consistently—it uses only a few more spaces than the original line. It's as readable as anything else, and it's as maintainable as anything else. In some cases you might be able to improve readability by fine-tuning the indentation or spacing, but be sure to keep the maintainability trade-off in mind when you consider fine-tuning.

Indent assignment continuation lines after the assignment operator. For its consistency with the other indentation guidelines, you might think that indenting continuation lines the standard number of spaces in a group of assignments is the preferred approach. Not so! Indenting the standard number of spaces disturbs the alignment of groups of assignment statements, as Listing 18-49 shows:

Listing 18-49. *Pascal example of standard indentation for assignment-statement continuation—bad practice.*

```
CustomerPurchases := CustomerPurchases + CustomerSales( CustomerID );
CustomerBill      := CustomerBill + CustomerPurchases;
TotalCustomerBill := CustomerBill + PreviousBalance( CustomerID ) +
   LateCharge( CustomerID );
CustomerRating    := Rating( CustomerID, TotalCustomerBill );
```

The goal is to have an alignment of the := operator to show that a group of statements is related. Indenting the continuation line, *LateCharge(CustomerID)*, by only the standard number of spaces interrupts the visual alignment of the group of assignments. The standard indentation scheme hurts readability without gaining in any other area. This is the one case in which endline layout is OK. Listing 18-50 on the next page shows how the formatted code looks.

Listing 18-50. *Pascal example of endline layout used for assignment-statement continuation—good practice.*

```
CustomerPurchases := CustomerPurchases + CustomerSales( CustomerID );
CustomerBill     := CustomerBill + CustomerPurchases;
TotalCustomerBill := CustomerBill + PreviousBalance( CustomerID ) +
                     LateCharge( CustomerID );
CustomerRating   := Rating( CustomerID, TotalCustomerBill );
```

Using Only One Statement per Line

Modern languages such as Pascal, C, and Ada allow multiple statements per line. Free formatting is a big improvement over Fortran's requirement that comments begin in column 1 and statements begin in column 7 or later.

The power of free formatting is a mixed blessing, however, when it comes to putting multiple statements on a line:

```
i = 0; j = 0; k = 0; DestroyBadLoopNames( i, j, k );
```

This line contains several statements that could logically be separated onto lines of their own.

One argument in favor of putting several statements on one line is that it requires fewer lines of screen space or printer paper, which allows more of the code to be viewed at once. It's also a way to group related statements, and some programmers believe that it provides optimization clues to the compiler.

These are good reasons, but the reasons to limit yourself to one statement per line are more compelling:

- Putting each statement on a line of its own provides an accurate view of a program's complexity. It doesn't hide complexity by making complex statements look trivial. Statements that are complex look complex. Statements that are easy look easy.

CROSS-REFERENCE
Code-level performance optimizations are discussed in Chapter 28, "Code-Tuning Strategies," and Chapter 29, "Code-Tuning Techniques."

- Putting several statements on one line doesn't provide optimization clues to modern compilers. Today's optimizing compilers don't depend on formatting clues to do their optimizations. This is illustrated later in this section.

- With statements on their own lines, the code reads from top to bottom, instead of top to bottom and left to right. When you're looking for a specific line of code, your eye should be able to follow the left margin of the code. It shouldn't have to dip into each and every line just because a single line might contain two statements.

- With statements on their own lines, it's easy to find syntax errors when your compiler provides only the line numbers of the errors. If you have multiple statements on a line, the line number doesn't tell you which statement is in error.

- With one statement to a line, it's easy to step through the code with line-oriented debuggers. If you have several statements on a line, the debugger executes them all at once, and you have to switch to assembler to step through individual statements.

- With one to a line, it's easy to edit individual statements—to delete a line or temporarily convert a line to a comment. If you have multiple statements on a line, you have to do your editing between other statements.

In C, avoid side effects. Side effects are consequences of a statement other than its main consequence. In C, the ++ operator on a line that contains other operations is a side effect. Likewise, assigning a value to a variable and using the left side of the assignment in a conditional is a side effect.

Side effects tend to make code difficult to read. For example, if *n* equals *4*, what is the printout of the statement shown in Listing 18-51?

Listing 18-51. *C example of an unpredictable side effect.*

```
printf( "%d  %d \n", ++n, n + 2 );
```

Is it *4* and *6*? Is it *5* and *7*? Is it *5* and *6*? The answer is None of the above. The first argument, *++n*, is *5*. But the C language does not define the order in which routine arguments are evaluated. So the compiler can evaluate the second argument, *n + 2*, either before or after the first argument; the result might be either *6* or *7*, depending on the compiler. Listing 18-52 shows how you should rewrite the statement so that the intent is clear:

Listing 18-52. *C example of avoiding an unpredictable side effect.*

```
++n;
printf( "%d  %d \n", n, n + 2 );
```

If you're still not convinced that you should put side effects on lines by themselves, try to figure out what the routine shown in Listing 18-53 does:

Listing 18-53. *C example of too many operations on a line.*

```
strcpy( char * t, char * s )
   {
   while ( *++t = *++s )
      ;
   }
```

Some experienced C programmers don't see the complexity in that example because it's a familiar function; they look at it and say, "That's *strcpy()*." In this case, however, it's not quite *strcpy()*. It contains an error. If you said, "That's *strcpy()*" when you saw the code, you were recognizing the code, not reading it. This is exactly the situation you're in when you debug a program: The code that you overlook because you "recognize" it rather than read it can contain the error that's harder to find than it needs to be.

The fragment shown in Listing 18-54 is functionally identical to the first and is more readable:

Listing 18-54. *C example of a readable number of operations on each line.*

```
strcpy( char * t, char * s )
   {
   do
      {
      ++t;
      ++s;
      *t = *s;
      }
   while ( *t != '\0' );
   }
```

In the reformatted code, the error is apparent. Clearly, *t* and *s* are incremented before *∗s* is copied to *∗t*. The first character is missed.

The second example looks more elaborate than the first, even though the operations performed in the second example are identical. The reason it looks more elaborate is that it doesn't hide the complexity of the operations.

CROSS-REFERENCE
For details on code tuning, see Chapter 28, "Code-Tuning Strategies," and Chapter 29, "Code-Tuning Techniques."

Improved performance doesn't justify putting multiple operations on the same line either. Because the two *strcpy()* routines are logically equivalent, you would expect the compiler to generate identical code for them. When both versions of the routine were profiled, however, the first version took 3.83 seconds to copy 50,000 strings and the second took 3.34 seconds. The first version also took 16 bytes instead of 11.

In this case, the "clever" version carries a 15 percent speed penalty and a 45 percent size penalty, which makes it look a lot less clever. The results vary from compiler to compiler, but in general they suggest that until you've measured performance gains, you're better off striving for clarity and correctness first, performance second.

Even if you read statements with side effects easily, take pity on other people who will read your code. Most good programmers need to think twice to understand expressions with side effects. Let them use their brain cells to understand the larger questions of how your code works rather than the syntactic details of a specific expression.

Laying Out Data Declarations

CROSS-REFERENCE
For details on documenting data declarations, see "Commenting Data Declarations" in Section 19.5. For aspects of data use, see Chapters 8 through 12.

Use alignment for data declarations. The main reason to align data declarations is different from the reason for aligning assignments. You already know that all the data declarations are related, so the benefit of alignment is a neater listing and quicker scanning of the right side of the list. The kind of information in the right side of the list varies from language to language. Sometimes the right side contains the variable types; sometimes it contains the variable names. If you're programming in Pascal, you'll put the data types on the right side of the list, as shown in Listing 18-55:

Listing 18-55. *Pascal example of aligning data declarations.*

```
SortBoundary:    Integer;
InsertPos:       Integer;
InsertVal:       SORT_STRING;
LowerBoundary:   SORT_STRING;
```

In this case, you could argue that it's not all that important to be able to scan the right side of the list—unless you often scan data declarations for something that's declared to be an *Integer* rather than for something declared as a *SORT_STRING*.

If you're programming in C, however, you'll put the data names on the right side of the list, as shown in Listing 18-56:

Listing 18-56. *C example of aligning data declarations.*

```
int           SortBoundary;
int           InsertPos;
SORT_STRING   InsertVal;
SORT_STRING   LowerBoundary;
```

In this case, it's highly useful to be able to scan the right side of the list because that's where the variable names are.

Use only one data declaration per line. As shown in the examples above, you should give each data declaration its own line. It's easier to put a comment next to each declaration if each one is on its own line. It's easier to modify declarations because each declaration is self-contained. It's easier to find specific variables because you can scan a single column rather than reading each line. It's easier to find and fix syntax errors because the line number the compiler gives you has only one declaration on it.

Quickly—in the data declaration in Listing 18-57, what type of variable is *CurrentBottom?*

Listing 18-57. *C example of crowding more than one variable declaration onto a line.*

CODING HORROR

```
int RowIdx, ColIdx; COLOR PreviousScreen, CurrentScreen, NextScreen;
    POINT PreviousTop, PreviousBottom, CurrentTop, CurrentBottom, NextTop,
    NextBottom; FONT PreviousFace, CurrentFace, NextFace;
    COLOR Choices[ NUM_COLORS ];
```

This is not an uncommon style of declaring variables, but the variable is hard to find because all the declarations are jammed together. The variable's type is hard to find too. This is the least readable style of declaration.

Now find the type of *NextFace* in Listing 18-58:

Listing 18-58. *Pascal example of crowding more than one variable declaration onto a line.*

```
RowIdx, ColIdx:        integer;

CurrentScreen,
NextScreen,
PreviousScreen:        COLOR;

CurrentBottom, CurrentTop,
NextBottom, NextTop,
PreviousBottom,
PreviousTop:           POINT ;

CurrentFace, NextFace,
PreviousFace:          FONT;

Choices:               array[ 1..NUM_COLORS ] of COLOR;
```

This is also a popular style, characterized by an attempt to align similar items, by one use of each type name, by an irregular number of items per line, by an aesthetically pleasing appearance, and by readability that isn't much better than in the first example.

Now, what is *NextScreen's* type in Listing 18-59?

The variable *NextScreen* was probably easier to find than *NextFace* was in Listing 18-58. This style is characterized by one declaration per line, a complete declaration including the variable type on each line, and aesthetically appealing alignment.

Admittedly, this style chews up a lot of screen space—20 lines instead of the 4 in the first example, although those 4 lines were pretty ugly. A comparison

Listing 18-59. *Pascal example of readability achieved by putting only one variable declaration on each line.*

```
RowIdx:            integer;
ColIdx:            integer;

CurrentBottom:     POINT;
CurrentTop:        POINT;
NextBottom:        POINT;
NextTop:           POINT;
PreviousBottom:    POINT;
PreviousTop:       POINT;

CurrentScreen:     COLOR;
NextScreen:        COLOR;
PreviousScreen:    COLOR;
Choices:           array[ 1..NUM_COLORS ] of COLOR;

CurrentFace:       FONT;
NextFace:          FONT;
PreviousFace:      FONT;
```

with the 17 lines in the second example is fairer. I can't point to any studies that show that this style leads to fewer bugs or greater comprehension. If Sally Programmer, Jr. asked me to review her code, however, and her data declarations looked like the first example, I'd say, "No way—too hard to read." If they looked like the second example, I'd say, "Uh...maybe I'll get back to you." If they looked like the final example, I would say, "Certainly—it's a pleasure."

Order declarations sensibly. In the example above, the declarations are grouped by types. Grouping by types is usually sensible since variables of the same type tend to be used in related operations. In other cases, you might choose to order them alphabetically by variable name. Although alphabetical ordering has many advocates, my feeling is that it's too much work for what it's worth. If your list of variables is so long that alphabetical ordering helps, your routine is probably too big. Break it up so that you have smaller routines with fewer variables.

In C, put the asterisk next to the type name in pointer declarations. It's common to see pointer declarations that have the asterisk next to the variable name rather than the type name, as in Listing 18-60:

Listing 18-60. *C example of misleading asterisks in pointer declarations.*

```
EMP_LIST    *Employees;
FILE        *InputFile;
```

437

Although it's common practice, it's misleading. The fact that a variable is a pointer is part of its type. When the asterisk is associated with the name, it looks as if the asterisk is part of the name. That's misleading because you can use the variable either with or without the asterisk. It makes more sense to put the asterisk next to the type, as in Listing 18-61:

Listing 18-61. *C example of accurate asterisks in pointer declarations.*

```
EMP_LIST *   Employees;
FILE *       InputFile;
```

The only problem with putting the asterisk next to the type name rather than the variable name crops up when you put more than one declaration on a line, in which case the asterisk applies to only the first variable. The best approach is to declare a type for the pointer and use that instead. An example is shown in Listing 18-62:

Listing 18-62. *C example of good uses of a pointer type in declarations.*

```
EMP_LIST_PTR  Employees;
FILE_PTR      InputFile;
```

18.6 Laying Out Comments

CROSS-REFERENCE
For details on other aspects of comments, see Chapter 19, "Self-Documenting Code."

Comments done well can greatly enhance a program's readability. Comments done poorly can actually hurt it. The layout of comments plays a large role in whether they help or hinder readability.

Indent a comment with its corresponding code. Visual indentation is a valuable aid to understanding a program's logical structure, and good comments don't interfere with the visual indentation. For example, what is the logical structure of the routine shown in Listing 18-63?

In this example you don't get much of a clue to the logical structure because the comments completely obscure the visual indentation of the code. You might find it hard to believe that anyone ever makes a conscious decision to use such an indentation style, but I've seen it in professional programs and know of at least one textbook that recommends it (Hughes, Pfleeger, and Rose 1978).

Listing 18-63. *Basic example of poorly indented comments.*

CODING HORROR

```
for TransactionID = 1 TO MaxRecords

'get transaction data
   read TransactionType
   read TransactionAmount

'process transaction based on transaction type
   if TransactionType = CustomerSale then
      AcceptCustomerSale( TransactionAmount )

   elseif TransactionType = CustomerReturn then

'either process return automatically or get manager approval,
'if required
      if TransactionAmount >= MgrApprovalRequired then

'try to get manager approval and then accept or reject the return
'based on whether approval is granted
         GetMgrApproval( Approval )
         if Approval = True then
            AcceptCustomerReturn( TransactionAmount )
         else
            RejectCustomerReturn( TransactionAmount )
         end if
      else

'manager approval not required, so accept return
         AcceptCustomerReturn( TransactionAmount )
      end if
   end if
next TransactionID
```

The code shown in Listing 18-64 on the next page is exactly the same as in Listing 18-63, except for the indentation of the comments.

In Listing 18-64, the logical structure is more apparent. One study of the effectiveness of commenting found that the benefit of having comments was not conclusive, and the author speculated that it was because they "disrupt visual scanning of the program" (Shneiderman 1980). From these examples, it's obvious that the *style* of commenting strongly influences whether comments are disruptive.

Listing 18-64. *Basic example of nicely indented comments.*

```
for TransactionID = 1 TO MaxRecords

    'read transaction data
    read TransactionType
    read TransactionAmount

    'process transaction based on transaction type
    if TransactionType = CustomerSale then
        AcceptCustomerSale( TransactionAmount )

    elseif TransactionType = CustomerReturn then

        'either process return automatically or get manager approval,
        'if required
        if TransactionAmount >= MgrApprovalRequired then

            'try to get manager approval and then accept or reject the return
            'based on whether approval is granted
            GetMgrApproval( Approval )
            if Approval = True then
                AcceptCustomerReturn( TransactionAmount )
            else
                RejectCustomerReturn( TransactionAmount )
            end if
        else

            'manager approval not required, so accept return
            AcceptCustomerReturn( TransactionAmount )
        end if
    end if
next TransactionID
```

Set off each comment with at least one blank line. If someone is trying to get an overview of your program, the most effective way to do it is to read the comments without reading the code. Setting comments off with blank lines helps a reader scan the code. An example is shown in Listing 18-65:

Listing 18-65. *Pascal example of setting off a comment with a blank line.*

```
{ comment zero }
CodeStatementZero;
CodeStatementOne;

{ comment one }
CodeStatementTwo;
CodeStatementThree;
```

Some people use a blank line both before and after the comment. Two blanks use more display space, but some people think the code looks better than with just one. An example is shown in Listing 18-66:

Listing 18-66. *Pascal example of setting off a comment with two blank lines.*

```
{ comment zero }

CodeStatementZero;
CodeStatementOne;

{ comment one }

CodeStatementTwo;
CodeStatementThree;
```

Unless your display space is at a premium, this is a purely aesthetic judgment and you can make it accordingly. In this, as in many other areas, the fact that a convention exists is more important than the convention's specific details.

18.7 Laying Out Routines

CROSS-REFERENCE
For details on documenting routines, see "Commenting Routines" in Section 19.5. For details on the process of writing a routine, see Chapter 4, "Steps in Building a Routine." For a discussion of the differences between good and bad routines, see Chapter 5, "Characteristics of High-Quality Routines."

Routines are composed of individual statements, data, control structures, comments—all the things discussed in the other parts of the chapter. This section provides layout guidelines unique to routines.

Use blank lines to separate parts of a routine. Use blank lines between the routine header, its data and named-constant declarations, and its body.

Use standard indentation for routine arguments. The options with routine-header layout are about the same as they are in a lot of other areas of layout: no conscious layout, endline layout, or standard indentation. As in most other cases, standard indentation does better in terms of accuracy, consistency, readability, and modifiability.

Listing 18-67 shows two examples of routine headers with no conscious layout:

Listing 18-67. *C examples of routine headers with no conscious layout.*

```
BOOLEAN ReadEmployeeData(int MaxEmployees,EMP_LIST * Employees,
    FILE * InputFile,int * EmployeeCount,BOOLEAN * IsInputError)
...

void InsertionSort(SORT_ARRAY Data,int FirstElmt,int LastElmt)
```

These routine headers are purely utilitarian. The computer can read them as well as it can read headers in any other format, but they cause trouble for humans. Without a conscious effort to make the headers hard to read, how could they be any worse?

The second approach in routine-header layout is the endline layout, which usually works all right. Listing 18-68 shows the same routine headers reformatted:

Listing 18-68. *C example of routine headers with mediocre endline layout.*

```
BOOLEAN ReadEmployeeData( int          MaxEmployees,
                         EMP_LIST *   Employees,
                         FILE *       InputFile,
                         int *        EmployeeCount,
                         BOOLEAN *    IsInputError )
...
void InsertionSort( SORT_ARRAY  Data,
                    int         FirstElmt,
                    int         LastElmt )
```

CROSS-REFERENCE
For more details on using routine parameters, see Section 5.7, "How to Use Routine Parameters."

The endline approach is neat and aesthetically appealing. The main problem is that it takes a lot of work to maintain, and styles that are hard to maintain aren't maintained. Suppose that the function name changes from *Read-EmployeeData()* to *ReadNewEmployeeData()*. That would throw the alignment of the first line off from the alignment of the other four lines. You'd have to reformat the other four lines of the parameter list to align with the new position of *MaxEmployees* caused by the longer function name. And you'd probably run out of space on the right side since the elements are so far to the right already.

The examples shown in Listing 18-69, formatted using standard indentation, are just as appealing aesthetically but take less work to maintain.

This style holds up better under modification. If the routine name changes, the change has no effect on any of the parameters. If parameters are added or deleted, only one line has to be modified—plus or minus a semicolon. The visual cues are similar to those in the indentation scheme for a loop or an *if* statement. Your eye doesn't have to scan different parts of the page for every individual routine to find meaningful information; it knows where the information is every time.

This style translates to Pascal in a straightforward way. It doesn't translate to Fortran at all since Fortran has the parameter declarations after the routine declaration.

Listing 18-69. *C example of routine headers with readable, maintainable standard indentation.*

```
BOOLEAN ReadEmployeeData
   (
   int         MaxEmployees;
   EMP_LIST *  Employees;
   FILE *      InputFile;
   int *       EmployeeCount;
   BOOLEAN *   IsInputError
   )
...

void InsertionSort
   (
   SORT_ARRAY  Data,
   int         FirstElmt,
   int         LastElmt
   )
```

In C, use new-style routine declarations. The style of routine headers adopted in the ANSI C standard is different from the original C header style, but most compilers and a few programmers still support the old style. Unfortunately, the old style has little to recommend it. Listing 18-70 shows a comparison of the old and new styles:

Listing 18-70. *C example of old-style and new-style routine headers.*

```
Old style —    void InsertionSort( Data, FirstElmt, LastElmt )
                  SORT_ARRAY  Data,
                  int         FirstElmt,
                  int         LastElmt
               {
               ...
               }

New style —    void InsertionSort
                  (
                  SORT_ARRAY  Data,
                  int         FirstElmt,
                  int         LastElmt
                  )
               {
               ...
               }
```

The difference between the two styles is that the old style lists the variable names once and then lists them again with their types where they are declared.

It takes extra effort to type the names twice in the first place, and they're harder to modify because you have to remember to modify both instances. In the second edition of *The C Programming Language*, Kernighan and Ritchie "strongly recommend" that you use the new style of declarations (1988).

In Fortran, declare parameters separately and in the same order in which they are listed in the subroutine's parameter list. Fortran unfortunately requires that variable names be given in the parameter list and repeated in a declaration following the parameter list--just as in old-style C declarations. Fortran also encourages mingling the declarations of parameters and local variables, giving rise to hodgepodges like the one shown in Listing 18-71:

Listing 18-71. *Fortran example of confusing parameter ordering.*

```
SUBROUTINE READEE( MAXEE, INFILE, INERR )
INTEGER    I, J
LOGICAL    INERR
INTEGER    MAXEE
CHARACTER  INFILE*8
```

This looks neat because a few things are aligned, but the neatness doesn't help solve its main problem. When I was a kid, I wouldn't let any of the food on my plate touch any of the other food on my plate. Now that I'm older, I enjoy the combinations of flavors that result from spilling a little maple syrup on my bacon and eggs. But I have yet to acquire a taste for mixing declarations of parameters with declarations of local variables. Listing 18-72 shows how the Fortran subroutine declaration should look:

Listing 18-72. *Fortran example of sensible parameter ordering.*

Parameters are —
declared first, in the
same order as in the
parameter list.

Local variables —
are declared second
and are separated
from parameter
declarations.

```
SUBROUTINE READEE( MAXEE, INFILE, INERR )
    INTEGER     MAXEE
    CHARACTER   INFILE*8
    LOGICAL     INERR

*   local variables

    INTEGER I
    INTEGER J
```

This example follows several of the other recommendations in this chapter by indenting the subroutine variables under the subroutine declaration, having only one declaration per line, aligning the columns of variable names, indenting the comment with its corresponding code, and setting off the comment and the parts of the routine with blank lines.

18.8 Laying Out Files, Modules, and Programs

CROSS-REFERENCE
For documentation details,
see "Commenting Files,
Modules, and Programs"
in Section 19.5.

Beyond the formatting techniques for routines is a larger formatting issue. How do you organize routines within a file, and how do you decide which routines to put in a file in the first place?

Put one module in one file. A file isn't just a bucket that holds some code. If your language allows it, a file should hold a collection of routines that supports one and only one purpose. A file is a way to package related routines into a module.

CROSS-REFERENCE
For details on the differences between modules and routines and how to make a collection of routines into a module, see Chapter 6, "Three out of Four Programmers Surveyed Prefer Modules."

All the routines within a file make up the module. The module might be one that the program really recognizes as such, or it might be just a logical entity that you've created as part of your design.

Modules are a semantic language concept. Files are a physical operating system concept. The correspondence between modules and files is coincidental. In the future, environments will tend to emphasize modules and de-emphasize files, but for now, the two are related, so treat them as though they are equivalent.

Separate routines within a file clearly. Separate each routine from other routines with at least two blank lines. The blank lines are as effective as big rows of asterisks or dashes, and they're a lot easier to type and maintain. Use two or three to produce a visual difference between blank lines that are part of a routine and blank lines that separate routines. An example is shown in Listing 18-73:

Listing 18-73. *Basic example of using blank lines between routines.*

Here's one blank line—typical of a blank line used within a routine.

At least two blank lines separate the two routines.

```
Function Max!( Arg1!, Arg2! )

'find the arithmetic maximum of Arg1 and Arg2
if ( Arg1! > Arg2! ) then
   Max! = Arg1!
else
   Max! = Arg2!
endif
end Function


Function Min!( Arg1!, Arg2! )

'find the arithmetic minimum of Arg1 and Arg2
if ( Arg1! < Arg2! ) then
   Max! = Arg1!
else
   Max! = Arg2!
endif
end Function
```

Blank lines are easier to type than any other kind of separator and look at least as good. Three blank lines are used here so that the separation between routines is more noticeable than the blank lines within each routine.

CROSS-REFERENCE
For details on creating modules in languages that support modules directly and languages that don't, see Section 6.4, "Implementing Modules in Any Language."

If you have more than one logical module in a file, identify each module clearly. Routines that are related should be grouped together into modules. A reader scanning your code should be able to tell easily which module is which. Identify each module clearly by using several blank lines between it and the modules next to it. A module is like a chapter in a book. In a book, you start each chapter on a new page and use big print for the chapter title. Emphasize the start of each module similarly. An example of separating modules is shown in Listing 18-74.

Avoid overemphasizing comments within modules. If you mark every routine and comment with a row of asterisks instead of blank lines, you'll have a hard time coming up with a device that effectively emphasizes the start of a new module. An example is shown in Listing 18-75 on page 448.

In this example, so many things are highlighted with asterisks that nothing is really emphasized. The program becomes a dense forest of asterisks. Although it's more an aesthetic than a technical judgment, in formatting, less is more.

If you must separate parts of a program with long lines of special characters, develop a hierarchy of characters (from densest to lightest) instead of relying exclusively on asterisks. For example, use asterisks for module divisions, dashes for routine divisions, and blank lines for important comments. Refrain from putting two rows of asterisks or dashes together. An example is shown in Listing 18-76 on page 449.

This advice about how to identify multiple modules within a single file applies only when your language restricts the number of files you can use in a program. If you're using C or a version of Pascal, Fortran, or Basic that supports multiple source files, put only one module in each file. Within a single module, however, you might still have subgroups of routines, and you can group them using techniques such as the ones shown here.

Sequence routines alphabetically. An alternative to grouping related routines in a file is to put them in alphabetical order. If you can't break a program up into modules or if your editor doesn't allow you to find functions easily, the alphabetical approach can save search time.

Listing 18-74. *Basic example of formatting the separation between modules.*

This is the last routine in a module.

```
Function ConvertBlanks$( MixedString$ )

'create a string identical to MixedString$ except that the
'blanks are replaced with underscores.

dim i%
dim StringLength%
dim WorkString$

WorkString$   = ""
StringLength% = Len( MixedString$ )
for i% = 1 to StringLength%
   if ( mid$( MixedString$, i%, 1 ) = " " ) then
      WorkString$ = WorkString$ + "_"
   else
      WorkString$ = WorkString$ + mid$( MixedString$, i%, 1 )
   endif
next i%
ConvertBlanks$ = WorkString$
end Function
```

The beginning of the new module is marked with several blank lines and the name of the module.

```
'---------------------------------------------------------------
' MATHEMATICAL FUNCTIONS
'
' This module contains the program's mathematical functions.
'---------------------------------------------------------------
```

This is the first routine in a new module.

```
Function Max!( Arg1!, Arg2! )

'find the arithmetic maximum of Arg1 and Arg2

if ( Arg1! > Arg2! ) then
   Max! = Arg1!
else
   Max! = Arg2!
endif
end Function
```

This routine is separated from the previous routine by blank lines only.

```
Function Min!( Arg1!, Arg2! )

'find the arithmetic minimum of Arg1 and Arg2

if ( Arg1! < Arg2! ) then
   Max! = Arg1!
else
   Max! = Arg2!
endif
end Function
```

Listing 18-75. *Basic example of overformatting a module.*

```
'********************************************************************
'********************************************************************
' MATHEMATICAL FUNCTIONS
'
' This module contains the program's mathematical functions.
'********************************************************************
'********************************************************************


'********************************************************************
Function Max!( Arg1!, Arg2! )
'********************************************************************
'find the arithmetic maximum of Arg1 and Arg2
'********************************************************************
if ( Arg1! > Arg2! ) then
    Max! = Arg1!
else
    Max! = Arg2!
endif
end Function


'********************************************************************
Function Min!( Arg1!, Arg2! )
'********************************************************************
'find the arithmetic maximum of Arg1 and Arg2
'********************************************************************
if ( Arg1! < Arg2! ) then
    Max! = Arg1!
else
    Max! = Arg2!
endif
end Function
```

In C, order the source file carefully. Here's the standard order of source-file contents in C:

> File-description comment
> *#include* files
> Constant definitions
> Macro function definitions
> Type definitions
> Global variables and functions imported
> Global variables and functions exported
> Variables and functions that are private to the file

Listing 18-76. *Basic example of good formatting with restraint.*

The lightness of this line compared to the line of asterisks visually reinforces the fact that the routine is subordinate to the module.

```
'*********************************************************************
' MATHEMATICAL FUNCTIONS
'
' This module contains the program's mathematical functions.
'*********************************************************************

'----------------------------        --------------------------------
Function Max!( Arg1!, Arg2! )
'--------------------------------------------------------------------

'find the arithmetic maximum of Arg1 and Arg2

if ( Arg1! > Arg2! ) then
   Max! = Arg1!
else
   Max! = Arg2!
endif
end Function


'--------------------------------------------------------------------
Function Min!( Arg1!, Arg2! )
'--------------------------------------------------------------------

'find the arithmetic minimum of Arg1 and Arg2

if ( Arg1! < Arg2! ) then
   Max! = Arg1!
else
   Max! = Arg2!
endif
end Function
```

CHECKLIST

Layout

GENERAL

❏ Is formatting done primarily to illuminate the logical structure of the code?

❏ Can the formatting scheme be used consistently?

❏ Does the formatting scheme result in code that's easy to maintain?

❏ Does the formatting scheme improve code readability?

CONTROL STRUCTURES

❏ Does the code avoid doubly indented *begin-end* pairs?

❏ Are sequential blocks separated from each other with blank lines?

❏ Are complicated expressions formatted for readability?

❏ Are single-statement blocks formatted consistently?

❏ Are *case* statements formatted in a way that's consistent with the formatting of other control structures?

❏ Have *goto*s been formatted in a way that makes their use obvious?

INDIVIDUAL STATEMENTS

❏ Do incomplete statements end the line in a way that's obviously incorrect?

❏ Are continuation lines indented sensibly?

❏ Are groups of related statements aligned?

❏ Are groups of *un*related statements *un*aligned?

❏ Does each line contain at most one statement?

❏ Is each statement written without side effects?

❏ Are data declarations aligned?

❏ Is there at most one data declaration per line?

COMMENTS

❏ Are the comments indented the same number of spaces as the code they comment?

❏ Is the commenting style easy to maintain?

(continued)

Layout checklist, *continued*

ROUTINES

❑ Are the arguments to each routine formatted so that each argument is easy to read, modify, and comment?

❑ In C, are new-style routine declarations used?

❑ In Fortran, are parameters declared separately from local variables?

FILES, MODULES, AND PROGRAMS

❑ In languages that permit more than one source file, does each file hold code for one and only one module?

❑ Are routines within a file clearly separated with blank lines?

❑ If a file does contain multiple modules, are all the routines in each module grouped together and is the module clearly identified?

❑ Alternatively, are all routines in alphabetical sequence?

Further Reading

Most programming textbooks say a few words about layout and style, but thorough discussions of programming style are rare; discussions of layout are rarer still. The following books talk about layout and programming style. The classic is Kernighan and Plauger's book, listed first.

Kernighan, Brian W., and P. J. Plauger. *The Elements of Programming Style,* 2d ed. New York: McGraw-Hill, 1978.

Kreitzberg, C. B., and B. Shneiderman. *The Elements of Fortran Style.* New York: Harcourt Brace Jovanovich, 1972.

Nevison, John M. *The Little Book of Basic Style.* Reading, Mass.: Addison-Wesley, 1978.

Plum, Thomas. *C Programming Guidelines.* Cardiff, N.J.: Plum Hall, 1984.

Software Productivity Consortium. *Ada Quality and Style: Guidelines for Professional Programmers.* New York: Van Nostrand Reinhold, 1989.

"A C Coding Standard." *Unix Review* 9, no. 9 (September 1991): 42–43.

Thomas, Edward J., and Paul W. Oman. "A Bibliography of Programming Style," *Sigplan Notices* 25, no. 2 (February 1990): 7–16. This article contains an exhaustive annotated bibliography of articles published about programming style.

For a substantially different approach to readability, see the discussion of Donald Knuth's "literate programming" in the two Jon Bentley "Programming Pearls" columns listed below, as well as in the T$_{E}$X book.

Bentley, Jon, and Donald Knuth. "Literate Programming." *Communications of the ACM* 29, no. 5 (May 1986): 364–69.

Bentley, Jon, Donald Knuth, and Doug McIlroy. "A Literate Program." *Communications of the ACM* 29, no. 6 (June 1986): 471–83. This article contains a small example of a literate program. It's pleasant to look at, with indentation, keywords in bold, massive commentary, and so on.

Knuth, Donald. *Computers and Typesetting, Volume B, T$_{E}$X: The Program*. Reading, Mass.: Addison-Wesley, 1986. Knuth's T$_{E}$X book contains the source code for T$_{E}$X, written as a literate program. Knuth has been writing about the virtues of literate programming for about 10 years, and in spite of his strong claim to the title Best Programmer on the Planet, literate programming isn't catching on. Read some of his code to form your own conclusions about the reason.

Key Points

- The first priority of visual layout is to illuminate the logical organization of the code. Criteria used to assess whether the priority is achieved include accuracy, consistency, readability, and maintainability.

- Looking good is secondary to the other criteria—a distant second. If the other criteria are met and the underlying code is good, however, the layout will look fine.

- Two layout styles that are effective in Pascal, C, and Basic are pure-block emulation and the use of *begin-end* block boundaries. Ada has pure blocks, so you can use a pure-block layout if you program in Ada.

- Structuring code is important for its own sake. The specific convention you follow may be less important than the fact that you follow some convention consistently. A layout convention that's followed inconsistently might actually hurt readability.

- Many aspects of layout are religious issues. Try to separate objective preferences from subjective ones. Use explicit criteria to help ground your discussions about style preferences.

19

Self-Documenting Code

Contents

19.1 External Documentation
19.2 Programming Style as Documentation
19.3 To Comment or Not to Comment
19.4 Keys to Effective Comments
19.5 Commenting Techniques

Related Topics

Layout: Chapter 18
The PDL-to-code process: Chapter 4
High-quality routines: Chapter 5
Programming as communication: Sections 31.5 and 32.3

MOST PROGRAMMERS ENJOY WRITING DOCUMENTATION if the documentation standards aren't unreasonable. Like layout, good documentation is a sign of the professional pride a programmer puts into a program. Software documentation can take many forms, and after describing the sweep of the documentation landscape, this chapter cultivates the specific patch of documentation known as "comments."

19.1 External Documentation

Documentation on a software project consists of information both inside the source-code listings and outside them—usually in the form of separate documents or unit development folders. On large, formal projects, most of the

HARD DATA

FURTHER READING
For a detailed description, see "The Unit Development Folder (UDF): An Effective Management Tool for Software Development" (Ingrassia 1976) or "The Unit Development Folder (UDF): A Ten-Year Perspective" (Ingrassia 1987).

documentation is outside the source code. In fact, about two-thirds of the total effort on a large project goes into creating documentation, rather than source code, as output (Boehm et al. 1984). External construction documentation tends to be at a high level compared to the code, at a low level compared to the documentation from phases prior to construction.

Unit development folders. A UDF, or software-development folder (SDF), is an informal document that contains notes used by a developer during construction. A "unit" is loosely defined, usually to mean either a routine or a module. The main purpose of a UDF is to provide a trail of design decisions that aren't documented elsewhere. Many projects have standards that specify the minimum content of a UDF, such as copies of the relevant requirements, the parts of the top-level design the unit implements, a copy of the development standards, a current code listing, and design notes from the unit's developer. Sometimes the customer requires a software developer to deliver the project's UDFs; often they are for internal use only.

Detailed-design document. The detailed-design document is the low-level design document. It describes the module-level or routine-level design decisions, the alternatives that were considered, and the reasons for selecting the approaches that were selected. Sometimes this information is contained in a formal document. In such cases, detailed design is usually considered to be separate from construction. Sometimes it consists mainly of developer's notes collected into a "Unit Development Folder" (UDF). Sometimes—often—it exists only in the code itself.

19.2 Programming Style as Documentation

In contrast to external documentation, internal documentation is found within the program listing itself. It's the most detailed kind of documentation, at the source-statement level. Because it's most closely associated with the code, internal documentation is also the kind of documentation most likely to remain correct as the code is modified.

The main contributor to code-level documentation isn't comments, but good programming style. Style includes good program structure, use of straightforward and easily understandable approaches, good variable names, good routine names, use of named constants instead of literals, clear layout, and minimization of control-flow and data-structure complexity.

Here's a code fragment with poor style:

Example of Poor Documentation Resulting from Bad Programming Style

```
for i := 1 to Num do
MeetsCriteria[ i ] := True;
for i := 2 to Num / 2 do
j := i + i;
while ( j <= Num ) do begin
MeetsCriteria[ j ] := False;
j := j + i;
end;
for i := 1 to Num do
if MeetsCriteria[ i ] then
writeln( i, ' meets criteria.' );
```

What do you think this routine does? It's unnecessarily cryptic. It's poorly documented not because it lacks comments, but because it lacks good programming style. The variable names are uninformative, and the layout is crude. Here's the same code improved—just improving the programming style makes its meaning much clearer:

CROSS-REFERENCE

In this code, the variable *FactorableNumber* is added solely for the sake of clarifying the operation. For details on adding variables to clarify operations, see "Making Complicated Expressions Simple" in Section 17.1.

Pascal Example of Documentation Without Comments (with Good Style)

```
for PrimeCandidate := 1 to Num do
   IsPrime[ PrimeCandidate ] := True;

for Factor := 2 to Num / 2 do begin
   FactorableNumber := Factor + Factor;
   while ( FactorableNumber <= Num ) do begin
      IsPrime[ FactorableNumber ] := False;
      FactorableNumber := FactorableNumber + Factor;
   end;
end;

for PrimeCandidate := 1 to Num do
   if IsPrime[ PrimeCandidate ] then
      writeln( PrimeCandidate, ' is prime.' );
```

Unlike the first piece of code, this one lets you know at first glance that it has something to do with prime numbers. A second glance reveals that it finds the prime numbers between *1* and *Num*. With the first code fragment, it takes more than two glances just to figure out where the loops end.

The difference between the two code fragments has nothing to with comments. Neither fragment has any. The second one is much more readable, however, and approaches the Holy Grail of legibility: self-documenting code. Such code relies on good programming style to carry the greater part of the documentation burden. In well-written code, comments are the icing on the readability cake.

━━ CHECKLIST ━━━━━━━━━━━━━━━━━━━━━━━━━━━

Self-Documenting Code

ROUTINES

❏ Does each routine's name describe exactly what the routine does?

❏ Does each routine perform one well-defined task?

❏ Have all parts of each routine that would benefit from being put into their own routines been put into their own routines?

❏ Is each routine's interface obvious and clear?

DATA NAMES

❏ Are type names descriptive enough to help document data declarations?

❏ Are variables named well?

❏ Are variables used only for the purpose for which they're named?

❏ Are loop counters given more informative names than i, j, and k?

❏ Are well-named enumerated types used instead of makeshift flags or boolean variables?

❏ Are named constants used instead of magic numbers or magic strings?

❏ Do naming conventions distinguish among type names, enumerated types, named constants, local variables, module variables, and global variables?

DATA ORGANIZATION

❏ Are extra variables used for clarity when needed?

❏ Are references to variables close together?

❏ Are data structures simple so that they minimize complexity?

❏ Is complicated data accessed through abstract access routines (abstract data types)?

(continued)

Self-Documenting Code checklist, *continued*

CONTROL

❑ Is the nominal path through the code clear?

❑ Are related statements grouped together?

❑ Have relatively independent groups of statements been packaged into their own routines?

❑ Does the normal case follow the *if* rather than the *else*?

❑ Are control structures simple so that they minimize complexity?

❑ Does each loop perform one and only one function, as a well-defined routine would?

❑ Is nesting minimized?

❑ Have boolean expressions been simplified by using additional boolean variables, boolean functions, and decision tables?

LAYOUT

❑ Does the program's layout show its logical structure?

DESIGN

❑ Is the code straightforward, and does it avoid cleverness?

❑ Are implementation details hidden as much as possible?

❑ Is the program written in terms of the problem domain as much as possible rather than in terms of computer-science or programming language structures?

19.3 To Comment or Not to Comment

Comments are easier to write poorly than well, and commenting can be more damaging than helpful. The heated discussions over the virtues of commenting often sound like philosophical debates over moral virtues, which makes me think that if Socrates had been a computer programmer, he and his students might have had the following discussion.

ॐ

THE COMMENTO

Characters:

THRASYMACHUS	A green, theoretical purist who believes everything he reads
CALLICLES	A battle-hardened veteran from the old school— a "real" programmer
GLAUCON	A young, confident, hot-shot computer jock
ISMENE	A senior programmer tired of big promises, just looking for a few practices that work
SOCRATES	The wise old programmer

Setting: THE WEEKLY TEAM MEETING

"I want to suggest a commenting standard for our projects," Thrasymachus said. "Some of our programmers barely comment their code, and everyone knows that code without comments is unreadable."

"You must be fresher out of college than I thought," Callicles responded. "Comments are an academic panacea, but everyone who's done any real programming knows that comments make the code harder to read, not easier. English is less precise than C or Pascal and makes for a lot of excess verbiage. Programming-language statements are short and to the point. If you can't make the code clear, how can you make the comments clear? Plus, comments get out of date as the code changes. If you believe an out-of-date comment, you're sunk."

"I agree with that," Glaucon joined in. "Heavily commented code is harder to read because it means more to read. I already have to read the code; why should I have to read a lot of comments too?"

"Wait a minute," Ismene said, putting down her coffee mug to put in her two drachmas' worth. "I know that commenting can be abused, but good comments are worth their weight in gold. I've had to maintain code that had comments and code that didn't, and I'd rather maintain code with comments. I don't think we should have a standard that says use one comment for every x lines of code, but we should encourage everyone to comment."

"If comments are a waste of time, why does anyone use them, Callicles?" Socrates asked.

"Either because they're required to or because they read somewhere that they're useful. No one who's thought about it could ever decide they're useful."

"Ismene thinks they're useful. She's been here three years, maintaining your code without comments and other code with comments, and she prefers the code with comments. What do you make of that?"

"Comments are useless because they just repeat the code in a more verbose—"

KEY POINT

"Wait right there," Thrasymachus interrupted. "Good comments don't repeat the code or explain it. They clarify its intent. Comments should explain, at a higher level of abstraction than the code, what you're trying to do."

"Right," Ismene said. "I scan the comments to find the section that does what I need to change or fix. You're right that comments that repeat the code don't help at all because the code says everything already. When I read comments, I want it to be like reading headings in a book, or a table of contents. Comments help me find the right section, and then I start reading the code. It's a lot faster to read one sentence in English than it is to parse 20 lines of code in a programming language." Ismene poured herself another cup of coffee.

"I think that people who refuse to write comments (1) think their code is clearer than it could possibly be; (2) think that other programmers are far more interested in their code than they really are; (3) think other programmers are smarter than they really are; (4) are lazy; or (5) are afraid someone else might figure out how their code works.

"Code reviews would be a big help here, Socrates," Ismene continued. "If someone claims they don't need to write comments and are bombarded by questions in a review—several peers start saying, 'What the heck are you trying to do in this piece of code?'—then they'll start putting in comments. If they don't do it on their own, at least their manager will have the ammo to make them do it.

"I'm not accusing you of being lazy or afraid that people will figure out your code, Callicles. I've worked on your code and you're one of the best programmers in the company. But have a heart, huh? Your code would be easier for me to work on if you used comments."

"But they're a waste of resources," Callicles countered. "A good programmer's code should be self-documenting; everything you need to know should be in the code."

"No way!" Thrasymachus was out of his chair. "Everything the compiler needs to know is in the code! You might as well argue that everything you need to know is in the binary executable file! If you were smart enough to read it! What is *meant* to happen is not in the code."

459

Thrasymachus realized he was standing up and sat down. "Socrates, this is ridiculous. Why do we have to argue about whether or not comments are valuable? Everything I've ever read says they're valuable and should be used liberally. We're wasting our time."

"Cool down, Thrasymachus. Ask Callicles how long he's been programming."

"How long, Callicles?"

"Well, I started on the Acropolis IV about 15 years ago. I guess I've seen about a dozen major systems from the time they were born to the time we gave them a cup of hemlock. And I've worked on major parts of a dozen more. Two of those systems had over half a million lines of code, so I know what I'm talking about. Comments are pretty useless."

Socrates looked at the younger programmer. "As Callicles says, comments have a lot of legitimate problems, and you won't realize that without more experience. If they're not done right, they're worse than useless."

"Even when they're done right, they're useless," Callicles said. "Comments are less precise than a programming language. I'd rather not have them at all."

"Ismene's point, though, Callicles, is that the reduced precision is a virtue of comments—it means you can say more with fewer words. You write comments for the same reason you use a high-level language. They give you a higher level of abstraction, and we all know that levels of abstraction are one of a programmer's most powerful tools."

"I don't agree with that. Instead of focusing on commenting, you should focus on making code more readable. A good programmer can read the intent from the code itself, and what good does it do to read about somebody's intent when you know the code has an error?" Glaucon was pleased with his contribution. Callicles nodded.

"It sounds like you guys have never had to modify someone else's code," Ismene said. Callicles suddenly seemed very interested in the pencil marks on the ceiling tiles. "Why don't you try reading your own code six months or a year after you write it? You can improve your code-reading ability and your commenting. You don't have to choose one or the other. I shouldn't have to switch into ultra-concentration mode and read hundreds of lines of code just to find the two lines I want to change."

"All right, I can see that it would be handy to be able to scan code," Glaucon said. He'd seen some of Ismene's programs and had been impressed. "But what about Callicles' other point, that comments get out of date as the code changes? I've only been programming for a couple of years, but even I know that nobody updates their comments."

> Clearly, at some level comments *have* to be useful. To believe otherwise would be to believe that the comprehensibility of a program is independent of how much information the reader might already have about it.
>
> *B. A. Sheil*

"Well, yes and no," Ismene said. "If you take the comment as sacred and the code as suspicious, you are in deep trouble. Actually, finding a disagreement between the comment and the code tends to mean that both are wrong. The fact that some comments are bad doesn't mean that commenting is bad. I'm going to the lunchroom to get another pot of coffee." Ismene left the room.

"My main objection to comments," Callicles said, "is that they're a waste of resources."

"Can anyone think of ways to minimize the time it takes to write the comments?" Socrates asked.

"Design routines in PDL, and then convert the PDL to comments and fill in the code between them," Glaucon said.

"OK, that would work as long as the comments don't repeat the code," Callicles said.

"Writing a comment makes you think harder about what your code is doing," Ismene said, returning from the lunchroom. "If it's hard to comment, either it's bad code or you don't understand it well enough. Either way, you need to spend more time on the code, so the time you spend commenting isn't wasted."

"All right," Socrates said. "I can't think of any more qustions, and I think Ismene got the best of you guys today. We'll encourage commenting, but we won't be naive about it. We'll have code reviews so that everyone will get a good sense of the kind of comments that actually help. If you have trouble understanding someone else's code, let them know how they can improve it."

19.4 Keys to Effective Comments

What docs the following routine do?

```
Mystery Routine Number One
{ write out the sums 1..n for all n from 1 to Num }
Crnt := 1;
Prev := 0;
Sum  := 1;
for i := 1 to Num do
   begin
   writeln( Sum );
   Sum    := Crnt + Prev;
   Prev   := Crnt;
   Crnt   := Sum;
   end;
```

Your best guess?

This routine computes the first *Num* fibonacci numbers. Its coding style is a little better than the style of the routine at the beginning of the chapter, but the comment is wrong, and if you blindly trust the comment, you head down the primrose path in the wrong direction.

What about this one?

```
Mystery Routine Number Two
{ set Product to "Base" }
Product := Base;

{ loop from 2 to "Num" }
for i := 2 to Num do
   begin

   { Multiply "Base" by "Product" }
   Product := Product * Base;
   end;
```

Your best guess?

This routine raises an integer *Base* to the integer power *Num*. The comments in this routine are accurate, but they add nothing to the code. They are merely a more verbose version of the code itself.

Here's one last routine:

```
Mystery Routine Number Three
{ compute the square root of Num using the Newton-Raphson approximation }
r := Num / 2;
while ( abs( r - (Num/r) ) < Tolerance ) do
   r := 0.5 * ( r + (Num/r) );
```

Your best guess?

This routine computes the square root of *Num*. The code isn't great, but the comment is accurate.

Which routine was easiest for you to figure out correctly? None of the routines is particularly well written—the variable names are especially poor. In a nutshell, however, these routines illustrate the strengths and weaknesses of internal comments. Routine One has an incorrect comment. Routine Two's commenting merely repeats the code and is therefore useless. Only Routine Three's commenting earns its rent. Poor comments are worse than no comments. Routines One and Two would be better with no comments than with the poor comments they have.

The following subsections describe keys to writing effective comments.

Kinds of Comments

Comments can be classified into five categories:

Repeat of the code

A repetitious comment restates what the code does in different words. It merely gives the reader of the code more to read without providing additional information.

Explanation of the code

Explanatory comments are typically used to explain complicated, tricky, or sensitive pieces of code. In such situations they are useful, but usually that's only because the code is confusing. If the code is so complicated that it needs to be explained, it's nearly always better to improve the code than it is to add comments. Make the code itself clearer, and then use summary or intent comments.

Marker in the code

A marker comment is one that isn't intended to be left in the code. It's a note to the developer that the work isn't done yet. Some developers type in a marker that's syntactically incorrect (******, for example) so that the compiler flags it and reminds them that they have more work to do. Other developers put a specified set of characters in comments so that they can search for them but they don't interfere with compilation.

Summary of the code

A comment that summarizes code does just that: It distills a few lines of code into one or two sentences. Such comments are more valuable than comments that merely repeat the code because a reader can scan them more quickly than the code. Summary comments are particularly useful when someone other than the code's original author tries to modify the code.

Description of the code's intent

A comment at the level of intent explains the purpose of a section of code. Intent comments operate more at the level of the problem than at the level of the solution. For example,

```
{ get current employee information }
```

is an intent comment, whereas

```
{ update EmpRec structure }
```

HARD DATA

is a summary comment in terms of the solution. A six-month study conducted by IBM found that maintenance programmers "most often said that understanding the original programmer's intent was the most difficult problem" (Fjelstad and Hamlen 1979). The distinction between intent and summary comments isn't always clear, and it's usually not important. Examples of intent comments are given throughout the chapter.

The only two kinds of comments that are acceptable for completed code are intent and summary comments.

Commenting Efficiently

Effective commenting isn't that time-consuming. Too many comments are as bad as too few, and you can achieve a middle ground economically.

Comments can take a lot of time to write for two common reasons. First, the commenting style might be time-consuming or tedious—a pain in the neck. If it is, find a new style. A commenting style that requires a lot of busy work is a maintenance headache: If the comments are hard to change, they won't be changed; they'll become inaccurate and misleading, which is worse than having no comments at all.

Second, commenting might be difficult because the words to describe what the program is doing don't come easily. That's usually a sign that you don't really understand what the program does. The time you spend "commenting" is really time spent understanding the program better, which is time that needs to be spent regardless of whether you comment.

Use styles that don't break down or discourage modification. Any style that's too fancy is annoying to maintain. For example, pick out the part of the comment below that won't be maintained:

Fortran Example of a Commenting Style That's Hard to Maintain

```
C     Variable        Meaning
C     --------        -------
C     XPOS .......... X Coordinate Position (in meters)
C     YPOS .......... Y Coordinate Position (in meters)
C     NDSCMP ........ Needs Computing (= 0 if no computation is needed,
C                                      = 1 if computation is needed)
C     PTGTTL ........ Point Grand Total
C     PTVLMX ........ Point Value Maximum
C     PSCRMX ........ Possible Score Maximum
```

If you said that the leader dots (.....) will be hard to maintain, you're right! They look nice, but the list is fine without them. They add busy work to the job of modifying comments, and you'd rather have accurate comments than nice-looking ones, if that's the choice—and it usually is.

Here's another example of a common style that's hard to maintain:

C Example of a Commenting Style That's Hard to Maintain

```
/*************************************************************************
 * module: GIGATRON.C                                                    *
 *                                                                       *
 * author: Dwight K. Coder                                               *
 * date:   July 4, 2014                                                  *
 *                                                                       *
 * Routines to control the twenty-first century's code evaluation        *
 * tool. The entry point to these routines is the EvaluateCode()         *
 * routine at the bottom of this file.                                   *
 *                                                                       *
 *************************************************************************/
```

This is a nice-looking block comment. It's clear that the whole block belongs together, and the beginning and ending of the block are obvious. What isn't clear about this block is how easy it is to change. If you have to add the name of a file to the bottom of the comment, chances are pretty good that you'll have to fuss with the pretty column of asterisks at the right. If you need to change the paragraph comments, you'll have to fuss with asterisks on both the left and the right. In practice, this means that the block won't be maintained because it will be too much work. If you can press a key and get neat columns of asterisks, that's great. Use it. The problem isn't the asterisks but that they're hard to maintain. The following comment looks almost as good and is a cinch to maintain:

C Example of a Commenting Style That's Easy to Maintain

```
/***********************************************************************
   module: GIGATRON.C

   author: Dwight K. Coder
   date:   July 4, 2014

   Routines to control the twenty-first century's code evaluation
   tool. The entry point to these routines is the EvaluateCode()
   routine at the bottom of this file.


 ***********************************************************************/
```

Here's a particularly hard style to maintain:

CODING HORROR

Basic Example of a Commenting Style That's Hard to Maintain

```
'   set up COLOR enumerated type
    +-----------------------------+
    ...

'   set up VEGETABLE enumerated type
    +-----------------------------+
    ...
```

It's hard to know what value the plus sign at the beginning and end of each dashed line adds to the comment, but easy to guess that every time a comment changes, the underline has to be adjusted so that the ending plus sign is in precisely the right place. And what do you do when a comment spills over into two lines? How do you align the plus signs? Take words out of the comment so that it takes up only one line? Make both lines the same length? The problems with this approach multiply when you try to apply it consistently.

The point is that you should pay attention to how you spend your time. If you spend a lot of time entering and deleting dashes to make plus signs line up, you're not programming; you're wasting time. Find a more efficient style. In the case of the underlines with plus signs, you could choose to have just the comments without any underlining. If you need to use underlines for emphasis, find some way other than underlines with plus signs to emphasize those comments. One way would be to have a standard underline that's always the same length regardless of the length of the comment. Such a line requires no maintenance, and you can use a text-editor macro to enter it in the first place.

CROSS-REFERENCE
For details on the
PDL-to-code process,
see Chapter 4, "Steps in
Building a Routine."

Use the PDL-to-code process to reduce commenting time. If you outline the code in comments before you write it, you win in several ways. When you finish the code, the comments are done. You don't have to dedicate time to comments. You also gain all the design benefits of writing in high-level PDL before filling in the low-level programming-language code.

Comment as you go along. The alternative to commenting as you go along, leaving commenting until the end of the project, has too many disadvantages. It becomes a task in its own right, which makes it seem like more work than when it's done a little bit at a time. Commenting done later takes more time because you have to remember or figure out what the code is doing instead of just writing down what you're already thinking about. It's also less accurate because you tend to forget assumptions or subtleties in the design.

The common argument against commenting as you go along is "When you're concentrating on the code you shouldn't break your concentration to write comments." The appropriate response is that, if you have to concentrate so hard on writing code that commenting interrupts your thinking, you need to design in PDL first and then convert the PDL to comments. Code that requires that much concentration is a warning sign. If your design is hard to code, simplify the design before you worry about comments or code. If you use PDL to clarify your thoughts, coding is straightforward and the comments are automatic.

Optimum Number of Comments

Projects sometimes adopt a standard such as "programs must have one comment at least every five lines." This standard addresses the symptom of programmers' not writing clear code, but it doesn't address the cause.

If you use the PDL-to-code process effectively, you'll probably end up with a comment for every few lines of code. The number of comments, however, will be a side effect of the process itself. Rather than focusing on the number of comments, focus on whether each comment is efficient. If the comments describe why the code was written and meet the other criteria established in this chapter, you'll have enough comments.

19.5 Commenting Techniques

Commenting is amenable to several different techniques depending on the level to which the comments apply: program, file, routine, paragraph, or individual line.

Commenting Individual Lines

In good code, the need to comment individual lines of code is rare. Here are two possible reasons a line of code would need a comment:

● The single line is complicated enough to need an explanation.

● The single line once had an error and you want a record of the error.

Here are some guidelines for commenting a line of code:

Avoid self-indulgent comments. Many years ago, I heard the story of a maintenance programmer who was called out of bed to fix a malfunctioning program. The program's author had left the company and couldn't be reached. The maintenance programmer hadn't worked on the program before, and after examining the documentation carefully, he found only one comment. It looked like this:

```
MOV AX, 723h     ; R. I. P. L. V. B.
```

After working with the program through the night and puzzling over the comment, the programmer made a successful patch and went home to bed. Months later, he met the program's author at a conference and found out that the comment stood for "Rest in peace, Ludwig van Beethoven." Beethoven died in 1827 (decimal), which is 723 (hexadecimal). The fact that 723h was needed in that spot had nothing to do with the comment. Aaarrrrghhhhh!

Endline comments and their problems

Endline comments are comments that appear at the ends of lines of code. Here's an example:

```
Basic Example of Endline Comments
for EmpID = 1 TO MaxRecords
   GetBonus( EmpID, EmpType, BonusAmt )
   if EmpType = Manager then
      PayMgrBonus( EmpID, BonusAmt )                ' pay intended, full amount
   elseif EmpType = Programmer then
      if BonusAmt >= MgrApprovalRequired then
         PayProgrBonus( EmpID, StdAmt() )           ' pay company std. amount
      else
         PayProgrBonus( EmpID, BonusAmt )           ' pay intended, full amount
      end if
next EmpID
```

Although useful in some circumstances, endline comments pose several problems. The comments have to be aligned to the right of the code so that they don't interfere with the visual structure of the code. If you don't align them neatly, they'll make your listing look like it's been through the washing machine.

Endline comments tend to be hard to format. If you use many of them, it takes time to align them. Such time is not spent learning more about the code; it's dedicated solely to the tedious task of pressing the spacebar or the tab key.

Endline comments are also hard to maintain. If the code on any line containing an endline comment grows, it bumps the comment farther out, and all the other endline comments will have to be bumped out to match. Styles that are hard to maintain aren't maintained, and the commenting deteriorates under modification rather than improving.

Endline comments also tend to be cryptic. The right side of the line usually doesn't offer much room, and the desire to keep the comment on one line means that the comment must be short. Work then goes into making the line as short as possible instead of as clear as possible. The comment usually ends up as cryptic as possible. You can eliminate this problem, unlike the others, with the use of 132-column monitors and printers.

Avoid endline comments on single lines. In addition to their practical problems, endline comments pose several conceptual problems. Here's an example of a set of endline comments:

Pascal Example of Useless Endline Comments

The comments merely repeat the code.

```pascal
MemToInit := MemoryAvailable();    { get amount of memory available }
Pointer := GetMem( MemToInit );    { get a ptr to the available memory }
ZeroMem( Pointer, MemToInit );     { set memory to 0 }
...
FreeMem( Pointer );                { free memory allocated }
```

A systemic problem with endline comments is that it's hard to write a meaningful comment for one line of code. Most endline comments just repeat the line of code, which hurts more than it helps.

Avoid endline comments for multiple lines of code. If an endline comment is intended to apply to more than one line of code, the formatting doesn't show which lines the comment applies to. Here's an example:

CODING HORROR

Pascal Example of a Confusing Endline Comment on Multiple Lines of Code

```pascal
for RateIdx := 1 to RateCount do begin    { Compute discounted rates }
   begin
   LookupRegularRate( RateIdx, RegularRate );
   Rate[ RateIdx ] := RegularRate * Discount[ RateIdx ];
   end;
```

Even though the content of this particular comment is fine, its placement isn't. You have to read the comment and the code to know whether the comment applies to a specific statement or to the entire loop.

When to use endline comments

Here are three exceptions to the recommendation against using endline comments:

CROSS-REFERENCE
Other aspects of endline comments on data declarations are described in "Commenting Data Declarations," later in this section.

Use endline comments to annotate data declarations. Endline comments are useful for annotating data declarations because they don't have the same systemic problems as endline comments on code, provided that you have enough width. With 132 columns, you can usually write a meaningful comment beside each data declaration. Here's an example:

Pascal Example of Good Endline Comments for Data Declarations

```
Boundary:  Integer;   { upper index of sorted part of array }
InsertVal: String;    { data elmt to insert in sorted part of array }
InsertPos: Integer;   { position to insert elmt in sorted part of array }
```

Use endline comments for maintenance notes. Endline comments are useful for recording modifications to code after its initial development. This kind of comment typically consists of a date and the programmer's initials, or possibly an error-report number. Here's an example:

```
for i := 1 to MaxElmts-1  { fixed error #A423 10/1/92 (scm) }
```

Such a comment is handled better by version-control software, but if you don't have the tool support for version control and you want to annotate a single-line fix, this is the way to do it.

CROSS-REFERENCE
Use of endline comments to mark ends of blocks is described further in "Commenting Control Structures," later in this section.

Use endline comments to mark ends of blocks. An endline comment is useful for marking the end of a long block of code—the end of a *while* loop or an *if* statement, for example. This is described in more detail later in this chapter.

Aside from a couple of special cases, endline comments have conceptual problems and tend to be used for code that's too complicated. They are also difficult to format and maintain. Overall, they're best avoided.

Commenting Paragraphs of Code

Most comments in a well-documented program are one- or two-sentence comments that describe paragraphs of code. Here's an example:

C Example of a Good Comment for a Paragraph of Code

```
/* swap the roots */

OldRoot  = root[0];
root[0]  = root[1];
root[1]  = OldRoot;
```

The comment doesn't repeat the code. It describes the code's intent. Such comments are relatively easy to maintain. Even if you find an error in the way the roots are swapped, for example, the comment won't need to be changed. Comments that aren't written at the level of intent are harder to maintain.

Write comments at the level of the code's intent. Describe the purpose of the block of code that follows the comment. Here's an example of a comment that's ineffective because it doesn't operate at the level of intent:

Pascal Example of an Ineffective Comment

```
{ check each character in "InputStr" until a dollar sign
  is found or all characters have been checked }

Done    := False;
MaxLen := Length( InputStr );
i       := 1;
while ( (not Done) and (i <= MaxLen) )
    begin
    if ( InputStr[ i ] = '$' ) then
        Done := True
    else
        i := i + 1
    end;
```

You can figure out that the loop looks for a $ by reading the code, and it's somewhat helpful to have that summarized in the comment. The problem with this comment is that it merely repeats the code and doesn't give you any insight into what the code is supposed to be doing. This comment would be a little better:

```
{ find '$' in InputStr }
```

This comment is better because it indicates that the goal of the loop is to find a $. But it still doesn't give you much insight into why the loop would need to find a $—in other words, into the deeper intent of the loop. Here's a comment that's better still:

```
{ find the command-word terminator }
```

This comment actually contains information that the code listing does not, namely that the *$* terminates a command word. In no way could you deduce that merely from reading the code fragment, so the comment is genuinely helpful.

Another way of thinking about commenting at the level of intent is to think about what you would name a routine that did the same thing as the code you want to comment. If you're writing paragraphs of code that have one purpose each, it isn't difficult. The comment in the code above is a good example. *FindCommandWordTerminator()* would be a decent routine name. The other options, *Find$InInputString()* and *CheckEachCharacterInInputStrUntil-ADollarSignIsFoundOrAllCharactersHaveBeenChecked()*, are poor names for obvious reasons. Type the description without shortening or abbreviating it, as you might for a routine name. That description is your comment, and it's probably at the level of intent.

If the code is part of another routine, take the next step and put the code into its own routine. If it performs a well-defined function and you name the routine well, you'll add to the readability and maintainability of your code.

KEY POINT

For the record, the code itself is always the first documentation you should check. In the case above, the literal, *$*, should be replaced with a named constant, and the variables should provide more of a clue about what's going on. If you want to push the edge of the readability envelope, add a variable to contain the result of the search. Doing that clearly distinguishes between the loop index and the result of the loop. Here's the code rewritten with good comments and good style:

Pascal Example of a Good Comment and Good Code

```
{ find the command-word terminator }

FoundTheEnd      := False;
MaxCommandLength := Length( InputStr );
Idx              := 1;
while ( (not FoundTheEnd) and (Idx <= MaxCommandLength) )
   begin
   if ( InputStr[ Idx ] = COMMAND_WORD_TERMINATOR ) then
      begin
      FoundTheEnd  := True;
      EndOfCommand := Idx
      end
   else
      Idx := Idx + 1
   end;
```

Here's the variable that contains the result of the search.

If the code is good enough, it begins to read at close to the level of intent, encroaching on the comment's explanation of the code's intent. At that point, the comment and the code might become somewhat redundant, but that's a problem few programs have.

Focus paragraph comments on the *why* rather than the *how*. Comments that explain how something is done usually operate at the programming-language level rather than the problem level. It's nearly impossible for a comment that focuses on how an operation is done to explain the intent of the operation, and comments that tell how are often redundant. What does the following comment tell you that the code doesn't?

CODING HORROR

C Example of a Comment That Focuses on *How*

```c
/* if allocation flag is zero */

if ( AllocFlag == 0 ) ...
```

The comment tells you nothing more than the code itself does. What about this comment?

C Example of a Comment That Focuses on *Why*

```c
/* if allocating new member */

if ( AllocFlag == 0 ) ...
```

This comment is a lot better because it tells you something you couldn't infer from the code itself. The code itself could still be improved by use of a meaningful named constant instead of *0*. Here's the best version of this comment and code:

C Example of Using Good Style in Addition to a "Why" Comment

```c
/* if allocating new member */

if ( AllocFlag == NEW_MEMBER ) ...
```

Use comments to prepare the reader for what is to follow. Good comments tell the person reading the code what to expect. A reader should be able to scan only the comments and get a good idea of what the code does and where to look for a specific activity. A corollary to this rule is that a comment should always precede the code it describes. This idea isn't always taught in programming classes, but it's a well-established convention in commercial practice.

Make every comment count. There's no virtue in excessive commenting. Too many comments obscure the code they're meant to clarify. Rather than writing more comments, put the extra effort into making the code itself more readable.

Document surprises. If you find anything that isn't obvious from the code itself, put it into a comment. If you have used a tricky technique instead of a straightforward one to improve performance, use comments to point out what the straightforward technique would be and quantify the performance gain achieved by using the tricky technique. Here's an example:

```
C Example of Documenting a Surprise
for ( i = 0; i < ElmtCount; i++ )
   {
   /* Use right shift to divide by two. Substituting the
      right-shift operation cuts the loop time by 75%. */

   Elmt[ i ] = Elmt[ i ] >> 1;
   }
```

The selection of the right shift in this example is intentional. Among experienced programmers, it's common knowledge that for integers, right shift is functionally equivalent to divide-by-two.

If it's common knowledge, why document it? Because the purpose of the operation is not to perform a right shift; it is to perform a divide-by-two. The fact that the code doesn't use the technique most suited to its purpose is significant. Moreover, most compilers optimize integer division-by-two to be a right shift anyway, meaning that the reduced clarity is usually unnecessary. In this particular case, the compiler evidently doesn't optimize the divide-by-two, and the time saved will be significant. With the documentation, a programmer reading the code would see the motivation for using the nonobvious technique. Without the comment, the same programmer would be inclined to grumble that the code is unnecessarily "clever" without any meaningful gain in performance. Usually such grumbling is justified, so it's important to document the exceptions.

Avoid abbreviations. Comments should be unambiguous, readable without the work of figuring out abbreviations. Avoid all but the most common abbreviations in comments.

Unless you're using endline comments, using abbreviations isn't usually a temptation. If you are, and it is, realize that abbreviations are another strike against a technique that struck out several pitches ago.

Differentiate between major and minor comments. In a few cases, you might want to differentiate between different levels of comments, indicating that a detailed comment is part of a previous, broader comment. You can handle this in a couple of ways.

You can try underlining the major comment and not underlining the minor comment, as in the following:

C Example of Differentiating Between Major and Minor Comments with Underlines—Not Recommended

```
/* copy the string portion of the table, along the way
   omitting strings that are to be deleted */
/*------------------------------------------------------------------*/

/* determine number of strings in the table */



...


/* mark the strings to be deleted */



...
```

The major comment is underlined. —

A minor comment that is part of the action described by the major comment isn't underlined here...

...or here. —

The weakness of this approach is that it forces you to underline more comments than you'd really like to. If you underline a comment, it's assumed that all the nonunderlined comments that follow it are subordinate to it. Consequently, when you write the first comment that isn't subordinate to the underlined comment, it too must be underlined and the cycle starts all over. The result is too much underlining, or inconsistently underlining in some places and not underlining in others.

This theme has several variations that all have the same problem. If you put the major comment in all caps and the minor comments in lowercase, you substitute the problem of too many all-caps comments for the problem of too many underlined comments. Some programmers use an initial cap on major statements and no initial cap on minor ones, but that's a subtle visual cue that's too easily overlooked.

A better approach is to use ellipses in front of the minor comments. Here's an example:

C Example of Differentiating Between Major and Minor Comments with Ellipses

The major comment is —
formatted normally.

```
/* copy the string portion of the table, along the way
   omitting strings that are to be deleted */
```

A minor comment that —
is part of the action
described by the major
comment is preceded
by an ellipsis here...

```
/* ... determine number of strings in the table */


...
```

...and here. —

```
/* ... mark the strings to be deleted */


...
```

Another approach that's often best is to put the major-comment operation into its own routine. Routines should be logically "flat," with all their activities on about the same logical level. If your code differentiates between major and minor activities within a routine, the routine isn't flat. Putting the complicated group of activities into its own routine makes for two logically flat routines instead of one logically lumpy one.

This discussion of major and minor comments doesn't apply to indented code within loops and conditionals. In such cases, you'll often have a broad comment at the top of the loop and more detailed comments about the operations within the indented code. In those cases, the indentation provides the clue to the logical organization of the comments. This discussion applies only to sequential paragraphs of code in which several paragraphs make up a complete operation and some paragraphs are subordinate to others.

Comment anything that gets around an error or an undocumented feature in a language or an environment. If it's an error, it's probably not documented. Even if it's documented somewhere, it doesn't hurt to document it again in your code. If it's an undocumented feature, by definition it isn't documented elsewhere, and it should be documented in your code.

Suppose you find that the library function *WriteData(Data, NumItems, BlockSize)* works properly except when *BlockSize* equals *500*. It works fine for *499*, *501*, and every other value you've ever tried, but you have found that the routine has a defect that appears only when *BlockSize* equals *500*. In code that uses *WriteData()*, document why you're making a special case when *BlockSize* is *500*. Here's an example of how it could look:

Pascal Example of Documenting the Workaround for an Error

```pascal
BlockSize := OptimalBlockSize( NumItems, SizePerItem );

{ The following code is necessary to work around an error in
  WriteData() that appears only when the third parameter
  equals 500. '500' has been replaced with a named constant
  for clarity. }

if ( BlockSize = WRITEDATA_BROKEN_SIZE )
   BlockSize := WRITEDATA_WORKAROUND_SIZE;

WriteData( File, Data, BlockSize );
```

Justify violations of good programming style. If you've had to violate good programming style, explain why. That will prevent a well-intentioned programmer from changing the code to a better style, possibly breaking your code. The explanation will make it clear that you knew what you were doing and weren't just sloppy—give yourself credit where credit is due!

FURTHER READING
For other perspectives on writing good comments, see *The Elements of Programming Style* (Kernighan and Plauger 1978).

Don't comment tricky code. One of the most prevalent and hazardous bits of programming folklore is that comments should be used to document especially "tricky" or "sensitive" sections of code. The reasoning is that people should know they need to be careful when they're working in certain areas.

This is a scary idea.

Commenting tricky code is exactly the wrong approach to take. Comments can't rescue difficult code. As Kernighan and Plauger emphasize, "Don't document bad code—rewrite it" (1978).

HARD DATA

One study found that areas of source code with large numbers of comments also tended to have the most defects and to consume the most development effort (Lind and Vairavan 1989). The authors hypothesized that programmers tended to comment difficult code heavily.

KEY POINT

When someone says, "This is really *tricky* code," I hear them say, "This is really *bad* code." If something seems tricky to you, it'll be incomprehensible to someone else. Even something that doesn't seem all that tricky to you can seem impossibly convoluted to another person who hasn't seen the trick before. If you have to ask yourself, "Is this tricky?", it is. You can always find a rewrite that's not tricky, so rewrite the code. Make your code so good that you don't need comments, and then comment it to make it even better.

This advice applies mainly to code you're writing for the first time. If you're maintaining a program and don't have the latitude to rewrite bad code, commenting the tricky parts is a good practice.

Commenting Data Declarations

CROSS-REFERENCE
For details on formatting data, see "Laying Out Data Declarations" in Section 18.5. For details on how to use data effectively, see Chapters 8 through 12.

Comments for variable declarations describe aspects of the variable that the variable name can't describe. It's important to document data carefully; at least one company that has studied its own practices has concluded that annotations on data are even more important than annotations on the processes in which the data is used (SDC, in Glass 1982). Here are some guidelines for commenting data:

Comment the units of numeric data. If a number represents length, indicate whether the length is expressed in inches, feet, meters, or kilometers. If it's time, indicate whether it's expressed in elapsed seconds since 1-1-1980, milliseconds since the start of the program, and so on. If it's coordinates, indicate whether they represent latitude, longitude, and altitude and whether they're in radians or degrees; whether they represent an X, Y, Z coordinate system with its origin at the earth's center; and so on. Don't assume that the units are obvious. To a new programmer, they won't be. To someone who's been working on another part of the system, they won't be. After the program has been substantially modified, they won't be.

Comment the range of allowable numeric values. If a variable has an expected range of values, document the expected range. If the language supports restricting the range—as Pascal and Ada do—restrict the range. If not, use a comment to document the expected range of values. For example, if a variable represents an amount of money in dollars, indicate that you expect it to be between $1 and $100. If a variable indicates a voltage, indicate that it should be between 105v and 125v.

Comment coded meanings. If your language supports enumerated types—as Pascal, C, and Ada do—use them to express coded meanings. If it doesn't, use comments to indicate what each value represents—and use a named constant rather than a literal for each of the values. If a variable represents kinds of electrical current, comment the fact that *1* represents alternating current, *2* represents direct current, and *3* represents *undefined*.

Here's an example of documenting variable declarations that illustrates the three preceding recommendations:

Basic Example of Nicely Documented Variable Declarations

```
DIM CursorX%  'horizontal cursor position; ranges from 1..MaxCols
DIM CursorY%  'vertical cursor position; ranges from 1..MaxRows

DIM AntennaLength!   'length of antenna in meters; range is >= 2
DIM SignalStrength%  'strength of signal in kilowatts; range is >= 1

DIM CharCode%    'ASCII character code; ranges from 0..255
DIM CharAttrib%  '0=Plain; 1=Italic; 2=Bold; 3=BoldItalic
DIM CharSize%    'size of character in points; ranges from 4..127
```

All the range information is given in comments. In a language that supports richer variable types, you can declare a few of the ranges with the variables. Here's an example:

This assumes that MaxCols and Max-Rows are named constants that are defined elsewhere.

Pascal Example of Nicely Documented Variable Declarations

```
var
    CursorX:    1..MaxCols;  { horizontal screen position of cursor }
    CursorY:    1..MaxRows;  { vertical position of cursor on screen }

    AntennaLength: Real;     { length of antenna in meters; >= 2 }
    SignalStrength: Integer; { strength of signal in kilowatts; >= 1 }

    CharCode:   0..255;   { ASCII character code }
    CharAttrib: Integer;  { 0=Plain; 1=Italic; 2=Bold; 3=BoldItalic }
    CharSize:   4..127;   { size of character in points }
```

This would often be handled with an enumerated type, but if the values are hard-coded (in a file, for example), you might hard-code the values rather than enumerate them.

Comment limitations on input data. Input data might come from an input parameter, a file, or direct user input. The guidelines above apply as much to routine-input parameters as to other kinds of data. Make sure that expected and unexpected values are documented. Comments are one way of documenting that a routine is never supposed to receive certain data. Assertions are another way, and if you can use them, the code becomes that much more self-checking.

Document flags to the bit level. If a variable is used as a bit field, document the meaning of each bit, as in the first example on the next page.

CROSS-REFERENCE
For details on naming flag variables, see "Naming Status Variables" in Section 9.2.

Pascal Example of Documenting Flags to the Bit Level

```
var
   { The meanings of the bits in StatusFlags are as follows:

      MSB   0      error detected: 1=yes, 0=no
            1-2    kind of error: 0=syntax, 1=warning, 2=severe, 3=fatal
            3      reserved (should be 0)
            4      printer status: 1=ready, 0=not ready
            ...
            14     not used (should be 0)
      LSB   15     not used (should be 0) }

   StatusFlags: integer;
```

If the example were written in C, it would call for bit-field syntax so that the bit-field meanings would be self-documenting.

Stamp comments related to a variable with the variable's name. If you have comments that refer to a specific variable, make sure that the comment is updated whenever the variable is updated. One way to improve the odds of a consistent modification is to stamp the comment with the name of the variable. That way, string searches for the variable name will find the comment as well as the variable.

CROSS-REFERENCE
For details on using global data, see Section 10.6, "Global Variables."

Document global data. If global data is used, annotate each piece well at the point at which it is declared. The annotation should indicate the purpose of the data and why it needs to be global. At each point at which the data is used, make it clear that the data is global. A naming convention is the first choice for highlighting a variable's global status. If a naming convention isn't used, comments can fill the gap.

Commenting Control Structures

CROSS-REFERENCE
For other details on control structures, see Section 18.3, "Layout Styles," Section 18.4, "Laying Out Control Structures," and Chapters 13 through 17.

The space before a control structure is usually a natural place to put a comment. If it's an *if* or a *case* statement, you can provide the reason for the decision and a summary of the outcome. If it's a loop, you can indicate the purpose of the loop. Here are a couple of examples:

C Example of Commenting the Purpose of a Control Structure

Purpose of the —
following loop

```
/* copy input field up to comma */

while ( *InputStr != ',' && *InputStr != END_OF_STRING )
   {
```

(continued)

*End of the loop —
(especially useful for
longer, nested loops)*

*Purpose of the —
conditional*

*Purpose of the loop. —
Position of comment
makes it clear that
InputStr is being
set up for the loop.*

```
    *Field = *InputStr;
    Field++;
    InputStr++;
    } /* while -- copy input field */

*Field = END_OF_STRING;

/* if at end of string, all actions are complete */

if ( *InputStr != END_OF_STRING )
    {
    /* read past comma and subsequent blanks to get to the
       next input field */

    *InputStr++;
    while ( *InputStr == ' ' && *InputStr != END_OF_STRING )
        InputStr++;
    } /* if -- at end of string */
```

This example suggests some guidelines.

Put a comment before each block of statements, *if*, *case*, or loop. Such a place is a natural spot for a comment, and these constructs often need explanation. Use a comment to clarify the purpose of the control structure.

Comment the end of each control structure. Use a comment to show what ended—for example,

```
end; { for ClientIdx -- process record for each client }
```

CROSS-REFERENCE
For details on naming
loops, see "Exiting the
Loop" in Section 15.2.

A comment is especially helpful at the end of long or nested loops. In languages that support named loops (Ada, for example), name the loops. In other languages, use comments to clarify loop nesting. Here's a Pascal example of using comments to clarify the ends of loop structures:

Pascal Example of Using Comments to Show Nesting

```
for TableIdx := 1 to TableCount
    begin
    while ( RecordIdx < RecordCount )
        begin
        if ( not IllegalRecNum( RecordIdx ) )
            begin
            ...
            end; { if }
        end; { while }
    end; { for }
```

*These comments
indicate which control —
structure is ending.*

This commenting technique supplements the visual clues about the logical structure given by the code's indentation. You don't need to use the technique for short loops that aren't nested. When the nesting is deep or the loops are long, however, the technique pays off.

Even though it's worthwhile, putting the comments in and maintaining them can get tedious, and the best way to avoid the tedious work is often to rewrite the complicated code that requires tedious documentation.

Commenting Routines

CROSS-REFERENCE
For details on formatting routines, see Section 18.7, "Laying Out Routines." For details on how to create high-quality routines, see Chapter 5, "Characteristics of High-Quality Routines."

CODING HORROR

Routine-level comments are the subject of some of the worst advice in typical computer-science textbooks. Many textbooks urge you to pile up a stack of information at the top of every routine, regardless of its size or complexity. Here's an example:

Basic Example of a Monolithic, Kitchen-Sink Routine Prolog

```
'******************************************************************
'
' Name: CopyString
'
' Purpose:       This routine copies a string from the source
'                string (Source$) to the target string (Target$).
'
' Algorithm:     It gets the length of Source$ and then copies each
'                character, one at a time, into Target$. It uses
'                the loop index as an array index into both Source$
'                and Target$ and increments the loop/array index
'                after each character is copied.
'
' Inputs:        Input$    The string to be copied
'
' Outputs:       Output$   The string to receive the copy of Input$
'
' Interface Assumptions: None
'
' Modification History: None
'
' Author:        Dwight K. Coder
' Date Created:  10/1/92
' Phone:         (222) 555-2255
' SSN:           111-22-3333
' Eye Color:     Green
' Maiden Name:   None
' Blood Type:    AB-
' Mother's Maiden Name: None
'
'******************************************************************
```

This is ridiculous. *CopyString* is presumably a trivial routine—probably fewer than five lines of code. The comment is totally out of proportion to the scale of the routine. The parts about the routine's *Purpose* and *Algorithm* are strained because it's hard to describe something as simple as *CopyString* at a level of detail that's between "copy a string" and the code itself. The boiler-plate comments *Interface Assumptions* and *Modification History* aren't useful either—they just take up space in the listing. To require all these ingredients for every routine is a recipe for inaccurate comments and maintenance failure. It's a lot of make-work that never pays off. Here are some guidelines for commenting routines:

Keep comments close to the code they describe. One reason that the prolog to a routine shouldn't contain voluminous documentation is that such a practice puts the comments far away from the parts of the routine they describe. During maintenance, comments that are far from the code tend not to be maintained with the code. The comments and the code start to disagree, and suddenly the comments are worthless.

Instead, follow the Principle of Proximity and put comments as close as possible to the code they describe. They're more likely to be maintained, and they'll continue to be worthwhile.

Several components of routine prologs are described below and should be included as needed. For your convenience, create a boilerplate documentation prolog. Just don't feel obliged to include all the information in every case. Fill out the parts that matter and delete the rest.

CROSS REFERENCE
Good routine names are key to routine documentation. For details on how to create them, see Section 5.2, "Good Routine Names."

Describe each routine in one or two sentences at the top of the routine. If you can't describe the routine in a short sentence or two, you probably need to think harder about what it's supposed to do. Difficulty in creating a short description is a sign that the design isn't as good as it should be. Go back to the design drawing board and try again. The short summary statement should be present in virtually all routines.

Document input and output variables where they are declared. If you're not using global data, the easiest way to document input and output variables is to put comments next to the parameter declarations. Here's an example:

Pascal Example of Documenting Input and Output Data Where It's Declared—Good Practice

```
procedure InsertionSort
   (
   Var Data:      tSortArray; { sort array elements FirstElmt..LastElmt }
       FirstElmt: Integer;    { index of first element to sort }
       LastElmt:  Integer     { index of last element to sort }
   );
```

CROSS-REFERENCE
Endline comments are discussed in more detail in "Endline comments and their problems," earlier in this section.

This practice is a good exception to the rule of not using endline comments; they are exceptionally useful in documenting input and output variables. This occasion for commenting is also a good illustration of the value of using standard indentation rather than endline indentation for routine parameter lists; you wouldn't have room for meaningful endline comments if you used endline indentation. The comments in the example are strained for space even with standard indentation, although it would be less a problem if the code in this book had more than 80 columns to work with. This example also demonstrates that comments aren't the only form of documentation. If your variable names are good enough, you might be able to skip commenting them. Finally, the need to document input and output variables is a good reason to avoid global data. Where do you document it? Presumably, you document the globals in the monster prolog. That makes for more work and unfortunately in practice usually means that the global data doesn't get documented. That's too bad because global data needs to be documented at least as much as anything else.

Differentiate between input and output data. It's useful to know which data is used as input and which is used as output. Pascal makes it relatively easy to tell because output data is preceded by the *var* keyword and input data isn't. If your language doesn't support such differentiation automatically, put it into comments. Here's an example in C:

CROSS-REFERENCE
The order of these parameters follows the standard order for C routines but conflicts with more general practices. For details, see "Put parameters in input-modify-output order" in Section 5.7. For details on using a naming convention to differentiate between input and output data, see Section 9.3, "The Power of Naming Conventions."

C Example of Differentiating Between Input and Output Data

```
void StringCopy
    (
    char *  Target,     /* out: string to copy to */
    char *  Source      /* in:  string to copy from */
    )
...
```

C-language routine declarations are a little tricky because some of the time the asterisk (*) indicates that the argument is an output argument, and a lot of the time it just means that the variable is easier to handle as a pointer than as a base type. You're usually better off identifying input and output arguments explicitly.

If your routines are short enough and you maintain a clear distinction between input and output data, documenting the data's input or output status is probably unnecessary. If the routine is longer, however, it's a useful service to anyone who reads the routine.

CROSS-REFERENCE
For details on other
considerations for routine
interfaces, see Section 5.7,
"How to Use Routine
Parameters."

Document interface assumptions. Documenting interface assumptions might be viewed as a subset of the other commenting recommendations. If you have made any assumptions about the state of variables you receive—legal and illegal values, arrays being in sorted order, data structures being initialized or containing only good data, and so on—document them either in the routine prolog or where the data is declared. This documentation should be present in virtually every routine.

Make sure that global data that's used is documented. A global variable is as much an interface to a routine as anything else and is all the more hazardous because it sometimes doesn't seem like one.

As you're writing the routine and realize that you're making an interface assumption, write it down immediately.

CROSS-REFERENCE
For details on the fact that
certain routines have a
disproportionate number of
errors, see "Which Routines
Contain the Most Errors?"
in Section 25.4.

Keep track of the routine's change history. Keep track of changes made to a routine after its initial construction. Changes are often made because of errors, and errors tend to be concentrated in a few troublesome routines. A lot of errors in a routine means that the same routine probably has even more errors. Keeping track of the errors detected in a routine means that if the number of errors reaches a certain point, you'll know it's time to redesign and rewrite the routine.

This isn't something you would expect to do for every routine, mainly because you wouldn't expect to see errors in every routine. Tracking a routine's change history can result in an annoying clutter of error-fix descriptions at the top of a routine, but the approach is self-correcting. If you get too many errors clogging up the top of the routine, your natural inclination will be to get rid of the distraction and rewrite the routine. Most programmers enjoy having an excuse to rewrite code they know could have been written better anyway, and this documentation is a good, visible justification for doing so.

Comment on the routine's limitations. If the routine provides a numeric result, indicate the accuracy of the result. If the computations are undefined under some conditions, document the conditions. If the routine has a default behavior when it gets into trouble, document the behavior. If the routine is expected to work only on arrays or tables of a certain size, indicate that. If you know of modifications to the program that would break the routine, document them. If you ran into gotchas during the development of the routine, document them too.

Document the routine's global effects. If the routine modifies global data, describe exactly what it does to the global data. As mentioned in Section 5.4, modifying global data is at least an order of magnitude more dangerous than merely reading it, so modifications should be performed carefully, part of the care being clear documentation. As usual, if documenting becomes too onerous, rewrite the code to reduce the use of global data.

Document the source of algorithms that are used. If you have used an algorithm from a book or magazine, document the volume and page number you took it from. If you developed the algorithm yourself, indicate where the reader can find the notes you've made about it.

Use comments to mark parts of your program. Some programmers use comments to mark parts of their program so that they can find them easily. One such technique in C is to mark the top of each routine with a comment such as

/***

This allows you to jump from routine to routine by doing a string search for /***.

A similar technique is to mark different kinds of comments differently, depending on what they describe. For example, in Pascal you could use {-X-, where X is a code you use to indicate the kind of comment. The comment {-R- could indicate that the comment describes a routine, {-I- input and output data, {-L- local data descriptions, and so on. This technique allows you to use tools to extract different kinds of information from your source files. For example, you could search for {-R- to retrieve descriptions of all the routines.

Commenting Files, Modules, and Programs

CROSS-REFERENCE
For layout details, see Section 18.8, "Laying Out Files, Modules, and Programs." For details on using modules, see Chapter 6, "Three out of Four Programmers Surveyed Prefer Modules."

Files, modules, and programs are all characterized by the fact that they contain multiple routines. A file or module should contain a collection of related routines. A program contains all the routines in a program. The documentation task in each case is to provide a meaningful, top-level view of the contents of the file, module, or program. The issues are similar in each case, so I'll just refer to documenting "files," and you can assume that the guidelines apply to modules and programs as well.

General guidelines for file documentation

At the top of a file, use a block comment to describe the contents of the file. Here are some guidelines for the block comment:

Describe the purpose of each file. If all the routines for a program are in one file, the purpose of the file is pretty obvious. If you're working on a program with multiple modules and the modules are separated into multiple files, explain why certain routines are put into certain files. Describe the purpose of each file. Since one file equals one module in this case, that will be sufficient documentation.

If the division into multiple source files is made for some reason other than modularity, a good description of the purpose of the file will be even more helpful to a programmer who is modifying the program. If someone is looking through the program's files for a routine that does x, can he or she tell whether this file contains such a routine?

Put your name and phone number in the block comment. Authorship is important information to have in a listing. It gives other programmers who work on the code a clue about the programming style, and it gives them someone to call if they need help. Depending on whether you work on individual routines, modules, or programs, you should include author information at the routine, module, or program level.

Include a copyright statement in the block comment. Many companies like to include copyright statements in their programs. If yours is one of them, include a line similar to this one:

> **C Example of a Copyright Statement**
>
> ```
> /* (c) Copyright 1993 Steve McConnell, Inc. All Rights Reserved. */
> ...
> ```

The Book Paradigm for program documentation

FURTHER READING
This discussion is adapted from "The Book Paradigm for Improved Maintenance" (Oman and Cook 1990a) and "Typographic Style Is More Than Cosmetic" (Oman and Cook 1990b). A similar analysis is presented in detail in *Human Factors and Typography for More Readable Programs* (Baecker and Marcus 1990).

Most experienced programmers agree that the documentation techniques described in the previous section are valuable. The hard, scientific evidence for the value of any one of the techniques is still weak. When the techniques are combined, however, evidence of their effectiveness is strong.

In 1990, Paul Oman and Curtis Cook published a pair of studies on the "Book Paradigm" for documentation (1990a, 1990b). They looked for a coding style that would support several different styles of code reading. One goal was to support top-down, bottom-up, and focused searches. Another was to break up the code into chunks that programmers could remember more easily than a long listing of homogeneous code. Oman and Cook wanted the style to provide for both high-level and low-level clues about code organization.

They found that by thinking of code as a special kind of book and formatting it accordingly, they could achieve their goals. In the Book Paradigm, code and its documentation are organized into several components similar to the components of a book to help programmers get a high-level view of the program.

The "preface" is a group of introductory comments such as those usually found at the beginning of a file. It functions as the preface to a book does. It gives the programmer an overview of the program.

The "table of contents" shows the files, modules, and routines (chapters). They might be shown in a list, as a traditional book's chapters are, or graphically, in a structure chart.

487

The "sections" are the divisions within routines—routine declarations, data declarations, and executable statements, for example.

The "cross-references" are cross-reference maps of the code, including line numbers.

The low-level techniques that Oman and Cook use to take advantage of the similarities between a book and a code listing are similar to the techniques described in Chapter 18, "Layout and Style," and in this chapter.

HARD DATA

The upshot of using their techniques to organize code was that when Oman and Cook gave a maintenance task to a group of experienced, professional programmers, the average time to perform a maintenance task in a 1000-line program was only about three-quarters of the time it took the programmers to do the same task in a traditional source listing (1990b). Moreover, the maintenance scores of programmers on code documented with the Book Paradigm averaged about 20 percent higher than on traditionally documented code. Similar results were obtained using both Pascal and C. Oman and Cook concluded that by paying attention to the typographic principles of book design, you can get a 10 to 20 percent improvement in comprehension. A study with student programmers at the University of Toronto produced similar results (Baecker and Marcus 1990).

The Book Paradigm emphasizes the importance of providing documentation that explains both the high-level and the low-level organization of your program.

CHECKLIST

Good Commenting Technique

GENERAL

❑ Does the source listing contain most of the information about the program?

❑ Can someone pick up the code and immediately start to understand it?

❑ Do comments explain the code's intent or summarize what the code does, rather than just repeating the code?

❑ Is the PDL-to-code process used to reduce commenting time?

❑ Has tricky code been rewritten rather than commented?

❑ Are comments up to date?

❑ Are comments clear and correct?

❑ Does the commenting style allow comments to be easily modified?

(continued)

Good Commenting Technique checklist, *continued*

STATEMENTS AND PARAGRAPHS

❏ Does the code avoid endline comments?

❏ Do comments focus on *why* rather than *how*?

❏ Do comments prepare the reader for the code to follow?

❏ Does every comment count? Have redundant, extraneous, and self-indulgent comments been removed or improved?

❏ Are surprises documented?

❏ Have abbreviations been avoided?

❏ Is the distinction between major and minor comments clear?

❏ Is code that works around an error or undocumented feature commented?

DATA DECLARATIONS

❏ Are units on data declarations commented?

❏ Are the ranges of values on numeric data commented?

❏ Are coded meanings commented?

❏ Are limitations on input data commented?

❏ Are flags documented to the bit level?

❏ Has each global variable been commented where it is declared?

❏ Has each global variable been identified as such at its use, by either a naming convention or a comment?

❏ Are magic numbers documented or, preferably, replaced with named constants or variables?

CONTROL STRUCTURES

❏ Is each control statement commented?

❏ Are the ends of long or complex control structures commented?

ROUTINES

❏ Is the purpose of each routine commented?

❏ Are other facts about each routine given in comments, when relevant, including input and output data, interface assumptions, limitations, error corrections, global effects, and sources of algorithms?

(continued)

Good Commenting Technique checklist, *continued*

FILES, MODULES, AND PROGRAMS

❏ Does the program have a short document such as that described in the Book Paradigm that gives an overall view of how the program is organized?

❏ Is the purpose of each file described?

❏ Are the author's name and phone number in the listing?

Further Reading on Documentation

CROSS-REFERENCE
For further reading on
programming style, see
the references in "Further
Reading" in Chapter 18,
page 451.

General information on commenting is scarce. The detailed references cited throughout the chapter are the best sources to consult for specific commenting information. Here are sources of information on other topics in software documentation:

IEEE Software Engineering Standards Collection, Spring 1991 Edition. New York: Institute of Electrical and Electronics Engineers (IEEE). This comprehensive volume contains the most recent ANSI/IEEE standards for software documents as of spring 1991. Each standard includes a document outline, a description of each component of the outline, and a rationale for that component. The document includes standards for quality-assurance plans, configuration-management plans, test documents, requirements specifications, verification and validation plans, design descriptions, project management plans, and user documentation. The book is a distillation of the expertise of hundreds of people at the top of their fields, and would be a bargain at virtually any price. Some of the standards are also available individually. All are available from the IEEE Computer Society in Los Alamitos, California.

Metzger, Philip W. *Managing a Programming Project,* 2d ed. Englewood Cliffs, N.J.: Prentice Hall, 1981. The second part of Metzger's book is an outline of a "project plan." It includes outlines for test, change-control, and documentation plans, as well as high-level outlines for requirements and design documents. (Metzger presents the outlines for requirements and design as part of his documentation plan). These outlines aren't as balanced, thorough, or authoritative as the ANSI/IEEE standards, but if the book is handy, it's a good place for you to start on an informal project.

Glass, Robert L. *Software Communication Skills*. Englewood Cliffs, N.J.: Prentice Hall, 1988. This book includes a general discussion of software documentation issues and several government documentation standards including the full text of two military standards: DOD-STD-2167 and DOD-STD-7935. These software-project documentation standards describe the documentation required on DoD projects, including extremely large ones.

Key Points

- The question of whether to comment is a legitimate one. Done poorly, commenting is a waste of time and sometimes harmful. Done well, commenting is worthwhile.

- The source-code listing should contain most of the critical information about the program. As long as the program is running, the listing is the only document that's guaranteed not to be lost or discarded, and it's useful to have important information bundled with the code.

- Good comments are written at the level of intent. They explain the *why* more than the *how*.

- Comments should say things about the code that the code can't say about itself. Good code is its own best documentation. As you're about to add a comment, ask yourself, "How can I improve the code so that this comment isn't needed?" Improve the code and then document it to make it even clearer.

20

Programming Tools

Contents

Related Topics

MODERN PROGRAMMING TOOLS DECREASE THE amount of time required for construction. Use of a leading-edge tool set can increase productivity by 50 percent or more (Jones 1986a, Boehm 1981). Programming tools can also reduce the amount of tedious detail work that programming requires.

HARD DATA

A dog might be man's best friend, but a few good tools are a programmer's best friends. As Barry Boehm points out, 20 percent of the tools account for 80 percent of the tool usage (1987b). If you're missing one of the most helpful tools, you're missing something that you could use a lot. The mission of this chapter is to describe tools you can make or buy to help construction.

This chapter is focused in two ways. First, it covers only construction tools. Requirements-specification, management, and end-to-end–development tools are outside the scope of the book. Refer to the "Further Reading" section at the end of the chapter for more information on tools for those aspects of software development. Second, this chapter covers kinds of tools rather than specific brands. A few tools are so common that they're discussed by name, but specific versions, products, and companies change so quickly that information about most of them would be out of date before the ink on these pages was dry. Ask your local vendor for specifics on the kinds of tools you find interesting.

If you're a tool expert, you won't find much new information in this chapter. You might skim the earlier parts of the chapter, read Section 20.6 on the ideal programming environment, and then move on to the next chapter.

20.1 Design Tools

CROSS-REFERENCE
For details on design, see Chapters 5 through 7.

Current design tools consist mainly of graphical tools that create design diagrams. Design tools are sometimes embedded in a CASE tool with broader functions; some vendors advertise standalone design tools as CASE tools.

Graphical design tools generally allow you to express a design in common graphical notations—hierarchy charts, Hierarchy Input Process Output (HIPO) diagrams, entity relationship diagrams, Jackson Structured Design, structure charts, or module diagrams. Some graphical design tools support only one notation. Others support a variety. Most also support PDL.

In one sense, these design tools are just fancy drawing packages. Using a simple graphics package or pencil and paper, you can draw everything that the tool can draw. But the tools offer valuable capabilities that a simple graphics package can't. If you've drawn a bubble chart and you delete a bubble, a graphical design tool will automatically rearrange the other bubbles, including connecting arrows and lower-level bubbles connected to the bubble. The tool takes care of the housekeeping when you add a bubble too. A design tool can enable you to move between higher and lower levels of abstraction. A design tool will check the consistency of your design, and some tools can create code directly from your design.

20.2 Source-Code Tools

The tools available for working with source code are richer and more mature than the tools available for working with designs.

Editing

This group of tools relates to editing source code.

Editors

HARD DATA

Some programmers estimate that they spend as much as 40 percent of their time editing source code (Ratliff 1987, Parikh 1986). If that's the case, spending a few extra dollars for the best possible editor is a good investment.

In addition to basic word-processing functions, good programming editors offer these features:

- Compilation and error detection from within the editor
- Compressed views of programs (routine names only or logical structures without their contents)
- Interactive help for the language being edited
- Brace or *begin-end* matching
- Templates for common language constructs (the editor completing the structure of a *for* loop after the programmer types *for*, for example)
- Smart indenting (including easily changing the indentation of a block of statements when logic changes)
- Macros programmable in a familiar programming language
- Memory of search strings so that commonly used strings don't need to be retyped
- Regular expressions in search-and-replace
- Search-and-replace across a group of files
- Editing multiple files simultaneously
- Multi-level undo

Considering the primitive editors that most people use, you might be surprised to learn that several editors include all of these capabilities.

Multiple-file string changers

It's often helpful to be able to change strings across multiple files. For example, if you want to give a routine, constant, or global variable a better name, you might have to change the name in several files. Utilities that allow string changes across multiple files make that easy to do, which is good because you should have as few obstructions as possible to creating excellent routine, constant, and global variable names.

FURTHER READING
For a description of AWK's capabilities, see *The AWK Programming Language* (Aho, Kernighan, and Weinberg 1977).

One commonly available tool that facilitates multiple-file search-and-replace is the AWK programming language. The AWK utility is somewhat hard to classify, and it's often described as using "associative arrays." Its main virtue, for purposes of this discussion, is that it's good at handling strings and groups of files. Consequently, it's handy for changing strings across groups of files. Other tools for handling multiple-file string changes include sed and perl.

File comparators

Programmers often need to compare two files. If you make several attempts to correct an error and need to remove the unsuccessful attempts, a file comparator will make a comparison of the original and modified files and list the lines you've changed. If you're working on a program with other people and want to see the changes they have made since the last time you worked on the code, a comparator will make a comparison of the current version with the last version of the code you worked on and show the differences. If you discover a new defect that you don't remember encountering in an older version of a program, rather than seeing a neurologist about amnesia, you can use a comparator to compare current and old versions of the source code, determine exactly what changed, and find the source of the problem.

Source-code beautifiers

CROSS-REFERENCE
For details on program layout, see Chapter 18, "Layout and Style."

Source-code beautifiers spruce up your source code so that it looks consistent. They standardize your indentation style, align variable declarations and routine headings, format comments consistently, and perform other similar functions. During printing, some beautifiers begin each routine at the top of a new page or perform even more dramatic formatting. Many beautifiers let you customize the way in which the code is beautified.

In addition to making code look nice, beautifiers are useful in several other ways. If you have code written by several programmers with several different styles, a code beautifier can convert the code to a standard form without putting a formatting burden on individual developers. Code indented by a machine also has a smaller chance of producing misleading indentation cues than code indented by a human. If you indent code in a *for* loop and forget to put the enclosing *begin* and *end* around the indented code, some human readers might be tricked into thinking that the code is subordinate to the loop. A code beautifier won't be tricked, and when it reformats the code without the misleading indentation, human readers won't be tricked either.

Templates

Templates help you exploit the simple idea of streamlining keyboarding tasks that you do often and want to do consistently. Suppose you want a standard comment prolog at the beginning of your routines. You could build a skeleton prolog with the correct syntax and places for all the items you want in the standard prolog. This skeleton would be a "template" you'd store in a file or a keyboard macro. When you created a new routine, you could easily insert the template into your source file. You can use the template technique for setting up larger entities, such as modules and files, or smaller entities, such as loops.

If you're working on a group project, templates are an easy way to encourage consistent coding and documentation styles. Make templates available to the whole team at the beginning of the project, and the team will use them because they make its job easier—you get the consistency as a side benefit.

Browsing

This group of tools helps you view source code. Editors also allow you to view source code, but browsers have a different role.

Browsers

Some tools are created specifically for browsing. In the rest of the world, browsing means you're window-shopping in a leisurely way, hoping you'll find something you like. In programming, browsing means that you know what you want to find and you want to find it right now. A browser is useful for making a consistent set of changes—making sure that you've accounted for all references to a routine or a variable, for instance. A good browser searches and replaces across groups of files. It shows cross-references and call structures.

A browser can find all the files that contain references to a particular variable or show every line that calls a routine. It can work with all the files in a project, all the files with a certain name, or all the files you have. It can search for variables and routine names intelligently, or it can perform simple string searches.

Multiple-file string searchers

FURTHER READING
For a good discussion of how to write a software tool to do multiple-file string searches, see *Software Tools* (Kernighan and Plauger 1976) or *Software Tools in Pascal* (Kernighan and Plauger 1981).

One specific kind of browser can search multiple files for occurrences of a designated string. You can use it to search for all occurrences of a global variable or routine name. You can use it to find all the files that a certain programmer has worked on, provided the programmer's name is somewhere in the file. When you find an error in your code, you can use it to check for similar errors in other files.

You can search for exact strings, similar strings (ignoring differences in capitalization), or regular expressions. Regular expressions are particularly powerful because they let you search for complex string patterns. If you wanted to find all the array references containing magic numbers (digits "0" through "9"), you could search for "[", followed by zero or more spaces, followed by one or more digits, followed by zero or more spaces, followed by "]". One widely available search tool is called "grep." A grep query for magic numbers would look like this:

```
grep "\[ *[0-9]* *\]" *.c
```

You can make the search criteria more sophisticated to fine-tune the search.

Cross-reference tools

A cross-reference tool lists variables and routines and all the places in which they're used in one gigantic listing. These batch-oriented tools have been largely supplanted by more interactive tools that produce information on demand for specific variables and routines.

Call-structure generators

A call-structure generator produces information about routines that call each other. This is sometimes useful in debugging but is more often used for analyzing a program's structure or packaging a program into modules or overlays. Some generators produce a voluminous listing of all the calls by all the routines. Others produce a diagram that shows all the calls emanating from the top routine. Still others trace calls from a routine forward or backward, listing all the routines that are called by the routine (directly or indirectly) and all the routines that call the routine (directly or indirectly).

Analyzing Code Quality

Tools in this category examine the static source code to assess its quality.

Picky syntax and semantics checkers

Syntax and semantics checkers supplement your compiler by checking code more thoroughly than the compiler normally does. Your compiler might check for only rudimentary syntax errors. A picky syntax checker might use nuances of the language to check for more subtle errors—things that aren't wrong from a compiler's point of view but that you probably didn't intend to write. For example, in C, the statement

```
while ( i = 0 ) ...
```

is a perfectly legal statement, but it's usually meant to be

```
while ( i == 0 ) ...
```

The first line is syntactically correct, but switching = and == is a common mistake and the line is probably wrong. Lint is a picky syntax and semantics checker you can find in many C environments. Lint warns you about uninitialized variables, completely unused variables, variables that are assigned values and never used, parameters of a routine that are passed out of the routine without being assigned a value, suspicious pointer operations, suspicious logical comparisons (like the one in the example above), inaccessible code, and many other common problems.

Metrics reporters

CROSS-REFERENCE
For more information on metrics, see Section 22.4, "Metrics."

Some tools analyze your code and report on its quality. For example, you can buy tools that report on the complexity of each routine so that you can target the most complicated routines for extra review, testing, or redesign. Some tools count lines of code, data declarations, comments, and blank lines in either entire programs or individual routines. They track defects and associate them with the programmers who made them, the changes that correct them, and the programmers who make the corrections. They count modifications to the software and note the routines that are modified the most often.

Restructuring Source Code

A few tools aid in converting source code from one format to another.

Restructurers

A restructurer will convert a plate of spaghetti code with *gotos* to a more nutritious entrée of structured code without *gotos*. A restructurer has to make a lot of assumptions when it converts code containing *gotos*, and if the logic is terrible in the original, it will still be terrible in the converted version. If you're doing a conversion manually, however, you can use a restructurer for the general case and hand-tune the hard cases. Alternatively, you can run the code through the restructurer and use it for inspiration for the hand conversion.

Code translators

Some tools translate code from one language to another. A translator is useful when you have a large code base that you're moving to another environment. The hazard in using a language translator is the same as the hazard in using a restructurer: If you start with bad code, the translator simply translates the bad code into an unfamiliar language.

Version Control

CROSS-REFERENCE
These tools and their benefits are described in "Software Code Changes" in Section 22.2.

You can better deal with proliferating software versions by using the version-control tools for

- Source-code control
- Make-style dependency control

Data Dictionaries

A data dictionary is a database of a program's variable names with descriptions. On large projects, a data dictionary is useful for keeping track of the thousands of variable definitions in a system. On database projects, it's useful for describing data stored in the database. On team projects, it's useful for avoiding naming clashes. A clash might be a direct, syntactic clash, in which the same name is used twice, or it might be a more subtle clash (or gap) in which different names are used to mean the same thing.

The data dictionary contains each variable's name, type, and attributes. The dictionary might also contain notes about how the variable is used. In a multiple-programmer environment, the dictionary should be readily available to all programmers. As programmer-support tools become more powerful, the data dictionary becomes more important; data is where all roads cross, and all the tools need to work with it.

20.3 Executable-Code Tools

Tools for working with executable code are as rich as the tools for working with source code.

Code Creation

The tools described in this section help with code creation.

Linkers

A standard linker links one or more object files, which the compiler has generated from your source files, with the standard code needed to make an executable program. More powerful linkers can link modules from multiple languages, allowing you to choose the language that's most appropriate for each part of your program without your having to handle the integration details yourself. An overlay linker helps you put 10 pounds in a 5-pound sack by developing programs that execute in less memory than the total amount of space they consume. An overlay linker creates an executable file that loads only part of itself into memory at any one time, leaving the rest on a disk until it's needed.

Code libraries

The best way to write high-quality code in a short amount of time is not to write it all—but to buy it instead. You can buy high-quality libraries in at least these areas:

- Keyboard and mouse input
- Windowed user-interface creation
- Screen and printer output

- Sophisticated graphics functions
- Multimedia application creation
- Data-file manipulation (including common database operations)
- Communications
- Networking
- Text editing and word processing
- Mathematical operations
- Sorting
- Data compression
- Compiler construction
- Platform-independent graphical tool sets. You might write code that executes in Microsoft Windows, OS/2 Presentation Manager, Apple Macintosh, and the X Window System just by recompiling for each environment.

Code generators

If you can't buy the code you want, how about getting someone else to write it instead? You don't have to put on your yellow plaid jacket and slip into a car salesman's patter to con someone else into writing your code. You can buy tools that write code for you. Code-generating tools tend to focus on database applications, but that includes a lot of applications. Commonly available code generators write code for databases, user interfaces, and compilers. The code they generate is rarely as good as code generated by a human programmer, but many applications don't require hand-crafted code. It's worth more to some users to have 10 working applications than to have one that works exceptionally well.

Code generators are also useful for making prototypes of production code. Using a code generator, you might be able to hack out a prototype in a few hours that demonstrates key aspects of a user interface or you might be able to experiment with various design approaches. It might take you several weeks to hand-code as much functionality. If you're just experimenting, why not do it in the cheapest possible way?

Macro preprocessors

CROSS-REFERENCE
For guidelines on using simple macro substitutions, see Section 11.7, "Named Constants." For guidelines on using macro routines, see Section 5.9, "Macro Routines."

If you've programmed in C using C's macro preprocessor, you probably find it hard to conceive of programming in a language without a preprocessor. Macros allow you to create simple named constants with no run-time penalty. For example, if you use *MAX_EMPS* instead of the literal *5000*, the preprocessor will substitute the literal value *5000* before the code is compiled.

A macro preprocessor will also allow you to create more complicated functional replacements for substitution at compile time—and again, without any run-time penalty. This gives you the twin advantages of readability and modifiability. Your code is more readable because you've used a macro that you have presumably given a good name. It's more modifiable because you've put all the code in one place, where you can easily change it.

CROSS-REFERENCE
For details on moving debugging aids in and out of the code, see "Planning to Remove Debugging Aids" in Section 5.6.

Preprocessor functions are good for debugging because they're easy to shift into development code and out of production code. During development, if you want to check memory fragmentation at the beginning of each routine, you can use a macro at the beginning of each routine. You might not want to leave the checks in production code, so for the production code you can redefine the macro so that it doesn't generate any code at all. For similar reasons, preprocessor macros are good for writing code that's targeted to be compiled in multiple environments—for example, in both MS-DOS and UNIX.

If you use a language with primitive control constructs, such as Fortran or assembler, you can write a control-flow preprocessor to emulate the structured constructs of *if-then-else* and *while* loops in your language.

If you're not fortunate enough to program in a language that has a preprocessor, you can write your own. For a description of how to write your own macro preprocessor, see Chapter 8 of *Software Tools* (Kernighan and Plauger 1976) or *Software Tools in Pascal* (Kernighan and Plauger 1981). *Software Tools* also describes how to build a control-flow preprocessor for Fortran, and you can adapt it to assembler.

Debugging

CROSS-REFERENCE
These tools and their benefits are described in Section 26.5, "Debugging Tools." For more information on debugging tools, see the "Further Reading" section at the end of Chapter 26.

These tools help in debugging:

- Compiler warning messages
- Scaffolding
- File comparators (for comparing different versions of source-code files)
- Execution profilers
- Interactive debuggers—both software and hardware.

Testing tools, discussed next, are related to debugging tools.

Testing

CROSS-REFERENCE
These tools and their benefits are described in Section 25.5, "Test-Support Tools."

These features and tools can help you do effective testing:

- Scaffolding
- Results comparators (for comparing data files, captured output, and screen images)
- Automated test generators

- Test-case record and playback utilities
- Coverage monitors (logic analyzers and execution profilers)
- Symbolic debuggers
- System perturbers (memory fillers, memory shakers, selective memory failers, memory-access checkers)
- Defect databases

Code Tuning

These tools can help you fine-tune your code.

Execution profilers

An execution profiler watches your code while it runs and tells you how many times each statement is executed or how much time the program spends on each statement. Profiling your code while it's running is like having a doctor press a stethoscope to your chest and tell you to cough. It gives you insight into how your program works, where the hot spots are, and where you should focus your code-tuning efforts.

Assembler listings and disassemblers

Some day you might want to look at the assembler code generated by your high-level language. Some high-level–language compilers generate assembler listings. Others don't, and you have to use a disassembler to recreate the assembler from the machine code that the compiler generates. Looking at the assembler code generated by your compiler shows you how efficiently your compiler translates high-level–language code into machine code. It can tell you why high-level code that looks fast runs slowly. In Chapter 29 on code-tuning techniques, several of the benchmark results are counterintuitive. While benchmarking that code, I frequently referred to the assembler listings to better understand the results that didn't make sense in the high-level language.

If you're not comfortable with assembly language and you want an introduction, you won't find a better one than comparing each high-level–language statement you write to the assembler instructions generated by the compiler. A first exposure to assembler is often a loss of innocence. When you see how much code the compiler creates—how much more than it needs to—you'll never look at your compiler in quite the same way again.

20.4 Tool-Oriented Environments

Some environments have proven to be better suited to tool-oriented programming than others. This section looks at three examples.

UNIX

UNIX and the philosophy of programming with small, sharp tools are inseparable. The UNIX environment is famous for its collection of small tools with funny names that work well together: grep, diff, sort, make, crypt, tar, lint, ctags, sed, awk, vi, and others. The C language, closely coupled with UNIX, embodies the same philosophy; the standard C library is composed of small functions that can easily be composed into larger functions because they work so well together.

Some programmers work so productively in UNIX that they take it with them. They use UNIX work-alike tools to support their UNIX habits in MS-DOS and other environments. One tribute to the success of the UNIX paradigm is the availability of tools that put a UNIX costume on an MS-DOS machine.

CASE

CASE is a catchall acronym for computer-aided software engineering. A CASE tool ideally is a program that provides end-to-end support for software development activities: requirements analysis, architecture, detailed design, coding, debugging, unit testing, system testing, and maintenance. A CASE tool that provided practical, integrated support for each of these activities would be a powerful tool indeed. Unfortunately, most CASE tools fall short in one or more of these areas:

- They support only part of the development cycle.
- They support all parts of the development cycle, but in some areas they're too weak to be useful.
- Their support of different parts of the life cycle isn't integrated.
- They require too much overhead. They try to do so much that they're huge and sluggish.
- They focus on one methodology religiously, excluding others and turning CASE into CASD: computer-aided software dogma.

HARD DATA

At the 1992 Achieving Software Quality Debates, Don Reifer reported the results of a survey on the effectiveness of CASE tools. He collected data from 45 companies in 10 industries representing over 100 million lines of code. Reifer found an average productivity gain with CASE of 9 to 12 percent but said that not a single firm could justify the cost of CASE using these gains alone as a reason (Myers 1992). A second report has also concluded that CASE tools have yet to meet the claims made for them in the popular press (Vessey, Jarvenpaa, and Tractinsky 1992).

APSE

APSE is an acronym for Ada Programming Support Environment. The goal of an APSE is to provide an integrated set of support tools for programming in Ada, with emphasis on software for embedded applications. The Department of Defense has identified a set of capabilities that an APSE is required to have, including

- Code-creation tools (an Ada-sensitive program editor, a pretty printer, a compiler)
- Code-analysis tools (static and dynamic code analyzers, performance measurers)
- Code-maintenance tools (a file administrator, a configuration manager)
- Project-support tools (a documentation system, a project-control system, a configuration-control system, a fault-report system, requirements tools, design tools)

Although some vendors currently offer an APSE, none of the support environments are outstanding yet. Because of the focus the DoD brings to the effort, however, this is an area to watch for exciting tool developments.

20.5 Building Your Own Programming Tools

FURTHER READING
For an excellent discussion of building your own toolset, see *Software Tools* (Kernighan and Plauger 1976) or *Software Tools in Pascal* (Kernighan and Plauger 1981).

Suppose you're given five hours to do the job and you have a choice:

1. Do the job comfortably in five hours, or
2. Spend four hours and 45 minutes feverishly building a tool to do the job, and then have the tool do the job in 15 minutes.

Most good programmers would choose the first option one time out of a million and the second option in every other case. Building tools is part of the warp and woof of programming. Nearly all large organizations (organizations with more than 1000 programmers) have internal tool and support groups. Many have proprietary analysis and design tools that are superior to those on the market (Jones 1986a).

KEY POINT

With a few exceptions, you can write most of the tools described in this chapter. It might not be cost effective to do it, but there aren't any mountainous technical barriers to doing it.

Project-specific tools

Most medium and large projects need special tools unique to the project. For example, you might need tools to generate special kinds of test data, to verify the quality of data files, or to emulate hardware that isn't yet available. Here are some examples of project-specific tool support:

- An aerospace team was responsible for developing in-flight software to control an infrared sensor and analyze its data. To verify the performance of the software, an in-flight data recorder documented the actions of the in-flight software. Engineers wrote custom data-analysis tools to analyze the performance of the in-flight systems. After each flight, they used the custom tools to check the primary systems.

- Microsoft planned to include a new font technology in a release of its Windows graphical environment. Since both the font data files and the software to display the fonts were new, errors could have arisen from either the data or the software. Microsoft developers wrote several custom tools to check for errors in the data files, which improved their ability to discriminate between font data errors and software errors.

- An insurance company developed an ambitious system to calculate its rate increases. Because the system was complicated and accuracy was essential, hundreds of computed rates needed to be checked carefully, even though hand-calculating a single rate took several minutes. The company wrote a separate software tool to compute rates one at a time. With the tool, the company could compute a single rate in a few seconds and check rates from the main program in a small fraction of the time it would have taken to check the main program's rates by hand.

Part of planning for a project should be thinking about the tools that might be needed and allocating time for building them.

Scripts

A script is a tool that automates a repetitive chore. In some systems, scripts are called batch files or macros. Scripts can be simple or complex, and some of the most useful are the easiest to write. For example, I keep a journal, and to protect my privacy, I encrypt it except when I'm writing in it. To make sure that I always encrypt and decrypt it properly, I have a script that decrypts my journal, executes the word processor, and then encrypts the journal. The script looks like this:

```
crypto c:\word\journal.* %1 /d /Es /s
word c:\word\journal.doc
crypto c:\word\journal.* %1 /Es /s
```

The *%1* is the field for my password which, for obvious reasons, isn't included in the script. The script saves me the work of typing all the parameters (and mistyping them) and ensures that I always perform all the operations and perform them in the right order.

If you find yourself typing something longer than about five characters more than a few times a day, it's a good candidate for a script or batch file. Examples include compile/link sequences, backup commands, and any command with a lot of parameters.

Batch-file enhancers

A batch file is an ASCII text file that contains a sequence of operating-system commands including commands supported by the batch language. Not all batch languages are created equal. Some are much more powerful than others. A few, like JCL, are legendary for being as complicated as the programming languages found on the same machines. Others lack important capabilities that would make them truly useful. If you find yourself using a weak batch language, look for a batch-file enhancer. It will give you more powerful batch capabilities than the standard batch language that comes with your computer.

20.6   Ideal Programming Environment

This section's description of an ideal programming environment is an excursion into programming fantasyland. Although such a vision is not immediately practical, this book about construction has a responsibility to define where construction tools should be going. All of the capabilities described in this section are easily within the reach of today's technology. Perhaps the description will serve as inspiration for an ambitious toolsmith who will create a programming environment that towers above the ones currently available.

For this discussion, the fantasy environment is called "Cobbler." The name is inspired by the old saying that the cobbler's children are the last to have new shoes, which is true of today's programmers and programming tools.

Integration

The Cobbler environment integrates the programming activities of detailed design, coding, and debugging. When source-code control is needed, Cobbler integrates source-code version control too. If the detailed-design practices suggested in this book are followed, the primary detailed-design tool required is PDL, which can be handled easily, even in text environments.

Language support

During code construction, Cobbler provides ready access to cross-referenced help on the programming language. Help discusses nuances of the language as well as the basics and mentions common problems in using features of the language. For error messages, Help lists the common problems that might give rise to each message.

The environment provides templates for language constructs so that you don't need to remember the precise syntax for a *case* statement, a *for* loop, or a more unusual construct. The help system provides a well-organized list of all available routines, and you can paste the template for a routine into your code.

Detailed cross-referencing

Cobbler enables you to generate a list of all the places in which a variable is used or receives a value. You can get help on a variable declaration the same way you'd get help on any other topic, with ready access to the variable definition and comments about it.

You can retrieve information on routines just as easily. You can follow a chain of calls to routines up and down—pointing at the name of the routine you want to view in more detail. You can check variable types in a call to a routine with the touch of a key.

Interactive views of program organization

The Cobbler environment radically changes the way you view program source text. Compilers read source files from beginning to end, and traditional development environments force you to view a program the same way. This is sequential and flat—far from what you need for a meaningful view of a program.

In Cobbler, you can view a tangle of routine names, graphically presented, and zoom in on any routine. You can choose the model that organizes the tangle of routines: hierarchy, network, modules, objects, or an alphabetical listing. Your high-level view isn't cluttered by a routine's details until you want to zoom in on them.

When looking at the guts of a routine, you can view them at any of several levels of detail. You can view only the routine's definition or only the comment prolog. You can view code only or comments only. You can view control structures with or without a display of the code they control. In languages with macro commands, you can view a program with the macros expanded or contracted. If they're contracted, you can expand an individual macro with the touch of a key.

In writing this book, I've used a word processor with a powerful outline view. Without the outline view and the ability to study an outline and then zoom in on its detailed contents, I'd have a weak sense of each chapter's structure. The only view I'd see of each chapter would be flat, and the only sense of structure I'd have would come from scrolling from beginning to end. The ability to zoom between low-level and high-level views gives me a sense of the topology of each chapter, and that's critical to organizing my writing.

Organizing source code is as difficult as organizing writing. It's hard to believe that I lack any capability whatsoever to view the topology of my programs, especially when I've had a similar capability in my writing tools for more than five years.

The kinds of components that make up a program can also be improved. The semantics of source files are hazy, and the concept is better replaced by the ideas of modules, packages, or objects. The concept of source files is obsolete. You should be able to think about the semantics of your programs without worrying about how the code is physically stored.

Interactive formatting

CROSS REFERENCE
For an idea of the potential of typographic code formatting, see Figure 18-1 in Section 18.1.

Cobbler provides more active formatting aids than existing environments do. For example, its graphical user interface makes outer parentheses larger than inner parentheses, as they have been displayed in mathematical texts for a hundred years.

The environment formats code according to user-specified parameters without resorting to a separate pretty-printer program. Any environment that knows about your program already knows where all your logical structures and variable declarations are. In Cobbler, you don't need to resort to a separate program to format your code. Some current environments provide feeble support for automatic indentation of control structures as you enter them. But when they're modified and 45 lines need to be shifted out six columns each, you're on your own. In the ideal programming environment, the environment formats the code according to the code's logical structure. If you change the logical structure, the environment reformats the code accordingly.

Documentation

Cobbler supports traditional commenting through extensive formatting and offers choices in the level of comments it displays. Cobbler also supports voice annotations. Rather than typing comments, you can record your thoughts by clicking the mouse and saying a few words. Cobbler also includes hypertext links to relevant sections of requirements and design documents.

Performance tuning

Cobbler automatically collects the performance metrics needed to fine-tune a program's performance. Where does the program spend 90 percent of its time? Which code is never executed? It collects detailed-design metrics for design improvements: Which areas of the program have the most complicated logic or the most detailed data or are most tightly coupled? It collects change metrics: Which parts of the program are relatively stable and which are volatile? The environment does all of this without requiring your assistance.

Environmental characteristics

The state of the environment is always saved from session to session—you don't lose the details of a debugging session just because the technician arrived to fix a flaky video card. You can pop right back into it. The same is true of your work with the editor: The editor has multi-level undo, memory of search strings, and regular-expression search-and-replace across single routines, modules, or entire programs—and all this information is associated with a specific project and reactivated when you work on that project again.

The Cobbler environment supports fully integrated debugging at a level comparable to that of today's best debuggers. Some of the current standalone debuggers are satisfactory in many respects. They offer robust abilities to inspect logic structures, data structures, changes to data, and objects. They offer backward execution and testing of individual routines, even within the context of a larger environment. In Cobbler, however, editing, compilation, and debugging are integrated into a single environment. You don't need to change "modes" to debug.

During program development, your program is always compiled as much as the environment is capable of compiling it. You can execute the program, change part of it, and continue execution without losing the state the program was in before you made the change. Cobbler figures out which parts of a program depend on which other parts and recompiles pieces as needed.

Of course, all the operations are instantaneous because Cobbler uses efficient background processing.

Finally, Cobbler supports a revolutionary distinction between development and production modes. In production mode, the emphasis is on small, fast programs. In development mode, however, the emphasis should be less on squeezing out every last machine cycle and more on maximizing the use of your time. The emphasis is on detecting and correcting errors as quickly and painlessly as possible. During development, the Cobbler environment detects and notifies you of common problems such as a dangling pointer, an uninitialized value, a bad array reference, or an overflowing or underflowing numeric value. A compiler can easily insert the extra code to check for such problems, and during development it should.

Cobbler's Key Advantages

Realization of this ideal development environment calls for a mental shift among tool writers. Here are the key differences between the ideal environment and the environments available today:

- Cobbler is completely interactive. Resources that used to be printed on paper—variable and routine cross-references, lists of routines, language reference manuals—are all available on line, instantly. Most of this capability is currently available in standalone tools but hasn't yet been integrated into a single tool.

- Cobbler is opportunistic. It anticipates your desires rather than waiting for you to ask. The environment knows that at some point you're going to request that your program be compiled and linked. Why should it wait until you ask? If it has spare time, it should compile routines in the background.

- Cobbler spends any amount of computer time to save any amount of your time. Computer time has become so cheap that it should be traded freely for your time. In the opportunistic-compile strategy, the computer might compile a routine that you know is not yet complete. Sometimes the compilation will be wasted. But so what? Other times you won't have to wait for the results when you ask for them.

- Cobbler abandons the pure source-code view. Although you want to know exactly what code you have, you don't necessarily want to look at it in exactly the same way that the compiler does. You want to look at it in varying degrees of detail, and you want to be able to distinguish among different kinds of information, such as executable code, data declarations, and comments. You want to be able to safely ignore administrative details such as which source file a routine is in; you just want to define objects or modules and restrict the interactions among them.

KEY POINT

All of these capabilities are within the grasp of current technology. Most are already in the Smalltalk or APL environment. Others are well-known hypertext ideas. None of them require changes to the underlying programming languages C, Pascal, Basic, Fortran, and Ada, and none of them loosen your direct grip on the code.

Further Reading

Kernighan, Brian W., and P. J. Plauger. *Software Tools.* Reading, Mass.: Addison-Wesley, 1976.

Kernighan, Brian W., and P. J. Plauger. *Software Tools in Pascal.* Reading, Mass.: Addison-Wesley, 1981. The two Kernighan and Plauger books cover the same ground—the first in Rational Fortran, the second in Pascal. The books have two agendas and meet both nicely. The first is to give you the source code for a useful set of programming tools. The tools include a multiple-file finder, a multiple-file changer, a macro pre-processor, a file comparator, an editor, and a print utility. The second agenda is to expose you to good programming practices by showing you how each of the tools is developed. Both authors are expert programmers, and the books are full of design-decision rationales and analyses of trade-offs, adding up to rare and valuable insight into how experienced designers and programmers approach their work.

Glass, Robert L. *Software Conflict: Essays on the Art and Science of Software Engineering.* Englewood Cliffs, N.J.: Yourdon Press, 1991. The chapter titled "Recommended: A Minimum Standard Software Toolset" provides a thoughtful counterpoint to the more-tools-is-better view. Glass argues for the identification of a minimum set of tools that should be available to all developers and proposes a starting kit.

Jones, T. Capers. *Programming Productivity.* New York: McGraw-Hill, 1986.

Boehm, Barry W. *Software Engineering Economics.* Englewood Cliffs, N.J.: Prentice-Hall, 1981. Both the Jones and the Boehm books devote sections to the impact of tool use on productivity.

IEEE Software 7, no. 3 (May 1990). The focus of this issue is a "Tools Fair," which presents 64 leading-edge software-engineering tools. The selection is heavily weighted toward front-end tools for multi-processing environments. It includes few construction tools, and the emphasis is on the new and novel rather than the tried and true. In spite of these biases, it's interesting to see the range of what people are working on, and this covers the map from PCs and workstations to mainframes.

Weber, Herbert, ed. *SIGSOFT '92: Proceedings of the Fifth ACM SIGSOFT Symposium on Software Development Environments,* aka *Software Engineering Notes* 17, no. 5 (December 1992). This special issue of *Software Engineering Notes* contains about 20 papers which explore leading-edge software-development environments. Topics range from hypermedia and groupware to theorem provers and reverse engineering.

Key Points

- Good tools can make your life a lot easier.
- You can make many of the tools you need.
- Huge advances in programming tools are possible with today's technology.

21

How Program Size Affects Construction

Contents

Related Topics

SCALING UP IN SOFTWARE DEVELOPMENT isn't a simple matter of taking a small project and making each part of it bigger. Suppose you wrote the 5000-line Gigatron software package in six work-months and found 25 errors in field testing. Suppose the Gigatron is successful, and you start work on the Gigatron Deluxe, a greatly enhanced version of the program that's expected to be 50,000 lines of code.

Even though it's 10 times as large as the original Gigatron, the Gigatron Deluxe won't take 10 times the effort to develop; it'll take 20 times the effort. Moreover, 20 times the total effort doesn't imply 20 times as much construction. It probably implies 12 times as much construction and 40 times as much integration and system testing. You won't have 10 times as many errors either; you'll have 15 times as many—or more.

If you've been accustomed to working on small projects, your first medium-to-large project can rage riotously out of control, becoming an uncontrollable beast instead of the pleasant success you had envisioned. This chapter tells you what kind of beast to expect and where to find the whip and chair to tame it. In contrast, if you're accustomed to working on large projects, you might use approaches that are too formal on your first small project. This chapter describes how you can economize to keep the project from toppling under the weight of its own overhead.

21.1 Range of Project Sizes

Is the size of the project you're working on typical? The wide range of project sizes means that you can't consider any single size to be typical. One way of thinking about project size is to think about the size of a project team. Here's a crude estimate of the percentages of all projects that are done by teams of various sizes:

Team Size	Percentage of Projects
1–3	50%
4–8	33%
8–12	6%
12–20	5%
20–50	3%
50+	2%

Source: "A Survey of Software Engineering Practice: Tools, Methods, and Results" (Beck and Perkins 1983).

One aspect of data on project size that might not be immediately apparent is the difference between the percentage of projects of various sizes and the percentage of programmers who work on projects of each size. Since larger projects use more programmers on each project than do small ones, they can make up a small percentage of the number of projects and still employ a large percentage of all programmers. Here's a rough estimate of the percentage of all programmers who work on projects of various sizes:

Program Size Expressed as Lines of Code	Percentage of Programmers
2K	5–10%
2K–16K	5–10%
16K–64K	10–20%
64K–512K	30–40%
512K+	30–40%

Source: Derived from data in "Program Quality and Programmer Productivity" (Jones 1977) and "A Survey of Software Engineering Practice: Tools, Methods, and Results" (Beck and Perkins 1983).

21.2 Effect of Project Size on Development Activities

If you are working on a 1-person project, the biggest influence on the project's success or failure is you. If you're working on a 25-person project, it's conceivable that you're still the biggest influence, but it's more likely that no one person will wear the medal for that distinction; your organization will be a stronger influence on the project's success or failure.

Communication and Size

If you're the only person on a project, the only communication path is between you and the customer, unless you count the path across your corpus callosum, the path that connects the left side of your brain to the right. As the number of people on a project increases, the number of communication paths increases too. The number doesn't increase additively, as the number of people increases. It increases multiplicatively, proportionally to the square of the number of people. Here's an illustration:

Communication path
with two programmers

Communication paths
with three programmers

Communication paths
with four programmers

Communication paths
with five programmers

Communication paths
with ten programmers

As you can see, a two-person project has only one path of communication. A five-person project has 10 paths. A ten-person project has 45 paths, assuming that every person talks to every other person. The 2 percent of projects that have fifty or more programmers have at least 1200 potential paths. The more communication paths you have, the more time you spend communicating and the more opportunities are created for communication mistakes. Larger-size projects demand organizational techniques that streamline communication or limit it in a sensible way.

The typical approach taken to streamlining communication is to formalize it in documents. Instead of having 50 people talk to each other in every conceivable combination, 50 people read and write documents. Some are text documents; some are graphic. Some are printed on paper; others are kept in electronic form.

Activity Proportions and Size

As project size increases and the need for formal communications increases, the kinds of activities a project needs change dramatically. Here's a chart that shows the proportions of development activities for projects of different sizes:

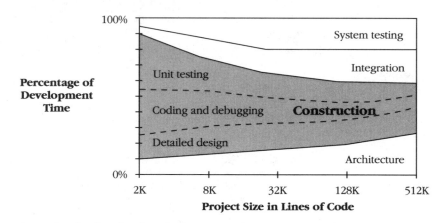

Sources: Brooks 1975; Albrecht 1979; Glass 1982; Boehm, Gray, and Seewaldt 1984; Boddie 1987; Card 1987; McGarry, Waligora, and McDermott 1989.

KEY POINT

On a small project, construction is the most prominent activity by far, taking up as much as 80 percent of the total development time. On a medium-size project, construction is still the dominant activity but its share of the total effort falls to about 50 percent. On very large projects, architecture, integration, and system testing each take up about as much time as construction. In short, as project size increases, construction becomes a smaller part of the total effort. The chart looks as though you could extend it to the right and make construction disappear altogether, so in the interest of protecting my job, I've cut it off at 512K.

Construction becomes less predominant because as project size increases, the construction activities—detailed design, coding, debugging, and unit testing—scale up linearly but many other activities scale up multiplicatively.

Here's an illustration:

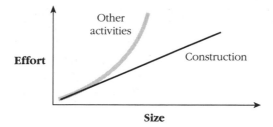

For example, if one project is twice as large as another—say, the Gigatron II compared to the Gigatron—it might take up twice as much effort in construction but four times as much in integration and system testing. When the Gigatron Deluxe comes out at 10 times the size of the original Gigatron, it will need 12 times more construction effort, but 100 times the planning effort and 40 times the integration effort. Here's a list of activities that grow at a more-than-linear rate as project size increases:

FURTHER READING
For more details on specific techniques that apply to projects of various sizes, see "Program Quality and Programmer Productivity" (Jones 1977).

- Planning
- Management
- Communication
- Requirements development
- System functional design
- Interface design and specification
- Architecture
- Integration
- Defect removal
- System testing
- Document production

Regardless of the size of a project, a few techniques are always valuable: structured coding, logic and code inspections by other programmers, online development support systems, and use of high-level languages (Jones 1977). On large projects, the techniques may not be enough by themselves, but they're not wasted on small ones.

Methodology and Size

Methodologies are used on projects of all sizes. On small projects, methodologies tend to be casual and instinctive. On large projects, they tend to be rigorous and carefully planned.

Some methodologies can be so loose that programmers aren't even aware that they're using them. A few programmers argue that methodologies are too rigid and say that they won't touch them. While it may be true that a programmer hasn't selected a methodology consciously, any approach to programming constitutes a methodology, no matter how unconscious or primitive the approach is. Merely getting out of bed and going to work in the morning is a rudimentary methodology though not a very creative one. The programmer who insists on avoiding methodologies is really only avoiding choosing one explicitly—no one can avoid using them altogether.

KEY POINT

Formal approaches aren't always fun, and if they are misapplied, their overhead gobbles up their other savings. The greater complexity of larger projects, however, requires a greater conscious attention to methodology. Building a skyscraper requires a different approach than building a doghouse. Different sizes of software projects work the same way. On large projects, unconscious choices are inadequate to the task. Successful project planners choose their strategies for large projects explicitly.

The Department of Defense has developed one method for determining the degree of formality required for a project. Regardless of whether you think that "military intelligence" is a contradiction in terms, realize that the Defense department is the largest user of computers and computer software in the world and is also one of the largest sponsors of programming research. Its approach to the question of formality involves scoring a programming project on the basis of points awarded in each of 12 categories. The DoD's Project Formality Worksheet is shown in Table 21-1.

A program can score between 12 and 60 points on the Project Formality Worksheet. A score of 12 means that the demands of the project are light and little formality is needed. A score of 60 means that the project is extremely demanding and needs as much structure as possible. In social settings, the more formal the event, the more uncomfortable your clothes have to be (high heels, neckties, and so on). In software development, the more formal the project, the more paper you have to generate to make sure you've done your homework. Depending on the score on the Project Formality Worksheet, documentation is recommended according to the breakdown in Table 21-2 on page 520.

Table 21-1. Project Formality Worksheet

	Factor	Points					Item Score
		1	**2**	**3**	**4**	**5**	
1	**Originality Required**	None; reprogram on different equipment.	Minimum; more stringent requirements.	Limited; apply new interfaces to the environment.	Considerable; apply existing state of the art.	Extensive; requires advance in state of the art.	_____
2	**Degree of Generality**	Highly restricted; single purpose.	Restricted; parameterized for a range of capabilities.	Limited flexibility; allows some change in format.	Multi-purpose; flexible format, range of subjects.	Very flexible; able to handle a broad range of subject matter on different equipment.	_____
3	**Span of Operation**	Local or utility.	Component command.	Single command.	Multi-command.	Defense department worldwide.	_____
4	**Change in Scope and Objective**	None.	Infrequent.	Occasional.	Frequent.	Continuous.	_____
5	**Equipment Complexity**	Single machine, routine processing.	Single machine, routine processing, extended peripheral system.	Multi-computer, standard peripheral system.	Multi-computer, advanced programming, complex peripheral system.	Master control system, multi-computer, auto input-output and display equipment.	_____
6	**Personnel Assigned**	1–2	3–5	5–10	10–18	18 and over	_____
7	**Development Cost**	3–15K	15–70K	70–200K	200–500K	Over 500K	_____
8	**Criticality**	Data processing.	Routine operations.	Personnel safety.	Unit survival.	National defense.	_____
9	**Average Response Time to Program Changes**	2 or more weeks	1–2 weeks	3–7 days	1–3 days	1–24 hours	_____
10	**Average Response Time to Data Inputs**	2 or more weeks	1–2 weeks	1–7 days	1–24 hours	9–60 minutes (interactive)	_____
11	**Programming Languages**	High-level language.	High-level and limited assembly language.	High-level and extensive assembly language.	Assembly language.	Machine language.	_____
12	**Software Is Developed Concurrently**	None.	Limited.	Moderate.	Extensive.	Exhaustive.	_____
	TOTAL						_____

Source: DOD-STD-7935 in *Wicked Problems, Righteous Solutions* (DeGrace and Stahl 1990).

Table 21-2. Documentation Recommendations

CROSS-REFERENCE
The documentation
described here is usually
kept outside the program
listing. For pointers to more
information on these kinds
of documentation, see
"Further Reading on
Documentation" at the
end of Chapter 19.

Formality Score	Recommended Documentation
12–15	*User Manual* and incidental program documentation

15–26	Documentation from lower level plus
	  Operations Manual
	  Maintenance Manual
	  Test Plan
	  Management Plan
	  Configuration-Management Plan

24–38	Documentation from lower levels plus
	  Functional Description
	  Quality-Assurance Plan

36–50	Documentation from lower levels plus
	  System and Subsystem Specifications
	  Test-Analysis Reports

48–60	Documentation from lower levels plus *Program Specification*

Sources: DOD-STD-7935 in *Wicked Problems, Righteous Solutions* (DeGrace and Stahl 1990) and *Guidelines for Documentation of Computer Programs and Automated Data Systems* (FIPS PUB 38).

Depending on the needs of the specific project, a *Data Requirements Document*, a *Database Specification*, and *Implementation Procedures* might also be recommended.

You don't create any of this documentation for its own sake. The point of your writing a configuration-management plan, for example, isn't to exercise your writing muscles. The point of your writing the plan is to force you to think carefully about configuration management and to force you to explain your plan to everyone else. The documentation is a tangible side effect of the real work you do as you plan and construct a software system. If you feel as though you're going through the motions and writing generic documents, something is wrong.

Programs, Products, Systems, and System Products

FURTHER READING
For another explanation of
this point, see Chapter 1 in
The Mythical Man-Month
(Brooks 1975).

Lines of code and team size aren't the only influences on a project's size. A more subtle influence is the quality and the complexity of the final software. The original Gigatron, the Gigatron Jr., might have taken only a month to write and debug. It was a single program written, tested, and documented by a single person. If the 2500-line Gigatron Jr. took one month, why did the full-fledged 5000-line Gigatron take six?

The simplest kind of software is a single "program" that's used by itself by the person who developed it or, informally, by a few others.

A more sophisticated kind of program is a software "product," a program that's intended for use by people other than the original developer. A software product is used in environments that differ to lesser or greater extents from the environment in which it was created. It's extensively tested before it's released, it's documented, and it's capable of being maintained by others. A software product costs about three times as much to develop as a software program.

Another level of sophistication is required to develop a group of programs that work together. Such a group is called a software "system." Development of a system is more complicated than development of a simple program because of the complexity of developing interfaces among the pieces and the care needed to integrate the pieces. On the whole, a system also costs about three times as much as a simple program.

HARD DATA

When a "system product" is developed, it has the polish of a product and the multiple parts of a system. System products cost about nine times as much as simple programs (Boehm 1987b).

A failure to appreciate the differences in polish and complexity among programs, products, systems, and system products is one common cause of estimation errors. Programmers who use their experience in building a program to estimate the schedule for building a system product can underestimate by a factor of almost 10. As you consider the following example, refer to the chart on page 516. If you used your experience in writing 2K lines of code to estimate the time it would take you to develop a 2K program, your estimate would be only 80 percent of the total time you'd actually need to perform all the activities that go into developing a program. Writing 2K lines of code doesn't take as long as creating a whole program that contains 2K lines of code. If you don't consider the time it takes to do nonconstruction activities, development will take 25 percent more time than you estimate.

As you scale up, construction becomes a smaller part of the total effort in a project. If you base your estimates solely on construction experience, the estimation error increases. If you used your own 2K construction experience to estimate the time it would take to develop a 32K program, your estimate would be only 50 percent of the total time required; development would take 100 percent more time than you would estimate.

The estimation error here would be completely attributable to your not understanding the effect of size on developing larger programs. If in addition you failed to consider the extra degree of polish required for a product rather than a mere program, the error could easily increase by a factor of 3 or more.

21.3   Effect of Project Size on Errors

CROSS-REFERENCE
For more details on
errors, see Section 25.4,
"Typical Errors."

Both the quantity and the kinds of errors are affected by project size. You might not think that the kinds of errors would be affected, but as project size increases, a larger percentage of errors can usually be attributed to mistakes in analysis and design. Here's an illustration:

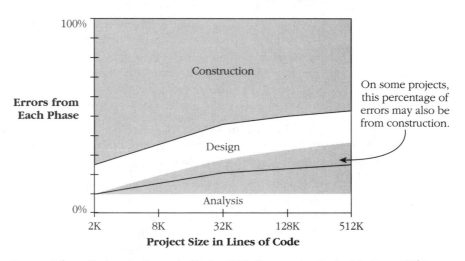

Sources: *Software Engineering Economics* (Boehm 1981), *Programming Productivity* (Jones 1986a), and "Measuring and Managing Software Maintenance" (Grady 1987).

On small projects, construction errors make up about 75 percent of all the errors found. Methodology has less influence on code quality, and the biggest influence on program quality is the skill of the individual writing the program (Jones 1977).

On larger projects, construction errors can taper off to about 50 percent of the total errors; analysis and architecture errors make up the difference. Presumably this is related to the fact that more analysis and architecture are required on large projects, so the opportunity for errors arising out of those activities is proportionally larger. In some very large projects, however, the proportion of construction errors remains high; sometimes even with 500,000 lines of code, up to 75 percent of the errors can be attributed to construction (Grady 1987).

KEY POINT

As the kinds of defects change with size, so do the numbers of defects. You would naturally expect a project that's twice as large as another to have twice as many errors. But the density of defects, the number of defects per line of code, increases. The product that's twice as large is likely to have more than twice as many errors. Table 21-3 shows the range of defect densities you can expect on projects of various sizes:

Table 21-3. Project Size and Error Density

CROSS-REFERENCE
The data in this table was reported in 1977. Since then, a few large projects have reported error rates lower than the minimums shown here. For examples, see "How Many Errors Should You Expect to Find?" in Section 25.4.

Project Size (in Lines of Code)	Error Density
Smaller than 2K	0–25 errors per thousand lines of code (KLOC)
2K–16K	0–40 errors per KLOC
16K–64K	0.5–50 errors per KLOC
64K–512K	2–70 errors per KLOC
512K or more	4–100 errors per KLOC

Source: "Program Quality and Programmer Productivity" (Jones 1977).

The data in this table was derived from specific projects, and the numbers may bear little resemblance to those for the projects you've worked on. As a snapshot of the industry, however, the data is illuminating. It indicates that the number of errors increases dramatically as project size increases, with very large projects having up to four times as many errors per line of code as small projects. The data also implies that up to a certain size, it's possible to write error-free code; above that size, errors creep in regardless of the measures you take to prevent them.

21.4 Effect of Project Size on Productivity

Productivity has a lot in common with software quality when it comes to project size. At small sizes (2000 lines of code or smaller), the single biggest influence on productivity is the skill of the individual programmer (Jones 1977). As project size increases, team size and organization quickly become greater influences on productivity.

HARD DATA

How big does a project need to be before team size begins to affect productivity? In "Prototyping Versus Specifying: A Multiproject Experiment," Boehm, Gray, and Seewaldt reported that smaller teams completed their projects with 39 percent higher productivity than larger teams. The size of the teams? Two people for the small projects, three for the large (1984).

Table 21-4 on the next page gives the inside scoop on the general relationship between project size and productivity.

Table 21-4. Project Size and Productivity

Project Size (in Lines of Code)	Lines of Code per Month
Smaller than 2K	333–2000
2K–16K	200–1250
16K–64K	125–1000
64K–512K	67–500
512K or more	36–250

Source: "Program Quality and Programmer Productivity" (Jones 1977).

Productivity is substantially determined by personnel quality, programming language, methodology, product complexity, programming environment, tool support, and many other factors, so it's likely that the data in Table 21-4 won't apply directly to your programming environment. Take the specific numbers with a grain of salt.

Realize, however, that the general trend the numbers indicate is significant. Productivity on the smallest projects is about 10 times the productivity on the largest ones. Even jumping from the middle of one range to the middle of the next—say, from a program of 1 KLOC to a program of 9 KLOC—you can expect productivity to be reduced by almost half.

Further Reading

Boehm, Barry W. *Software Engineering Economics*. Englewood Cliffs, N.J.: Prentice Hall, 1981. Boehm's book is an extensive treatment of the cost, productivity, and quality ramifications of project size and other variables in the software-development process. It includes discussions of the effect of size on construction and other activities. Chapter 11 is an excellent explanation of software's diseconomies of scale. Other information on project size is spread throughout the book.

Jones, Capers. *Programming Productivity*. New York: McGraw-Hill, 1986. Jones's book is perhaps the most condensed source of quantitative data on software development available. At about a third the size of Boehm's book, it provides numerous comparisons of projects of different sizes. The section titled "The Impact of Program Size" in Chapter 3 addresses size directly.

Brooks, Frederick P., Jr. *The Mythical Man-Month*. Reading, Mass.: Addison-Wesley, 1975. Brooks was the manager of IBM's OS/360 development, a mammoth project that took 5000 work-years. He discusses management issues pertaining to small and large teams and presents a particularly vivid account of chief-programmer teams in this engaging collection of essays.

DeGrace, Peter, and Leslie Stahl. *Wicked Problems, Righteous Solutions: A Catalogue of Modern Software Engineering Paradigms*. Englewood Cliffs, N.J.: Yourdon Press, 1990. As the title suggests, this book catalogs approaches to developing software. As noted throughout this chapter, your approach needs to vary as the size of the project varies, and DeGrace and Stahl make that point clearly. The section titled "Attenuating and Truncating" in Chapter 5 discusses customizing software-development processes based on project size and formality. The book includes descriptions of models from NASA and the Department of Defense and a remarkable number of edifying illustrations.

Jones, T. Capers. "Program Quality and Programmer Productivity." *IBM Technical Report TR 02.764* (January 1977): 42–78. Also available in Jones's *Tutorial: Programming Productivity: Issues for the Eighties,* 2d ed., Los Angeles: IEEE Computer Society Press, 1986. This paper contains the first in-depth analysis of the reasons large projects have different spending patterns than small ones. It's a thorough discussion of the differences between large and small projects, including requirements and quality-assurance measures. It's somewhat dated now, but it's still interesting.

Key Points

- Activities that are taken for granted on a small project must be carefully planned on larger ones. Construction becomes less predominant as project size increases.

- As project size increases, communication needs to be streamlined. The point of most methodologies is to reduce communications problems, and a methodology should live or die on its merits as a communication facilitator.

- All other things being equal, productivity will be lower on a large project than on a small one.

- All other things being equal, a large project will have more errors per line of code than a small one.

22

Managing Construction

Contents

Related Topics

MANAGING SOFTWARE DEVELOPMENT HAS BECOME one of the formidable challenges of the late twentieth century. The general topic of software-project management is beyond the scope of this book, but a few specific management topics that apply directly to construction are discussed here. Because the chapter covers a broad collection of topics, several other sections also describe where you can go for more information.

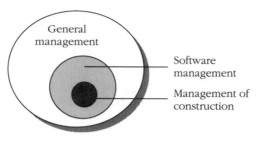

This chapter covers the software-management topics related to construction.

22.1 Encouraging Good Coding

Since code is the primary output of construction, a key question in managing construction is "How do you encourage good coding practices?" In general, mandating a strict set of standards from the top isn't a good idea. Programmers tend to view managers as being at a lower level of technical evolution, somewhere between single-celled organisms and the woolly mammoths that died out during the Ice Age, and if there are going to be programming standards, programmers need to buy into them.

Considerations in Setting Standards

Standards shouldn't be imposed at all, if you can avoid them. Consider the alternatives to standards: flexible guidelines, a collection of suggestions rather than guidelines, or a set of examples that embody the best practices.

Techniques

Here are several techniques for achieving good coding practices, techniques that aren't as heavy-handed as laying down rigid coding standards:

Assign two people to every part of the project. If two people have to work on each line of code, you'll guarantee that at least two people think it works and is readable. The mechanisms for teaming two people can range from team development to mentor-trainee pairs to buddy-system reviews.

CROSS-REFERENCE
For details on reviews, see Chapter 24, "Reviews."

Review every line of code. A code review typically involves the programmer and at least two reviewers. That means that at least three people read every line of code. Another name for peer review is "peer pressure." In addition to providing a safety net in case the original programmer leaves the project, reviews improve code quality because the programmer knows that the code will be read by others. Even if your shop hasn't created explicit coding standards, reviews provide a subtle way of moving toward a group coding standard—decisions are made by the group during reviews, and, over time, the group will derive its own standards.

Require code sign-offs. In other fields, technical drawings are approved and signed by the managing engineer. The signature means that to the best of the engineer's knowledge, the drawings are technically competent and error-free. Some companies treat code the same way. Before code is considered to be complete, senior technical personnel must sign the code listing.

Route good code examples for review. A big part of good management is communicating your objectives clearly. One way to communicate your objectives is to circulate good code to your programmers or post it for public display. In doing so, you provide a clear example of the quality you're aiming for. Similarly, a coding-standards manual can consist mainly of a set of "best code listings." Identifying certain listings as "best" sets an example for others to follow. Such a manual is easier to update than an English-language standards manual and effortlessly presents subtleties in coding style that are hard to capture point by point in prose descriptions.

CROSS-REFERENCE
A large part of programming is communicating your work to other people. For details, see Section 31.5, "Communication and Cooperation," and Section 32.3, "Write Programs for People First, Computers Second."

Emphasize that code listings are public assets. Programmers sometimes feel that the code they've written is "their code," as if it were private property. Although it is the result of their work, code is part of the project and should be freely available to anyone else on the project who needs it. It should be seen by others during reviews and maintenance, even if at no other time.

One of the most successful projects ever reported developed 83,000 lines of code in 11 work-years of effort. Only one error that resulted in system failure was detected in the first 13 months of operation. This accomplishment is even more dramatic when you realize that the project was completed in the late 1960s, without online compilation or interactive debugging. Productivity on the project, 7500 lines of code per work-year in the late 1960s, is still twice today's average productivity of 3750 lines per work-year. The chief programmer on the project reported that one key to the project's success was the identification of all computer runs (erroneous and otherwise) as public rather than private assets (Baker and Mills 1973).

HARD DATA

Reward good code. Use your organization's reward system to reinforce good coding practices. Keep these considerations in mind as you develop your reinforcement system:

● The reward should be something that the programmer wants. (Many programmers find "attaboy" rewards distasteful, especially when they come from nontechnical managers.)

- Code that receives an award should be exceptionally good. If you give an award to a programmer everyone else knows does bad work, you look like Charlie Chaplin trying to run a cake factory. It doesn't matter that the programmer has a cooperative attitude or always comes to work on time. You lose credibility if your reward doesn't match the technical merits of the situation. If you're not technically skilled enough to make the good-code judgment, don't! Don't make the award at all, or let your team choose the recipient.

One easy standard. If you're managing a programming project and you have a programming background, an easy and effective technique for eliciting good work is to say "I must be able to read and understand any code written for the project." That the manager isn't the hottest technical hotshot can be an advantage in that it may discourage "clever" or tricky code.

The Role of This Book

Most of this book is a discussion of good programming practices. It isn't intended to be used to justify rigid standards, and it's intended even less to be used as a set of rigid standards. Using it in such a way would contradict some of its most important themes. Use this book as a basis for discussion, as a sourcebook of good programming practices, and for identifying practices that could be beneficial in your environment.

22.2 Configuration Management

A software project is dynamic. The code changes; the design changes; the requirements change. What's more, changes in the requirements lead to more changes in the design; changes in the design lead to even more changes in the code and test cases.

What Is Configuration Management?

Configuration management is the practice of handling changes systematically so that a system can maintain its integrity over time. Another name for it is "change control." It includes techniques for evaluating proposed changes, tracking changes, and keeping copies of the system as it existed at various points in time.

If you don't control changes to design, you can end up writing code for parts of the design that are eventually eliminated. You can write code that's incompatible with new parts of the design. You might not detect many of the incompatibilities until integration time, which will become finger-pointing time because nobody will really know what's going on.

If changes to code aren't controlled, you might change a routine that someone else is changing at the same time; successfully combining your changes with theirs will be problematic. Uncontrolled code changes can make code seem more tested than it is. The version that's been tested will probably be the old, unchanged version; the modified version might not have been tested. Without good change control, you can make changes to a routine, find new errors, and not be able to back up to the old, working routine.

The problems go on indefinitely. If changes aren't handled systematically, you're taking random steps in the fog rather than moving directly toward a clear destination. Without good change control, rather than developing code you're wasting your time thrashing. Configuration management helps you use your time effectively.

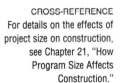

In spite of the obvious need for configuration management, many programmers don't use it. One survey found that over a third of programmers weren't even familiar with the idea (Beck and Perkins 1983).

Configuration management wasn't invented by programmers. But because programming projects are so volatile, it's especially useful to programmers. Applied to software projects, configuration management is usually called software configuration management, or SCM (commonly pronounced "scum"). SCM focuses on a program's source code, documentation, and test data.

The systemic problem with SCM is overcontrol. The surest way to stop auto accidents is to prevent everyone from driving, and one sure way to prevent software-development problems is to stop all software development. Although that's one way to control changes, it's a terrible way to develop software. You have to plan SCM carefully so that it's an asset rather than an albatross around your neck.

CROSS-REFERENCE
For details on the effects of project size on construction, see Chapter 21, "How Program Size Affects Construction."

On a small 1-person project, you can probably do well with no SCM beyond planning for informal periodic backups. On a large 50-person project, you'll probably need a full-blown SCM scheme including fairly formal procedures for backups, change control for requirements and design, and document, source-code, and test-case control.

If your project is neither very large nor very small, you'll have to settle on a degree of formality somewhere between the two extremes. The following subsections describe some of the options in implementing SCM.

Software Design Changes

During development, you're bound to be bristling with ideas about how to improve the design of the system. If you implement each change as it occurs to you, you'll soon find yourself walking on a software treadmill—for all that the system will be changing, it won't be moving closer to completion. Here are some guidelines for controlling design changes:

CROSS-REFERENCE
An alternative to minimizing change is making change a planned-for part of your development process by using evolutionary delivery. For details, see Section 27.4, "Evolutionary Delivery."

Follow a formal change-control procedure. As Chapter 3 noted, a formal change-control procedure is a godsend when you have a lot of change requests. By establishing a formal procedure, you make it clear that changes will be considered in the context of what's best for the project overall.

Establish a change-control board. The job of a change-control board is to separate the wheat from the chaff in change requests. Anyone who wants to propose a change submits the change request to the change-control board. The term "change request" refers to any request that would change the software: an idea for a new feature, a change to an existing feature, an "error report" that might or might not be reporting a real error, and so on. The board meets periodically to review proposed changes. It either approves, disapproves, or defers each change.

Handle change requests in groups. It's tempting to implement easy changes as ideas arise. The problem with handling changes in this way is that good changes can get lost. If you think of a simple change 25 percent of the way through the project and you're on schedule, you'll make it. If you think of another simple change 90 percent of the way through the project and you're already behind, you won't. When you start to run out of time at the end of the project, it won't matter that the second change is 10 times as good as the first—you won't be in a position to make any nonessential changes. Some of the best changes can slip through the cracks merely because you thought of them later rather than sooner.

The informal solution to this problem is to write down all ideas and suggestions, no matter how easy they would be to implement, and save them until you have time to work on them. Then, viewing them as a group, choose the ones that will be the most beneficial.

Estimate the cost of each change. Whenever your customer, your boss, or you are tempted to change the system, estimate the time it would take to make the change, including review of the code for the change and retesting the whole system. Include in your estimate time for dealing with the change's ripple effect through requirements to design to code to test to changes in the user documentation. Let all the interested parties know that software is intricately interwoven and that time estimation is necessary even if the change appears small at first glance.

Regardless of how optimistic you feel when the change is first suggested, refrain from giving an off-the-cuff estimate. Handwaving estimates are often mistaken by a factor of 10 or 100.

CROSS-REFERENCE
For another angle on handling changes, see "Handling Requirements Changes During Construction" in Section 3.3.

Be wary of major changes. If your customer suggests major changes, that's a warning that you're not yet done with requirements. If the suggestions come up during high-level design, stop work on design and back up to requirements. Wait until change requests have become less dramatic before proceeding with design.

If you get persistent requests for major design changes during coding, sit down with your customer and point out the implications of the changes for the work that's already been done. One obvious implication is that some of the early work will be thrown out.

Software Code Changes

Another configuration-management issue is controlling source code. If you change the code and a new error surfaces that seems unrelated to the change you made, you'll probably want to compare the new version of the code to the old in your search for the source of the error. If that doesn't tell you anything, you might want to look at a version that's even older. This kind of excursion through history is easy if you have version-control tools that keep track of multiple versions of source code.

KEY POINT

Version-control software. Good version-control software works so easily that you barely notice you're using it. It's especially helpful on team projects. Typically, when you need to work on source code in a particular file, you check the file out of version control. If someone else has already checked it out, you're notified that you can't check it out. When you can check the file out, you work on it just as you would without version control until you're ready to check it in. When you check the file in, version control asks why you changed it, and you type in a reason.

For this modest investment of effort, you get several big benefits:

- You don't step on anyone's toes by working on a file while someone else is working on it.
- You can easily update your copies of all the project's files to the current versions, usually by issuing a single command.
- You can backtrack to any version of any file that was ever checked into version control.
- You can get a list of the changes made to any version of any file.
- You don't have to worry about personal backups because the version-control copy is a safety net.

Version control is indispensable on team projects. It's so effective that the applications division of Microsoft has found source-code version control to be a "major competitive advantage" (Moore 1992).

Make. A special kind of version-control tool is the "make" utility that's associated with UNIX and the C language. The purpose of make is to minimize the time needed to create current versions of all your object files. For each object file in your project, you specify the files that the object file depends on and how to make it.

Suppose you have an object file named *userface.obj*. In the make file, you indicate that to make *userface.obj*, you have to compile the file *userface.c*. You also indicate that *userface.c* depends on *userface.h*, *stdlib.h*, and *project.h*. The concept of "depends on" simply means that if *userface.h*, *stdlib.h*, or *project.h* changes, *userface.c* needs to be recompiled.

When you build your program, make checks all the dependencies you've described and determines the files that need to be recompiled. If 5 of your 25 source files depend on data definitions in *userface.h* and it changes, make automatically recompiles the 5 files that depend on it. It doesn't recompile the 20 files that don't depend on *userface.h*. Using make beats the alternatives of recompiling all 25 files or recompiling each file manually, forgetting one, and getting weird out-of-synch errors. Overall, make substantially improves the time and reliability of the average compile-link-run cycle.

Backup Plan

A backup plan isn't a dramatic new concept; it's the idea of backing up your work periodically. If you were writing a book by hand, you wouldn't leave the pages in a pile on your porch. If you did, they might get rained on or blown away, or your neighbor's dog might borrow them for a little bedtime reading. You'd put them somewhere safe. Software is less tangible, so it's easier to forget that you have something of enormous value on one machine.

Many things can happen to computerized data. A disk can fail. You or someone else can delete key files accidentally. An angry employee can sabotage your machine. You could lose a machine to theft, flood, or fire.

Take steps to safeguard your work. Your backup plan should include making backups on a periodic basis and periodic transfer of backups to off-site storage, and it should encompass all the important materials on your project— documents, graphics, and notes—in addition to source code.

One often-overlooked aspect of devising a backup plan is a test of your backup procedure. Try doing a restore at some point to make sure that the backup contains everything you need and that the recovery works.

When you finish a project, make a project archive. Save a copy of everything: source code, compilers, tools, requirements, design, documentation—everything you need to re-create the product. Keep it all in a safe place.

CHECKLIST

Configuration Management

GENERAL

❑ Is your software-configuration-management plan designed to help programmers and minimize overhead?

❑ Does your SCM approach avoid overcontrolling the project?

❑ Do you group change requests, either through informal means such as a list of pending changes or through a more formal approach such as a change-control board?

❑ Do you formally estimate the effect of each proposed change?

❑ Do you view major changes as a warning that requirements analysis isn't yet complete?

TOOLS

❑ Do you use version-control software to facilitate configuration management?

❑ Do you use version-control software to reduce coordination problems of working in teams?

❑ Do you use make or other dependency-control software to build programs efficiently and reliably?

BACKUP

❑ Do you back up all project materials periodically?

❑ Are project backups transferred to off-site storage periodically?

❑ Are all materials backed up, including source code, documents, graphics, and important notes?

❑ Have you tested the backup-recovery procedure?

Further Reading

Because this book is about construction, this section has focused on change control from a construction point of view. But changes affect projects at all levels, and a comprehensive change-control strategy needs to do the same.

Bersoff, Edward H., et al. *Software Configuration Management.* Englewood Cliffs, N.J.: Prentice Hall, 1980.

Babich, W. *Software Configuration Management.* Reading, Mass.: Addison-Wesley, 1986. The Bersoff and the Babich books thoroughly cover the SCM topic.

Bersoff, Edward H., and Alan M. Davis. "Impacts of Life Cycle Models on Software Configuration Management." *Communications of the ACM* 34, no. 8 (August 1991): 104–118. This article describes how SCM is affected by newer approaches to software development, especially prototyping approaches.

22.3 Estimating a Construction Schedule

HARD DATA

Managing a software project is one of the formidable challenges of the late twentieth century, and estimating the size of a project and the effort required to complete it is one of the most challenging aspects of software-project management. The average large software project is one year late and 100 percent over budget (Jones 1986a). This has as much to do with poor size and effort estimates as with poor development efforts. This section outlines the issues involved in estimating software projects and indicates where to look for more information.

Estimation Approaches

FURTHER READING
For further reading on schedule-estimation techniques, see *Software Engineering Metrics and Models* (Conte, Dunsmore, and Shen 1986) or *Software Engineering Economics* (Boehm 1981).

You can estimate the size of a project and the effort required to complete it in any of several ways:

- Use scheduling software.

- Use an algorithmic approach, such as COCOMO, Barry Boehm's estimation model (1981).

- Have outside estimation experts estimate the project.

- Have a walkthrough meeting for estimates.

- Estimate pieces of the project, and then add the pieces together.

- Have people estimate their own pieces, and then add the pieces together.

- Estimate the time needed for the whole project, and then divide up the time among the pieces.

- Refer to experience on previous projects.

- Keep previous estimates and see how accurate they were. Use them to adjust new estimates.

Pointers to more information on these approaches are given in the "Further Reading" subsection at the end of this section. Here's a good approach to estimating a project:

FURTHER READING
This approach is adapted from Software Engineering Economics (Boehm 1981).

CROSS-REFERENCE
For more information on software requirements, see Section 3.3, "Requirements Prerequisite."

CROSS REFERENCE
It's hard to find an area of software development in which iteration is not a valuable technique. This is one case in which iteration is useful. For a summary of iterative techniques, see Section 32.7, "Iterate, Repeatedly, Again and Again."

Establish objectives. What are you estimating? Why do you need an estimate? How accurate does the estimate need to be to meet your objectives? What degree of certainty needs to be associated with the estimate? Would an optimistic or a pessimistic estimate produce substantially different results?

Allow time for the estimate, and plan it. Rushed estimates are inaccurate estimates. If you're estimating a large project, treat estimation as a miniproject and take the time to miniplan the estimate so that you can do it well.

Formalize software requirements. Just as an architect can't estimate how much a "pretty big" house will cost, you can't reliably estimate a "pretty big" software project. It's unreasonable for anyone to expect you to be able to estimate the amount of work required to build something when "something" has not yet been defined. Define requirements or plan a preliminary exploration phase before making an estimate.

Estimate at a low level of detail. Depending on the objectives you identified, base the estimate on a detailed examination of project activities. In general, the more detailed your examination is, the more accurate your estimate will be. The Law of Large Numbers says that the error of sums is greater than the sum of errors. In other words, a 10 percent error on one big piece is 10 percent high or 10 percent low. On 50 small pieces, 10 percent errors are both high and low and tend to cancel each other out.

Use several different estimation techniques, and compare the results. The list of estimation approaches at the beginning of the section identified several techniques. They won't all produce the same results, so try several of them. Study the different results from the different approaches.

Children learn early that if they ask each parent individually for a third bowl of ice cream, they have a better chance of getting at least one "yes" than if they ask only one parent. Sometimes the parents wise up and give the same answer; sometimes they don't. See what different answers you can get from different estimation techniques. No approach is best in all circumstances, and the differences among them can be illuminating.

Re-estimate periodically. Factors on a software project change after the initial estimate, so plan to update your estimate periodically. As the project moves closer to completion, you can estimate better and evaluate your initial estimates. Use the results of your evaluation to refine future estimates. The accuracy of your estimates should improve as you move toward completing the project.

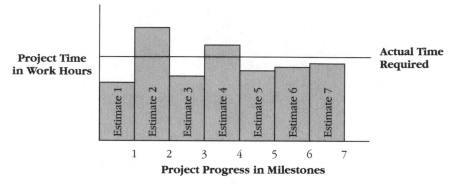

Re-estimate periodically throughout a project. Use what you learn during each activity to improve your estimate for the next activity. As the project progresses, the accuracy of your estimates should improve.

Estimating the Amount of Construction

CROSS-REFERENCE
For details on the amount of coding for projects of various sizes, see "Activity Proportions and Size" in Section 21.2.

The extent to which construction will be a major influence on a project's schedule depends in part on the proportion of the project that will be devoted to construction—understood as detailed design, coding, debugging, and unit testing. As this chart from Chapter 21 shows, the proportion varies by project size.

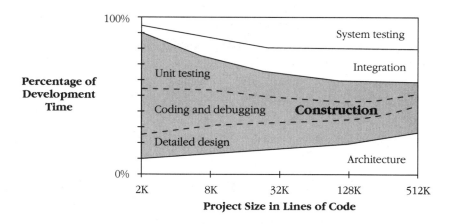

Until your company has project-history data of its own, the proportion of time devoted to each activity shown in the chart is a good place to start estimates for your projects.

The best answer to the question of how much construction a project will call for is that the proportion will vary from project to project and organization to organization. Keep records of your organization's experience on projects and use them to estimate the time future projects will take.

Influences on Schedule

CROSS-REFERENCE
The effect of a program's size on productivity and quality isn't always intuitively apparent. See Chapter 21, "How Program Size Affects Construction," for an explanation of how size affects the construction phase.

The largest influence on a software project's schedule is the size of the program to be produced. But many other factors also influence a software-development schedule. Studies of commercial programs have quantified some of the factors, and they're shown in Table 22-1 on the next pages. To make use of the table, first come up with a base effort estimate for a project of your project's size. Then adjust the effort estimate by multiplying the base estimate by the appropriate factor from each row of the table.

Here are some of the less easily quantified factors that can influence a software-development schedule. These ideas are drawn from Barry Boehm's *Software Engineering Economics* (1981) and C. E. Walston and C. P. Felix's "A Method of Programming Measurement and Estimation" (1977).

- Team motivation
- Management quality
- Amount of code reused
- Personnel turnover
- Language level (high-level language vs. assembler)
- Requirements volatility
- Quality of relationship with customer
- User participation in requirements
- Customer experience with the type of application
- Extent to which programmers participate in requirements analysis
- Classified security environment for computer, programs, and data
- Amount of documentation
- Project objectives (schedule vs. quality vs. usability vs. the many other possible objectives)

Even though these factors aren't easily quantified, they're significant, so consider them along with the quantitative factors shown in Table 22-1.

Table 22-1. Factors That Influence Software-Project Effort

Cost Driver	Ratings						Possible Range of Factor's Influence
	Very low	Low	Nominal	High	Very high	Extra high	
Reliability required (effect of unreliability)	.75 Slight inconvenience	.88 Low, easily recoverable losses	1.00 Moderate, recoverable losses	1.15 High financial loss	1.40 Risk to human life		1.87
Database Size		.94 $\frac{DB\ Bytes}{Lines\ of\ Code} < 10$	1.00 $10 \leq \frac{DB\ Bytes}{Code} < 100$	1.08 $100 \leq \frac{DB\ Bytes}{Code} < 1000$	1.16 $\frac{DB\ Bytes}{Lines\ of\ Code} \geq 1000$		1.23
Product complexity	.70 Very simple contol computations, device-dependent operations, and data management	.85 Simple control, computations, device-dependent operations, and data management	1.00 Average control, computations, device-dependent operations, and data management	1.15 Moderately complex control, computations, device-dependent operations, and datamanagement	1.30 Complex control, computations, device-dependent operations, and data management	1.65 Extremely complex control, computations, device-dependent operations, and data management	2.36
Execution time required			1.00 ≤50% use of available execution time	1.11 ≤70% use of available execution time	1.30 ≤85% use of available execution time	1.66 About 95% use of available execution time	1.66
Main storage constraint			1.00 ≤50% use of available storage	1.06 ≤70% use of available storage	1.21 ≤85% use of available storage	1.56 About 95% use of available storage	1.56
Volatility of underlying hardware and software (operating system)		.87 Major change every 12 months; minor every 1 month	1.00 Major change every 6 months; minor every 2 weeks	1.15 Major change every 2 months; minor every 1 week	1.30 Major change every 2 weeks; minor every 2 days		1.49
Turnaround time on development computer		.87 Interactive	1.00 Average turnaround ≤4 hours	1.07 Average turnaround 4–12 hours	1.15 Average turnaround 12 hours		1.32
Analyst team capability: ability, efficiency, communication, cooperation	1.46 15th percentile	1.19 35th percentile	1.00 55th percentile	.86 75th percentile	.71 90th percentile		2.06

(continued)

Table 22-1. Factors That Influence Software-Project Effort, *continued*

Cost Driver	Ratings						Possible Range of Factor's Influence
	Very low	Low	Nominal	High	Very high	Extra high	
Team's experience in applications area	1.29 ≤4 months	1.13 1 year	1.00 3 years	.91 6 years	.82 12 years		1.57
Programmer team capability: ability, efficiency, communication, cooperation	1.42 15th percentile	1.17 35th percentile	1.00 55th percentile	.86 75th percentile	.70 90th percentile		2.03
Programmers' experience with underlying hardware and software (operating system)	1.21 ≤1 months	1.10 4 months	1.00 1 year	.90 3 years			1.34
Team's programming language experience	1.14 ≤1 months	1.07 4 months	1.00 1 year	.95 3 years			1.20
Use of modern programming practices	1.24 No use	1.10 Beginning use	1.00 Some use	.91 General use	.82 Routine use		1.51
Use of software tools	1.24 Basic micro-processor tools	1.10 Basic mini tools	1.00 Basic mini/maxi tools	.91 Strong maxi programming, test tools	.83 Add requirements, design, management, documentation tools		1.49
Required development schedule	1.23 75% of nominal	1.08 85% of nominal	1.00 100% of nominal	1.04 130% of nominal	1.10 160% of nominal		1.23

Source: *Software Engineering Economics* (Boehm 1981).

Estimation vs. Control

The important question is, do you want prediction, or do you want control?

Tom Gilb

Estimation is an important part of planning to complete a software project on time. Once you have a delivery date and a product specification, the main problem is how to control the expenditure of human and technical resources for an on-time delivery of the product. In that sense, the accuracy of the initial estimate is much less important than your subsequent success at controlling resources to meet the schedule.

What to Do If You're Behind

HARD DATA

Most software projects fall behind. Surveys of estimated vs. actual schedules have shown that estimates tend to have an optimism factor of 20 to 30 percent (van Genuchten 1991).

When you're behind, increasing the amount of time usually isn't an option. If it is, do it. Otherwise, you can try one or more of these solutions:

Hope that you'll catch up. Hopeful optimism is a common response to a project's falling behind schedule. The rationalization typically goes like this: "Requirements took a little longer than we expected, but now they're solid, so we're bound to save time later. We'll make up the shortfall during coding and testing." This is hardly ever the case. One survey of over 300 software projects concluded that delays and overruns generally increase toward the end of a project (van Genuchten 1991). Projects don't make up lost time later; they fall further behind.

HARD DATA

Expand the team. According to Fred Brooks's law, adding people to a late software project makes it later (1975). It's like adding gas to a fire. Brooks's explanation is convincing: New people need time to familiarize themselves with a project before they can become productive. Their training takes up the time of the people who have already been trained. And merely increasing the number of people increases the complexity and amount of project communication. Brooks points out that the fact that one woman can have a baby in nine months does not imply that nine women can have a baby in one month.

Undoubtedly the warning in Brooks's law should be heeded more often than it is. It's tempting to throw people at a project and hope that they'll bring it in on time. Managers need to understand that developing software isn't like riveting sheet metal: More workers working doesn't necessarily mean more work will get done.

The simple statement that adding programmers to a late project makes it later, however, masks the fact that under some circumstances it's possible to add people to a late project and speed it up. As Brooks points out in the analysis of his law, adding people to software projects in which the tasks can't be divided and performed independently doesn't help. But if a project's tasks are partitionable, you can divide them further and assign them to different people, even to people who are added late in the project. Other researchers have formally identified circumstances under which you can add people to a late project without making it later (Abdel-Hamid 1989).

Reduce the scope of the project. The powerful technique of reducing the scope of the project is often overlooked. If you eliminate a feature, you eliminate the design, coding, debugging, testing, and documentation of that feature. You eliminate that feature's interface to other features.

FURTHER READING
For a cogent argument in favor of building only the most-needed features, see Section 11.7, "The Best Way to Combat Diseconomies of Scale," in *Software Engineering Economics* (Boehm 1981).

When you plan the product initially, partition the product's capabilities into "must haves," "nice to haves," and "optionals." If you fall behind, prioritize the "optionals" and "nice to haves" and drop the ones that are the least important.

Short of dropping a feature altogether, you can provide a cheaper version of the same functionality. You might provide a version that's on time but that hasn't been tuned for performance. You might provide a version in which the least important functionality is implemented crudely. You might decide to back off on a speed requirement because it's much easier to provide a slow version. You might back off on a space requirement because it's easier to provide a memory-intensive version.

Re-estimate development time for the least important features. What functionality can you provide in two hours, two days, or two weeks? What do you gain by building the two-week version rather than the two-day version, or the two-day version rather than the two-hour version?

Further Reading

Boehm, Barry W. *Software Engineering Economics.* Englewood Cliffs, N.J.: Prentice Hall, 1981. This book is an exhaustive treatment of software-project estimation. If you want data on the effect on software development of virtually any factor, you'll find it somewhere in this book. You'll probably also find a survey of all the studies done on that factor and a good summary of how the factor should be assimilated into an overall estimate. This is unquestionably the best source of information on the topic of estimating software projects.

Humphrey, Watts S. *Managing the Software Process.* Reading, Mass.: Addison-Wesley, 1989. Section 6.4 looks at how to estimate a software project.

Conte, S. D., H. E. Dunsmore, and V. Y. Shen. *Software Engineering Metrics and Models*. Menlo Park, Calif.: Benjamin/Cummings, 1986. Chapter 6 contains a good survey of estimation techniques including a history of estimation, statistical models, theoretically based models, and composite models. The book also demonstrates the use of each estimation technique on a database of projects and compares the estimates to the projects' actual lengths.

Gilb, Tom. *Principles of Software Engineering Management*. Wokingham, England: Addison-Wesley, 1988. The title of Chapter 16, "Ten Principles for Estimating Software Attributes," is somewhat tongue-in-cheek. Gilb argues against project estimation and in favor of project control. Pointing out that people don't really want to predict accurately but do want to control final results, Gilb lays out 10 principles you can use to steer a project to meet a calendar deadline, a cost goal, or another project objective.

22.4 Metrics

The term "metrics" refers to any measurement related to software development. Lines of code, number of defects, defects per thousand lines of code, defects per module, number of global variables, hours to complete a project—these are all metrics, as are all other measurable aspects of the software-development process. Here are two solid reasons to measure your process:

KEY POINT

Any way of measuring the process is superior to not measuring it at all. The measurement may not be perfectly precise; it may be difficult to make; it may need to be refined over time; but any measurement gives you a handle on your software-development process that you don't have without it (Gilb, in DeMarco and Lister 1985).

If data is to be used in a scientific experiment, it must be quantified. Can you imagine an FDA scientist recommending a ban on a new food product because a group of white rats "just seemed to get sicker" than another group? That's absurd. You'd demand a quantified reason, like "Rats that ate the new food product were sick 3.7 more days per month than rats that didn't." To evaluate software-development methods, you must measure them. Statements like "This new method seems more productive" aren't good enough.

To argue against metrics is to argue that it's better not to know what's really happening on your project. When you measure an aspect of a project, you know something about it that you didn't know before. You can see whether the aspect gets bigger or smaller or stays the same. The measurement gives you a window into at least that aspect of your project. The window might be small and cloudy until you refine your measurements, but it will be better than no window at all. To argue against all metrics because some are inconclusive is to argue against windows because some happen to be cloudy.

You can measure virtually any aspect of the software-development process. Table 22-2 lists some metrics that other practitioners have found to be useful:

Table 22-2. Useful Metrics

Size
Total lines of code written
Total comment lines
Total data declarations
Total blank lines

Productivity
Work-hours spent on the project
Work-hours spent on each routine
Number of times each routine changed
Dollars spent on project
Dollars spent per line of code
Dollars spent per defect

Defect Tracking
Severity of each defect
Location of each defect
Way in which each defect is corrected
Person responsible for each defect
Number of lines affected by each
  defect correction
Work hours spent correcting each
  defect
Average time required to find a defect
Average time required to fix a defect
Number of attempts made to correct
  each defect
Number of new errors resulting from
  defect correction

Overall Quality
Total number of defects
Number of defects in each routine
Average defects per thousand lines of
  code
Mean time between failures
Compiler-detected errors

Maintainability
Number of parameters passed to each
  routine
Number of local variables used by each
  routine
Number of routines called by each
  routine
Number of decision points in each
  routine
Control-flow complexity in each
  routine
Lines of code in each routine
Lines of comments in each routine
Number of data declarations in each
  routine
Number of blank lines in each routine
Number of *gotos* in each routine
Number of input/output statements in
  each routine

You can collect most of these measurements with software tools that are currently available. Discussions throughout the book indicate the reasons that each measurement is useful. At this time, most of the measurements aren't useful for making fine distinctions among programs, modules, and routines (Shepperd and Ince 1989). They're useful mainly for identifying routines that are "outliers"; abnormal metrics in a routine are a warning sign that you should re-examine that routine, checking for unusually low quality.

Don't start by collecting data on all possible metrics—you'll bury yourself in data so complex that you won't be able to figure out what any of it means. Start with a simple set of metrics such as the number of defects, the number of work-months, the total dollars, and the total lines of code. Standardize the measurements across your projects, and then refine them and add to them as your understanding of what you want to measure improves (Pietrasanta 1990).

Make sure you're collecting data for a reason. Set goals; determine the questions you need to ask to meet the goals; and then measure to answer the questions (Basili and Weiss 1984). A review of data collection at NASA's Software Engineering Laboratory concluded that the most important lesson learned in 15 years was that you need to define measurement goals before you measure (Valett and McGarry 1989).

Further Reading

Conte, S. D., H. E. Dunsmore, and V. Y. Shen. *Software Engineering Metrics and Models*. Menlo Park, Calif.: Benjamin/Cummings, 1986. This book catalogs current knowledge of software measurement circa 1986, including commonly used measurements, experimental techniques, and criteria for evaluating experimental results.

Grady, Robert B., and Deborah L. Caswell. *Software Metrics: Establishing a Company-Wide Program*, Englewood Cliffs, N.J.: Prentice Hall, 1987. Grady and Caswell describe their experience in establishing a software-metrics program at Hewlett-Packard and tell you how to establish a software-metrics program in your organization.

Card, David N., with Robert L. Glass. *Measuring Software Design Quality*. Englewood Cliffs, N.J.: Prentice Hall, 1990. Rather than cataloging all possible metrics, Card describes ways in which you can use a small set of design metrics to control a software project from design to completion. This short book (129 pages) contains many helpful diagrams.

Jones, Capers. *Applied Software Measurement*. New York: McGraw-Hill, 1991. Jones is a leader in software metrics, and his book is an accumulation of knowledge in this area. It provides the definitive theory and practice of current measurement techniques and describes problems with traditional metrics. It lays out a full program for collecting "function-point metrics," the metric that will probably replace lines of code as the standard measure of program size. Jones has collected and analyzed a huge amount of quality and productivity data, and this book distills the results in one place—including a fascinating chapter on averages for U.S. software development.

Jones, Capers. *Programming Productivity*. New York: McGraw-Hill, 1986. This earlier book by Jones focuses on metrics based on lines of code. Although it's been outdated by Jones's newer book, it's still a good introduction to the idea that "any measurement is better than no measurement at all."

22.5 Treating Programmers as People

KEY POINT

The abstractness of the programming activity calls for an offsetting naturalness in the office environment and rich contacts among coworkers. Highly technical companies offer parklike corporate campuses, organic organizational structures, comfortable offices, and other "high-touch" environmental features to balance the intense, sometimes arid intellectuality of the work itself. The most successful technical companies combine elements of high-tech and high-touch (Naisbitt 1982). This section describes ways in which programmers are more than organic reflections of their silicon alter egos.

How Do Programmers Spend Their Time?

Programmers spend their time programming, but they also spend time in meetings, on training, on reading their mail, and on just thinking. A 1964 study at Bell Laboratories found that programmers spent their time this way:

Activity	Source Code	Business	Personal	Meetings	Training	Mail/Misc. Documents	Technical Manuals	Operating Procedures, Misc.	Program Test	Totals
Talk or listen	4%	17%	7%	3%				1%		**32%**
Talk with manager		1%								**1%**
Telephone		2%	1%							**3%**
Read	14%					2%	2%			**18%**
Write/record	13%					1%				**14%**
Away or out		4%	1%	4%	6%					**15%**
Walking	2%	2%	1%			1%				**6%**
Miscellaneous	2%	3%	3%			1%		1%	1%	**11%**
Totals	**35%**	**29%**	**13%**	**7%**	**6%**	**5%**	**2%**	**2%**	**1%**	**100%**

Source: "Research Studies of Programmers and Programming" (Bairdain 1964, reported in Boehm 1981).

This data is based on a time-and-motion study of 70 programmers. It's pretty old, and the proportions of time spent in the different activities would vary among programmers, but the results are nonetheless illuminating. About 30 percent of a programmer's time is spent in activities that don't directly help the project: walking, personal business, and so on. Programmers in this study spent 6 percent of their time walking; that's about 2.5 hours a week, about 125 hours a year. That might not seem like much until you realize that programmers spend as much time each year walking as they spend in training, three times as much time as they spend reading technical manuals, and six times as much as they spend talking with their managers.

Variation in Performance and Quality

HARD DATA

Talent and effort among individual programmers vary tremendously, as they do in all fields. One study found that in a variety of professions—writing, football, invention, police work, and aircraft piloting—the top 20 percent of the people produced about 50 percent of the output (Augustine 1979). The results of the study are based on an analysis of productivity data such as touchdowns, patents, solved cases, and so on. Since some people make no tangible contribution whatsoever (football players who make no touchdowns, inventors who own no patents, detectives who don't close cases, and so on), the data probably understates the actual variation in productivity.

In programming specifically, many studies have shown order-of-magnitude differences in the quality of the programs written, the sizes of the programs written, and the productivity of programmers.

Individual variation

HARD DATA

The original study that showed huge variations in individual programming productivity was conducted in the late 1960s by Sackman, Erikson, and Grant (1968). They studied professional programmers with an average of 7 years' experience and found that the ratio of initial coding time between the best and worst programmers was about 20 to 1; the ratio of debugging times over 25 to 1; of program size 5 to 1; and of program execution speed about 10 to 1. They found no relationship between a programmer's amount of experience and code quality or productivity.

HARD DATA

Although specific ratios such as 25 to 1 aren't particularly meaningful, more general statements such as "There are order-of-magnitude differences among programmers" are meaningful and have been confirmed by many other studies of professional programmers (Curtis 1981, Mills 1983, DeMarco and Lister 1985, Curtis et al. 1986, Card 1987, Boehm and Papaccio 1988, Valett and McGarry 1989).

Team variation

Programming teams also exhibit sizable differences in software quality and productivity. Good programmers tend to cluster, as do bad programmers, an observation that has been confirmed by a study of 166 professional programmers from 18 organizations (Demarco and Lister 1985).

HARD DATA

In one study of seven identical projects, the efforts expended varied by a factor of 3.4 to 1 and program sizes by a factor of 3 to 1 (Boehm, Gray, and Seewaldt 1984). In spite of the productivity range, the programmers in this study were not a diverse group. They were all professional programmers with several years of experience who were enrolled in a computer-science graduate program. It's reasonable to assume that a study of a less homogeneous group would turn up even greater differences.

An earlier study of programming teams observed a 5-to-1 difference in program size and a 2.6-to-1 variation in the time required for a team to complete the same project (Weinberg and Schulman 1974).

After reviewing data from programs at TRW, Barry Boehm concluded that developing a program with a team in the 15th percentile of programmers ranked by ability typically requires over four times the number of work-months that developing a program with a team in the 90th percentile does (1981). Boehm and other researchers have found that 80 percent of the contribution comes from 20 percent of the contributors (1987b).

The implication for recruiting and hiring is clear. If you have to pay twice as much to get a top-10-percent programmer rather than a bottom-10-percent programmer, jump at the chance. You'll get an immediate payoff in the quality and productivity of the programmer you hire, and a residual effect in the quality and productivity of the other programmers your organization is able to retain because good programmers tend to cluster.

Religious Issues

Managers of programming projects aren't always aware that certain programming issues are matters of religion. If you try to require compliance with certain programming practices, you're inviting your programmers' ire. Here's a list of religious issues:

- Use of *goto*s
- Programming language
- Indentation style
- Placing of braces or *begin-end* keywords

- Choice of text editor
- Commenting style
- Efficiency vs. readability trade-offs
- Choice of methodology—for example, object-oriented design vs. structured design
- Programming utilities
- Variable naming convention
- Use of global variables
- Metrics, especially productivity measures such as lines of code per day

The common denominator among these topics is that a programmer's position on each is a reflection of personal style. If you think you need to control a programmer in any of these religious areas, consider these points:

Be aware that you're dealing with a sensitive area. Sound out the programmer on each emotional topic before jumping in with both feet.

Use "suggestions" or "guidelines" with respect to the area. Avoid setting rigid "rules" or "standards."

Finesse the issues you can by sidestepping explicit mandates. To finesse indentation style or brace placement, require source code to be run through a pretty-printer formatter before it's declared finished. Let the pretty printer do the formatting. To finesse commenting style, require that all code be reviewed and that unclear code be modified until it's clear.

Have your programmers develop their own standards. As mentioned elsewhere, the details of a specific standard are often less important than the fact that some standard exists. Don't set standards for your programmers, but do insist they standardize in the areas that are important to you.

Which of the religious topics are important enough to warrant going to the mat? Conformity in minor matters of style in any area probably won't produce enough benefit to offset the effects of lower morale. If you find indiscriminate use of *goto*s or global variables, unreadable styles, or other practices that affect whole projects, be prepared to put up with some friction in order to improve code quality. If your programmers are conscientious, this is rarely a problem. The biggest battles tend to be over nuances of coding style, and you can stay out of those with no loss to the project.

Physical Environment

Here's an experiment: Go out to the country. Find a farm. Find a farmer. Ask how much money in equipment the farmer has for each worker. The farmer will look at the barn and see a few tractors, some wagons, a combine for wheat, and a peaviner for peas and will tell you that it's over $100,000 per employee.

Next go to the city. Find a programming shop. Find a programming manager. Ask how much money in equipment the programming manager has for each worker. The programming manager will look at an office and see a desk, a chair, a few books, and a computer and will tell you that it's under $25,000 per employee.

Physical environment makes a big difference in productivity. DeMarco and Lister asked 166 programmers from 35 organizations about the quality of their physical environments. Most employees rated their workplaces as not acceptable. In a subsequent programming competition, the programmers who performed in the top 25 percent had bigger, quieter, more private offices and fewer interruptions from people and phone calls. Here's a summary of the differences in office space between the best and worst performers:

Environmental Factor	Top 25%	Bottom 25%
Dedicated floor space	78 sq. ft.	46 sq. ft.
Acceptably quiet workspace	57% yes	29% yes
Acceptably private workspace	62% yes	19% yes
Ability to silence phone	52% yes	10% yes
Ability to divert calls	76% yes	19% yes
Frequent needless interruptions	38% yes	76% yes
Workspace that makes programmer feel appreciated	57% yes	29% yes

Source: "Programmer Performance and the Effects of the Workplace" (DeMarco and Lister 1985).

HARD DATA

The data shows a strong correlation between productivity and the quality of the workplace. Programmers in the top 25 percent were 2.6 times more productive than programmers in the bottom 25 percent. DeMarco and Lister thought that the better programmers might naturally have better offices because they had been promoted, but further examination revealed that this wasn't the case. Programmers from the same organizations had similar facilities, regardless of differences in their performance.

Large software-intensive organizations have had similar experiences. Xerox, TRW, IBM, and Bell Labs have indicated that they realize significantly improved productivity with a $10,000 to $30,000 capital investment per person, sums that were more than recaptured in improved productivity (Boehm 1987a). With "productivity offices," self-reported estimates ranged from 39 to 47 percent improvement in productivity (Boehm et al. 1984).

In summary, bringing your workplace from a bottom-25-percent to a top-25-percent environment is likely to result in at least a 100 percent improvement in productivity.

Further Reading

Weinberg, Gerald M. *The Psychology of Computer Programming*. New York: Van Nostrand Reinhold, 1971. This is the first book to explicitly identify programmers as human beings, and it's still the best on programming as a human activity. It's crammed with acute observations about the human nature of programmers and its implications.

DeMarco, Tom, and Timothy Lister. *Peopleware: Productive Projects and Teams*. New York: Dorset House, 1987. As the title suggests, this book also deals with the human factor in the programming equation. It's filled with anecdotes about managing people, the office environment, hiring and developing the right people, growing teams, and enjoying work. The authors lean on the anecdotes to support some uncommon viewpoints, and the logic is thin in places, but the people-centered spirit of the book is what's important, and the authors deliver that message without faltering.

McCue, Gerald M. "IBM's Santa Teresa Laboratory—Architectural Design for Program Development," *IBM Systems Journal* 17, no. 1 (1978): 4–25. McCue describes the process that IBM used to create its Santa Teresa office complex. IBM studied programmer needs, created architectural guidelines, and designed the facility with programmers in mind. Programmers participated throughout. The result is that in annual opinion surveys each year, the physical facilities at the Santa Teresa facility are rated the highest in the company.

Carnegie, Dale. *How to Win Friends and Influence People*, Revised Edition. New York: Pocket Books, 1981. When Dale Carnegie wrote the title for the first edition of this book in 1936, he couldn't have realized the connotation it would carry today. It sounds like a book Machiavelli would have displayed on his shelf. The spirit of the book is diametrically opposed to Machiavellian manipulation, however, and one of Carnegie's key points is the importance of developing a genuine interest in other people. Carnegie has a keen insight into everyday relationships and explains how to work with other people by understanding them better. The book is filled with memorable anecdotes, sometimes two or three to a page. Anyone who works with people should read it at some point, and anyone who manages people should read it now.

22.6 Managing Your Manager

In software development, nontechnical managers seem to be the rule rather than the exception. The most common exception to the rule is the manager who has technical experience but is 10 years behind the times. Technically competent, technically current managers are rare. If you work for one, do whatever you can to keep your job. It's an unusual treat.

In a Hierarchy Every Employee Tends to Rise to His Level of Incompetence.

The Peter Principle

If you don't have an unusual manager, you're faced with the unenviable task of managing your manager. "Managing your manager" means that you need to tell your manager what to do rather than the other way around. The trick is to do it in a way that allows your manager to continue believing that you are the one being managed. Here are some approaches to dealing with your manager:

- Refuse to do what your manager tells you, and insist on doing your job the right way.

- Pretend to do what your manager wants you to do, and secretly do it the right way.

- Plant ideas for what you want to do, and then wait for your manager to have a brainstorm (your idea) about doing what you want to do.

- Educate your manager about the right way to do things. This is an ongoing job because managers are often promoted, transferred, or fired.

- Find another job.

The best long-term solution is to try to educate your manager. That's not always an easy task, but one way you can prepare for it is by reading Dale Carnegie's *How to Win Friends and Influence People*.

Further Reading

Here are a few books that cover issues of general concern in managing software projects.

Humphrey, Watts S. *Managing the Software Process*. Reading, Mass.: Addison-Wesley, 1989. This book is a thorough, responsible discussion of software-project–management issues. Humphrey takes the middle of the software-engineering road throughout the book, making this a collection of generally accepted software-management techniques.

Gilb, Tom. *Principles of Software Engineering Management*. Wokingham, England: Addison-Wesley, 1988. Gilb doesn't walk the party line as straight as Humphrey does, which is both a weakness and a strength. It's a weakness because if you read Gilb's book first, you won't necessarily know all the standard lingo that a well-read software manager knows. It's a strength because Gilb is incredibly pragmatic and you'll probably avoid learning a lot of lingo that isn't very useful anyway. The titles of the book's three parts summarize its contents well: "Why Do It?"; "How to Do It"; and "Advanced Insights and Practical Experiences."

DeMarco, Tom. *Controlling Software Projects*. New York: Yourdon Press, 1982. DeMarco's book is a good alternative to Humphrey's or Gilb's. It's organized as a workbook and covers the essential bases pragmatically.

Brooks, Frederick P., Jr. *The Mythical Man-Month*. Reading, Mass.: Addison-Wesley, 1975. This book is a hodgepodge of metaphors and folklore related to managing programming projects. It's entertaining, and it will give you many illuminating insights into your own projects. It's based on Brooks's failures in developing the OS/360 operating system, which gives me some reservations. It's full of advice along the lines of "We did this and it failed" and "We should have done this because it would have worked." Brooks's observations about techniques that failed are well grounded, but his claims that other techniques would have worked are too speculative. Read the book critically to separate the observations from the speculations. This warning doesn't diminish the book's basic value. It's still cited in computing literature more often than any other book, and even though it was written in 1975, it seems fresh today. It's hard to read it without saying "Right on!" every couple of pages.

Thayer, Richard H., ed. *Tutorial: Software Engineering Project Management*. Los Alamitos, Calif.: IEEE Computer Society Press, 1990. This collection of about 45 papers on the topic of managing software projects contains some of the best discussions available on software engineering; project management; and planning, organizing, staffing, directing, and controlling a software project. Thayer provides an introduction to each topic and comments briefly on each paper.

Key Points

- Configuration management, when properly applied, makes programmers' work easier.
- You can find ways to measure any aspect of a project that are better than not measuring it at all. Accurate measurement is a key to accurate scheduling, to quality control, and to improving your development process.
- Programmers and managers are people, and they work best when treated with care.
- Accurately estimating a software project is one of the most challenging aspects of managing software development. Try several alternative approaches, and then study the differences in the resulting estimates to gain insight into your project.

23

The Software-Quality Landscape

Contents

Related Topics

THIS CHAPTER SURVEYS SOFTWARE-QUALITY techniques. The whole book is about improving software quality, of course, but this chapter focuses on quality and quality assurance per se. It focuses more on big-picture issues than it does on hands-on techniques. If you're looking for practical advice about reviews, testing, and debugging, move on to the next three chapters.

23.1 Characteristics of Software Quality

FURTHER READING
For a classic discussion of quality attributes, see *Characteristics of Software Quality* (Boehm et al. 1978).

Software has both external and internal quality characteristics. External characteristics are characteristics that a user of the software product is aware of, including

- Correctness. The degree to which a system is free from faults in its specification, design, and implementation.

- Usability. The ease with which users can learn and use a system.

557

- Efficiency. Minimal use of system resources, including memory and execution time.

- Reliability. The ability of a system to perform its required functions under stated conditions whenever required—having a long mean time between failures.

- Integrity. The degree to which a system prevents unauthorized or improper access to its programs and its data. The idea of integrity includes restricting unauthorized user accesses as well as ensuring that data is accessed properly—that is, that tables with parallel data are modified in parallel, that date fields contain only valid dates, and so on.

- Adaptability. The extent to which a system can be used, without modification, in applications or environments other than those for which it was specifically designed.

- Accuracy. The degree to which a system, as built, is free from error, especially with respect to quantitative outputs. Accuracy differs from correctness; it is a determination of how well a system does the job it's built for rather than whether it was built correctly.

- Robustness. The degree to which a system continues to function in the presence of invalid inputs or stressful environmental conditions.

Some of these characteristics overlap, but all have different shades of meaning that are applicable more in some cases, less in others.

External characteristics of quality are the only kind of software characteristics that users care about. Users care about whether the software is easy to use, not about whether it's easy for you to modify. They care about whether the software works correctly, not about whether the code is readable or well structured.

Programmers care about the internal characteristics of the software as well as the external ones. This book is code-centered, so it focuses on the internal quality characteristics. They include

- Maintainability. The ease with which you can modify a software system to change or add capabilities, improve performance, or correct defects.

- Flexibility. The extent to which you can modify a system for uses or environments other than those for which it was specifically designed.

- Portability. The ease with which you can modify a system to operate in an environment different from that for which it was specifically designed.

- Reusability. The extent to which and the ease with which you can use parts of a system in other systems.

- Readability. The ease with which you can read and understand the source code of a system, especially at the detailed-statement level.

- Testability. The degree to which you can unit-test and system-test a system; the degree to which you can verify that the system meets its requirements.

- Understandability. The ease with which you can comprehend a system at both the system-organizational and detailed-statement levels. Understandability has to do with the coherence of the system at a more general level than readability does.

As in the list of external quality characteristics, some of these internal characteristics overlap, but they too each have different shades of meaning that are valuable.

The internal aspects of system quality are the main subject of this book and aren't discussed further in this chapter.

The difference between internal and external characteristics isn't completely clear-cut because at some level internal characteristics affect external ones. Software that isn't internally understandable or maintainable impairs your ability to correct defects, which in turn affects the external characteristics of correctness and reliability. Software that isn't flexible can't be enhanced in response to user requests, which in turn affects the external characteristic of usability. The point is that some quality characteristics are emphasized to make life easier for the user and some are emphasized to make life easier for the programmer. Try to know which is which.

The attempt to maximize certain characteristics invariably conflicts with the attempt to maximize others. Finding an optimal solution from a set of competing objectives is one activity that makes software development a true engineering discipline. Figure 23-1 on the next page shows the way in which focusing on some external quality characteristics affects others. The same kinds of relationships can be found among the internal characteristics of software quality.

The most interesting aspect of this chart is that focusing on a specific characteristic doesn't always mean a trade-off with another characteristic. Sometimes one hurts another, sometimes one helps another, and sometimes one neither hurts nor helps another. For example, correctness is the characteristic of functioning exactly to specification. Robustness is the ability to continue functioning even under unanticipated conditions. Focusing on correctness hurts robustness and vice versa. In contrast, focusing on adaptability helps robustness and vice versa.

The chart shows only typical relationships among the quality characteristics. On any given project, two characteristics might have a relationship that's different from their typical relationship. It's useful to think about your specific quality goals and whether each pair of goals is mutually beneficial or antagonistic.

How focusing on the factor below affects the factor to the right	Correctness	Usability	Efficiency	Reliability	Integrity	Adaptability	Accuracy	Robustness
Correctness	↑		↑	↑			↑	↓
Usability		↑				↑	↑	
Efficiency	↓		↑	↓	↓	↓	↓	↓
Reliability	↑	↑		↑	↑		↑	↓
Integrity			↓	↑	↑			
Adaptability						↓	↑		↑
Accuracy	↑		↓	↑		↓	↑	↓
Robustness	↓	↑	↓	↓	↓	↑	↓	↑

Helps ↑

Hurts ↓

Figure 23-1. *Focusing on one external characteristic of software quality can affect other characteristics positively, adversely, or not at all.*

23.2 Techniques for Improving Software Quality

Software quality assurance is a planned and systematic program of activities designed to ensure that a system has the desired characteristics. Although it might seem that the best way to develop a high-quality product would be to focus on the product itself, in software quality assurance the best place to focus is on the process. Here are some of the elements of a software-quality program:

Software-quality objectives. One powerful technique for improving software quality is setting explicit quality objectives from among the external and internal characteristics described in the last section. Without explicit goals, programmers can work to maximize characteristics different from the ones you expect them to maximize. The power of setting explicit goals is discussed in more detail later in this section.

Explicit quality-assurance activity. One common problem in assuring quality is that quality is perceived as a secondary goal. Indeed, in some organizations, quick and dirty programming is the rule rather than the exception. Programmers like Gary Goto, who litter their code with defects and "complete" their programs quickly, are rewarded more than programmers like High-Quality Henry, who write excellent programs and make sure that they are usable before releasing them. In such organizations, it shouldn't be surprising that programmers don't make quality their first priority. The organization must show programmers that quality is a priority. Making the quality-assurance activity independent makes the priority clear, and programmers will respond accordingly.

Testing strategy. Execution testing can provide a detailed assessment of a product's reliability. Developers on many projects rely on testing as the primary method of both quality assessment and quality improvement. The rest of this chapter demonstrates in more detail that this is too heavy a burden for testing to bear by itself. Testing does have a role in the construction of high-quality software, however, and part of quality assurance is developing a test strategy in conjunction with the product requirements, the architecture, and the design.

CROSS-REFERENCE
For details on testing, see Chapter 25, "Unit Testing."

Software-engineering guidelines. These are guidelines that control the technical character of the software as it's developed. Such guidelines apply to all phases of development including problem definition, requirements analysis, architecture, construction, and system testing. The guidelines in this book are, in one sense, a set of software-engineering guidelines for construction (detailed design, coding, unit testing, and integration).

CROSS-REFERENCE
For a discussion of one class of software-engineering guidelines appropriate for construction, see Section 3.6, "Programming Conventions."

Informal technical reviews. Many software developers review their work before turning it over for formal review. Informal reviews include desk-checking the design or the code or walking through the code with a few peers.

Formal technical reviews. One part of managing a software-engineering process is catching problems at the "lowest-value" stage—that is, at the stage in which problems cost the least to correct. To achieve such a goal, developers on most software-engineering projects use "quality gates," periodic tests that determine whether the quality of the product at one stage is sufficient to justify moving on to the next. Quality gates are usually used between requirements analysis and architecture, architecture and detailed design, detailed design and coding, and coding and testing. The "gate" can be a peer review, a customer review, an inspection, a walkthrough, or an audit.

CROSS-REFERENCE
Reviews and inspections are discussed in Chapter 24, "Reviews."

External audits. An external audit is a specific kind of technical review used to determine the status of a project or the quality of a product being developed. An audit team is brought in from outside the organization and reports its findings to whoever commissioned the audit, usually management.

Development process. Each of the elements mentioned so far has something to do explicitly with assuring software quality and implicitly with the process of software development. Development efforts that include quality-assurance activities produce better software than those that do not. Other processes that aren't explicitly quality-assurance activities also affect software quality.

FURTHER READING
For a discussion of software development as a process, see Watts Humphrey's book *Managing the Software Process* (1989).

An example of a development process that is not explicitly a quality-assurance activity but that still affects quality is the use of effective risk management. If risks are handled in a predictable, reliable way, the software will be predictable and reliable. If risks are handled on an ad hoc basis, the software will be poorly organized and chaotic, reflecting the structure of the organization that built it.

CROSS-REFERENCE
For details on change control, see Section 22.2, "Configuration Management."

Change-control procedures. One big obstacle to achieving software quality is uncontrolled changes. Uncontrolled changes in requirements can result in disruption to design and coding. Uncontrolled changes in architecture or design can result in code that doesn't agree with its design, inconsistencies in the code, or the use of more time in modifying code to meet the changing design than in moving the project forward. Uncontrolled changes in the code itself can result in internal inconsistencies and uncertainties about which code has been fully reviewed and tested and which hasn't. Uncontrolled changes in documentation--as an expression of requirements, architecture, design, or code--can have all of these effects. Consequently, handling changes effectively is a key to effective product development.

Measurement of results. Unless results of a quality-assurance plan are measured, you'll have no way of knowing whether the plan is working. Measurement tells you whether your plan is a success or a failure and also allows you to vary your process in a controlled way to see whether it can be improved.

> **What gets measured, gets done.**
> *Tom Peters*

Measurement has a second, motivational, effect. People pay attention to whatever is measured, assuming that it's used to evaluate them. Choose what you measure carefully. People tend to focus on work that's measured and to ignore work that isn't.

HARD DATA

Prototyping. Prototyping is the development of realistic models of a system's key functions. A developer can prototype parts of a user interface to determine usability, critical calculations to determine execution time, or typical data sets to determine memory requirements. A survey of 16 published and 8 unpublished case studies compared prototyping to traditional, specification-development methods. The comparison revealed that prototyping can lead to better designs, better matches with user needs, and improved maintainability (Gordon and Bieman 1991).

Setting Objectives

Explicitly setting quality objectives is a simple, obvious step in achieving quality software, but it's easy to overlook. You might wonder whether, if you set explicit quality objectives, programmers will actually work to achieve them? The answer is, yes, they will, if they know what the objectives are and the objectives are reasonable. Programmers can't respond to a set of objectives that change daily or that are impossible to meet.

Gerald Weinberg and Edward Schulman conducted a fascinating experiment to investigate the effect on programmer performance of setting quality objectives (1974). They had five teams of programmers work on five versions of the same program. The same five quality objectives were given to each of the five teams, and each team was told to maximize a different objective. One team was told to minimize the memory required, another was told to produce the clearest possible output, another was told to build the most readable code, another was told to use the minimum number of statements, and the last group was told to complete the program in the least amount of time possible. Here are the results:

	Team Ranking on Each Objective				
Objective Team Was Told to Optimize	**Minimum memory**	**Output readability**	**Program readability**	**Minimum statements**	**Minimum programming time**
Minimum memory	**1**	4	4	2	5
Output readability	5	**1**	1	5	3
Program readability	3	2	**2**	3	4
Minimum statements	2	5	3	**1**	3
Minimum programming time	4	3	5	4	**1**

Source: "Goals and Performance in Computer Programming" (Weinberg and Schulman 1974)

HARD DATA

The results of this study were remarkable. Four of the five teams finished first in the objective they were told to optimize. The other team finished second in its objective. None of the teams did consistently well in all objectives.

The surprising implication is that people actually do what you ask them to do. Programmers have high achievement motivation: They will work to the objectives specified, but they must be told what the objectives are. The second implication is that, as expected, objectives conflict and it's generally not possible to do well on all of them.

23.3 Relative Effectiveness of the Techniques

The various quality-assurance practices don't all have the same effectiveness. Many techniques have been studied, and their effectiveness at detecting and removing defects is known. This and several other aspects of the "effectiveness" of the quality-assurance practices are discussed in this section.

Percentage of Defects Detected

> If builders built buildings the way programmers wrote programs, then the first woodpecker that came along would destroy civilization.
>
> *Gerald Weinberg*

Some practices are better at detecting defects than others, and different methods find different kinds of defects. One way to evaluate defect-detection methods is to determine the percentage of defects they find out of the total defects found over the life of a product. Table 23-1 on the next page, taken from Capers Jones's *Programming Productivity,* shows the percentages of defects detected by each of 10 common defect-detection techniques.

Table 23-1. Defect-Detection Rates

Removal Step	Lowest Rate	Modal Rate	Highest Rate
Personal checking of design documents	15%	35%	70%
Informal group design reviews	30%	40%	60%
Formal design inspections	35%	55%	75%
Formal code inspections	30%	60%	70%
Modeling or prototyping	35%	65%	80%
Personal desk-checking of code	20%	40%	60%
Unit testing (single routines)	10%	25%	50%
Function testing (related routines)	20%	35%	55%
Integration testing (complete system)	25%	45%	60%
Field testing (live data)	35%	50%	65%
Cumulative effect of complete series	**93%**	**99%**	**99%**

Source: *Programming Productivity* (Jones 1986a).

HARD DATA

The most interesting fact that this data reveals is that the modal rates don't rise above 65 percent for any single technique. Moreover, for the most common kind of defect detection, unit testing, the modal rate is only 25 percent.

The strong implication is that if project developers are striving for a higher defect-detection rate, they need to use a combination of techniques. A study by Glenford Myers confirmed this implication (Myers 1978b). Myers studied a group of programmers with a minimum of 7 and an average of 11 years of professional experience. Using a program with 15 known errors, he had each programmer look for errors using one of these techniques:

- Execution testing against the specification
- Execution testing against the specification with the source code
- Walkthrough/inspection using the specification and the source code

HARD DATA

Myers found a huge variation in the number of defects detected in the program, ranging from 1.0 to 9.0 defects found. The average number found was 5.1, or about a third of those known.

When used individually, no method had a statistically significant advantage over any of the others. The variety of errors people found was so great, however, that any combination of two methods (including having two independent groups using the same method) increased the total number of defects found by a factor of almost 2. A study at NASA's Software Engineering Laboratory also reported that different people tend to find different defects. Only 29 percent of the errors found by code reading were found by both of two code readers (Kouchakdjian, Green, and Basili 1989).

Glenford Myers points out that human processes (inspections and walkthroughs, for instance) tend to be better than computer-based testing at finding certain kinds of errors and that the opposite is true for other kinds of errors (1979). This result was confirmed in a later study, which found that code reading detected more interface defects and functional testing detected more control defects (Basili, Selby, and Hutchens 1986).

KEY POINT

The upshot is that defect-detection methods work better in pairs than they do singly. Jones made the same point when he observed that cumulative defect-detection efficiency is significantly higher than that of any individual technique. The outlook for the effectiveness of testing used by itself is bleak. Jones points out that a combination of unit testing, functional testing, and system testing often results in a cumulative defect detection of less than 60 percent, which is usually inadequate for commercial software.

Cost of Finding Defects

Some defect-detection practices cost more than others. The most economical practices result in the least cost per defect found, all other things being equal. The qualification that all other things must be equal is important because per-defect cost is influenced by the total number of defects found, the stage at which each defect is found, and other factors besides the economics of a specific defect-detection technique.

In the 1978 Myers study cited earlier, the difference in cost per defect between the two execution-testing methods (with and without source code) wasn't statistically significant, but the walkthrough/inspection method cost over twice as much per defect found as the test methods (Myers 1978). Unfortunately, that result isn't conclusive because the subjects in the test lacked experience in inspections.

HARD DATA

Organizations tend to become more effective at doing inspections as they gain experience. Consequently, more recent studies have shown conclusively that inspections are cheaper than testing. One study of three releases of a system showed that on the first release, inspections found only 15 percent of the errors found with all techniques. On the second release, inspections found 41 percent, and on the third, 61 percent (Humphrey 1989). If this history were applied to Myers's study, it might turn out that inspections would eventually cost half as much per defect as testing instead of twice as much. A study at the

Software Engineering Laboratory found that code reading detected about 80 percent more faults per hour than testing (Basili and Selby 1987).

Cost of Fixing Defects

CROSS-REFERENCE
For details on the fact that defects become more expensive the longer they stay in a system, see "Appeal to data" in Section 3.1. For an up-close look at errors themselves, see Section 25.4, "Typical Errors."

The cost of finding defects is only one part of the cost equation. The other is the cost of fixing defects. It might seem at first glance that how the defect is found wouldn't matter—it would always cost the same amount to fix.

That isn't true because the longer a defect remains in the system, the more expensive it becomes to remove. A detection technique that finds the error earlier therefore results in a lower cost of fixing it. Even more important, some techniques, such as inspections, find and fix defects in one step; others, such as testing, find defects but require additional work to diagnose and fix the problems. The result is that one-step techniques are substantially cheaper overall than two-step ones. Microsoft's applications division has found that it takes 3 hours to find and fix a defect using code inspection, a one-step technique, and 12 hours to find and fix a defect using testing, a two-step technique (Moore 1992). Collofello and Woodfield reported on a 700,000-line program built by over 400 developers (1989). They found that code reviews were several times as cost-effective as testing—1.38 return on investment vs. 0.17.

HARD DATA

The bottom line is that an effective software-quality program must include a combination of techniques that apply to all stages of development. Here's a recommended combination:

- Formal design inspections of the critical parts of a system
- Modeling or prototyping using a rapid prototyping technique
- Code reading or inspections
- Execution testing

23.4 When to Do Quality Assurance

CROSS-REFERENCE
Quality assurance of upstream activities—analysis and architecture, for instance—is outside the scope of this book. The "Further Reading" section at the end of the chapter describes books you can turn to for more information about them.

As Chapter 3 noted, the earlier an error is inserted into software, the more embedded it becomes in other parts of the software and the more expensive it becomes to remove. A fault in analysis can produce one or more corresponding faults in design, which can produce many corresponding faults in code. An analysis error can result in extra architecture or in bad architectural decisions. The extra architecture results in extra code, test cases, and documentation. Just as it's a good idea to work out the defects in the blueprints for a house before pouring the foundation in concrete, it's a good idea to catch analysis and architecture errors before they affect later activities.

In addition, errors made during requirements analysis or architecture tend to be more sweeping than errors made during construction. A single architectural error can affect several modules and dozens of routines, whereas a single construction error is unlikely to affect more than one routine or module. For this reason, too, it's cost-effective to catch errors as early as you can.

KEY POINT

Defects creep into software at all stages. Consequently, you should emphasize quality-assurance work in the early stages and throughout the rest of the project. It should be planned into the project as work begins; it should be part of the technical fiber of the project as work continues; and it should punctuate the end of the project, verifying the quality of the product as work ends.

23.5 The General Principle of Software Quality

KEY POINT

There's no such thing as a free lunch, and even if there were, there's no guarantee that it would be any good. Software development is a far cry from *haute cuisine*, however, and software quality is unusual in a significant way. The General Principle of Software Quality is that improving quality reduces development costs.

Understanding this principle depends on understanding a key observation: The best way to improve productivity and quality is to reduce the time spent reworking code, whether the rework is from changes in requirements, changes in design, or debugging. The industry-average productivity for a software product is about 8 to 20 of lines of code per person per day. It takes only a matter of minutes to type in 8 to 20 lines of code, so how is the rest of the day spent?

CROSS-REFERENCE
For details on the difference between writing an individual program and writing a software product, see "Programs, Products, Systems, and System Products" in Section 21.2.

A software product takes much longer to develop than a simple program and involves a lot more than merely typing in the code. But that's not what usually fills the rest of the day.

The rest of the day is usually spent debugging. Debugging takes about 50 percent of the time spent in a traditional, naive software-development cycle. Getting rid of debugging by preventing errors improves productivity. Therefore, the most obvious method of shortening a development schedule is to improve the quality of the product and decrease the amount of time spent debugging and reworking the software.

HARD DATA

This analysis is confirmed by field data. In a review of 50 development projects involving over 400 work-years of effort and almost 3 million lines of code, a study at NASA's Software Engineering Laboratory found that increased quality assurance was associated with decreased error rate but no increase or decrease in overall development cost (Card 1987).

A study at IBM had produced similar findings:

> Projects that aim from the beginning at achieving the shortest possible schedules regardless of quality considerations, tend to have fairly high frequencies of both schedule and cost overruns. Software projects that aim initially at achieving the highest possible levels of quality and reliability tend to have the best schedule adherence records, the highest productivity, and even the best marketplace success. (Jones 1986a)

HARD DATA

The same effect holds true on a smaller scale. In a 1985 study, 166 professional programmers wrote programs from the same specification. The resulting programs averaged 220 lines of code and a little under five hours to write. The fascinating result was that programmers who took the median time to complete their programs produced programs with the greatest number of errors. The programmers who took more or less than the median time produced programs with significantly fewer errors (DeMarco and Lister 1985). Figure 23-2 graphs the results:

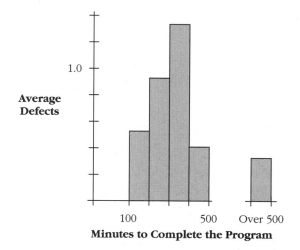

Figure 23-2. *Neither the fastest nor the slowest development approach produces the software with the most defects.*

The two slowest groups took about five times as long to achieve roughly the same defect rate as the fastest group. It's not necessarily the case that writing software without defects takes more time than writing software with defects. As the graph shows, it can take less.

Admittedly, on certain kinds of projects, quality assurance costs money. If you're writing code for the space shuttle or for a medical life-support system, the degree of reliability required makes the project more expensive.

Compared to the traditional code-test-debug cycle, however, an enlightened software-quality program saves money. It redistributes resources away from debugging and into upstream quality-assurance activities. Upstream activities have more leverage on product quality than downstream activities, so the time you invest upstream saves more time downstream. The net effect is fewer defects, shorter development time, and lower costs. You'll see several more examples of the General Principle of Software Quality in the next two chapters.

CHECKLIST

A Quality-Assurance Program

❑ Have you identified specific quality characteristics that are important to your project?

❑ Have you made others aware of the project's quality objectives?

❑ Have you differentiated between external and internal quality characteristics?

❑ Have you thought about the ways in which some characteristics may compete with or complement others?

❑ Does your project call for the use of several different error-detection techniques suited to finding several different kinds of errors?

❑ Does your project include a plan to take steps to assure software quality during each stage of software development?

❑ Is the quality measured in some way so that you can tell whether it's improving or degrading?

❑ Does management understand that quality assurance incurs additional costs up front in order to save costs later?

Further Reading

It's not hard to list books in this section because virtually any book on effective software methodologies describes techniques that result in improved quality and productivity. The difficulty is finding books that deal with software quality per se. Here are a few:

Chow, Tsun S., ed. *Tutorial: Software Quality Assurance: A Practical Approach.* Silver Spring, Md.: IEEE Computer Society Press, 1985. These 45 or so papers cluster around the idea of software quality. Sections focus on software-quality definitions, measurements, and applications; on the managerial issues of planning, organization, standards, and conventions; on the technical issues of requirements, design, coding, and testing; and on the implementation of a software-quality-assurance program. The book contains many of the classic papers on this subject, and its breadth makes it especially valuable.

IEEE Std 730.1-1989: IEEE Standard for Software Quality Assurance Plans. IEEE Software Engineering Standards Collection, Spring 1991. New York: Institute of Electrical and Electronics Engineers.

IEEE Std 983-1986: IEEE Guide for Software Quality Assurance Planning. IEEE Software Engineering Standards Collection, Spring 1991. New York: Institute of Electrical and Electronics Engineers. These two IEEE standards provide the IEEE guidelines for creating software-quality-assurance plans.

Glass, Robert L. *Building Quality Software.* Englewood Cliffs, N.J.: Prentice Hall, 1992. This book examines quality considerations during all phases of software development including requirements, design, implementation, checkout, maintenance, and management. It describes and evaluates a wide variety of quality-assurance methods and offers numerous capsule descriptions of other books and articles about software quality.

Schulmeyer, G. Gordon. *Zero Defect Software.* New York: McGraw-Hill, 1990. This book is a thorough and up-to-date treatment of all aspects of software quality assurance. It contains a little too much religion for my tastes—it focuses on only one methodology—but it is nonetheless a good reference.

Schulmeyer, G. Gordon, ed. *Handbook of Software Quality Assurance.* New York: Van Nostrand Reinhold, 1987. This book is a collection of 17 essays written by leaders in the software-quality-assurance field. Some of the discussions are more abstract than practical, but like the Chow tutorial, it's a good survey of various software-quality-assurance issues. The essays are more focused on software quality assurance and more up-to-date than those in the Chow tutorial.

Myers, Glenford J. *Software Reliability.* New York: John Wiley, 1976. This book takes a code-focused approach to software quality that's heavy on testing as a means of quality assurance. Part 4, "Additional Topics in Software Reliability," is the gem of the book. Among other things, it describes several techniques you can use to answer the age-old question "Based on the errors we've found, how many can we estimate are left in the program?"

Key Points

- Not all quality-assurance goals are simultaneously achievable. Explicitly decide which goals you want to achieve, and communicate the goals to other people on your team.

- No single defect-detection technique is effective by itself. Testing by itself is particularly ineffective at removing errors. Successful quality-assurance programs use several different techniques to detect different kinds of errors.

- You can apply effective techniques during construction and many equally powerful techniques before construction. The earlier you find a defect, the less damage it will cause.

- Quality assurance in the software arena is process-oriented. Software development doesn't have a repetitive manufacturing phase that affects the final product, so the process used for product development controls the quality of the result.

- Quality is free, in the end, but it requires a reallocation of resources so that defects are prevented cheaply instead of fixed expensively.

24

Reviews

Contents

Related Topics

YOU MIGHT HAVE HAD AN EXPERIENCE common to many programmers. You prepared carefully for a demonstration to a client and were sure that you'd eliminated all the errors from your program. During the demonstration, the client suggested an odd combination of inputs, pushed the keys in the wrong order, or ran the program 10 times in a row. Suddenly bugs appeared out of nowhere. In one way or another, all reviews are attempts to formalize the process of showing your work to someone before the client sees it. If you've read about inspections and walkthroughs before, you won't find much new information in this chapter. The hard data about the effectiveness of inspections in Section 24.1 might surprise you, and you might not have considered the code-reading alternative described in Section 24.3. But if your knowledge is all from your own experience, read on! Other people have had different experiences, and you'll find some new ideas.

24.1 Role of Reviews in Software Quality Assurance

All technical reviews, despite their differences, are based on the idea that developers are blind to some of the trouble spots in their work, that other people don't have the same blind spots, and that it's beneficial to have someone else look at their work.

The mere act of explaining a problem is often enough to show you where the problem is. It's commonly reported that a programmer will walk into another programmer's cubicle and say, "Would you mind looking at this? I'm having some trouble." Then the programmer will start to explain the problem, get three minutes into it, and figure it out before the "helper" has said a word.

Some people use the word "review" in a specific, technical sense. In this chapter, "review" is a catchall term for inspections, walkthroughs, code readings, and other practices in which someone else looks at your work.

Reviews Complement Other Quality-Assurance Techniques

KEY POINT

The primary purpose of technical reviews is to improve software quality. As noted in Chapter 23, software testing alone has limited effectiveness—the average defect-detection rate is only 25 percent for unit testing, 35 percent for function testing, and 45 percent for integration testing. In contrast, the average effectivenesses of design and code inspections are 55 and 60 percent (Jones 1986a). The auxiliary benefit of reviews is that they decrease development time, which in turn lowers development costs. Case studies of review results have been impressive:

HARD DATA

- In a software-maintenance organization, 55 percent of one-line maintenance changes were in error before code reviews were introduced. After reviews were introduced, only 2 percent of the changes were in error (Freedman and Weinberg 1982). When all changes were considered, 95 percent were correct the first time after reviews were introduced. Before reviews were introduced, under 20 percent were correct the first time.

- In a group of 11 programs developed by the same group of people, the first 5 were developed without reviews. The remaining 6 were developed with reviews. After all the programs were released to production, the first 5 had an average of 4.5 errors per 100 lines of code. The 6 that had been inspected had an average of only 0.82 errors per 100. Reviews cut the errors by over 80 percent (Freedman and Weinberg 1982).

- The Aetna Insurance Company found 82 percent of the errors in a program by using inspections and was able to decrease its development resources by 25 percent (Fagan 1976).

- IBM's 500,000-line Orbit project used 11 levels of inspections. It was delivered early and had only about 1 percent of the errors that would normally be expected (Gilb 1988).

- A study of an organization at AT&T with more than 200 people reported a 14 percent increase in productivity and a 90 percent decrease in defects after the organization introduced reviews (Fowler 1986).

- Jet Propulsion Laboratories estimates that it saves about $25,000 per inspection by finding and fixing defects at an early stage (Bush and Kelly 1989).

These results dramatically illustrate the General Principle of Software Quality, which holds that reducing the number of defects in the software also improves development time.

KEY POINT

Various studies have shown that in addition to being more effective at catching errors than testing, reviews find different kinds of errors than testing does (Myers 1978; Basili, Selby, and Hutchens 1986). A secondary effect is that when people know their work will be reviewed, they scrutinize it more carefully. Thus, even when testing is done effectively, reviews are needed for a comprehensive quality program.

Reviews Disseminate Corporate Culture and Programming Experience

Informal review procedures were passed on from person to person in the general culture of computing for many years before they were acknowledged in print. The need for reviewing was so obvious to the best programmers that they rarely mentioned it in print, while the worst programmers believed they were so good that their *work did not need reviewing.*

Daniel Freedman and Gerald Weinberg

Software standards can be written down and distributed, but if no one talks about them or encourages others to use them, they won't be followed. Reviews are an important mechanism for giving programmers feedback about their code. The code, the standards, and the reasons for making the code meet the standards are good topics for review discussions.

In addition to feedback about how well they follow standards, programmers need feedback about more subjective aspects of programming—formatting, comments, variable names, local and global variable use, design approaches, the-way-we-do-things-around-here, and so on. Programmers who are still wet behind the ears need guidance from those who are more knowledgeable. More knowledgeable programmers tend to be busy and need to be encouraged to spend time sharing what they know. Reviews create a venue for more experienced and less experienced programmers to communicate about technical issues. As such, reviews are an opportunity for cultivating quality improvements in the future as much as in the present.

Reviews Assess Quality and Progress

Reviews generally come in two kinds: managerial and technical. Managerial reviews assess progress and recommend corrective action. They focus on issues of cost and schedule. Managerial reviews are important, but they are the subject of other books, not this one.

Technical reviews can also be used for assessing progress, but it is the technical progress that is assessed. That usually means answering two questions: (1) Is the technical work being done? and (2) Is the technical work being done *well?* The answers to both questions are by-products of technical reviews.

Reviews Apply As Much Before Construction As After

This book is about construction, so reviews of detailed design and code are the focus of this chapter. However, most of the comments about reviews in this chapter apply to management, planning, requirements-analysis, architectural, and maintenance reviews as well. By reading between the lines and studying the references at the end of the chapter, you can apply reviews to any stage of software development.

24.2 Inspections

FURTHER READING
If you want to read the original article on inspections, see "Design and Code Inspections to Reduce Errors in Program Development" (Fagan 1976).

An inspection is a specific kind of review that has been shown to be extremely effective in detecting defects and to be relatively economical compared to testing. Inspections were developed by Michael Fagan and used at IBM for several years before Fagan published the paper that made them public. Although any review involves reading designs or code, an inspection differs from a run-of-the-mill review in several key ways:

- Checklists focus the reviewers' attention on areas that have been problems in the past.
- The emphasis is on defect detection, not correction.
- Reviewers prepare for the inspection meeting beforehand and arrive with a list of the problems they've discovered.
- Distinct roles are assigned to all participants.
- The moderator of the inspection isn't the author of the work product under inspection.
- The moderator has received specific training in moderating inspections.
- Data is collected at each inspection and is fed into future inspections to improve them.
- General management doesn't attend the inspection meeting. Technical leaders might.

What Results Can You Expect from Inspections?

HARD DATA

The general experience with inspections has been that the combination of design and code inspections usually removes 60 percent or more of the defects in a product (Fagan 1976). Inspections identify error-prone routines early, and Fagan reports that they result in about 30 percent fewer defects per 1000 lines of code than walkthroughs do. Designers and coders learn to improve their work through participating in inspections, and inspections increase productivity by about 20 percent. On a project that uses inspections for design and code, the inspections will take up about 15 percent of project cost.

Roles During an Inspection

One key characteristic of an inspection is that each person involved has a distinct role to play. Here are the roles:

FURTHER READING
The Advanced Learning Technologies project has developed a highly interactive, high-fidelity simulator for training in inspections. For details, see "Intelligent Interactive Video Simulation of a Code Inspection" (Stevens 1989).

Moderator. The moderator is responsible for keeping the inspection moving at a rate that's fast enough to be productive but slow enough to find the most errors possible. The moderator must be technically competent—not necessarily an expert in the particular design or code under inspection, but capable of understanding relevant details. This person manages other aspects of the inspection, such as distributing the design or code to be reviewed and the inspection checklist, setting up a meeting room, reporting inspection results, and following up on the action items assigned at the inspection meeting.

Author. The person who wrote the design or code plays a relatively minor role in the inspection. Part of the goal of an inspection is to be sure that the design or code speaks for itself. If the design or code under inspection turns out to be unclear, the author will be assigned the job of making it clearer. Otherwise, the author's duties are to explain parts of the design or code that are unclear and, occasionally, to explain why things that seem like errors are actually acceptable. If the project is unfamiliar to the reviewers, the author might present an overview of the project in preparation for the inspection meeting.

Reviewer. A reviewer is anyone who has a direct interest in the design or code but who is not the author. A reviewer of a design might be the programmer who will implement the design. A tester or higher-level architect might also be involved. The role of the reviewers is to find defects. They usually find defects during preparation, and, as the design or code is discussed at the inspection meeting, the group should find considerably more defects.

Scribe. The scribe records errors that are detected and the assignments of action items during the inspection meeting. Sometimes the scribe's role is performed by the moderator and sometimes by another person. Neither the author nor a reviewer should be the scribe.

Management. No way. The point of a software inspection is that it is a purely technical review. Management's presence changes the technical interactions; people feel that they, instead of the review materials, are under evaluation, which changes the focus from technical to political. Management has a right to know the results of an inspection, and an inspection report is prepared to keep management informed.

Similarly, under no circumstances should inspection results be used for performance appraisals. Don't kill the goose that lays the golden eggs. Code examined in an inspection is still under development. Evaluation of performance should be based on final products, not on work that isn't finished.

Overall, an inspection should have no fewer than three participants. It's not possible to have a separate moderator, author, and reviewer with fewer than three people, and those roles shouldn't be combined. Traditional advice is to limit an inspection to about six people because with any more, the group becomes too large to manage. Experience at Jet Propulsion Laboratories has indicated that having more than three inspectors doesn't appear to improve the number of defects found (Bush and Kelly 1989).

General Procedure for an Inspection

An inspection consists of several distinct stages:

Planning. The author gives the design or code to the moderator. The moderator decides who will review the material and when and where the inspection meeting will occur, and then distributes the design or code and a checklist that focuses the attention of the inspectors.

Overview. When the reviewers aren't familiar with the project they are reviewing, the author can spend up to an hour or so describing the technical environment within which the design or code has been created. Having an overview tends to be a dangerous practice because it can lead to a glossing over of unclear points in the design or code under inspection. The design or code should speak for itself; the overview shouldn't speak for it.

Preparation. Each reviewer works alone for about 90 minutes to become familiar with the design or code. The reviewers use the checklist to stimulate and direct their examination of the review materials.

For a review of application code written in a high-level language, reviewers can prepare at about 700 lines of code per hour. For a review of system code written in a high-level language, reviewers can prepare at only about 125 lines of code per hour (Humphrey 1989). The most effective rate of review varies a great deal, so keep records of preparation rates in your organization to determine the rate that's most effective in your environment.

Inspection meeting. The moderator chooses someone—usually the author—to paraphrase the design or read the code. All logic is explained, including each branch of each logical structure. During this presentation, the scribe records errors as they are detected, but discussion of an error stops as soon as it's recognized as an error. The scribe notes the type and the severity of the error, and the inspection moves on.

The rate at which the design or the code is considered should be neither too slow nor too fast. If it's too slow, attention can lag and the meeting won't be productive. If it's too fast, the group can overlook errors it would otherwise catch. Optimal inspection rates vary from environment to environment, as preparation rates do. Keep records so that over time you can determine the optimal rate for your environment. Other organizations have found that for system code, an inspection rate of 90 lines of code per hour is optimal. For applications code, the inspection rate can be as rapid as 500 lines of code per hour (Humphrey 1989).

Don't discuss solutions during the meeting. The group should stay focused on identifying defects. Some inspection groups don't even allow discussion about whether a defect is really a defect. They assume that if someone is confused enough to think it's a defect, the design, code, or documentation needs to be clarified.

The meeting generally should not last more than two hours. This doesn't mean that you have to fake a fire alarm to get everyone out at the two-hour mark, but experience at IBM and other companies has been that reviewers can't concentrate for much more than about two hours at a time. For the same reason, it's unwise to schedule more than one inspection on the same day.

Inspection report. Within a day of the inspection meeting, the moderator produces an inspection report that lists each defect, including its type and severity. The inspection report helps to ensure that all defects will be corrected and is used to develop a checklist that emphasizes problems specific to the organization. If you collect data on the time spent and the number of errors found over time, you can respond to challenges about inspection's efficacy with hard data. Otherwise, you'll be limited to saying that inspections seem better. That won't be as convincing to someone who thinks testing seems better. You'll also be able to tell if inspections aren't working in your environment and modify or abandon them, as appropriate. Data collection is also important because any new methodology needs to justify its existence.

Rework. The moderator assigns defects to someone, usually the author, for repair. The assignee resolves each defect on the list.

Follow-up. The moderator is responsible for seeing that all rework assigned during the inspection is carried out. If more than 5 percent of the design or code needs to be reworked, the whole inspection process should be repeated. If less, the moderator may still call for a re-inspection or choose to verify the rework personally.

Third-hour meeting. Even though during the inspection participants aren't allowed to discuss solutions to the problems raised, some might still want to. You can hold an informal, third-hour meeting to allow interested parties to discuss solutions after the official inspection is over.

Fine-tuning the inspection. Once you become skilled at performing inspections "by the book," you can usually find several ways to improve them. Don't introduce changes willy-nilly, though. "Instrument" the inspection process so that you know whether your changes are beneficial.

All the parts of the inspection process are necessary. Companies have found that removing or combining any of the parts costs more than is saved (Fagan 1986). If you're tempted to change the inspection process without measuring the effect of the change, don't. If you have measured the process and you know that your changed process works better than the one described here, go right ahead.

As you do inspections, you'll notice that certain kinds of errors occur more frequently than other kinds. Create a checklist that calls attention to those kinds of errors so that reviewers will focus on them. Over time, you'll find kinds of errors that aren't on the checklist; add those to it. You might find that some errors on the initial checklist cease to occur; remove those. After a few inspections, your organization will have a checklist for inspections customized to its needs and will also have a good idea of trouble areas in which its programmers need more training or support. Limit your checklist to one page or less. Longer ones are hard to use at the level of detail needed in an inspection.

Egos in Inspections

FURTHER READING
For a discussion of egoless programming, see *The Psychology of Computer Programming* (Weinberg 1971).

The point of the inspection itself is to discover defects in the design or code. It is not to explore alternatives or to debate about who is right and who is wrong. The point is most certainly not to criticize the author of the design or code. The experience should be a positive one for the author in which it's obvious that group participation improves the program and is a learning experience for all involved. It should not convince the author that some people in the group are jerks or that it's time to look for a new job. Comments like "Anyone who knows Pascal knows that it's more efficient to loop from *Num* to *0*" are totally inappropriate, and if they occur, the moderator should make their inappropriateness unmistakably clear.

Because the design or code is being criticized and the author probably feels somewhat attached to it, the author will naturally feel some of the heat directed at the code. The author should anticipate hearing criticisms of several defects that aren't really defects and several more that seem debatable. In spite of that, the author should acknowledge each alleged defect and move on. Acknowledging a criticism doesn't imply that the author agrees it's true. The author should not try to defend the work under review. After the review, the author can think about each point in private and decide whether it's valid.

Reviewers must remember that the author has the ultimate responsibility for deciding what to do about a defect. It's fine to enjoy finding defects (and outside the review, to enjoy proposing solutions), but each reviewer must respect the author's ultimate right to decide how to resolve an error.

CHECKLIST

Effective Inspections

❑ Do you have checklists that focus reviewer attention on areas that have been problems in the past?

❑ Is the emphasis on defect detection rather than correction?

❑ Are inspectors given enough time to prepare before the inspection meeting, and is each one prepared?

❑ Does each participant have a distinct role to play?

❑ Does the meeting move at a productive rate?

❑ Is the meeting limited to two hours?

❑ Has the moderator received specific training in conducting inspections?

❑ Is data about error types collected at each inspection so that you can tailor future checklists to your organization?

❑ Is data about preparation and inspection rates collected so that you can optimize future preparation and inspections?

❑ Are the action items assigned at each inspection followed up, either personally by the moderator or with a re-inspection?

❑ Does management understand why it should not attend inspection meetings?

Inspection Summary

Inspection checklists encourage focused concentration. The inspection process is systematic because of its standard checklists and standard roles. It is also self-optimizing because it uses a formal feedback loop to improve the checklists and to monitor preparation and inspection rates. With this control over the process and continuing optimization, inspection quickly becomes a powerful technique almost no matter how it begins.

FURTHER READING
For more details on the SEI's concept of developmental maturity, see *Managing the Software Process* (Humphrey 1989).

The Software Engineering Institute (SEI) has defined an Organizational Maturity Scale that measures the effectiveness of an organization's software-development process. The inspection process demonstrates what the highest level is like. The process is systematic and repeatable and uses measured feedback to improve itself. You can apply the same ideas to virtually any technique described in this book. When generalized to an entire development organization, these ideas are, in a nutshell, what it takes to move the organization to the highest possible level of quality and productivity.

24.3 Other Kinds of Reviews

Other kinds of reviews haven't accumulated the body of empirical support that inspections have, so they're covered in less depth here. The kinds covered in this section include walkthroughs, code reading, and dog-and-pony shows.

Walkthroughs

A walkthrough is a popular kind of review. The term is loosely defined, and at least some of its popularity can be attributed to the fact that people can call virtually any kind of review a "walkthrough."

Because the term is so loosely defined, it's hard to say exactly what a walkthrough is. Certainly, a walkthrough involves two or more people discussing a design or code. It might be as informal as an impromptu bull session around a whiteboard; it might be as formal as a scheduled meeting with overhead transparencies prepared by the art department and a formal summary sent to management. In one sense, "where two or three are gathered together," there is a walkthrough. Proponents of walkthroughs like the looseness of such a definition, so I'll just point out a few things that all walkthroughs have in common and leave the rest of the details to you:

KEY POINT

- The walkthrough is usually hosted and moderated by the author of the design or code under review.
- The purpose of the walkthrough is to improve the technical quality of a program rather than to assess it. It's a working meeting.
- All participants prepare for the walkthrough by reading the design or code and looking for errors.
- The walkthrough is a chance for senior programmers to pass on experience and corporate culture to junior programmers. It's also a chance for junior programmers to present new methodologies and to challenge timeworn, possibly obsolete, assumptions.

- A walkthrough usually lasts 30 to 60 minutes.
- The emphasis is on error detection, not correction.
- Management doesn't attend.
- The walkthrough concept is flexible and can be adapted to the specific needs of the organization using it.

What results can you expect from a walkthrough?

Used intelligently, a walkthrough can produce results similar to those of an inspection—that is, it can typically find between 30 and 70 percent of the errors in a program (Myers 1979, Boehm 1987b, Yourdon 1989b). Walkthroughs have been shown to be marginally less effective than inspections, but in some circumstances, they can be preferable.

HARD DATA

Used unintelligently, walkthroughs are more trouble than they're worth. The low end of their effectiveness, 30 percent, isn't worth much, and at least one organization (Boeing Computer Services) found peer reviews of code to be "extremely expensive." Boeing found it was difficult to motivate project personnel to apply walkthrough techniques consistently, and when project pressures increased, walkthroughs became nearly impossible (Glass 1982).

Comparison of inspections and walkthroughs

What are the differences between inspections and walkthroughs? Here's a summary:

Properties	Inspection	Walkthrough
Formal moderator training	Yes	No
Distinct participant roles	Yes	No
Who "drives" the inspection or walkthrough	Moderator	Author, usually
"How to Find Errors" checklists	Yes	No
Focused review effort—looks for the most frequently found kinds of errors	Yes	No
Formal follow-up to reduce bad fixes	Yes	No
Fewer future errors because of detailed error feedback to individual programmers	Yes	Incidental
Improved inspection efficiency from analysis of results	Yes	No
Analysis of data leading to detection of problems in the process, which in turn leads to improvements in the process	Yes	No

Source: "Design and Code Inspections to Reduce Errors in Program Development" (Fagan 1976).

Inspections seem to be more effective than walkthroughs at removing errors. So why would anyone choose to use walkthroughs?

If you have a large review group, a walkthrough is a good review choice because it brings many diverse viewpoints to bear on the item under review. If everyone involved in the walkthrough can be convinced that the solution is all right, it probably doesn't have any major flaws.

If reviewers from other organizations are involved, a walkthrough might also be preferable. Roles in an inspection are more formalized and require some practice before people perform them effectively. Reviewers who haven't participated in inspections before are at a disadvantage. If you want to solicit their contributions, a walkthrough might be the best choice.

KEY POINT

Inspections are more focused than walkthroughs and generally pay off better. Consequently, if you're choosing a review standard for your organization, think hard about choosing inspections.

Code Reading

Code reading is an alternative to inspections and walkthroughs. In code reading, you read source code and look for errors. You also comment on qualitative aspects of the code such as its design, style, readability, maintainability, and efficiency.

HARD DATA

A study at NASA's Software Engineering Laboratory found that code reading detected about 3.3 defects per hour of effort. Testing detected about 1.8 errors per hour (Card 1987). Code reading also found 20 to 60 percent more errors over the life of the project than the various kinds of testing did.

Like the idea of a walkthrough, the concept of code reading is loosely defined. A code reading usually involves two or more people reading code independently and then meeting with the author of the code to discuss it. Here's how code reading goes:

- In preparation for the meeting, the author of the code hands out source listings to the code readers. The listings are from 1000 to 10,000 lines of code; 4000 lines is typical.

- Two or more people read the code. Use at least two people to encourage competition between the reviewers. If you use more than two, measure everyone's contribution so that you know how much the extra people contribute.

- Reviewers read the code independently. Estimate a rate of about 1000 lines a day.

- When the reviewers have finished reading the code, the code-reading meeting is hosted by the author of the code. The meeting lasts one or two hours and focuses on problems discovered by the code readers. No one makes any attempt to walk through the code line by line. The meeting is not even strictly necessary.

- The author of the code fixes the problems identified by the reviewers.

KEY POINT

The difference between code reading on the one hand and inspections and walkthroughs on the other is that code reading focuses more on individual review of the code than on the meeting. The result is that each reviewer's time is focused on finding problems in the code. Less time is spent in meetings in which each person contributes only part of the time and in which a substantial amount of the effort goes into moderating group dynamics. Less time is spent delaying meetings until each person in the group can meet for two hours. Code readings are especially valuable in situations in which reviewers are geographically dispersed.

HARD DATA

A study of 13 reviews at AT&T found that the importance of the review meeting itself was overrated; 90 percent of the defects were found in preparation for the review meeting, and only about 10 percent were found during the review itself (Votta 1991).

Dog-and-Pony Shows

Dog-and-pony shows are reviews in which a software product is demonstrated to a customer. Customer reviews are common in software developed for government contracts, which often stipulate that reviews will be held for requirements, design, and code. The purpose of a dog-and-pony show is to demonstrate to the customer that the project is OK, so it's a management review rather than a technical review.

Don't rely on dog-and-pony shows to improve the technical quality of your products. Preparing for them might have an indirect effect on technical quality, but usually more time is spent in making good-looking viewfoils than in improving the quality of the software. Rely on inspections, walkthroughs, or code reading for technical quality improvements.

Further Reading

Inspections

The Software Engineering Institute provides video training tapes on software inspections. For details, contact The Software Engineering Institute, Carnegie-Mellon University, Pittsburgh, PA 15213, 412-268-5800. Alternatively, you can contact the clearing house for SEI technical materials: Research Access, 3400 Forbes Avenue, Suite 302, Pittsburgh, PA 15213, 800-685-6510, fax 412-682-6530. Here are other sources of information on inspections:

Fagan, Michael E. "Design and Code Inspections to Reduce Errors in Program Development." *IBM Systems Journal* 15, no. 3 (1976): 182–211.

Fagan, Michael E. "Advances in Software Inspections." *IEEE Transactions on Software Engineering,* SE-12, no. 7 (July 1986): 744–51. These two articles were written by the developer of inspections. They contain the meat of what you need to know to run an inspection, including all the standard inspection forms.

Humphrey, Watts S. *Managing the Software Process.* Reading, Mass.: Addison-Wesley, 1989. In Chapter 10 and Appendix C of this book, Humphrey describes inspections in detail. The book includes many detailed inspection checklists and inspection report forms.

Gilb, Tom. *Principles of Software Engineering Management.* Wokingham, England: Addison-Wesley, 1988. In Chapter 12 of this book, Gilb describes the general practice of inspections, including a lot of practical detail. Chapter 21 provides a detailed case study of the use of inspections on a real project.

Walkthroughs

Yourdon, Edward. *Structured Walk-Throughs,* 4th ed. New York: Yourdon Press, 1989. This book explains all the ins and outs of walkthroughs, including the many variations resulting from the looseness of the concept. It's thorough, easy to read, and relatively short (192 pages). Unfortunately, the book itself could have used a walkthrough to avert its many minor imperfections. My copy came with eight pages of corrections, and the page numbers in the table of contents and index are often wrong by one, two, or three pages.

Reviews in general

Freedman, Daniel P., and Gerald M. Weinberg. *Handbook of Walkthroughs, Inspections and Technical Reviews,* 3d ed. New York: Dorset House, 1990. This is an excellent sourcebook on reviews of all kinds, including inspections and walkthroughs. Its question-and-answer format makes the information easy to read. Weinberg is the original proponent of "egoless programming," the idea upon which most review techniques are based, which gives the book substantial credibility. Its advice is practical, and it includes many useful checklists, reports on the success of reviews in other companies, and entertaining anecdotes.

IEEE Std 1028-1988: IEEE Standard for Software Reviews and Audits, in IEEE 1991. *IEEE Software Engineering Standards Collection,* Spring 1991 ed. New York: Institute of Electrical and Electronics Engineers. Section 6 of the standard discusses inspections (briefly), and Section 7 discusses walkthroughs (also briefly). The document provides a good, albeit bone-dry, overview of reviews and audits.

Hollocker, Charles P. *Software Reviews and Audits Handbook.* New York: John Wiley, 1990. Hollocker was the chairman of the IEEE committee that published *Std 1028-1988,* mentioned above. His book is a thorough treatment of reviews and audits, including 60 pages of review checklists, 10 pages of audit and inspection forms, and about 40 pages of sample review and audit documentation.

Key Points

- Overall, reviews are usually better at finding defects than testing is.
- Reviews focus on error detection rather than error correction.
- Reviews tend to find different kinds of errors than testing does, implying that you need to use both reviews and testing to ensure the quality of your software.
- Inspections use checklists, preparation, well-defined roles, and continual process improvement to maximize error-detection efficiency. They tend to find more defects than walkthroughs.
- Walkthroughs and code reading are alternatives to inspections. Code reading offers the advantage of using each person's time effectively.

25

Unit Testing

Contents

Related Topics

TESTING IS THE MOST POPULAR quality-improvement activity—a practice supported by a wealth of industrial and academic research and by commercial experience. In this chapter, the word "testing" refers to unit testing by the developer—the testing of individual routines and possibly modules but not whole systems. "Testing" in this chapter refers to "glass-box" testing, the kind of testing you as a developer use to test your own code—as opposed to functional testing, in which an independent tester uses a functional specification as a basis for checking out a program.

If a system is small enough, you can adapt the techniques in this chapter to testing the entire system. If the system is larger, it will probably be tested by an independent testing organization, and the main testing that you'll do is the unit testing of each routine before it's integrated into the overall system.

Some programmers use the terms "testing" and "debugging" interchangeably, but careful programmers distinguish between the two activities. Testing is a means of detecting errors. Debugging is a means of diagnosing and correcting their root causes. This chapter deals exclusively with error detection. Error correction is discussed in detail in Chapter 26, "Debugging."

25.1 Role of Unit Testing in Software Quality

CROSS-REFERENCE
For details on reviews, see
Chapter 24, "Reviews."

Testing is an important part of any software-quality program, and in many cases it's the only part. This is unfortunate, because reviews in their various forms have been shown to find a higher percentage of errors than testing does, and reviews cost only about half as much per error found as testing does (Card 1987). Individual testing steps (unit test, functional test, component test, and system test) typically find less than 50 percent of the errors present each. The combination of testing steps often finds less than 60 percent of the errors present (Jones 1986a). Nevertheless, because testing is an entrenched practice in many organizations and because testing is capable of finding different kinds of errors than reviews do, it should be a part of the software development cycle.

Programs do not acquire bugs as people acquire germs, by hanging around other buggy programs. Programmers must insert them.

Harlan Mills

If you were to list a set of software-development activities on "Sesame Street" and ask, "Which of these things is not like the others?", the answer would be "Testing." Testing is a hard activity for most developers to swallow for several reasons:

- Testing's goal runs counter to the goals of other development activities. The goal is to find errors. A successful test is one that breaks the software. The goal of every other development activity is to prevent errors and keep the software from breaking.

- Testing can never prove the absence of errors—only their presence. If you have tested extensively and found thousands of errors, does it mean that you've found all the errors or that you have thousands more to find? An absence of errors could mean ineffective or incomplete test cases as easily as it could mean perfect software.

- Testing by itself does not improve software quality. Test results are an indicator of quality, but in and of themselves, they don't improve it. Trying to improve software quality by increasing the amount of testing is like trying to lose weight by weighing yourself more often. What you eat before you step onto the scale determines how much you will weigh, and the software-development techniques you use determine how many errors testing will find. If you want to lose weight, don't buy a new scale; change your diet. If you want to improve your software, don't test more; develop better.

HARD DATA

- Testing requires you to assume that you'll find errors in your code. If you assume you won't, you probably won't, but only because you'll have set up a self-fulfilling prophecy. If you execute the program hoping that it won't have any errors, it will be too easy to overlook the errors you find. Glenford Myers had a group of experienced programmers test a program with 15 known defects. The average programmer found only 5 of the 15 errors. The best found only 9. The main source of undetected errors was that erroneous output was not examined carefully enough. The errors were visible but the programmers didn't notice them (Myers 1978).

  You must hope to find errors in your code. Such a hope might seem like an unnatural act, but you should hope that it's you who finds the errors and not someone else.

A key question is, How much time should be spent in unit testing on a typical project? A commonly cited figure for all testing is 50 percent of the time spent on the project (Myers 1979), but that's misleading for several reasons. First, that particular figure combines testing and debugging; testing alone takes less time. Second, that figure represents the amount of time that's typically spent rather than the time that should be spent. Third, the figure includes system testing as well as unit testing.

As Figure 25-1 shows, depending on the project's size and complexity, unit testing should probably take 8 to 35 percent of the total project time. This is consistent with much of the data that has been reported.

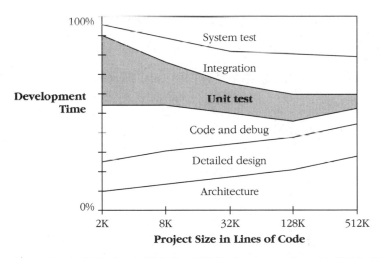

Sources: Brooks 1975; Albrecht 1979; Glass 1982; Boehm, Gray, and Seewaldt 1984; Boddie 1987; and Card 1987.

Figure 25-1. *As the size of the project increases, unit testing consumes a smaller percentage of the total development time.*

A second question is, What do you do with the results of unit testing? Most immediately, you can use the results to assess the reliability of the product under development. Even if you never correct the defects that testing finds, testing describes how reliable the software is. Another use for the results is that they can and usually do guide corrections to the software. Finally, over time, the record of defects found through testing helps reveal the kinds of errors that are most common. You can use this information to select appropriate training classes, direct future technical review activities, and design future test cases.

Testing During Construction

KEY POINT

As the introduction to this chapter noted, the whole topic of testing is much larger than the subject of testing during construction. This book doesn't address the big, wide world of testing: System testing, functional testing, black-box testing, and so on are discussed only in the "Further Reading" section at the end of the chapter.

The big, wide world of testing sometimes ignores the subject of this chapter: "glass-box," or "white-box," testing. You generally want to design a routine to be a black box—a user of the routine won't have to look past the interface to know what the routine does. In testing the routine, however, it's advantageous to treat it as a glass box, to look at the internal source code of the routine as well as its inputs and outputs. If you know what's inside the box, you can test the routine more thoroughly, or at least with a better chance of detecting errors. Compared to someone who's a stranger to the code, you're in a stronger position to find its problems.

CROSS-REFERENCE
Top-down, bottom-up, incremental, and partitioned builds used to be thought of as alternative approaches to testing, but they are really techniques for integrating a program. These alternatives are discussed in Chapter 27, "System Integration."

During construction you generally write a routine, check it mentally, and then review it or test it. Regardless of your integration or system-testing strategy, you should test each unit thoroughly before you combine it with any others. If you're writing several routines, you should test them one at a time. Routines aren't really any easier to test individually, but they're much easier to debug. If you throw several untested routines together at once and find an error, any of the several routines might be guilty. If you add one routine at a time to a collection of previously tested routines, you know that any new errors are the result of the new routine or of interactions with the new routine. The debugging job is easier.

25.2 General Approach to Unit Testing

A systematic approach to unit testing maximizes your ability to detect errors of all kinds with a minimum of effort. Be sure to cover this ground:

- Test for each relevant requirement to make sure that the requirements have been implemented. Plan the test cases for this step at the requirements stage or as early as possible—preferably before you begin writing the unit to be tested. Consider testing for common omissions in requirements. The level of security, storage, the installation procedure, and system reliability are all fair game for testing and are often overlooked at requirements time.

- Test for each relevant design concern to make sure that the design has been implemented. Plan the test cases for this step at the design stage or as early as possible—before you begin the detailed coding of the routine to be tested.

- Use basis testing to add detailed test cases to those that test the requirements and the design. Add data-flow tests, and then add the remaining test cases needed to thoroughly exercise the code. At a minimum, you should test every line of code. Basis testing and data-flow testing are described in the next section.

Build the test cases along with the product. This can help avoid errors in requirements and design, which tend to be more expensive than coding errors. Plan to test and find defects as early as possible because it's cheaper to fix defects early.

25.3 Bag of Testing Tricks

Why isn't it possible to prove that a program is correct by testing it? To use testing to prove that a program works, you'd have to test every conceivable input value to the program and every conceivable combination of input values. Even for simple programs, such an undertaking would become massively prohibitive. Suppose, for example, that you have a program that takes a name, an address, and a phone number and stores them in a file. This is certainly a simple program, much simpler than any whose correctness you'd really be worried about. Suppose further that each of the possible names and addresses is 20 characters long and that there are 26 possible characters to be used in them. This would be the number of possible inputs:

Name	26^{20} (20 characters, each with 26 possible choices)
Address	26^{20} (20 characters, each with 26 possible choices)
Phone Number	10^{10} (10 digits, each with 10 possible choices)
Total Possibilities	$= 26^{20} * 26^{20} * 10^{10} \approx 10^{66}$

Even with this relatively small amount of input, you have one-with-66-zeros possible test cases. To put this in perspective: If Noah had gotten off the ark and started testing this program at the rate of a trillion test cases per second, he would be far less than 1 percent of the way done today. Obviously, if you added a more realistic amount of data, the task of exhaustively testing all possibilities would become even more impossible.

Incomplete Testing

CROSS-REFERENCE
One way of telling whether you've covered all the code is to use a coverage monitor. For details, see "Coverage Monitors" in Section 25.5, later in this chapter.

Since exhaustive testing is impossible, practically speaking, the art of testing is that of picking the test cases most likely to find errors. Of the 10^{66} possible test cases, only a few are likely to disclose errors that the others don't. You need to concentrate on picking a few that tell you different things rather than a set that tells you the same thing over and over.

When you're planning tests, eliminate those that don't tell you anything new—that is, tests on new data that probably won't produce an error if other, similar data didn't produce an error. Various people have proposed various methods of covering the bases efficiently, and several of these methods are discussed next.

Structured Basis Testing

In spite of the hairy name, structured basis testing is a fairly simple concept. The idea is that you need to test each statement in a program at least once. If the statement is a logical statement, say an *if* or a *while*, you need to vary the testing according to how complicated the expression inside the *if* or *while* is to make sure that the statement is fully tested. The easiest way to make sure that you've gotten all the bases covered is to calculate the number of paths through the program and then develop the minimum number of test cases that will exercise every path through the program.

You might have heard of "code coverage" testing or "logic coverage" testing. They are approaches in which you test all the paths through a program. Since they cover all paths, they're similar to structured basis testing, but they don't include the idea of covering all paths with a *minimal* set of test cases. If you use code coverage or logic coverage testing, you might create many more test cases than you would need to cover the same logic with structured basis testing.

You can compute the minimum number of cases needed for basis testing in the straightforward way outlined in Table 25-1.

Table 25-1. Determining the Number of Test Cases Needed for Structured Basis Testing

CROSS-REFERENCE
This procedure is similar
to the one for measuring
complexity in Section 17.7.

1. Start with 1 for the straight path through the routine.
2. Add 1 for each of the following keywords, or their equivalents: *if, while, repeat, for, and,* and *or.*
3. Add 1 for each case in a *case* statement. If the *case* statement doesn't have a default case, add 1 more.

Here's an example:

Count "1" for the routine itself. —

Count "2" for the if. —

Simple Example of Computing the Number of Paths Through a Pascal Program

```
Statement1;
Statement2;
if X < 10 then
    begin
    Statement3;
    end;
Statement4;
```

In this instance, you start with one and count the *if* once to make a total of two. That means that you need to have at least two test cases to cover all the paths through the program. In this example, you'd need to have the following test cases:

- Statements controlled by *if* are executed (*X < 10*).
- Statements controlled by *if* aren't executed (*X >= 10*).

The sample code needs to be a little more realistic to give you an accurate idea of how this kind of testing works. Realism in this case includes code containing defects.

The listing below is a slightly more complicated example. This piece of code is used throughout the chapter and contains a few possible errors.

Example of Computing the Number of Cases Needed for Basis Testing of a Pascal Program

Count "1" for the routine itself.

Count "2" for the for.

Count "3" for the if.

Count "4" for the if and "5" for the and.

Count "6" for the if.

```
1 { Compute Net Pay }
2
3 TtlWithholdings := 0;
4
5 for ID := 1 to NumEmployees
6    begin
7
8      { compute social security withholding, if below the maximum }
9      if ( Employee[ ID ].SSWithheld < MAX_SOCIAL_SECURITY ) then
10        begin
11        SocialSecurity := ComputeSocialSecurity( Employee[ ID ] )
12        end;
13
14     { set default to no retirement contribution }
15     Retirement := 0;
16
17     { determine discretionary employee retirement contribution }
18     if ( Employee[ ID ].WantsRetirement ) and
19        ( EligibleForRetirement( Employee [ ID ] ) ) then
20        begin
21        Retirement := GetRetirement( Employee[ ID ] )
22        end;
23
24     GrossPay := ComputeGrossPay( Employee[ ID ] );
25
26     { determine IRA contribution }
27     IRA := 0;
28     if ( EligibleForIRA( Employee[ ID ] ) ) then
29        begin
30        IRA := IRAContribution( Employee[ ID ], Retirement, GrossPay )
31        end;
32
33     { make weekly paycheck }
34     Withholding := ComputeWithholding( Employee[ ID ] );
35     NetPay      := GrossPay - Withholding - Retirement -
36                      SocialSecurity - IRA;
37     PayEmployee( Employee[ ID ], NetPay );
38
39     { add this employee's paycheck to total for accounting }
40     TtlWithholdings   := TtlWithholdings + Withholding;
41     TtlSocialSecurity := TtlSocialSecurity + SocialSecurity;
42     TtlRetirement     := TtlRetirement + Retirement;
43     end; { for }
44
45 SavePayRecords( TtlWithholdings, TtlSocialSecurity, TtlRetirement );
```

In this example, you'll need one initial test case plus one for each of the five keywords, for a total of six. That doesn't mean that any six test cases will cover all the bases. It means that, at a minimum, six cases are required. Unless the cases are constructed carefully, they almost surely won't cover all the bases. The trick is to pay attention to the same keywords you used when counting the number of cases needed. Each keyword in the code represents something that can be either true or false; make sure you have at least one test case for each true and at least one for each false.

Here is a set of test cases that covers all the bases in this example:

Case	Test Description	Test Data
1	Nominal case	All boolean conditions are true
2	The initial *for* condition is false	*NumEmployees < 1*
3	The first *if* is false	*Employee[ID].SSWithheld >= MAX_SOCIAL_SECURITY*
4	The second *if* is false because the first part of the *and* is false	*not Employee[ID].WantsRetirement*
5	The second *if* is false because the second part of the *and* is false	*not EligibleForRetirement(Employee [ID])*
6	The third *if* is false	*not EligibleForIRA(Employee[ID])*

Note: This table will be extended with additional test cases throughout the chapter.

If the routine were much more complicated than this, the number of test cases you'd have to use just to cover all the paths would increase pretty quickly. Shorter routines tend to have fewer paths to test. Boolean expressions without a lot of *and*s and *or*s have fewer variations to test. Ease of testing is another good reason to keep your routines short and your boolean expressions simple.

Now that you've created six test cases for the routine and satisfied the demands of structured basis testing, can you consider the routine to be fully tested? Probably not. This kind of testing assures you only that all of the code will be executed. It does not account for variations in data.

Data-Flow Testing

Viewing the last subsection and this one together gives you another example illustrating that control flow and data flow are equally important in computer programming.

Data-flow testing is based on the idea that data usage is at least as error-prone as control flow. Boris Beizer claims that at least half of all modern code consists of data declarations and initializations (1990).

Data can exist in one of three states:

Defined. The data has been initialized, but it hasn't been used yet.

Used. The data has been used for computation, as an argument to a routine, or for something else.

Killed. The data was once defined, but it has been undefined in some way. For example, if the data is a pointer, perhaps the pointer has been freed. If it's a *for*-loop index, perhaps the program is out of the loop and the programming language doesn't define the value of a *for*-loop index once it's outside the loop. If it's a pointer to a record in a file, maybe the file has been closed and the record pointer is no longer valid.

In addition to having the terms "defined," "used," and "killed," it's convenient to have terms that describe entering or exiting a routine immediately before or after doing something to a variable:

Entered. The control flow enters the routine immediately before the variable is acted upon.

Exited. The control flow leaves the routine immediately after the variable is acted upon.

Combinations of data states

The normal combination of data states is that a variable is defined, used one or more times, and perhaps killed. View the following patterns suspiciously:

Defined-Defined. If you have to define a variable twice before the value sticks, you don't need a better program, you need a better computer. It's wasteful and error-prone, even if not actually wrong.

Defined-Exited. If the variable is a local variable, it doesn't make sense to define it and exit without using it. If it's a routine parameter or a global variable, it might be all right.

Defined-Killed. Defining a variable and then killing it without using it is wasted effort. If you have variables to spare, maybe you need to make your program smaller.

Entered-Killed. This is a problem if the variable is a local variable. It wouldn't need to be killed if it hasn't been defined or used. If, on the other hand, it's a routine parameter or a global variable, this pattern is all right as long as the variable is defined somewhere else before it's killed.

Entered-Used. Again, this is a problem if the variable is a local variable. The variable needs to be defined before it's used. If, on the other hand, it's a routine parameter or a global variable, the pattern is all right if the variable is defined somewhere else before it's used.

Killed-Killed. A variable shouldn't need to be killed twice. Variables don't come back to life, unless you need a new computer; otherwise, a resurrected variable indicates sloppy programming. Double kills are also fatal for pointers—one of the best ways to hang your machine is to kill (free) a pointer twice.

Killed-Used. Using a variable after it has been killed might work sometimes, but it's always a logical error. If the code seems to work anyway, that's an accident, and it will stop working at the time when it will cause the most mayhem.

Used-Defined. Using and then defining a variable might or might not be a problem, depending on whether the variable was also defined before it was used. Certainly if you see a used-defined pattern, it's worthwhile to check for a previous definition.

Check for these anomalous sequences of data states before testing begins. After you've checked for the anomalous sequences, the key to writing data-flow test cases is to exercise all possible defined-used paths. You can do this to various degrees of thoroughness, including

- All definitions. Test every definition of every variable (that is, every place at which any variable receives a value). This is a weak strategy because if you try to exercise every line of code you'll do this by default.

- All defined-used combinations. Test every combination of defining a variable in one place and using it in another. This is a stronger strategy than testing all definitions because merely executing every line of code does not guarantee that every defined-used combination will be tested.

Here's an example:

C Example of a Program Whose Data Flow Is to Be Tested

```
if ( Condition 1 )
    x = a;
else
    x = b;

if ( Condition 2 )
    y = x + 1;
else
    y = x - 1;
```

To cover every path in the program, you need one test case in which *Condition 1* is true and one in which it's false. You also need a test case in which *Condition 2* is true and one in which it's false. This can be handled by two test cases: Case 1 (*Condition 1=True, Condition 2=True*) and Case 2 (*Condition 1=False, Condition 2=False*). Those two cases are all you need for structured basis testing. They're also all you need to exercise every line of code that defines a variable; they give you the weak form of data-flow testing automatically.

To cover every defined-used combination, however, you need to add a few more cases. Right now you have the cases created by having *Condition 1* and *Condition 2* true at the same time and *Condition 1* and *Condition 2* false at the same time:

```
x = a;
...
y = x + 1;
```

and

```
x = b;
...
y = x - 1;
```

But you need two more cases to test every defined-used combination. You need: (1) $x = a$ and then $y = x - 1$ and (2) $x = b$ and then $y = x + 1$. In this example, you can get these combinations by adding two more cases: Case 3 (*Condition 1=True, Condition 2=False*) and Case 4 (*Condition 1=False, Condition 2=True*).

A good way to develop test cases is to start with structured basis testing, which gives you some if not all of the defined-used data flows. Then add the cases you still need to have a complete set of defined-used data-flow test cases.

As discussed in the previous subsection, structured basis testing provided six test cases for the routine on page 596. Data-flow testing of each defined-used pair requires several more test cases, some of which are covered by existing test cases and some of which aren't. Here are all the data-flow combinations that add test cases beyond the ones generated by structured basis testing:

Case	Test Description
7	Define *Retirement* in line 15 and use it first in line 30. This isn't necessarily covered by any of the previous test cases.
8	Define *Retirement* in line 15 and use it first in line 35. This isn't necessarily covered by any of the previous test cases.
9	Define *Retirement* in line 21 and use it first in line 35. This isn't necessarily covered by any of the previous test cases.

Once you run through the process of listing data-flow test cases a few times, you'll get a sense of which cases are fruitful and which are already covered. When you get stuck, list all the defined-used combinations. That might seem like a lot of work, but it's guaranteed to show you any cases that you didn't test for free in the basis-testing approach.

Equivalence Partitioning

CROSS-REFERENCE
Equivalence partitioning is discussed in far more depth in the books listed in the "Further Reading" section at the end of this chapter.

A good test case covers a large part of the possible input data. If two test cases flush out exactly the same errors, you need only one of them. The concept of "equivalence partitioning" is a formalization of this idea and helps reduce the number of test cases required.

In the listing on page 596, line 9 is a good place to use equivalence partitioning. The condition to be tested is *Employee[ID].SSWithheld < MAX_ SOCIAL_ SECURITY.* This case has two equivalence classes: the class in which *Employee[ID].SSWithheld* is less than *MAX_ SOCIAL_ SECURITY* and the class in which it's greater than or equal to *MAX_ SOCIAL_ SECURITY.* Other parts of the program may have other, related equivalence classes that imply that you need to test more than two possible values of *Employee[ID].SSWithheld,* but as far as this part of the program is concerned, only two are needed.

Thinking about equivalence partitioning won't give you a lot of new insight into a program when you have already covered the program with basis and data-flow testing. It's especially helpful, however, when you're looking at a routine from the outside (from a specification rather than the source code), or when the data is complicated and the complications aren't all reflected in the program's logic.

Error Guessing

CROSS-REFERENCE
For details on heuristics, see Section 2.2, "How to Use Software Metaphors."

In addition to the formal test techniques, good programmers use a variety of less formal, heuristic techniques to expose errors in their code. For application programming, virtually all differences among tests boil down to differences in test data. The exception to the rule is real-time processing, which is beyond the scope of this discussion.

One heuristic is the technique of error guessing. The term "error guessing" is a lowbrow name for a sensible concept. It means creating test cases based upon guesses about where the program might have errors, although it implies a certain amount of sophistication in the guessing.

You can base guesses on intuition or on past experience. Chapter 24 on reviews points out that one virtue of inspections is that they produce and maintain a list of common errors. The list is used to check new code. When you keep records of the kinds of errors you've made before, you improve the likelihood that your "error guess" will discover an error.

The next few subsections describe specific kinds of errors that lend themselves to error guessing.

Boundary Analysis

One of the most fruitful areas for testing is boundary conditions—off-by-one errors. Saying *Num−1* when you mean *Num* and saying *>=* when you mean *>* are common mistakes.

The idea of boundary analysis is to write test cases that exercise the boundary conditions. Pictorially, if you're testing for a range of values that are less than *Max*, you have three possible conditions:

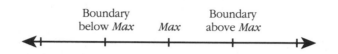

As shown, there are three boundary cases: just less than *Max*, *Max* itself, and just greater than *Max*. It takes three cases to ensure that none of the common mistakes has been made.

The example on page 596 contains a test for *Employee[ID].SSWithheld > MAX_SOCIAL_SECURITY*. According to the principles of boundary analysis, three cases should be examined:

Case	Test Description
1	Case 1 is defined so that the true boolean condition for *Employee[ID]. SSWithheld < MAX_SOCIAL_SECURITY* is the true side of the boundary. Thus, the Case 1 test case sets *Employee[ID].SSWithheld* to *MAX_SOCIAL_SECURITY − 1*. This test case was already generated.
3	Case 3 is defined so that the false boolean condition for *Employee[ID]. SSWithheld < MAX_SOCIAL_SECURITY* is the false side of the boundary. Thus, the Case 3 test case sets *Employee[ID].SSWithheld* to *MAX_SOCIAL_SECURITY + 1*. This test case was also already generated.
10	An additional test case is added for the dead-on case in which *Employee [ID].SSWithheld = MAX_SOCIAL_SECURITY*.

Compound Boundaries

Boundary analysis also applies to minimum and maximum allowable values. In this example, it might be minimum or maximum *GrossPay*, *Retirement*, or *IRAContribution*, but since calculations of those values are outside the scope of the routine, test cases for them aren't discussed further here.

A more subtle kind of boundary condition occurs when the boundary involves a combination of variables. For example, if two variables are multiplied together, what happens when both are large positive numbers? Large negative numbers? *0*? What if all the strings passed to a routine are uncommonly long?

In the running example, you might want to see what happens to the variables *TtlWithholdings*, *TtlSocialSecurity*, and *TtlRetirement* when every member of a large group of employees has a large salary—say, a group of programmers at $250,000 each. (We can always hope!) This calls for another test case:

Case	Test Description
11	A large group of employees, each of whom has a large salary—for the sake of example (what constitutes "large" depends on the specific system being developed), 1000 employees each with a salary of $250,000, none of whom have had any social security tax withheld and all of whom want retirement withholding.

A test case in the same vein but on the opposite side of the looking glass would be a small group of employees, each of whom has a salary of $0.00.

Case	Test Description
12	A group of 10 employees, each of whom has a salary of $0.00.

Classes of Bad Data

Aside from guessing that errors show up around boundary conditions, you can guess about and test for several other classes of bad data. Typical bad-data test cases include

- Too little data (or no data)
- Too much data
- The wrong kind of data (invalid data)
- The wrong size of data
- Uninitialized data

Some of the test cases you would think of if you followed these suggestions have already been covered. For example, "too little data" is covered by Cases 2 and 12, and it's hard to come up with anything for "wrong size of data." This fertile area nonetheless gives rise to a few more cases:

Case	Test Description
13	An array of 32,768 employees. Tests for too much data. Of course, how much is too much would vary from system to system, but for the sake of the example assume that this is far too much.
14	A negative salary. Wrong kind of data.
15	A negative number of employees. Wrong kind of data.

Classes of Good Data

When you try to find errors in a program, it's easy to overlook the fact that the nominal case might contain an error. Usually the nominal cases described in the basis-testing section represent one kind of good data. Here are other kinds of good data that are worth checking:

- Nominal cases—middle-of-the-road, expected values
- Minimum normal configuration
- Maximum normal configuration
- Compatibility with old data

Checking each of these kinds of data can reveal errors, depending on the item being tested.

The minimum normal configuration is useful for testing not just one item, but a group of items. It's similar in spirit to the boundary condition of many minimal values, but it's different in that it creates the set of minimum values out of the set of what is normally expected. One example would be to save an empty spreadsheet when testing a spreadsheet. For testing a word processor, it would be saving an empty document. In the case of the running example, testing the minimum normal configuration would add the following test case:

Case	Test Description
16	A group of one employee. To test the minimum normal configuration.

The maximum normal configuration is the opposite of the minimum. It's similar in spirit to boundary testing, but again, it creates a set of maximum values out of the set of expected values. An example of this would be saving a spreadsheet that's as large as the "maximum spreadsheet size" advertised on the product's packaging. Or printing the maximum-size spreadsheet. For a word processor, it would be saving a document of the largest recommended size. In the case of the running example, testing the maximum normal configuration depends on the maximum normal number of employees. Assuming it's 500, you would add the following test case:

Case	Test Description
17	A group of 500 employees. To test the maximum normal configuration.

The last kind of normal data testing, testing for compatibility with old data, comes into play when the program or routine is a replacement for an older program or routine. The new routine should produce the same results with old data that the old routine did, except in cases in which the old routine was defective. This kind of continuity between versions is the basis for regression testing, the purpose of which is to ensure that corrections and enhancements maintain previous levels of quality without backsliding. In the case of the running example, the compatibility criterion wouldn't add any test cases.

CHECKLIST

Test Cases

❏ Does each requirement that applies to the routine have its own test case?

❏ Does each element from the design that applies to the routine have its own test case?

❏ Has each line of code been tested with at least one test case? Has this been verified by computing the minimum number of tests necessary to exercise each line of code?

❏ Have all defined-used data-flow paths been tested with at least one test case?

❏ Has the code been checked for data-flow patterns that are unlikely to be correct, such as defined-defined, defined-exited, and defined-killed?

❏ Has a list of common errors been used to write test cases to detect errors that have occurred frequently in the past?

❏ Have all simple boundaries been tested—maximum, minimum, and off-by-one boundaries?

❏ Have compound boundaries been tested—that is, combinations of input data that might result in a computed variable that's too small or too large?

❏ Do test cases check for the wrong kind of data—for example, a negative number of employees in a payroll program?

❏ Are representative, middle-of-the-road values tested?

❏ Is the minimum normal configuration tested?

❏ Is the maximum normal configuration tested?

❏ Is compatibility with old data tested? And are old hardware, old versions of the operating system, and interfaces with old versions of other software tested?

❏ Do the test cases make hand-checks easy?

Use Test Cases That Make Hand-Checks Convenient

Let's suppose you're writing a test case for a nominal salary; you need a nominal salary, and the way you get one is to type in whatever numbers your hands land on. I'll try it:

1239078382346

OK. That's a pretty high salary, a little over a trillion dollars, in fact, but if I trim it so that it's somewhat realistic, I get *$39,078.38.*

Now, further suppose that this test case succeeds, that is, it finds an error. How do you know that it's found an error? Well, presumably, you know what the answer is and what it should be because you calculated the correct answer by hand. When you try to do hand-calculations with an ugly number like *$39,078.38*, however, you're as likely to make an error in the hand-calc as you are to discover one in your program. On the other hand, a nice, even number like *$20,000* makes number crunching a snap. The *0*s are easy to punch into the calculator, and multiplying by *2* is something most programmers can do without using their fingers and toes.

You might think that an ugly number like *$39,078.38* would be more likely to reveal errors, but it's no more likely to than any other number in its equivalence class.

25.4 Typical Errors

This section is dedicated to the proposition that you can test best when you know as much as possible about your enemy: errors.

Which Routines Contain the Most Errors?

KEY POINT

It's natural to assume that defects are distributed evenly throughout your source code. If you have an average of 10 defects per 1000 lines of code, you might assume that you'll have 1 defect in a routine that's 100 lines long. This is a natural assumption, but it's wrong. Most errors tend to be concentrated in a few highly defective routines. Here is the general relationship between errors and code:

HARD DATA

- Eighty percent of the errors are found in 20 percent of a project's routines (Endres 1975, Gremillion 1984, Boehm 1987b).

- Fifty percent of the errors are found in 10 percent of a project's routines (Endres 1975, Gremillion 1984).

These relationships might not seem so important until you recognize a few corollaries.

First, 20 percent of a project's routines contribute 80 percent of the cost of development (Boehm 1987b). That doesn't necessarily mean that the 20 percent that cost the most are the same as the 20 percent with the most defects, but it's pretty doggone suggestive.

HARD DATA

Second, regardless of the exact proportion of the cost contributed by highly defective routines, highly defective routines are extremely expensive. In the 1960s, IBM performed a study of its OS/360 operating system and found that errors were not distributed evenly across all routines but were concentrated into a few. Those error-prone routines were found to be "the most expensive entities in programming" (Jones 1986a). They contained as many as 50 defects per 1000 lines of code, and fixing them often cost 10 times what it took to develop the whole system. (The costs included customer support and in-the-field maintenance.)

CROSS-REFERENCE
Another class of routines that tend to contain a lot of errors is the class of overly complex routines. For details on identifying and simplifying routines, see "General Guidelines for Reducing Complexity" in Section 17.7.

Third, the implication of expensive routines for development is clear. As the old expression goes, "time is money." The corollary is that "money is time," and if you can cut close to 80 percent of the cost by avoiding troublesome routines, you can cut a substantial amount of the schedule as well. This is a clear illustration of the General Principle of Software Quality, that improving quality improves the development schedule.

Fourth, the implication of avoiding troublesome routines for maintenance is equally clear. Maintenance activities should be focused on identifying, redesigning, and rewriting from the ground up those routines that have been identified as error-prone. Gerald Weinberg reported a case in which maintenance programmers were allowed to spend a small amount of time selecting and rewriting the routines that produced the most problems. In a surprisingly short time, the overall error rates and maintenance efforts were substantially reduced (Gilb 1977).

Errors by Classification

CROSS-REFERENCE
For a list of all the checklists in the book, see the list of checklists following the table of contents.

Several researchers have tried to classify errors by type and determine the extent to which each kind of error occurs. Every programmer has a list of errors that have been particularly troublesome: off-by-one errors, forgetting to reinitialize a loop variable, and so on. The checklists presented throughout the book provide more details.

Boris Beizer combined data from several studies, arriving at an unbelievably detailed error taxonomy (1990). On the next page is a summary of his results.

25.18%	Structural
22.44%	Data
16.19%	Functionality as implemented
9.88%	Implementation
8.98%	Integration
8.12%	Functional requirements
2.76%	Test definition or execution
1.74%	System, software architecture
4.71%	Unspecified

Beizer has reported his results to a confident two decimal places, but the research into error types has generally been inconclusive. Different studies report wildly different kinds of errors, and studies that report on similar kinds of errors arrive at wildly different results, results that differ by 50 percent rather than by hundredths of a percentage point. (For examples, see Brown and Sampson 1973; Youngs 1974; Endres 1975; Weiss 1975; and Curtis, Krasner, and Iscoe 1988.) Given the wide variations in reports, combining results from multiple studies as Beizer has done probably doesn't produce meaningful data. But even if the data isn't conclusive, some of it is suggestive. Here are some of the suggestions that can be derived from it:

HARD DATA

The scope of most errors is fairly limited. One study found that 85 percent of errors could be corrected without modifying more than one routine (Endres 1975).

Many errors are outside the domain of construction. Researchers conducting a series of 97 interviews found that the three most common sources of errors were thin application-domain knowledge, fluctuating and conflicting requirements, and communication and coordination breakdown (Curtis, Krasner, and Iscoe 1988).

Most implementation errors are the programmers' fault. Of total errors reported, roughly 95 percent are caused by programmers, 2 percent by systems software (the compiler and the operating system), 2 percent by some other software, and 1 percent by the hardware (Brown and Sampson 1973, Ostrand and Weyuker 1984).

Clerical errors are a surprisingly common source of problems. One study found that 36 percent of all implementation errors were clerical mistakes (Weiss 1975). A 1987 study of almost 3 million lines of flight-dynamics software found that 18 percent of all errors were clerical (Card 1987). Another study found that 4 percent of all errors were spelling errors in messages (Endres 1975). In one of my programs, a colleague found several spelling errors simply by running all the strings from the executable file through a spelling

HARD DATA

checker. Attention to detail counts. If you doubt that, consider the three most expensive programming errors ever made. Gerald Weinberg reports that the top three cost $1.6 billion, $900 million, and $245 million. Each one involved the change of a *single digit* in a previously correct program (Weinberg 1983).

Misunderstanding the design is a recurring theme in studies of programmer errors. Beizer's compilation study, for what it's worth, found that 16.19 percent of the errors grew out of misinterpretations of the design (1990). Another study found that 19 percent of the errors resulted from misunderstood design (Weiss 1975). It's worthwhile to take the time you need to understand the design thoroughly. Such time doesn't produce immediate dividends (you don't necessarily look like you're working), but it pays off over the life of the project.

Avoiding errors in assignment statements is a key to quality. One study found that 41 percent of all errors were in assignment statements; that's in contradiction to the notion that most errors are off-by-one errors or loop problems (Youngs 1974). When this statistic is coupled with the fact that errors in assignment statements tend to be about three times as hard to find as other kinds of errors (Gould 1975), it suggests a major blind spot. The prevailing wisdom might not give assignment errors the status of off-by-one errors, but it's worth your time to think about how to avoid them.

Most errors are easy to fix. About 85 percent of errors can be fixed in less than a few hours. About 15 percent can be fixed in a few hours to a few days. And about 1 percent take longer (Weiss 1975, Ostrand and Weyuker 1984). This result is supported by Barry Boehm's observation that about 20 percent of the errors take about 80 percent of the resources to fix (1987b). Avoid as many of the hard errors as you can by doing analysis and design reviews upstream. Handle the numerous small errors as efficiently as you can.

It's a good idea to measure your own organization's experiences with errors. The diversity of results cited in this section indicates that people in different organizations have tremendously different experiences. That makes it hard to apply other organizations' experiences to yours. Some results go against common intuition; you might need to supplement your intuition with other tools. A good first step is to start measuring your process so that you know where the problems are.

Proportion of Errors Resulting from Faulty Construction

If the data that classifies errors is inconclusive, so is much of the data that attributes errors to the various development activities. One certainty is that construction always results in a significant number of errors. Sometimes people argue that the errors caused by construction are cheaper to fix than the errors caused by analysis or design. Fixing individual construction errors might be cheaper, but the evidence doesn't support such a claim about the total cost.

Here are my conclusions:

HARD DATA

- On small projects, implementation defects make up the vast bulk of all errors. In one study of coding errors on a small project (1000 lines of code), 75 percent of defects resulted from coding, compared to 10 percent from analysis and 15 percent from design (Jones 1986a). This error breakdown appears to be representative of many small projects.

- Implementation defects account for at least 40 percent of all defects. Although the proportion of implementation defects is smaller on large projects, they still account for at least 40 percent of all defects (Jones 1986a). Some researchers have reported proportions in the 75 percent range even on very large projects (Grady 1987). In general, the better the application area is understood, the better the overall architecture is. Errors then tend to be concentrated in detailed design and coding (Basili and Perricone 1984).

- Construction errors, though cheaper to fix than analysis and design errors, are still expensive. A study of two very large projects at Hewlett-Packard found that the average construction defect cost 25 to 50 percent as much to fix as the average design error (Grady 1987). When the greater number of construction defects was figured into the overall equation, the total cost to fix construction defects was one to two times as much as the cost attributed to design defects.

Figure 25-2 provides a rough idea of the relationship between project size and the source of errors.

How Many Errors Should You Expect to Find?

The number of errors you should expect to find varies according to the quality of the development process you use. Here's the range of possibility:

HARD DATA

- Industry average experience is about 15 to 50 errors per 1000 lines of code for delivered software. The software has usually been developed using a hodgepodge of techniques, probably including structured programming (Boehm 1981, Gremillion 1984, Jones 1986a, Yourdon 1989a). Cases that have one-tenth as many errors as this are rare; cases that have 10 times more tend not to be reported. (They probably aren't ever completed!)

- The Applications Division at Microsoft experiences about 10 to 20 defects per 1000 lines of code during in-house testing, and 0.5 defect per 1000 lines of code in released product (Moore 1992). The technique used to achieve this level is a combination of the code-reading techniques described in Section 24.3 and independent testing.

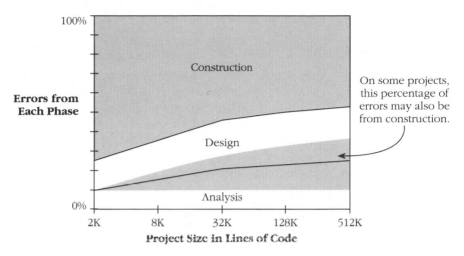

On some projects, this percentage of errors may also be from construction.

Sources: Boehm 1981, Jones 1986a, and Grady 1987.

Figure 25-2. *As the size of the project increases, the proportion of errors committed during construction decreases. Nevertheless, construction errors account for 45–75 percent of all errors on even the largest projects.*

HARD DATA

- Harlan Mills pioneered "cleanroom development," a technique that has been able to achieve rates as low as 3 defects per 1000 lines of code during in-house testing, and 0.1 defect per 1000 lines of code in released product (Cobb and Mills 1990). A few projects — for example, the space-shuttle software—have achieved a level of 0 defects in 500,000 lines of code using a system of formal development methods, peer reviews, and statistical testing.

FURTHER READING
For details on clean-room development, see "Cleanroom Software Engineering" (Mills, Dyer, and Linger 1987).

The results of the cleanroom projects confirm the General Principle of Software Quality: It's cheaper to build high-quality software than it is to build and fix low-quality software. Productivity for a fully checked-out, 80,000-line cleanroom project was 740 lines of code per work-month. The industry average rate for fully checked out code is closer to 150 lines per work-month. The cost savings and productivity come from the fact that virtually no time is devoted to debugging on cleanroom projects. Mills claims that after a team has completed three or four cleanroom development projects, it should be able to reduce the density of errors in its code by a factor of 100 and simultaneously increase its productivity by a factor of 10. That is truly a worthy goal!

Errors in Testing Itself

KEY POINT

You may have had an experience like this: The software is found to be in error. You have a few immediate hunches about which part of the code might be wrong, but all that code seems to be correct. You run several more test cases to try to refine the error, but all the new test cases produce correct results. You spend several hours reading and rereading the code and hand-calculating the results. They all check out. After a few more hours, something causes you to re-examine the test data. Eureka! The error's in the test data! How idiotic it feels to waste hours tracking down an error in the test data rather than in the code!

HARD DATA

This is a common experience. Test cases are often more likely to contain errors than the code being tested (Weiland 1983, Jones 1986a). The reasons are easy to find—especially when the developer writes the test cases. Test cases tend to be created on the fly rather than through a careful design and implementation process. They are often viewed as one-time tests and are developed with the care commensurate with something to be thrown away.

You can do several things to reduce the number of errors in your test cases:

Check your work. Develop test cases as carefully as you develop code. Such care certainly includes double-checking your own testing. Step through test code in a debugger, line by line, just as you would production code. Walkthroughs and inspections of test data are appropriate.

Plan test cases as you develop your software. Effective planning for testing should start at the requirements stage or as soon as you get the assignment for the program. This helps to avoid test cases that are based on mistaken assumptions.

Keep your test cases. Spend a little quality time with your test cases. Save them for regression testing and for work on version 2. It's easy to justify the trouble if you know you're going to keep them rather than throw them away.

25.5 Test-Support Tools

This section surveys the kinds of testing tools you can buy commercially or build yourself. It won't name specific products because they could easily be out of date by the time you read this. Refer to your favorite programmer's magazine for the most recent specifics.

Building Scaffolding to Test Individual Routines

The term "scaffolding" comes from building construction. Scaffolding is built so that workers can reach parts of a building they couldn't reach otherwise. Software scaffolding is built for the sole purpose of making it easy to exercise code.

FURTHER READING
For several good examples of scaffolding, see Jon Bentley's essay "Confessions of a Coder" in *More Programming Pearls* (1988).

One kind of scaffolding is a low-level routine that's dummied up so that it can be called by a higher-level routine that's being tested. Such a routine is called a "stub." You can make a stub more or less realistic, depending on how much veracity you need. It can

- Return control immediately, having taken no action
- Test the data fed to it
- Print a diagnostic message, perhaps an echo of the input parameters
- Get return values from interactive input
- Return a standard answer regardless of the input
- Burn up the number of clock cycles allocated to the real routine
- Function as a slow, fat, simple, or less accurate version of the real routine.

Another kind of scaffolding is a fake routine that calls the real routine being tested. This is called a "driver" or, sometimes, a "test harness." It can

- Call the routine with a fixed set of inputs
- Prompt for input interactively and call the routine with it
- Take arguments from the command line (in operating systems that support it) and call the routine
- Read arguments from a file and call the routine
- Run through predefined sets of input data in multiple calls to the routine

CROSS REFERENCE
The line between testing tools and debugging tools is fuzzy. For details on debugging tools, see Section 26.5, "Debugging Tools."

A final kind of scaffolding is the dummy file, a small version of the real thing that has the same types of components that a full-size file has. A small dummy file offers a couple of advantages. Since it's small, you can know its exact contents and can be reasonably sure that the file itself is error-free. And since you create it specifically for testing, you can design its contents so that any error in using it is conspicuous.

Obviously, building scaffolding requires some work, but if an error is ever detected in a routine, you can reuse the scaffolding. If you use scaffolding, the routine can also be tested without the risk of its being affected by interactions with other routines. Scaffolding is particularly useful when subtle algorithms are involved. It's easy to get stuck in a rut in which it takes several minutes to execute each test case because the code being exercised is embedded in other code. Scaffolding allows you to exercise the code directly. The few minutes that you spend building scaffolding to exercise the deeply buried code can save hours of debugging time.

You can write a few routines in a file and include a *main()* scaffolding routine in the file, even though the routines being tested aren't intended to stand by themselves. The *main()* routine reads arguments from the command line and passes them to the routine being tested so that you can exercise the routine on its own before integrating it with the rest of the program. When you integrate the code, leave the routines and the scaffolding code that exercises them in the file and use preprocessor commands or comments to deactivate the scaffolding code. Since it's preprocessed out, it doesn't affect the executable code, and since it's at the bottom of the file, it's not in the way visually. No harm is done by leaving it in. It's there if you need it again, and it doesn't burn up the time it would take to remove and archive it.

Results Comparators

CROSS-REFERENCE
For details on regression testing, see "Retesting (Regression Testing)" in Section 25.6.

Regression testing, or retesting, is a lot easier if you have automated tools to check the actual output against the expected output. One easy way to check printed output is to redirect the output to a file and use a file-comparison tool to compare the new output against the expected output that was sent to a file previously. If the outputs aren't the same, you have detected a regression error.

Test-Data Generators

You can also write code to exercise selected pieces of a program systematically. A few years ago, I developed a proprietary encryption algorithm and wrote a file-encryption program to use it. The intent of the program was to encode a file so that it could be decoded only with the right password. The encryption didn't just change the file superficially; it altered the entire contents. It was critical that the program be able to decode a file properly, since the file would be ruined otherwise.

I set up a test-data generator that fully exercised the encryption and decryption parts of the program. It generated files of random characters in random sizes, from 0K through 500K. It generated passwords of random characters in random lengths from 1 through 255. For each random case, it generated two copies of the random file; encrypted one copy; reinitialized itself; decrypted the copy; and then compared each byte in the decrypted copy to the unaltered copy. If any bytes were different, the generator printed all the information I needed to reproduce the error.

I weighted the test cases toward the average length of my files, 30K, which was considerably shorter than the maximum length of 500K. If I had not weighted the test cases toward a shorter length, file lengths would have been uniformly distributed between 0K and 500K. The average tested file length would have been 250K. The shorter average length meant that I could test more files, passwords, end-of-file conditions, odd file lengths, and other circumstances that might produce errors than I could have with uniformly random lengths.

The results were gratifying. After running only about 100 test cases, I found two errors in the program. Both arose from special cases that might never have shown up in practice, but they were errors nonetheless, and I was glad to find them. After fixing them, I ran the program for weeks, encrypting and decrypting over 100,000 files without an error. Given the range in file contents, lengths, and passwords I tested, I could confidently assert that the program was correct.

Here are the lessons from this story:

- Properly designed random-data generators can generate unusual combinations of test data that you wouldn't think of.
- Random-data generators can exercise your program more thoroughly than you can.
- You can refine randomly generated test cases over time so that they emphasize a realistic range of input. This concentrates testing in the areas most likely to be exercised by users, maximizing reliability in those areas.
- Modular design pays off during testing. I was able to pull out the encryption and decryption code and use it independently of the user-interface code, making the job of writing a test driver straightforward.
- You can reuse a test driver if the code it tests ever has to be changed. Once I had corrected the two early errors, I was able to start retesting immediately.

Coverage Monitors

HARD DATA

Robert Grady of Hewlett-Packard reports that testing done without measuring code coverage typically exercises only about 55 percent of the code (1993). A coverage monitor is a tool that keeps track of the code that's exercised and the code that isn't. A coverage monitor is especially useful for systematic testing because it tells you whether a set of test cases fully exercises the code. If you run your full set of test cases and the coverage monitor indicates that some code still hasn't been executed, you know that you need more tests.

Symbolic Debuggers

A symbolic debugger is a technological supplement to code walkthroughs and inspections. A debugger has the capacity to step through code line by line, keep track of variables' values, and always interpret the code the same way the computer does. The process of stepping through a piece of code in a debugger and watching it work is enormously valuable.

Walking through code in a debugger is in many respects the same process as having other programmers step through your code in a review. Neither your peers nor the debugger has the same blind spots that you do. The additional benefit with a debugger is that it's less labor-intensive then a team review. Watching your code execute under a variety of input-data sets is good assurance that you've implemented the code you intended to.

A good debugger is even a good tool for learning about your language because you can see exactly how the code executes. You can toggle back and forth between a view of your high-level language code and a view of the assembler code to see how the high-level code is translated into assembler. You can watch registers and the stack to see how arguments are passed. You can look at code your compiler has optimized to see the kinds of optimizations that are performed. None of these benefits has much to do with the debugger's intended use—diagnosing errors that have already been detected—but imaginative use of a debugger produces benefits far beyond its initial charter.

System Perturbers

Another class of test-support tools are designed to perturb a system. Many people have stories of programs that work 99 times out of 100 but fail on the hundredth run-through with the same data. The problem is nearly always a failure to initialize a variable somewhere, and it's usually hard to reproduce because 99 times out of 100 the uninitialized variable happens to be *0*.

This class includes tools that have a variety of capabilities:

- Memory filling. You want to be sure you don't have any uninitialized variables. Some tools fill memory with arbitrary values before you run your program so that uninitialized variables aren't set to *0* accidentally. In some cases, the memory may be set to a specific value. For example, on the 80x86 processor, the value *0xCC* is the machine-language code for a breakpoint interrupt. If you fill memory with *0xCC* and have an error that causes you to execute something you shouldn't, you'll hit a breakpoint in the debugger and detect the error.
- Memory shaking. In multi-tasking sytems, some tools can rearrange memory as your program operates so that you can be sure you haven't written any code that depends on data being in absolute rather than relative locations.

- Selective memory failing. A memory driver can simulate low-memory conditions in which a program might be running out of memory, fail on a memory request, grant an arbitrary number of memory requests before failing, or fail on an arbitrary number of requests before granting one. This is especially useful for testing complicated programs that work with dynamically allocated memory.

- Memory-access checking (bounds checking). If you work in a protected-mode operating system such as OS/2, you have the luxury of knowing when a pointer error occurs. The operating system doesn't allow a pointer to reference memory outside its program's area. If you work in a real-mode operating system such as MS-DOS or the Apple Macintosh, you don't necessarily know when pointers are referencing memory they shouldn't be. The operating system doesn't check for memory violations. Fortunately, you can buy a memory-access checker that watches pointer operations to make sure your pointers behave themselves. Such a tool is useful for detecting uninitialized or dangling pointers.

Error Databases

One powerful test tool is a database of errors that have been reported. Such a database is both a management and a technical tool. It allows you to check for recurring errors, track the rate at which new errors are being detected and corrected, and track the status of open and closed errors and their severity. For details on what information you should keep in an error database, see Section 25.7, "Keeping Test Records."

25.6 Improving Your Testing

The steps for improving your testing are similar to the steps for improving any other process. You have to know exactly what the process does so that you can vary it slightly and observe the effects of the variation. When you observe a change that has a positive effect, you modify the process so that it becomes a little better. The following subsections describe how to do this with testing.

Planning to Test

CROSS-REFERENCE
Part of planning to test is formalizing your plans in writing. To find further information on test documentation, refer to the "Further Reading" section at the end of Chapter 19.

One key to effective testing is planning from the beginning of the project to test. Putting testing on the same level of importance as design or coding means that time will be allocated to it, it will be viewed as important, and it will be a high-quality process. Test planning is also an element of making the testing process *repeatable*. If you can't repeat it, you can't improve it.

Retesting (Regression Testing)

Suppose that you've tested a product thoroughly and found no errors. Suppose that the product is then changed in one area and you want to be sure that it still passes all the tests it did before the change—that the change didn't introduce any new defects. Testing designed to make sure the software hasn't taken a step backwards, or "regressed," is called "regression testing."

HARD DATA

One survey of data-processing personnel found that 52 percent of those surveyed weren't familiar with this concept (Beck and Perkins 1983). That's unfortunate because it's nearly impossible to produce a high-quality software product unless you can systematically retest it after changes have been made. If you run different tests after each change, you have no way of knowing for sure that no new defects have been introduced. Consequently, regression testing must run the same tests each time. Sometimes new tests are added as the product matures, but the old tests are kept too.

The only practical way to manage regression testing is to automate it. People become numbed from running the same tests many times and seeing the same test results many times. It becomes too easy to overlook errors, which defeats the purpose of regression testing.

The main tools used to support automatic testing generate input, capture output, and compare actual output with expected output. The variety of tools discussed in the preceding section will perform some or all of these functions.

25.7 Keeping Test Records

KEY POINT

Aside from making the testing process repeatable, you need to measure the project so that you can tell for sure whether changes improve or damage it. Here are a few kinds of data you can collect to measure your project:

- Administrative description of the defect (the date reported, the person who reported it, a title or description, the date fixed)
- Full description of the problem
- Steps to take to repeat the problem
- Suggested workaround for the problem
- Related defects
- Severity of the problem—for example, fatal, bothersome, or cosmetic
- Classification of the defect—analysis, design, coding, or testing
- Subclassification of a coding defect—off-by-one, bad assignment, bad array index, bad routine call, and so on

- Location of the fix for the defect
- Modules and routines changed by the fix
- Person responsible for the defect (this can be controversial and might be bad for morale)
- Lines of code affected by the defect
- Hours to find the defect
- Hours to fix the defect

Once you collect the data, you can crunch a few numbers to determine whether your project is getting sicker or healthier:

- Number of defects in each routine, sorted from worst routine to best
- Average number of testing hours per defect found
- Average number of test cases per defect found
- Average number of programming hours per defect fixed
- Percentage of code covered by test cases
- Number of outstanding defects in each severity classification

Further Reading

Federal truth-in-advising statutes compel me to disclose that several other books cover testing in more depth than this chapter does. Books that are devoted to testing discuss system and black-box testing, which haven't been discussed in this chapter. They also go into more depth on unit-testing topics. They discuss formal approaches such as cause-effect graphing and the ins and outs of establishing an independent test organization.

Myers, Glenford J. *The Art of Software Testing*. New York: John Wiley, 1979. After more than 10 years, this is probably still the best testing book available. Myers knows his subject, and the contents of the book are straightforward: A Self-Assessment Test; The Psychology and Economics of Program Testing; Program Inspections, Walkthroughs, and Reviews; Test-Case Design; Module Testing; Higher-Order Testing; Debugging; Test Tools and Other Techniques. It's short (177 pages) and readable. The quiz at the beginning gets you started thinking like a tester and demonstrates how many ways there are to break a piece of code.

Hetzel, Bill. *The Complete Guide to Software Testing*, 2d ed. Wellesley, Mass.: QED Information Systems, 1988. A good alternative to Myers's book, Hetzel's is a more modern treatment of the same territory. In addition to what Myers covers, Hetzel discusses testing of requirements and designs, regression testing, purchased software, and management considerations. At 284 pages, this book is also relatively short, and the author has a knack for presenting powerful technical concepts understandably.

Beizer, Boris. *Software Testing Techniques,* 2d ed. New York: Van Nostrand Reinhold, 1990. This book is a long treatment of testing (550 pages). Whereas Myers and Hetzel touch on related topics like reviews and inspections, Beizer sticks strictly to testing and covers a few kinds of testing that aren't discussed in other books, such as data-flow testing. In spite of its scope, the eccentric contents often neglect mainstream testing ideas for the sake of more idiosyncratic concerns. For example, it doesn't include any significant discussion of testing documentation or of the IEEE/ANSI testing standards, but it does include an argument that most variables should be made global rather than local. Inspections and walkthroughs aren't defined in the glossary, but "Incredible Hulk" is. If Myers's or Hetzel's book is available, read it first. When you want to explore testing in more depth, Beizer's book is worth having as an auxiliary reference.

IEEE Std 1008-1987: IEEE Standard for Software Unit Testing. IEEE Software Engineering Standards Collection, Spring 1991. New York: Institute of Electrical and Electronics Engineers.

IEEE Std 829-1983: IEEE Standard for Software Test Documentation. IEEE Software Engineering Standards Collection, Spring 1991. New York: Institute of Electrical and Electronics Engineers. The two standards are the IEEE recommendations for software test documentation and unit testing practices.

Weeks, Kevin. "Is Your Code Done Yet?" *Computer Language* 9, no. 4 (April 1992): 63–72. This article steps through the process of building a set of test cases. Weeks describes the general testing strategy and tips for testing effectively and efficiently.

Rettig, Marc. "Testing Made Palatable." *Communications of the ACM* 34, no. 5 (May 1991): 25–29. This article describes how a programming team made glass-box unit testing part of its development process.

Key Points

- Unit testing by the developer is a key part of a full testing strategy. Module and system testing are also important but are outside the scope of this book.

- The combination of all kinds of testing is only one part of a good software-quality program. High-quality development methods, including orderly creation of requirements and design, are at least as important. Inspections and walkthroughs are also at least as effective at detecting errors as testing and detect different kinds of errors.

- You can generate many test cases deterministically, using basis testing, data-flow analysis, and error guessing.

- Errors tend to cluster in a few error-prone routines. Find the routines, redesign them, and rewrite them.

- Test data tends to have a higher error density than the code being tested. Because hunting for such errors wastes time without improving the code, test-data errors are more aggravating than programming errors. Avoid them by developing your tests as carefully as your code.

- In the long run, the best way to improve your testing process is to make it regular, measure it, and use what you learn to improve it.

26

Debugging

Contents

Related Topics

DEBUGGING IS THE PROCESS OF IDENTIFYING the root cause of an error and correcting it. It contrasts with testing, which is the process of detecting the error initially. On some projects, debugging occupies as much as 50 percent of the total development time. For many programmers, debugging is the hardest part of programming.

Debugging doesn't have to be the hardest part. If you follow the advice in this book, debugging can be the easiest part. You'll have few errors to debug. Most of the errors you will have will be minor oversights and typos, easily found by looking at a source-code listing or stepping through the code in a debugger.

26.1 Overview of Debugging Issues

The late Rear Admiral Grace Hopper, co-inventor of COBOL, always said that the word "bug" dated back to the first large-scale digital computer, the Mark I (IEEE 1992). Programmers traced a circuit malfunction to the presence of a large moth that had found its way into the computer, and from that time on, computer problems were blamed on "bugs."

The word "bug" is a cute word and conjures up images like this one:

The reality of software defects, however, is that bugs aren't organisms that sneak into your code when you forget to spray it with pesticide. They are errors. A bug in software means that a programmer made a mistake. The result of the mistake isn't like the cute picture shown above. It's more likely a note like this one:

In this context, technical accuracy requires that mistakes in the code be called "errors" or "defects."

Role of Debugging in Software Quality

Like testing, debugging isn't a way to improve the quality of your software; it's a way to repair defects. Software quality must be built in from the start. The best way to build a quality product is to follow a careful requirements analysis or prototyping, have an excellent design, and use high-quality coding practices. Debugging is a last resort.

Variations in Debugging Performance

Why talk about debugging? Doesn't everyone know how to debug?

KEY POINT

No, not everyone knows how to debug. Studies of experienced programmers have found roughly a 20-to-1 difference in the time it takes experienced programmers to find the same set of errors. Moreover, some programmers find more errors and make corrections more accurately. Here are the results of one study that examined how effectively professional programmers with at least four years of experience debugged a program with 12 errors:

	Fastest Three Programmers	Slowest Three Programmers
Average debug time (minutes)	5.0	14.1
Average number of errors not found	0.7	1.7
Average number of errors made correcting errors	3.0	7.7

Source: "Some Psychological Evidence on How People Debug Computer Programs" (Gould 1975).

HARD DATA

The three programmers who were best at debugging were able to find the defects in about one-third the time and made only about two-fifths as many errors as the three who were the worst. The best programmer found all the defects and didn't make any errors in correcting them. The worst missed 4 of the 12 defects and made 11 errors in correcting the 8 defects he found. This wide variation has been confirmed by other studies (Gilb 1977, Curtis 1981).

CROSS-REFERENCE
For details on the relationship between quality and cost, see Section 23.5, "The General Principle of Software Quality."

In addition to providing insight into debugging, the evidence supports the General Principle of Software Quality: Improving quality reduces development costs. The best programmers found the most errors, found the errors most quickly, and made correct modifications most often. You don't have to choose between quality, cost, and time—they all go hand in hand.

Errors as Opportunities

What does having an error mean? Assuming that you don't want the program to have errors, it means that you don't fully understand what the program does. The idea of not understanding what the program does is unsettling. After all, if you created the program, it should do your bidding. If you don't know exactly what you're telling the computer to do, you're merely trying different things until something seems to work. If you're programming by trial and error, errors are guaranteed. You don't need to learn how to fix errors; you need to learn how to avoid them in the first place.

Most people are somewhat fallible, however, and you might be an excellent programmer who has simply made a modest oversight. If this is the case, an error in your program represents a powerful opportunity. You can:

Learn about the program you're working on. You have something to learn about the program because if you already knew it perfectly, it wouldn't have an error. You would have corrected it already.

625

Learn about the kind of mistakes you make. If you wrote the program, you inserted the error. It's not every day that a spotlight exposes a weakness with glaring clarity, but this particular day you have an opportunity to learn about your mistakes. Once you find the mistake, ask why did you make it? How could you have found it more quickly? How could you have prevented it? Does the code have other mistakes just like it? Can you can correct them before they cause problems of their own?

Learn about the quality of your code from the point of view of someone who has to read it. You'll have to read your code to find the error. This is an opportunity to look critically at the quality of your code. Is it easy to read? How could it be better? Use your discoveries to improve the code you write next.

Learn about how you solve problems. Does your approach to solving debugging problems give you confidence? Does your approach work? Do you find errors quickly? Or is your approach to debugging weak? Do you feel anguish and frustration? Do you guess randomly? Do you need to improve? Considering the amount of time many projects spend on debugging, you definitely won't waste time if you observe how you debug. Taking time to analyze and change the way you debug might be the quickest way to decrease the total amount of time it takes you to develop a program.

Learn about how you fix errors. In addition to learning how you find errors, you can learn about how you fix them. Do you make the easiest possible correction, by applying *goto* Band-Aids and special-case makeup that changes the symptom but not the problem? Or do you make systemic corrections, demanding an accurate diagnosis and prescribing treatment for the heart of the problem?

All things considered, debugging is an extraordinarily rich soil in which to plant the seeds of your own improvement. It's where all construction roads cross: readability, design, code quality—you name it. This is where building good code pays off—especially if you do it well enough that you don't have to debug very often.

An Ineffective Approach

Unfortunately, programming classes in colleges and universities hardly ever offer instruction in debugging. If you studied programming in college, you might have had a lecture devoted to debugging. Although my computer-science education was excellent, the extent of the debugging advice I received was to "put print statements in the program to find the error." This is not adequate. If other programmers' educational experiences are like mine, a great many programmers are being forced to reinvent debugging concepts on their own. What a waste!

The Devil's Guide to Debugging

In Dante's vision of hell, the lowest circle is reserved for Satan himself. In modern times, Old Scratch has agreed to share the lowest circle with programmers who don't learn to debug effectively. He tortures programmers by making them use this common debugging approach:

Find the error by guessing. To find the error, scatter print statements randomly throughout a program. Examine the output to see where the error is. If you can't find the error with print statements, try changing things in the program until something seems to work. Don't back up the original version of the program, and don't keep a record of the changes you've made. Programming is more exciting when you're not quite sure what the program is doing. Stock up on Jolt cola and Twinkies because you're in for a long night in front of the terminal.

Don't waste time trying to understand the problem. It's likely that the problem is trivial, and you don't need to understand it completely to fix it. Simply finding it is enough.

Fix the error with the most obvious fix. It's usually good just to fix the specific problem you see, rather than wasting a lot of time making some big, ambitious correction that's going to affect the whole program. This is a perfect example:

```
X = Compute( Y )
if ( Y = 17 )
   X = $25.15        { Compute() doesn't work for Y = 17, so fix it }
```

Who needs to dig all the way into *Compute()* for an obscure problem with the value of *17* when you can just write a special case for it in the obvious place?

Debugging by superstition

Satan has leased part of hell to programmers who debug by superstition. Every group has one programmer who has endless problems with demon machines, mysterious compiler errors, hidden language defects that appear when the moon is full, bad data, losing important changes, a vindictive, possessed editor that saves programs incorrectly—you name it. This is "programming by superstition."

If you have a problem with a program you've written, it's your fault. It's not the computer's fault, and it's not the compiler's fault. The program doesn't do something different every time. It didn't write itself; you wrote it, so take responsibility for it.

Even if an error at first appears not to be your fault, it's strongly in your interest to assume that it is. That assumption helps you debug: It's hard enough to find an error in your code when you're looking for it; it's even harder when you've

> Programmers do not always use available data to constrain their reasoning. They carry out minor and irrational repairs, and they often don't undo the *in*correct repairs.
>
> *Iris Vessey*

assumed your code is error-free. It improves your credibility because when you do claim that an error arose in someone else's code, other programmers will believe that you have checked out the problem carefully. Assuming the error is your fault also saves you the embarrassment of claiming that an error is someone else's fault and then having to recant publicly later when you find out that it was your error after all.

26.2 Finding an Error

Debugging consists of finding the error and fixing it. Finding the error (and understanding it) is usually 90 percent of the work.

Fortunately, you don't have to make a pact with Satan in order to find an approach to debugging that's better than random guessing. Contrary to what the Devil wants you to believe, debugging by thinking about the problem is much more effective and interesting than debugging with an eye of newt and the dust of a frog's ear.

Suppose you were asked to solve a murder mystery. Which would be more interesting: going door to door throughout the county, checking every person's alibi for the night of October 17, or finding a few clues and deducing the murderer's identity? Most people would rather deduce the person's identity, and most programmers find the intellectual approach to debugging more satisfying. Even better, the effective programmers who debug in one-twentieth the time of the ineffective programmers aren't randomly guessing about how to fix the program. They're using the scientific method.

The Scientific Method of Debugging

Here are the steps you go through when you use the scientific method:

1. Gather data through repeatable experiments.
2. Form a hypothesis that accounts for as much of the relevant data as possible.
3. Design an experiment to prove or disprove the hypothesis.
4. Prove or disprove the hypothesis.
5. Repeat as needed.

KEY POINT

This process has many parallels in debugging. Here's an effective approach for finding an error:

1. Stabilize the error.
2. Locate the source of the error.
3. Fix the error.

4. Test the fix.

5. Look for similar errors.

The first step is similar to the scientific method's first step in that it relies on repeatability. The defect is easier to diagnose if you can make it occur reliably. The second step uses all the steps of the scientific method. You gather the test data that divulged the error, analyze the data that has been produced, and form a hypothesis about the source of the error. You design a test case or an inspection to evaluate the hypothesis and then declare success or renew your efforts, as appropriate.

Let's look at each of the steps in conjunction with an example.

Assume that you have an employee database program that has an intermittent error. The program is supposed to print a list of employees and their income-tax withholdings in alphabetical order. Here's part of the output:

```
Formatting, Fred Freeform    $5,877
Goto, Gary                   $1,666
Modula, Mildred             $10,788
Many-Loop, Mavis             $8,889
Statement, Sue Switch        $4,000
Whileloop, Wendy             $7,860
```

The error is that *Many-Loop, Mavis* and *Modula, Mildred* are out of order.

Stabilize the error

If a defect doesn't occur reliably, it's almost impossible to diagnose. Making an intermittent defect occur predictably is one of the most challenging tasks in debugging.

CROSS-REFERENCE
For details on using pointers safely, see Section 11.9, "Pointers."

An error that doesn't occur predictably is usually an initialization error or a dangling-pointer problem. If the calculation of a sum is right sometimes and wrong sometimes, a variable involved in the calculation probably isn't being initialized properly—most of the time it just happens to start at *0*. If the problem is a strange and unpredictable phenomenon and you're using pointers, you almost certainly have an uninitialized pointer or are using a pointer after the memory that it points to has been deallocated.

Stabilizing an error usually requires more than finding a test case that produces the error. It includes narrowing the test case to the simplest one that still produces the error. If you work in an organization that has an independent test team, sometimes it's the team's job to make the test cases simple. Most of the time, it's your job.

To simplify the test case, you bring the scientific method into play again. Suppose you have 10 factors that, used in combination, produce the error. Form a hypothesis about which factors were irrelevant to producing the error. Change the supposedly irrelevant factors, and rerun the test case. If you still get the error, you can eliminate those factors and you've simplified the test. Then you can try to simplify the test further. If you don't get the error, you've disproven that specific hypothesis, and you know more than you did before. It might be that some subtly different change would still produce the error, but you know at least one specific change that does not.

In the employee withholdings example, when the program is run initially, *Many-Loop, Mavis* is listed after *Modula, Mildred.* When the program is run a second time, however, the list is fine:

```
Formatting, Fred Freeform    $5,877
Goto, Gary                   $1,666
Many-Loop, Mavis             $8,889
Modula, Mildred             $10,788
Statement, Sue Switch        $4,000
Whileloop, Wendy             $7,860
```

It isn't until *Fruit-Loop, Frita* is entered and shows up in an incorrect position that you remember that *Modula, Mildred* had been entered just before she showed up in the wrong spot too. What's odd about both cases is that they were entered singly. Usually, employees are entered in groups.

You hypothesize: The problem has something to do with entering a single new employee.

If this is true, running the program again should put *Fruit-Loop, Frita* in the right position. Here's the result of a second run:

```
Formatting, Fred Freeform    $5,877
Fruit-Loop, Frita            $5,771
Goto, Gary                   $1,666
Many-Loop, Mavis             $8,889
Modula, Mildred             $10,788
Statement, Sue Switch        $4,000
Whileloop, Wendy             $7,860
```

This successful run supports the hypothesis. To confirm it, you want to try adding a few new employees, one at a time, to see whether they show up in the wrong order and whether the order changes on the second run.

Locate the source of the error

The goal of simplifying the test case is to make it so simple that changing any aspect of it changes the behavior of the error. Then, by changing the test case carefully and watching the program's behavior under controlled conditions, you can diagnose the problem.

Locating the source of the error also calls for using the scientific method. You might suspect that the defect is a result of a specific problem, say an off-by-one error. You could then vary the parameter you suspect is causing the problem—one below the boundary, on the boundary, and one above the boundary—and determine whether your hypothesis is correct.

In the running example, the source of the problem could be an off-by-one error that occurs when you add one new employee but not when you add two or more. Examining the code, you don't find an obvious off-by-one error. Resorting to Plan B, you run a test case with a single new employee to see whether that's the problem. You add *Hardcase, Henry* as a single employee and hypothesize that his record will be out of order. Here's what you find:

```
Formatting, Fred Freeform      $5,877
Fruit-Loop, Frita              $5,771
Goto, Gary                     $1,666
Hardcase, Henry                  $493
Many-Loop, Mavis               $8,889
Modula, Mildred               $10,788
Statement, Sue Switch          $4,000
Whileloop, Wendy               $7,860
```

The line for *Hardcase, Henry* is exactly where it should be, which means that your first hypothesis is false. The problem isn't caused simply by adding one employee at a time. It's either a more complicated problem or something completely different.

Examining the test-run output again, you notice that *Fruit-Loop, Frita* and *Many-Loop, Mavis* are the only names containing hyphens. *Fruit-Loop* was out of order when she was first entered, but *Many-Loop* wasn't, was she? Although you don't have a printout from the original entry, in the original error *Modula, Mildred* appeared to be out of order, but she was next to *Many-Loop*. Maybe *Many-Loop* was out of order and *Modula* was all right.

You hypothesize: The problem arises from names with hyphens, not names that are entered singly.

But how does that account for the fact that the problem shows up only the first time an employee is entered? You look at the code and find that two different sorting routines are used. One is used when an employee is entered, and another is used when the data is saved. A closer look at the routine used when an employee is first entered shows that it isn't supposed to sort the data completely. It only puts the data in approximate order to speed up the save routine's sorting. Thus, the problem is that the data is printed before it's sorted. The problem with hyphenated names arises because the rough-sort routine doesn't handle niceties such as punctuation characters. Now, you can refine the hypothesis even further.

You hypothesize: Names with punctuation characters aren't sorted correctly until they're saved.

You later confirm this hypothesis with additional test cases.

Tips for Finding Errors

Once you've stabilized an error and refined the test case that produces it, finding its source can be either trivial or challenging, depending on how well you've written your code. If you're having a hard time finding an error, it's probably because the code isn't well written. You might not want to hear that, but it's true. If you're having trouble, consider these tips:

Use all the data available to make your hypothesis. When creating a hypothesis about the source of a defect, account for as much of the data as you can in your hypothesis. In the example, you might have noticed that *Fruit-Loop, Frita* was out of order and created a hypothesis that names beginning with an "F" are sorted incorrectly. That's a poor hypothesis because it doesn't account for the fact that *Modula, Mildred* was out of order or that names are sorted correctly the second time around. If the data doesn't fit the hypothesis, don't discard the data—ask why it doesn't fit, and create a new hypothesis.

The second hypothesis in the example, that the problem arises from names with hyphens, not names that are entered singly, didn't seem initially to account for the fact that names were sorted correctly the second time around either. In this case, however, the second hypothesis led to a more refined hypothesis that proved to be correct. It's all right that the hypothesis doesn't account for all of the data at first as long as you keep refining the hypothesis so that it does eventually.

Refine the test cases that produce the error. If you can't find the source of an error, try to refine the test cases further than you already have. You might be able to vary one parameter more than you had assumed, and focusing on one of the parameters might provide the crucial breakthrough.

Reproduce the error several different ways. Sometimes trying cases that are similar to the error-producing case, but not exactly the same, is instructive. Think of this approach as triangulating the error. If you can get a fix on it from one point and a fix on it from another, you can determine exactly where it is.

Reproducing the error several different ways helps diagnose the cause of the error. Once you think you've identified the error, run a case that's close to the cases that produce errors but that should not produce an error itself. If it does produce an error, you don't completely understand the problem yet. Errors often arise from combinations of factors, and trying to diagnose the problem with only one test case sometimes doesn't diagnose the root problem.

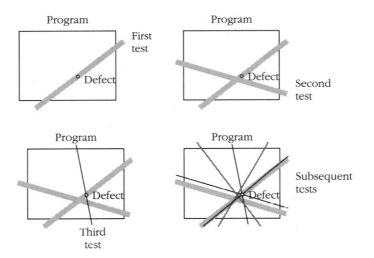

Try to reproduce an error several different ways to determine its exact cause.

Generate more data to generate more hypotheses. Choose test cases that are different from the test cases you already know to be erroneous or correct. Run them to generate more data, and use the new data to add to your list of possible hypotheses.

Use the results of negative tests. Suppose you create a hypothesis and run a test case to prove it. Suppose the test case disproves the hypothesis, so that you still don't know the source of the error. You still know something you didn't before—namely, that the error is not in the area in which you thought it was. That narrows your search field and the set of possible hypotheses.

Brainstorm for possible hypotheses. Rather than limiting yourself to the first hypothesis you think of, try to come up with several. Don't analyze them at first—just come up with as many as you can in a few minutes. Then look at each hypothesis and think about test cases that would prove or disprove it. This mental exercise is helpful in breaking the debugging logjam that results from concentrating too hard on a single line of reasoning.

Narrow the suspicious region of the code. If you've been testing the whole program, or a whole module or routine, test a smaller part instead. Systematically remove parts of the program, and see whether the error still occurs. If it doesn't, you know it's in the part you took away. If it does, you know it's in the part you've kept.

Rather than removing regions haphazardly, divide and conquer. Use a binary search algorithm to focus your search. Try to remove about half the code the first time. Determine the half the error is in, and then divide that section. Again, determine which half contains the error, and again, chop that section in half. Continue until you find the error.

If you use many small routines, you'll be able to chop out sections of code simply by commenting out calls to the routines. Otherwise, you can use comments or preprocessor commands to remove code.

If you're using a debugger, you don't necessarily have to remove pieces of code. You can set a breakpoint partway through the program and check for the error that way instead. If your debugger allows you to skip calls to routines, eliminate suspects by skipping the execution of certain routines and seeing whether the error still occurs. The process with a debugger is otherwise similar to the one in which pieces of a program are physically removed.

CROSS-REFERENCE
For more details on error-prone routines, see "Which Routines Contain the Most Errors?" in Section 25.4.

Be suspicious of routines that have had errors before. Routines that have had errors before are likely to continue to have errors. A routine that has been troublesome in the past is more likely to contain a new error than a routine that has been error-free. Re-examine error-prone routines.

Check code that's changed recently. If you have a new error that's hard to diagnose, it's usually related to code that's changed recently. It could be in completely new code or in changes to old code. If you can't find an error, run an old version of the program to see whether the error occurs. If it doesn't, you know the error's in the new version or is caused by an interaction with the new version. Scrutinize the differences between the old and new versions.

Expand the suspicious region of the code. It's easy to focus on a small section of code, sure that "the error *must* be in this section." If you don't find it in the section, consider the possibility that the error isn't in the section. Expand the area of code you suspect, and then focus on pieces of it using the binary search technique described above.

CROSS-REFERENCE
For a full discussion of integration, see Chapter 27, "System Integration."

Integrate incrementally. Debugging is easy if you add pieces to a system one at a time. If you add a piece to a system and encounter a new error, remove the piece and test it separately. Strap on a test harness and exercise the routine by itself to determine what's wrong.

Use brute force. If you've used incremental integration and a new error raises its ugly head, you'll have a small section of code in which to check for the error. It's sometimes tempting to run the integrated code to find the error rather than dis-integrating the code and checking the new routine by itself. Running a test case through the integrated system, however, might require a few minutes whereas running one through the specific code you're integrating takes only a few seconds. If you don't find the error the first or second time you run the whole system, bite the bullet, dis-integrate the code, and debug the new code separately.

Set a maximum time for quick and dirty debugging. It's always tempting to try for a quick guess rather than systematically instrumenting the code and giving the error no place to hide. The gambler in each of us would rather use a risky approach that might find the error in five minutes than the surefire approach that will find the error in half an hour. The risk is that if the five-minute approach doesn't work, you get stubborn. Finding the error the "easy" way becomes a matter of principle, and hours pass unproductively.

When you decide to go for the quick victory, set a maximum time limit for trying the quick way. If you go past the time limit, resign yourself to the idea that the error is going to be harder to diagnose than you originally thought, and flush it out the hard way. This approach allows you to get the easy errors right away and the hard errors after a bit longer.

Check for common errors. Use code-quality checklists to stimulate your thinking about possible errors. If you're following the inspection practices described in Section 24.2, you'll have your own fine-tuned checklist of the common problems in your environment. You can also use the checklists that appear throughout this book. See the "List of Checklists" following the table of contents.

CROSS REFERENCE
For details on how reviews put a beneficial distance between you and the problem, see Section 24.1, "Role of Reviews in Software Quality Assurance."

Talk to someone else about the problem. Some people call this "confessional debugging." You often discover your own error in the act of explaining it to another person. For example, if you were explaining the problem in the salary example, you might sound like this:

"Hey, Jennifer, have you got a minute? I'm having a problem. I've got this list of employee salaries that's supposed to be sorted, but some names are out of order. They're sorted all right the second time I print them out but not the first. I checked to see if it was new names, but I tried some that worked. I know they should be sorted the first time I print them because the program sorts all the names as they're entered and again when they're saved—wait a minute—no, it doesn't sort them when they're entered. That's right. It only orders them roughly. Thanks, Jennifer. You've been a big help."

Jennifer didn't say a word, and you solved your problem. This result is typical, and this approach is perhaps your most potent tool for solving difficult errors.

Take a break from the problem. Sometimes you concentrate so hard you can't think. How many times have you paused for a cup of coffee and figured out the problem on your way to the coffee machine? Or in the middle of lunch? Or on the way home? If you're debugging and making no progress, once you've tried all the options, let it rest. Go for a walk. Work on something else. Let your subconscious mind tease a solution out of the problem.

The auxiliary benefit of giving up temporarily is that it reduces the anxiety associated with debugging. The onset of anxiety is a clear sign that it's time to take a break.

Syntax Errors

Syntax-error problems are going the way of the woolly mammoth and the saber-toothed tiger. Compilers are getting better at diagnostic messages, and the days when you had to spend two hours finding a misplaced semicolon in a Pascal listing are almost gone. Here's a list of guidelines you can use to hasten the extinction of this endangered species:

Don't trust line numbers in compiler messages. When your compiler reports a mysterious syntax error, look immediately before and immediately after the error—the compiler could have misunderstood the problem or simply have poor diagnostics. Once you find the real error, try to determine the reason the compiler put the message on the wrong statement. Understanding your compiler better can help you find future errors.

Don't trust compiler messages. Compilers try to tell you exactly what's wrong, but compilers are dissembling little rascals, and you often have to read between the lines to know what one really means. For example, in UNIX C, you can get a message that says "floating exception" for an integer divide-by-0. In Fortran, you can get an error message that says "No END terminator in subroutine CRIBAG," which really means that you don't have an END terminator in subroutine NXTHND. You can probably come up with many examples of your own.

Don't trust the compiler's second message. Some compilers are better than others at detecting multiple errors. Some compilers get so excited after detecting the first error that they become giddy and overconfident; they prattle on with dozens of error messages that don't mean anything. Other compilers are more level-headed, and although they must feel a sense of accomplishment when they detect an error, they refrain from spewing out inaccurate messages. If you can't quickly find the source of the second or third error message, don't worry about it. Fix the first one and recompile.

Divide and conquer. The idea of dividing the program into sections to help detect errors works especially well for syntax errors. If you have a troublesome syntax error, remove part of the code and compile again. You'll either get no error (because the error's in the part you removed), get the same error (meaning you need to remove a different part), or get a different error (because you'll have tricked the compiler into producing a message that makes more sense).

CROSS-REFERENCE
Many programming text
editors can automatically
find matching braces or
begin-end pairs. For details
on programming editors,
see "Editing" in Section 20.2.

Find extra comments and quotation marks. If your code is tripping up the compiler because it contains an extra quotation mark or beginning comment somewhere, insert the following sequence systematically into your code to help locate the error:

```
C                /*"/**/
```

or

```
Pascal           {'{}
```

This, fortunately, is not a problem with Fortran, which is the only aspect of Fortran I can think of that recommends it over C or Pascal. It isn't a problem with Basic either.

26.3 Fixing an Error

HARD DATA

The hard part is finding the error. Fixing the error is the easy part. But as with many easy tasks, the fact that it's easy makes it especially error-prone. As Chapter 30 on software evolution points out, defect corrections have more than a 50 percent chance of being wrong the first time (Yourdon 1986b). Here are a few guidelines for reducing the chance of error:

KEY POINT

Understand the problem before you fix it. "The Devil's Guide to Debugging" is right: The best way to make your life difficult and corrode the quality of your program is to fix problems without really understanding them. Before you fix a problem, make sure you understand it to the core. Triangulate the error both with cases that should reproduce the error and with cases that shouldn't reproduce the error. Keep at it until you understand the problem well enough to predict its occurrence correctly every time.

HARD DATA

Understand the program, not just the problem. If you understand the context in which a problem occurs, you're more likely to solve the problem completely rather than only one aspect of it. A study done with short programs found that programmers who achieve a global understanding of program behavior have a better chance of modifying it successfully than programmers who focus on local behavior, learning about the program only as they need to (Littman et al. 1986). Because the program in this study was small (280 lines), it doesn't prove that you should try to understand a 50,000-line program completely before you fix a defect. It does suggest that you should understand at least the code in the vicinity of the error correction—the "vicinity" being not a few lines but a few hundred.

Confirm the error diagnosis. Before you rush to fix an error, make sure that you've diagnosed the problem correctly. Take the time to run test cases that prove your hypothesis and disprove competing hypotheses. If you've proven only that the error could be the result of one of several causes, you don't yet have enough evidence to work on the one cause; rule out the others first.

Relax. A programmer was ready for a ski trip. His product was ready to ship, he was already late, and he had only one more error to correct. He changed the source file and checked it into version control. He didn't recompile the program and didn't verify that the change was correct.

Never debug standing up.

Gerald Weinberg

In fact, the change was not correct, and his manager was outraged. How could he change code in a product that was ready to ship without checking it? What could be worse? Isn't this the pinnacle of professional recklessness?

If this isn't the height of recklessness, it's close, and it's common. Hurrying to solve a problem is one of the most time-ineffective things you can do. It leads to rushed judgments, incomplete error diagnosis, and incomplete corrections. Wishful thinking can lead you to see solutions where there are none. The pressure—often self-imposed—encourages haphazard trial-and-error solutions, sometimes assuming that a solution works without verifying that it does.

Relax long enough to make sure your solution is right. Don't be tempted to take shortcuts. It might take more time, but it'll probably take less. If nothing else, you'll fix the problem correctly and your manager won't call you back from your ski trip.

CROSS-REFERENCE
General issues involved in changing code are discussed in depth in Chapter 30, "Software Evolution."

Save the original source code. Before you begin fixing the error, be sure to archive a version of the code that you can return to later. It's easy to forget which change in a group of changes is the significant one. If you have the original source code, at least you can compare the old and the new files and see where the changes are.

Fix the problem, not the symptom. You should fix the symptom too, but the focus should be on fixing the underlying problem rather than wrapping it in programming duct tape. If you don't thoroughly understand the problem, you're not fixing the code. You're fixing the symptom and making the code worse. Suppose you have this code:

Pascal Example of Code That Needs to Be Fixed

```pascal
for ClaimNumber := 1 to NumClaims[ Client ] do
   begin
   Sum[ Client ] := Sum[ Client ] + ClaimAmount[ ClaimNumber ]
   end;
```

Further suppose that when *Client* equals *45*, *Sum* turns out to be wrong by $3.45. Here's the wrong way to fix the problem:

CODING HORROR

Pascal Example of Making the Code Worse by "Fixing" It

```
for ClaimNumber := 1 to NumClaims[ Client ] do
   begin
   Sum[ Client ] := Sum[ Client ] + ClaimAmount[ ClaimNumber ]
   end;
```

Here's the "fix." ──
```
if ( Client = 45 ) then
   Sum[ 45 ] := Sum[ 45 ] + 3.45;
```

Now suppose that when *Client* equals *37* and the number of claims for the client is *0*, you're not getting *0*. Here's the wrong way to fix the problem:

CODING HORROR

Pascal Example of Making the Code Worse by "Fixing" It (continued)

```
for ClaimNumber := 1 to NumClaims[ Client ] do
   begin
   Sum[ Client ] := Sum[ Client ] + ClaimAmount[ ClaimNumber ]
   end;

if ( Client = 45 ) then
   Sum[ 45 ] :- Sum[ 45 ] + 3.45
```
Here's the ──
second "fix."
```
else if ( Client = 37 ) and ( NumClaims[ Client ] = 0.0 ) then
   Sum[ 37 ] :- 0.0;
```

If this doesn't send a cold chill down your spine, you won't be affected by anything else in this book either. It's impossible to list all the problems with this approach in a book that's only a little over 800 pages long, but here are the top three:

- The fixes won't work most of the time. The problems look as though they're the result of initialization errors. Initialization errors are, by definition, unpredictable, so the fact that the sum for client 45 is off by $3.45 today doesn't tell you anything about tomorrow. It could be off by $10,000.02, or it could be correct. That's the nature of initialization errors.

- It's unmaintainable. When code is special-cased to work around errors, the special cases become the code's most prominent feature. The $3.45 won't always be $3.45, and another error will show up later. The code will be modified again to handle the new special case, and the special case for $3.45 won't be removed. The code will become increasingly barnacled with special cases. Eventually the barnacles will be too heavy for the code to support, and the code will sink to the bottom of the ocean— a fitting place for it.

- It uses the computer for something that's better done by hand. Computers are good at predictable, systematic calculations, but humans are better at fudging data creatively. You'd be wiser to treat the output with White-out and a typewriter than to monkey with the code.

Change the code only for good reason. Related to fixing symptoms is the technique of changing code at random until it seems to work. The typical line of reasoning goes like this: "This loop seems to contain an error. It's probably an off-by-one error, so I'll just put a −1 here and try it. OK. That didn't work, so I'll just put a +1 in instead. OK. That seems to work. I'll say it's fixed."

As popular as this practice is, it isn't effective. Making changes to code randomly is like poking a jellyfish with a stick to see if it moves. You're not learning anything; you're just goofing around. By changing the program randomly, you say in effect, "I don't know what's happening here, but I'll try this change and hope it works." Don't change code randomly. The more different you make it without understanding it, the less confidence you'll have that it works correctly.

Before you make a change, be confident that it will work. Being wrong about a change should leave you astonished. It should cause self-doubt, personal re-evaluation, and deep soul-searching. It should happen rarely.

Make one change at a time. Changes are tricky enough when they're done one at a time. When done two at a time, they can introduce subtle errors that look like the original errors. Then you're in the awkward position of not knowing whether (1) you didn't correct the error, (2) you corrected the error but introduced a new one that looks similar, or (3) you didn't correct the error and you introduced a similar new error. Keep it simple: Make just one change at a time.

CROSS-REFERENCE
For details on automated regression testing, see "Retesting (Regression Testing)" in Section 25.6.

Check your fix. Check the program yourself, have someone else check it for you, or walk through it with someone else. Run the same triangulation test cases you used to diagnose the problem to make sure that all aspects of the problem have been resolved. If you've solved only part of the problem, you'll find out that you still have work to do.

Rerun the whole program to check for side effects of your changes. The easiest and most effective way to check for side effects is to run the program through an automated suite of regression tests.

Look for similar errors. When you find one error, look for others that are similar. Errors tend to occur in groups, and one of the values of paying attention to the kinds of errors you make is that you can correct all the errors of that kind. Looking for similar errors requires you to have a thorough understanding of the problem. Watch for the warning sign: If you can't figure out how to look for similar errors, that's a sign that you don't yet completely understand the problem.

26.4 Psychological Considerations in Debugging

FURTHER READING
For an excellent discussion of psychological issues in debugging, as well as many other areas of software development, see *The Psychology of Computer Programming* (Weinberg 1971).

Debugging is as intellectually demanding as any other software-development activity. Your ego tells you that your code is good and doesn't have an error even when you have seen that it has one. You have to think precisely—forming hypotheses, collecting data, analyzing hypotheses, and methodically rejecting them—with a formality that's unnatural to many people. If you're both building code and debugging it, you have to switch quickly between the fluid, creative thinking that goes with design and the rigidly critical thinking that goes with debugging. As you read your code, you have to battle the code's familiarity and guard against seeing what you expect to see.

How "Psychological Set" Contributes to Debugging Blindness

When you see a token in a program that says *Num*, what do you see? Do you see a misspelling of the word "Numb"? Or do you see the abbreviation for "Number"? Most likely, you see the abbreviation for "Number." This is the phenomenon of "psychological set"—seeing what you expect to see. What does this sign say?

Paris in the
the Spring

In this classic puzzle, people often see only one "the." People see what they expect to see. Consider the following:

- Students who are taught the three structured-control constructs expect all programs to operate that way. When they see code containing *goto*s, they expect the *goto*s to follow one of the three patterns they already know; it doesn't occur to them that the *goto*s might not (Lewis 1979).

- Students learning *while* loops often expect a loop to be continuously evaluated; that is, they expect the loop to terminate as soon as the *while* condition becomes false, rather than only at the top or bottom (Curtis et al. 1986). They expect a *while* loop to act as "while" does in natural language.

- Errors in assignment statements are about three times as hard to find as errors in arrays or "interaction errors" (Gould 1975). Programmers look for off-by-one errors and side-effects but overlook problems in simple statements.

- A programmer who unintentionally used both the variable SYSTSTS and the variable SYSSTSTS thought he was using a single variable. He didn't discover the problem until the program had been run hundreds of times, and a book was written containing the erroneous results (Weinberg 1971).

- A programmer looking at code like this code:

```
if ( X < Y ) then
   Swap := X
   X := Y
   Y := Swap
```

sometimes sees code like this code:

```
if ( X < Y ) then
   begin
   Swap := X
   X := Y
   Y := Swap
   end
```

People expect a new phenomenon to resemble similar phenomena they've seen before. They expect a new control construct to work the same as old constructs; programming-langauge *while* statements to work the same as real-life "while" statements; and variable names to be the same as they've been before. You see what you expect to see and thus overlook differences, like the misspelling of the word "language" in the previous sentence.

What does psychological set have to do with debugging? First, it speaks to the importance of good programming practices. Good formatting, commenting, variable names, routine names, and other elements of programming style help structure the programming background so that likely defects appear as variations and stand out.

The second impact of psychological set is in selecting parts of the program to examine when an error is found. Research has shown that the programmers who debug most effectively mentally slice away parts of the program that aren't relevant during debugging (Basili, Selby, and Hutchens 1986). In general, the practice allows excellent programmers to narrow their search fields and find errors more quickly. Sometimes, however, the part of the program that contains the error is mistakenly sliced away. You spend time scouring a section of code for an error, and you ignore the section that contains the error.

You took a wrong turn at the fork in the road and need to back up before you can go forward again. Some of the suggestions in Section 26.2's discussion of tips for finding errors are designed to overcome this "debugging blindness."

How "Psychological Distance" Can Help

CROSS-REFERENCE
For details on creating variable names that won't be confusing, see Section 9.7, "Kinds of Names to Avoid."

Psychological distance can be defined as the ease with which two items can be differentiated. If you are looking at a long list of words and have been told that they're all about ducks, you could easily mistake "Queck" for "Quack" because the two words look similar. The psychological distance between the words is small. You would be much less likely to mistake "Tuack" for "Quack" even though the difference is only one letter again. "Tuack" is less like "Quack" than "Queck" is because the first letter in a word is more prominent than the one in the middle.

Here are examples of psychological distances between variable names:

First Variable	Second Variable	Psychological Distance
STOPPT	STOPPT	Almost invisible
SHIFTRF	SHIFTRT	Almost none
CLAIMS1	CLAIMS2	Small
GCOUNT	CCOUNT	Small
PRODUCT	SUM	Large

As you debug, be ready for the problems caused by insufficient psychological distance between similar variable names and between similar routine names. As you construct code, choose names with large differences so that you avoid the problem.

26.5 Debugging Tools

CROSS-REFERENCE
The line between testing tools and debugging tools is fuzzy. For details on testing tools, see Section 25.5, "Test-Support Tools." For details on tools for other software-development activities, see Chapter 20, "Programming Tools."

You can do much of the detailed, brain-busting work of debugging with debugging tools that are readily available. The tool that will drive the final stake through the heart of the defect vampire isn't yet available, but each year brings an incremental improvement in available capabilities.

Source-Code Comparator

A source-code comparator is useful when you're modifying a program in response to errors. If you make several changes and need to remove some that you can't quite remember, a comparator can pinpoint the differences and jog your memory. If you discover a defect in a new version that you don't remember in an older version, you can compare the files to determine exactly what changed.

Compiler Warning Messages

KEY POINT

One of the simplest and most effective debugging tools is your own compiler.

Set your compiler's warning level to the highest, pickiest level possible and fix the code so that it doesn't produce any compiler warnings. It's sloppy to ignore compiler errors. It's even sloppier to turn off the warnings so that you can't even see them. Children sometimes think that if they close their eyes and can't see you, they've made you go away. Setting a switch on the compiler to turn off warnings just means you can't see the errors. It doesn't make them go away any more than closing your eyes makes an adult go away.

Assume that the people who wrote the compiler know a great deal more about your language than you do. If they're warning you about something, it usually means you have an opportunity to learn something new about your language. Make the effort to understand what the warning really means.

Treat warnings as errors. Some compilers let you treat warnings as errors. One reason to use the feature is that it elevates the apparent importance of a warning. Just as setting your watch five minutes fast tricks you into thinking it's five minutes later than it is, setting your compiler to treat warnings as errors tricks you into taking them more seriously. Another reason to treat warnings as errors is that they often affect how your program compiles. When you compile and link a program, warnings typically won't stop the program from linking but errors typically will. If you want to check warnings before you link, set the compiler switch that treats warnings as errors.

Initiate projectwide standards for compile-time settings. Set a standard that requires everyone on your team to compile code using the same compiler settings. Otherwise, when you try to integrate code compiled by different people with different settings, you'll get a flood of error messages and an integration nightmare.

Extended Syntax and Logic Checking

You can buy additional tools to check your code more thoroughly than your compiler does. For example, for C programmers, the lint utility painstakingly checks for use of uninitialized variables, writing = when you mean = =, and similarly subtle problems.

Execution Profiler

You might not think of an execution profiler as a debugging tool, but a few minutes spent studying a program profile can uncover some surprising (and hidden) errors.

For example, I had suspected that a memory-management routine in one of my programs was a performance bottleneck. Memory management had originally been a small component using a linearly ordered array of pointers to memory. I replaced the linearly ordered array with a hash table in the expectation that execution time would drop by at least half. But after profiling the code, I found no change in performance at all. I examined the code more closely and found an error that was wasting a huge amount of time in the allocation algorithm. The bottleneck hadn't been the linear-search technique; it was the error. I hadn't needed to optimize the search after all. Examine the output of an execution profiler to satisfy yourself that your program spends a reasonable amount of time in each area.

Scaffolding

CROSS-REFERENCE
For details on scaffolding, see "Building Scaffolding to Test Individual Routines" in Section 25.5.

As mentioned in Section 26.2 on finding errors, pulling out a troublesome piece of code, writing code to test it, and executing it by itself is often the most effective way to exorcise the demons from an error-prone program.

Debugger

High-level symbolic debuggers are far more efficient than print statements, even if the print statements aren't scattered randomly. Commercially available debuggers have advanced rapidly in the last 10 years, and the capabilities available today can change the way you program.

Good debuggers allow you to set breakpoints to break when execution reaches a specific line, or the nth time it reaches a specific line, or when a global variable changes, or when a variable is assigned a specific value. They allow you to step through code line by line, stepping through or over routines. They allow the program to be executed backwards, stepping back to the point where an error originated. They allow you to log the execution of specific statements—similar to scattering "I'm here!" print statements throughout a program.

Good debuggers allow full examination of data, including structured and dynamically allocated data. They make it easy to view the contents of a linked list of pointers or a dynamically allocated array. They're intelligent about user-defined data types. They allow you to make ad hoc queries about data, assign new values, and continue program execution.

You can look at the high-level language or the assembly language generated by your compiler. If you're using several languages, the debugger automatically displays the correct language for each section of code. You can look at a chain of calls to routines and quickly view the source code of any routine. You can change parameters to a program within the debugger environment. A good debugger should allow you to pick a routine and exercise it directly from the debugger, but I don't know of any debuggers that currently support that capability.

The best of today's debuggers also remember debugging parameters (breakpoints, variables being watched, and so on) for each individual program so that you don't have to re-create them for each program you debug.

Hardware debuggers operate in hardware rather than software so that they don't interfere with the execution of the program being debugged. They're essential when you are debugging programs that are sensitive to timing or the amount of memory available.

An interactive debugger is an outstanding example of what is not needed—it encourages trial-and-error hacking rather than systematic design, and also hides marginal people barely qualified for precision programming.

Harlan Mills

Given the enormous power offered by modern debuggers, you might be surprised that anyone would criticize them. But some of the most respected people in computer science recommend not using them. They recommend using your brain and avoiding debugging tools altogether. Their argument is that debugging tools are a crutch and that you find problems faster by thinking about them than by relying on tools. They argue that you, rather than the debugger, should mentally execute the program to flush out errors.

Research on the effectiveness of interactive debuggers is scarce, and I don't know of any that has been done using the powerful debuggers developed within the last five years. Some research done earlier, however, suggests that mental execution of a program isn't necessarily required for effective debugging (Vessey 1986).

Regardless of the empirical evidence, the basic argument against debuggers isn't valid. The fact that a tool can be misused doesn't imply that it should be rejected. You wouldn't avoid taking aspirin merely because it's possible to overdose. You wouldn't avoid mowing your lawn with a power mower just because it's possible to cut yourself. Any other powerful tool can be used or abused, and so can a debugger.

KEY POINT

The debugger isn't a substitute for good thinking. But, in some cases, thinking isn't a substitute for a good debugger either. The most effective combination is good thinking and a good debugger.

CHECKLIST

Debugging

TECHNIQUES FOR FINDING ERRORS

❑ Use all the data available to form a hypothesis.

❑ Refine the test cases that produce the error.

❑ Reproduce the error several different ways.

❑ Generate more data to generate more hypotheses.

❑ Use the results of negative tests.

❑ Brainstorm for possible hypotheses.

❑ Narrow the suspicious region of the code.

❑ Check code that's changed recently.

❑ Expand the suspicious region of the code.

❑ Integrate incrementally.

❑ Be suspicious of routines that have had errors before.

❑ Use brute force.

❑ Set a maximum time for quick and dirty debugging.

❑ Check for common errors.

❑ Use confessional debugging.

❑ Take a break from the problem.

TECHNIQUES FOR FIXING ERRORS

❑ Understand the problem.

❑ Understand the program as well as the problem.

❑ Confirm the error diagnosis.

❑ Relax.

❑ Save the original source code.

❑ Fix the problem, not just the symptom.

❑ Change the code only for good reason.

❑ Make one change at a time.

❑ Check your work. Verify that the fix is correct.

❑ Look for similar errors.

(continued)

Debugging checklist, *continued*

GENERAL APPROACH TO DEBUGGING

❑ Do you use debugging as an opportunity to learn more about your program, mistakes, code quality, and problem-solving approach?

❑ Do you avoid the trial-and-error, superstitious approach to debugging?

❑ Do you assume that errors are your fault?

❑ Do you use the scientific method to stabilize intermittent errors?

❑ Do you use the scientific method to find errors?

❑ Rather than using the same approach every time, do you use several different techniques to find errors?

❑ Do you verify that the fix is correct?

❑ Do you use warning messages, execution profiling, scaffolding, and interactive debugging?

Further Reading

Stitt, Martin. *Debugging: Creative Techniques and Tools for Software Repair.* New York: John Wiley, 1992. This enormously practical book includes sections on how errors arise, how to find errors, how to fix errors, and how to program in ways that avoid errors. It includes an extensive discussion of debugging tools and a unique appendix that allows you to look up the symptoms of a problem and find appropriate debugging approaches. Most of the techniques and tool suggestions apply to UNIX, the Macintosh, and other environments as well as they apply to the MS-DOS environment the book uses as a vehicle for its discussions.

Ward, Robert. *A Programmer's Introduction to Debugging C.* Lawrence, Kans.: R & D Publications, 1989. This book focuses on debugging techniques that are especially useful for dealing with the specific problems of C—pointers, macros, lack of array bounds checking, misplaced equals signs, and so on. It's a thoughtful and thorough explanation of debugging but is less generally applicable to non-C programming than Stitt's book.

IEEE Software 8, no. 3 (May 1991). This issue is ostensibly devoted to the topic of debugging. It includes seven strongly academic articles that focus on the future of debugging tools. Some of the articles are out of touch with current debugging technology. For example, one article claims that no researchers have "produced debuggers that are effective enough for high-level debugging" and cites a debugging symposium held in 1983 as proof. I didn't like the debuggers that were available in 1983 either, but the tools I use now are several generations beyond what was available then. In spite of some weak spots, other articles genuinely represent the state of the art and provide an exciting forecast of what might be commercially available within a few years.

Myers, Glenford J. *The Art of Software Testing.* New York: John Wiley, 1979. Chapter 7 of this classic book is devoted to debugging.

Key Points

- Debugging is a make-or-break aspect of software development. The best approach is to use other techniques described in this book to avoid errors in the first place. It's still worth your time to improve your debugging skills, however, because the difference between good and poor debugging performance is at least 10 to 1 and probably greater.

- Set your compiler warning to the pickiest level possible, and fix the errors it reports. It's hard to fix subtle errors if you ignore the obvious ones.

- A systematic approach to finding and fixing errors is critical to success. Focus your debugging so that each test moves you a step forward.

- Understand the root problem before you fix the program. Random guesses about the sources of errors and random corrections will leave the program in worse condition than when you started.

- Debugging tools are powerful aids to software development. Find them and use them. Remember to use your brain at the same time.

27

System Integration

Contents

Related Topics

THE TERM "INTEGRATION" REFERS TO the software-development activity in which you combine separate software components into a single system. On small projects, integration might consist of a morning spent hooking a handful of routines together. On large projects, it might consist of weeks or months of hooking sets of programs together. Regardless of the size of the task, common principles apply.

27.1 Importance of the Integration Method

In engineering fields other than software, the importance of proper integration is well known. The Pacific Northwest, where I live, saw a dramatic illustration of the hazards of poor integration when the football stadium at the University of Washington collapsed partway through construction.

The football stadium add-on at the University of Washington collapsed because it wasn't strong enough to support itself during construction. It likely would have been strong enough when completed, but it was constructed in the wrong order— an integration error.

The structure wasn't strong enough to support itself as it was being built. It doesn't matter that it would have been strong enough by the time it was done; it needed to be strong enough at each step. If you integrate software in the wrong order, it's hard to code, hard to test, and hard to debug. If none of it will work until all of it works, it can seem as though it will never be finished. It too can collapse under its own weight during construction—even though the finished product would work.

Because it's done after a developer has finished unit testing and in conjunction with system testing, integration is sometimes thought of as a testing activity. It's complex enough, however, that it should be viewed as an independent activity. Here are some of the benefits you can expect from careful integration:

KEY POINT

- Easier defect diagnosis
- Fewer defects
- Less scaffolding
- Shorter time to first working product
- Shorter overall development schedules

- Better customer relations
- Improved morale
- Improved chance of project completion
- More reliable schedule estimates
- More accurate status reporting
- Improved code quality
- Less documentation

These might seem like elevated claims for system testing's forgotten child, but the fact that it's overlooked in spite of its importance is precisely the reason integration has its own chapter in this book.

27.2 Phased vs. Incremental Integration

Programs are integrated by means of either the phased or the incremental approach.

Phased Integration

Until a few years ago, phased integration was the norm. It follows these well-defined steps:

1. Design, code, test, and debug each routine. This step is called "unit development."
2. Combine the routines into one whopping-big system. This is called "system integration."
3. Test and debug the whole system. This is called "system dis-integration." (Thanks to Meilir Page-Jones for this witty observation.)

CROSS-REFERENCE
Many integration problems arise from using global data. For techniques on working with global data safely, see Section 10.6, "Global Variables."

One problem with phased integration is that when the routines in a system are put together for the first time, new problems inevitably surface and the causes of the problems could be anywhere. Since you have a large number of routines that have never worked together before, the culprit might be a poorly tested routine, an error in the interface between two routines, or an error caused by an interaction between two routines. All routines are suspect.

The uncertainty about the location of any of the specific problems is compounded by the fact that all the problems suddenly present themselves at once. This forces you to deal not only with problems caused by interactions between routines but with problems that are hard to diagnose because the problems themselves interact. For this reason, another name for phased integration is "big bang integration."

Phased Integration

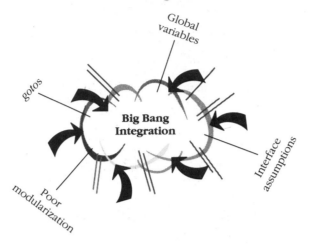

Phased integration can't begin until late in the project, after all the routines have been unit-tested. When the routines are finally combined and errors surface by the score, programmers immediately go into panicky debugging mode rather than methodical error detection and correction.

For small programs—no, for tiny programs—phased integration might be the best approach. If the program has only two or three routines, phased integration might save you time, if you're lucky. But in most cases, another approach is better.

Incremental Integration

CROSS-REFERENCE
Metaphors appropriate for incremental integration are discussed in "Software Oyster Farming: System Accretion" and "Software Construction: Building Software" in Section 2.3.

The metaphors chapter mentioned that it was unfortunate that no one had ever written a book about incremental approaches to software development because it would be a potent collection of techniques. Incremental integration is one such technique.

General approach

In incremental integration, you write and test a program in small pieces and then combine the pieces one at a time. In this one-piece-at-a-time approach to integration, you follow these steps:

1. Develop a small, functional part of the system. It can be the smallest functional part, the hardest part, or a key part. Thoroughly test and debug it. It will serve as a skeleton on which to hang the muscles, nerves, and skin that make up the remaining parts of the system.

2. Design, code, test, and debug a routine.

3. Integrate the new routine with the skeleton. Test and debug the combination of skeleton and new routine. Make sure the combination works before you add any new routines. If work remains to be done, repeat the process starting at step 2.

Occasionally, you might want to integrate units larger than a routine. If a module has been thoroughly tested, for example, and each of its component routines put through a mini-integration, you can integrate the whole module and still be doing incremental integration. The system grows and gains momentum as you add pieces to it in the same way that a snowball grows and gains momentum when it rolls down a hill.

Incremental Integration

Snowballing Integration

Benefits of incremental integration

The incremental approach offers many advantages over the traditional phased approach regardless of which incremental strategy you use.

Errors are easy to locate. When new problems surface during incremental integration, the new routine is obviously at fault. Either its interface to the rest of the program contains an error or its interaction with a previously integrated routine produces an error. Either way, you know exactly where to look. Moreover, simply because you have fewer problems at once, you reduce the risk that multiple problems will interact or that one problem will mask another. The more interface errors you tend to have, the more this benefit of incremental integration will help your projects. A record of errors for one project revealed that 39 percent were intermodule interface errors (Basili and Perricone 1984). Since developers on many projects spend up to 50 percent of their time debugging, maximizing debugging effectiveness by making errors easy to locate provides benefits in quality and productivity.

HARD DATA

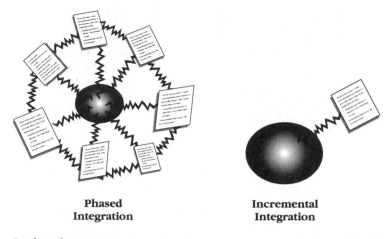

**Phased
Integration**

**Incremental
Integration**

In phased integration, you integrate so many components at once that it's hard to know where the error is. It might be in in any of the components or in any of their connections. In incremental integration, the error is either in the new component or in the connection between the new component and the system.

The system succeeds early in the project. When code is integrated and running, even if the system isn't usable, it's apparent that it soon will be. With incremental integration, programmers see early results from their work, so their morale is better than when they suspect that their project will never draw its first breath. Management also has a more tangible sense of progress from seeing a system working with 50 percent of its capability than from hearing that coding is "99 percent complete."

The units of the system are tested more fully. Integration starts early in the project. You integrate each routine as it's developed, rather than waiting for one magnificent binge of integration at the end. Routines are unit-tested in both cases, but each routine is exercised as a part of the overall system more often with incremental integration than it is with phased integration.

You can build the system with a shorter development schedule. If integration is planned carefully, you can design part of the system while another part is being coded. This doesn't reduce the total number of work-hours required to develop the complete design and code, but it allows some work to be done in parallel, an advantage when calendar time is at a premium.

Incremental integration supports and encourages other incremental strategies. The advantages of incrementalism applied to integration are the tip of the iceberg. A more complete incremental approach is described in Section 27.4, "Evolutionary Delivery."

27.3 Incremental Integration Strategies

With phased integration, you don't have to plan the order in which project components are built. All components are integrated at the same time, so you can build them in any order as long as they're all ready by D-day.

With incremental integration, you have to plan more carefully. Most systems will call for the integration of some components before the integration of others. Planning for integration thus affects planning for construction; the order in which components are constructed has to support the order in which they will be integrated.

Integration-order strategies come in a variety of shapes and sizes, and none is best in every case. The best integration approach varies from project to project, and the best solution is always the one that you create to meet the specific demands of a specific project. Knowing the points on the methodological numberline will give you insight into the possible solutions.

Top-Down Integration

In top-down integration, the routine at the top of the hierarchy is written and integrated first. Stubs have to be written to exercise the top routine. Then, as routines are integrated from the top down, stub routines are replaced with real ones. Here's how this kind of integration proceeds:

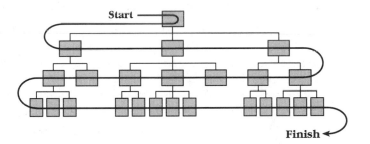

In top-down integration, you add routines at the top first, at the bottom last.

An important aspect of top-down integration is that the interfaces between routines and modules must be carefully specified. The most troublesome errors to debug are not the ones that affect single routines but those that arise from subtle interactions between routines. Careful interface specification can reduce the problem. Interface specification isn't especially an integration activity, but making sure that the interfaces have been specified well is.

In addition to the advantages you get from any kind of incremental integration, an advantage of top-down integration is that the control logic of the system is tested relatively early. All the routines at the top of the hierarchy are exercised a lot, so that big, conceptual, design problems are exposed quickly.

Another advantage of top-down integration is that, if you plan it carefully, you can complete a partially working system early in the project. If the user-interface parts are at the top, you can get a basic interface working quickly and flesh out the details later. The morale of both users and programmers benefits from getting something visible working early.

Top-down incremental integration also allows you to begin coding before the low-level design details are complete. Once the design has been driven down to a fairly low level of detail in all areas, you can begin implementation and integration of the routines at the higher levels without waiting to dot every "i" and cross every "t."

In spite of these advantages, pure top-down integration usually involves disadvantages that are more troublesome than you'll want to put up with.

Pure top-down integration leaves exercising the tricky hardware interfaces until last. If hardware interfaces are buggy or a performance problem, you'd usually like to get to them long before the end of the project. It's not unusual for a low-level problem to bubble its way to the top of the system, causing high-level changes and reducing the benefit of earlier integration work. Minimize the bubbling problem through early careful unit testing and performance analysis of the routines that exercise hardware interfaces.

Another problem with pure top-down integration is that it takes a dump truck full of stubs to integrate from the top down. Many low-level routines haven't been integrated, which implies that a large number of stubs will be needed during intermediate steps in integration. Stubs are problematic in that, as test code, they are more likely to contain errors than the more carefully designed production code. Errors in the new stubs that support a new routine defeat the purpose of incremental integration, which is to restrict the source of errors to one new routine.

CROSS-REFERENCE
Top-down integration is related to top-down design in name only. For details on top-down design, see "Top-down decomposition" in Section 7.2.

Top-down integration is also nearly impossible to implement purely. In top-down integration done by the book, you start at the top (call it Level 1) and then integrate all the routines at the next level (Level 2). When you've integrated all the routines from Level 2, and not before, you integrate the routines from Level 3. The rigidity in pure top-down integration is completely arbitrary. It's hard to imagine anyone going to the trouble of using pure top-down integration. Most people use a hybrid approach such as integrating from the top down in sections instead.

Finally, you can't use top-down integration if the collection of routines doesn't have a top. If you use object-oriented design, the collection won't have a top

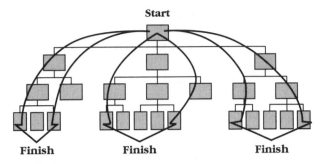

As an alternative to proceeding strictly top to bottom, you can integrate from the top down in sections.

and you'll need a different integration strategy. In many interactive systems, the location of the "top" is subjective. Although top-down integration isn't the same thing as top-down design, they do have one thing in common—a top. If you design a system using top-down design, at least you know that it has a top, and you can integrate it from the top down.

Even though pure top-down integration isn't workable, thinking about it will help you decide on a general approach. Some of the benefits and hazards that apply to a pure top-down approach apply, less obviously, to a looser top-down approach, so keep them in mind.

Bottom-Up Integration

In bottom-up integration, you write and integrate the routines at the bottom of the hierarchy first. Adding the low-level routines one at a time rather than all at once is what makes bottom-up integration an incremental integration strategy. You write test drivers to exercise the low-level routines initially and add routines to the test-driver scaffolding as they're developed. As you add higher-level routines, you replace driver routines with real ones. Here's the order in which routines are integrated in the bottom-up approach:

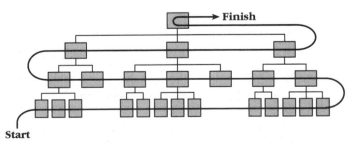

In bottom-up integration, you integrate routines at the bottom first, at the top last.

659

Bottom-up integration provides a limited set of incremental-integration advantages. It restricts the possible sources of error to the single routine being integrated, so errors are easy to locate. Integration can start early in the project.

Bottom-up integration also exercises potentially troublesome hardware interfaces early. Since hardware limitations often determine whether you can meet the system's goals, making sure the hardware has done a full set of calisthenics is worth the trouble.

What are the problems with bottom-up integration? The main problem is that it leaves integration of the major, high-level system interfaces until last. If the system has conceptual design problems at the higher levels, the implementation activity won't find them until all the detailed work has been done. If the design must be changed significantly, some of the low-level work might have to be discarded.

Bottom-up integration requires you to complete the design of the whole system before you start integration. If you don't, assumptions that needn't have controlled the design might end up deeply embedded in low-level code, giving rise to the awkward situation in which you design high-level routines to work around problems in low-level ones. Letting low-level details drive the design of higher-level routines contradicts principles of information hiding and structured design. The problems of integrating higher-level routines are but a teardrop in a rainstorm compared to the problems you'll have if you don't complete the design of high-level routines before you begin low-level coding.

As with top-down integration, pure bottom-up integration is rare, and you can use a hybrid approach instead, including integrating in sections.

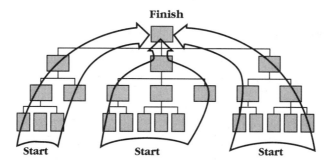

As an alternative to proceeding purely bottom to top, you can integrate from the bottom up in sections. This blurs the line between bottom-up integration and feature-oriented integration, which is described later in this chapter.

Sandwich Integration

The problems with pure top-down and pure bottom-up integration have led some programmers to recommend a sandwich approach (Myers 1976). You first integrate the control routines at the top of the hierarchy. Then you integrate the device-interface routines and widely used utility routines at the bottom. These high-level and low-level routines are the bread of the sandwich.

You leave the middle-level routines until later. These make up the meat, cheese, and tomatoes of the sandwich. If you're a vegetarian, they might make up the tofu and bean sprouts of the sandwich, but the author of sandwich integration is silent on this point—maybe his mouth was full.

Here's an illustration of the sandwich approach:

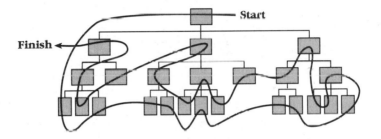

In sandwich integration, you integrate top-level and widely used bottom-level routines first, and save middle-level routines for last.

This approach avoids the rigidity of pure bottom-up or top-down integration. It integrates the often-troublesome routines first and has the potential to minimize the amount of scaffolding you'll need. It's a realistic, practical approach.

The next approach is similar and more sophisticated.

Risk-Oriented Integration

Risk-oriented integration is also called "hard part first" integration. It's like sandwich integration in that it seeks to avoid the problems inherent in pure top-down or pure bottom-up integration. Coincidentally, it also tends to integrate the routines at the top and the bottom first, saving the middle-level routines for last. The motivation, however, is different.

In risk-oriented integration, you identify the level of risk associated with each routine. You decide which will be the most challenging parts to implement, and you implement them first. Experience indicates that top-level interfaces are risky, so they are often at the top of the risk list. Hardware interfaces, usually at the bottom level of the hierarchy, are also risky, so they're also at the top of the risk list. In addition, you might know of routines in the middle that will be challenging. Perhaps a routine implements a poorly understood algorithm or has ambitious performance goals. Such routines can also be identified as high risks and integrated relatively early.

The remainder of the code, the easy stuff, can wait until later. Some of it will probably turn out to be harder than you thought, but that's unavoidable. Here's an illustration of risk-oriented integration:

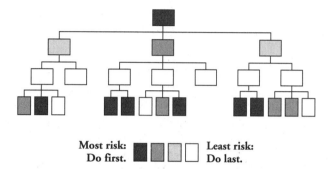

Most risk: ■■□□ **Least risk:**
Do first. **Do last.**

In risk-oriented integration, you integrate routines that you expect to be most troublesome first; you implement easier routines later.

Feature-Oriented Integration

A final kind of incremental integration is integrating one feature at a time. The term "feature" doesn't refer to anything fancy—just an identifiable function of the system you're integrating. If you're writing a word processor, a feature might be displaying underlining on the screen or reformatting the document automatically—something like that.

CROSS-REFERENCE
Feature-oriented integration is a good strategy to use in conjunction with evolutionary delivery, described in Section 27.4.
Many features must be implemented in multiple routines, which puts a twist on the one-routine-at-a-time aspect of incremental integration. When the feature to be integrated is bigger than a single routine, the "increment" in incremental integration is bigger than a single routine. This diminishes the benefit of incrementalism a little in that it reduces your certainty about the source of new errors, but if you have thoroughly tested the routines that implement the new feature before you integrate them, that's only a small disadvantage. You can use the incremental integration strategies recursively by integrating small pieces to form features and then incrementally integrating features to form a system.

You'll usually want to start with a skeleton you've chosen for its ability to support the other features. In an interactive system, the first feature might be the interactive menu system. You can hang the rest of the features on the feature that you integrate first. Here's how it looks graphically:

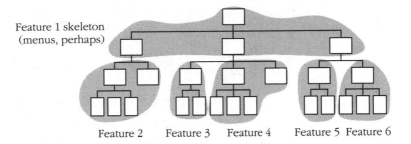

In feature-oriented integration, you integrate routines in groups that make up identifiable features—usually, but not always, more than one routine at a time.

Components are added in "feature trees," hierarchical collections of routines that make up a feature. Integration is easier if each feature is relatively independent, perhaps calling the same low-level library code as the routines for other features, but having no calls to middle-level code in common with other features. (The shared, low-level library routines aren't shown in the illustration above.)

Feature-oriented integration offers three main advantages. First, it eliminates scaffolding for virtually everything except low-level library routines. The skeleton might need a little scaffolding, or some parts of the skeleton might simply not be operational until particular features have been added. When each feature has been hung on the structure, however, no additional scaffolding is needed. Since each feature is self-contained, each feature contains all the support code it needs.

The second main advantage is that each newly integrated feature brings about an incremental addition in functionality. This provides evidence that the project is moving steadily forward, and such incremental additions are the essence of evolutionary delivery, discussed later in the chapter.

A third advantage is that feature-oriented integration works well with object-oriented design. Objects tend to map well to features, which makes feature-oriented integration a natural choice for object-oriented systems.

Pure feature-oriented integration is as difficult to pursue as pure top-down or bottom-up integration. Usually some of the low-level code must be integrated before certain significant features can be.

Bottom-up, top-down, sandwich, risk-oriented, feature-oriented—do you get the feeling that people are making these names up as they go along? They are.

None of these approaches are robust procedures that you should follow methodically from step 1 to step 47 and then declare yourself to be done. Like software-design approaches, they are heuristics more than algorithms, and rather than following any procedure dogmatically, you come out ahead by making up a unique strategy tailored to your specific project.

CHECKLIST

Incremental Integration Strategy

❑ Does the strategy identify the optimal order in which routines and modules should be integrated?

❑ Is the integration order coordinated with the construction order so that routines will be ready for integration at the right time?

❑ Does the strategy lead to easy diagnosis of defects?

❑ Does the strategy keep scaffolding to a minimum?

❑ Is the strategy better than other approaches?

❑ Have the interfaces between components been specified well? (Specifying interfaces isn't an integration task, but verifying that they have been specified well is.)

When used thoughtfully, incremental integration is a powerful asset to a software project. The evolutionary-delivery strategy described in the next section is an example of the power of incremental strategies when applied throughout a project.

27.4 Evolutionary Delivery

Evolutionary delivery is an incremental approach to delivering software. In some ways, it's a broader concept than incremental integration, but its main technical features are incremental integration and an exceptionally careful ordering of construction activities.

Expedition Analogies

The approaches of different explorers to planning their expeditions suggest some possibilities for approaches to planning software development.

The first approach to planning is to map out everything to the nth detail. This is similar to the approach Roald Amundsen used in planning his quest for the South Pole. In this approach, you plan every aspect of the trip: the number of explorers and dogs, the amount of equipment and food, the route you'll take, when you'll eat the food, the number of miles you'll travel per day, when you'll get to the South Pole, how long you'll stay there, and what you'll do. You leave little to chance.

If your planning is accurate enough, you'll have a predictable project. If you're working in a familiar area, your customer knows exactly what's needed, and you have a strict schedule, Amundsen's kind of planning is effective. On some projects, your customer might require a detailed schedule of activities, essentially forcing an Amundsen-style mission.

This approach can have several disadvantages, though—all arising from the rigidity of the plan. Simple changes in the working environment can cause major problems in your plan. Amundsen could have encountered an unexpected storm, an illness, or mechanical problems with the dogsleds. A delay two days longer than planned could have meant a failed mission. You might have computer downtime, a steeper learning curve than you anticipated, or turnover in personnel that makes you late.

Amundsen planning also inhibits your ability to respond to changes in the customer environment. If Amundsen had found the Abominable Snowman, he wouldn't have had time to take its picture. The parallel in software development is especially strong. Rigid planning assumes that when your customer has accepted a requirements document, no more changes will be needed. However, before the code is written, the customer usually can't reliably describe what is needed. It might be therapeutic to moan about customers who don't know what they really want, but that aspect of software development won't go away. The longer customers work with the problem, the more they learn about what they need—just as the longer you work with a problem, the more you learn about the solution. Any flexibility you can provide the customer is a competitive advantage.

The second approach is to plan to respond to changing circumstances as best you can. This is similar to the approach Meriwether Lewis and William Clark took to their expedition.

FURTHER READING
Software isn't the only industry that benefits from flexible planning. For more information on working well in any business climate that's remarkable for its volatility, see *Thriving on Chaos* by Tom Peters (1987).

In this approach, resources are chosen carefully: the quantity of wagons, whiskey, horses, personnel, food, cigars, trinkets, and so on. The plan assumes that the explorers will be called upon to respond to unexpected circumstances in ways that work toward the overall project goal. In some respects the goal is well defined—find a route to the Pacific Ocean—but other important parts of the expedition are left to the ingenuity and resourcefulness of the explorers: the specific route, how long it takes, and how many coonskin caps are made along the way.

In software, Lewis and Clark's kind of planning is similar to setting a goal of writing the most usable word processor on the market. The rest of the project is an exploration of what "most usable" means. It could mean excellent printing ability, execution speed, or customer support. It could mean an unusually simple or an unusually powerful user interface. The specifics of the goal aren't defined in advance. You plan to be prepared for as many possibilities as possible. The purpose of planning is to make sure that nobody starves or freezes during the trip; it isn't to map out each step in advance. The plan is to embrace the unexpected and capitalize on unforeseen opportunities. It's a good approach to a market characterized by rapidly changing tools, personnel, and standards of excellence.

General Approach

The essence of evolutionary delivery is that you produce and deliver a program at successive levels of completeness, and each level is a version of the program that's to some extent usable. For example, if you were developing a spreadsheet program, you could plan several levels of releases:

Delivery 1   The basic interface is available. Arithmetic calculations work. Simple data entry is supported, but many more sophisticated features are not.

Delivery 2   Formulas and more sophisticated data-entry functions are available.

Delivery 3   The ability to save and load files is available.

Delivery 4   Database operations are available.

Delivery 5   Graphing capabilities are available.

Delivery 6   Interfaces to other products (databases, ASCII text files, other spreadsheets) are available. The product is fully functional.

Delivery 7   The performance-tuned product is available. Performance bottlenecks in the previous versions have been identified and ameliorated.

Delivery 8   The fully system-tested product is available.

The point of evolutionary delivery is that the first delivery is the core of the product you will ultimately deliver. Subsequent releases add more capabilities in a carefully planned way.

Part of planning for an evolutionary-delivery approach is deciding how responsive you intend to be to user-requested changes. Users might suggest changes in the user interface, in functionality, or in performance. If you want to be responsive to their requests, plan the flexibility to respond into your process.

Here's an illustration of the difference between traditional and evolutionary approaches:

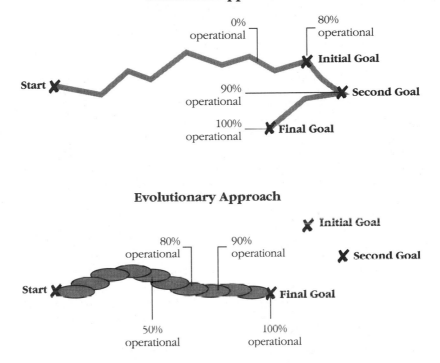

Evolutionary delivery builds flexibility into the development process, encouraging small mid-course corrections rather than large end-course ones.

In the traditional approach the project meets the initial goal, then the second goal, and then the final goal. In the evolutionary approach the project doesn't have to work all the way to the initial goal to realize that it should change course and head toward a slightly different goal. Similarly, it doesn't have to reach the second goal to change course again to reach the final goal. Because the evolutionary approach is incremental, it makes course corrections more frequently than a less incremental approach, and the overall course toward the final goal is straighter.

In a traditional approach, you develop the whole product at once in the sense that none of the product is operational until most or all of the product is operational. Multiple releases such as alpha, beta, and final releases are used primarily for improving the reliability of the product—its testedness—not its functionality.

667

In the evolutionary approach, complete detailed design, coding, and testing are done for each release. Because each release is small, you can treat each one as a small project. The extent to which you do analysis and design all at once rather than for each release depends on how much flexibility you want to build into your process. If you don't need much flexibility, you might be better off doing most of the design before beginning coding.

In the evolutionary approach, planning for each release is done toward the end of the previous release. This gives the process a certain amount of flexibility regardless of how you treat analysis and design.

Planning for the first release is unique in that it always needs to include some global architectural thinking about things like "Is the software architecture open enough to support modifications, including many that we haven't fully anticipated?" It's also a good idea to plot a general direction for the software at the beginning of the project, but, depending on how much flexibility you build into the process, it might merely be a best guess that you'll override later.

CROSS-REFERENCE
For details on ensuring that software quality improves with modifications, see Chapter 30, "Software Evolution."

Evolutionary delivery isn't limited to completely new systems. Each new release can replace part of the old system and can develop new capabilities. At some point, you'll have replaced so much of the old system that you'll actually have a new system. The architecture of the new system needs to be designed carefully so that you can transition to it without infecting it with the old system's restrictions. This might mean that you can't add certain parts of the new system directly to the old system; doing so might require inelegant kludges, and you might prefer to wait until the new system can support those parts more gracefully.

Benefits

The evolutionary method is hard to describe without describing its benefits—the benefits and the process are intertwined.

Integration takes care of itself. The likelihood that software will have serious problems during integration is directly proportional to the time between successive integration attempts. If the time between attempts is long, the chance of problems is large. When you deliver software early and often, as you do with evolutionary delivery, you must also perform integration early and often. This ensures that you exercise the main interfaces and minimizes problems.

The developers in Microsoft's applications division have used this technique successfully. When they develop a new product, they compile the whole product every night. A quick test is run each morning to make sure that no one has integrated bad code and broken the system. Since the product is known to work at all times, the motto in the applications division is "We can ship the product every day." The product might not have all the functionality it will ultimately have, but what it has, works.

Product-shipping cycles are shorter. In a typical development approach for mass-market software, you define version 1 and design, code, and test until you complete it. If development takes longer than you planned, the product ships late and revenue from the product is also late. In the extreme but not uncommon case, if you're slow in releasing version 1, you might never get to version 2.

In the evolutionary-delivery approach, you can define internal versions at a finer granularity than version 1 and version 2. You can define versions 2a through 2f and plan to have them ready at one-month intervals after a certain amount of time. You might plan to have 2a ready seven months into a one-year schedule, 2b ready at eight, 2c ready at nine, and so on. If you meet your one year schedule, you'll have 2f ready and you can ship the "full" product. If you don't complete 2f, you'll still have a working product in 2a, 2b, or 2c. Any of those versions will be an improvement over version 1, and you can ship it instead of 2f. Once you ship it, you can define new increments for version 3 and continue.

This approach enables more frequent and predictable product releases. From your customer's point of view, you've released two versions of the software, 1 and 2. From your point of view, you've developed ten versions but released only two of them—the two that were ready at the time your company needed them. This approach requires sophisticated coordination with marketing and user-documentation efforts, but if you're working in the highly competitive world of packaged software, it can be an effective way to stabilize product development cycles.

Customer satisfaction is built into the process. An important criterion for the success of any project is how well it's received by customers. With evolutionary delivery, once the system opens its eyes and blinks a few times, users get excited about having a system that's working. They see the system early and can start suggesting changes early, when it's most changeable. They have more time to adjust to the working system, and they'll adopt it more readily. In addition, because the software is designed to be delivered in several releases, its architecture assumes that changes will be made, which, again, improves your ability to respond to change requests.

Project status is easier to assess. One reason technical projects are difficult to manage is that it's hard to know the real status of the project. If code is "90 percent complete," does that mean that 10 percent more will make it 100 percent complete? Or does it mean that 10 percent more will make hundreds of errors visible, delaying the project for months? Rather than the ubiquitous and empty "90 percent complete," evolutionary delivery provides frequent, indisputable milestones. Either the release is done or it isn't. The work's quality is obvious from the release's quality. If a development team is in trouble, you find out within the first couple of releases; you don't have to wait until the project is 100 percent complete and not working.

HARD DATA

Estimation error is reduced. The problem of erroneous software-project estimates is one of the biggest problems facing the software industry. Capers Jones estimates that the average large project is a year late and 100 percent over budget (Jones 1986a). It's not clear whether the main problem is bad original estimates, poorly controlled projects, or both. The evolutionary approach sidesteps the issue by delivering early and often. Instead of making one large estimate for the whole project, you make several smaller estimates for several smaller releases. With each release, you learn from your mistakes in the way you estimated it, recalibrate your approach, and improve the accuracy of future estimates.

Development and testing resources are more evenly distributed. A typical evolutionary-delivery project consists of many minicycles of planning, requirements analysis, design, coding, and testing. Analysis isn't bunched up at the beginning, programming isn't bunched up in the middle, and testing isn't bunched up at the end. You can distribute analysis, programming, and testing resources more or less uniformly throughout the development cycle.

Morale improves. With evolutionary delivery, after the first release, at least part of the product always works. A working product gives everyone reason to believe that the project will be a success, which is a powerful morale booster.

Project completion is more likely. Completion of the project is more likely in several senses:

- The project won't be abandoned. If it runs into funding trouble, it's less likely to be cancelled if it's 50 percent complete and 50 percent operational than if it's 90 percent complete and doesn't work at all.

- The project will be partially complete even if your customer runs out of money. Depending on the point at which the well runs dry, the project might be largely usable. In many cases, the last 10 or 20 percent of the project consists of optional capabilities that aren't part of the product core. Thus, even if a few frills are missing, the customer can get most of the necessary capabilities. Imagine how much happier your customer will be with a mostly functioning product than if you had used an all-at-once method and "90 percent complete" had meant "0 percent operational."

- You and your customer can agree to finish early. In some cases, you get to the 80 percent mark and your customer says, "This is exactly what I need. I don't know what the last 20 percent was supposed to be for, but this suits me fine." If this happens, both you and the customer will be heroes to your companies. Your customer will have saved money by stopping the project at the 80 percent mark, and you will have completed a project early.

Evolutionary delivery improves overall code quality. In traditional approaches, you know that "someone" has to read your code and maintain it. This is an abstract motivation to write good code. With evolutionary delivery, you know that *you* will need to read and modify the code many times. Naturally, the incentive to write maintainable, modifiable code is more compelling (Basili and Turner 1975).

You find out early whether the program supports modifications. In projects that deliver software all at once, the design and coding practices might or might not support future modifications. With evolutionary delivery, you place a premium on modifiability throughout the project. If software is to be delivered in multiple releases, the design must support modifications. If it doesn't, you find out within a few releases and can change it accordingly.

The code needs less documentation. As discussed in Chapter 21 on program size, larger projects require a disproportionately larger documentation effort. Because each evolutionary release represents a small coding effort, you can approach each as a small project with modest documentation requirements. The total documentation required for a set of small projects is less than that required for one large project. This savings is significant since document production chews up as much as two-thirds of the total effort on a large project (Boehm et al. 1984).

HARD DATA

Relationship to Prototyping

Is evolutionary delivery a form of prototyping? No. It's different in several ways. Prototyping is always exploratory. Its goal might be to determine the functionality that the customer really wants. The point might be to explore the user interface or to refine the calculations engine, the feature set, or some other function of the software.

The point of evolutionary delivery is less exploratory. Each version of the product is supposed to be acceptable, and each version is supposed to be a step toward a final product. You might or might not plan to respond to the customer's requests for changes. The point might simply be to get an initial version of the software into the customer's hands more quickly.

Most prototyping is in line with Fred Brooks's suggestion that you "build one to throw away." The idea is to build a cheap version to refine the software concept and then build the fast, small, robust version using a traditional development cycle. With evolutionary delivery, you don't build one to throw away. You simply sequence the construction tasks so that a part of the system is available sooner rather than later.

Some forms of prototyping include a plan to keep the protoype, eventually evolving it into finished software. Such an approach can be tantamount to an evolutionary-delivery approach. It's nonetheless useful to remember that, in general, protoyping can occur without evolutionary delivery, and evolutionary delivery can occur without prototyping.

Limitations of Evolutionary Delivery

Evolutionary delivery isn't a panacea. Bear these limitations in mind:

Evolutionary delivery requires more planning. Multiple releases of a product require more planning than traditional projects in which all the planning is clustered at the beginning of the project. This is not much of a disadvantage since clustering all planning at the beginning of the project usually isn't effective. To the extent that a project managed traditionally should involve revising plans and estimates as you gain insight into the project anyway, evolutionary delivery doesn't require significantly more effort than an enlightened traditional approach.

Evolutionary delivery requires more technical overhead. Multiple releases of a product require that the product be clean enough for release at several points in the development cycle. A traditional approach requires that it be clean only at the point at which it's released to the public.

If the application area isn't well understood at the outset, this isn't much of a disadvantage either. Frequent integration and frequent releases ensure that the coding cattle are all moving in the same direction. If you wait until the end of the project, you sometimes find that the coding cattle have wandered far from where you thought they were going, and it's much harder to round them up and put them in the same corral.

If the application area is well understood, the overhead of multiple deliveries might be wasted. If you're sure that everyone agrees on where to be at the end of the project, you might be able to develop more efficiently by planning for only one delivery.

Evolutionary delivery is sometimes used as an excuse for skimping on planning, analysis, or design. A final weakness of evolutionary delivery is that it's sometimes used to rationalize incomplete requirements or an unstable design. If you use the evolutionary approach, make sure that you're not shortchanging the prerequisites to construction.

CHECKLIST

Evolutionary Delivery

❏ Have you planned for several releases of the software before the full, final capabilities will be present?

❏ Does the first release contain the core of the program, the seed from which the rest of the program will be developed?

❏ Will the first release be made as early as possible to get the ball rolling?

❏ Is the first release usable, at least at some minimal level?

❏ Have you defined what each evolutionary stage will deliver as best as you can in the hazy dawn of the project?

❏ Will each release add significant capabilities?

❏ Is the process flexible enough to respond to user feedback? If not, is the inflexibility intentional?

❏ Is the architecture open enough to support many changes through several releases?

❏ Will each release be treated as a small project with its own coding and testing and, in some cases, its own requirements analysis and design?

❏ Have you considered basing the evolutionary-delivery process on modifications to an existing program?

❏ Will you use the results of each stage to improve your estimates and planning for the next stage?

Further Reading

Integration

Myers, Glenford J. *The Art of Software Testing*. New York: John Wiley, 1979. The integration topic hasn't received a lot of attention, and it's often described as a testing activity. Myers discusses phased and incremental integration as approaches to testing.

Evolutionary delivery

Gilb, Tom. *Principles of Software Engineering Management*. Wokingham, England: Addison-Wesley, 1988. Chapters 7 and 15 contain thorough discussions of evolutionary delivery. Gilb has firsthand experience using the technique on large projects, and much of the management approach described in the rest of his book assumes the use of evolutionary delivery.

Incrementalism

DeGrace, Peter, and Leslie Stahl. *Wicked Problems, Righteous Solutions: A Catalogue of Modern Software Engineering Paradigms*. Englewood Cliffs, N.J.: Yourdon Press, 1990. This excellent survey of software-development paradigms covers traditional, incremental, and other approaches. It discusses trade-offs required among various development strategies and is valuable for both technical and nontechnical readers. It's well written, and most key points are illustrated with charts, graphs, and pictures.

Boehm, Barry W. "A Spiral Model of Software Development and Enhancement." *Computer,* May 1988: 61–72. In this paper, Boehm describes his "spiral model" of software development. He presents the model as an approach to managing risk in a software-development project, so the paper is about development generally rather than about integration specifically. Boehm is probably the world's foremost expert on the big-picture issues of software development, and the clarity of his explanations reflects the quality of his understanding.

Key Points

- Integration planning affects the order in which routines and modules are designed, coded, and tested. It also affects the ease with which you can test and debug them.

- Incremental integration comes in several varieties, and, unless the project is trivial, any one of them is better than phased integration.

- A good incremental approach is more like the Lewis and Clark expedition than like Amundsen's trip to the South Pole. It assumes that parts of the course are uncharted and that flexibility is important. It plans to respond to unexpected opportunities.

- Evolutionary delivery puts working software into the customer's hands early in the project; traditional approaches make the customer wait until the end before anything is delivered.

- Evolutionary delivery is an approach that benefits everyone. It gives the customer early assurances that the project will succeed. It gives management a clear sense of the project's progress. It lets developers see what it's like to maintain their own code and results in improved code quality.

28

Code-Tuning Strategies

Contents

Related Topics

THIS CHAPTER DISCUSSES THE QUESTION of performance improvement—historically, a controversial issue. Computer resources were severely limited in the 1960s, and efficiency was a paramount concern. As computers became more powerful in the 1970s, programmers realized how much their focus on performance had hurt readability and maintainability, and code tuning received less attention. The return of performance limitations with the microcomputer revolution of the 1980s again brought efficiency to the fore.

You can address performance concerns at two levels: strategic and tactical. This chapter addresses strategic performance issues: what performance is, how important it is, and the general approach for achieving it. If you already have a good grip on performance strategies and are looking for specific code-level techniques for improving performance, move on to the next chapter. Before you begin any major performance work, however, at least skim the information in this chapter so that you don't waste time optimizing when you should be doing other kinds of work.

28.1   Performance Overview

More computing sins
are committed in the
name of efficiency
(without necessarily
achieving it) than for
any other single
reason—including
blind stupidity.

W. A. Wulf

Code tuning is one way of improving a program's performance. You can usually find another way to improve performance more, in less time and with less harm to the code, than by code tuning. This section describes the options.

Quality Characteristics and Performance

Some people look at the world through rose-colored glasses. Programmers like you and me tend to look at the world through code-colored glasses. We assume that the better we make the code, the more our clients and customers will like our software.

This point of view might have a mailing address somewhere in reality, but it doesn't have a street number, and it certainly doesn't own any real estate. Users are more interested in tangible program characteristics than they are in code quality. Sometimes users are interested in raw performance, but only when it affects their work. Users tend to be more interested in program throughput than raw performance. Delivering software on time, providing a clean user interface, and avoiding downtime may all be more significant.

Here's an illustration: I write about 10 letters a week, and I hate to address them by hand, so I feed the envelopes through my printer. A year ago, to print an envelope from my word processor, I had to open my "envelope" file, change the address, call up a dialog box, switch my printer to landscape mode, close the dialog box, print the envelope, call up the dialog box again, switch back to portrait mode, and close the dialog box. To do this 10 times a week was tedious.

Earlier this year, I upgraded my word processor, and now it has an envelope button. Instead of going through the envelope-file, landscape-portrait, dialog-box rigmarole, I press the button. As a user of the word processor, I don't care whether the printing is twice as slow as it used to be because my throughput is faster. I don't know whether the code in the word-processor upgrade is faster or slower; its performance is better.

KEY POINT

Performance is only loosely related to code speed. To the extent that you work on your code's speed, you're not working on other quality characteristics. Be wary of sacrificing other characteristics in order to make your code faster. Your work on speed may hurt performance rather than help it.

Performance and Code Tuning

Once you've chosen efficiency as a priority, whether its emphasis is on speed or on size, you should consider several options before choosing to improve either speed or size at the code level. Think about efficiency from each of these viewpoints:

- Program design
- Module and routine design
- Operating-system interactions
- Code compilation
- Hardware
- Code tuning

Program design

CROSS-REFERENCE
For details on designing
performance into a
program, see the "Further
Reading" section at the end
of the chapter.

This level includes the major strokes of the design for a single program, mainly the way in which a program is divided into modules. Some program designs make it difficult to write a high-performance system. Others make it hard not to.

Consider the example of a real-world data-acquisition program for which the high-level design had identified measurement throughput as a key product attribute. Each measurement included time to make an electrical measurement, calibrate the value, scale the value, and convert it from sensor data units (such as millivolts) into engineering data units (such as degrees).

In this case, without addressing the risk in the high-level design, the programmers would have found themselves trying to optimize the math to evaluate a 13th-order polynomial in software — that is, a polynomial with 14 terms including variables raised to the 13th power. Instead, they addressed the problem with different hardware and a high-level design that used dozens of 3rd-order polynomials. This change could not have been effected through code tuning, and it's unlikely that any amount of code tuning would have solved the problem. This is an example of a problem that had to be addressed at the program-design level.

CROSS-REFERENCE
For details on the way programmers work toward
objectives, see "Setting
Objectives" in Section 23.2.

If you know that a program's size and speed are important, design the program's architecture so that you can reasonably meet your size and speed goals. Design a performance-oriented architecture, and then set space and speed goals for individual subsystems and modules. This will help in several ways:

- Setting individual space and speed goals makes the system's ultimate performance predictable. If each subsection meets its space and speed goals, the whole system will meet its goals. You can identify subsystems that have trouble meeting their goals early and target them for redesign or code tuning.
- The mere act of making goals explicit improves the likelihood that they'll be achieved. Programmers work to objectives when they know what they are; the more explicit the objectives, the easier they are to work to.

KEY POINT

- You can set goals that don't achieve efficiency directly but promote efficiency in the long run. Efficiency is often best treated in the context of other issues. For example, achieving a high degree of modifiability can provide a better basis for meeting efficiency goals than explicitly setting an efficiency target. With a highly modular, modifiable design, you can easily swap less-efficient components for more-efficient ones.

Module and routine design

CROSS-REFERENCE
For more information about data structures and algorithms, see the "Further Reading" section at the end of the chapter.

Once you've identified modules at the program-design level, you design the internals of modules and routines. This is another opportunity to design for performance. One key to performance that comes into play at this level is the choice of data structures and algorithms, which usually affect both the memory use and the execution speed of a program.

Operating-system interactions

CROSS-REFERENCE
For code-level strategies for dealing with slow or fat operating-system routines, see Chapter 29, "Code-Tuning Techniques."

If your program works with external files, dynamic memory, or output devices, it's probably interacting with the operating system. If performance isn't good, it might be because the operating-system routines are slow or fat. You might not be aware that the program is interacting with the operating system; sometimes your compiler generates system calls you would never dream of.

Code compilation

CROSS-REFERENCE
The optimization results reported in Chapter 29, "Code-Tuning Techniques," provide numerous examples of compiler optimizations that produce more efficient code than manual code tuning does.

Good compilers turn clear, high-level language code into optimized machine code. If you choose the right language and the right compiler, you might not need to think about optimizing speed any further. If your compiler-linker combination supports overlays, you might be able to avoid size problems too.

Hardware

Sometimes the cheapest and best way to improve a program's performance is to buy new hardware. If you're distributing a program for nationwide use by hundreds of thousands of customers, buying new hardware isn't a realistic option. But if you're developing custom software for a few in-house users, a hardware upgrade might be the cheapest option. It saves the cost of initial performance work. It saves the cost of future maintenance problems caused by performance work. It improves the performance of every other program that runs on that hardware too.

Code tuning

Code tuning is the practice of modifying correct code in ways that make it run more efficiently, and it is the subject of the rest of this chapter. Tuning doesn't change the design; it changes only the implementation.

Since you can make dramatic improvements at each level, from program design through code tuning, Jon Bentley cites an argument that in some systems, the improvements at each level can be multiplied (1982). Since you can achieve a 10-fold improvement in each of the six levels, that implies a potential performance improvement of a millionfold. Although such a multiplication of improvements requires a program in which gains at one level are independent of gains at other levels, which is rare, the potential is inspiring.

28.2 Introduction to Code Tuning

What is the appeal of code tuning? It's not the most effective way to improve performance. Program design, data-structure selection, and algorithm selection usually produce more dramatic improvements. Nor is it the easiest way to improve performance. Buying new hardware or a compiler with a better optimizer is easier. It's not the cheapest way to improve performance either. It takes more time to hand-tune code initially, and hand-tuned code is harder to read later.

Code tuning is appealing for several reasons. One attraction is that it seems to defy the laws of nature. It's incredibly satisfying to take a routine that executes in 500 milliseconds, tweak a few lines, and reduce the execution speed to 100 milliseconds.

It's also appealing because mastering the art of writing efficient code is a rite of passage to becoming a serious programmer. In tennis, you don't get any points for the way you pick up a tennis ball, but you still need to learn the right way to do it. You can't just lean over and pick it up with your hand. If you're good, you whack it with the head of your racket until it bounces waist high and then you catch it. Whacking it more than three times or not bouncing it the first time are both serious failings. It doesn't really matter how you pick up a tennis ball, but within the tennis culture the way you pick it up carries a certain cachet. Similarly, no one but you and other programmers usually cares how tight your code is. Nonetheless, within the programming culture, writing micro-efficient code proves you're cool.

The problem with code tuning is that efficient code isn't necessarily "better" code. That's the subject of the next few subsections.

Old Wives' Tales

Much of what you've heard about code tuning is false. Here are some common misapprehensions:

Reducing the lines of code in a high-level language improves the speed or size of the resulting machine code—false! Many programmers cling tenaciously to the belief that if they can write code in one or two lines, it will be

CROSS-REFERENCE
Both these code fragments
violate several rules of good
programming. Readability
and maintenance are
usually more important
than execution speed or
size, but in this chapter the
topic is performance, and
that implies a trade-off with
the other objectives. You'll
see many examples of cod-
ing practices here that
aren't recommended in
other parts of this book.

the most efficient possible. Consider the following line that initializes a five-element array:

```
for i = 1 to 5 do a[ i ] = i
```

Would you guess that the line is faster or slower than the following five lines that do the same job?

```
a[ 1 ] = 1
a[ 2 ] = 2
a[ 3 ] = 3
a[ 4 ] = 4
a[ 5 ] = 5
```

If you follow the old "fewer lines are faster" dogma, you'll guess that the first code is faster because it has four fewer lines. Hah! Tests in Pascal and Basic have shown that the second fragment is over 80 percent faster than the first. Here are the numbers:

Language	*for*-Loop Time	Straight-Code Time	Time Savings	Performance Ratio
Pascal	0.660	0.110	83%	6:1
Basic	0.379	0.051	87%	7:1

Note: (1) Times in this and the following tables in this chapter are given in seconds and are meaningful only for comparisons across rows in each table. Actual times will vary according to the compiler and compiler options used and the environment in which each test is run. (2) Benchmark results are typically made up of several hundred to several thousand executions of the code fragments to smooth out sample-to-sample fluctuations in the results. (3) Specific brands and versions of compilers aren't indicated. Performance characteristics vary significantly from brand to brand and from version to version. (4) Comparisons among results from different languages aren't always meaningful because compilers for different languages don't always offer comparable code-generation options.

In addition to providing the dramatic speed improvement, in Pascal the first fragment consumes 47 bytes whereas the second fragment takes up only 30 bytes—a size savings of 36 percent. This certainly doesn't imply the conclusion that increasing the number of lines of high-level language code always improves speed or reduces size. It does imply that regardless of the aesthetic appeal of writing something with the fewest lines of code, there's no predictable relationship between the number of lines of code in a high-level language and a program's ultimate size and speed.

Certain operations are probably faster or smaller than others—false! There's no room for "probably" when you're talking about performance. You must always measure performance to know whether your changes helped or hurt your program. The rules of the game change every time you change languages, compilers, or even versions of compilers. What was true on one machine with one compiler is probably false on another machine with another compiler.

This phenomenon suggests several reasons not to improve performance by code tuning. If you want your program to be portable, techniques that improve performance in one environment can degrade it in others. If you change compilers or upgrade, the new compiler might automatically optimize code the way you were hand-tuning it, and your work will have been wasted. Even worse, your code tuning might defeat compiler optimizations that have been designed to work with more straightforward code.

We should forget about small efficiencies, say about 97% of the time: premature optimization is the root of all evil.

Donald Knuth

You should optimize as you go—false! One theory is that if you strive to write the fastest and smallest possible code as you write each routine, your program will be fast and small. This approach creates a forest-for-the-trees situation in which programmers ignore significant global optimizations because they're too busy with micro-optimizations. Here are the main problems with optimizing as you go along:

- It's almost impossible to identify performance bottlenecks before a program is working completely. Programmers almost never target the right area ahead of time. This leads to time spent optimizing the wrong area and a program with inferior performance because the time needed for effective optimization has been wasted.

- In the rare case in which developers identify the bottlenecks correctly, they overkill the ones they've identified and allow others to become critical. Again, the ultimate effect is a reduction in performance. Optimizations done after a system is complete can identify each problem area and its relative importance so that optimization time is allocated effectively.

- Focusing on optimization during initial development detracts from achieving other program objectives. Developers immerse themselves in algorithm analysis and arcane debates that in the end don't contribute much value to the user. Concerns such as correctness, modularity, information hiding, and readability become secondary goals, even though performance is easier to improve later than they are. Post-hoc performance work typically affects only about 5 percent of a program's code. Would you rather go back and do performance work on 5 percent of the code or readability work on 100 percent?

HARD DATA

If the development time saved by implementing the simplest program is devoted to optimizing the running program, the result will always be a faster-running program than one in which optimization efforts have been exerted indiscriminately as the program was developed (Stevens 1981).

In short, premature optimization's primary drawback is its lack of perspective. Final performance, program quality, and thus the user end up suffering.

In an occasional project, post-hoc optimization won't be sufficient to meet performance goals, and you'll have to make major changes in the completed code. In those cases, small, localized optimizations wouldn't have provided the gains needed anyway. The problem in such cases isn't inadequate code quality—it's inadequate software architecture.

If you need to optimize before a program is complete, minimize the risks by building perspective into your process. One way is to spec size and speed goals for routines or subsystems and then optimize to meet the goals as you go along. Setting such goals in a spec is a way to keep one eye on the forest while you figure out how big your particular tree is.

FURTHER READING
For many other entertaining and enlightening anecdotes, see Gerald Weinberg's *Psychology of Computer Programming* (1971).

A fast program is just as important as a correct one—false! It's hardly ever true that programs need to be fast or small before they need to be correct. Gerald Weinberg tells the story of a programmer who was flown to Detroit to help debug a troubled program. The programmer worked with the team who had developed the program and concluded after several days that the situation was hopeless.

On the flight home, he mulled over the situation and realized what the problem was. By the end of the flight, he had an outline for the new code. He tested the code for several days and was about to return to Detroit when he got a telegram saying that the project had been cancelled because the program was impossible to write. He headed back to Detroit anyway and convinced the executives that the project could be completed.

Then he had to convince the project's original programmers. They listened to his presentation, and when he'd finished, the creator of the old system asked, "And how long does your program take?"

"That varies, but about ten seconds per input."

"Aha! But my program takes only one second per input." The veteran leaned back, satisfied that he'd stumped the upstart. The other programmers seemed to agree, but the new programmer wasn't intimidated.

"Yes, but your program *doesn't work*. If mine doesn't have to work, I can make it run instantly and take up no memory."

For a certain class of projects, size or speed is a major concern. This class is the minority and is much smaller than most people think. For these projects, the performance risks must be addressed by up-front design. For other projects, early optimization poses a significant threat to overall software quality, including performance.

The Pareto Principle

The Pareto Principle, also known as the 80/20 rule, states that you can get 80 percent of the result with 20 percent of the effort. The principle applies to a lot of areas other than programming, but it definitely applies to program optimization.

Barry Boehm reports that 20 percent of a program's routines consume 80 percent of its execution time (1987b). In his classic paper "An Empirical Study of FORTRAN Programs," Donald Knuth found that less than 4 percent of a program usually accounts for more than 50 percent of its run time (1971).

Knuth used a line-count profiler to discover this surprising relationship, and the implications for optimization are clear. You should measure the code to find the hot spots and then put your resources into optimizing the few percent that are used the most. Knuth profiled his line-count program and found that it was spending half its execution time in two loops. He changed a few lines of code and doubled the speed of the profiler in less than an hour.

Jon Bentley describes a case in which a thousand-line program spent 80 percent of its time in a five-line square-root routine. By tripling the speed of the square-root routine, he doubled the speed of the program (1988).

Bentley also reports the case of a team who discovered that half an operating system's time was spent in a small loop. They rewrote the loop in microcode and made the loop 10 times faster, but it didn't change the system's performance—they had rewritten the system's idle loop.

The team who designed the ALGOL language—the precursor to Pascal, C, and Ada and one of the most influential languages ever—received the following advice: The best is the enemy of the good. Working toward perfection may prevent completion. Complete it first, and then perfect it. The part that needs to be perfect is usually small.

Measurement

Since small parts of a program usually take a disproportionate share of the run time, measure your code to find the hot spots.

Once you've found the hot spots and optimized them, measure the code again to assess how much you've improved it. Many aspects of performance are counterintuitive. The earlier case in this chapter, in which five lines of code were significantly faster and smaller than one line, is one example of the ways that code can surprise you.

Experience doesn't help much with optimization either. A person's experience might have come from an old machine, language, or compiler—and when any of those things changes, all bets are off. You can never be sure about the effect of an optimization until you measure the effect.

A few years ago I wrote a program that summed the elements in a matrix. The original code looked like the example on the next page.

C Example of Straightforward Code to Sum the Elements in a Matrix

```
Sum = 0;
for ( Row = 0; Row < RowCount; Row++ )
   {
   for ( Column = 0; Column < ColumnCount; Column++ )
      {
      Sum = Sum + Matrix[ Row ][ Column ];
      }
   }
```

This code was straightforward, but performance of the matrix-summation routine was critical, and I knew that all the array accesses and loop tests had to be expensive. I knew from computer-science classes that every time the code accessed a two-dimensional array, it performed expensive multiplications and additions. For a 10-by-10 matrix, that totaled 100 multiplications and additions plus the loop overhead. By converting to pointer notation, I reasoned, I could increment a pointer and replace 100 expensive multiplications with 100 relatively cheap increment operations. I carefully converted the code to pointer notation and got this:

C Example of an Attempt to Tune Code to Sum the Elements in a Matrix

```
Sum            = 0;
ElementPtr     = Matrix;
LastElementPtr = Matrix[ RowCount-1 ][ ColumnCount-1 ] + 1;
while ( ElementPtr < LastElementPtr )
   {
   Sum += *ElementPtr++;
   }
```

FURTHER READING Jon Bentley reported a similar experience in which converting to pointers hurt performance by about 10 percent. The same conversion had—in another setting—improved performance more than 50 percent. See "Software Exploratorium: Writing Efficient C Programs" (Bentley 1991).

Even though the code wasn't as readable as the first code, especially to programmers who aren't C experts, I was magnificently pleased with myself. For a 10-by-10 matrix, I calculated that I had saved 100 multiplications and a lot of loop overhead. I was so pleased that I decided to measure the speed improvement, something I didn't always do back then, so that I could pat myself on the back more quantitatively.

Do you know what I found?

No improvement whatsoever. Not with a 10-by-10 matrix. Not with a 3-by-3 matrix. Not with a 25-by-25 matrix. The compiler's optimizer had optimized the first code well enough that my optimization didn't help at all. I was powerfully disappointed, and I learned that the only result of optimization you can usually be sure of without measuring performance is that you've made your code harder to read. If it's not worth measuring to prove it's more efficient, it's not worth sacrificing clarity for a performance gamble.

Measurements need to be precise

CROSS-REFERENCE
For a discussion of profiling
tools, see "Code Tuning" in
Section 20.3.

Performance measurements need to be precise. Timing your program with a stopwatch or by counting "one elephant, two elephant, three elephant" isn't precise enough. Profiling tools are useful, or you can use your system's clock and routines that record the elapsed times for computing operations.

Whether you use someone else's tool or write your own code to make the measurements, make sure that you're measuring only the execution time of the code you're tuning. If you're working on a multi-user or multi-tasking system, use the number of CPU clock ticks allocated to your program rather than the time of day. Otherwise, when the system swaps your program out and another one in, one of your routines will be penalized for the time spent executing another program. Likewise, try to factor out measurement overhead so that neither the original code nor the tuning attempt is unfairly penalized.

Compiler Optimizations

Modern compiler optimizations might be more powerful than you expect. In the case I described earlier, my compiler did as good a job of optimizing a nested loop as I was able to do by rewriting the code in a supposedly more efficient style.

When shopping for a compiler, compare the performance of each compiler on your program. Each compiler has different strengths and weaknesses, and some will be better suited to your program than others.

Optimizing compilers are better at optimizing straightforward code than they are at tricky code. If you do "clever" things like fooling around with loop indexes, your compiler can't do its job and your program suffers. See "Using Only One Statement per Line" in Section 18.5 for an example in which a straightforward approach resulted in compiler-optimized code that was 15 percent faster and 45 percent smaller than comparable "tricky" code.

With a good optimizing compiler, your code speed can improve 30 percent or more across the board. Many of the techniques described in the next chapter produce gains of only about 20 percent. Why not just write clear code and let the compiler do the work? Here are the results of a few tests to check how much an optimizer speeded up an insertion-sort routine:

Language	Time Without Compiler Optimizations	Time with Compiler Optimizations	Time Savings	Performance Ratio
Ada	2.80	1.60	43%	2:1
C compiler 1	2.25	1.65	27%	4:3
C compiler 2	2.58	2.58	0%	1:1
C compiler 3	2.31	0.99	57%	2:1

The only difference between versions of the routine was that compiler optimization was turned off for the first compile, on for the second. Clearly, some compilers optimize better than others, and you'll have to check your own compiler to measure its effect. The differences among the three C-compiler times show the difficulty of generalizing about the efficiency of any particular language over another. The Ada compiler produced faster optimized code than two of the three C compilers but slower code than the third.

When to Tune

Jackson's Rules of Optimization: Rule 1. Don't do it. Rule 2 (for experts only). Don't do it yet—that is, not until you have a perfectly clear and unoptimized solution.

M. A. Jackson

Use a high-quality design. Make the program right. Make it modular and easily modifiable so that it's easy to work on later. When it's complete and correct, check the performance. If the program lumbers, make it fast and small. Don't optimize until you know you need to.

Iteration

Once you've identified a performance bottleneck, you'll be amazed at how much you can improve performance by code tuning. You'll rarely get a 10-fold improvement from one technique, but you can effectively combine techniques; so keep trying, even after you find one that works.

I once wrote a software implementation of the Data Encryption Standard, or DES. Actually, I didn't write it once—I wrote it about 30 times. Encryption according to DES encodes digital data so that it can't be unscrambled without a password. The encryption algorithm is so convoluted that it seems like it's been used on itself. The performance goal for my DES implementation was to encrypt an 18K file in 37 seconds on an original IBM PC. My first implementation executed in 21 minutes and 40 seconds, so I had a long row to hoe.

Even though most individual optimizations were small, cumulatively they were significant. To judge from the percentage improvements, no three or even four optimizations would have met my performance goal. But the final combination was effective. The moral of the story is that if you dig deep enough, you can make some surprising gains.

The code tuning I did in this case is the most aggressive code tuning I've ever done. At the same time, the final code is the most unreadable, unmaintainable code I've ever written. The initial algorithm is complicated. The code resulting from the high-level language transformation was barely readable. The translation to assembler produced a single 500-line routine that I'm afraid to look at. In general, this relationship between code tuning and code quality holds true. Here's a table that shows a history of the optimizations:

CROSS-REFERENCE
The techniques listed in this table are described in Chapter 29, "Code-Tuning Techniques."

Optimization	Benchmark Time	Improvement
Implement initially—straightforward	21:40	—
Convert from bit fields to arrays	7:30	65%
Unroll innermost *for* loop	6:00	20%
Remove final permutation	5:24	10%
Combine two variables	5:06	5%
Use a logical identity to combine the first two steps of the DES algorithm	4:30	12%
Make two variables share the same memory to reduce data shuttling in inner loop	3:36	20%
Make two variables share the same memory to reduce data shuttling in outer loop	3:09	13%
Unfold all loops and use literal array subscripts	1:36	49%
Remove routine calls and put all the code in line	0:45	53%
Rewrite the whole routine in assembler	0:22	51%
Final	**0:22**	**98%**

Note: The steady progress of optimizations in this table doesn't imply that all optimizations work. I haven't shown all the things I tried that doubled the run time.

28.3 Kinds of Fat and Molasses

In code tuning you find the parts of a program that are as slow as molasses in winter and as big as Fat Albert and change them so that they run like greased lightning and are so skinny they can hide in the cracks between the other bytes in RAM. You always have to profile the program to know with any confidence which parts are slow and fat, but some operations have a long history of laziness and obesity, and you can start by investigating them.

Common Sources of Inefficiency

Here are several common sources of inefficiency:

Input/output operations. One of the most significant sources of inefficiency is unnecessary i/o. If you have a small file and a choice of storing it either in memory or on disk (or of reading it into memory before using it), use an in-memory data structure unless space is critical. Here's a performance comparison between code that accesses random elements in a 100-element in-memory array and code that accesses random elements of the same size in a 100-record disk file:

Language	External File Time	In-Memory Data Time	Time Savings	Performance Ratio
C	54.29	0.066	99.9%	800:1
Fortran	56.78	0.159	99.7%	350:1

According to this data, in-memory access is on the order of 1000 times faster than accessing data in an external file. If the test had used a slower medium for external access—a floppy disk or hard disk without disk caching—the difference would have been even greater. If the array had had 1000 elements instead of 100, the effect would also have been greater.

The performance comparison for sequential accesses is similar but a little less dramatic:

Language	External File Time	In-Memory Data Time	Time Savings	Performance Ratio
C	5.65	0.066	98.8%	85:1
Fortran	38.32	0.159	99.6%	250:1

The effect of in-memory access isn't quite as great on sequential accesses as on random accesses, but it's still on the order of 100 times faster—enough to make you think twice about having i/o in a speed-critical part of a program.

Formatted printing routines. Formatted printing routines tend to incur both size and speed penalties. Code for statements like C's *printf()*, Basic's *PRINT USING*, and Fortran's *FORMAT()* tends to be complicated, and using one formatted print statement pulls in the whole bag of complicated code. Here are some figures on the extra space formatting can take up:

Language	Unformatted Print Size (Bytes)	Formatted Print Size (Bytes)	Extra Bytes
Basic	12,310	15,614	3,304
C	7,308	8,921	1,613

Each of these programs simply printed the word "Hi" to the standard output device. The only difference between them was whether the print statements were formatted or unformatted. If space is at a premium, formatted printing is a good place to look for space savings.

Floating-point operations. On machines that don't support floating-point operations in hardware—many PCs, for example—floating-point operations are expensive in terms of both space and speed. Speed is discussed in detail in the next section. When thinking about space, realize that a single floating-point operation can pull in the entire floating-point library. If you don't use any floating-point operations, you won't get the floating-point library. If you use even one floating-point statement, however, you'll get the whole thing. Here are the results of changing a formatted print statement from an integer *10* to a floating-point *10.0*:

Language	Integer Size (Bytes)	Floating-Point Size (Bytes)	Extra Bytes
C	8,921	23,821	14,900
Pascal	8,216	20,664	12,448

With both compilers, the difference is startling. In both cases, if you could replace all floating-point operations with integer operations, you'd save 12K to 15K. This doesn't mean that you'd save 15K every time you eliminated a floating-point operation. The first floating-point operation pulls in the whole library. Subsequent operations don't have any additional effect.

Can you depend on this savings? The results with a Basic compiler are quite different:

Language	Integer Size (Bytes)	Floating-Point Size (Bytes)	Extra Bytes
Basic	15,614	15,614	0

In this case, changing from integer to floating point makes no difference at all. This particular Basic compiler includes the floating-point library automatically, regardless of whether your program contains any floating-point operations. This isn't an inherent difference between C and Pascal on the one hand and Basic on the other; it's a characteristic of different compilers. It reinforces the importance of measuring to verify that an optimization does what you want it to.

Paging. An operation that causes the operating system to swap pages of memory is much slower than an operation that works on only one page of memory. Sometimes a simple change makes a huge difference. In the example on the next page, one programmer wrote an initialization loop that produced many page faults on a system that used 2K pages.

Pascal Example of an Initialization Loop That Causes Many Page Faults

```
for Column := 1 to 1000 do
   begin
   for Row := 1 to 5 do
      begin
      Table[ Row, Column ] := 0
      end
   end;
```

This is a nicely formatted loop with good variable names, so what's the problem? The problem is that each element of *Table* is 2 bytes long. Since each row of *Table* is 1000 elements long, that means each row of *Table* is 2000 bytes long, or about a page long. Every time the program accesses a different row, the operating system has to switch memory pages. The way the loop is structured, every single array access switches rows, which means that every single array access causes a page fault. If a page fault costs 1 millisecond, the initialization code takes 5 seconds to run.

The programmer restructured the loop this way:

Pascal Example of an Initialization Loop That Causes Few Page Faults

```
for Row := 1 to 5 do
   begin
   for Column := 1 to 1000 do
      begin
      Table[ Row, Column ] := 0
      end
   end;
```

This code still causes a page fault every time it switches rows, but it switches rows only 5 times instead of 5000, so it performs in a total time of a few milliseconds rather than several thousand milliseconds.

System calls. Calls to system routines are often expensive. System routines include input/output operations to disk, keyboard, screen, printer, or other device; memory-management routines; and certain utility routines. If you're working in an environment that's laid on top of an operating system, such as Microsoft Windows, find out how expensive your system calls are. If they're expensive, consider these options:

● Write your own services. Sometimes you need only a small part of the functionality offered by a system routine and can build your own from lower-level system routines. Writing your own replacement gives you something that's smaller, faster, and better suited to your needs.

- Avoid going to the system.

- Work with the system vendor to make the call faster. Most vendors want to improve their products and are glad to learn about parts of their systems with weak performance. (They may seem a little grouchy about it at first, but they really are interested.)

Relative Performance Costs of Common Operations

Although you can't count on some operations being more expensive than others without measuring them, certain operations tend to be more expensive. When you look for the molasses in your program, use Table 28-1 to help make some initial guesses about the sticky parts of your program.

Table 28-1. Costs of Common Operations

Operation	Example	Relative Time Consumed	
		Pascal	C
Integer assignment	i = j	1	1
Integer addition/ subtraction	i = j + k	2	1.3
Integer multiplication	i = j * k	3	2
Integer division	i = j div k	5	4
Access integer array with constant subscript	i = a[5]	3	2
Access integer array with variable subscript	i = a[j]	3	4
Access two-dimensional integer array with constant subscripts	i = a[3, 5]	3	2
Access two-dimensional integer array with variable subscripts	i = a[j, k]	6	4
Access field of structured variable	i = rec.num	1	1
Access singly dereferenced pointer	i = rec^.num	2.5	2
Access doubly dereferenced pointer	i = rec^.next^.num	3.8	2.6
Each additional dereference	i = rec^.next^.next^...	1.3	0.6
Floating-point assignment	x = y	5	85
Floating-point addition/ subtraction	x = y + z	300	150

(continued)

Table 28-1. Costs of Common Operations, *continued*

Operation	Example	Relative Time Consumed	
		Pascal	**C**
Floating-point multiplication/division	x = y * z	300	150
Floating-point square root	x = sqrt(y)	500	300
Floating-point sine	x = sin(y)	1000	700
Floating-point logarithm	x = log(y)	1800	1200
Floating-point e^x	x = exp(y)	2000	1300
Access floating-point array with constant subscript	x = z[5]	5	100
Access floating-point array with integer-variable subscript	x = z[j]	8	100
Access two-dimensional floating-point array with constant subscripts	x = z[3, 5]	5	100
Access two-dimensional floating-point array with integer-variable subscripts	x = z[j, k]	10	100
Routine call with no parameters	foo()	6	6
Routine call with 1 parameter	foo(i)	6	6
Routine call with 2 parameters	foo(i, j)	8	8

Note: Measurements in this table are highly sensitive to local code circumstances, compiler optimizations, and code generated by specific compilers.

You might spot a few patterns in Table 28-1. Floating-point operations are generally more expensive than integer operations. (Floating-point operations are performed in software rather than hardware in this example.) Multiplication and division are more expensive than addition and subtraction. Transcendental math functions are extremely expensive.

As interesting as the patterns are, the surprises are even more interesting. The two compilers have comparable times for integer operations. In floating-point math operations, the C compiler is about twice as fast as the Pascal compiler. To perform a floating-point variable assignment, however, the C compiler takes more than 10 times as long as the Pascal compiler. This discrepancy is extraordinary: 5 for Pascal, 85 for C. If you were working with this C compiler, you'd have a hefty incentive to avoid floating-point operations. Logically, a floating-point assignment shouldn't take much longer than an integer assignment. The fact that it actually does illustrates the importance of measuring performance instead of making assumptions about it.

Considering the order-of-magnitude differences between compilers in the complicated operations, treat the numbers in Table 28-1 mainly as a curiosity. Test the operations you're interested in within your own environment.

This table, or a similar one that you make, is the key that unlocks all the speed improvements described in Chapter 29, "Code-Tuning Techniques." In every case, improving speed comes from replacing an expensive operation with a cheaper one. The next chapter provides examples of how to do so.

28.4 Summary of the Approach to Code Tuning

Here are the steps you should take as you consider whether code tuning can help you improve the performance of a program:

1. Develop the software using a good design with highly modular code that's easy to understand and modify.
2. If performance is poor, measure the system to find hot spots.
3. Determine whether the weak performance comes from inadequate design, data structures, or algorithms and whether code tuning is appropriate. If code tuning isn't appropriate, go back to step 1.
4. Tune the bottleneck identified in step 3. Measure each improvement, and if it doesn't improve the code, take it out.
5. Repeat from step 2.

Further Reading

Performance

Smith, Connie U. *Performance Engineering of Software Systems.* Reading, Mass.: Addison-Wesley, 1990. This book covers software performance engineering, an approach for building performance into software systems at all stages of development. It makes extensive use of examples and case studies for several kinds of programs.

Armenise, Pasquale. "A Structured Approach to Program Optimization." *IEEE Transactions on Software Engineering* SE-15, no. 2 (February 1989): 101–8. This article sets out an approach for optimizing programs in a structured development environment.

Algorithms and data structures

Sedgewick, Robert. *Algorithms,* 2d ed. Reading, Mass.: Addison-Wesley, 1988. This book's 45 chapters contain a survey of the best methods of solving a wide variety of problems. Its subject areas include fundamentals, sorting, searching, string processing, geometric algorithms, graph algorithms, mathematical algorithms, and advanced topics.

Reingold, Edward M., and Wilfred J. Hansen. *Data Structures.* Boston: Little, Brown, 1983. This book provides a good, textbook introduction to data structures including arrays, records, pointers, lists, and trees.

Knuth, Donald. *The Art of Computer Programming,* vol. 1, *Fundamental Algorithms,* 2d ed. Reading, Mass.: Addison-Wesley, 1973.

Knuth, Donald. *The Art of Computer Programming,* vol. 3, *Sorting and Searching.* Reading, Mass.: Addison-Wesley, 1973.

Knuth, Donald. *The Art of Computer Programming,* vol. 2, *Seminumerical Algorithms,* 2d ed. Reading, Mass.: Addison-Wesley, 1981. These are the first three volumes of a series that was originally intended to grow to seven volumes. They can be somewhat intimidating. In addition to the English description of the algorithms, they're described in mathematical notation or MIX, an assembly language for the imaginary MIX computer. The books contain exhaustive details on a huge number of topics, and if you have an intense interest in a particular algorithm, you won't find a better reference.

Key Points

- Performance is only one aspect of overall software quality, and it's probably not the most influential aspect. Finely tuned code is only one aspect of overall performance, and it's probably not the most influential aspect. Program architecture, detailed design, and data-structure and algorithm selection usually have more influence on a program's size and execution speed than the efficiency of its code does.

- Quantitative measurement is a key to maximizing performance. It's needed to find the areas in which performance improvements will really count, and it's needed again to verify that optimizations improve rather than degrade the software.

- Most programs spend most of their time in a small fraction of their code. You won't know which code that is until the program is functioning and you can measure it.

- The best way to prepare for performance work during initial coding is to write clean code that's easy to understand and modify.

29

Code-Tuning Techniques

Contents

Related Topics

ALTHOUGH CODE TUNING HAS BEEN neglected in recent years, it has been a popular topic during most of the history of computer programming. Consequently, once you've decided that you need to improve performance and that you want to do it at the code level, you have a rich set of techniques at your disposal.

This chapter focuses on improving speed and includes a few tips for making code smaller. Performance usually refers to both speed and size, but size reductions tend to come more from redesigning data structures than from tuning code. Code tuning refers to changing the implementation of a design rather than changing the design itself.

Few of the techniques in this chapter are so generally applicable that you'll be able to copy the example code directly into your programs. The main purpose of the discussion here is to illustrate a handful of techniques that you can adapt to your situation.

29.1 Loops

CROSS-REFERENCE
For other details on loops,
see Chapter 15,
"Controlling Loops."

Because loops are executed many times, the hot spots in a program are often inside loops. The techniques in this section make the loop itself faster.

Unswitching

Switching refers to making a decision inside a loop every time it's executed. If the decision doesn't change while the loop is executing, you can unswitch the loop by making the decision outside the loop. Usually this requires turning the loop inside out, putting loops inside the conditional rather than putting the conditional inside the loop. Here's an example of a loop before unswitching:

C Example of a Switched Loop

```c
for ( i = 0; i < Count; i++ )
   {
   if ( SumType == Net )
      {
      NetSum = NetSum + Amount[ i ];
      }
   else /* SumType == Gross */
      {
      GrossSum = GrossSum + Amount[ i ];
      }
   }
```

In this code, the test *if (SumType == Net)* is repeated through each iteration even though it'll be the same each time through the loop. You can rewrite the code for a speed gain this way:

C Example of an Unswitched Loop

```c
if ( SumType == Net )
   {
   for ( i = 0; i < Count; i++ )
      {
      NetSum = NetSum + Amount[ i ];
      }
   }
else /* SumType == Gross */
   {
   for ( i = 0; i < Count; i++ )
      {
      GrossSum = GrossSum + Amount[ i ];
      }
   }
```

The *for* statement is repeated, so the code uses more space, but the time savings speak for themselves:

Language	Straight Time	Code-Tuned Time	Time Savings
C	1.81	1.43	21%
Basic	4.07	3.30	19%

Note: (1) Times in these tables are given in seconds and are meaningful only for comparisons across rows of each table. Actual times will vary according to the compiler and compiler options used and the environment in which each test is run. (2) Benchmark results are typically made up of several hundred to several thousand executions of the code fragments to smooth out the sample-to-sample fluctuations in the results. (3) Specific brands and versions of compilers aren't indicated. Performance characteristics vary significantly from brand to brand and version to version. (4) Comparisons among results from different languages aren't always meaningful because compilers for different languages don't always offer comparable code-generation options.

The hazard in this case is that the two loops have to be maintained in parallel. If *Count* changes to *ClientCount*, you have to remember to change it in both places, which is an annoyance for you and a maintenance headache for anyone else who has to work with the code.

If your code were really this simple, you could sidestep the maintenance issue and get the code-tuning benefit by introducing a new variable, using it in the loop, and assigning it to *NetSum* or *GrossSum* after the loop.

Jamming

Jamming, or "fusion," is the result of combining two loops that operate on the same set of elements. The gain lies in cutting the loop overhead from two loops to one. Here's a candidate for loop jamming:

Basic Example of Separate Loops That Could Be Jammed

```
for i = 1 to Num
   EmployeeName( i ) = ""
next i
...

for i = 1 to Num
   EmployeeEarnings( i ) = 0
next i
```

When you jam loops, you find code in two loops that you can combine into one. Usually, that means the loop counters have to be the same. In this example, both loops run from *1* to *Num*, so you can jam them. Here's how:

CODING HORROR

Basic Example of a Jammed Loop

```
for i = 1 to Num
    EmployeeName( i ) = ""
    EmployeeEarnings( i ) = 0
next i
```

Here are the savings:

Language	Straight Time	Code-Tuned Time	Time Savings
Basic	6.54	6.31	4%
C	4.83	4.72	2%
Fortran	6.15	5.88	4%

Note: Benchmarked for the case in which *Num* equals *100*.

As you can see, the savings aren't earthshaking in these cases. They might be more significant in other environments, but you'd have to measure to know whether they were.

Loop jamming has two main hazards. First, the indexes for the two parts that have been jammed might change so that they're no longer compatible. Second, the location of each loop might be significant. Before you combine the loops, make sure they'll still be in the right order with respect to the rest of the code.

Unrolling

The goal of loop unrolling is to reduce the amount of loop housekeeping. In Chapter 28, a loop was completely unrolled, and five lines of code were shown to be faster than one. In that case, the loop that went from one to five lines was unrolled so that all five array accesses were done individually.

Although completely unrolling a loop is a fast solution and works well when you're dealing with a small number of elements, it's not practical when you have a large number of elements or when you don't know in advance how many elements you'll have. Here's an example of a general loop:

Normally, you'd probably use a for loop for a job like this, but to optimize, you'd have to convert to a while loop. For clarity, a while loop is shown here.

Ada Example of a Loop That Can Be Unrolled

```
i := 1;
while ( i <= Num ) loop
    a( i ) := i;
    i := i + 1;
end loop
```

To unroll the loop partially, you handle two or more cases in each pass through the loop instead of one. This unrolling hurts readability but doesn't hurt the generality of the loop. Here's the loop unrolled once:

CODING HORROR

These lines pick up the case that might fall through the cracks if the loop went by twos instead of by ones.

Ada Example of a Loop That's Been Unrolled Once

```
i := 1;
while ( i < Num ) loop
    a( i )     := i;
    a( i + 1 ) := i + 1;
    i          := i + 2;
end loop

if ( i = Num ) then
    a( Num ) := Num;
end if;
```

When five lines of straightforward code expand to nine lines of tricky code, the code becomes harder to read and maintain. Except for the gain in speed, its quality is poor. Part of any design discipline, however, is making necessary trade-offs. So, even though a particular technique generally represents poor coding practice, specific circumstances may make it the best one to use.

The technique replaced the original $a(i) := i$ line with two lines, and i is incremented by *2* rather than by *1*. The extra code after the *while* loop is needed when *Num* is odd and the loop has one iteration left after the loop terminates. Here are the results of unrolling the loop:

Language	Straight Time	Code-Tuned Time	Time Savings
Ada	1.04	0.82	21%
C	1.59	1.15	28%

Note: Benchmarked for the case in which *Num* equals *100*.

A gain of 21 to 28 percent is respectable. The main hazard of loop unrolling is an off-by-one error in the code after the loop that picks up the last case.

What if you unroll the loop even further, going for two or more unrollings? Do you get more benefit? Here's the code for a loop unrolled twice:

CODING HORROR

Ada Example of a Loop That's Been Unrolled Twice

```ada
i := 1;
while ( i < Num-1 ) loop
   a( i )       := i;
   a( i + 1 )   := i + 1;
   a( i + 2 )   := i + 2;
   i := i + 3;
end loop;

if ( i <= Num ) then
   a( Num ) := Num;
end if;
if ( i = Num-1 ) then
   a( Num-1 ) := Num-1;
end if;
```

Here are the results of unrolling the loop the second time:

Language	Straight Time	Single Unrolled Time	Double Unrolled Time	Additional Time Savings
Ada	1.04	0.82	0.72	10%
C	1.59	1.15	0.99	10%

Note: Benchmarked for the case in which *Num* equals *100*.

The results indicate that further loop unrolling can result in further time savings. The main concern is how Byzantine your code becomes. When you look at the code above, you might not think it looks incredibly complicated, but when you realize that it started life a couple of pages ago as a five-line loop, you can appreciate the trade-off between performance and readability.

Minimizing the Work Inside Loops

One key to writing effective loops is to minimize the work done inside a loop. If you can evaluate a statement or part of a statement outside a loop so that only the result is used inside the loop, do so. It's good programming practice, and, in some cases, it improves readability.

Suppose you have a complicated pointer expression inside a hot loop that looks like this:

C Example of a Complicated Pointer Expression Inside a Loop

```
for ( i = 0; i < Num; i++ )
   {
   NetRate[ i ] = BaseRate[ i ] * Rates->Discounts->Factors->Net;
   }
```

In this case, assigning the complicated pointer expression to a well-named variable improves readability and often improves performance.

C Example of Simplifying a Complicated Pointer Expression

```
QuantityDiscount = Rates->Discounts->Factors->Net;
for ( i = 0; i < Num; i++ )
   {
   NetRate[ i ] = BaseRate[ i ] * QuantityDiscount;
   }
```

The extra variable, *QuantityDiscount*, makes it clear that the *BaseRate* array is being multiplied by a quantity-discount factor to compute the net rate. That wasn't at all clear from the original expression in the loop. Putting the complicated pointer expression into a variable outside the loop also saves the pointer from being dereferenced three times for each pass through the loop, resulting in the following savings:

Language	Straight Time	Code-Tuned Time	Time Savings
C	9.56	8.29	13%
C++	8.51	8.40	1%
Pascal	10.44	10.33	1%

Note: Benchmarked for the case in which *Num* equals *100*.

Except for the C compiler, the savings aren't anything to crow about, implying that during initial coding you can use whichever technique is more readable without worrying about the speed of the code until later.

Sentinel Values

When you have a loop with a compound test, you can often save time by simplifying the test. If the loop is a search loop, one way to simplify the test is to use a sentinel value, a value that you put just past the end of the search range and that's guaranteed to terminate the search.

The classic example of a compound test that is improved by use of a sentinel is the search loop that checks both whether it has found the value it is seeking and whether it has run out of values. Here's the code:

C Example of Compound Tests in a Search Loop

Here's the ──
compound test.

```
Found = FALSE;
i     = 0;
while ( (! Found) && (i < ElementCount) )
    {
    if ( Item[ i ] == TestValue )
        Found = TRUE;
    else
        i++;
    }

if ( Found )
...
```

In this code, each iteration of the loop tests for *! Found* and for *i < Element-Count*. The purpose of the *! Found* test is to determine when the desired element has been found. The purpose of the *i < ElementCount* test is to avoid running past the end of the array. Inside the loop, each value of *Item* is tested individually, so the loop really has three tests for each iteration.

In this kind of search loop, you can combine the three tests so that you test only once per iteration by putting a sentinel at the end of the search range to stop the loop. In this case, you can simply assign the value you're looking for to the element just beyond the end of the search range. You then check each element, and if the first element you find is the one you stuck at the end, you know that the value you're looking for isn't really there. Here's the code:

C Example of Using a Sentinel Value to Speed Up a Loop

Remember to allow ──
space for the sentinel
value at the end
of the array.

```
/* set sentinel value, preserving the original value */
InitialValue = Item[ ElementCount ];
Item[ ElementCount ] = TestValue;

i = 0;
while ( Item[ i ] != TestValue )
    {
    i++;
    }

/* restore the value displaced by the sentinel */
Item[ ElementCount ] = InitialValue;
```

(continued)

```
/* check if value was found */
if ( i < ElementCount )
...
```

When *Item* is an array of integers, the savings are dramatic:

Language	Straight Time	Code-Tuned Time	Time Savings	Performance Ratio
C++	6.21	4.45	28%	1:1
Pascal	0.21	0.10	52%	2:1
Basic	6.65	0.60	91%	11:1

Note: Search is of a 100 element array of integers.

The Basic-compiler results are particularly dramatic, but all the results are good. When the kind of array changes, however, the results also change. Here are the results when *Item* is an array of single-precision floating-point numbers:

Language	Straight Time	Code-Tuned Time	Time Savings	Performance Ratio
C++	20.93	21.48	−3%	1:1
Pascal	21.42	21.97	−3%	1:1
Basic	59.84	30.07	49%	2:1

Note: Search is of a 100-element array of 4-byte floating-point numbers.

In this case, the results vary significantly, which shows once again that you have to measure the effect in your particular environment before you can be sure your optimization will help.

The sentinel technique can be applied to virtually any situation in which you use a linear search—to linked lists as well as arrays. The only caveats are that you must choose the sentinel value carefully and that you must be careful about how you put the sentinel value into the array or linked list, remembering to preserve the original value and replace it.

Putting the Busiest Loop on the Inside

When you have nested loops, think about which loop you want on the outside and which you want on the inside. On the next page is an example of a nested loop that can be improved.

Pascal Example of a Nested Loop That Can Be Improved

```pascal
for column := 1 to 100 do
   begin
   for row := 1 to 5 do
      begin
      Sum := Sum + Table[ row, column ]
      end
   end;
```

The key to improving the loop is that the outer loop executes much more often than the inner loop. Each time the loop executes, it has to initialize the loop index, increment it on each pass through the loop, and check it after each pass. The total number of loop executions is 100 for the outer loop and 100 * 5 = 500 for the inner loop, for a total of 600 iterations. By merely switching the inner and outer loops, you can change the total number of iterations to 5 for the outer loop and 5 * 100 = 500 for the inner loop, for a total of 505 iterations. Analytically, you'd expect to save about (600 − 505) / 600 = 16 percent by switching the loops. Here's the measured difference in performance:

Language	Straight Time	Code-Tuned Time	Time Savings	Performance Ratio
Pascal	2.53	2.42	4%	1:1
Ada	2.14	2.03	5%	1:1
Fortran	1.97	3.57	−81%	1:2

These results are instructive in two senses. First, the loop overhead might have decreased by 16 percent, but the loop has other, more time-consuming activities that dilute the effect of the optimization—resulting in modest 4 and 5 percent savings with the Pascal and Ada compilers.

KEY POINT

The wild card in this case is the Fortran compiler. Reordering the loops caused the performance police to fine the program 81 percent. Since the Fortran code's straight time is faster than any of the other compilers' optimized times, apparently the Fortran compiler's optimization should be left alone. This counterintuitive result illustrates again that you have to measure the effects of code tuning before you put your savings in the bank.

Strength Reduction

Reducing strength means replacing an expensive operation such as multiplication with a cheaper operation such as addition. Sometimes you'll have an expression inside a loop that depends on multiplying the loop index by a factor. Addition is usually faster than multiplication, and if you can compute the same number by adding the amount on each iteration of the loop rather than by multiplying, the code will run faster. Here's an example of code that uses multiplication:

Basic Example of Multiplying a Loop Index

```
for i = 1 to Num
    Commission( i ) = i * Revenue * BaseCommission * Discount
next i
```

This code is straightforward but expensive. You can rewrite the loop so that you accumulate multiples rather than computing them each time. This reduces the strength of the operations from multiplication to addition. Here's the code:

Basic Example of Adding Rather Than Multiplying

```
Increment = Revenue * BaseCommission * Discount
TotalCommission = Increment
for i = 1 to Num
    Commission( i ) = TotalCommission
    TotalCommission = TotalCommission + Increment
next i
```

Multiplication is expensive, and this kind of change is like a manufacturer's coupon that gives you a discount on the cost of the loop. The original code incremented *i* each time and multiplied it by *Revenue * BaseCommission * Discount*—first by 1, then by 2, then by 3, and so on. The optimized code sets *Increment* equal to *Revenue * BaseCommission * Discount*. It then adds *Increment* to *TotalCommission* on each pass through the loop. On the first pass, it's been added once; on the second pass, it's been added twice; on the third pass, it's been added three times; and so on. The effect is the same as multiplying *Increment* by 1, then by 2, then by 3, and so on, but it's cheaper.

The key is that the original multiplication has to depend on the loop index. In this case, the loop index was the only part of the expression that varied, so the expression could be recoded more economically. Here's how much the rewrite helped in some test cases:

Language	Straight Time	Code-Tuned Time	Time Savings
Basic	3.85	2.85	26%
C	3.35	2.64	21%

Note: Benchmark performed with *Num* equals *20*. All computed variables are floating point.

29.2 Logic

CROSS-REFERENCE
For other details on using
control structures, see
Chapters 13 through 17.

Much of programming consists of manipulating logic. This section describes how to manipulate logical expressions to your advantage.

Stop Testing When You Know the Answer

Suppose you have a statement like

```
if ( 5 < x ) and ( x < 10 ) then ...
```

Once you've determined that x is less than 5, you don't need to perform the second half of the test.

Some languages provide a form of expression evaluation known as "short-circuit evaluation," which means that the compiler generates code that automatically stops testing as soon as it knows the answer. Short-circuit evaluation is part of ANSI-standard C. Ada supports explicit short-circuit comparisons with the *and then* and *or else* keywords. A short-circuit version of the previous example would look like this:

```
if ( 5 < x ) and then ( x < 10 ) then ...
```

In other languages, either short-circuit evaluation is compiler dependent or you're on your own. If you want to stop testing when you know the answer, you have to avoid using *and* and *or*, adding logic instead. With short-circuit evaluation, the code above changes to this:

```
if ( 5 < x ) then
   if ( x < 10 ) then ...
```

The principle of not testing after you know the answer is a good one for many other kinds of cases as well. A search loop is a common case. If you're scanning an array of input numbers for a negative value and you simply need to know whether a negative value is present, one approach is to check every value, setting a *NegativeFound* variable when you find one. Here's how the search loop would look:

C Example of Not Stopping After You Know the Answer

```c
NegativeFound = False;
for ( i = 0; i < Num; i++ )
   {
   if ( Input[ i ] < 0 )
      {
      NegativeFound = True;
      }
   }
```

A better approach would be to stop scanning as soon as you find a negative value. Here are the approaches you could use to solve the problem:

- Add a *break* statement after the *NegativeFound = True* line. In Ada, you would use *exit*.
- If your language doesn't have *break*, emulate a *break* with a *goto* that goes to the first statement after the loop.
- Change the *for* loop to a *while* loop and check for *NegativeFound* as well as for incrementing the loop counter past *Num*.
- Change the *for* loop to a *while* loop, put a negative sentinel value in the first array element after the last value entry, and simply check for a negative value in the *while* test. After the loop terminates, see whether the position of the negative value is in the array or one past the end. Sentinels were discussed in more detail earlier in the chapter.

Here are the results of using the *break* keyword in C and a standard *while* test in Pascal:

Language	Straight Time	Code-Tuned Time	Time Savings
C	2.03	1.48	27%
Pascal	2.97	2.69	9%

Note: The impact of this change varies a great deal depending on how many values you have and how often you expect to find a negative value. This test assumed an average of 100 values and assumed that a negative value would be found 50 percent of the time. The Pascal example used a standard *while* test without a sentinel.

Order Tests by Frequency

Arrange tests so that the one that's fastest and most likely to be true is performed first. It should be easy to drop through the normal case, and if there are inefficiencies, they should be in processing the exceptions. This principle applies to *case* statements and to chains of *if-then-else*s.

Here's a *case* statement that responds to keyboard input in a word processor:

Pascal Example of a Poorly Ordered Logical Test

```
case( InputChar ) of
    '+',
    '=':        ProcessMathSymbol( InputChar );
    '.',
    '.',
    ':',
```

(continued)

```
  ';',
  '!',
  '?':        ProcessPunctuation( InputChar );
  '0'..'9':   ProcessDigit( InputChar );
  ' ':        ProcessSpace( InputChar );
  'A'..'Z',
  'a'..'z':   ProcessAlpha( InputChar );
  else        ProcessError( InputChar )
end;
```

The cases in this *case* statement are ordered in something close to the ASCII sort order. In a *case* statement, however, the effect is often the same as if you had written a big set of *if-then-else*s, so if you get an *'a'* as an input character, the program tests whether it's a math symbol, a punctuation mark, a digit, or a space before determining that it's an alphabetic character. If you know the likely frequency of your input characters, you can put the most common cases first. Here's the reordered *case* statement:

Pascal Example of a Well-Ordered Logical Test

```
case( InputChar ) of
  'A'..'Z',
  'a'..'z':   ProcessAlpha( InputChar );
  ' ':        ProcessSpace( InputChar );
  ',',
  '.',
  ':',
  ';',
  '!',
  '?':        ProcessPunctuation( InputChar );
  '0'..'9':   ProcessDigit( InputChar );
  '+',
  '=':        ProcessMathSymbol( InputChar );
  else        ProcessError( InputChar )
end;
```

Since the most common case is usually found sooner in the optimized code, the net effect will be the performance of fewer tests. Here are the results of this optimization with a typical mix of characters:

Language	Straight Time	Code-Tuned Time	Time Savings
Pascal	3.13	1.97	37%
C	5.17	3.47	33%

Note: Benchmarked with an input mix of 78 percent alphabetic characters, 17 percent spaces, and 5 percent punctuation symbols.

Substitute Table Lookups for Complicated Expressions

CROSS-REFERENCE
For details on using table lookups to replace complicated logic, see Section 12.2, "Table-Driven Methods."

In some circumstances, a table lookup may be quicker than traversing a complicated chain of logic. The point of a complicated chain is usually to categorize something and then to take an action based on its category. As an abstract example, suppose you want to assign a class number to something based on which of Groups *A*, *B*, and *C* it falls into:

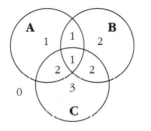

Here's an example of the complicated logic chain that assigns the class numbers:

C Example of a Complicated Chain of Logic

```c
if ( ( A && !C ) || ( A && B && C ) )
   Class = 1;
else if ( ( B && !A ) || ( A && C && !B ) )
   Class = 2;
else if ( C && !A && !B )
   Class = 3;
else
   Class = 0;
```

You can replace this test with a more modifiable and higher-performance lookup table. Here's how:

C Example of Using a Table Lookup to Replace Complicated Logic

This table definition is somewhat difficult to understand. Any commenting you can do to make table definitions readable helps.

```c
/* define ClassTable */
static int ClassTable[ 2 ][ 2 ][ 2 ] =
   /* !B!C  !BC   B!C   BC        */
   {  0,    3,    2,    2,  /* !A */
      1,    2,    1,    1 }; /*  A */
...

Class = ClassTable[ A ][ B ][ C ];
```

Although the definition of the table is hard to read, if it's well documented, it won't be any harder to read than the code for the complicated chain of logic was. If the definition changes, the table will be much easier to maintain than the earlier logic would have been. Here are the performance results:

Language	Straight Time	Code-Tuned Time	Time Savings	Performance Ratio
C	2.31	1.59	31%	1:1
Basic	58.88	23.00	60%	3:1

In this case, the table-lookup version also reaps a small size advantage. The logic-chain version uses 88 bytes in C, and the table version uses only 43 including the space for the table.

Use Lazy Evaluation

One of my former roommates was a great procrastinator. He justified his laziness by saying that many of the things people feel rushed to do simply don't need to be done. If he waited long enough, he claimed, the things that weren't important would be procrastinated into oblivion, and he wouldn't waste his time doing them.

Lazy evaluation is based on the principle my roommate used. If a program uses lazy evaluation, it avoids doing any work until the work is needed. Lazy evaluation is similar to just-in-time strategies that do the work closest to when it's needed.

Suppose, for example, that your program contains a table of 5000 values, generates the whole table at startup time, and then uses it as the program executes. If the program uses only a small percentage of the entries in the table, it might make more sense to compute them as they're needed rather than all at once. Once an entry is computed, it can still be stored for future reference ("cached").

29.3 Data Transformations

Changes in data structures can be a powerful aid in reducing program size and improving execution speed. Data-structure design is outside the scope of this book, but modest changes in the implementation of a specific data structure can also benefit performance. Here are a few ways to tune your data structures.

Use Integers Rather Than Floating-Point Numbers

CROSS-REFERENCE
For details on using integers and floating point, see Chapter 11, "Fundamental Data Types."

As the data in Table 28-1 on the cost of common operations suggests, integer addition and multiplication tend to be much faster than floating point, at least when floating point is implemented in software rather than hardware. Changing a loop index from a floating point to an integer, for example, can save time. Floating point isn't a problem in many languages, but in some, like Basic, all variables default to single-precision floating-point numbers, and explicitly making them integers can help. Here's an example:

Basic Example of a Loop That Uses a Time-Consuming Floating-Point Loop Index

```
for i = 1 to 100
   x( i ) = 0
next i
```

Unless *i* is declared to be an integer, in Basic it's a floating-point number. Contrast this with a similar Basic loop that explicitly uses integer subscripts:

Basic Example of a Loop That Uses a Timesaving Integer Loop Index

The variable i% is —
an integer.
```
for i% = 1 to 100
   x( i% ) = 0
next i%
```

How much difference does it make? Here are the results for this Basic code and for similar code in Fortran:

Language	Straight Time	Code-Tuned Time	Time Savings	Performance Ratio
Basic	5.54	0.94	83%	6:1
Fortran	5.51	0.93	83%	6:1

Use the Fewest Array Dimensions Possible

CROSS-REFERENCE
For details on arrays, see Chapter 11, "Fundamental Data Types."

Conventional wisdom maintains that multiple dimensions on arrays are expensive. If you can structure your data so that it's in a one-dimensional array rather than a two-dimensional or three-dimensional array, you might be able to save some time.

Suppose you have initialization code like this:

Pascal Example of a Standard, Two-Dimensional Array Initialization

```
for Row := 1 to NumRows do
   begin
   for Col := 1 to NumCols do
      begin
      Matrix[ Row, Col ] := 0
      end;
   end;
```

When this code is run with 50 rows and 20 columns, it takes 3.32 milliseconds. But when the array is restructured so that it's one-dimensional instead of two-dimensional, it takes only 2.28 milliseconds. Here's how the revised code would look:

Pascal Example of a One-Dimensional Representation of an Array

```
for Entry := 1 to NumRows * NumCols do
   begin
   Matrix[ Entry ] := 0
   end;
```

Here's a summary of the results, with the addition of comparable results in C and C++:

Language	Straight Time	Code-Tuned Time	Time Savings	Performance Ratio
Pascal	6.64	4.55	32%	4:3
C	7.57	5.71	25%	5:4
C++	4.29	7.69	−79%	1:2

Note: Times for the Pascal case don't match the times in the text discussion because the performance benchmarks are run many times (in this case 2000 times) in order to smooth out sample-to-sample fluctuations in the results.

The results are good in Pascal and C but terrible in C++. You might wonder whether the negative savings is an upshot of some defect in the C++ compiler, but the initial, unoptimized, C++ code is faster than either of the optimized versions from the other two compilers, so you can't be too hard on it. More likely, the code tuning thwarted automatic compiler optimizations, which in this case seem to be more effective than manual ones.

These results also show the hazard of following any code-tuning advice blindly. You can never be sure until you try the advice in your specific circumstances.

A hazard of this particular technique—turning a two-dimensional array into a one-dimensional array—is the possibility that the computation of *NumRows* * *NumCols* will inadvertently overflow the *Entry* index. You can solve the problem by making *Entry* a long integer, which avoids the overflow problem but might bring you full circle with an adverse effect on performance. Here's what happens to performance when you change *Entry* from an integer to a long integer:

Language	Initial Time	Time for *Entry* as an Integer	Time for *Entry* as a Long Integer	Total Time Savings
Pascal	6.64	4.55	7.25	−9%
C	7.57	5.71	15.43	−104%
C++	4.29	7.69	9.62	−124%

Note: "Total Time Savings" is the difference between *Entry* as a long integer and the initial, two-dimensional array time.

The penalty for switching to long integers ranges from 9 through 124 percent, but in none of these cases is the optimization better than the initial time for a two-dimensional array.

Minimize Array References

In addition to minimizing accesses to doubly or triply dimensioned arrays, it's often advantageous to minimize array accesses, period. A loop that repeatedly uses one element of an array is a good candidate for the application of this technique. Here's an example of an unnecessary array access:

```
C Example of Unnecessarily Referencing an Array Inside a Loop
for ( DiscountLevel = 0; DiscountLevel < NumLevels; DiscountLevel++ )
   {
   for ( RateIdx = 0; RateIdx < NumRates; RateIdx++ )
      {
      Rate[ RateIdx ] = Rate[ RateIdx ] * Discount[ DiscountLevel ];
      }
   }
```

The reference to *Discount[DiscountLevel]* doesn't change when *RateIdx* changes in the inner loop. Consequently, you can move it out of the inner loop so that you'll have only one array access per execution of the outer loop rather than one for each execution of the inner loop. The next example shows the revised code.

C Example of Moving an Array Reference Outside a Loop

```
for ( DiscountLevel = 0; DiscountLevel < NumLevels; DiscountLevel++ )
   {
   ThisDiscount = Discount[ DiscountLevel ];
   for ( RateIdx = 0; RateIdx < NumRates; RateIdx++ )
      {
      Rate[ RateIdx ] = Rate[ RateIdx ] * ThisDiscount;
      }
   }
```

Here are the results:

Language	Straight Time	Code-Tuned Time	Time Savings
C	16.09	13.51	16%
C++	15.16	15.16	0%
Basic	31.09	21.37	31%

Note: Benchmark times were computed for the case in which *NumLevels* equals *10* and *NumRates* equals *100*.

Once again, the results vary significantly from compiler to compiler.

Use Supplementary Indexes

Using a supplementary index means adding related data that makes accessing a data structure more efficient. You can add the related data to the main data structure, or you can store it in a parallel structure.

String-length index

In C, strings are terminated by a byte that's set to *0*. In Pascal, a length byte hidden at the beginning of each string indicates how long the string is. To determine the length of a string in C, a program has to start at the beginning of the string and count each byte until it finds the byte that's set to *0*. In Pascal, the program just looks at the length byte. Pascal's length byte is an example of augmenting a data structure with an index to make certain operations—like computing the length of a string—faster.

You can apply the idea of indexing for length to any variable-length data structure. It's often more efficient to keep track of the length of the structure rather than computing the length each time you need it.

Index for an ordered list of one-way pointers

FURTHER READING
For an extended discussion
of tuning linked-list code,
see "Software Explora-
torium: Writing Efficient C
Programs" (Bentley 1991).

If you want to find a specific entry in an ordered list of one-way pointers, you have to start at the beginning and check each pointer until you find the one you need. If the list is long, say 1000 pointers, you'll have to check an average of half the pointers before you find the one you want.

If performance is an issue, you can augment the linked list with another, smaller, linked list that acts as an index into the main list. Suppose the index has 10 entries. The first entry would point to the beginning of the main list. The second would point one-tenth of the way through the list; the third, two-tenths; the fourth, three-tenths; and so on. When you search for a pointer in the main linked list, you go first to the index list. You'll check an average of half the index pointers before you figure out which tenth of the main list the value is in. Then you check the values in that tenth, an average of half of them, to find the value you want.

If the list is 1000 links long, the 10-pointer augmentation reduces the average number of pointers you have to check from 500 to 55. The augmentation increases the amount of time required to insert an element, however, so you have to weigh the trade-offs between search time, insertion time, and storage.

This idea is useful for linked lists and even more useful for accessing disk-based data structures. A similar scheme is used for storing B-trees.

Independent, parallel index structure

Sometimes it's more efficient to manipulate an index to a data structure than it is to manipulate the data structure itself. If the items in the data structure are big or hard to move (on disk, perhaps), sorting and searching index references is faster than working with the data directly. If each data item is large, you can create an auxiliary structure that consists of key values and pointers to the detailed information. If the difference in size between the data-structure item and the auxiliary-structure item is great enough, sometimes you can store the key item in memory even when the data item has to be stored externally. All searching and sorting is done in memory, and you have to access the disk only once, when you know the exact location of the item you want.

Use Caching

Caching means saving a few values in such a way that you can retrieve the most commonly used values more easily than the less commonly used values. If a program randomly reads records from a disk, for example, a routine might use a cache to save the records most frequently read. When the routine receives a request for a record, it checks the cache to see whether it has the record. If it does, the record is returned directly from memory rather than from disk.

In addition to caching records on disk, you can apply caching in other areas. In a Microsoft Windows font-proofing program, the performance bottleneck was in retrieving the width of each character as it was displayed. Caching the most recently used character width roughly doubled the display speed. Jon Bentley reports a spelling-correction program that cached the 1000 most frequently used words in memory (1982). The program had a 500,000-word dictionary on disk, but the in-memory cache made disk accesses rare.

You can cache the results of time-consuming computations too—especially if the parameters to the calculation are simple. Suppose, for example, that you need to compute the length of the hypotenuse of a right triangle, given the lengths of the other two sides. The straightforward implementation of the routine would look like this:

Pascal Example of a Routine That's Conducive to Caching

```pascal
function Hypotenuse
   (
   SideA:   real;
   SideB:   real
   ): real;
begin
   Hypotenuse := sqrt( SideA * SideA + SideB * SideB );
end;
```

If you know that the same values tend to be requested repeatedly, you can cache values this way:

Pascal Example of Caching to Avoid an Expensive Computation

A typed constant is a nonstandard feature of Pascal. It acts as a local variable that retains its value between calls to the routine. —

```pascal
function Hypotenuse
   (
   SideA:   real;
   SideB:   real
   ): real;
const
   CachedHypotenuse: real = 0;
   CachedSideA:      real = 0;
   CachedSideB:      real = 0;
begin
   { check to see if the triangle is already in the cache }
```

(continued)

```
      if ( (SideA = CachedSideA) and
           (SideB = CachedSideB) ) then
        begin
        Hypotenuse := CachedHypotenuse;
        exit;
        end;

    { compute new hypotenuse and cache it }

    CachedHypotenuse := sqrt( SideA * SideA + SideB * SideB );
    CachedSideA      := SideA;
    CachedSideB      := SideB;

    Hypotenuse       := CachedHypotenuse;
  end;
```

The second version of the routine is more complicated than the first and takes up more space, so speed has to be at a premium to justify it. Many caching schemes cache more than one element, so they have even more overhead. Here's the speed difference between these two versions:

Language	Straight Time	Code-Tuned Time	Time Savings
Pascal	2.63	2.25	14%
C	1.99	1.93	3%
Basic	1.75	2.52	−44%

Note: The results shown assume that the cache is hit twice for each time it's set. The break-even point was 1 hit for the Pascal routine, 2 for the C, and 19 for the Basic.

Once again, the results from different compilers vary wildly. The success of the cache depends on the relative costs of accessing a cached element, creating an uncached element, and saving a new element in the cache. Success also depends on how often the cached information is requested. In some cases, success might also depend on caching done by the hardware. Generally, the more it costs to generate a new element and the more times the same information is requested, the more valuable a cache is. The cheaper it is to access a cached element and save new elements in the cache, the more valuable a cache is.

29.4 Expressions

CROSS-REFERENCE
For more information on expressions, see Section 17.1, "Boolean Expressions."

Much of the work in a program is done inside mathematical or logical expressions. Complicated expressions tend to be expensive, so this section looks at ways to make them cheaper.

Exploit Algebraic Identities

You can use algebraic identities to replace costly operations with cheaper ones. For example, the following expressions are logically equivalent:

```
not A and not B
not (A or B)
```

If you choose the second expression instead of the first, you can save a *not* operation. If you can reverse the polarity of the test—for example, by using a *repeat-until* loop instead of a *while-do* loop in Pascal—you can drop the *not* from the second option and save two *not*s.

Although the savings from avoiding a single *not* operation are probably slight, the general principle is powerful. Jon Bentley describes a program that tested whether $sqrt(x) < sqrt(y)$ (1982). Since $sqrt(x)$ is less than $sqrt(y)$ only when x is less than y, you can replace the first test with $x < y$. Given the cost of the $sqrt()$ routine, you'd expect the savings to be dramatic, and they are. Here are the results:

Language	Straight Time	Code-Tuned Time	Time Savings	Performance Ratio
C	3.63	0.71	80%	5:1
Basic	2.37	0.94	60%	3:1

Use Strength Reduction

As mentioned earlier, strength reduction means replacing an expensive operation with a cheaper one. Here are some possible substitutions:

- Replace multiplication with addition.
- Replace exponentiation with multiplication.
- Replace trigonometric routines with their trigonometric identities.
- Replace long integers with short integers.
- Replace floating-point numbers with fixed-point numbers or integers.
- Replace double-precision floating points with single-precision numbers.
- Replace integer multiplication and division by two with shift operations.

Here is a detailed example. Suppose you have to evaluate a polynomial. If you're rusty on polynomials, they're the things that look like

$Ax^2 + Bx + C$

The letters A, B, and C are coefficients, and x is a variable. General code to evaluate an nth-order polynomial looks like this:

Basic Example of Evaluating a Polynomial

```
Value = Coefficient( 0 )
for Power = 1 to Order
   Value = Value + Coefficient( Power ) * x^Power
next Power
```

If you're thinking about strength reduction, you'll look at the exponentiation operator with a jaundiced eye. One solution would be to replace the exponentiation with a multiplication on each pass through the loop, which is analogous to the strength-reduction case a few sections ago in which a multiplication was replaced with an addition. Here's how the reduced-strength polynomial evaluation would look:

Basic Example of a Reduced-Strength Method of Evaluating a Polynomial

```
Value = Coefficient( 0 )
PowerOfX = x
for Power = 1 to Order
   Value = Value + Coefficient( Power ) * PowerOfX
   PowerOfX = PowerOfX * x
next Power
```

This produces a noticeable advantage if you're working with second order polynomials (polynomials in which the highest-power term is squared) or higher-order polynomials.

Language	Straight Time	Code-Tuned Time	Time Savings	Performance Ratio
Basic	25.43	3.24	87%	8:1
Ada	28.72	11.42	60%	3:1

If you're serious about strength reduction, you still won't care for those two floating-point multiplications. You can further reduce the strength of the operations in the loop by accumulating powers rather than multiplying them each time. Here's that code:

Basic Example of Further Reducing the Strength Required to Evaluate a Polynomial

```
Value = 0
for Power = Order to 1 Step -1
   Value = ( Value + Coefficient( Power ) ) * X
next Power
Value = Value + Coefficient( 0 )
```

This method eliminates the extra *PowerOfX* variable and replaces the two multiplications in each pass through the loop with one. It's not exactly straightforward, but that's the penalty you pay for code tuning. The code is considerably faster.

Language	Straight Time	First Optimization	Second Optimization	Savings over First Optimization
Basic	25.43	3.24	1.98	39%
Ada	28.72	11.42	6.97	39%

The lesson to be learned here is Don't stop after the first optimization. Even though the first produced a nice benefit, the second was better.

Initialize at Compile Time

If you're using a named constant or a magic number in a routine call and it's the only argument, that's a clue that you could precompute the number, put it into a constant, and avoid the routine call. The same principle applies to multiplications, divisions, additions, and other operations.

I once needed to compute the base-two logarithm of an integer, truncated to the nearest integer. The system didn't have a log–base-two routine, so I wrote my own. The quick and easy approach was to use the fact that

$$\log(x)_{base} = \log(x) \;/\; \log(base)$$

Given this identity, I could write a routine like this one:

CROSS-REFERENCE
For details on binding variables to their values, see Section 10.3, "Binding Time."

C Example of a Log–Base-Two Routine Based on System Routines

```c
unsigned int log2( unsigned int x )
   {
   return( (unsigned int) (log( x ) / log( 2 )) );
   }
```

This routine was really slow, and since the value of *log(2)* never changed, I replaced *log(2)* with its computed value, *0.69314718.* Then the code looked like this:

C Example of a Log–Base-Two Routine Based on a System Routine and a Constant

LOG2 is a named constant equal to 0.69314718. ——

```c
unsigned int log2( unsigned int x )
   {
   return( (unsigned int) (log( x ) / LOG2) );
   }
```

Since *log()* tends to be an expensive routine, much more expensive than type conversions or division, you'd expect that cutting the calls to the *log()* function by half would cut the time required for the routine by about half. Here are the measured results:

Language	Straight Time	Code-Tuned Time	Time Savings
C	29.00	21.74	25%
Fortran	43.06	32.95	23%

The savings is not as large as expected, apparently because a floating-point division and two type conversions dilute the effect of the optimization. The educated guess about the relative importance of the division and type conversions and the estimate of 50 percent were simply wrong, as educated guesses often are when optimization is concerned.

Be Wary of System Routines

System routines are expensive and provide accuracy that's often wasted. The system math routines, for example, are designed to put an astronaut on the moon within $\pm$ 2 feet of the target. If you don't need that degree of accuracy, you don't need to spend the time to compute it either.

In the previous example, the *log2()* routine returned an integer value but used a floating-point *log()* routine to compute it. That was overkill for an integer result, so after my first attempt, I wrote a series of integer tests that were perfectly accurate for calculating an integer $\log_2$. Here's the code:

C Example of a Log–Base-Two Routine Based on Integers

```
unsigned int log2( unsigned int x )
   {
   if ( x < 2 )        return( 0 );
   if ( x < 4 )        return( 1 );
   if ( x < 8 )        return( 2 );
   if ( x < 16 )       return( 3 );
   if ( x < 32 )       return( 4 );
   if ( x < 64 )       return( 5 );
   if ( x < 128 )      return( 6 );
   if ( x < 256 )      return( 7 );
   if ( x < 512 )      return( 8 );
   if ( x < 1024 )     return( 9 );
   if ( x < 2048 )     return( 10 );
   if ( x < 4096 )     return( 11 );
```

(continued)

```
if ( x < 8192 )     return( 12 );
if ( x < 16384 )    return( 13 );
if ( x < 32768 )    return( 14 );
return( 15 );
}
```

This routine uses integer operations, never converts to floating point, and blows the doors off both floating-point versions. Here are the results:

Language	Straight Time	Code-Tuned Time	Time Savings	Performance Ratio
C	29.00	0.15	99.5%	200:1
Fortran	43.06	0.44	98.9%	100:1

Most of the so-called "transcendental" functions are designed for the worst case—that is, they convert to double-precision floating point internally even if you give them an integer argument. If you find one in a tight section of code and don't need that much accuracy, give it your immediate attention.

Another option is to take advantage of the fact that a right-shift operation is the same as dividing by two. The number of times you can divide a number by two and still have a nonzero value is the same as the $\log_2$ of that number. Here's how code based on that observation looks:

CODING HORROR

C Example of an Alternative Log–Base-Two Routine Based on the Right-Shift Operator

```
unsigned int log2( unsigned int x )
   {
   unsigned int i = 0;
   while ( (x = (x >> 1)) != 0 )
      {
      i++;
      }
   return( i );
   }
```

To non-C programmers, this code is particularly hard to read. The complicated expression in the *while* condition is an example of a coding practice you should avoid unless you have a good reason to use it.

This routine takes about 40 percent longer than the longer version above, executing in 0.21 seconds rather than 0.15 seconds. It takes only about one-sixth of the memory (27 vs. 174 bytes), however, so you might prefer it in some circumstances.

This example highlights the value of not stopping after one successful optimization. The first optimization earned a respectable 25 percent savings but had nowhere near the impact of the second or third optimization. An additional attempt produced a compromise between speed and memory use.

Use the Correct Type of Constants

Use named constants and literals that are the same type as the variables they're assigned to. When a constant and its related variable are different types, the compiler has to do a type conversion to assign the constant to the variable. A good compiler does the type conversion at compile time so that it doesn't affect run-time performance.

A less advanced compiler or an interpreter, however, generates code for a run-time conversion, so you might be stuck. Here are some differences in performance between the initializations of a floating-point variable x and an integer variable i in two cases. In the first case, the initializations look like this:

```
x - 5
i = 3.14
```

and require type conversions. In the second case, they look like this:

```
x = 3.14
i = 5
```

and don't require type conversions. Here are the results:

Language	Straight Time	Code-Tuned Time	Time Savings	Performance Ratio
Compiled Basic	5.38	5.38	0%	1:1
Interpreted Basic	15.27	6.42	58%	2:1
C	20.65	5.45	74%	4:1
C++	4.94	4.94	0%	1:1
Fortran	3.07	3.07	0%	1:1

It's not surprising that all but one of the compilers produced no savings or that the Basic interpreter's time improved. It is surprising that the C compiler—the current, third generation of a popular product—did such an abysmal job. The lesson is that each compiler has specific strengths and weaknesses, and sometimes the weaknesses are surprising.

Precompute Results

A common low-level design decision is the choice of whether to compute results on the fly or compute them once, save them, and look them up as needed. If the results are used many times, it's often cheaper to compute them once and look them up.

This choice manifests itself in several ways. At the simplest level, you might compute part of an expression outside a loop rather than inside. An example of this appeared earlier in the chapter. At a more complicated level, you might compute a lookup table once when program execution begins, using it every time thereafter, or you might store results in a data file or embed them in a program.

In a space-wars video game, for example, the programmers initially computed gravity coefficients for different distances from the sun. The computation for the gravity coefficients was expensive and affected performance. The program recognized relatively few distinct distances from the sun, however, so the programmers were able to precompute the gravity coefficients and store them in a 10-element array. The array lookup was much faster than the expensive computation.

Suppose you have a routine that computes payment amounts on automobile loans. The code for such a routine would look like this:

Pascal Example of a Complex Computation That Could Be Precomputed

```pascal
function ComputePayment
    (
    LoanAmount:     longint;
    Months:         integer;
    InterestRate:   real;
    ): real;

begin
    Payment := LoanAmount /
                (
                ( 1.0 - Power( 1.0+(InterestRate/12.0), - Months ) ) /
                ( InterestRate/12.0 )
                )
end;
```

The formula for computing loan payments is complicated and fairly expensive. Putting the information in a table instead of computing it each time would probably be cheaper.

How big would the table be? The widest-ranging variable is *LoanAmount*. The variable *InterestRate* might range from 5% through 20% by quarter points, but that's only 61 distinct rates. *Months* might range from 12 through 72, but that's only 61 distinct periods. *LoanAmount* could conceivably range from $1000 through $100,000, which is more entries than you'd generally want to handle in a lookup table.

Most of the computation doesn't depend on *LoanAmount*, however, so you can put the really ugly part of the computation (the denominator of the larger expression) into a table that's indexed by *InterestRate* and *Months*. You re-compute the *LoanAmount* part each time. Here's the revised code:

Pascal Example of Precomputing a Complex Computation

```pascal
function ComputePayment
    (
    LoanAmount:    longint;
    Months:        integer;
    InterestRate:  real;
    ): real;
var
    InterestIdx: integer;
begin
    InterestIdx :=
        Round( (InterestRate - LOWEST_RATE) * GRANULARITY * 100.00 );
    Payment := LoanAmount / LoanDivisor[ InterestIdx, Months ]
end:
```

The new variable — *InterestIdx needs to be created to have a subscript for the LoanDivisor array.*

In this code, the hairy calculation has been replaced with the computation of an array index and a single array access. Here are the results of the change:

Language	Straight Time	Code-Tuned Time	Time Savings	Performance Ratio
Pascal	3.13	0.82	74%	4:1
Ada	9.39	2.09	78%	4:1

Note: The Ada compiler's results are considerably slower than the Pascal compiler's, but they're not comparable because the Pascal program didn't perform range checking on its array accesses. To the Ada compiler's credit, its optimizer is the only one that fully optimized any of the test programs in this chapter. In this case, it detected the fact that the *Payment* variable was never used and removed all the code that computed it—resulting in initial benchmark times of *0.0* and *0.0*.

Depending on your circumstances, you would need to precompute the *Loan-Divisor* array at program initialization time or read it from a disk file. Alternatively, you could initialize it to *0*, compute each element the first time it's requested, store it, and look it up each time it's requested subsequently. That would be a form of caching, discussed earlier.

You don't have to create a table to take advantage of the performance gains you can achieve by precomputing an expression. Code similar to the code in the previous examples raises the possibility of a different kind of precomputation. Suppose you have code that computes payments for many loan amounts, as shown on the next page.

Pascal Example of a Second Complex Computation That Could Be Precomputed

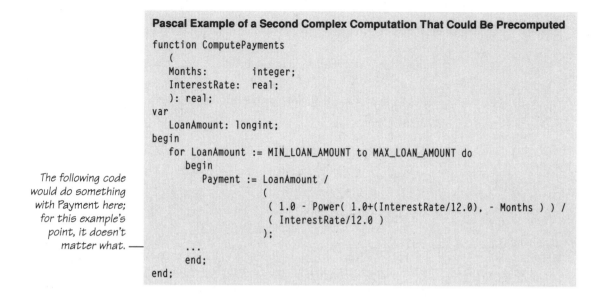

```
function ComputePayments
   (
   Months:       integer;
   InterestRate: real;
   ): real;
var
   LoanAmount: longint;
begin
   for LoanAmount := MIN_LOAN_AMOUNT to MAX_LOAN_AMOUNT do
      begin
         Payment := LoanAmount /
            (
            ( 1.0 - Power( 1.0+(InterestRate/12.0), - Months ) ) /
            ( InterestRate/12.0 )
            );
      ...
      end;
end;
```

The following code would do something with Payment here; for this example's point, it doesn't matter what.

Even without precomputing a table, you can precompute the complicated part of the computation outside the loop and use it inside the loop. Here's how it would look:

Pascal Example of Precomputing the Second Complex Computation

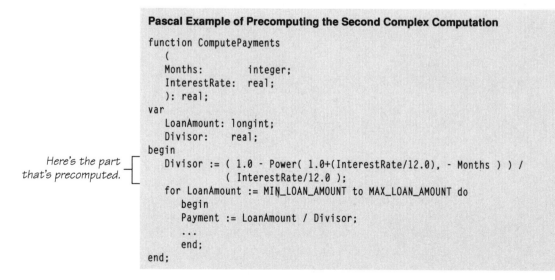

```
function ComputePayments
   (
   Months:       integer;
   InterestRate: real;
   ): real;
var
   LoanAmount: longint;
   Divisor:    real;
begin
   Divisor := ( 1.0 - Power( 1.0+(InterestRate/12.0), - Months ) ) /
            ( InterestRate/12.0 );
   for LoanAmount := MIN_LOAN_AMOUNT to MAX_LOAN_AMOUNT do
      begin
      Payment := LoanAmount / Divisor;
      ...
      end;
end;
```

Here's the part that's precomputed.

This is similar to the techniques suggested earlier of putting array references and pointer dereferences outside a loop. The results in this case are comparable to the results of using the precomputed table in the first optimization:

Language	Straight Time	Code-Tuned Time	Time Savings	Performance Ratio
Pascal	3.51	0.77	78%	5:1
Ada	10.33	1.70	84%	6:1

Optimizing a program by precomputation can take several forms:

- Computing results before the program executes and wiring them into constants that are assigned at compile time
- Computing results before the program executes and hard-coding them into variables used at run time
- Computing results before the program executes and putting them into a file that's loaded at run time
- Computing results once, at program startup, and then referencing them each time they're needed
- Computing as much as possible before a loop begins, minimizing the work done inside the loop
- Computing results the first time they're needed and storing them so that you can retrieve them when they're needed again

Eliminate Common Subexpressions

If you find an expression that's repeated several times, assign it to a variable and refer to the variable rather than recomputing the expression in several places. The loan-calculation example has a common subexpression that you could eliminate. Here's the original code:

Pascal Example of a Common Subexpression

```
Payment := LoanAmount /
          (
            ( 1.0 - Power( 1.0+(InterestRate/12.0), - Months ) ) /
            ( InterestRate/12.0 )
          );
```

In this sample, you can assign *InterestRate/12.0* to a variable that is then referenced twice rather than computing the expression twice. If you have chosen the variable name well, this optimization can improve the code's readability at the same time that it improves performance. The next example shows the revised code.

Pascal Example of Eliminating a Common Subexpression
```
MonthlyInterest := InterestRate / 12.0;
Payment := LoanAmount /
          (
              ( 1.0 - Power( 1.0+MonthlyInterest, - Months ) ) /
              MonthlyInterest
          );
```

The savings in this case don't seem impressive:

Language	Straight Time	Code-Tuned Time	Time Savings
Pascal	3.13	3.08	2%
Ada	9.56	9.33	2%

It appears that the *Power()* routine is so costly that it overshadows the savings from subexpression elimination. In other cases, if the subexpression were a bigger part of the cost of the whole expression, the optimization would have more impact.

Not all subexpression eliminations are created equal. For example, suppose you wanted to eliminate the *Mtx[InsertPos–1]* expression in the following code fragment:

C Example of a Candidate for Subexpression Removal
```
for ( Boundary = 1; Boundary < NUM; Boundary++ )
   {
   InsertPos = Boundary;
   while ( InsertPos > 0 && Mtx[ InsertPos ] < Mtx[ InsertPos-1 ] )
      {
      SwapVal           = Mtx[ InsertPos ];
      Mtx[ InsertPos ]  = Mtx[ InsertPos-1 ];
      Mtx[ InsertPos-1 ] = SwapVal;
      InsertPos--;
      }
   }
```

You could replace the common expression in a couple of ways. The most common way would be to assign it a value and use the value, where possible. In this example, you could replace *Mtx[InsertPos–1]* with *TestVal*. That code would look like this:

C Example of a Subexpression Removal That Doesn't Work Well

```
for ( Boundary = 1; Boundary < NUM; Boundary++ )
   {
   InsertPos = Boundary;
   TestVal    = Mtx[ InsertPos-1 ];
   while ( InsertPos > 0 && Mtx[ InsertPos ] < TestVal )
      {
      SwapVal            = Mtx[ InsertPos ];
      Mtx[ InsertPos ]   = TestVal;
      Mtx[ InsertPos-1 ] = SwapVal;
      InsertPos--;
      TestVal = Mtx[ InsertPos-1 ];
      }
   }
```

TestVal is substituted here... —

...and here. —

This approach eliminates only one array reference and one computation of *InsertPos–1* for each pass through the loop. The results aren't impressive:

Language	Straight Time	Code-Tuned Time	Time Savings
C	1.53	1.58	−3%
Ada	1.43	1.59	−11%

The technique actually hurt performance. But C does support a different kind of subexpression—namely, a pointer. Here is an example of how to use a pointer, *TestValPtr*, to remove the common subexpression:

C Example of a Subexpression Removal That Works Better

```
for ( Boundary = 1; Boundary < NUM; Boundary++ )
   {
   InsertPos = Boundary;
   TestValPtr = &Mtx[ InsertPos-1 ];
   while ( InsertPos > 0 && Mtx[ InsertPos ] < *TestValPtr )
      {
      SwapVal          = Mtx[ InsertPos ];
      Mtx[ InsertPos ] = *TestValPtr;
      *TestValPtr      = SwapVal;
      InsertPos--;
      TestValPtr--;
      }
   }
```

This approach eliminates three array references and three computations of *InsertPos–1* for each pass through the loop. The results are correspondingly more impressive:

Language	Straight Time	Code-Tuned Time	Time Savings
C	1.53	1.33	13%

29.5 Routines

CROSS-REFERENCE
For details on working with routines, see Chapter 5, "Characteristics of High-Quality Routines."

One of the most powerful tools in code tuning is a good routine decomposition. Small, well-defined routines save space because they take the place of doing jobs separately in multiple places. They make a program easy to optimize because you can adjust one routine and thus improve every routine that calls it. Small routines are relatively easy to rewrite in assembler. Long, tortuous routines are hard enough to understand on their own; in assembler they're impossible. For well-defined tasks, you may be able to buy routines from a vendor who has probably had more time to polish the routines than you're likely to have.

Rewrite Routines In Line

In the early days of computer programming, some machines imposed prohibitive performance penalties for using a routine. A call to a routine meant that the operating system had to swap out the program, swap in a directory of routines, swap in the particular routine, execute the routine, swap out the routine, and swap the calling routine back in. All this swapping chewed up resources and made the program slow. Modern machines—and "modern" means any machine you're ever likely to work on—impose virtually no penalty for calling a routine. Moreover, because of the increased code size resulting from putting code in line and the extra swapping that's associated with increased code size on demand-paged virtual-memory machines, a recent study found a slight timing *penalty* for using inline code rather than routines (Davidson and Holler 1992).

In some cases, you might be able to save a few microseconds by putting the code from a routine into the program directly where it's needed. If you're working in a language with a macro preprocessor, you can use a macro to put the code in, switching it in and out as needed. Here are the results of putting a string-copy routine in line:

Language	Routine Time	Inline-Code Time	Time Savings
C	1.81	1.65	9%
Pascal	1.20	1.04	13%

The percentage gains shown in this table are probably higher than those you'd normally see. String copying is simple, so the ratio of routine-call overhead to work is higher than it is for other kinds of operations. The less work a routine does, the greater the potential benefit from putting it in line. If a routine does a lot of work, don't expect much improvement.

29.6 Recoding in Assembler

One piece of conventional wisdom that shouldn't be left unmentioned is the advice that when you run into a performance bottleneck, you should recode in assembler. Recoding in assembler tends to improve both speed and code size. Here is a typical approach to optimizing with assembler:

1. Write 100 percent of an application in a high-level language.

2. Fully test the application, and verify that it's in compliance with the requirements.

CROSS-REFERENCE
For details on the phenomenon of a small percentage of a program accounting for most of its run time, see "The Pareto Principle" in Section 28.2.

3. If performance improvements are needed after that, profile the application to identify hot spots. Since about 5 percent of a program usually accounts for about 50 percent of the running time, you can usually identify small pieces of the program as hot spots.

4. Recode a few small pieces in assembler to improve overall performance.

Whether you follow this well-beaten path depends on how comfortable you are with assembler and on your level of desperation.

I got my first exposure to assembler on the DES encryption program I mentioned in the previous chapter. I had tried every optimization I'd ever heard of, and the program was still twice as slow as the speed goal. Recoding part of the program in assembler was the only remaining option. As an assembler novice, about all I could do was make a straight translation from a high-level language to assembler, but I got a 50 percent improvement even at that rudimentary level.

Suppose you have a routine that converts binary data to uppercase ASCII characters for transmission over a modem. The next example shows the Pascal code to do it.

Pascal Example of Code That's Better Suited to Assembler

```
procedure HexGrow
   (
   var Source:  ByteArray;
   var Target:  WordArray;
       num:     word
   );
var
   Index:       integer;
   LowerByte:   byte;
   UpperByte:   byte;
   TgtIndex:    integer;
begin
   TgtIndex := 1;
   for Index := 1 to Num do
      begin
      Target[ TgtIndex ]   := ( (Source[ Index ] and $F0) shr 4 ) + $41;
      Target[ TgtIndex+1 ] := (Source[ Index ] and $0f) + $41;
      TgtIndex := TgtIndex + 2;
      end;
end;
```

Although it's hard to see where the fat is in this code, it contains a lot of bit manipulation, which isn't exactly Pascal's forte. Bit manipulation is assembler's forte, however, so this code is a good candidate for recoding. Here's the assembler code:

Example of a Routine Recoded in Assembler

```
HexExpand    PROC    NEAR

        MOV    BX,SP                ; get stack pointer for routine arg's
        MOV    CX,SS:[BX+2]         ; load number of bytes to expand
        MOV    SI,SS:[BX+8]         ; load source offset
        MOV    DI,SS:[BX+4]         ; load target offset

        XOR    AX,AX                ; zero-out array offset

EXPAND:

        MOV    BX,AX                ; array offset
        MOV    DL,DS:[SI+BX]        ; get source byte
        MOV    DH,DL                ; copy source byte
```

(continued)

```
        AND     DH,15                   ; get msb's
        ADD     DH,65                   ; add 65 to make modem ready

        SHR     DL,1                    ; move lsb's into position
        SHR     DL,1                    ; move lsb's into position
        SHR     DL,1                    ; move lsb's into position
        SHR     DL,1                    ; move lsb's into position
        AND     DL,15                   ; get lsb's
        ADD     DL,65                   ; add 65 to make modem ready

        SHL     BX,1                    ; double offset for target array index
        MOV     DS:[DI+BX],DX           ; put target word

        INC     AX                      ; increment array offset
        LOOP    EXPAND                  ; repeat until finished

        RET     10                      ; pop arg's off stack and return

HexExpand       ENDP
```

Rewriting in assembler in this case was profitable, resulting in a time savings of 65 percent. It's logical to assume that code in a language that's more suited to bit manipulation—C, for instance—would have less to gain than Pascal code would, but as is often the case, real-world optimization results don't pay much attention to logical assumptions. Here are the results:

Language	High-Level Time	Assembler Time	Time Savings	Performance Ratio
Pascal	1.59	0.55	65%	3:1
C	0.83	0.38	54%	2:1

The assembler routine shows that rewriting in assembler doesn't have to produce a huge, ugly routine. Such routines are often quite modest, as this one is. Sometimes assembler code is almost as compact as its high-level–language equivalent.

A relatively easy and effective strategy for recoding in assembler is to start with a compiler that generates assembler listings as a by-product of compilation. Extract the assembler code for the routine you need to tune, and save it in a separate source file. Using the compiler's assembler code as a base, hand-optimize the code, checking for correctness and measuring improvements at each step. Some compilers intersperse the high-level–language statements as comments in the assembler code. If yours does, keep them in the assembler code as documentation.

29.7 Quick Reference to Tuning Techniques

Depending on the circumstances, you might try any of the techniques in Table 29-1 to optimize your code.

Table 29-1. Summary of Code-Tuning Techniques

Technique	See Page
Improve Both Speed and Size	
Jam loops	697
Substitute table lookups for complicated logic	709
Use integer instead of floating-point variables	711
Initialize data at compile time	720
Use constants of the correct type	723
Precompute results	723
Eliminate common subexpressions	727
Translate key routines to assembler	731
Improve Speed Only	
Unswitch loops that contain *if* tests	696
Unroll loops	698
Minimize work performed inside loops	700
Use sentinels in search loops	701
Put the busiest loop on the inside of nested loops	703
Reduce the strength of operations performed inside loops	704
Stop testing when you know the answer	706
Order tests in *case* statements and *if-then-else* chains by frequency	707
Use lazy evaluation	710
Change multiple-dimension arrays to a single dimension	711
Minimize array references	713
Augment data structures with indexes	714
Cache frequently used values	715
Exploit algebraic identities	718
Reduce strength in logical and mathematical expressions	720
Be wary of system routines	721
Rewrite routines in line	730

Further Reading

Bentley, Jon. *Writing Efficient Programs*. Englewood Cliffs, N.J.: Prentice Hall, 1982. This book is an expert treatment of code tuning, broadly considered. Bentley describes techniques that trade time for space and space for time. He provides several examples of redesigning data structures to reduce both space and time. His approach is a little more anecdotal than the one taken here, and his anecdotes are interesting. He takes a few routines through several optimization steps so that you can see the effects of first, second, and third attempts on a single problem. Bentley strolls through the primary contents of the book in 135 pages. The book has an unusually high signal-to-noise ratio—it's one of the rare gems that every practicing programmer should own.

Abrash, Michael. "Flooring It. The Optimization Challenge." *PC Techniques* 2, no. 6 (February/March 1992): 82–88. This is an interesting report on the top entries in an assembler code-tuning contest. The winning entry was about 4 times faster than the original hand-tuned assembler code and about 13 times as fast as the original code in C. The report illustrated some of the techniques described in this chapter.

Key Points

- Results of optimizations vary widely with different languages, compilers, and environments. Without measuring a specific optimization, you'll have no idea whether it will help or hurt your program.

- The first optimization is often not the best. Even after you find a good one, keep looking for one that's better.

- Code tuning is a little like nuclear energy. It's a controversial, emotional topic. Some people think it's so detrimental to reliability and maintainability that they won't do it at all. Others think that with proper safeguards, it's beneficial. If you decide to use the techniques in this chapter, apply them with the utmost care.

30

Software Evolution

Contents

Related Topics

MYTH: A WELL-MANAGED SOFTWARE PROJECT conducts a careful analysis of the program's requirements and sets a stable list of the operations the program must perform. Design follows requirements, and it is done carefully so that coding can proceed linearly, from start to finish, implying that most of the code can be written once, tested, and forgotten. According to the myth, the only time that the code is significantly modified is during the software-maintenance phase, something that happens only after the initial version of a system has been delivered.

HARD DATA

Reality: Code evolves substantially during its initial development. Many of the changes seen during initial coding are at least as dramatic as changes seen during maintenance. Coding, debugging, and unit testing consume between 25 and 70 percent of the effort on a typical project, depending on the project's size. (See Chapter 21, "How Program Size Affects Construction," for details.) If coding and unit testing were straightforward processes, they would consume no more than 20 percent of the total effort on a project. Even on well-managed projects, however, requirements change by about 25 percent over the project's initial development (Boehm 1981). Requirements changes invariably affect the code, sometimes substantially.

KEY POINT

Another Reality: Modern development practices increase the potential for code changes during construction. In the traditional life cycle, the focus—successful or not—is on avoiding code changes. More modern approaches—evolutionary delivery and prototyping, for example—move away from coding predictability. The new approaches are more code-centered, and over the life of a project, you can expect code to evolve more than ever.

30.1 Kinds of Software Evolution

Software evolution is like biological evolution in that some mutations are beneficial and many mutations are not. Good software evolution produces code whose development mimics the ascent from monkeys to Neanderthals to our current exalted state as computer programmers. Evolutionary forces sometimes beat on a program the other way, however, knocking the program into a de-evolutionary spiral.

KEY POINT

The key distinction between kinds of software evolution is whether the program's quality improves or degrades under modification. If you fix errors with logical duct tape and superstition, quality degrades. If you treat modifications as opportunities to tighten up the original design of the program, quality improves. If you see that program quality is degrading, that's like a canary in a mine shaft that has stopped singing. It's a warning that the program is evolving in the wrong direction.

> There is no code so big, twisted, or complex that maintenance can't make it worse.
>
> *Gerald Weinberg*

A second distinction in the kinds of software evolution is the one between changes made during construction and those made during maintenance. These two kinds of evolution differ in several ways. Construction changes are usually made by the original developer, usually before the program has been completely forgotten. The system isn't yet on line, so the pressure to finish changes is only schedule pressure—it's not 500 angry users wondering why their system isn't working. For the same reason, changes during construction can be more freewheeling—the system is in a more dynamic state, and the penalty for making mistakes is low. These circumstances imply a style of software evolution that's different from what you'd find during software maintenance.

30.2 General Guidelines for Software Evolution

One common weakness in programmers' approaches to software evolution is that it goes on as an un-self-conscious process. If you recognize that evolution during development is an inevitable and important phenomenon and plan for it, you can use it to your advantage.

The Cardinal Rule of Software Evolution is that evolution should improve the internal quality of the program. Here are some guidelines:

CROSS-REFERENCE
For other details on how to construct effective routines, see Chapter 5, "Characteristics of High-Quality Routines."

Develop more, smaller routines. One way to improve a system is to increase its modularity—increase the number of well-defined, well-named routines that do one thing and do it well. When changes lead you to revisit a section of code, take the opportunity to check the modularity of the routines in that section. If a routine would be cleaner if part of it were made into a separate routine, create a separate routine. This process is discussed in much more depth in Section 30.3, "Making New Routines."

CROSS-REFERENCE
For guidelines on the use of global variables, see Section 10.6, "Global Variables." For an explanation of the differences between global data and module data, see "Module data mistaken for global data" in Section 6.2.

Reduce the number of global variables. When you revisit a section of code that uses global variables, take time to re-examine them. You might have thought of a way to avoid using global variables since the last time you visited that part of the code. Because you're less familiar with the code than when you first wrote it, you might now find the global variables sufficiently confusing that you're willing to develop a cleaner approach. You might also have a better sense of how to isolate global variables in access routines and a keener sense of the pain caused by not doing so. Bite the bullet and make the beneficial modifications. The initial coding will be far enough in the past that you can be objective about your work yet close enough that you will still remember most of what you need in order to make the revisions correctly. The time during early revisions is the perfect time to improve the code.

Improve your programming style. When you go back for changes, that's a good time to clean up variable names, routine names, layout, comments—to work on all aspects of good programming style.

CROSS-REFERENCE
For details on change control and pointers to further reading, see Section 22.2, "Configuration Management."

Manage changes. During development you'll be faced with requests for new features and with error fixes that require you to change source code. If you change the code and a new error surfaces that seems unrelated to the change you made, you'll probably want to compare the new version of the code with the old to find the source of the error. If that doesn't work, you might want to try a version that's even older. You can handle such comparisons easily with version-control tools that keep track of multiple versions of source code. These are discussed more in Chapter 22, "Managing Construction."

CROSS-REFERENCE
For details on reviews, see Chapter 24, "Reviews."

Review code changes. If reviews are important the first time through, they are even more important the second. Ed Yourdon reports that when programmers make changes to a program, they typically have more than a 50 percent chance of making an error the first time (Yourdon 1986b). Interestingly, if programmers work with a substantial portion of the code, rather than just a few lines, the chance of making a correct modification improves. Specifically, as the number of lines changed increases from one to five lines, the chance of making a bad change increases. After that, the chance of making a bad change decreases.

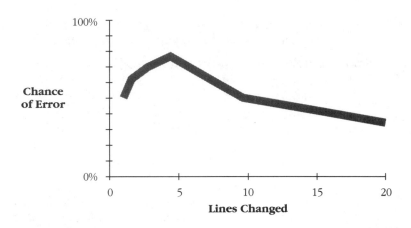

Source: "Kill That Code!" (Weinberg 1983).

Programmers treat small changes casually. They don't desk-check them, they don't have others review them, and they sometimes don't even run the code to verify that the fix works properly.

HARD DATA

The moral is simple. Treat simple changes as if they were complicated. One organization that introduced reviews for one-line changes found that its error rate went from 55 percent before reviews to 2 percent afterward (Freedman and Weinberg 1982).

HARD DATA

Retest. Reviews of changed code should be complemented by retests. This "regression testing" is described in more detail in Chapter 25, "Unit Testing." Gerald Weinberg reports that the ten most expensive programming errors of all time each involved changes to existing code. The top three each cost hundreds of millions of dollars, and each was a one-line change (Weinberg 1983).

Philosophy of Software Evolution

KEY POINT

Evolution is at once hazardous and an opportunity to approach perfection. When you have to make a change, strive to improve the code so that future changes are easier. You never know as much while you're writing a program initially as you do afterward. When you have a chance to revise a program, use what you've learned to improve it. Make both your initial code and your changes with future changes in mind.

30.3 Making New Routines

One activity that heavily influences whether a program improves or degrades under modification is turning an old routine into two or more new routines.

Many of the other activities that lead to successful software evolution don't require any great skill or are described elsewhere in this book. This topic deserves its own treatment.

A program with numerous small, well-named routines is as close as you'll get to a self-documenting program. Well-named routines are preferable to comments because readers can look at code only, rather than code and comments, and routine names are less likely to get out of date than comments are. In their *Software Maintenance Guidebook,* Glass and Noiseux point out that the modularity of code is by far the most important factor in easing maintenance (1981).

Creating New Routines to Reduce Complexity

Perhaps the kind of routine you'll create most frequently when you revisit your code is the kind you use solely to improve the readability of a complicated routine. A routine might be complicated because it has difficult logic or simply because it's long. The point isn't to save code space or improve performance. You're simply trying to make a complicated routine easier to understand.

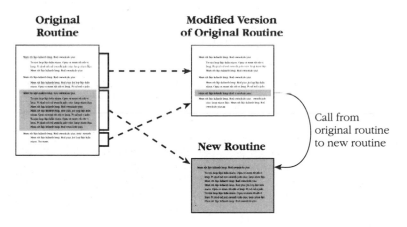

Making a new routine is often as simple as pulling code from an existing routine and adding a routine header.

Making new routines should be something that you can do almost without thinking about it. If you ever find yourself thinking, "Is it worth the trouble to break up this routine?"—break it up. It's virtually always worth the effort.

Reduce complexity by shortening a routine

Another way to reduce complexity is to shorten a routine. Suppose you initially have a routine that displays one of four commands, based on a coded command string, like the one shown on the next page.

Pascal Example of a Routine That Will Be Modified

```pascal
procedure DisplayCommand
   (
      CommandSentence:    string;
   Var Command:           COMMAND_TYPE;
   Var Error:             ERROR_TYPE
   );

{ Display a readable version of a coded command string.
  Command strings are of the form "# CA @AT arg1 @AT arg2 ..."
    '#'    indicates the beginning of a command
    'CA'   is the command abbreviation--one character
    '@'    is the beginning of an argument
    'AT'   is the argument type--one character
    'arg1' is an argument to the command }

var
   Idx:                integer;
   CommandChar:        char;
   CommandWord:        string;
   Argument:           array[ 1..MAX_ARGUMENTS ] of string;
   ArgCount:           integer;

begin

   { check for valid command }
   if ( ( CommandSentence[ 1 ] <> COMMAND_SIGN ) or
      ( Length( CommandSentence ) < MIN_COMMAND_LENGTH ) ) then begin
      Error := InvalidCommandString;
      exit
   end;

   { expand the command abbreviation to a meaningful command word }
   case CommandSentence[ 2 ] of
      'L': CommandWord := 'Left';
      'R': CommandWord := 'Right';
      'U': CommandWord := 'Up';
      'D': CommandWord := 'Down';
      else FatalError( 'Unexpected command in DisplayCommand.' )
   end; { case }

   { extract arguments }
   ArgCount := 0;
   for Idx := 3 to Length( CommandSentence ) do begin
      CommandChar := CommandSentence[ Idx ];

      { begin new argument }
      if ( CommandChar = ARGUMENT_SIGN ) then begin
         ArgCount               := ArgCount + 1;
         Argument[ ArgCount ] := ''
      end
```

Watch this part. It's going to be expanded.

(continued)

```
      { add next character to existing argument }
      else begin
          Argument[ ArgCount ] := Argument[ ArgCount ] + CommandChar
      end
   end; { for }

   { display the command and its arguments in a pleasing format }
   writeln( 'Command: ', CommandWord );
   for Idx := 1 to ArgCount do begin
      writeln( '                ', Argument[ Idx ] )
   end

end; { DisplayCommand }
```

Now suppose that the program is changed, and instead of handling four commands in the routine, it needs to handle twelve. The *case* statement in the middle of the routine suddenly expands to this:

Pascal Example of a *case* Statement That Has Expanded

```
   { expand the command abbreviation to a meaningful command word }
   case CommandSentence[ 2 ] of
      'L': CommandWord := 'Left';
      'R': CommandWord := 'Right';
      'U': CommandWord := 'Up';
      'D': CommandWord := 'Down';
      'E': CommandWord := 'Enter';
      'X': CommandWord := 'Delete';
      '*': CommandWord := 'Undo';
      'J': CommandWord := 'Join';
      'B': CommandWord := 'Break';
      'S': CommandWord := 'Save';
      'O': CommandWord := 'Open';
      'C': CommandWord := 'Close';
      else FatalError( 'Unexpected command in DisplayCommand.' )
   end; { case }
```

This case and those that follow are new.

You could leave the *case* statement in the routine, or you could put it into its own routine. Giving the new routine a meaningful name would help to document the initial routine and make the flow of the initial routine clearer. The next page shows the new routine.

Pascal Example of a Routine That Has Been Changed to Two Routines

This is the new —
routine.

```
function CommandFromWord( CommandCode: char ): string;
begin

   { expand the command abbreviation to a meaningful command word }
   case CommandCode of
      'L': CommandFromWord := 'Left';
      'R': CommandFromWord := 'Right';
      'U': CommandFromWord := 'Up';
      'D': CommandFromWord := 'Down';
      'E': CommandFromWord := 'Enter';
      'X': CommandFromWord := 'Delete';
      '*': CommandFromWord := 'Undo';
      'J': CommandFromWord := 'Join';
      'B': CommandFromWord := 'Break';
      'S': CommandFromWord := 'Save';
      'O': CommandFromWord := 'Open';
      'C': CommandFromWord := 'Close';
      else FatalError( 'Unexpected command in CommandFromWord.' )
   end; { case }

end; { CommandFromWord }
```

The name of the —
routine in this
message had to
be changed.

In the old routine, *DisplayCommand()*, you replace the *case* statement with a call to *CommandFromWord()*:

```
CommandWord := CommandFromWord( CommandSentence[ 2 ] );
```

This is perhaps the most typical way in which new routines are created during modification—by pulling out the contents of a nested logical construct. Such code is generally a sensible candidate for its own routine because code that's nested inside a logical structure typically performs a single, well-defined function and makes sense as a routine.

Reduce complexity by reducing nesting

CROSS-REFERENCE
For details on nesting level,
see Section 17.4, "Taming
Dangerously Deep Nesting."

In addition to making a routine shorter, pulling code out of a nested logical construct makes the routine less complex—a second reason the code will be more readable. Here's an example of a routine with nested code that's begging to be put into its own routine:

C Example of Nested Code That Should Be Broken Out into Its Own Routine

```
void ReadEmployeeData
   (
   EMPLOYEE    Employee[ MAX_EMPLOYEES ];
   int *       EmployeeCount;
   )
```

(continued)

```
{
EMPLOYEE    NewEmployee;
BOOLEAN     ValidRecord;
char        TestChar;
int         FieldIdx;
int         CharIdx;
FILE *      EmployeeFile;
int         Length;

EmployeeFile = OpenEmployeeFile( EmployeeFile );

{ read and check each employee record }
*EmployeeCount = 0;
ReadEmployeeRec( &NewEmployee );
do
   {
   /* check each record's validity */
   ValidRecord = TRUE;
   for ( FieldIdx = 0; FieldIdx < NewEmployee.NumFields; FieldIdx++ )
      {
      /* check each field's validity */
      Length = strlen( NewEmployee.Field[ FieldIdx ] );

      for ( CharIdx = 0; CharIdx < Length; CharIdx++ )
         {
         TestChar = NewEmployee.Field[ FieldIdx ][ CharIdx ];
         if ( !
            ( 'a' <= TestChar && TestChar <= 'z' ||
              'A' <= TestChar && TestChar <= 'Z' ||
              '0' <= TestChar && TestChar <= '9' ) )
         ValidRecord = FALSE;
         } /* for */
      } /* for */
   if ( ValidRecord )
      {
      Employee[ *EmployeeCount ] = NewEmployee;
      (*EmployeeCount)++;
      }
   ReadEmployeeRec( NewEmployee );
   } /* do */
while ( *EmployeeCount < MAX_EMPLOYEES && ! feof( EmployeeFile ) );
...
} /* ReadEmployeeData() */
```

The content of either of these loops (with the related loop-initialization code) would be a good candidate for its own routine.

If you're forced to change the routine so that the inner loops become even more complex or if you get the chance to polish this routine, converting either of the loops (with its initialization code) into its own routine will make the code more modular, readable, and maintainable. You could turn the larger loop into a routine you called *ValidateEmployeeRec()*. You could turn the smaller loop into a routine called *ValidateInputField()*. The next example shows how the larger loop would look if it were turned into its own routine.

C Example of Putting Code from a Nested Loop into Its Own Routine

```
BOOLEAN ValidateEmployeeRec( EMPLOYEE   Employee )
   {
   int      FieldIdx;
   int      CharIdx;
   FILE *   EmployeeFile;
   char     TestChar;
   BOOLEAN  ValidRecord;
   int      Length;

   ValidRecord = TRUE;
   for ( FieldIdx = 0; FieldIdx < Employee.NumFields; FieldIdx++ )
      {
      Length = strlen( Employee.Field[ FieldIdx ] );
      for ( CharIdx = 0; CharIdx < Length; CharIdx++ )
         {
         TestChar = Employee.Field[ FieldIdx ][ CharIdx ];
         if ( !
            ( 'a' <= TestChar && TestChar <= 'z' ||
              'A' <= TestChar && TestChar <= 'Z' ||
              '0' <= TestChar && TestChar <= '9' ) )
         ValidRecord = FALSE;
         } /* for */
      } /* for */
   return( ValidRecord );
   }
```

The large *for* loop in the old routine has been replaced by a call to the new routine:

C Example of Calling New Code from Its Former Routine

```
void ReadEmployeeData
   ...
   { read and check each employee record }
   *EmployeeCount = 0;
   ReadEmployeeRec( &NewEmployee );
   do
      {
      /* check each record's validity */
      ValidRecord = ValidateEmployeeRec( NewEmployee );
      if ( Valid Record )
         ...
```

Here's the call to the routine that has the code that used to be in this routine.

The most important advantages of the modified code are that both of the routines are now short and the nesting is shallower.

The point at which code evolves and simple loops become more complex is an especially good time to consider moving code from loops into routines. This example didn't incorporate a functional change but shows a good technique to use when code is modified: Clean up the routine without changing its functionality. Then, with your increased understanding of the routine and the routine's increased readability, modifiability, and modularity, make your changes. You can use the same technique to simplify *case* statements.

Changing Routines to Share Code

As a program evolves, you commonly find routines that do almost what you want them to do but not quite. The instinctive way to address this problem is to add new code to the existing routine and then pass a flag to it to tell it whether to do its original job or the new job.

This is rarely the best approach. Try to be more generic. Rather than modifying one routine slightly, break out the functionality needed by both the old and the new operations and put the shared functionality into its own routine. Then make two new routines that contain the differences between the old and the new operations. The routines you create with this kind of modification are often usable in more places than you initially imagine. Giving the new routines clear names explains your intent and moves you a step closer to self-documenting code.

Since you're making these changes during software evolution, the original design won't have called for the two routines to have code in common. Consequently, you're faced with the question of how to share the code.

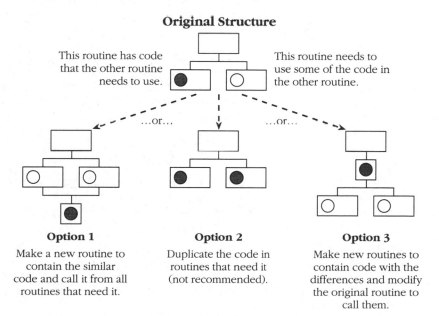

Original Structure

This routine has code that the other routine needs to use.

This routine needs to use some of the code in the other routine.

...or...   ...or...

Option 1
Make a new routine to contain the similar code and call it from all routines that need it.

Option 2
Duplicate the code in routines that need it (not recommended).

Option 3
Make new routines to contain code with the differences and modify the original routine to call them.

This diagram shows the three possible modification strategies.

Consider these options:

CROSS-REFERENCE
For details on organizing
collections of routines, see
Chapter 6, "Three out of
Four Programmers Sur-
veyed Prefer Modules" and
Chapter 7, "High-Level
Design in Construction."

- Emphasize similarities at a low level. Create a new routine for the shared code. Take the code out of the original routine and call it from the original routine and from other routines that need to share the code. This is the most common solution and tends to improve modularity.

- Emphasize similarities separately in each case. Duplicate the code in all routines that need it. You can copy the code out of the first routine and place it manually in other routines, as you need to. This approach wastes space because code appears multiple times rather than once. It's a maintenance headache because any change to the algorithm in the duplicated code must be made in multiple places rather than in one. This is hardly ever a good approach.

- Emphasize similarities at a high level. Create a new routine that contains the shared code. Write new, low-level routines to handle the differences. The original, higher-level routine handles the general case—the commonalities—and calls the new lower-level routines to handle the differences.

An example of sharing code in a low-level routine

Suppose you're working on software for a a nuclear-reactor cooling system, on the code that shuts down the reactor in case of nuclear meltdown:

Pascal Example of Code That's Ready to Be Shared

```
...
AllowableTemperature := MaxAllowableTemperature( Environment );

/* get most recent temperature from top of stack */

Temperature                      := Stack.Temperature[ Stack.Top ];
Stack.Temperature[ Stack.Top ] := INITIAL_TEMPERATURE;
if ( Stack.Top > 0 ) then
    begin
    Stack.Top := Stack.Top - 1
    end;

if ( Temperature > AllowableTemperature) then
    begin
    ShutdownReactor( Environment, Temperature )
    end;
...
```

This stack-manipulation code is ripe for sharing.

Further suppose that you have another routine that needs to know the most recent temperature. You could duplicate the stack-popping code, but the logical way to do it would be to pull out the stack-manipulation code, put it into its own routine, and call it from both routines that need it. Graphically, the process looks like this:

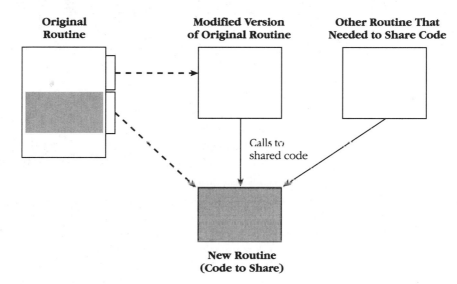

Here's the new routine to be shared:

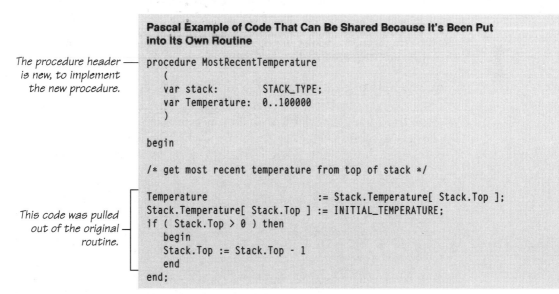

Pascal Example of Code That Can Be Shared Because It's Been Put into Its Own Routine

The procedure header is new, to implement the new procedure.

```
procedure MostRecentTemperature
    (
    var stack:          STACK_TYPE;
    var Temperature:    0..100000
    )

begin

/* get most recent temperature from top of stack */

Temperature                          := Stack.Temperature[ Stack.Top ];
Stack.Temperature[ Stack.Top ] := INITIAL_TEMPERATURE;
if ( Stack.Top > 0 ) then
    begin
    Stack.Top := Stack.Top - 1
    end
end;
```

This code was pulled out of the original routine.

749

Now that you've put the code for getting the most recent temperature into its own routine, here's how you can call it from the original location:

*Here's the call to the —
new routine.*

```
AllowableTemperature := MaxAllowableTemperature( Environment );
MostRecentTemperature( Stack, Temperature );
if ( Temperature > AllowableTemperature) then
    begin
    ShutdownReactor( Environment, Temperature )
    end;
...
```

Now you can also call this code from the other routine that needed it. In addition to sharing the code, you've documented that the point of all the stack popping was to get the most recent temperature—the new routine's name makes that clear.

CROSS-REFERENCE
For details on information hiding, see Section 6.2, "Information Hiding."

You've also hidden the details of how the data structure that keeps track of temperatures is implemented. The whole program doesn't need to know that the data structure is in a stack. Only selected access routines should know, and you've just created such an access routine. You have a minor problem in that the data used by the high-level routines is named *Stack*, and that name is computer-sciencey rather than problem-oriented. In high-level routines that don't manipulate the data structure directly, a better name for the variable would be *TemperatureRecord*; you could still call it *Stack* in the low-level access routine.

All in all, the new routine improves the code substantially. It promotes code sharing and improves the level of abstraction and information hiding.

An example of sharing code in a high-level routine

Suppose you're a rocket scientist working for an aerospace company, and you're developing a routine that catalogs messages about a missile. At first, the only messages the routine deals with record the missile's position in "missile-position" messages. Here are the steps you follow to catalog a message:

- Read the message.
- Check the message ID to verify that the message is a missile-position message.
- Check all the fields in the message.
- Save the message.

If all these operations are simple, you can combine them into one routine called *CatalogMissilePositionMessage()*. For purposes of this example, assume that they are simple. The calling hierarchy would look like this:

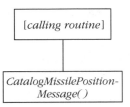

Now suppose you learn that in addition to missile-position messages, you need to catalog "new-missile" messages, "missile-update" messages, and "missile-identification" messages. The code you've written already does most of what is needed; the new messages have to be read, have their IDs checked, have each of their fields checked, and then be saved. How do you convert the code so that you share as much as you can?

Share code at a lower level. The first way to share code is to write new, lower-level routines based on the similarities between the original routine and the new ones. The new code is to be shared by higher-level routines. In general, this is a good approach. It's similar to the approach discussed earlier in this chapter when a big *case* statement or a deeply nested inner loop was pulled out of one routine and made into its own routine.

In the case of the missile-position-message routine, you might pull code out of *CatalogMissilePositionMessage()* and create the new routines *ReadMessage()*, *CheckMessageID()*, *CheckMessageFields()*, and *SaveMessage()* to handle the new kinds of messages. Then you would write new routines for each new message, and have *CatalogMissilePositionMessage()* and each of the new routines call the new lower-level routines. Somewhere toward the top of the hierarchy you'd also have to write code to identify the kind of message and shuttle the message off to the right routine.

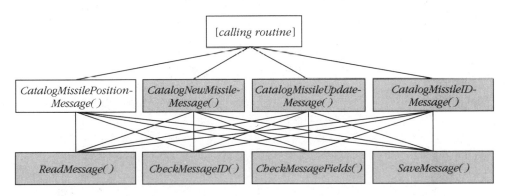

In this illustration, the new routines are shown in gray boxes. As you can see, you have to write several new routines to use this approach and they're heavily interconnected.

CROSS-REFERENCE
Object-oriented-
programming aficionados
might point out that you
could handle this problem
more elegantly in an object-
oriented environment. You
could treat each missile-
message type as a different
kind of object, inheriting
the generic characteristics
of a "message" object and
specifying the differences
needed to check the specific
missile message's fields.
For details on object-
oriented design and pointers to further reading,
see Section 7.3, "Object-
Oriented Design."

Share code at a higher level. A second way to share code is to write new, lower-level routines based on the differences between the original routine and the new ones. Instead of having new code called from multiple places, you have multiple places called from new code.

The tasks of reading a message, checking a message ID, and saving a message might be general enough that they wouldn't need to be modified to support the new kinds of messages. You might be able to leave them as they are, in *CatalogMissilePositionMessage()*. If the only task that needs to know about differences in the messages is checking the message fields, you can write low-level routines to account for differences in the fields and then call them from the routine that used to have the name *CatalogMissilePositionMessage()*. This would result in a much simpler design than creating several new higher-level routines would. The new name of the *CatalogMissilePositionMessage()* routine should reflect its more general function, but other than that, the only change is calling a specific routine to handle checking the message fields for the various kinds of messages.

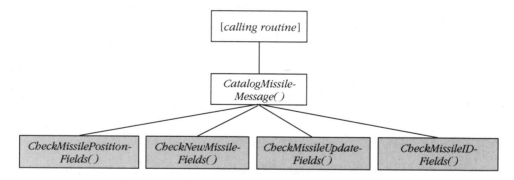

The new routines are again shown in gray boxes, and there aren't as many as last time. More significantly, they're less heavily interconnected.

Obviously, there's a substantial difference between sharing code at a lower level and sharing it at a higher one. In most cases, unlike this one, you'll benefit from sharing code at a lower level, but always consider the possibility of sharing at the higher level instead. In the few cases in which it's appropriate, you'll be glad you did.

CHECKLIST

Making Changes

- ❏ Is each change part of a systematic change strategy?
- ❏ Has the change been reviewed as thoroughly as initial development would be?
- ❏ Has the software been regression-tested to establish that the change has not degraded it?
- ❏ Does the change enhance the program's internal quality rather than degrading it?
- ❏ Have you improved the system's modularity by breaking routines into smaller routines when possible?
- ❏ Have you reduced the use of global variables when possible?
- ❏ Have you improved the program's style—variable names, routine names, formatting, comments, and so on?
- ❏ If changes cause you to look for ways to share code, have you considered putting the shared code at a higher level and considered putting it at a lower level?
- ❏ Does this change make the next change easier?

Further Reading

Evolution during development is an issue that hasn't received much attention in its own right. With the rise of code-centered approaches such as prototyping and evolutionary delivery, it's likely to receive an increasing amount of attention. For now, the best sources of information are software-maintenance books—read between the lines, remember the differences between evolution during construction and during maintenance, and you'll probably find some valuable information.

Glass, Robert L., and Ronald A. Noiseux. *Software Maintenance Guidebook*. Englewood Cliffs, N.J.: Prentice-Hall, 1981. This practical, short (193 pages) book nicely lays out the groundwork for software maintenance.

Arthur, Lowell J. *Software Evolution: The Software Maintenance Challenge*. New York: John Wiley, 1988. In spite of the title, the book isn't about evolution in the same sense that this chapter is. It contains appealing, readable discussions of change management, kinds of maintenance, improving online programs while the motor is running, and issues in managing maintenance. Its approach is more formal (in the more-starch-in-the-collar sense) than that of the *Software Maintenance Guidebook*.

Lientz, B. P., and E. B. Swanson. *Software Maintenance Management*. Reading, Mass.: Addison-Wesley, 1980. This comprehensive study of program-maintenance practices summarizes maintenance data from almost 500 organizations and is filled with fascinating statistics—for example, two-thirds of all systems are maintained by one or two people; almost a third of all systems are maintained by people with no experience in their development; and so on.

Longstreet, David H., ed. *Software Maintenance and Computers*. Los Alamitos, Calif.: IEEE Computer Society Press, 1990.

Parikh, G., and N. Zvegintzov, eds. *Tutorial on Software Maintenance*. Los Alamitos, Calif.: IEEE Computer Society Press, 1983. These two IEEE tutorials contain excellent collections of papers, as IEEE tutorials usually do. The papers survey software-maintenance issues and are written by some of the most prominent people in the field.

Spier, Michael J. "Software Malpractice—A Distasteful Experience." *Software—Practice and Experience* 6 (1976): 293–99. This is a graphic description of the worst that can happen as a program deteriorates under modification.

Key Points

- Evolution during initial development has been a fact of life with traditional development approaches and is likely to become even more prominent with newer approaches.

- Under evolution, software can either improve or degrade. The Cardinal Rule of Software Evolution is that internal quality should improve with age. Although software degradation is hard to avoid during extended maintenance, software that degrades during construction is in trouble.

- Evolution during development is the best chance you'll get to improve your program, to make all the changes you'll wish you'd made the first time. Take advantage of it!

- The way in which you create new routines as you modify a program is the greatest influence on whether you make the program healthier or sicker. Create new routines in such a way that you smooth out the rough edges in a design rather than poke holes in it.

31

Personal Character

Contents

Related Topics

PERSONAL CHARACTER HAS RECEIVED A RARE DEGREE of attention in software development. Ever since Edsger Dijkstra's landmark 1965 article "Programming Considered as a Human Activity," programmer character has been regarded as a legitimate and fruitful area of inquiry. Although titles such as *The Psychology of Bridge Construction* and "Exploratory Experiments in Attorney Behavior" might seem absurd, in the computer field *The Psychology of Computer Programming,* "Exploratory Experiments in Programmer Behavior," and similar titles are classics.

Engineers in every discipline learn the limits of the tools and materials they work with. If you're an electrical engineer, you know the conductivity of various metals and a hundred ways to use a voltmeter. If you're a structural engineer, you know the load-bearing properties of wood, concrete, and steel.

If you're a software engineer, your basic building material is human intellect and your primary tool is *you*. Rather than designing a structure to the last detail and then handing the blueprints to someone else for construction, you know that once you've designed a piece of software to the last detail, it's done. The whole job of programming is building air castles—it's one of the most purely mental activities you can do. Consequently, when software engineers study the essential properties of their tools and raw materials, they find that they're studying people—intellect, character, and other attributes that are less tangible than wood, concrete, and steel.

If you're looking for concrete programming tips, this chapter might seem too abstract to be useful. Once you've absorbed the specific advice in the rest of the book, however, this chapter spells out what you need to do to continue improving. Read the next section, and then decide whether you want to skip the chapter.

31.1 Isn't Personal Character Off the Topic?

The intense inwardness of programming makes personal character especially important. You know how difficult it is to put in eight concentrated hours in one day. You've probably had the experience of being burned out one day from concentrating too hard the day before, or burned out one month from concentrating too hard the month before. You've probably had days on which you've worked well from 8:00 A.M. to 2:00 P.M. and then felt like quitting. You didn't quit, though; you pushed on from 2:00 P.M. to 5:00 P.M. and then spent the rest of the week fixing what you wrote from 2:00 to 5:00.

Programming work is essentially unsupervisable because no one ever really knows what you're working on. We've all had projects in which we spent 80 percent of the time working on a small piece we found interesting and 20 percent of the time building the other 80 percent of the program.

Your employer can't force you to be a good programmer; a lot of times your employer isn't even in a position to judge whether you're good. If you want to be great, you're responsible for making yourself great. It's a matter of your personal character.

HARD DATA

Once you decide to make yourself a superior programmer, the potential for improvement is huge. Study after study has found differences on the order of 10 to 1 in the time required to create a program. They have also found differences on the order of 10 to 1 in the time required to debug a program and 10 to 1 in the resulting size, speed, error rate, and number of errors detected (Sackman, Erikson, and Grant 1968; Curtis 1981; Mills 1983; DeMarco and Lister 1985; Curtis et al. 1986; Card 1987; Valett and McGarry 1989).

You can't do anything about your intelligence, so the classical wisdom goes, but you can do something about your character. It turns out that character is the more decisive factor in the makeup of a superior programmer.

31.2   Intelligence and Humility

We become authorities and experts in the practical and scientific spheres by so many separate acts and hours of work. If a person keeps faithfully busy each hour of the working day, he can count on waking up some morning to find himself one of the competent ones of his generation.

William James

Intelligence doesn't seem like an aspect of personal character, and it isn't. Coincidentally, great intelligence is only loosely connected to being a good programmer.

What? You don't have to be superintelligent?

No, you don't. Nobody is really smart enough to program computers. Fully understanding an average program requires an almost limitless capacity to absorb details and an equal capacity to comprehend them all at the same time. The way you focus your intelligence is more important than how much intelligence you have.

At the 1972 Turing Award Lecture, Edsger Dijkstra delivered a paper titled "The Humble Programmer." He argued that most of programming is an attempt to compensate for the strictly limited size of our skulls. The people who are best at programming are the people who realize how small their brains are. They are humble. The people who are the worst at programming are the people who refuse to accept the fact that their brains aren't equal to the task. Their egos keep them from being great programmers. The more you learn to compensate for your small brain, the better a programmer you'll be. The more humble you are, the faster you'll improve.

The purpose of many good programming practices is to reduce the load on your gray cells. Here are a few examples:

- The point of "decomposing" a system is to make it simpler to understand. Humans have an easier time comprehending several simple pieces of information than one complicated piece. The goal of all software-design techniques is to break a complicated problem into simple pieces. Whether you're using structured, top-down, or object-oriented design, the goal is the same.

- Conducting reviews, inspections, and tests is a way of compensating for anticipated human fallibilities. These review techniques originated as part of "egoless programming" (Weinberg 1971). If you never made mistakes, you wouldn't need to review your software. But you know that your intellectual capacity is limited, so you augment it with someone else's.

- Keeping routines short helps reduce your mental workload.

- Writing programs in terms of the problem domain rather than in computer-science terms and working at the highest level of abstraction reduce the load on your brain.

- Using conventions of all sorts frees your brain from the relatively mundane aspects of programming, which offer little payback.

757

You might think that the high road would be to develop better mental abilities so that you wouldn't need these programming crutches. You might think that a programmer who uses mental crutches is taking the low road. Empirically, however, it's been shown that humble programmers who compensate for their fallibilities write code that's easier for themselves and others to understand and that has fewer errors. The real low road is the road of errors and delayed schedules.

31.3 Curiosity

Once you admit that your brain is too small to understand most programs and you realize that effective programming is a search for ways to offset that fact, you begin a careerlong search for ways to compensate.

In the development of a superior programmer, curiosity about technical subjects must be a priority. The relevant technical information changes continually. Many PC programmers have never had to program on a CP/M machine, and many CP/M programmers never had to deal with punch cards. Specific features of the technical environment change every 5 to 10 years. If you aren't curious enough to keep up with the changes, you may find yourself down at the old-programmers' home playing cards with T-Bone Rex and the Brontosaurus sisters.

Programmers are so busy working they often don't have time to be curious about how they might do their jobs better. If this is true for you, you're not alone. The following subsections describe a few specific actions you can take to exercise your curiosity and make learning a priority.

CROSS-REFERENCE
For a fuller discussion of the importance of process in software development, see Section 32.2, "Pick Your Process."

Build your awareness of the development process. The more aware you are of the development process, whether from reading or from your own observations about software development, the better position you're in to understand changes and to move your group in a good direction.

If your workload consists entirely of short-term assignments that don't develop your skills, be dissatisfied. If you're working in a competitive software market, half of what you now need to know in order to do your job will be out of date in three years. If you're not learning, you're turning into a dinosaur.

HARD DATA

You're in too much demand to spend time working for management that doesn't have your interests in mind. The average number of jobs available in the U.S. is expected to increase by 11 to 19 percent between 1988 and 2000. Jobs for computer systems analysts are expected to increase by 53 percent, for computer programmers by 48 percent, and for computer operators by 29 percent—a total of 556,000 new jobs beyond the 1,237,000 that currently exist (U.S. Department of Labor 1990). If you can't learn at your job, find a new one.

CROSS-REFERENCE
Some key aspects of programming other than personal character revolve around the idea of experimentation. For details, see "Experimentation" in Section 32.8.

Experiment. One effective way to learn about programming is to experiment with programming and the development process. If you don't know how a feature of your language works, write a short program to exercise the feature, and see how it works. Watch the program execute in the debugger. You're better off working with a short program to test a concept than you are writing a larger program with a feature you don't quite understand.

What if the short program shows that the feature doesn't work the way you want it to? That's what you wanted to find out. Better to find it out in a small program than a large one. One key to effective programming is learning to make mistakes quickly, learning from them each time. Making a mistake is no sin. Failing to learn from a mistake is.

FURTHER READING
A great book that teaches problem solving is James Adams's *Conceptual Blockbusting* (1980).

Read about problem solving. Problem solving is the core activity in building computer software. Herbert Simon reported a series of experiments on human problem solving. They found that human beings don't always discover clever problem-solving strategies themselves, even though the same strategies could readily be taught to the same people (1969). The implication is that even if you want to reinvent the wheel, you can't count on success. You might reinvent the square instead.

Analyze and plan before you act. You'll find that there's a tension between analysis and action. At some point you have to quit gathering data and act. The problem for most programmers, however, isn't an excess of analysis. The pendulum is currently so far on the "acting" side of the arc that you can wait until it's at least partway to the middle before worrying about getting stuck on the "analysis-paralysis" side.

Learn about successful projects. One especially good way to learn about programming is to study the work of the great programmers. Jon Bentley thinks that you should be able to sit down with a glass of brandy and a good cigar and read a program the way you would a good novel. That might not be as far-fetched as it sounds. Most people wouldn't want to use their recreational time to scrutinize a 500-page source listing, but many people would enjoy studying a high-level design and dipping into more detailed source listings for selected areas.

The software-engineering field makes extraordinarily limited use of examples of past successes and failures. If you were interested in architecture, you'd study the drawings of Louis Sullivan, Frank Lloyd Wright, and I. M. Pei. You'd probably visit some of their buildings. If you were interested in structural engineering, you'd study the Brooklyn bridge, the Tacoma Narrows bridge, and a variety of other concrete, steel, and wood structures. You would study examples of successes and failures in your field.

Thomas Kuhn points out that a part of any mature science is a set of solved problems that are commonly recognized as examples of good work in the field and serve as examples for future work (1970). Software engineering is only beginning to mature to this level. In 1990, the Computer Science and Technology Board concluded that there were few documented case studies of either successes or failures in the software field (CSTB 1990). An article in the March 1992 issue of *Communications of the ACM* argued for learning from case studies of programming problems (Linn and Clancy 1992). The fact that someone has to argue for this is significant.

That one of the most popular computing columns, "Programming Pearls," was built around case studies of programming problems is suggestive. The most popular book in software engineering is *The Mythical Man-Month*, a postmortem on the IBM OS/360 project, a case study in programming management.

With or without a book of case studies in programming, find code written by superior programmers and read it. Ask to look at the code of programmers you respect. Ask to look at the code of programmers you don't. Compare their code, and compare their code to your own. What are the differences? Why are they different? Which way is better? Why?

In addition to reading other people's code, develop a desire to know what expert programmers think about your code. Find world-class programmers who'll give you their criticism. As you listen to the criticism, filter out points that have to do with their personal idiosyncrasies and concentrate on the points that matter. Then change your programming so that it's better.

Read manuals. Manual phobia is rampant among programmers. Manuals tend to be poorly written and poorly organized, but for all their problems, there's much to gain from overcoming an excessive fear of paper products. Manuals contain the keys to the castle, and it's worth spending time reading them. Overlooking information that's in the manual is such a common oversight that a familiar acronym on newsgroups and bulletin boards is "RTFM!," which stands for "Read the !#*%*@ Manual!"

A modern language product is usually bundled with an enormous set of library routines. Time spent browsing through the reference manual is well invested. Often the company that provides the language product has already created many of the routines you need to use. If it has, make sure you know about them. Skim the manuals every couple of months.

CROSS-REFERENCE
For books you can use in a personal reading program, see Section 33.1, "The Library of a Software Professional."

Read other books and periodicals. Pat yourself on the back for reading this book. You're already learning more than most people in the software industry because one book is more than most programmers read each year (DeMarco and Lister 1987). A little reading goes a long way toward professional advancement. If you read even one good programming book every two months, roughly 35 pages a week, you'll soon have a firm grasp on the industry and distinguish yourself from nearly everyone around you.

31.4 Intellectual Honesty

Part of maturing as a programming professional is developing an uncompromising sense of intellectual honesty. Intellectual honesty commonly manifests itself in several ways:

- Refusing to pretend you're an expert when you're not
- Readily admitting your mistakes
- Trying to understand a compiler warning rather than suppressing the message
- Clearly understanding your program   not compiling it to see if it works
- Providing realistic status reports
- Providing realistic schedule estimates and holding your ground when management asks you to adjust them

The first two items on this list—admitting that you don't know something or that you made a mistake—echo the theme of intellectual humility discussed earlier. How can you learn anything new if you pretend that you know everything already? You'd be better off pretending that you don't know anything. Listen to people's explanations, learn something new from them, and assess whether *they* know what *they* are talking about.

Be ready to quantify your degree of certainty on any issue. If it's usually 100 percent, that's a warning sign.

> Any fool can defend his or her mistakes— and most fools do.
> *Dale Carnegie*

Refusing to admit mistakes is a particularly annoying habit. If Sally refuses to admit a mistake, she apparently believes that not admitting the mistake will trick others into believing that she didn't make it. The opposite is true. Everyone will know she made a mistake. Mistakes are accepted as part of the ebb and flow of complex intellectual activities, and as long as she hasn't been negligent, no one will hold mistakes against her.

If she refuses to admit a mistake, the only person she'll fool is herself. Everyone else will learn that they're working with a prideful programmer who's not completely honest. That's a more damning fault than making a simple error. If you make a mistake, admit it quickly and emphatically.

Pretending to understand compiler messages when you don't is another common blind spot. If you don't understand a compiler warning or if you think you know what it means but are too pressed for time to check it, guess what's really a waste of time? You'll probably end up trying to solve the problem from the ground up while the compiler waves the solution in your face. I've had several people ask for help in debugging programs. I'll ask if they have a clean compile, and they'll say yes. Then they'll start to explain the symptoms of the problem, and I'll say, "Hmmmm. That sounds like it would be an uninitialized pointer, but the compiler should have warned you about that." Then they'll say, "Oh yeah—it did warn about that. We thought it meant something else." It's hard to fool other people about your mistakes. It's even harder to fool the computer, so don't waste your time trying.

A related kind of intellectual sloppiness occurs when you don't quite understand your program and "just compile it to see if it works." In that situation, it doesn't really matter whether the program works because you don't understand it well enough to know whether it works or not. Remember that testing can only show the presence of errors, not their absence. If you don't understand the program, you can't test it thoroughly. Feeling tempted to compile a program to "see what happens" is a warning sign. It might mean that you need to back up to design or that you began coding before you were sure you knew what you were doing. Make sure you have a strong intellectual grip on the program before you relinquish it to the compiler.

> The first 90 percent of the code accounts for the first 90 percent of the development time. The remaining 10 percent of the code accounts for the other 90 percent of the development time.
>
> *Tom Cargill*

Status reporting is an area of scandalous duplicity. Programmers are notorious for saying that a program is "90 percent complete" during the last 50 percent of the project. If your problem is that you have a poor sense of your own progress, you can solve it by learning more about how you work. But if your problem is that you don't speak your mind because you want to give the answer your manager wants to hear, that's a different story. A manager usually appreciates honest observations about the status of a project, even if they're not the opinions the manager wants to hear. If your observations are well thought out, give them as dispassionately as you can and in private. Management needs to have accurate information to coordinate development activities, and full cooperation is essential.

An issue related to inaccurate status reporting is inaccurate estimation. The typical scenario goes like this: Management asks Bert for an estimate of how long it would take to develop a new database product. Bert talks to a few programmers, crunches some numbers, and comes back with an estimate of eight programmers and six months. His manager says, "That's not really what we're looking for. Can you do it in a shorter time, with fewer programmers?" Bert goes away and thinks about it and decides that for a short period he could cut training and vacation time and have everyone work a little overtime. He comes back with an estimate of six programmers and four months. His manager says, "That's great. This is a relatively low-priority project, so try to keep it on time without any overtime because the budget won't allow it."

The mistake Bert made was not realizing that estimates aren't negotiable. He can revise an estimate to be more accurate, but negotiating with his boss won't change the time it takes to develop a software project. IBM's Bill Weimer says, "We found that technical people, in general, were actually very good at estimating project requirements and schedules. The problem they had was defending their decisions; they needed to learn how to hold their ground" (Weimer in Metzger 1981). Bert's not going to make his manager any happier by promising to deliver a project in four months and delivering it in six than he would by promising and delivering it in six. In the long run, he'll lose credibility by compromising. In the short run, he'll gain respect by standing firm on his estimate.

If management applies pressure to change your estimate, realize that it's within management's purview to decide whether to do a project. Say "Look. This is how much it's going to cost. I can't say whether it's worth this price to the company—that's your job. But I can tell you how long it takes to develop a piece of software—that's my job. I can't 'negotiate' how long it will take; that's like negotiating how many feet are in a mile. You can't negotiate laws of nature. We can, however, negotiate other aspects of the project that affect the schedule and then reestimate the schedule. We can eliminate features, reduce performance, develop the project in stages, or use fewer people and a longer schedule or more people and a shorter schedule."

One of the scariest exchanges I've ever heard was at a lecture on managing software projects. The speaker was the author of a best-selling software-project–management book. A member of the audience asked, "What do you do if management asks for an estimate and you know that if you give them an accurate estimate they'll say it's too high and decide not to do the project?" The speaker responded that that was one of those tricky areas in which you had to get management to buy into the project by underestimating it. He said that once they'd invested in the first part of the project, they'd see it through to the end.

Wrong answer! Management is responsible for the big-picture issues of running a company. If a certain software capability is worth $100K to a company and you estimate it will cost $200K to develop, the company shouldn't develop the software. It's management's responsibility to make such judgments. When the speaker advocated lying about the project's cost, telling management it would cost less than it really would, he advocated covertly stealing management's authority. If you think a project is interesting, breaks important new ground for the company, or provides valuable training, say so. Management can weigh those factors too. But tricking management into making the wrong decision could literally cost the company hundreds of thousands of dollars. If it costs you your job, you'll have gotten what you deserve.

31.5   Communication and Cooperation

Truly excellent programmers learn how to work and play well with others. Writing readable code is part of being a team player.

The computer probably reads your program as often as other people do, but it's a lot better at reading poor code than people are. As a readability guideline, keep the person who has to modify your code in mind. Programming is communicating with another programmer first, communicating with the computer second.

Most good programmers enjoy making their programs readable, given sufficient time to do so. There are a few holdouts, though, and some of them are good coders. A look at the levels of programmer development helps explain where the holdouts fit in.

FURTHER READING
For other discussions of programmer levels, see "Programmers: The Amateur vs. the Professional" (Ledgard 1985) and "A Taxonomy of Programmers" (Boundy 1991).

Level 1: Beginner

A beginner is a programmer capable of using the basic capabilities of one language. Such a person can write routines, loops, and conditionals and use many of the features of a language.

Level 2: Intermediate

An intermediate programmer is capable of using the basic capabilities of multiple languages and is very comfortable in at least one language.

Level 3: Specialist

A programming specialist has expertise in a language or an environment or both. Programmers at this level are valuable to their companies, and some programmers never move beyond this level.

Level 4: Guru

HARD DATA

A guru has the expertise of a Level 3 specialist and recognizes that programming is only 15 percent communicating with the computer, that it's 85 percent communicating with people. Only 30 percent of an average programmer's time is spent working alone (McCue 1978). Even less time is spent communicating with the computer. The guru writes code for an audience of people rather than machines. True guru-level programmers write code that's crystal-clear, and they document it too. They don't want to waste their valuable gray cells reconstructing the logic of a section of code that they could have read in a one-sentence comment.

A great coder who doesn't emphasize readability is probably stuck at Level 3, but even that isn't usually the case. In my experience, the main reason people write unreadable code is that their code is bad. They don't say to themselves, "My code is bad, so I'll make it hard to read." They just don't understand their code well enough to make it readable, which puts them at Level 1 or Level 2.

The worst code I've ever seen was written by someone who wouldn't let anyone go near her programs. Finally, her manager threatened to fire her if she didn't cooperate. Her code was uncommented and littered with variables like *X*, *XX*, *XXX*, *XX1*, and *XX2*, all of which were global. Her manager's boss thought she was a great programmer because she fixed errors quickly. The quality of her code gave her abundant opportunities to demonstrate her error-correcting ability.

It's no sin to be a beginner or an intermediate. It's no sin to be a specialist instead of a guru. The sin is in how long you remain a beginner or a specialist after you know what you have to do to improve.

31.6 Creativity and Discipline

When I got out of school, I thought I was the best programmer in the world. I could write an unbeatable tic-tac-toe program, use five different computer languages, and create 1000-line programs that WORKED (really)!!! Then I got out into the Real World. My first task in the Real World was to read and understand a 200,000-line Fortran program, then speed it up by a factor of two. Any Real Programmer will tell you that all the Structured Coding in the world won't help you solve a problem like that—it takes actual talent.

"Real Programmers Don't Write Pascal"

It's hard to explain to a fresh computer-science graduate why you need conventions and engineering discipline. When I was an undergraduate, the largest program I wrote was about 500 lines of executable code. As a professional, I've written dozens of utilities that have been smaller than 500 lines, but the average main-project size has been 5,000 to 25,000 lines, and I've participated in projects with over a half million lines of code. This type of effort requires not the same skills on a larger scale, but a new set of skills altogether.

Some creative programmers view the discipline of standards and conventions as stifling to their creativity. The opposite is true. Without standards and conventions on large projects, project completion itself is impossible. Creativity isn't even imaginable. Don't waste your creativity on things that don't matter. Establish conventions in noncritical areas so that you can focus your creative energies in the places that count.

In a 15-year retrospective on work at NASA's Software Engineering Laboratory, McGarry and Pajerski reported that methods and tools that emphasize human discipline have been especially effective (1990). Many highly creative

765

people have been extremely disciplined. "Form is liberating," as the saying goes. Great architects work within the constraints of physical materials, time, and cost. Great artists do too. Anyone who has examined Leonardo's drawings has to admire his disciplined attention to detail. When Michelangelo designed the ceiling of the Sistine Chapel, he divided it into symmetric collections of geometric forms such as triangles, circles, and squares. He designed it in three zones corresponding to three Platonic stages. Without this self-imposed structure and discipline, the 300 human figures would have been merely chaotic rather than the coherent elements of an artistic masterpiece.

A programming masterpiece requires just as much discipline. If you don't try to analyze requirements and design before you begin coding, much of your learning about the project will occur during coding, and the result of your labors will look more like a three-year-old's finger painting than a work of art.

31.7 Laziness

Laziness manifests itself in several ways:

- Deferring an unpleasant task
- Doing an unpleasant task quickly to get it out of the way
- Writing a tool to do the unpleasant task so that you never have to do the task again

Some of these manifestations of laziness are better than others. The first is hardly ever beneficial. You've probably had the experience of spending several hours futzing with jobs that didn't really need to be done so that you wouldn't have to face a relatively minor job that you couldn't avoid. I detest data entry, and many programs require a small amount of data entry. I've been known to delay working on a program for days just to delay the inevitable task of entering several pages of numbers by hand. This habit is "true laziness." It manifests itself again in the habit of compiling a routine to see if it works so that you can avoid the exercise of checking the routine with your mind.

The small tasks are never as bad as they seem. If you develop the habit of doing them right away, you can avoid the procrastinating kind of laziness. This habit is "enlightened laziness"—the second kind of laziness. You're still lazy, but you're getting around the problem by spending the smallest possible amount of time on something that's unpleasant.

The third option is to write a tool to do the unpleasant task. This is "long-term laziness." It is undoubtedly the most productive kind of laziness, provided that you ultimately save time by having written the tool. In these contexts, a certain amount of laziness is beneficial.

When you step through the looking glass, you see the other side of the laziness picture. "Hustle" or "making an effort" doesn't have the rosy glow it does in high-school phys-ed class. Hustle is extra, unnecessary effort. It shows that you're eager but not that you're getting your work done. The most important work in effective programming is thinking, and people tend not to look busy when they're thinking. If I worked with a programmer who looked busy all the time, I'd assume that he was not a good programmer because he wasn't using his most valuable tool, his brain.

31.8 Characteristics That Don't Matter As Much As You Might Think

Hustle isn't the only characteristic that you might admire in other aspects of your life but that doesn't work very well in software development.

Persistence

Depending on the situation, persistence can be either an asset or a liability. Like most value-laden concepts, it's identified by different words depending on whether you think it's a good quality or a bad one. If you want to identify persistence as a bad quality, you say it's "stubbornness" or "pigheadedness." If you want it to be a good quality, you call it "tenacity" or "perseverance."

Most of the time, persistence in software development is pigheadedness—it has little value. Persistence when you're stuck on a piece of new code is hardly ever a virtue. Try redesigning the routine, try an alternative coding approach, or try coming back to it later. When one approach isn't working, that's a good time to try an alternative.

In debugging, it can be mighty satisfying to track down the error that has been annoying you for four hours, but it's often better to give up on the error after a certain amount of time with no progress—say 15 minutes. Let your subconscious chew on the problem for a while. Try to think of an alternative approach that would circumvent the problem altogether. Rewrite the troublesome section of code from scratch. Come back to it later when your mind is fresh. Fighting computer problems is no virtue. Avoiding them is better.

It's hard to know when to give up, but it's essential that you ask. When you notice that you're frustrated, that's a good time to ask the question. Asking doesn't necessarily mean that it's time to give up, but it probably means that it's time to set some parameters on the activity: "If I don't solve the problem using this approach within the next 30 minutes, I'll take 10 minutes to brainstorm about different approaches and try the best one for the next hour."

Experience

The value of hands-on experience as compared to book learning is smaller in software development than in many other fields for several reasons. In many other fields, basic knowledge changes slowly enough that someone who graduated from college 10 years after you did probably learned the same basic material that you did. In software development, even basic knowledge changes rapidly. The person who graduated from college 10 years after you did probably learned twice as much about effective programming techniques. Older programmers tend to be viewed with suspicion not just because they might be out of touch with specific technology but because they might never have been exposed to basic programming concepts that became well known after they left school.

In other fields, what you learn about your job today is likely to help you in your job tomorrow. In software, if you can't shake the habits of thinking you developed while using your former programming language or the code-tuning techniques that worked on your old machine, your experience will be worse than none at all. A lot of software people spend their time preparing to fight the last war rather than the next one. If you can't change with the times, experience is more a handicap than a help.

Aside from the rapid changes in software development, people often draw the wrong conclusions from their experiences. It's hard to view your own life objectively. You can overlook key elements of your experience that would cause you to draw different conclusions if you recognized them. Reading studies of other programmers is helpful because the studies reveal other people's experience—filtered enough that you can examine it objectively.

People also put an absurd emphasis on the *amount* of experience programmers have. "We want a programmer with five years of C programming experience" is a silly statement. If a programmer hasn't learned C after a year or two, the next three years won't make much difference. This kind of "experience" has little relationship to performance.

The fact that information changes quickly in programming makes for weird dynamics in the area of "experience." In many fields, a professional who has a history of achievement can coast—relaxing and enjoying the respect earned by a string of successes. In software development, anyone who coasts quickly becomes out of touch. To stay valuable, you have to stay current. For young, hungry programmers, this is an advantage. Older programmers sometimes feel they've already earned their stripes and resent having to prove themselves year after year.

The bottom line on experience is this: If you work for 10 years, do you get 10 years of experience or do you get 1 year of experience 10 times? You have to reflect on your activities to get true experience. If you make learning a continuous commitment, you'll get experience. If you don't, you won't, no matter how many years you have under your belt.

Gonzo Programming

If you haven't spent at least a month working on the same program—working 16 hours a day, dreaming about it during the remaining 8 hours of restless sleep, working several nights straight through trying to eliminate that "one last bug" from the program—then you haven't really written a complicated computer program. And you may not have the sense that there is something exhilarating about programming.

Edward Yourdon

This lusty tribute to programming machismo is pure B.S. and an almost certain recipe for failure. Those all-night programming stints make you feel like the greatest programmer in the world, but then you have to spend several weeks correcting the defects you installed during your blaze of glory. By all means, get excited about programming. But learn how to handle the firearm before you shoot yourself in the foot.

31.9 Habits

The moral virtues, then, are engendered in us neither by nor contrary to nature...their full development in us is due to habit....Anything that we have to learn to do we learn by the actual doing of it....Men will become good builders as a result of building well and bad ones as a result of building badly....So it is a matter of no little importance what sort of habits we form from the earliest age—it makes a vast difference, or rather all the difference in the world.

Aristotle

Good habits matter because most of what you do as a programmer you do without consciously thinking about it. For example, at one time, you might have thought about how you wanted to format indented loops, but now you don't think about it again each time you write a new loop. You do it the way you do it out of habit. This is true of virtually all aspects of program formatting. When was the last time you seriously questioned your formatting style? Chances are good that if you've been programming for five years, you last questioned it four and a half years ago. The rest has been habit.

CROSS-REFERENCE
For details on errors in
assignment statements, see
"Errors by Classification" in
Section 25.4.

You have habits in many areas. For example, programmers tend to check loop indexes carefully and not to check assignment statements, making errors in assignment statements much harder to find than errors in loop indexes (Gould 1975). You respond to criticism in a friendly way or in an unfriendly way. You're always looking for ways to make code readable or fast, or you're not. If you have to choose between making code fast and making it readable, and you make the same choice every time, you're not really choosing; you're responding out of habit.

Study the quotation from Aristotle and substitute "programming virtues" for "moral virtues." He points out that you are not predisposed to either good or bad behavior but are constituted in such a way that you can become either a good or a bad programmer. The main way you become good or bad at what you do is by doing—builders by building and programmers by programming. What you do becomes habit, and what you do by habit determines whether you have the "programming virtues." Over time, your good and bad habits determine whether you're a good or a bad programmer.

Bill Gates, Chairman and CEO of Microsoft Corporation, says that any programmer who will ever be good is good in the first few years. After that, whether a programmer is good or not is cast in concrete (Lammers 1986). After you've been programming a long time, it's hard to suddenly start saying, "How do I make this loop faster?" or "How do I make this code more readable?" These are habits that good programmers develop early.

When you first learn something, learn it the right way. When you first do it, you're actively thinking about it and you still have an easy choice between doing it in a good way and doing it in a bad way. After you've done it a few times, you pay less attention to what you're doing and "force of habit" takes over. Make sure that the habits that take over are the ones you want to have.

What if you don't already have the most effective habits? How do you change a bad habit? If I had the definitive answer to that, I could sell self-help tapes on late-night TV. But here's at least part of an answer. You can't replace a bad habit with no habit at all. That's why people who suddenly stop smoking or swearing or overeating have such a hard time unless they substitute something else, like chewing gum. It's easier to replace an old habit with a new one than it is to eliminate one altogether. In programming, try to develop new habits that work. Develop the habit of writing a routine in PDL before coding it and carefully reading the code before compiling it, for instance. You won't have to worry about losing the bad habits; they'll naturally drop by the wayside as new habits take their places.

Further Reading

Dijkstra, Edsger. "The Humble Programmer." Turing Award Lecture. *Communications of the ACM* 15, no. 10 (October 1972): 859–66. This classic paper helped begin the inquiry into how much computer programming depends on the programmer's mental abilities. Dijkstra has persistently stressed the message that the essential task of programming is mastering the enormous complexity of computer science. He argues that programming is the only activity in which humans have to master nine orders of magnitude of difference between the lowest level of detail and the highest. This paper would be interesting reading solely for its historical value, but many of its themes sound fresh 20 years later. It also conveys a good sense of what it was like to be a programmer in the early days of computer science.

Weinberg, Gerald M. *The Psychology of Computer Programming.* New York: Van Nostrand Reinhold, 1971. This classic book contains a detailed exposition of the idea of egoless programming and of many other aspects of the human side of computer programming. It contains many entertaining anecdotes and is one of the most readable books yet written about software development.

Curtis, Bill, ed. *Tutorial: Human Factors in Software Development.* Los Angeles: IEEE Computer Society Press, 1985. This is an excellent collection of papers that address the human aspects of creating computer programs. The 45 papers are divided into sections on mental models of programming knowledge, learning to program, problem solving and design, effects of design representations, language characteristics, error diagnosis, and methodology. If programming is one of the most difficult intellectual challenges that humankind has ever faced, learning more about human mental capacities is critical to the success of the endeavor. These papers about psychological factors also help you to turn your mind inward and learn about how you individually can program more effectively.

Key Points

- Your personal character directly affects your ability to write computer programs.

- The characteristics that matter most are humility, curiosity, intellectual honesty, creativity and discipline, and enlightened laziness.

- The characteristics of a superior programmer have almost nothing to do with talent and everything to do with a commitment to personal development.

- Surprisingly, raw intelligence, experience, persistence, and guts hurt as much as they help.

- Many programmers stop actively seeking new information and techniques and instead rely on accidental, on-the-job exposure to new information. If you devote a small percentage of your time to reading and learning about programming, after a few months or years you'll dramatically distinguish yourself from the programming mainstream.

- Good character is mainly a matter of having the right habits. To be a great programmer, develop the right habits, and the rest will come naturally.

32

Themes in Software Craftsmanship

Contents

THIS BOOK IS MOSTLY ABOUT the details of software construction: high-quality routines, variable names, loops, source-code layout, system integration, and so on. This book has de-emphasized abstract topics in order to emphasize subjects that are more concrete.

Once the earlier parts of the book have put the concrete topics on the table, all you have to do to appreciate the abstract concepts is to pick up the topics from the various chapters and see how they're related. This chapter makes the abstract themes explicit: complexity, abstraction, process, readability, iteration, and so on. These themes account in large part for the difference between hacking and software craftsmanship.

32.1 Conquer Complexity

Computing is the only profession in which a single mind is obliged to span the distance from a bit to a few hundred megabytes, a ratio of 1 to 10^9, or nine orders of magnitude. This gigantic ratio is staggering. Edsger Dijkstra put it this way: "Compared to that number of semantic levels, the average mathematical theory is almost flat. By evoking the need for deep conceptual hierarchies, the automatic computer confronts us with a radically new intellectual challenge that has no precedent in our history" (1989).

CROSS-REFERENCE
For details on the importance of attitude in conquering complexity, see Section 31.2, "Intelligence and Humility."

The drive to reduce complexity is at the heart of computer science. Although it's tempting to try to be a hero and deal with computer-science problems at all levels, no one's brain is really capable of spanning nine orders of magnitude of detail. Computer science and software engineering have developed many intellectual tools for handling such complexity, and discussions of other topics in this book have brushed up against several of them.

Ways to Reduce Complexity

At the software-architecture level, the complexity of a problem is reduced by dividing the system into subsystems. The more independent the subsystems are, the more you reduce the complexity. Carefully defined modules separate concerns so that you can focus on one thing at a time. Packaging code into objects produces much the same benefit.

Global data is harmful because it weakens your ability to focus on one thing at a time. By the same token, module data isn't harmful because it doesn't shift your attention away from the module you're working on.

If you have data leaks between subsystems in the form of shared global data or sloppily defined interfaces, you have a flood of complexity as well, and the result is a dilution of the intellectual benefit of dividing the system into smaller subsystems.

Complexity should be minimized for the sake of good design, and minimizing complexity is a motive for many code-level improvements too. The point of limiting control structures to *for* and *if* statements (or their equivalents) and straight-line code is to reduce the number of different control patterns your brain has to deal with. *goto*s are particularly harmful because they don't necessarily follow a specific pattern; your brain can't simplify their operation in any way that reduces their complexity. Keeping routines short, limiting the nesting of loops and *if* statements, and restricting the number of parameters passed to routines are additional tools in managing complexity.

When you put a complicated test into a boolean function and abstract the purpose of the test, you make the code less complex. When you substitute a table lookup for a complicated chain of logic, you do the same thing. When you create access routines for major data structures, you eliminate the need to worry about implementation details of the data structures at the higher level and simplify your job overall.

The point of having coding conventions is also, to some extent, to reduce complexity. When you can standardize decisions about formatting, loops, and variable names, you release mental resources that you need to focus on more challenging aspects of the programming problem. One reason coding conventions are so controversial is that choices among the options have some limited aesthetic base but are essentially arbitrary. People have the most heated arguments over their smallest differences. Conventions are the most useful when they spare you the trouble of making and defending arbitrary decisions. They're less valuable when they impose restrictions in more meaningful areas.

Hierarchies and Complexity

A hierarchy minimizes complexity by handling different details at different levels. It frees your brain from worrying about all the details at any particular level. The details don't go away completely; they're simply pushed to another level so that you can think about them when you want to rather than thinking about all the details all of the time.

Using hierarchies comes naturally to most people. When they draw a complex object such as a house, they draw it hierarchically. First they draw the outline of the house, then the windows and doors, and then more details (Simon 1969). They don't draw the house brick by brick, shingle by shingle, or nail by nail.

CROSS-REFERENCE
For details on creating your own levels of hierarchy, see "Separating a Program into Levels of Abstraction" in Section 32.5, later in this chapter.

In a typical computer system, you'll have at the very least the ascending levels from machine instructions, through operating-system operations and high-level–language programming, to user-interface operations. As a high-level–language programmer, you only have to know about high-level programming and user-interface operations. That saves you the grief of dealing with the machine instructions and operating-system calls at the lowest levels of the hierarchy.

If you're smart about designing a software system, you'll create your own hierarchical levels in addition to the ones you get automatically by writing a program in a high-level language.

Abstraction and Complexity

Abstraction is another means of reducing complexity by handling different details at different levels. Any time you work with an aggregate, you're working with an abstraction. If you refer to an object as a "house" rather than a combination of glass, wood, and nails, you're making an abstraction. If you refer to a collection of houses as a "town," you're making another abstraction.

Abstraction is a more general concept than hierarchy. Hierarchy implies a tiered, structured organization in which levels are ordered and have ranks. Abstraction doesn't necessarily imply a hierarchically structured organization. Abstraction can reduce complexity by spreading details across a network of components, for example, rather than among the levels of a tiered hierarchy.

Programming is advancing largely through increasing the abstractness of program components. Fred Brooks argues that the biggest single gain ever made in computer science was in the jump from machine language to higher-level languages—it freed programmers from worrying about the detailed quirks of individual pieces of hardware and allowed them to focus on programming (1987). The idea of routines was another big step. And DBMSs were a big step because they essentially abstract data, enabling you to work with records and tables rather than individual data items.

Naming variables functionally, for the "what" of the problem rather than the "how" of the computer-science solution, increases the level of abstraction. If you say, "OK, I'm popping the stack and that means that I'm getting the most recent employee," abstraction can save you the mental step "I'm popping the stack." You simply say, "I'm getting the most recent employee." This is a small gain, but when you're trying to reduce a range in complexity of 1 to 10^9, every step counts. Using named constants rather than literals also increases the level of abstraction. Abstract data types reduce complexity because they allow you to work with characteristics of a problem-domain data type rather than a computer-science structure. Object-oriented programming provides a level of abstraction that applies to algorithms and data at the same time, a kind of abstraction that functional decomposition alone doesn't provide.

In summary, a primary goal of software design and coding is conquering complexity. The motivation behind many programming practices is to reduce a program's complexity. Reducing complexity is a key to being an effective programmer.

32.2   Pick Your Process

A second major thread in this book is the idea that the process you use to develop software matters a surprising amount.

On a small project, the talents of the individual programmer are the biggest influence on the quality of the software. Part of what makes an individual programmer successful is his or her choice of processes.

On projects with more than one programmer, organizational characteristics make a bigger difference than the skills of the individuals involved do. Even if you have a great team, its collective ability isn't simply the sum of the team members' individual abilities. The way in which people work together determines whether their abilities are added to each other or subtracted from each other. The process the team uses determines whether one person's work supports the work of the rest of the team or undercuts it.

CROSS-REFERENCE
For details on making requirements stable, see Section 3.3, "Requirements Prerequisite." For details on evolutionary delivery, see Section 27.4, "Evolutionary Delivery."

One example of the way in which process matters is the consequence of not making requirements stable before you begin designing and coding. If you don't know what you're building, you can't very well create a superior design for it. If the requirements and subsequently the design change while the software is under development, the code must change too, degrading the quality of the system.

"Sure," you say, "but in the real world, you never really have stable requirements, so that's a red herring." Again, the process you use determines both how stable your requirements are and how stable they need to be. If you want to build more flexibility into the requirements, you can set up an evolutionary delivery in which you plan to deliver the software in several stages rather than all at once. This is an attention to process, and it's the process you use that ultimately determines whether your project succeeds or fails. Table 3-1 in Section 3.1 makes it clear that analysis errors are far more costly than design or coding errors, so focusing on that part of the process also affects cost and schedule.

> **My message to the serious programmer is: spend a part of your working day examining and refining your own methods. Even though programmers are always struggling to meet some future or past deadline, methodological abstraction is a wise long term investment.**
>
> *Robert W. Floyd*

The same principle of consciously attending to process applies to design. You have to lay a solid foundation before you can begin building on it. If you rush to coding before the foundation is complete, it will be harder to make fundamental changes in the system's architecture. People will have an emotional investment in the design because they will have already written code for it. It's hard to throw away a bad foundation once you've started building a house on it.

The main reason the process matters is that in software, quality must be built in from the first step onward. This flies in the face of the folk wisdom that you can code like hell and then test all the mistakes out of the software. That idea is dead wrong. Testing merely tells you the specific ways in which your software is defective. Testing won't make your program more usable, faster, smaller, more readable, or more extensible.

Premature optimization is another kind of process error. In an effective process, you make coarse adjustments at the beginning and fine adjustments at the end. If you were a sculptor, you'd rough out the general shape before you started polishing individual features. Premature optimization wastes time because you spend time polishing sections of code that don't need to be polished. You might polish sections that are small enough and fast enough as they are; you might polish code that you later throw away; you might fail to throw away bad code because you've already spent time polishing it. Always be thinking, "Am I doing this in the right order? Would changing the order make a difference?" Consciously follow a good process.

CROSS-REFERENCE
For details on iteration, see Section 32.7, "Iterate, Repeatedly, Again and Again," later in this chapter.

Low-level processes matter too. If you follow the process of writing PDL and then filling in the code around the PDL, you reap the benefits of designing from the top down. You're also guaranteed to have comments in the code without having to put them in later.

Observing large processes and small processes means pausing to pay attention to how you create software. It's time well spent. Saying that "code is what matters; you have to focus on how good the code is, not some abstract process" is shortsighted and ignores mountains of experimental and practical evidence to the contrary. Software development is a creative exercise. If you don't understand the creative process, you're not getting the most out of the primary tool you use to create software—your brain. A bad process wastes your brain cycles. A good process leverages them to maximum advantage.

32.3 Write Programs for People First, Computers Second

your program *n.* A maze of non sequiturs littered with clever-clever tricks and irrelevant comments. *Compare* MY PROGRAM.
my program *n.* A gem of algoristic precision, offering the most sublime balance between compact, efficient coding on the one hand and fully commented legibility for posterity on the other. *Compare* YOUR PROGRAM.

Stan Kelly-Bootle

Another theme that runs throughout this book is an emphasis on code readability. Communication with other people is the motivation behind the quest for the Holy Grail of self-documenting code.

The computer doesn't care whether your code is readable. It's better at reading binary machine instructions than it is at reading high-level–language statements. You write readable code because it helps other people to read your code. Readability has a positive effect on all these aspects of a program:

- Comprehensibility
- Reviewability
- Error rate
- Debugging
- Modifiability
- Development time—a consequence of all of the above
- External quality—a consequence of all of the above

In the early years of programming, a program was regarded as the private property of the programmer. One would no more think of reading a colleague's program unbidden than of picking up a love letter and reading it. This is essentially what a program was, a love letter from the programmer to the hardware, full of the intimate details known only to partners in an affair. Consequently, programs became larded with the pet names and verbal shorthand so popular with lovers who live in the blissful abstraction that assumes that theirs is the only existence in the universe. Such programs are unintelligible to those outside the partnership.
Michael Marcotty

Readable code doesn't take any longer to write than confusing code does, and the effort to make it readable justifies itself during initial work on the code. It's easier to be sure your code works if you can easily read what you wrote. That should be a sufficient reason to write readable code. But code is also read during reviews. It's read when you or someone else fixes an error. It's read when the code is modified. It's read when someone tries to use part of your code in a similar program.

Making code readable is not an optional part of the development process. You should go to the effort of writing good code, which you can do once, rather than the effort of reading bad code, which you'd have to do again and again.

"What if I'm just writing code for myself? Why should I make it readable?" Because a week or two from now you're going to be working on another program and think, "Hey! I already wrote this routine last week. I'll just drop in my old tested, debugged code and save some time." If the code isn't readable, good luck!

The idea of writing unreadable code because you're the Lone Ranger on a project is disturbing. It's like not stealing because you might get caught. The Lone Ranger never steals, period. A professional programmer writes readable code, period.

Your mother used to say, "What if your face froze in that expression?" Habits affect all your work; you can't turn them on and off at will, so be sure that what you're doing is something you want to become a habit.

It's also good to recognize that whether a piece of code ever belongs exclusively to you is debatable. Douglas Comer came up with a useful distinction between private and public programs (1981): "Private programs" are programs for a programmer's own use. They aren't used by others. They aren't modified by others. Others don't even know the programs exist. They are usually trivial, and they are the rare exception. "Public programs" are programs used or modified by someone other than the author.

**Programming can
be fun, so can cryp-
tography; however
they should not be
combined.**
*Kreitzberg
and Shneiderman*

Standards for public and for private programs can be different. Private programs can be sloppily written and full of limitations without affecting anyone but the author. Public programs must be written more carefully: Their limitations should be documented; they should be reliable; and they should be modifiable. Beware of a private program's becoming public, as private programs often do. You need to convert the program to a public program before it goes into general circulation. Part of making a private program public is making it readable.

Even if you think you're the only one who will read your code, in the real world chances are good that someone else will need to modify your code. One study found that 10 generations of maintenance programmers work on an average program before it gets rewritten (Thomas 1984). Maintenance programmers spend 50 to 60 percent of their time trying to understand the code they have to maintain, and they appreciate the time you put into documenting it (Parikh and Zvegintzov 1983).

HARD DATA

Earlier chapters examined the techniques that help you achieve readability: good variable names, careful formatting, good routine names, small routines, hiding complex boolean tests in boolean functions, assigning intermediate results to variables for clarity in complicated calculations, and so on. No individual application of a technique can make the difference between a readable program and an illegible one. But the accumulation of many small readability improvements will be significant.

If you think you don't need to make your code readable because no one else ever looks at it, make sure you're not confusing cause and effect.

32.4 Focus Your Attention with the Help of Conventions

CROSS-REFERENCE
For an analysis of the
value of conventions as they
apply to program layout,
see "How Much Is Good
Layout Worth?" and
"Objectives of Good
Layout" in Section 18.1.

A set of conventions is one of the intellectual tools used to manage complexity. Earlier chapters talk about specific conventions. This section lays out the benefits of conventions with many examples.

Many of the details of programming are somewhat arbitrary. How many spaces do you indent a loop? How do you format a comment? How should you order routine parameters? Most of the questions like these have several right answers. The specific way in which such a question is answered is less important than that it be answered consistently each time. Conventions save programmers the trouble of answering the same questions—making the same arbitrary decisions—again and again. On projects with many programmers, using conventions prevents the confusion that results when different programmers make the arbitrary decisions differently.

A convention conveys important information concisely. In naming conventions, a single character can differentiate among local, module, and global variables; capitalization can concisely differentiate among types, named constants, and variables. Indentation conventions can concisely show the logical structure of a program. Alignment conventions can indicate concisely that statements are related.

Conventions protect against known hazards. You can establish conventions to eliminate the use of dangerous practices, to restrict such practices to cases in which they're needed, or to compensate for their known hazards. You could eliminate a dangerous practice, for example, by prohibiting global variables or prohibiting multiple statements on a line. You could restrict a dangerous practice by requiring that *goto*s go only to the end of a routine. You could compensate for a hazardous practice by requiring parentheses around complicated expressions or requiring pointers to be cleared immediately after they're freed to help prevent dangling pointers.

Conventions add predictability to low-level tasks. Having conventional ways of handling memory requests, error processing, input/output, and routine interfaces adds a meaningful structure to your code and makes it easier for another programmer to figure out—as long as the programmer knows your conventions. As mentioned in an earlier chapter, one of the biggest benefits of eliminating *goto*s is that you eliminate an unconventional control structure. A reader knows roughly what to expect from a *for*, an *if*, or a *case* statement. But it's hard to tell whether a *goto* jumps up or down, five lines or half the program. The *goto* increases the reader's uncertainty. With good conventions, you and your readers can take more for granted. The amount of detail that has to be assimilated will be reduced, and that in turn will improve program comprehension.

Conventions can compensate for language weaknesses. In languages that don't support named constants, a convention can differentiate between variables intended to be both read and written and those that are intended to emulate read-only constants. Conventions for the disciplined use of *goto*s and pointers are other examples of compensating for language weaknesses with conventions.

Programmers on large projects sometimes go overboard with conventions. They establish so many standards and guidelines that remembering them becomes a full-time job. But programmers on small projects tend to go "underboard," not realizing the full benefits of intelligently conceived conventions.

Understand their real value and take advantage of them. Use them to provide structure in areas in which structure is needed.

32.5 Program in Terms of the Problem Domain

Another specific method of dealing with complexity is to work at the highest possible level of abstraction. One way of working at a high level of abstraction is to work in terms of the programming problem rather than the computer-science solution.

Top-level code shouldn't be filled with details about files and stacks and queues and arrays and characters whose parents couldn't think of better names for them than *i*, *j*, and *k*. Top-level code should describe the problem that's being solved. It should be packed with descriptive routine calls that indicate exactly what the program is doing, not cluttered with details about opening a file as "read only." Top-level code shouldn't contain clumps of comments that say "*i* is a variable that represents the index of the record from the employee file here, and then a little later it's used to index the client account file there..."

That's clumsy programming practice. At the top level of the program, you don't need to know that the employee data comes as records or that it's stored as a file. Information at that level of detail should be hidden. At the highest level, you shouldn't have any idea how the data is stored. Nor do you need to read a comment that explains what *i* means and that it's used for two purposes. You should see a variable named something like *EmployeeIdx* so that you don't need a verbose comment about *i*. If *i* has been used for two purposes, you should see different variable names for the two purposes instead, and they should also have distinctive names such as *EmployeeIdx* and *ClientIdx*.

Separating a Program into Levels of Abstraction

Obviously, you have to work in computer-science terms at some level, but you can isolate the part of the program that works in computer-science terms from the part that works in problem-domain terms.

If you're working in a high-level language, you don't have to worry about the lowest level—your language takes care of it automatically. You should worry about the higher levels, however, even though most programmers don't. If you're designing a program, design it so that it has at least these levels of abstraction:

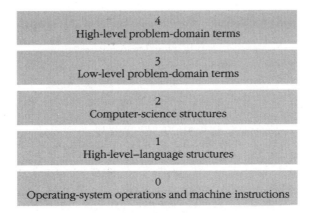

Level 4
High-level problem-domain terms

Level 3
Low-level problem-domain terms

Level 2
Computer-science structures

Level 1
High-level–language structures

Level 0
Operating-system operations and machine instructions

Level 1: High-level–language structures

High-level language structures are the language's primitive data types, control structures, and so on. Using them comes naturally since you can't write a program in a high-level language without them. Many programmers never work above this level of abstraction, which makes their lives much harder than they need to be.

Level 2: Computer-science structures

Computer-science structures are slightly higher-level structures than those provided by the language itself. They tend to be the operations and data structures you learn about in college courses in algorithms and data structures—stacks, queues, linked lists, trees, indexed files, sequential files, sort algorithms, search algorithms, and so on. Although this level represents an improvement in abstraction over high-level–language structures, it still contains too much detail to be able to win the battle against complexity.

Level 3: Low-level problem-domain terms

At this level, you have the primitives you need in order to work in terms of the problem domain. It's a glue layer between the computer-science structures below and the high-level problem-domain code above. To write code at this level, you need to figure out the vocabulary of the problem area and the building blocks you need in order to work with the problem the program solves. Routines at this level provide the vocabulary and the building blocks. At this level, the routines might be too primitive to be used to solve the problem directly, but they provide an Erector set that higher-level routines can use to build a solution to the problem.

Level 4: High-level problem-domain terms

This level provides the abstractive power to work with a problem on its own terms. Your code at this level should be somewhat readable by someone who's not a computer-science whiz. Code at this level won't depend much on the specific features of your programming language because you'll have built your own set of tools to work with the problem. Consequently, at this level your code depends more on the tools you've built than on the capabilities of the language you're using.

Implementation details should be hidden two layers below this one, in a layer of computer-science structures, so that changes in hardware or the operating system don't affect this layer at all. Embody the user's view of the world in the program at this level because when the program changes, it will change in terms of the user's view. Changes in the problem domain should affect this layer a lot, but they should be easy to accommodate by programming in the problem-domain building blocks from the layer below.

Low-Level Techniques for Working in the Problem Domain

Even without a complete, architectural approach to working in the problem area's vocabulary, you can use many of the techniques in this book to work in terms of the real-world problem rather than the computer-science solution:

- Use abstract data types to implement structures that are meaningful in problem-domain terms.

- Hide information about the computer-science structures and their implementation details.

- In object-oriented programs, design a component that refers directly to the problem domain. Encapsulate information about the problem domain in this component.

- Use named constants to document the meanings of strings and of numeric literals.

- Assign intermediate variables to document the results of intermediate calculations.

- Use boolean functions to clarify complex boolean tests.

32.6   Watch for Falling Rocks

Programming is neither fully an art nor fully a science. Thus far, it's been an unholy combination, a "craft" that's somewhere between the two. It still takes plenty of individual judgment to create a working software product. And part of having good judgment in computer programming is being sensitive to a wide array of warning signs, subtle indications of problems in your program. Warning signs in programming alert you to the possibility of problems, but they're usually not as blatant as a road sign that says "Watch for falling rocks."

When you or someone else says "This is a really tricky routine," that's a warning sign, usually of poor code. "Tricky routine" is a code phrase for "bad routine." If you think a routine is tricky, think about rewriting it so that it's not.

A routine's having more errors than average is a warning sign. A few error-prone routines tend to be the most expensive part of a program. If you have a routine that has had more errors than average, it will probably continue to have more errors than average. Think about rewriting it.

If programming were a science, each warning sign would imply a specific, well-defined corrective action. Because programming is still a craft, however, a warning sign merely points to an issue that you should consider. You can't necessarily rewrite tricky code or improve an error-prone routine.

Just as an abnormal number of defects in a routine warns you that the routine has low quality, an abnormal number of defects in a program implies that your process is defective. A good process wouldn't allow error-prone code to be developed. It would include the checks and balances of architecture followed by architecture reviews, design followed by design reviews, and code followed by code reviews. By the time the code was ready for testing, most errors would have been eliminated. Exceptional performance requires working smart in addition to working hard. Lots of debugging on a project is a warning sign that implies people aren't working smart. Writing a lot of code in a day and then spending two weeks debugging it is not working smart.

You can use design metrics as another kind of warning sign. Most design metrics are heuristics that give an indication of the quality of a design. The fact that a routine is longer than two printed pages doesn't necessarily mean that it's poorly designed, but it's a warning that the routine is complicated. Similarly, more than about 10 decision points in a routine, more than three levels of logical nesting, an unusual number of variables, high coupling to other routines, or low internal cohesion should raise a warning flag. None of these signs necessarily means that a routine is poorly designed, but the presence of any of them should cause you to look at the routine skeptically.

Any warning sign should cause you to doubt the quality of your program. As Charles Saunders Peirce says, "Doubt is an uneasy and dissatisfied state from which we struggle to free ourselves and pass into the state of belief." Treat a warning sign as an "irritation of doubt" that prompts you to look for the more satisfied state of belief.

If you find yourself working on repetitious code or making similar modifications in several areas, you should feel "uneasy and dissatisfied," doubting that control has been adequately centralized in routines or macros. If you find it hard to create scaffolding for test cases because you can't call an individual routine easily, you should feel the "irritation of doubt" and ask whether the routine is coupled too tightly to other routines. If you can't reuse code in other programs because some routines are too interdependent, that's another warning sign that the routines are coupled too tightly.

When you're deep into a program, pay attention to warning signs that indicate that part of the program design isn't defined well enough to code. Difficulties in writing comments, naming variables, and decomposing the problem into small, well-defined routines all indicate that you need to think harder about the design before coding. Wishy-washy routine names and difficulty in describing routines in one-line comments are other signs of trouble. When the design is clear in your mind, the low-level details come easily.

Be sensitive to indications that your program is hard to understand. Any discomfort is a clue. If it's hard for you, it will be even harder for the next programmers. They'll appreciate the extra effort you make to improve it. If you're figuring out code instead of reading it, it's too complicated. If it's hard, it's wrong. Make it simpler.

HARD DATA

If you want to take full advantage of warning signs, program in such a way that you create your own warnings. This is useful because even after you know what the signs are, it's surprisingly easy to overlook them. Glenford Myers conducted a study of defect correction in which he found that the single most common cause of not finding errors was simply overlooking them. The errors were visible on test output but not noticed (1978b).

Make it hard to overlook problems in your program. One example is setting pointers to NULL or NIL after you free them so that they'll cause ugly problems if you mistakenly use one. A freed pointer might point to a valid memory location even after it's been freed. Setting it to NULL or NIL guarantees that it points to an invalid location, making the error harder to overlook.

Compiler warnings are literal warning signs that are often overlooked. If your program generates warnings or errors, fix it so that it doesn't. You don't have much chance of noticing subtle warning signs when you're ignoring those that have "WARNING" printed directly on them.

Why is paying attention to intellectual warning signs especially important in software development? The quality of the thinking that goes into a program largely determines the quality of the program, so paying attention to warnings about the quality of thinking directly affects the final product.

32.7 Iterate, Repeatedly, Again and Again

Iteration is appropriate for many software-development activities. When you first specify a system, you work with the user through several versions of requirements until you're sure you agree on them. That's an iterative process. If you've chosen to build more flexibility into your process by using evolutionary development, you deliver a system in several stages. That's an iterative process. If you use prototyping to develop several alternative solutions quickly and cheaply before crafting the final product, that's another form of iteration. At this initial stage, iteration is perhaps as important as any other aspect of the development process. Projects fail because they commit themselves to a solution before exploring alternatives. Iteration provides a way to learn about a product before you build it.

As Chapter 22 on managing construction points out, during initial project planning, schedule estimates can vary greatly depending on the estimation technique you use. Using an iterative approach for estimation produces a more accurate estimate than relying on a single technique.

Software design is a heuristic process and, like all heuristic processes, is subject to iterative revision and improvement. Software tends to be validated rather than proven, which means that it's tested and developed iteratively until it answers questions correctly. Both high-level and low-level design attempts should be repeated. A first attempt might produce a solution that works, but it's unlikely to produce the best solution. Taking several repeated and different approaches produces insight into the problem that's unlikely with a single approach.

The idea of iteration appears again in code tuning. Once the software is operational, you can rewrite small parts of it to greatly improve overall system performance. Many of the attempts at optimization, however, hurt the code more than they help it. It's not an intuitive process, and some techniques that seem likely to make a system smaller and faster actually make it larger and slower. The uncertainty about the effect of any optimization technique creates a need for tuning, measuring, and tuning again. If a bottleneck is critical to system performance, you can tune the code several times, and several of your later attempts may be more successful than your first.

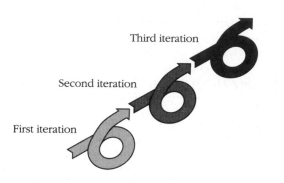

At the least, iteration helps improve product specifications, planning, design, code quality, and performance.

Reviews cut across the grain of the development process, inserting iterations at any stage in which they're conducted. The purpose of a review is to check the quality of the work at a particular point. If the product fails the review, it's sent back for rework. If it succeeds, it doesn't need further iteration.

When you take iteration to the extreme, you get Fred Brooks's advice: "Build one to throw away; you will, anyhow" (1975). One definition of engineering is to do for a dime what anyone can do for a dollar. Throwing a whole system away is doing for two dollars what anyone can do for one dollar. The trick of software engineering is to build the disposable version as quickly and inexpensively as possible, which is the point of iterating in the early stages.

32.8 Thou Shalt Rend Software and Religion Asunder

Religion appears in software development in numerous incarnations—as dogmatic adherence to a single design method, as unswerving belief in a specific formatting or commenting style, as a zealous avoidance of *goto*s. It's always inappropriate.

Software Oracles

CROSS-REFERENCE
For details on handling programming religion as a manager, see "Religious Issues" in Section 22.5.

Unfortunately, the religious attitude is decreed from on high by some of the more prominent people in the profession. It's important to popularize new methods before they can be fully proven. The dissemination of research results to practitioners is called "technology transfer" and is important for advancing the state of the practice of software development. There's a difference, however, between disseminating a new methodology and selling object-structured snake oil. The idea of technology transfer is poorly served by dogmatic methodology peddlers who try to convince you that their new one-size-fits-all, object-structured cow pies will solve all your problems. Forget everything you've already learned because this new method is so great it will improve your productivity 100 percent in everything!

When you run into one of these clowns, ask how long it's been since he wrote a system in his method-o-matic. He'll say, "Well, I've been consulting for 15 years and have thousands of clients who can attest to the veracity of my claims." Bull! He has thousands of clients who don't want to admit they've wasted $800 on his seminar. Press him again. Ask how long it's been since he personally used one of these methods he's peddling. Chances are good that not only has he not written a significant system with this new method, but he also hasn't written one with the old method he wants you to throw away!

Rather than latching on to the latest miracle fad, use a mixture of methods. Experiment with the exciting, recent methods, but bank on the old and dependable ones.

Eclecticism

CROSS-REFERENCE
For more on the difference between algorithmic and heuristic approaches, see Section 2.2, "How to Use Software Metaphors." For information on eclecticism in design, see Section 7.5, "Round-Trip Design."

Blind faith in one method precludes the selectivity you need if you're to find the most effective solutions to programming problems. If software development were a deterministic, algorithmic process, you could follow a rigid methodology to your solution. Software development isn't a deterministic process, however. It's heuristic—which means that rigid processes are inappropriate and have little hope of success. In design, for example, sometimes top-down decomposition works well. Sometimes an object-oriented approach, a bottom-up composition, or a data-structure approach works better. You have to be willing to try several approaches, knowing that some will fail and some will succeed but not knowing which ones will work until after you try them. You have to be eclectic.

Adherence to a single method is also harmful in that it makes you force-fit the problem to the solution. If you decide on the solution method before you fully understand the problem, you act prematurely. You over-constrain the set of possible solutions, and you might rule out the most effective solution.

You'll be uncomfortable with any new methodology initially, and the advice that you avoid religion in programming isn't meant to suggest that you should stop using a new method as soon as you have a little trouble solving a problem with it. Give the new method a fair shake, but give the old methods their fair shakes too.

Eclecticism is a useful attitude to bring to the techniques presented in this book as much as to techniques described in other sources. Discussions of several topics have advanced alternative approaches that you can't use at the

CROSS-REFERENCE
For a more detailed
description of the toolbox
metaphor, see "Applying
Software Techniques:
The Intellectual Toolbox"
in Section 2.3.

same time. You have to choose one or the other for each specific problem. You have to treat the techniques as tools in a toolbox and use your own judgment to select the best tool for the job. Most of the time, the tool choice doesn't matter very much. You can use a box wrench, vise-grip pliers, or a crescent wrench. In some cases, however, the tool selection matters a lot, so you should always make your selection carefully. Engineering is in part a discipline of making trade-offs among competing techniques. You can't make a trade-off if you've prematurely limited your choices to a single tool.

The toolbox metaphor is useful because it makes the abstract idea of eclecticism concrete. Suppose you were a general contractor and your buddy Simple Simon always used vise-grip pliers. Suppose he refused to use a box wrench or a crescent wrench. You'd probably think he was odd because he wouldn't use all the tools at his disposal. The same is true in software development. At a high level, you have alternative design methods. At a more detailed level, you can choose one of several data structures to represent any given design. At an even more detailed level, you can choose several different schemes for formatting and commenting code, naming variables, and passing routine parameters.

A dogmatic stance conflicts with the eclectic toolbox approach to software construction. It's incompatible with the attitude needed to build high-quality software.

Experimentation

Eclecticism has a close relative in experimentation. You need to experiment throughout the development process, but the religious attitude hobbles the impulse. To experiment effectively, you must be willing to change your beliefs based on the results of the experiment. If you're not willing, experimentation is a gratuitous waste of time.

Many of the religious approaches to software development are based on a fear of making mistakes. A blanket attempt to avoid mistakes is the biggest mistake of all. Design is a process of carefully planning small mistakes in order to avoid making big ones. Experimentation in software development is a process of setting up tests so that you learn whether an approach fails or succeeds—the experiment itself is a success as long as it resolves the issue.

Experimentation is appropriate at as many levels as eclecticism is. At each level at which you are ready to make an eclectic choice, you can probably come up with a corresponding experiment to determine which approach works best. At the architectural-design level, an experiment might consist of sketching software architectures using three different design approaches. At the detailed-design level, an experiment might consist of following the implications of a higher-level architecture using three different low-level design approaches. At the programming-language level, an experiment might consist of writing a short experimental program to exercise the operation of a part of the language you're not completely familiar with. The experiment might consist of tuning a piece of code and benchmarking it to verify that it's really smaller or faster. At the overall software-development–process level, an experiment might consist of collecting quality and productivity data so that you can see whether inspections really find more errors than walkthroughs.

The point is that you have to keep an open mind about all aspects of software development. Rather than being religious, you have to get technical about your process as well as your product. Open-minded experimentation and religious adherence to a predefined approach don't mix.

Key Points

- One primary goal of programming is managing complexity.

- The programming process affects the final product more than many people realize.

- Team programming is more an exercise in communicating with people than in communicating with a computer. Individual programming is more an exercise in communicating with yourself than with a computer.

- When abused, a convention is a cure that's worse than the disease. Used thoughtfully, a convention adds valuable structure to the development environment and helps with managing complexity and communication.

- Programming in terms of the problem rather than the solution helps to manage complexity.

- Paying attention to intellectual warning signs like the "irritation of doubt" is especially important in programming because programming is almost purely a mental activity.

- The more you iterate in each development activity, the better the product of that activity will be.

- Dogmatic methodologies and high-quality software development don't mix. Fill your intellectual toolbox with programming alternatives and improve your skill at choosing the right tool for the job.

33

Where to Go for More Information

Contents

IF YOU'VE READ THIS FAR, you already know that a lot has been written about the software-development process. Much more information is available than most people realize. People have already made all the mistakes that you're making now, and unless you're a glutton for punishment, you'll prefer reading their books and avoiding their mistakes to inventing new versions of old problems.

33.1 The Library of a Software Professional

Because this book describes hundreds of other books and articles that contain articles on software development, it's hard to know what to read first.

A software-development library is made up of several kinds of information. A core of programming books explains fundamental concepts of effective programming. Ancillary books explain the larger technical, management, and intellectual context within which programming goes on. And detailed references on the languages, operating systems, environments, and hardware contain information that's useful for specific projects.

Books in the last category generally have a life span of about one project; they're more temporary and aren't discussed here.

Of the other kinds of books, it's useful to have a core set that discusses each of the major software-development activities in depth—books on analysis, design, construction, management, and testing.

Top-Ten List

The following books make up a solid foundation for a software professional's permanent library.

1. *The Psychology of Computer Programming*. Gerald Weinberg's *The Psychology of Computer Programming* (1971) is packed with fascinating anecdotes about programming. It's far-ranging because it was written at a time when anything related to software was considered to be about programming. The advice in the original review of the book in the *ACM Computing Reviews* is as good today as it was when the review was written:

> Every manager of programmers should have his own copy. He should read it, take it to heart, act on the precepts, and leave the copy on his desk to be stolen by his programmers. He should continue replacing the stolen copies until equilibrium is established (Weiss 1972).

If you can't find *The Psychology of Computer Programming,* look for *The Mythical Man-Month* (Brooks 1975) or *PeopleWare* (DeMarco and Lister 1987). They both drive home the theme that programming is first and foremost something done by people and only secondarily something that happens to involve computers.

2. *Programming Pearls*. Jon Bentley's *Programming Pearls* (1986) is the first of a pair of "Programming Pearls" books. It's a vigorous discussion of programming that articulates the reasons some of us find programming so interesting. The fact that the book isn't comprehensive or rigidly organized doesn't prevent it from conveying powerful insights that you'll read about in a few minutes and use for many years.

Another excellent book in the same spirit by the same author is *Writing Efficient Programs* (1982). It's a nearly exhaustive treatment of code tuning with loads of examples. Although Bentley doesn't present many more techniques than Chapters 28 and 29 of this book do, he's a master of interesting examples and supports his code-tuning techniques with many memorable anecdotes.

3. *Classics in Software Engineering*. Ed Yourdon's *Classics in Software Engineering* (1979) is a collection of the seminal papers in software engineering. Every programmer should read Edsger Dijkstra's papers "Go To Statement Considered Harmful" and "The Humble Programmer" along with several others. They contain in a nutshell the accumulated wisdom of the programming community as of about 1975.

4. *Principles of Software Engineering Management.* Even if you plan to avoid management your entire career, it's a good idea to learn something about it for two reasons. It gives you insight into what your manager does (or what your manager should do), and it helps you self-manage your own projects. Tom Gilb's *Principles of Software Engineering Management* (1988) is a good place to start. Gilb is a good writer, a metrics hotshot, and a master of quantitative approaches to management. He is keenly aware of leading-edge approaches. After the first couple of chapters you can pick and choose your way through his book.

Tom DeMarco's *Controlling Software Projects* (1982) is a good alternative to Gilb's book. DeMarco also takes a quantitative approach, and both he and Gilb are unusual in that they emphasize controlling projects rather than predicting what they will do.

5. *Structured Design.* The first book on structured design was *Structured Design: Fundamentals of a Discipline of Computer Program and Systems Design* (Yourdon and Constantine 1979). It was cowritten by Larry Constantine, who developed most of the key ideas in the structured-design approach. Other books have provided easier explanations, but this book is readable enough, and you can't beat hearing about a body of ideas from the person who came up with them.

A good companion to *Structured Design* is Grady Booch's *Object Oriented Design: With Applications* (1991). Even though object-oriented design doesn't have structured design's track record, it promises to be truly useful in composing systems at a higher level of abstraction than structured design provides for. Booch is a pioneer in the use of Ada and in object-oriented methods, and his experience shows throughout this book.

6. *The Art of Software Testing.* Every programmer should have a book on testing. This isn't to say that testing is the most valuable quality-assurance activity— just that testing is something a programmer should understand. Glenford Myers's *The Art of Software Testing* (1979) was the first book devoted to the topic and is still one of the best. If you can find it, a good alternative is Bill Hetzel's *The Complete Guide to Software Testing* (1988).

In addition to the specific books in the first part of this top-ten list, you should have others that cover these general topics:

7. A book on requirements analysis. You have a choice among several first-rate books on requirements analysis. The first really good book on the topic was Tom DeMarco's *Structured Analysis and Systems Specification: Tools and Techniques* (1979). A more recent treatment is Ed Yourdon's *Modern Structured Analysis* (1989a). For real-time programmers, *Strategies for Real-Time System Specification* (Hatley and Pirbhai 1988) is a good choice. Once you've read the standard analysis books, check out Gerald Weinberg's *Rethinking Systems Analysis and Design* (1988) for its entertaining departures from the conventional wisdom.

8. A book on quantitative project planning and productivity. After years of wondering why no one was publishing quantitative data about software-development methods, I came across a paper on the topic by Barry Boehm. If I could have only one software-engineering reference book, it would be Boehm's *Software Engineering Economics* (1981). Ostensibly about how to do estimates for software projects—work-months, number of programmers, calendar time, manpower loading, and so on—it describes just about every important factor that goes into making software projects productive or unproductive. Boehm has a passion for quantitative data, and he has summarized much of the data available in this volume. Don't be put off by its size or the enormous number of charts and tables. You don't need to read most of them, but they'll be there whenever you're curious. Try starting with Section 33.6, "Personnel Attributes," a pointedly human overview of the reasons software-project estimation is characterized by so much variation and unpredictability. For a short introduction to the same information, see Boehm's paper "Software Engineering Economics" (1984).

A good companion or alternative to Boehm's book is *Applied Software Measurement* (Jones 1991). Capers Jones is just as dedicated to the quest for quantitative data as Boehm, and you could view the material in his book as an updated subset of the information in Boehm's. Chapter 3 on United States averages for software productivity and quality is especially fascinating. Jones's earlier book, *Programming Productivity* (1986a), is just as interesting but has been superseded to some extent by the publication of his more recent book.

9. A book on data structures and algorithms. Every programmer should have a good book on data structures and algorithms. It's better to pull clever algorithms out of a book than to invent them yourself. The advantages are (1) that you know the algorithm works and (2) that it probably works better than any you'd have the time to come up with. Robert Sedgewick's *Algorithms* (1988) is one good choice. Others are *Data Structures* (Reingold and Hansen 1983) and the three volumes of Donald Knuth's *The Art of Computer Programming* (1973a, 1973b, 1981).

10. An overview of the software-development process. It's useful to know what a software-development cycle looks like from a larger perspective. If you've been all the way through a few smaller projects, you might have an intuitive sense of the cycle. If you've worked on small parts of large projects, you might have no sense of it at all.

One excellent overview is *Wicked Problems, Righteous Solutions* (DeGrace and Stahl 1990), a catalog of alternative software life cycles. The authors cover this relatively small topic thoroughly and include lots of tables and diagrams. In exposing you to several different project life cycles, the book gives you a good perspective on planning or analyzing your own projects or other people's.

A second choice, covering different ground, is Watts Humphrey's *Managing the Software Process* (1989). Humphrey describes software development as a process and outlines the activities in each of its parts. Unlike DeGrace and Stahl, Humphrey offers firm opinions about which methods are better than others, but you'll get the big picture from either book.

For an even broader view, not of software processes but of how software processes come into being, take a look at Fred Brooks's "No Silver Bullets— Essence and Accidents of Software Engineering" (1987). It's a witty and informative discussion of what's needed to improve software development now that all the really big improvements have already been made.

33.2 Information About Software Construction

I wrote this book because I couldn't find a thorough discussion of software construction. While I was writing it, Prentice Hall published Michael Marcotty's book on construction. In *Software Implementation* (1991), Marcotty covers the general construction issues by focusing on the themes of abstraction, complexity, readability, and correctness. In the first part of his book, Marcotty examines the history of programming, the programming subculture, the makeup of programming teams, and how typical programmers spend their time. The book is written with wit and style, and the first 100 pages on "the business of programming" are especially well done.

The book is in Prentice Hall's "Practical Software Engineering" series, but the focus isn't entirely practical. It spends 13 pages on the theoretical underpinnings of structured programming (flowgraphs and D-structures) but only lightly discusses the practical issues of variable naming, layout, commenting style, and code tuning. If you want a hands-on reference to code construction, you can probably live without this book. But if you're interested in implementation and aren't alarmed by a little theory, it's well worth reading.

A few other books at least touch on software-construction issues. Brian Kernighan and P. J. Plauger wrote the classic coding-style guide, *The Elements of Programming Style* (1978). It's an excellent reference that focuses on Fortran.

Jon Bentley's *Programming Pearls* (1986) and *More Programming Pearls: Confessions of a Coder* (1988) are collections of essays on coding. Each essay presents a valuable idea concisely and memorably. I use something I learned from Bentley's essays nearly every day that I program.

Henry Ledgard's books with John Tauer, *C With Excellence: Programming Proverbs* (1987a) and *Professional Software,* vol. 2, *Programming Practice* (1987b), and Ledgard's *Programming Proverbs* books are about the coding part of implementation. They contain commonsense programming advice about routines and modules, global variables, comments, variable and constant names, and structured programming. Aside from a little religion in the *goto* area, the books stick to practical advice for making code better. They're short (about 150 pages plus extended program listings) and well written.

Programmers at Work by Susan Lammers (1986) contains interviews with the industry's high-profile programmers. The interviews explore their personalities, work habits, and programming philosophies. The luminaries interviewed include Bill Gates (founder of Microsoft), John Warnock (founder of Adobe), Andy Hertzfeld (principal developer of the Macintosh operating system), Butler Lampson (a senior engineer at DEC), Toru Iwatani (one of the original Pac Man programmers), Wayne Ratliff (inventor of dBase), Dan Bricklin (inventor of VisiCalc), and a dozen others.

33.3 Topics Beyond Construction

Beyond the core books described in the last two sections, here are some books that range further afield from the topic of software construction.

Software in General

Ed Yourdon has done the software-development community a service in bringing together the collection of articles in *Classics in Software Engineering* (1979). The book contains many of the papers that set the course for software engineering today: Dijkstra's "Humble Programmer" and "Go To Statement Considered Harmful" papers, the original "Structured Design" paper, Boehm's famous "Software Engineering" paper, two key papers on chief programmer teams, and Parnas's classic article on information hiding. Yourdon introduces each paper nicely, setting the historical context and explaining its contribution to the field.

The articles in Yourdon's second collection, *Writings of the Revolution: Selected Readings on Software Engineering* (1982), are probably not as seminal as those in the first, but they're still mighty interesting. The collection includes Wirth's paper on "Program Development by Stepwise Refinement," Fagan's original paper on inspections, and Hoare's 1980 Turing Award Lecture, "The Emperor's Old Clothes." It contains "Exploratory Experimental Studies Comparing Online and Offline Programming Performance," the paper that first reported the 10-to-1 or 20-to-1 difference in programmer productivity and resulting program quality. It also contains key papers on quantifying software quality and productivity by Boehm, Jones, and Walston and Felix.

If there's a difference between Yourdon's first and second collections, it's one between explaining how to program and explaining how to figure out how to program. There's a loss of innocence between the first set of papers and the second. The writers of the first set believed they'd found the answers whereas the writers of the second set understood all too clearly that the answers were still somewhere over the horizon. The first collection of papers is full of direct advice and says, in effect, "Do this and your program will be better." The second collection is more deeply reflective, saying, in effect, "When we know this, we will have taken the first steps toward genuine improvement."

Capers Jones collected the excellent papers in *Tutorial: Programming Productivity: Issues for the Eighties* (1986). The 35 articles are grouped into categories: measurement, life-cycle analysis, requirements and design, environments, and case studies that scientifically measure programming productivity. The papers identify an extraordinary range of factors that have been shown to affect productivity in at least a few circumstances: caliber of personnel, design method, coding method, language, physical environment, and management approach, to name just a few.

In Robert L. Glass's *Software Conflict: Essays on the Art and Science of Software Engineering* (1991), an energetic collection of essays provides a valuable counterpoint to some of the current software-engineering groupthink. Glass addresses quality assurance, methodologies, tools, languages, management, education, and the difference between theory and practice, among other topics. His treatment isn't thorough or even systematic, but it brings a perspective that's been missing from other, more euphoric books and articles.

Software-Engineering Overviews

Every practicing computer programmer or software engineer should have a high-level reference on software engineering. Such books survey the methodological landscape rather than painting specific features in detail. They provide an overview of effective software-engineering practices and capsule descriptions of specific software-engineering techniques. The capsule descriptions aren't detailed enough to train you in the techniques, but a single book would have to be several thousand pages long to do that. They provide enough information so that you can learn how the techniques fit together and can choose techniques for further investigation.

The third edition of Ian Sommerville's *Software Engineering* (1989) is a balanced treatment of requirements, design, quality validation, and management. Its 650 pages slight programming practice, but that is a minor defect, especially if you have a book on construction such as the one you're reading.

The book contains helpful diagrams and an annotated further-reading section on each subject.

Roger S. Pressman's *Software Engineering: A Practitioner's Approach* (1987) is a good alternative to Sommerville's book, similar in scope and size. It's not at all clear that the "Practitioner's Approach" makes the book any more practical than Sommerville's. For example, it contains only five pages on coding style and two on efficiency. As a high-level overview, however, it provides a good perspective on the software-development process.

N. D. Birrell and M. A. Ould wrote *A Practical Handbook for Software Development* (1985) with a focus on practical techniques useful for a one-person or two-person programming team and with an emphasis on construction. The book discusses the development process, requirements, design, construction, testing, and maintenance in a handbook format. Even though it's only 250 pages long, its discussion of each topic is practical and thorough, and it contains several useful checklists. A little less theoretical than Pressman's and Sommerville's books, it doesn't acknowledge that it's a software-engineering book, even though it covers that territory. It's not quite as up-to-date as the Sommerville and Pressman books—for example, it doesn't mention object-oriented methods—but it does cover older methods that can still be useful in some circumstances and that the other books don't discuss—HIPO charts, for example.

A second book by Roger Pressman, *Making Software Engineering Happen: A Guide for Instituting the Technology* (1988), is oriented toward software managers who want to implement software engineering in their environments. It contains a complete discussion of the benefits of software engineering, sources of resistance to software engineering, and strategies for implementing software engineering within an organization.

User-Interface Design

Ben Shneiderman's book *Designing the User Interface: Strategies for Effective Human-Computer Interaction* (1987) and Paul Heckel's *The Elements of Friendly Software Design: The New Edition* (1991) cover similar territory in different ways. Shneiderman proposes specific, detailed engineering guidelines for use of color, response time, command structures, menu layouts, and many other aspects of user-interface design. He suggests specific procedures for improving designs including prototyping and iterative testing. Most of his recommendations have been validated by scientific tests. Shneiderman's approach is careful, methodical, and scientific.

Heckel's approach is more freewheeling. Rather than providing detailed procedures, he provides a set of 30 inspirational design heuristics. Heckel argues that interface design is essentially a communication exercise like writing, speaking, or filmmaking, and he draws an elaborate, thought-provoking analogy between designing a user interface and making a movie. In contrast to Shneiderman's emphasis on current laboratory results, Heckel provides an adventurous look into the possibilities of the art.

Both books are valuable on their own terms. Heckel's is more fun. Shneiderman's is on more solid ground. They make a good, complementary pair.

Brenda Laurel collected articles written by people prominent in interface design into *The Art of Human-Computer Interface Design* (1990). As in any collection, some people's ideas are better than others', but this collection contains some gems. My favorite is the article by Alan Kay, the researcher who pioneered Smalltalk, icons, graphical windows, and other interface technologies that make up the heart of modern computing. Kay's article resonates with the force of his creative energy and glimpses into what he's planning for computing's future.

Donald A. Norman's *The Psychology of Everyday Things* (1988) isn't explicitly about software design. It's about the user-interface design of everyday things: doors, pitchers, radios, stoves, and so on. Even so, it's hard to find any part of the book that doesn't apply directly to designing software user interfaces. Norman isn't obliged to focus on software examples, and the range of topics is inspirational. I'd read it again just for the description of opening doors the wrong way. If you've ever felt foolish for pulling a door that says "PUSH," read this book—it's not your fault!

Database Design

An Introduction to Database Systems by Chris Date (1977) and *Fundamentals of Database Systems* by Ramez Elmasri and Shamkant B. Navathe (1989) are two good books on database design and construction. Regardless of how small or informal your program is and of whether you use a "database," you'll benefit from knowing database concepts. If you use files in your programs, you're using a database, and every programmer should be familiar with key database concepts such as "normal form."

Formal Methods

Formal methods prove programs correct through logical arguments rather than through execution testing. Formal methods thus give programs an almost mathematical correctness. Formal methods have so far been applied to only a few projects, but some of them have displayed impressive gains in quality and productivity (Mills, Dyer, and Linger 1987; Cobb and Mills 1990). Here are a few sources of information on formal methods.

The September 1990 issue of *IEEE Software* focuses on formal methods with a collection of articles that are generally supportive of the techniques.

Anyone who cannot cope with mathematics is not fully human. At best, he is a tolerable subhuman who has learned to dress himself, bathe, and not make messes in the house.

Robert Heinlein

Software Engineering Mathematics by Jim Woodcock and Martin Loomes (1988) introduces formal methods to both students and professionals. The first few chapters lay the foundation for formal methods, and examples and exercises in the later chapters are more directly applicable to programming. The notation used in the book is Z (pronounced "zed"), which seems to be headed for ascendancy in the world of formal methods and is a good notation to learn.

Structured Programming: Theory and Practice by Richard C. Linger, Harlan D. Mills, and Bernard I. Witt (1979) is similar to other books on formal methods in that it lays out a rigorous, mathematical foundation for a formal approach to programming, using a formal notation to work with programming concepts. It's different, however, in that it has a relentlessly practical emphasis. Not an "academic exercise," it lays down the foundation for the cleanroom-development approach that has displayed an impressive record of quality and productivity—in the space-shuttle software, for example.

Thus, far from being an exercise in reason, a convincing certification of truth, or a device for enhancing the understanding, a proof in a textbook on advanced topics is often a stylized minuet in which the author dances with his readers to achieve certain social ends. What begins as reason soon becomes aesthetics and winds up as anaesthetics.

P. J. Davis

The subject of formal methods is controversial. Here are two papers that have expressed critical viewpoints:

In "Social Processes and Proofs of Theorems and Programs" (1979), Richard A. DeMillo, Richard J. Lipton, and Alan J. Perlis question whether formal methods can bring certainty to software engineering. Their premise is that mathematics is fallible and that a mathematical approach doesn't always guarantee correctness.

In "Program Verification: The Very Idea" (1988), James H. Fetzer argues that DeMillo, Lipton, and Perlis offered bad arguments for good positions. Fetzer reviews their arguments, reviews counterarguments, and further supports their conclusions. In a sense, he puts their arguments on a more formal footing—a strange way to go about arguing against formal methods.

Further Reading

Good computing bibliographies are rare. Here are a few that justify the effort it takes to obtain them.

Ed Yourdon has been active in the computing literature for over 20 years and has read much more than most of us ever will. His article "The 63 Greatest Software Books" (1988) is an excellent list of key books on a wide variety of computing topics. Yourdon comments on most of the books, at least on his more surprising selections. A copy of the report is included as an appendix to *Decline & Fall of the American Programmer* (Yourdon 1992).

ACM Computing Reviews is a special-interest publication of the ACM that's dedicated to reviewing books about all aspects of computers and computer programming. The reviews are organized according to an extensive classification scheme, making it easy to find books in your area of interest. For information on this publication and on membership in the ACM, write: ACM, PO Box 12114, Church Street Station, New York, NY 10257.

P. J. Plauger's "A Designer's Bibliography" (1988) is a candid description of some of the better books a programmer should read, and as the title suggests, it focuses on program design. Plauger is one of the software-publishing world's insiders; he knows many of the authors whose books he recommends and strays into interesting comments about their personal backgrounds.

33.4 Periodicals

Lowbrow Programmer Magazines

These magazines are often available at local newsstands.

BYTE. One Phoenix Mill Lane, Peterborough, NH 03458. This large magazine covers the microcomputer industry from A to Z including hardware and software development, programming tips, product reviews, and news. Over the past few years, it's evolved from a code-intensive programmer magazine to a general-audience publication that also prints programming articles.

Software Development. PO Box 5032, Brentwood, TN 37204-5032. 800-950-0523. This magazine focuses on programming issues—less on tips for specific environments than on the general issues you face as a professional programmer. The quality of the articles is quite good. It also includes product reviews.

Datamation. 275 Washington Street, Newton, MA 02158. 800-323-4958. This magazine focuses on programming from a data-processing perspective and is written for corporate computing professionals. It ranges far and wide, covering PC and Macintosh topics in addition to mainframe topics. It's also one of the oldest programmer journals.

Dr. Dobb's Journal. PO Box 56188, Boulder, CO 80322-6188. 800-456-1215. This magazine is oriented toward hard-core C and assembler programmers. Its articles tend to deal with lower-level issues that would otherwise be lost in the cracks between C and assembler. It includes lots of code.

If you can't find these magazines at your local newsstand, many publishers will send you a complimentary issue.

Highbrow Programmer Journals

You don't usually buy these magazines at the newsstand. You usually have to go to a major university library or subscribe to them for yourself or your company.

IEEE Software. IEEE Computer Society Publications Office, 10662 Los Vaqueros Circle, PO Box 3014, Los Alamitos, CA 90720-1264. 714-821-8380. This bimonthly magazine focuses on software-development methods and other leading-edge software topics. It publishes many articles by researchers and makes an earnest attempt to print research on practical topics that are of use to professional programmers. It isn't always as practical as I'd like it to be, but in my opinion, it's still the most valuable magazine a programmer can subscribe to.

IEEE Computer. IEEE Computer Society Publications Office, 10662 Los Vaqueros Circle, PO Box 3014, Los Alamitos, CA 90720-1264. 714-821-8380. This monthly magazine is the flagship publication of the IEEE Computer Society. It publishes articles on a wide spectrum of computer topics and has scrupulous review standards to ensure the quality of the articles it publishes. Because of its breadth, you'll probably find fewer articles that interest you than you will in *IEEE Software.*

Communications of the ACM. ACM, 1515 Broadway, New York, NY 10036. 212-869-7440. (This is the address for membership information since a subscription to *CACM* comes free with a membership in the ACM.) This magazine is one of the oldest and most respected computer publications available. It has the broad charter of publishing about the length and breadth of computerology, a subject that's much vaster than it was even a few years ago. As with *IEEE Computer,* because of its breadth, you'll probably find that many of the articles are outside your area of interest. The magazine tends to have an academic flavor, which has both a bad side and a good side. The bad side is that some of the authors write in an obfuscatory academic style. The good side is that it contains leading-edge information that won't filter down to the lowbrow magazines for years.

Boutique Publications

These publications contain articles focused on programming topics and reach a much smaller audience than the highbrow programmer journals just described. They tend to be expensive.

American Programmer. 161 West 86th Street, New York, NY 10024-3411. 212-769-9460. This magazine is published 10 times a year by Ed Yourdon and focuses on programming issues. Recent themes include software quality assurance, creativity and innovation, pen computing, structured methods, object orientation, and software metrics. The good news about this magazine is that the articles are well written and practical and don't try to dazzle you with technobabble. They're written by many of the heaviest heavyweights in the software-consulting industry. The bad news is that the magazine costs about $400 a year. Write for a sample copy.

The Software Practitioner. PO Box 213, State College, PA 16804. This new magazine, started in 1991, is published six times a year by Robert L. Glass. Recent topics include formal methods, re-engineering, process maturity, and reports on software conferences. It's heavy on reviews—reviews of books, conferences, periodicals, and popular methodologies. It doesn't generally publish articles describing the nuts and bolts of new methods—that knowledge is assumed. It reads as if you were sitting in your living room with an old friend, chewing the fat about issues in contemporary programming. This one costs about $55 a year for a personal subscription.

Software Practice and Experience. Subscription Department, John Wiley & Sons, Limited, Baffins Lane, Chichester, Sussex, PO19 1UD, England. This highly regarded British publication focuses on case studies and other topics of interest to programming practitioners. It tends to have a lot of hands-on "here's how I solved my concurrent-update problem" articles. It's published 12 times a year and costs about $500 annually.

Special-Interest Publications

Several publications provide in-depth coverage of specialized topics.

Professional publications

The ACM has special-interest groups in Ada, artificial intelligence, business information technology, biomedical computing, computers and society, computers and human interaction, data communication, computer-personnel research, graphics, measurement and evaluation, programming languages, software engineering, and other topics. Write the ACM for full descriptions.

The IEEE has special-interest groups too and publishes transactions on software engineering, computer graphics and animation, and other topics similar to those in the ACM publications. Write the IEEE Computer Society at the address given in Section 33.5 for more information.

Popular-market publications

These magazines all cover what their names suggest they cover.

The C Users Journal. R&D Publications, Inc., 1601 West 23rd Street, Suite 200, PO Box 3127, Lawrence, KS 66046-0127. 913-841-1631.

DBMS: Developing Corporate Applications. M&T Publishing Inc., PO Box 57511, Boulder, CO 80322-7511. 800-456-1859.

Embedded Systems Programming. Miller Freeman Inc., 600 Harrison Street, San Francisco, CA 94107. 800-950-0523.

LAN Technology: The Technical Resource for Network Specialists. M&T Publishing Inc., PO Box 56456, Boulder, CO 80322-6456. 800-456-1654.

LAN: The Local Area Network Magazine. Miller Freeman Inc., 600 Harrison Street, San Francisco, CA 94107. 800-933-3321.

MacWorld. MacWorld Communications Inc., 501 Second Street, San Francisco, CA 94107.

PC Techniques. 7721 East Gray Road, Suite 204, Scottsdale, AZ 85260. 602-483-0192.

Personal Workstation: Configuring Windowed Networked Computers. Computer Metrics, Inc., 501 Galveston Drive, Redwood City, CA 94063.

Unix Review. Miller Freeman Inc., 500 Howard Street, San Francisco, CA 94105. 415-397-1881.

Software Management News. 141 St. Marks Place, #5F, Staten Island, NY 10301.

Windows Tech Journal. Oakley Publishing Company, 150 North Fourth Street, Springfield, OR 97477. 800-234-0386.

33.5 Joining a Professional Organization

One of the best ways to learn more about programming is to get in touch with other programmers who are as dedicated to the profession as you are. Local user groups for specific hardware and language products are one kind of group. Other kinds are national and international professional organizations. The original professional organization was the Association for Computing Machinery, or ACM. The ACM publishes *Communications of the ACM* and many special-interest magazines. To reach the ACM, write to ACM, PO Box 12114, Church Street Station, New York, NY 10257.

A professional organization that's just as active as the ACM is the Institute of Electrical and Electronics Engineers, or IEEE. The IEEE Computer Society publishes the *IEEE Computer* and *IEEE Software* magazines and is less academically oriented than the ACM. To reach the computer society, write to IEEE Computer Society Headquarters, 1730 Massachusetts Avenue NW, Washington, DC 20036-1903.

33.6 Book Sources

You can obtain many of the books described in this chapter and elsewhere from the following sources:

ACM Books. 1515 Broadway, New York, NY 10036-9998. 800-342-6626.

IEEE Computer Society Press. Customer Service Center, 10662 Los Vaqueros Circle, PO Box 3014, Los Alamitos, CA 90720-1264. 800-272-6657.

Computer Literacy Bookshops, Inc. 2590 North First Street, San Jose, CA 95131. Phone: 408-435-0744, fax: 408-435-1823, e-mail: info@clbooks.com. This company has 13,000 computer and electronics titles in stock and can special-order about 20,000 more. After some preliminary bookkeeping, you can send in orders via e-mail.

Software Engineering Institute, Carnegie-Mellon University, Pittsburgh, PA 15213. 412-268-5800.

Bibliography

Abdel-Hamid, Tarek K. 1989. "The Dynamics of Software Project Staffing: A System Dynamics Based Simulation Approach." *IEEE Transactions on Software Engineering* SE-15, no. 2 (February): 109–19.

Abrash, Michael. 1992. "Flooring It: The Optimization Challenge." *PC Techniques* 2, no. 6 (February/March): 82–88.

Adams, James L. 1980. *Conceptual Blockbusting: A Guide to Better Ideas,* 2d ed. New York: Norton.

Aho, Alfred V., and Jeffrey D. Ullman. 1977. *Principles of Compiler Design.* Reading, Mass.: Addison-Wesley.

Aho, Alfred V., Brian W. Kernighan, and Peter J. Weinberg. 1977. *The AWK Programming Language.* Reading, Mass.: Addison-Wesley.

Aho, Alfred V., John E. Hopcroft, and Jeffrey D. Ullman. 1983. *Data Structures and Algorithms.* Reading, Mass.: Addison-Wesley.

Albrecht, Allan J. 1979. "Measuring Application Development Productivity." *Proceedings of the Joint SHARE/GUIDE/IBM Application Development Symposium, October 1979*: 83–92.

Anand, N. 1988. "Clarify Function!" *ACM Sigplan Notices* 23, no. 6 (June): 69–79.

Aristotle. *The Ethics of Aristotle: The Nicomachean Ethics.* Trans. by J.A.K. Thomson. Rev. by Hugh Tredennick. Harmondsworth, Middlesex, England: Penguin, 1976.

Armenise, Pasquale. 1989. "A Structured Approach to Program Optimization." *IEEE Transactions on Software Engineering* SE-15, no. 2 (February): 101–8.

Arthur, Lowell J. 1988. *Software Evolution: The Software Maintenance Challenge.* New York: John Wiley.

Augustine, N. R. 1979. "Augustine's Laws and Major System Development Programs." *Defense Systems Management Review*: 50–76.

Babich, W. 1986. *Software Configuration Management.* Reading, Mass.: Addison-Wesley.

Bachman, Charles W. 1973. "The Programmer as Navigator." Turing Award Lecture. *Communications of the ACM* 16, no. 11 (November): 653.

Baecker, Ronald M., and Aaron Marcus. 1990. *Human Factors and Typography for More Readable Programs.* Reading, Mass.: Addison-Wesley.

Bairdain, E. F. 1964. "Research Studies of Programmers and Programming." Unpublished studies reported in Boehm 1981.

Baker, F. Terry, and Harlan D. Mills. 1973. "Chief Programmer Teams." *Datamation* 19, no. 12 (December): 58–61.

Barbour, Ian G. 1966. *Issues in Science and Religion*. New York: Harper & Row.

Barbour, Ian G. 1974. *Myths, Models, and Paradigms: A Comparative Study in Science and Religion*. New York: Harper & Row.

Basili, V. R., and B. T. Perricone. 1984. "Software Errors and Complexity: An Empirical Investigation." *Communications of the ACM* 27, no. 1 (January): 42–52.

Basili, Victor R., and David M. Weiss. 1984. "A Methodology for Collecting Valid Software Engineering Data." *IEEE Transactions on Software Engineering* SE-10, no. 6 (November): 728–38.

Basili, Victor R., and Richard W. Selby. 1987. "Comparing the Effectiveness of Software Testing Strategies." *IEEE Transactions on Software Engineering* SE-13, no. 12 (December): 1278–96.

Basili, Victor R., and Albert J. Turner. 1975. "Iterative Enhancement: A Practical Technique for Software Development." *IEEE Transactions on Software Engineering* SE-1, no. 4 (December): 390–96.

Basili, Victor R., Richard W. Selby, and David H. Hutchens. 1986. "Experimentation in Software Engineering." *IEEE Transactions on Software Engineering* SE-12, no. 7 (July): 733–43.

Bastani, Farokh, and Sitharama Iyengar. 1987. "The Effect of Data Structures on the Logical Complexity of Programs." *Communications of the ACM* 30, no. 3 (March): 250–59.

Beck, Kent. 1991. "Think Like An Object." *Unix Review* 9, no. 10 (October): 39–43.

Beck, Leland L., and Thomas E. Perkins. 1983. "A Survey of Software Engineering Practice: Tools, Methods, and Results." *IEEE Transactions on Software Engineering* SE-9, no. 5 (September): 541–61.

Beizer, Boris. 1990. *Software Testing Techniques,* 2d ed. New York: Van Nostrand Reinhold.

Bentley, Jon. 1982. *Writing Efficient Programs*. Englewood Cliffs, N.J.: Prentice Hall.

Bentley, Jon. 1986. *Programming Pearls*. Reading, Mass.: Addison-Wesley.

Bentley, Jon. 1988. *More Programming Pearls: Confessions of a Coder*. Reading, Mass.: Addison-Wesley.

Bentley, Jon. 1991. "Software Exploratorium: Writing Efficient C Programs." *Unix Review* 9, no. 8 (August): 62–73.

Bentley, Jon, and Donald Knuth. 1986. "Literate Programming." *Communications of the ACM* 29, no. 5 (May): 364–69.

Bentley, Jon, Donald Knuth, and Doug McIlroy. 1986. "A Literate Program." *Communications of the ACM* 29, no. 5 (May): 471–83.

Berry, R. E., and B. A. E. Meekings. 1985. "A Style Analysis of C Programs." *Communications of the ACM* 28, no. 1 (January): 80–88.

Bersoff, Edward H. 1984. "Elements of Software Configuration Management." *IEEE Transactions on Software Engineering* SE-10, no. 1 (January): 79–87.

Bersoff, Edward H., et al. 1980. *Software Configuration Management.* Englewood Cliffs, N.J.: Prentice Hall.

Bersoff, Edward H., and Alan M. Davis. 1991. "Impacts of Life Cycle Models on Software Configuration Management." *Communications of the ACM* 34, no. 8 (August): 104–18.

Birrell, N. D., and M. A. Ould. 1985. *A Practical Handbook for Software Development.* Cambridge, England: Cambridge University Press.

Blum, Bruce I. 1989. "A Software Environment: Some Surprising Empirical Results." *Proceedings of the Fourteenth Annual Software Engineering Workshop, November 29, 1989.* Greenbelt, Md.: Goddard Space Flight Center. Document SEL-89-007.

Boddie, John. 1987. *Crunch Mode.* New York: Yourdon Press.

Boehm, Barry W. 1981. *Software Engineering Economics.* Englewood Cliffs, N.J.: Prentice Hall.

Boehm, Barry W. 1984. "Software Engineering Economics." *IEEE Transactions on Software Engineering* SE-10, no. 1 (January): 4–21.

Boehm, Barry W. 1987a. "Improving Software Productivity." *IEEE Computer,* September, 43–57.

Boehm, Barry W. 1987b. "Industrial Software Metrics Top 10 List." *IEEE Software* 4, no. 9 (September): 84–85.

Boehm, Barry W. 1988. "A Spiral Model of Software Development and Enhancement." *Computer,* May, 61–72.

Boehm, Barry W., ed. 1989. *Tutorial: Software Risk Management.* Washington, D.C.: IEEE Computer Society Press.

Boehm, Barry W., et al. 1978. *Characteristics of Software Quality.* New York: North-Holland.

Boehm, Barry W., et al. 1984. "A Software Development Environment for Improving Productivity." *Computer,* June, 30–44.

Boehm, Barry W., T. E. Gray, and T. Seewaldt. 1984. "Prototyping Versus Specifying: A Multiproject Experiment." *IEEE Transactions on Software Engineering* SE-10, no. 3 (May): 290–303. Also in Jones 1986b.

Boehm, Barry W., and Philip N. Papaccio. 1988. "Understanding and Controlling Software Costs." *IEEE Transactions on Software Engineering* SE-14, no. 10 (October): 1462–77.

Boehm-Davis, Deborah, Sylvia Sheppard, and John Bailey. 1987. "Program Design Languages: How Much Detail Should They Include?" *International Journal of Man-Machine Studies* 27, no. 4: 337–47.

Böhm, C., and G. Jacopini. 1966. "Flow Diagrams, Turing Machines and Languages with Only Two Formation Rules." *Communications of the ACM* 9, no. 5 (May): 366–71.

Booch, Grady. 1987. *Software Engineering with Ada,* 2d ed. Menlo Park, Calif.: Benjamin/Cummings.

Booch, Grady. 1991. *Object Oriented Design: With Applications.* Redwood City, Calif.: Benjamin/Cummings.

Boundy, David. 1991. "A Taxonomy of Programmers." *ACM SIGSOFT Software Engineering Notes* 16, no. 4 (October): 23–30.

Branstad, Martha A., John C. Cherniavsky, and W. Richards Adrion. 1980. "Validation, Verification, and Testing for the Individual Programmer." *Computer,* December, 24–30.

Brockmann, R. John. *Writing Better Computer User Documentation: From Paper to Hypertext: Version 2.0.* New York: John Wiley.

Brooks, Frederick P., Jr. 1975. *The Mythical Man-Month,* Reading, Mass.: Addison-Wesley.

Brooks, Frederick P., Jr. 1987. "No Silver Bullets—Essence and Accidents of Software Engineering." *Computer,* April, 10–19.

Brooks, Ruven. 1977. "Towards a Theory of the Cognitive Processes in Computer Programming." *International Journal of Man-Machine Studies* 9:737–51.

Brooks, W. Douglas. 1981. "Software Technology Payoff—Some Statistical Evidence." *The Journal of Systems and Software* 2:3–9.

Brown, A. R., and W. A. Sampson. 1973. *Program Debugging.* New York: American Elsevier.

Bush, Marilyn, and John Kelly. 1989. "The Jet Propulsion Laboratory's Experience with Formal Inspections." *Proceedings of the Fourteenth Annual Software Engineering Workshop, November 29, 1989.* Greenbelt, Md.: Goddard Space Flight Center. Document SEL-89-007.

Caine, S. H., and E. K. Gordon. 1975. "PDL—A Tool for Software Design." *AFIPS Proceedings of the 1975 National Computer Conference 44.* Montvale, N.J.: AFIPS Press, 271–76.

Card, David N. 1987. "A Software Technology Evaluation Program." *Information and Software Technology* 29, no. 6 (July/August): 291–300.

Card, David, Gerald Page, and Frank McGarry. 1985. "Criteria for Software Modularization." *Proceedings of the 8th International Conference on Software Engineering.* Washington, D.C.: IEEE Computer Society Press, 372–77.

Card, David N., Victor E. Church, and William W. Agresti. 1986. "An Empirical Study of Software Design Practices." *IEEE Transactions on Software Engineering* SE-12, no. 2 (February): 264–71.

Card, David N., Frank E. McGarry, and Gerald T. Page. 1987. "Evaluating Software Engineering Technologies." *IEEE Transactions on Software Engineering* SE-13, no. 7 (July): 845–51.

Card, David N., with Robert L. Glass, 1990. *Measuring Software Design Quality,* Englewood Cliffs, N.J.: Prentice Hall.

Carnegie, Dale. 1981. *How to Win Friends and Influence People,* Revised Edition. New York: Pocket Books.

Chase, William G., and Herbert A. Simon. 1973. "Perception in Chess." *Cognitive Psychology* 4:55–81.

Chow, Tsun S., ed. 1985. *Tutorial: Software Quality Assurance: A Practical Approach*. Silver Spring, Md.: IEEE Computer Society Press.

Coad, Peter, and Edward Yourdon. 1991. *Object-Oriented Design*. Englewood Cliffs, N.J.: Yourdon Press.

Cobb, Richard H., and Harlan D. Mills. 1990. "Engineering Software Under Statistical Quality Control." *IEEE Software* 7, no. 6 (November): 45–54.

Collofello, Jim, and Scott Woodfield. 1989. "Evaluating the Effectiveness of Reliability Assurance Techniques." *Journal of Systems and Software* 9, no. 3 (March).

Comer, Douglas. 1981. "Principles of Program Design Induced from Experience with Small Public Programs." *IEEE Transactions on Software Engineering* SE-7, no. 2 (March): 169–74.

Constantine, Larry L. 1990a. "Comments on 'On Criteria for Module Interfaces.'" *IEEE Transactions on Software Engineering* SE-16, no. 12 (December): 1440.

Constantine, Larry L. 1990b. "Objects, Functions, and Program Extensibility." *Computer Language,* January, 34–56.

Conte, S. D., H. E. Dunsmore, and V. Y. Shen. 1986. *Software Engineering Metrics and Models*. Menlo Park, Calif.: Benjamin/Cummings.

Cooper, Doug, and Michael Clancy. 1982. *Oh! Pascal!* 2d ed. New York: Norton.

Corbató, Fernando J. 1991. "On Building Systems That Will Fail." 1991 Turing Award Lecture. *Communications of the ACM* 34, no. 9 (September): 72–81.

Corwin, Al. 1991. Private communication.

CSTB 1990. "Scaling Up: A Research Agenda for Software Engineering." Excerpts from a report by the Computer Science and Technology Board. *Communications of the ACM* 33, no. 3 (March): 281–93.

Curtis, Bill. 1981. "Substantiating Programmer Variability." *Proceedings of the IEEE* 69, no. 7: 846.

Curtis, Bill, ed. 1985. *Tutorial: Human Factors in Software Development*. Los Angeles: IEEE Computer Society Press.

Curtis, Bill, et al. 1986. "Software Psychology: The Need for an Interdisciplinary Program." *Proceedings of the IEEE* 74, no. 8: 1092–1106.

Curtis, Bill, H. Krasner, and N. Iscoe. 1988. "A Field Study of the Software Design Process for Large Systems." *Communications of the ACM* 31, no. 11 (November): 1268–87.

Curtis, Bill, et al. 1989. "Experimentation of Software Documentation Formats." *Journal of Systems and Software* 9, no. 2 (February): 167–207.

Dahl, O. J., E. W. Dijkstra, and C. A. R. Hoare. 1972. *Structured Programming*. New York: Academic Press.

Date, Chris. 1977. *An Introduction to Database Systems*. Reading, Mass.: Addison-Wesley.

Davidson, Jack W., and Anne M. Holler. 1992. "Subprogram Inlining: A Study of Its Effects on Program Execution Time." *IEEE Transactions on Software Engineering* SE-18, no. 2 (February): 89–102.

Davis, P. J. 1972. "Fidelity in Mathematical Discourse: Is One and One Really Two?" *American Mathematical Monthly,* March, 252–63.

DeGrace, Peter, and Leslie Stahl. 1990. *Wicked Problems, Righteous Solutions: A Catalogue of Modern Software Engineering Paradigms.* Englewood Cliffs, N.J.: Yourdon Press.

DeMarco, Tom. 1979. *Structured Analysis and Systems Specification: Tools and Techniques.* Englewood Cliffs, N.J.: Prentice Hall.

DeMarco, Tom. 1982. *Controlling Software Projects.* New York: Yourdon Press.

DeMarco, Tom, and Timothy Lister. 1985. "Programmer Performance and the Effects of the Workplace." *Proceedings of the 8th International Conference on Software Engineering.* Washington, D.C.: IEEE Computer Society Press, 268–72.

DeMarco, Tom, and Timothy Lister. 1987. *Peopleware: Productive Projects and Teams.* New York: Dorset House.

DeMillo, Richard A., Richard J. Lipton, and Alan J. Perlis. 1979. "Social Processes and Proofs of Theorems and Programs." *Communications of the ACM* 22, no. 5 (May): 271–80.

Dijkstra, Edsger. 1965. "Programming Considered as a Human Activity." *Proceedings of the 1965 IFIP Congress.* Amsterdam: North-Holland, 213–17. Reprinted in Yourdon 1982.

Dijkstra, Edsger. 1968. "Go To Statement Considered Harmful." *Communications of the ACM* 11, no. 3 (March): 147–48.

Dijkstra, Edsger. 1969. "Structured Programming." Reprinted in Yourdon 1979.

Dijkstra, Edsger. 1972. "The Humble Programmer." *Communications of the ACM* 15, no. 10 (October): 859–66.

Dijkstra, Edsger. 1985. "Fruits of Misunderstanding." *Datamation,* February 15, 86–87.

Dijkstra, Edsger. 1989. "On the Cruelty of Really Teaching Computer Science." *Communications of the ACM* 32, no. 12 (December): 1397–1414.

Dunn, Robert H. 1984. *Software Defect Removal.* New York: McGraw-Hill.

Elmasri, Ramez, and Shamkant B. Navathe. 1989. *Fundamentals of Database Systems.* Redwood City, Calif.: Benjamin/Cummings.

Elshoff, James L. 1976. "An Analysis of Some Commercial PL/I Programs." *IEEE Transactions on Software Engineering* SE-2, no. 2 (June): 113–20.

Elshoff, James L. 1977. "The Influence of Structured Programming on PL/I Program Profiles." *IEEE Transactions on Software Engineering* SE-3, no. 5 (September): 364–68.

Elshoff, James L., and Michael Marcotty. 1982. "Improving Computer Program Readability to Aid Modification." *Communications of the ACM* 25, no. 8 (August): 512–21.

Endres, Albert. 1975. "An Analysis of Errors and Their Causes in System Programs." *IEEE Transactions on Software Engineering* SE-1, no. 2 (June): 140–49.

Evangelist, Michael. 1984. "Program Complexity and Programming Style." *Proceedings of the First International Conference on Data Engineering*. New York: IEEE Computer Society Press, 534–41.

Fagan, Michael E. 1976. "Design and Code Inspections to Reduce Errors in Program Development." *IBM Systems Journal* 15, no. 3: 182–211.

Fagan, Michael E. 1986. "Advances in Software Inspections." *IEEE Transactions on Software Engineering* SE-12, no. 7 (July): 744–51.

Federal Software Management Support Center. 1986. *Programmers Workbench Handbook*. Falls Church, Va.: Office of Software Development and Information Technology.

Fetzer, James H. 1988. "Program Verification: The Very Idea." *Communications of the ACM* 31, no. 9 (September): 1048–63.

FIPS PUB 38, *Guidelines for Documentation of Computer Programs and Automated Data Systems*. 1976. U.S. Department of Commerce. National Bureau of Standards. Washington, D.C.: U.S. Government Printing Office, Feb. 15.

Fjelstad, R. K., and W. T. Hamlen. 1979. "Applications Program Maintenance Study: Report to our Respondents." *Proceedings Guide 48,* Philadelphia. Reprinted in *Tutorial on Software Maintenance,* G. Parikh and N. Zvegintzov, eds. Los Alamitos, Calif.: CS Press, 1983: 13–27.

Floyd, Robert. 1979. "The Paradigms of Programming." *Communications of the ACM* 22, no. 8 (August): 455–60.

Fowler, Priscilla J. 1986. "In-Process Inspections of Work Products at AT&T." *AT&T Technical Journal,* March/April, 102–12.

Freedman, Daniel P., and Gerald M. Weinberg. 1990. *Handbook of Walkthroughs, Inspections and Technical Reviews,* 3d ed. New York: Dorset House.

Freeman, Peter, and Anthony I. Wasserman, eds. 1983. *Tutorial on Software Design Techniques,* 4th ed. Silver Spring, Md.: IEEE Computer Society Press.

Gibson, Elizabeth. 1990. "Objects—Born and Bred." *BYTE,* October, 245–54.

Gilb, Tom. 1977. *Software Metrics*. Cambridge, Mass.: Winthrop.

Gilb, Tom. 1988. *Principles of Software Engineering Management*. Wokingham, England: Addison-Wesley.

Glass, Robert L. 1982. *Modern Programming Practices: A Report from Industry*. Englewood Cliffs, N.J.: Prentice Hall.

Glass, Robert L. 1988. *Software Communication Skills*. Englewood Cliffs, N.J.: Prentice Hall.

Glass, Robert L. 1991. *Software Conflict: Essays on the Art and Science of Software Engineering*. Englewood Cliffs, N.J.: Yourdon Press.

Glass, Robert L. 1992. *Building Quality Software*. Englewood Cliffs, N.J.: Prentice Hall.

Glass, Robert L., and Ronald A. Noiseux. 1981. *Software Maintenance Guidebook*. Englewood Cliffs, N.J.: Prentice Hall.

Gordon, Ronald D. 1979. "Measuring Improvements in Program Clarity." *IEEE Transactions on Software Engineering* SE-5, no. 2 (March): 79–90.

Gordon, Scott V., and James M. Bieman. 1991. "Rapid Prototyping and Software Quality: Lessons from Industry." *Ninth Annual Pacific Northwest Software Quality Conference, October 7–8*. Oregon Convention Center, Portland, Ore.

Gorla, N., A. C. Benander, and B. A. Benander. 1990. "Debugging Effort Estimation Using Software Metrics." *IEEE Transactions on Software Engineering* SE-16, no. 2 (February): 223–31.

Gould, John D. 1975. "Some Psychological Evidence on How People Debug Computer Programs." *International Journal of Man-Machine Studies* 7:151–82.

Grady, Robert B. 1987. "Measuring and Managing Software Maintenance." *IEEE Software* 4, no. 9 (September): 34–45.

Grady, Robert B., and Deborah L. Caswell. 1987. *Software Metrics: Establishing a Company-Wide Program,* Englewood Cliffs, N.J.: Prentice Hall.

Grady, Robert B. 1993. "Practical Rules of Thumb for Software Managers." *The Software Practitioner* 3, no. 1 (January/February): 4–6.

Green, Paul. 1987. "Human Factors in Computer Systems, Some Useful Readings." *Sigchi Bulletin* 19, no. 2: 15–20.

Gremillion, Lee L. 1984. "Determinants of Program Repair Maintenance Requirements." *Communications of the ACM* 27, no. 8 (August): 826–32.

Gries, David. 1981. *The Science of Programming*. New York: Springer-Verlag.

Grove, Andrew S. 1983. *High Output Management*. New York: Random House.

Hansen, John C., and Roger Yim. 1987. "Indentation Styles in C." *SIGSMALL/PC Notes* 13, no. 3 (August): 20–23.

Hanson, Dines. 1984. *Up and Running*. New York: Yourdon Press.

Harrison, Warren, and Curtis Cook. 1986. "Are Deeply Nested Conditionals Less Readable?" *Journal of Systems and Software* 6, no. 4 (November): 335–42.

Hatley, Derek J., and Imtiaz A. Pirbhai. 1988. *Strategies for Real-Time System Specification*. New York: Dorset House.

Hecht, Alan. 1990. "Cute Object-oriented Acronyms Considered FOOlish." *Software Engineering Notes,* January, 48.

Heckel, Paul. 1991. *The Elements of Friendly Software Design*. New York: Warner Books.

Henry, Sallie, and Dennis Kafura. 1984. "The Evaluation of Software Systems' Structure Using Quantitative Software Metrics." *Software—Practice and Experience* 14, no. 6 (June): 561–73.

Hetzel, Bill. 1988. *The Complete Guide to Software Testing,* 2d ed. Wellesley, Mass.: QED Information Systems.

Hildebrand, J. D. 1989. "An Engineer's Approach." *Computer Language,* October, 5–7.

Hollocker, Charles P. 1990. *Software Reviews and Audits Handbook.* New York: John Wiley.

Houghton, Raymond C. 1990. "An Office Library for Software Engineering Professionals." *Software Engineering: Tools, Techniques, Practice,* May/June, 35–38.

Hughes, Charles E., Charles P. Pfleeger, and Lawrence L. Rose. 1978. *Advanced Programming Techniques: A Second Course in Programming Using Fortran.* New York: John Wiley.

Humphrey, Watts S. 1989. *Managing the Software Process.* Reading, Mass.: Addison-Wesley.

Humphrey, Watts S., Terry R. Snyder, and Ronald R. Willis. 1991. "Software Process Improvement at Hughes Aircraft." *IEEE Software* 8, no. 4 (July): 11–23.

Ichbiah, Jean D., et al. 1986. *Rationale for Design of the Ada Programming Language.* Minneapolis, Minn.: Honeywell Systems and Research Center.

IEEE Software 7, no. 3 (May 1990).

IEEE, 1991. *IEEE Software Engineering Standards Collection, Spring 1991 Edition.* New York: Institute of Electrical and Electronics Engineers.

IEEE, 1992. "Rear Adm. Grace Hopper dies at 85." *IEEE Computer,* February, 84.

Ingrassia, Frank S. 1976. "The Unit Development Folder (UDF): An Effective Management Tool for Software Development." TRW Technical Report TRW-SS-76-11. Also reprinted in Reifer 1986, 366–79.

Ingrassia, Frank S. 1987. "The Unit Development Folder (UDF): A Ten-Year Perspective." *Tutorial: Software Engineering Project Management,* ed. Richard H. Thayer. Los Alamitos, Calif.: IEEE Computer Society Press, 405–15.

Jackson, Michael A. 1975. *Principles of Program Design.* New York: Academic Press.

Johnson, Walter L. 1987. "Some Comments on Coding Practice." *ACM SIGSOFT Software Engineering Notes* 12, no. 2 (April): 32–35.

Jones, T. Capers. 1977. "Program Quality and Programmer Productivity." *IBM Technical Report TR 02.764,* January, 42–78. Also in Jones 1986b.

Jones, Capers. 1986a. *Programming Productivity.* New York: McGraw-Hill.

Jones, T. Capers, ed. 1986b. *Tutorial: Programming Productivity: Issues for the Eighties,* 2d ed. Los Angeles: IEEE Computer Society Press.

Jones, Capers. 1991. *Applied Software Measurement.* New York: McGraw-Hill.

Jonsson, Dan. 1989. "Next: The Elimination of GoTo-Patches?" *ACM Sigplan Notices* 24, no. 3 (March): 85–92.

Kaelbling, Michael. 1988. "Programming Languages Should NOT Have Comment Statements." *ACM Sigplan Notices* 23, no. 10 (October): 59–60.

Keller, Daniel. 1990. "A Guide to Natural Naming." *ACM Sigplan Notices* 25, no. 5 (May): 95–102.

Kelly, John C. 1987. "A Comparison of Four Design Methods for Real-Time Systems." *Proceedings of the Ninth International Conference on Software Engineering.* 238–52.

Kelly-Bootle, Stan. 1981. *The Devil's DP Dictionary.* New York: McGraw-Hill.

Kernighan, Brian W., and P. J. Plauger. 1976. *Software Tools.* Reading, Mass.: Addison-Wesley.

Kernighan, Brian W., and P. J. Plauger. 1978. *The Elements of Programming Style.* 2d ed. New York: McGraw-Hill.

Kernighan, Brian W., and P. J. Plauger. 1981. *Software Tools in Pascal.* Reading, Mass.: Addison-Wesley.

Kernighan, Brian W., and Dennis M. Ritchie. 1988. *The C Programming Language,* 2d ed. Englewood Cliffs, N.J.: Prentice Hall.

King, David. 1988. *Creating Effective Software: Computer Program Design Using the Jackson Methodology.* New York: Yourdon Press.

Knuth, Donald. 1971. "An Empirical Study of FORTRAN programs," *Software—Practice and Experience* 1:105–33.

Knuth, Donald. 1973a. *The Art of Computer Programming,* vol. 1, *Fundamental Algorithms,* 2d ed. Reading, Mass.: Addison-Wesley.

Knuth, Donald. 1973b. *The Art of Computer Programming,* vol. 3, *Sorting and Searching.* Reading, Mass.: Addison-Wesley.

Knuth, Donald. 1974. "Structured Programming with go to Statements." In *Classics in Software Engineering,* edited by Edward Yourdon. Englewood Cliffs, N.J.: Yourdon Press, 1979.

Knuth, Donald. 1981. *The Art of Computer Programming,* vol. 2, *Seminumerical Algorithms,* 2d ed. Reading, Mass.: Addison-Wesley.

Knuth, Donald. 1986. *Computers and Typesetting, Volume B, T$_E$X: The Program.* Reading, Mass.: Addison-Wesley.

Korson, Timothy D., and Vijay K. Vaishnavi. 1986. "An Empirical Study of Modularity on Program Modifiability." In Soloway and Iyengar 1986: 168–86.

Kouchakdjian, Ara, Scott Green, and Victor Basili. 1989. "Evaluation of the Cleanroom Methodology in the Software Engineering Laboratory." *Proceedings of the Fourteenth Annual Software Engineering Workshop, November 29, 1989.* Greenbelt, Md.: Goddard Space Flight Center. Document SEL-89-007.

Kreitzberg, C. B., and B. Shneiderman. 1972. *The Elements of Fortran Style.* New York: Harcourt Brace Jovanovich.

Kuhn, Thomas S. 1970. *The Structure of Scientific Revolutions,* 2d ed. Chicago: University of Chicago Press.

Lammers, Susan. 1986. *Programmers at Work*. Redmond, Wash.: Microsoft Press.

Lampson, Butler. 1984. "Hints for Computer System Design." *IEEE Software* 1, no. 1 (January): 11–28.

Laurel, Brenda, ed. 1990. *The Art of Human-Computer Interface Design*. Reading, Mass.: Addison-Wesley.

Ledgard, Henry. 1985. "Programmers: The Amateur vs. the Professional." *Abacus* 2, no. 4 (Summer): 29–35.

Ledgard, Henry, and Michael Marcotty. 1986. *The Programming Language Landscape: Syntax, Semantics, and Implementation,* 2d ed. Chicago: Science Research Associates.

Ledgard, Henry F., with John Tauer. 1987a. *C With Excellence: Programming Proverbs*. Indianapolis: Hayden Books.

Ledgard, Henry F., with John Tauer. 1987b. *Professional Software*, vol. 2, *Programming Practice*. Indianapolis: Hayden Books.

Leveson, Nancy G. 1986. "Software Safety: Why, What, and How." *Computing Surveys* 18, no. 2 (June): 125–63.

Lewis, Daniel W. 1979. "A Review of Approaches to Teaching Fortran." *IEEE Transactions on Education,* E-22, no. 1: 23–25.

Lientz, B. P., and E. B. Swanson. 1980. *Software Maintenance Management*. Reading, Mass.: Addison-Wesley.

Lind, Randy K., and K. Vairavan. 1989. "An Experimental Investigation of Software Metrics and Their Relationship to Software Development Effort." *IEEE Transactions on Software Engineering* SE-15, no. 5 (May): 649–53.

Linger, Richard C., Harlan D. Mills, and Bernard I. Witt. 1979. *Structured Programming: Theory and Practice*. Reading, Mass.: Addison-Wesley.

Linn, Marcia C., and Michael J. Clancy. 1992. "The Case for Case Studies of Programming Problems." *Communications of the ACM* 35, no. 3 (March): 121–32.

Liskov, Barbara, and Stephen Zilles. 1974. "Programming with Abstract Data Types." *ACM Sigplan Notices* 9, no. 4: 50–59.

Littman, David C., et al. 1986. "Mental Models and Software Maintenance." In Soloway and Iyengar 1986: 80–98.

Longstreet, David H., ed. 1990. *Software Maintenance and Computers*. Los Alamitos, Calif.: IEEE Computer Society Press.

Loy, Patrick H. 1990. "A Comparison of Object-Oriented and Structured Development Methods." *Software Engineering Notes* 15, no. 1 (January): 44–48.

Mannino, P. 1987. "A Presentation and Comparison of Four Information System Development Methodologies." *Software Engineering Notes* 12, no. 2 (April): 26–29.

Marca, David. 1981. "Some Pascal Style Guidelines." *ACM Sigplan Notices* 16, no. 4 (April): 70–80.

Marcotty, Michael. 1991. *Software Implementation.* New York: Prentice Hall.

McCabe, Tom. 1976. "A Complexity Measure." *IEEE Transactions on Software Engineering,* SE-2, no. 4 (December): 308–20.

McCue, Gerald M. 1978. "IBM's Santa Teresa Laboratory—Architectural Design for Program Development." *IBM Systems Journal* 17, no. 1: 4–25.

McGarry, Frank, Sharon Waligora, and Tim McDermott. 1989. "Experiences in the Software Engineering Laboratory (SEL) Applying Software Measurement." *Proceedings of the Fourteenth Annual Software Engineering Workshop, November 29, 1989.* Greenbelt, Md.: Goddard Space Flight Center. Document SEL-89-007.

McGarry, Frank, and Rose Pajerski. 1990. "Towards Understanding Software—15 Years in the SEL." *Proceedings of the Fifteenth Annual Software Engineering Workshop, November 28–29, 1990.* Greenbelt, Md.: Goddard Space Flight Center. Document SEL-90-006.

McKeithen, Katherine B., et al. 1981. "Knowledge Organization and Skill Differences in Computer Programmers." *Cognitive Psychology* 13:307–25.

Metzger, Philip W. 1981. *Managing a Programming Project,* 2d ed. Englewood Cliffs, N.J.: Prentice Hall.

Meyer, Bertrand. 1988. *Object-Oriented Software Construction.* New York: Prentice Hall.

Miaria, Richard J., et al. 1983. "Program Indentation and Comprehensibility." *Communications of the ACM* 26, no. 11 (November): 861–67.

Miller, G. A. 1956. "The Magical Number Seven, Plus or Minus Two: Some Limits on Our Capacity for Processing Information." *The Psychological Review* 63, no. 2 (March): 81–97.

Mills, Harlan D. 1983. *Software Productivity.* Boston, Mass.: Little, Brown.

Mills, Harlan D. 1986. "Structured Programming: Retrospect and Prospect." *IEEE Software,* November, 58–66.

Mills, Harlan D., and Richard C. Linger. 1986. "Data Structured Programming: Program Design Without Arrays and Pointers." *IEEE Transactions on Software Engineering* SE-12, no. 2 (February): 192–97.

Mills, Harlan D., Michael Dyer, and Richard C. Linger. 1987. "Cleanroom Software Engineering." *IEEE Software,* September, 19–25.

Mitchell, Jeffrey, Joseph Urban, and Robert McDonald. 1987. "The Effect of Abstract Data Types on Program Development." *IEEE Computer* 20, no. 9 (September): 85–88.

Mody, R. P. 1991. "C in Education and Software Engineering." *SIGCSE Bulletin* 23, no. 3 (September): 45–56.

Moore, Dave. 1992. Private communication.

Myers, Glenford J. 1976. *Software Reliability.* New York: John Wiley.

Myers, Glenford J. 1978a. *Composite/Structural Design.* New York: Van Nostrand Reinhold.

Myers, Glenford J. 1978b. "A Controlled Experiment in Program Testing and Code Walkthroughs/Inspections." *Communications of the ACM* 21, no. 9 (September): 760–68.

Myers, Glenford J. 1979. *The Art of Software Testing*. New York: John Wiley.

Myers, Ware. 1992. "Good Software Practices Pay Off—Or Do They?" *IEEE Software,* March, 96–97.

Naisbitt, John. 1982. *Megatrends*. New York: Warner Books.

NCES 1991. *Digest of Education Statistics*. National Center for Education Statistics, U.S. Department of Education. Washington, D.C.: Office of Educational Research and Improvement. Document NCES 91-697.

Nevison, John M. 1978. *The Little Book of BASIC Style*. Reading, Mass.: Addison-Wesley.

Norcio, A. F. 1982. "Indentation, Documentation and Programmer Comprehension." *Proceedings: Human Factors in Computer Systems, March 15–17, 1982, Gaithersburg, Md.:* 118–20.

Norman, Donald A. 1988. *The Psychology of Everyday Things*. New York: Basic Books. (Also published in paperback as *The Design of Everyday Things*. New York: Doubleday, 1990.)

Oman, Paul W., and Curtis R. Cook. 1990a. "The Book Paradigm for Improved Maintenance." *IEEE Software,* January, 39–45.

Oman, Paul W., and Curtis R. Cook. 1990b. "Typographic Style Is More Than Cosmetic." *Communications of the ACM* 33, no. 5 (May): 506–20.

Ostrand, Thomas J., and Elaine J. Weyuker. 1984. "Collecting and Categorizing Software Error Data in an Industrial Environment." *Journal of Systems and Software* 4, no. 4 (November): 289–300.

Page-Jones, Meilir. 1988. *The Practical Guide to Structured Systems Design*. Englewood Cliffs, N.J.: Yourdon Press.

Parikh, Girish. 1986. *Handbook of Software Maintenance*. New York: John Wiley.

Parikh, G., and N. Zvegintzov, eds. 1983. *Tutorial on Software Maintenance*. Los Alamitos, Calif.: IEEE Computer Society Press.

Parnas, David L. 1972. "On the Criteria to Be Used in Decomposing Systems into Modules." *Communications of the ACM* 5, no. 12 (December): 1053–58.

Parnas, David L. 1979. "Designing Software for Ease of Extension and Contraction." *IEEE Transactions on Software Engineering* SE-5, no. 2 (March): 128–38.

Parnas, David L., Paul C. Clements, and D. M. Weiss. 1985. "The Modular Structure of Complex Systems." *IEEE Transactions on Software Engineering* SE-11, no. 3 (March): 259–66.

Parnas, David L., and Paul C. Clements. 1986. "A Rational Design Process: How and Why to Fake It." *IEEE Transactions on Software Engineering* SE-12, no. 2 (February): 251–57.

Peters, Lawrence J. 1981. *Handbook of Software Design: Methods and Techniques.* New York: Yourdon Press.

Peters, Lawrence J., and Leonard L. Tripp. 1977. "Comparing Software Design Methodologies." *Datamation,* November, 89–94.

Peters, Tom. 1987. *Thriving on Chaos: Handbook for a Management Revolution.* New York: Knopf.

Pietrasanta, Alfred M. 1990. "Alfred M. Pietrasanta on Improving the Software Process." *Software Engineering: Tools, Techniques, Practices* 1, no. 1 (May/June): 29–34.

Pietrasanta, Alfred M. 1991a. "A Strategy for Software Process Improvement." *Ninth Annual Pacific Northwest Software Quality Conference, October 7–8, 1991.* Oregon Convention Center, Portland, Ore.

Pietrasanta, Alfred M. 1991b. "Implementing Software Engineering in IBM." Keynote address. *Ninth Annual Pacific Northwest Software Quality Conference, October 7–8, 1991.* Oregon Convention Center, Portland, Ore.

Plauger, P. J. 1988. "A Designer's Bibliography." *Computer Language,* July, 17–22.

Plum, Thomas. 1984. *C Programming Guidelines.* Cardiff, N.J.: Plum Hall.

Polya, G. 1957. *How to Solve It: A New Aspect of Mathematical Method,* 2d ed. Princeton, N.J.: Princeton University Press.

Pressman, Roger S. 1987. *Software Engineering: A Practitioner's Approach.* New York: McGraw-Hill.

Pressman, Roger S. 1988. *Making Software Engineering Happen: A Guide for Instituting the Technology.* Englewood Cliffs, N.J.: Prentice Hall.

Raghavan, Sridhar A., and Donald R. Chand. 1989. "Diffusing Software-Engineering Methods." *IEEE Software,* July, 81–90.

Ramsey, H. Rudy, Michael E. Atwood, and James R. Van Doren. 1983. "Flowcharts Versus Program Design Languages: An Experimental Comparison." *Communications of the ACM* 26, no. 6 (June): 445–49.

Ratliff, Wayne. 1987. Interview in *Solution Systems 1987.*

Rees, Michael J. 1982. "Automatic Assessment Aids for Pascal Programs." *ACM Sigplan Notices* 17, no. 10 (October): 33–42.

Reingold, Edward M., and Wilfred J. Hansen. 1983. *Data Structures.* Boston, Mass.: Little, Brown.

Rettig, Marc. 1991. "Testing Made Palatable." *Communications of the ACM* 34, no. 5 (May): 25–29.

Rittel, Horst, and Melvin Webber. 1973. "Dilemmas in a General Theory of Planning." *Policy Sciences* 4:155–69.

Rombach, H. Dieter. 1990. "Design Measurements: Some Lessons Learned." *IEEE Software,* March, 17–25.

Rubin, Frank. 1987. " 'GOTO Considered Harmful' Considered Harmful." Letter to the editor. *Communications of the ACM* 30, no. 3 (March): 195–96. Follow-up letters in 30, no. 5 (May 1987) 351–55; 30, no. 6 (June 1987) 475–78; 30, no. 7 (July 1987) 632–34; 30, no. 8 (August 1987) 659–62; 30, no. 12 (December 1987) 997, 1085.

Sackman, H., W. J. Erikson, and E. E. Grant. 1968. "Exploratory Experimental Studies Comparing Online and Offline Programming Performance." *Communications of the ACM* 11, no. 1 (January): 3–11.

Schulmeyer, G. Gordon, ed. 1987. *Handbook of Software Quality Assurance.* New York: Van Nostrand Reinhold.

Schulmeyer, G. Gordon. 1990. *Zero Defect Software.* New York: McGraw-Hill.

Sedgewick, Robert. 1988. *Algorithms,* 2d ed. Reading, Mass.: Addison-Wesley.

Selby, Richard W., and Victor R. Basili. 1991. "Analyzing Error-Prone System Structure." *IEEE Transactions on Software Engineering* SE-17, no. 2 (February): 141–52.

Sheil, B. A. 1981. "The Psychological Study of Programming." *Computing Surveys* 13, no. 1 (March): 101–20.

Shen, Vincent Y., et al. 1985. "Identifying Error-Prone Software—An Empirical Study." *IEEE Transactions on Software Engineering* SE-11, no. 4 (April): 317–24.

Sheppard, S. B., et al. 1978. "Predicting Programmers' Ability to Modify Software." *TR 78-388100-3,* General Electric Company, May.

Sheppard, S. B., et al. 1979. "Modern Coding Practices and Programmer Performance." *IEEE Computer* 12, no. 12 (December): 41–49.

Shepperd, M., and D. Ince. 1989. "Metrics, Outlier Analysis and the Software Design Process." *Information and Software Technology* 31, no. 2 (March): 91–98.

Shlaer, Sally, and Stephen J. Mellor. 1988. *Object Oriented Systems Analysis—Modeling the World in Data.* Englewood Cliffs, N.J.: Prentice Hall.

Shneiderman, Ben. 1976. "Exploratory Experiments in Programmer Behavior." *International Journal of Computing and Information Science* 5:123–43.

Shneiderman, Ben. 1980. *Software Psychology: Human Factors in Computer and Information Systems.* Cambridge, Mass.: Winthrop.

Shneiderman, Ben. 1987. *Designing the User Interface: Strategies for Effective Human-Computer Interaction.* Reading, Mass.: Addison-Wesley.

Shneiderman, Ben, and Richard Mayer. 1979. "Syntactic/Semantic Interactions in Programmer Behavior: A Model and Experimental Results." *International Journal of Computer and Information Sciences* 8, no. 3: 219–38.

Simon, Herbert. 1969. *The Sciences of the Artificial.* Cambridge, Mass.: MIT Press.

Simonyi, Charles, and Martin Heller. 1991. "The Hungarian Revolution." *BYTE,* August, 131–38.

Smith, Connie U. 1990. *Performance Engineering of Software Systems.* Reading, Mass.: Addison-Wesley.

Software Productivity Consortium. 1989. *Ada Quality and Style: Guidelines for Professional Programmers.* New York: Van Nostrand Reinhold.

Soloway, Elliot, and Sitharama Iyengar, eds. 1986. *Empirical Studies of Programmers.* Norwood, N.J.: Ablex.

Soloway, Elliot, and Kate Ehrlich. 1984. "Empirical Studies of Programming Knowledge." *IEEE Transactions on Software Engineering* SE-10, no. 5 (September): 595–609.

Soloway, Elliot, Jeffrey Bonar, and Kate Ehrlich. 1983. "Cognitive Strategies and Looping Constructs: An Empirical Study." *Communications of the ACM* 26, no. 11 (November): 853–60.

Solution Systems. 1987. *World-Class Programmers' Editing Techniques: Interviews with Seven Programmers.* South Weymouth, Mass.: Solution Systems.

Sommerville, Ian. 1989. *Software Engineering,* 3d ed. Reading, Mass.: Addison-Wesley.

Spier, Michael J. 1976. "Software Malpractice—A Distasteful Experience." *Software—Practice and Experience* 6:293–99.

Spinrad, Mark, and Curt Abraham. 1985. "The Wild-West Lifecycle (WILI)." *ACM SIGSOFT Software Engineering Notes* 10, no. 3 (July): 47–48.

Stevens, Scott M. 1989. "Intelligent Interactive Video Simulation of a Code Inspection." *Communications of the ACM* 32, no. 7 (July): 832–43.

Stevens, W., G. Myers, and L. Constantine. 1974. "Structured Design." *IBM Systems Journal* 13, no. 2 (May): 115–39.

Stevens, Wayne. 1981. *Using Structured Design.* New York: John Wiley.

Stitt, Martin. 1992. *Debugging: Creative Techniques and Tools for Software Repair.* New York: John Wiley.

Tenny, Ted. 1988. "Program Readability: Procedures versus Comments." *IEEE Transactions on Software Engineering* SE-14, no. 9 (September): 1271–79.

Thayer, Richard H., ed. 1990. *Tutorial: Software Engineering Project Management.* Los Alamitos, Calif.: IEEE Computer Society Press.

Thimbleby, Harold. 1988. "Delaying Commitment." *IEEE Software,* May, 78–86.

Thomas, Edward J., and Paul W. Oman. 1990. "A Bibliography of Programming Style." *ACM Sigplan Notices* 25, no. 2 (February): 7–16.

Thomas, Richard A. 1984. "Using Comments to Aid Program Maintenance." *BYTE,* May, 415–22.

U.S. Department of Labor. 1990. "The 1990–91 Job Outlook in Brief." *Occupational Outlook Quarterly, Spring.* U.S. Government Printing Office. Document 1990-282-086/20007.

"A C Coding Standard." 1991. *Unix Review* 9, no. 9 (September): 42–43.

Valett, J., and F. E. McGarry. 1989. "A Summary of Software Measurement Experiences in the Software Engineering Laboratory." *Journal of Systems and Software* 9, no. 2 (February): 137–48.

van Genuchten, Michiel. 1991. "Why Is Software Late? An Empirical Study of Reasons for Delay in Software Development." *IEEE Transactions on Software Engineering* SE-17, no. 6 (June): 582–90.

Van Tassel, Dennie. 1978. *Program Style, Design, Efficiency, Debugging, and Testing,* 2d ed. Englewood Cliffs, N.J.: Prentice Hall.

Vessey, Iris. 1986. "Expertise in Debugging Computer Programs: An Analysis of the Content of Verbal Protocols." *IEEE Transactions on Systems, Man, and Cybernetics* SMC-16, no. 5 (September/October): 621–37.

Vessey, Iris, Sirkka L. Jarvenpaa, and Noam Tractinsky. 1992. "Evaluation of Vendor Products: CASE Tools as Methodological Companions." *Communications of the ACM* 35, no. 4 (April): 91–105.

Votta, Lawrence G., et al. 1991. "Investigating the Application of Capture-Recapture Techniques to Requirements and Design Reviews." *Proceedings of the Sixteenth Annual Software Engineering Workshop, December 4–5, 1991.* Greenbelt, Md.: Goddard Space Flight Center. Document SEL-91-006.

Walston, C. E., and C. P. Felix. 1977. "A Method of Programming Measurement and Estimation." *IBM Systems Journal* 16, no. 1: 54–73.

Ward, Robert. 1989. *A Programmer's Introduction to Debugging C.* Lawrence, Kans.: R & D Publications.

Ward, William T. 1989. "Software Defect Prevention Using McCabe's Complexity Metric." *Hewlett-Packard Journal,* April, 64–68.

Webster, Dallas E. 1988. "Mapping the Design Information Representation Terrain." *IEEE Computer,* December, 8–23.

Weeks, Kevin. 1992. "Is Your Code Done Yet?" *Computer Language,* April, 63–72.

Weiland, Richard J. 1983. *The Programmer's Craft: Program Construction, Computer Architecture, and Data Management.* Reston, Va.: Reston Publishing.

Weinberg, Gerald M. 1971. *The Psychology of Computer Programming.* New York: Van Nostrand Reinhold.

Weinberg, Gerald M. 1983. "Kill That Code!" *Infosystems,* August, 48–49.

Weinberg, Gerald. 1988. *Rethinking Systems Analysis and Design.* New York: Dorset House.

Weinberg, Gerald M., and Edward L. Schulman. 1974. "Goals and Performance in Computer Programming." *Human Factors* 16, no. 1 (February): 70–77.

Weiss, David M. 1975. "Evaluating Software Development by Error Analysis: The Data from the Architecture Research Facility." *Journal of Systems and Software* 1, no. 2 (June): 57–70.

Weiss, Eric A. 1972. "Review of *The Psychology of Computer Programming,* by Gerald M. Weinberg." *ACM Computing Reviews* 13, no. 4 (April): 175–76.

Whorf, Benjamin. 1956. *Language, Thought and Reality.* Cambridge, Mass.: MIT Press.

Wirth, Niklaus. 1971. "Program Development by Stepwise Refinement." *Communications of the ACM* 14, no. 4 (April): 221–27.

Wirth, Niklaus. 1986. *Algorithms and Data Structures.* Englewood Cliffs, N.J.: Prentice Hall.

Woodcock, Jim, and Martin Loomes. 1988. *Software Engineering Mathematics.* Reading, Mass.: Addison-Wesley.

Woodfield, S. N., H. E. Dunsmore, and V. Y. Shen. 1981. "The Effect of Modularization and Comments on Program Comprehension." *Proceedings of the Fifth International Conference on Software Engineering,* March 1981, 215–23.

Wulf, W. A. 1972. "A Case Against the GOTO." *Proceedings of the 25th National ACM Conference,* August 1972, 791–97.

Youngs, Edward A. 1974. "Human Errors in Programming." *International Journal of Man-Machine Studies* 6:361–76.

Yourdon, Edward, ed. 1979. *Classics in Software Engineering.* Englewood Cliffs, N.J.: Yourdon Press.

Yourdon, Edward, ed. 1982. *Writings of the Revolution: Selected Readings on Software Engineering.* New York: Yourdon Press.

Yourdon, Edward. 1986a. *Managing the Structured Techniques: Strategies for Software Development in the 1990s,* 3d ed. New York: Yourdon Press.

Yourdon, Edward. 1986b. *Nations at Risk.* New York: Yourdon Press.

Yourdon, Edward. 1988. "The 63 Greatest Software Books." *American Programmer,* September.

Yourdon, Edward. 1989a. *Modern Structured Analysis.* New York: Yourdon Press.

Yourdon, Edward. 1989b. *Structured Walk-Throughs,* 4th ed. New York: Yourdon Press.

Yourdon, Edward. 1992. *Decline & Fall of the American Programmer.* Englewood Cliffs, N. J.: Yourdon Press.

Yourdon, Edward, and Larry L. Constantine. 1979. *Structured Design: Fundamentals of a Discipline of Computer Program and Systems Design.* Englewood Cliffs, N.J.: Yourdon Press.

Zahniser, Richard A. 1992. "A Massively Parallel Software Development Approach." *American Programmer,* January, 34–41.

Index

Page numbers in italics refer to tables or code examples.

O

About the Author

Steve McConnell is a consultant to software-intensive companies in the Puget Sound area including Microsoft. His primary focus has been on the development of mass-distribution commercial microcomputer software. In addition to more theoretical projects such as writing this book, he has personally written more than 50,000 lines of production code in the last five years. McConnell earned a bachelor's degree from Whitman College in Walla Walla, Washington, and a master's degree in software engineering from Seattle University. He is a member of the IEEE Computer Society and the ACM.

The manuscript for this book was prepared and submitted to Microsoft Press in electronic form. Text files were prepared using Microsoft Word for Windows 2.0.

Principal editorial compositor: Barb Runyan
Principal proofreader/copy editor: Alice Copp Smith
Principal typographer: Katherine Erickson
Interior designer: Peggy Herman
Principal illustrators: Mark Monlux and Lisa Sandburg
Cover designer: Rebecca Geisler
Cover color separator: Color Service
Indexer: Julie Kawabata

Text composition by Microsoft Press in Garamond Light with display type in Helvetica Bold, using the Magna composition system and the Linotronic 300 laser imagesetter.

Printed on recycled paper stock.

STEVE MAGUIRE'S *WRITING SOLID CODE*, the companion volume to *Debugging the Development Process*, covers techniques and strategies that programmers can use immediately to reduce their bug rates and write bug-free code.

Steve Maguire maintains that the most critical requirement for writing bug-free code is to become attuned to what causes bugs. All of the techniques and strategies Maguire presents in *Writing Solid Code* are the result of programmers asking themselves two questions over and over, year after year, every time they find a bug in their code:

◆ How could I have *automatically* detected this bug?

◆ How could I have *prevented* this bug?

The easy answer to both questions would be "better testing," but that's not automatic, nor is it really preventive. Maguire says that answers like "better testing" are so general they have no muscle—they're effectively worthless. He insists that good answers to the two questions result in the specific techniques that will eliminate the kind of bug you've just found.

Writing Solid Code is devoted to the techniques and strategies that have been found to reduce or completely eliminate entire classes of bugs. Some of the book's points smack right up against common coding practices, but all have been effective in reducing the number of bugs in code. The book also covers techniques that programmers can use to automatically detect bugs—techniques other than using test applications. By building "debug code" directly into their programs, code that monitors a program from the inside, programmers can automatically detect numerous types of otherwise hard-to-find bugs. *Writing Solid Code* covers the most effective ways to write such debug code.

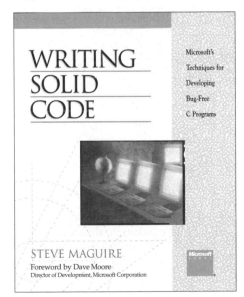

The book is written in the same format and style as *Debugging the Development Process*. Its examples are written in the C programming language, but its good advice is generally applicable—regardless of whether you're using C, FORTRAN, or some other programming language. The next few pages contain an excerpt from *Writing Solid Code*'s Chapter 5, "Candy-Machine Interfaces."

HERE'S WHAT THE CRITICS HAVE SAID about the bestselling
Writing Solid Code, winner of a 1994 *Software Development* Jolt Productivity
Award and of awards from the Society for Technical Communication.

Maguire's writing style is fluid and clear, and the content is
intended to provoke both thought and action (namely changes
in your bad habits).

—Ray Valdés, **Dr. Dobb's Journal**

This unique volume gathers a wealth of coding wisdom
developed over the years inside Microsoft. These aren't coding
techniques so much as coding and testing *philosophies*—
mindsets that help Microsoft's programmers produce better
code with fewer bugs in less time than their competitors.

—Jeff Duntemann, **PC Techniques**

Writing Solid Code is superbly written and offers a variety of
sound practical coding guidelines at a level suitable for the
professional C coder. The author's experience, coupled with
an obvious enthusiasm for the subject, has resulted in a book
which is both informative and easy to read. . . You'll find
historical notes about the development of programs such as
[Microsoft] Excel and Word. . . You do not, incidentally, need to
be an MSDOS, Windows, or Apple Mac programmer to appreciate the wisdom in this book or to follow the code. . . An
excellent book and one of those relatively rare offerings
that all C programmers would do well to read.

—Paul Overaa, **Computing**

If you are serious about developing C code, read this book.
Consider it carefully. Reject it if you will, but I think you
would be foolish to do so. This is easily my 'Book of the Year.'

—Ian Cargill, **C Vu**

5

CANDY-MACHINE INTERFACES

One of the perks that Microsoft gives its employees is free soft drinks, flavored seltzer water, milk (chocolate too!), and those little cartons of fruit juices. As much as you want. But, darn it, if you want candy, you have to pay for that yourself. Occasionally, I would get the munchies and stroll down to a vending machine. I'd plunk in my quarters, press 4 and then 5 on the selection keypad, and watch in horror as the machine spit out jalapeño-flavored bubble gum instead of the Grandma's Peanut Butter Cookie I thought I'd asked for. Of course, the machine was right and I was wrong—number 45 was the gum. A quick look at the little sign by the cookie would always verify my mistake: No. 21, 45¢.

That candy machine always infuriated me because if the engineers had spent an extra 30 seconds thinking about their design, they could have saved me, and I'm sure countless others, from getting something they didn't want. If one of the engineers had thought, "Hmm. People are going to be thinking '45¢' as they deposit their money—I'll bet some of them are going to turn to the keypad and mistakenly enter the price instead of the selection number. To prevent that from happening, we should use an alphabetic keypad instead of a numeric one."

The machine wouldn't have cost any more to make, and the improvement wouldn't have changed the design in any appreciable way, but every time I turned to the keypad to punch in 45¢, I would find I couldn't and so be reminded to punch in the letter code. The interface design would have led people to do the right thing.

When you design function interfaces, you face similar problems. Unfortunately, programmers aren't often trained to think about how other programmers will use their functions, but as with the candy machine, a trivial difference in design can either cause bugs or prevent them. It's not enough that your functions be bug-free; they must also be safe to use.

getchar GETS AN *int*, OF COURSE

Many of the standard C library functions, and thousands of functions patterned after them, have candy-machine interfaces that can trip you up. Think about the *getchar* function, for instance. The interface for *getchar* is risky for several reasons, but the most severe problem is that its design encourages programmers to write buggy code. Look at what Brian Kernighan and Dennis Ritchie have to say about it in *The C Programming Language*:

> Consider the code
>
> ```
> char c;
>
> c = getchar();
> if (c == EOF)
>     ...
> ```
>
> On a machine which does not do sign extension, c is always positive because it is a char, yet EOF is negative. As a result, the test always fails. To avoid this, we have been careful to use int instead of char for any variable which holds a value returned by getchar.

With a name such as *getchar* it's natural to define *c* to be a character, and that's why programmers get caught by this bug. But really, is there any reason *getchar* should be so hazardous? It's not doing anything complex; it's simply trying to read a character from a device and returning a possible error condition.

The code below shows another problem common in many function interfaces:

```
/* strdup -- allocate a duplicate of a string. */

char *strdup(char *str)
{
    char *strNew;

    strNew = (char *)malloc(strlen(str)+1);
    strcpy(strNew, str);

    return (strNew);
}
```

This code will work fine until you run out of memory and *malloc* fails, returning *NULL* instead of a pointer to memory. Who knows what *strcpy* will do when the destination pointer, *strNew*, is *NULL*, but whether *strcpy* crashes or quietly trashes memory, the result won't be what the programmer intended.

Programmers have trouble using *getchar* and *malloc* because they can write code that appears to work correctly even though it's flawed. It's not until weeks or months later that the code crashes unexpectedly because, as in the sinking of the *Titanic*, a precise series of improbable events takes place and leads to disaster. Neither *getchar* nor *malloc* leads programmers to write correct code; both lead programmers to ignore the error condition.

The problem with *getchar* and *malloc* is that their return values are imprecise. Sometimes they return the valid data that you expect, but other times they return magic error values.

If *getchar* didn't return the funny *EOF* value, declaring *c* to be a character would be correct and programmers wouldn't run into the bug that Kernighan and Ritchie talk about. Similarly, if *malloc* didn't return *NULL* as though it were a pointer to memory, programmers wouldn't forget to handle the error condition. The problem with these functions is not that they return errors, but that they bury those errors in normal return values where it's easy for programmers to overlook them.

What if you redesigned *getchar* so that it returned both outputs separately? It could return *TRUE* or *FALSE* depending upon whether it successfully read a new character, and the character itself could be returned in a variable that you pass by reference:

```
flag fGetChar(char *pch);      /* prototype */
```

With the interface above, it would be natural to write

```
char ch;

if (fGetChar(&ch))
    ch has the next character;
else
    hit EOF, ch is garbage;
```

The problem with *char* vs. *int* goes away, and it's unlikely that any programmer, no matter how green, would accidentally forget to test the error return value. Compare the return values for *getchar* and *fGetChar*. Do you see that *getchar* emphasizes the character being returned, whereas *fGetChar* emphasizes the error condition? Where do you think the emphasis should be if your goal is to write bug-free code?

True, you do lose the flexibility to write code such as

```
putchar(getchar());
```

but how often are you certain that *getchar* won't fail? In almost all cases, the code above would be wrong.

Some programmers might think, "Sure, *fGetChar* may be a safer interface, but you waste code because you have to pass an extra argument when you call it. And what if a programmer passes *ch* instead of *&ch*? After all, forgetting the *&* is an age-old source of bugs when programmers use the *scanf* function."

Good questions.

Whether the compiler will generate better or worse code is actually compiler dependent, but granted, most compilers will generate slightly more code at each call. Still, the minor difference in code size is probably not worth worrying about when you consider that the cost of disk and memory storage is plummeting while program complexity and associated bug rates are climbing. This gap will only get larger in the future.

The second concern—passing a character to *fGetChar* instead of a pointer to a character—shouldn't worry you if you're using function prototypes as suggested in Chapter 1. If you pass *fGetChar* anything but a pointer to a character, the compiler will automatically generate an error and show you your mistake.

The reality is that combining mutually exclusive outputs into a single return value is a carryover from assembly language, where you have a limited number of machine registers to manipulate and pass data. In that environment, using a single register to return two mutually exclusive values is not only efficient but often necessary. Coding in C is another matter—even though C lets you "get close to the machine," that doesn't mean you should write high-level assembly language.

When you design your function interfaces, choose designs that lead programmers to write correct code *the first time*. Don't use confusing dual-purpose return values—each output should represent exactly one data type. Make it hard to ignore important details by making them explicit in the design.

———◆———

Make it hard to ignore error conditions.
Don't bury error codes in return values.

———◆———

Writing Solid Code
Microsoft's Techniques for Developing Bug-Free C Programs
Steve Maguire

Foreword by Dave Moore
Director of Development, Microsoft Corporation

288 pages, softcover
$24.95 ($32.95 Canada)
ISBN 1-55615-551-4

IN *DEBUGGING THE DEVELOPMENT PROCESS*, the companion to *Writing Solid Code*, Steve Maguire shows leads and programmers how to fine-tune the development process itself with proven techniques and strategies they can use to organize and run their software projects without the turmoil, long hours, and slipped schedules so common in the software industry.

Maguire's premise in *Writing Solid Code* is that programmers can write code with far fewer bugs than they typically do. His premise in *Debugging the Development Process* is that "it *is* possible to ship high-quality, bug-free software on schedule, without working long hours—and to have fun doing it."

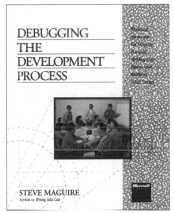

Debugging the Development Process lays out the sometimes controversial but inarguably successful practices Maguire used to retrain teams at Microsoft whose projects were in trouble for one reason or another: their projects were overdue, or the quality of their code wasn't up to company standards, or they were working crazy hours and making no headway.

Maguire believes that for a team to be successful every team member, not just the lead, needs to understand the principles, guidelines, and strategies that result in the timely shipping of quality software. That's why he addresses *Debugging the Development Process* to the whole software development team.

Maguire's experience has been that most software development leads haven't been trained to be leads, that most of them simply wake up one day to discover they've been given the reins. That's why he addresses *Debugging the Development Process* to both present-day leads and present-day programmers.

Debugging the Development Process contains many examples drawn from Maguire's experiences at Microsoft, and to make the examples easier to follow, Maguire provides in the introduction a "snapshot" of the organization of software projects at Microsoft. With the refreshing candor reviewers admired in *Writing Solid Code*, subsequent chapters talk about what did and didn't work at Microsoft and tell you

- ◆ How to energize software teams to work effectively—and to enjoy their work
- ◆ Why a lead might want to kick a star programmer off the team
- ◆ How to avoid corporate snares and overblown corporate processes
- ◆ Which tiny changes produce major results
- ◆ How to deliver on schedule and without overwork
- ◆ How to pull twice the value out of everything you do
- ◆ How to get your team going on a creative roll
- ◆ How to raise the average programmer level at your company

The next few pages contain an excerpt from Chapter 8 of *Debugging the Development Process*, "That Sinking Feeling."

Here's what the critics have said about *Debugging the Development Process*, winner of a 1995 *Software Development* Jolt Productivity Award.

Following on the heels of *Writing Solid Code,* his 1993 Productivity Award winner, Steve Maguire has come out with another brilliant work. Simply put, *Debugging the Development Process* is down-to-earth, sensible management advice for project leaders. This work provides strategic and tactical advice in completing your projects on time, within budget, without alienating your development team. Here at *Software Development,* we felt it was so valuable to readers that we reprinted a chapter . . . Maguire relates plenty of good stories from his years at Microsoft, which in itself makes this book worth a read. Once you pick this book up, you'll have a hard time putting it down.

—Alex Dunne, *Software Development*

Maguire has an authoritative but friendly style which I find extremely easy to read. I read this book in virtually a single session without any effort at all, something I very rarely find with technical books. Maguire achieves a nice balance between a friendly, conversational style and a voice of authority. He has also achieved a nice balance between the main thread of the text and the real-world examples he uses to illustrate his points . . . I think anyone but the most neophyte programmer could benefit from reading this book. For team leaders and managers, it should be compulsory reading.

—Ian Cargill, *C Vu*

I will be ordering this book for my students, and I urge every teacher of software engineering to read it themselves. It should also be a requirement for keeping a job in the software industry in general . . . Liberally illustrated with actual examples, well-organized and designed, this book is a milestone in the game of hitting milestones. I only wish I were an alien with more arms. I'd give it three thumbs up.

—James Tomayko, *ACM Computing Reviews*

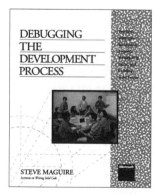

Debugging the Development Process
Practical Strategies for Staying Focused, Hitting Ship Dates, and Building Solid Teams
Steve Maguire

216 pages, softcover
$24.95 ($32.95 Canada)
ISBN 1-55615-650-2

Microsoft Press books are available wherever quality computer books are sold. Or call 1-800-MSPRESS for ordering information. Outside the U.S., write to International Coordinator, Microsoft Press, One Microsoft Way, Redmond, WA 98052-6399.

8

THAT SINKING FEELING

When projects start slipping, the first two actions leads often take are the easy, obvious ones: hire more people, and force the team to work longer hours. These may seem like reasonable responses, but in fact they're probably the worst approaches leads can take to turning around a troubled project.

Imagine a sixteenth century merchant galleon crossing the Atlantic Ocean from the Old World to the New World. When the galleon is far out in the ocean, the first mate notices that the ship is taking on water and alerts the captain. The captain orders members of the crew to bail water, but despite their efforts, the water continues to rise. The captain orders more crew members to bail water—to no avail. Soon the captain has the entire crew bailing water in shifts, but the water continues to rise . . .

Realizing that he has no more sailors to call on, and with the ship continuing to take on water, the captain orders all crew members to bail ever longer hours, their days and nights becoming nothing but bailing water, collapsing from exhaustion, waking up, and going back to bailing. It works. The sailors are not only able to prevent the water from rising, but they're able to make headway, bailing water out faster than it's coming in. The captain is happy. Through his brilliant management of human resources, he has prevented the ship from sinking.

At least for the first week.

Soon the crew members get bone weary and bail less water than they did when they worked in shifts and were well rested. The ship again starts taking on more water than they can bail out. The first mate tries to convince the captain that he must allow the crew members to rest if he wants them to be effective. But because the ship is sinking the captain rejects all talk of giving the crew a break. "We're *sinking*. The crew *must* work long hours," the captain shouts. "*We—are—sinking!*"

The water continues to rise and the ship eventually sinks, taking everybody with her.

Could there have been a better approach to saving that ship than putting all the crew members on the bailing task and then forcing them to work long, hard hours? If you were on a ship that was taking on water, what would you do? I can tell you what I'd do: *I'd search for the leaks.* Wouldn't you?

This is such an obvious point, but why then do so many leads run their projects as if they were sinking ships? When a project starts to slip, many a lead will first throw more people onto the job. If the project continues to slip and the lead can't get more people, he or she will demand that the developers put in longer hours. Just as that ship captain did. The project can be waist-deep in water, but the lead won't stop to look for and fix the leaks. Fortunately for their companies, most project teams can bail water slightly faster than it comes in, and they end up shipping their products, but often not without an enormous amount of misplaced effort.

In Chapter 1, I described a user interface library team that had been working 80-hour weeks for more than a year, with no end in sight. Water was gushing in on that project, but nobody stopped to look for leaks.

The team was fully staffed, and they were working 12-hour days, seven days a week. What more could they do? But as I pointed out in Chapter 1, that team was spending most of its time on work they shouldn't have been doing. They were ignoring what should have been their primary goal: *to provide a library that contains only functionality that is useful to all groups who will use the library.* That was a leak.

In Chapter 3, I talked about a dialog manager team that was working hard to speed up their library for the Word for Windows team. Despite all their hard work, they kept falling short of the quality bar for speed that the Word team had set. Word's swapping hack that kicked out all "unnecessary" code segments was kicking out every byte of the library code, so that physically reloading the code, to say nothing of executing the code, took more time than Word's quality bar allowed. But nobody was looking at load issues. The dialog manager team members were focused on optimizing the code to make it run faster.

And in Chapter 5, I described the Excel team's working 80-hour weeks to meet an unrealistic and demoralizing schedule.

In all of those cases, the need to work long hours should have been a red flag, a clear indication that something, somewhere, was seriously wrong. Unfortunately, many leads take the two obvious steps when projects start to slip their schedules—hiring more people and demanding longer hours—instead of looking for the causes of the schedule slips.

Have a Life

As I've said, for several years at Microsoft, my job was to take floundering projects and make them functional again. In every case, the team members had been working long hours, seven days a week, in a desperate attempt to catch a ship date that was moving ever further away. Team morale was usually low, and often programmers had come to detest their jobs.

On my first day as the new lead, my initial actions were always to put a stop to the long hours and start looking for the causes of the slipping schedule. I would walk down the halls in the early evening and kick people out. "Get outta here. Go have a life."

Programmers would protest: "I can't leave—I'm behind on this feature."

"That's OK," I'd say. "The entire team has been working insane hours for nearly a year, and all that effort hasn't kept the project from regularly slipping. Working long hours won't bring this project under control. There's something fundamentally wrong here, something we need to find and fix, and continuing to work long hours is not going to help us find the problem. Go home. Get some rest. We'll look for the problem first thing tomorrow."

At first the team members would think I was joking. The message they had been getting—in some cases for more than a year—was work harder, longer hours, and I was telling them to go home while the sun was still out. They thought I was nuts. If the project was slipping so badly now, they thought, what would it look like if they stopped working those long hours?

But over the next few weeks, I'd hit the project with all the strategies I've described in the first seven chapters of this book. I'd put a stop to unnecessary reports and meetings and all other unnecessary interruptions. I'd toss out the existing task-list–driven schedule and replace it with a win-able schedule made up of subproject milestones of the type I've described in Chapter 5, cutting all nonstrategic features in the process. I'd promote the attitudes I've presented in Chapter 7, such as the attitude that it's crucial that the team fix bugs the moment they're found. I'd make sure that the project goals were clear and that the programmers understood that one of my goals as a lead was to help create large blocks of time during the day for them to work uninterrupted. I'd do all of the things I've encouraged you to do. A hard month or two later, the team would hit their first milestone, as planned, but they'd do it without working 80-hour weeks. They'd have their first win. In the following months, hitting those subproject milestones would get progressively easier as new work skills became habits.

———◆———

If your project is slipping, something is wrong. Don't ignore the causes and demand long hours of the team members. Find and fix the problems.

———◆———

The Commitment Myth

Some teams work long hours, not to meet an ever slipping schedule, but because an upper-level manager demands that they work 80-hour weeks, believing that development teams must work long hours to get products out the door. When such a manager sees a team working 40-hour weeks, his or her immediate interpretation is that the team is not committed to the company. If you point out that the team hits all its drop dates, the upper-level manager will counter with the statement that the team must be padding its schedules with gobs of free time. That same manager will hold up a team whose members work 80-hour weeks as an example for other teams to follow. "This team shows commitment!" If the team isn't hitting its deadlines, well, that's just because the project's schedule is unattainable, just as a schedule should be if you want programmers to work as hard as possible.

Obviously, I disagree with that point of view. If I held that view, I would have to conclude that the user interface library project, the dialog manager project, and the Excel project were model projects to be emulated. And I'd have to conclude that any team who had concrete goals and objectives, who focused on strategic features, who constantly invested in training, and who as a consequence always hit their drop dates while working efficient 40-hour weeks was a team who were screwing up.

It sounds silly when I put it that way, but that's effectively what that manager is saying when he sees a team working only 40-hour weeks and demands that the lead force the team members to put in more hours: "This is *not* a company of clock-watchers. You tell your team they're expected to put in more hours. I want to see some commitment!"

What nonsense. Managers like that praise the teams who work inefficiently and think the worst of the teams who work well. Compare such a manager with a manager who looks at a 40-hour-per-week team and is grateful that at least one project is running smoothly. That manager asks the team what they're doing to achieve such success and works to get other teams to duplicate that success.

Why such opposite reactions to the same event? In a word, attitudes.

The two upper-level managers respond differently because their primary attitudes about projects that run smoothly are polar opposites: one manager assumes that teams who work only 40-hour weeks and who consistently meet their schedules are doing something *wrong*; the other type of manager assumes those teams are doing something *right*. Either manager could be mistaken in the case of a particular project, but what good does it do to start out assuming the worst of a team?

Just as some leads ask first for long hours instead of looking for the real problem and then solving it, some upper-level managers have glommed onto that same uninventive approach, believing that long hours are good for the project and the corporate culture. Such managers forget that the business purpose of a development team is to contribute value to the company. A team can contribute value in numerous ways: reducing their cost-of-goods and thereby increasing the profit per box shipped, writing shareable code that saves development time, and so on. A manager who demands long hours focuses on one obvious way it might seem that programmers can add value to the company: giving the company all of their waking—and some of their sleeping—time.

It might seem logical that having the programmers work all of those hours would enable them to finish the product sooner. Unfortunately, it doesn't work that way, not in software development. If the company made widgets and managers demanded that workers run the widget-making machines for three extra hours every day, the company would get three hours' worth more of widgets—added value. There's a direct correlation between the number of hours worked and the amount of product produced, a correlation that in my experience doesn't exist in software development.

Don't Blame the Programmers

I've been picking on the user interface library and dialog manager projects, but the problems with those projects and with the Excel project were not the programmers. In all of these cases, the programmers were working hard, trying to do their best in a frustrating situation. It's easy to make the mistake of blaming the programmers when a project is slipping and not running smoothly, but if the entire team is in trouble, that indicates a management problem.

Microsoft® Windows NT™ Resource Kit

Microsoft Corporation

This exclusive three-volume Microsoft collection is a comprehensive source of technical information and tools necessary for self-support of Windows NT installations. The *Microsoft Windows NT Resource Kit* includes *Windows NT Resource Guide* (with four 3.5-inch disks), *Windows NT Messages* (with three 3.5-inch disks), and *Optimizing Windows NT* (with one 3.5-inch disk). These volumes are also available separately.

BONUS! The three-volume set also includes a CD-ROM containing all the disk-based utilities PLUS tools and utilities for RISC-based computers.

Three-volume set boxed with eight 3.5-inch disks and one CD-ROM
$109.95 ($148.95 Canada)   ISBN 1-55615-602-2

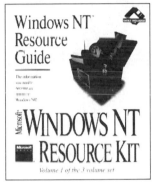

Volume 1:
Windows NT Resource Guide

This complete technical guide to Windows NT features information about installing, configuring, customizing, and troubleshooting Windows NT. It also includes information on applications compatibility and migration from Windows 3.1, MS-DOS, OS/2, and LAN Manager, and using database services with Windows NT. The four disks include more than 50 tools, utilities, and value-added software, including tools to manage users and groups of servers, a Computer Profile Setup tool for easily installing Windows NT on large groups of workstations, an adapter card Help file, an online registry Help filer, and utilities for the POSIX subsystem.

1024 pages, with four 3.5-inch disks
$49.95 ($67.95 Canada)
ISBN 1-55615-598-0

Volume 2:
Windows NT Messages

An alphabetic reference and online database that provides in-depth, accessible information about Windows NT and Windows NT Advanced Server error and system-information messages. Also includes detailed discussions about Windows NT executive messages and an extensive glossary of common message terms and user actions. The messages have been loaded into a Microsoft Access database with a simple user interface, which enables the user to search the database, add personal notes under a message, back up the database, and print a selected group of messages. The three disks contain a runtime version of Microsoft Access and the Messages database.

624 pages, with three 3.5-inch disks
$39.95 ($53.95 Canada)
ISBN 1-55615-600-6

Volume 3:
Optimizing Windows NT

The one resource that provides all the information needed to maximize the capacity and speed of Windows NT, including information on bottleneck detection and capacity planning for the desktop and network. Also includes information on designing and tuning your Windows NT applications for high performance. Included with the book is one disk full of software accessories and utilities for troubleshooting, fine-tuning, and optimizing PC performance.

608 pages, with one 3.5-inch disk
$34.95 ($46.95 Canada)
ISBN 1-55615-619-7

Microsoft Press books are available wherever quality books are sold and through CompuServe's Electronic Mall—GO MSP.
Call 1-800-MSPRESS for direct ordering information or for placing credit card orders.*
Please refer to BBK when placing your order. Prices subject to change.

*In Canada, contact Macmillan Canada, Attn: Microsoft Press Dept., 164 Commander Blvd., Agincourt, Ontario, Canada M1S 3C7, or call (416) 293-8464, ext. 340.
Outside the U.S. and Canada, write to International Coordinator, Microsoft Press, One Microsoft Way, Redmond, WA 98052-6399

Register Today!

Return the
Code Complete
registration card for:

- ✔ a Microsoft Press catalog
- ✔ exclusive offers on specially priced books

Fill in information below and mail postage free. Please mail only the bottom half of this page.

NAME

COMPANY

ADDRESS

CITY   STATE   ZIP

Your feedback is important to us.

Include your daytime telephone number, and we may call to find out how you use *Code Complete* and what we can do to make future editions even more useful. If we call you, we'll send you a **FREE GIFT** for your time!

(   )

DAYTIME TELEPHONE NUMBER

1-55615-484-4A

XILX

Microsoft Techniques for Developing Bug-Free C Programs

Writing Solid Code
Steve Maguire

Foreword by Dave Moore,
Director of Development, Microsoft Corporation

"Writing Solid Code is a worthwhile addition to the shelves of any full-time programmer." **Peter Coffee, PC WEEK**

Written by a former Microsoft developer and troubleshooter, this book is an insider's view of the most important aspect of the commercial development process: preventing and detecting bugs. Maguire identifies the places developers typically make mistakes and offers practical advice for detecting costly mistakes. Includes proven programming techniques for producing solid, shippable code.
288 pages, softcover $24.95 ($32.95 Canada)   ISBN 1-55615-551-4

Microsoft Press

NO POSTAGE
NECESSARY
IF MAILED
IN THE
UNITED STATES

BUSINESS REPLY MAIL
FIRST-CLASS MAIL   PERMIT NO. 53   BOTHELL, WA

POSTAGE WILL BE PAID BY ADDRESSEE

MICROSOFT PRESS REGISTRATION
CODE COMPLETE
PO BOX 3019
BOTHELL WA   98041-9910